WINDOWS 2000

ONE WEEK LOAN

)00:

Guide

WINDOWS 2000

Windows 2000: A Beginner's Guide

MARTIN S. **MATTHEWS**

Osborne/**McGraw-Hill**

Berkeley   New York   St. Louis   San Francisco
Auckland   Bogotá   Hamburg   London   Madrid
Mexico City   Milan   Montreal   New Delhi   Panama City
Paris   São Paulo   Singapore   Sydney
Tokyo   Toronto

Osborne/**McGraw-Hill**
2600 Tenth Street
Berkeley, California 94710
U.S.A.

For information on translations or book distributors outside the U.S.A., or to arrange bulk purchase discounts for sales promotions, premiums, or fund-raisers, please contact Osborne/**McGraw-Hill** at the above address.

Windows 2000: A Beginner's Guide

1234567890 DOC DOC 019876543210

ISBN 0-07-212324-9

Publisher
  Brandon A. Nordin

Vice President and Associate Publisher
  Scott Rogers

Acquisitions Editor
  Jane Brownlow

Project Editor
  Janet Walden

Acquisitions Coordinator
  Tara Davis

Technical Editor
  John Cronan

Copy Editor
  William McManus

Proofreader
  Mike McGee

Indexer
  Claire Splan

Computer Designers
  Jim Kussow
  Lauren McCarthy
  Roberta Steele

Illustrators
  Robert Hansen
  Michael Mueller
  Beth Young

Series Design
  Peter F. Hancik

This book was composed with Corel VENTURA ™ Publisher.

To Tom Sheldon, one super computer book author and one super friend.
Thanks Tom, for always being there.

ABOUT THE AUTHOR

Martin Matthews (Marty) has used computers for over 30 years, from some of the early mainframe computers to recent personal computers. He has done this as a programmer, systems analyst, manager, vice president, and president of a software firm. As a result, he has first-hand knowledge of not only how to program and use a computer, but also how to make the best use of the information a computer can produce.

Over 20 years ago Marty wrote his first computer book on how to buy mini-computers. Sixteen years ago Marty and his wife Carole began writing books as a major part of their occupation. In the intervening years they have written over 50 books including ones on desktop publishing, web publishing, Microsoft Office, and Microsoft operating systems from MS-DOS through Windows 2000. Recent books published by Osborne/McGraw-Hill include *FrontPage 2000: The Complete Reference*, *Windows 98 Answers! Certified Tech Support*, *Office 2000 Answers! Certified Tech Support*, and *Outlook 98 Made Easy*.

Marty, Carole, and their son live on an island in Puget Sound where, on the rare moments when they can look up from their computers, they look west across seven miles of water and the main shipping channel to the snow-capped Olympic mountains.

ABOUT THE CONTRIBUTING AUTHORS

John Cronan cut his teeth as a writer and technical editor under the tutelage of the author, Martin Matthews, and Osborne/McGraw-Hill in the early 1990s. He has since worked on dozens of books for several publishing houses and contracts regularly for Microsoft Corporation as a technical writer. John lives in the Seattle area with his significant other, Faye, and significant Newfoundland, Louise.

Michael Cooper (MCSE + I, MCT, CNE, CCP, CCNA, CCDA) has been part of the computer industry his entire life. Before he reached his 21st birthday Michael was a technical support supervisor for the world's eighth largest computer company. He has served in various technical roles since then, including WAN/LAN administrator for the world's third largest custom manufacturer. Currently Michael is a senior system's engineer and senior technical instructor at CTG, Idaho's largest consulting group. A tested and certified expert in Microsoft, Novell, Citrix, and Cisco technologies, Michael has led Windows NT and 2000 integrations and migrations that have spanned city, county, state, and international borders, and works in partnership with Microsoft Consulting Services on the majority of his current projects. Michael can be reached via e-mail at MCooper@MCooper.com.

Craig Zacker is a writer, editor, and networker whose computing experience began in the halcyon days of teletypes and paper tape. After making the move from minicomputers to PCs, he worked as an administrator of Novell NetWare networks and as a PC support technician while operating a freelance desktop publishing business. After earning a masters degree in English and American literature from NYU, Craig worked extensively on the integration of Windows NT into existing NetWare internetworks, and was employed as a technical writer, content provider, and webmaster for the online services group of a large software company. Since devoting himself to writing and editing full time, Craig has authored or contributed to many books on operating systems and networking topics and has published articles with top industry publications including *Windows NT Magazine*, for which he is a contributing editor.

James Murray is an MCSE, MCT, CNA, CTM and has degrees including a BS in MIS, MBA* (*pending in the next 30 to 60 days...waiting for final acceptance of his masters thesis). James has been working for nine years in the networking field, presently as a consultant for Best consulting in Seattle, WA. His specialty is network design and installation and administration, as well as technical training in Microsoft systems. He can be contacted at jamesmu@bestnet.com.

AT A GLANCE

CONTENTS

Part III

Networking Windows 2000

Part IV

Communications and the Internet

Part V
Administering Windows 2000 Server

Part VI

Using Windows 2000 Professional

ACKNOWLEDGMENTS

▼

t takes a number of people to create a book like this and especially to make it a really good book. The following people, and others I do not know, have added much to the book and have made my job manageable.

Tom Sheldon, the author of *The Encyclopedia of Networking* and many other books and a great friend, spent many hours on the phone and through e-mail answering my many questions. (See the book's dedication.) Thanks Tom!

John Cronan wrote Chapters 16, 17, and 18 on Windows 2000 Professional and was the technical editor for the rest of the book. John corrected many errors, added many tips and notes, and generally improved the book. John is also a great friend. Thanks John!

Craig Zacker, **Michael Cooper**, and **James Murray** wrote Chapters 8, 9, and 11 respectively adding a lot of outside expertise, and did so in a short time span and without a lot of guidance. Thanks Craig, Michael, and James!

Thomas Beard, CNE, and another one of my great friends who goes way beyond friendship, in this case to try and educate me on Novell NetWare and to read and comment on the Novell chapter. Thanks Tom!

Jane Brownlow, acquisitions editor, provided a lot of support, as well as a lot of latitude. Thanks Jane!

Janet Walden, project editor, although we are locked in an epochal struggle over the quantity of screen shots, Janet added greatly to the readability and understandability of the book while always listening to my considerations and generally making working with her a joy. Thanks Janet!

Tara Davis, acquisitions coordinator, kept the project organized and on track while correcting formatting problems and identifying lost screen shots. Throughout it all Tara has been a delight to work with. Thanks Tara!

Carole Matthews, my life partner, my very best friend, and sharer of our parenting adventure, provided the necessary support without which this book would not have been possible. Thanks my love!

INTRODUCTION

I n a very real sense Windows 2000 is a new operating system that takes the very best of Windows NT and Windows 98 and upgrades it for the latest operating system technology. The net result is an extremely capable client/server operating system that is more reliable, easier to install, faster, and more scalable. It also has an excellent directory service, supports most current hardware, is easier to manage, provides better security, and delivers exceptional mobile computer support.

The purpose of this book is to show you how to use these features and many others, and get the attendant benefits.

How This Book is Organized

Windows 2000: A Beginner's Guide is written the way most people learn. It starts by reviewing the basic concepts and then uses a learn-by-doing method to demonstrate the major features of the product. Throughout, the book uses detailed examples and clear explanations with many line drawings and screenshots to give you the insight needed to make the fullest use of Windows 2000. *Windows 2000: A Beginner's Guide* has six parts, each providing a complete discussion of one major aspect of Windows 2000.

Part I: The Windows 2000 Environment

Part I introduces you to the Windows 2000 environment, and what's new about it. This part establishes the foundation for the rest of the book.

▼ **Chapter 1, "Exploring Windows 2000,"** provides an overview of Windows 2000 and serves as a guide to the more in-depth discussions that take place in the later chapters.

▲ **Chapter 2, "Migrating to Windows 2000,"** explores the pros and cons of migrating to Windows 2000 and how an organization might go through the evaluation for themselves.

Part II: Deploying Windows 2000

Part II covers the planning for and carrying out of the deployment of Windows 2000 across an organization. The purpose of this part is to assist you in going though the planning process and then actually doing a detail installation.

▼ **Chapter 3, "Getting Ready for Windows 2000,"** looks at all the steps that must be carried out prior to installing Windows 2000, including the possible pitfalls to stir clear of.

■ **Chapter 4, "Installing Windows 2000 Server,"** takes you through the various steps necessary to install the Server from different starting points, as well as if you are upgrading or doing a clean install.

▲ **Chapter 5, "Rolling Out Windows 2000 Professional,"** describes both the manual and automated approach to the installation of Professional.

Part III: Networking Windows 2000

Part III devotes four chapters to networking, the single most important function within Windows 2000.

▼ **Chapter 6, "Windows 2000 Networking Environment,"** provides a comprehensive foundation on networking by describing the schemes, hardware, and protocols or standards that are used to make it function.

■ **Chapter 7, "Setting Up and Managing a Windows 2000 Netowrk,"** describes how networking is set up and managed in Windows 2000.

■ **Chapter 8, "Working with NetWare,"** discusses how Novell NetWare works with Windows 2000 and how to migrate from NetWare to Windows 2000.

▲ **Chapter 9, "Using Active Directory and Domains,"** looks at how domains are used in Windows 2000 and the central role that Active Directory plays in managing networking.

Part IV: Communications and the Internet

Part IV covers the ways that you and your organization can reach out from your LAN to connect to others or allow others to connect to you, both on the Internet and through direct communications.

▼ **Chapter 10, "Communications and Internet Services,"** provides an overview of communications and how to set it up, including using a dial-up connection with the Remote Access Service (RAS), and using an Internet connection with Internet Explorer and Outlook Express.

▲ **Chapter 11, "Internet Information Services Version 5,"** describes Internet Information Services (IIS), and how is it set up and managed.

Part V: Administering Windows 2000 Server

The purpose of Part V is to explore the numerous administrative tools that are available within Windows 2000 Server and discuss how they can best be used.

▼ **Chapter 12, "Storage and File System Management,"** looks at the extensive set of tools that are available in Windows 2000 to handle the various types of storage systems and the files and folders they contain.

■ **Chapter 13, "Setting Up and Managing Printing,"** describes what constitutes Windows 2000 printing, how to set it up, how to manage it, and how to manage the fonts that are required for printing.

■ **Chapter 14, "Windows 2000 Management Tools,"** discusses the system management tools and user management tools that are not part of setting up, networking, file management, or printing.

▲ **Chapter 15, "Windows 2000 Security Services,"** describes each of the security demands and the Windows 2000 facilities that address that demand, as well as the ways to implement those facilities.

Part VI: Using Windows 2000 Professional

Part VI describes how Windows 2000 Professional gives the business user a computing platform to handle their applications, communications, and processing needs in a powerful, reliable, and secure way.

▼ **Chapter 16, "Working with Windows 2000 Professional,"** takes you on a tour of Professional and describes how to use the major components.

■ **Chapter 17, "Customizing Windows 2000 Professional"** shows you how to customize Windows 2000 to your needs and how to set up and install applications to fit your requirements.

▲ **Chapter 18, "Mobile Computing with Windows 2000"** explores the powerful features that Windows 2000 has for laptop and notebook computers.

CONVENTIONS USED IN THIS BOOK

Windows 2000: A Beginner's Guide uses several conventions designed to make the book easier for you to follow. Among these are

▼ **Bold type** is used for text that you are to type from the keyboard.

■ *Italic type* is used for a word or phrase that is being defined or otherwise deserves special emphasis.

■ A monospaced typeface is used for command listings either produced by Windows 2000 or entered by the user.

▲ SMALL CAPITAL LETTERS are used for keys on the keyboard such as ENTER and SHIFT.

When you are expected to enter a command, you are told to press the key(s). If you are to enter text or numbers, you are told to type them.

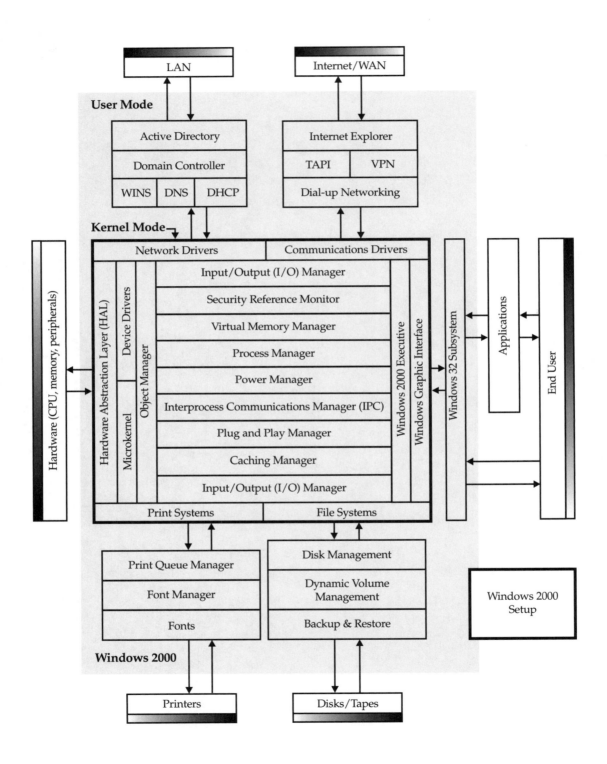

PART I

The Windows 2000 Environment

Part I introduces you to the Windows 2000 environment and what's new about it. This part establishes the foundation for the rest of the book. It provides an overview of Windows 2000 and serves as a guide to the more in-depth discussions that will take place in the later chapters.

CHAPTER 1

Exploring Windows 2000

Windows 2000 is a very significant and worthwhile upgrade from Windows NT 4, both Server and Workstation, and from Windows 95/98. There are many reasons for saying this, but among the more outstanding ones are the following:

▼ **More reliable** My own experience confirms what numerous sources other than Microsoft have said about Windows 2000: it is more reliable than Windows NT 4 and a lot more reliable than Windows 95/98.

■ **Easier to install** Plug and Play capability and a large driver database, plus an improved Setup program, make Windows 2000 significantly easier to install than Windows NT 4 and at least equal in ease to Window 98.

■ **Faster** Across the many ways that processing speed can be measured, outside sources and my experience show that Windows 2000 is generally faster than Windows NT and Windows 98, and Windows 2000 can make better use of memory that's added, further improving the speed.

■ **More scalable** The Windows 2000 Server line can smoothly grow from a single computer with a single processor and 128MB of memory to a cluster of up to 32 computers each with up to 32 processors and up to 64GB of memory. Windows 2000 Professional can grow from a single computer with a single processor and 32MB of memory to a single computer with 2 processors and 4GB of memory.

■ **Better directory** Windows 2000's Active Directory is a very significant improvement over Windows NT's limited domain structure, and is at least equal to Novell Directory Services (NDS) 4.*x*.

■ **More hardware supported** Windows 2000 provides support for many new hardware devices, including Firewire (IEEE 1394) used with camcorders and other high-speed serial devices; universal serial bus (USB) used with keyboards, mice, and scanners; and infrared devices for communications between notebook computers.

■ **Easier to manage** Windows 2000 includes the Microsoft Management Console (MMC), which enables you to group a number of controls, such as comprehensive computer and storage management, in one place with a standard interface; IntelliMirror, which enables settings and files to follow a user from machine to machine across a network; and Remote Storage and Removable Storage, enabling you to track and better handle removable media, such as tape and removable disks.

■ **Better security** Windows 2000 Active Directory enables you to encrypt files, use Kerberos standard authentication, and use smart cards. Also, a public key infrastructure (PKI) is now built into Windows 2000 and Active Directory and is supported by a complete set of certificate services.

▲ **Improved mobile support**   Windows 2000 Professional is the best thing that has happened to mobile (laptop/notebook) computers in a while. Among the reasons for this are greatly improved battery management; a real hibernate mode that lets you close the lid for an extended period with very little power drain, and then open the lid to the same screen you had without rebooting; and Offline Files that let you work with server files offline and then automatically synchronize with them when you reconnect.

The purpose of this book is to show you how to use these features and many others, and get the attendant benefits. In this chapter, you will take a tour of Windows 2000, looking briefly at each area of the product, including a description of its function and how it relates to the rest of the product.

WINDOWS 2000 OVERVIEW

Windows 2000 is really four independent and separately sold products:

▼ **Windows 2000 Professional**   A workstation client operating system that is meant for business users and is an upgrade for Windows NT Workstation 3.51 and 4, and Windows 95 and 98.

■ **Windows 2000 Server**   A network server operating system that is meant for smaller organizations and is an upgrade for Windows NT Server 3.51 and 4.

■ **Windows 2000 Advanced Server**   A network server operating system that is meant for larger organizations, especially those involved in e-commerce, and is an upgrade for Windows NT Server 4 Enterprise Edition.

▲ **Windows 2000 Datacenter Server**   A network server operating system that is meant for the largest organizations, especially those involved in data warehousing and online transaction processing.

Hardware Differences

The hardware usage differs significantly among the versions of Windows 2000, as shown in Table 1-1.

This book discusses only Windows 2000 Professional and Windows 2000 Server.

Windows 2000	Concurrent CPUs	Max. Memory	Min. Memory	Cluster Nodes
Professional	2	4GB	32MB	1
Server	4	4GB	128MB	1
Advanced Server	8	8GB	256MB	2-node failover, 32-node load balancing
Datacenter Server	32	64GB	N/A	4-node failover, 32-node load balancing

Table 1-1. Hardware Differences Among Windows 2000 Versions

Windows 2000 Components

Windows 2000 is a very complex operating system with numerous components that work together to perform the necessary functions. Figure 1-1 shows the key components of Windows 2000 in an idealized block diagram. The central square marked Kernel Mode is the kernel of the operating system and interfaces with the outside world of users, applications, and hardware through the components in the remaining shaded area or gray area labeled User Mode. User Mode has five main component areas. These are, going clockwise from the upper left in Figure 1-1, as follows:

▼ Networking over a local area network (LAN)

■ Communications and the Internet over a wide area network (WAN)

■ User and application interface

■ Storage and file management system

▲ Printing system

The focus of this book is to fully understand how to use these components in the User Mode plus Windows 2000 Setup. The components in the Kernel Mode are discussed only to the extent to which you need to understand them to be able to use the User Mode components.

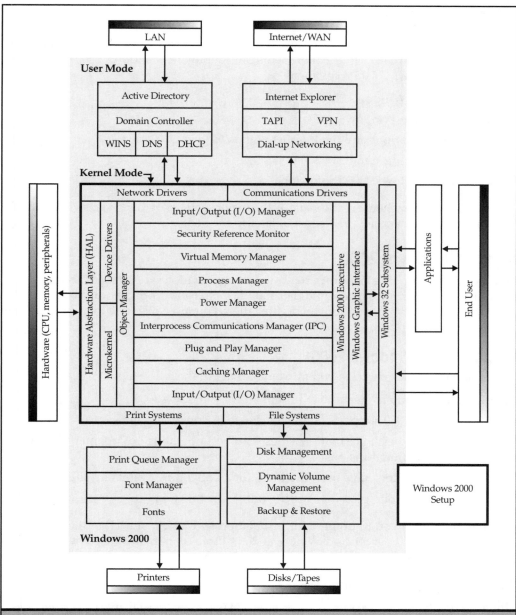

Figure 1-1.   Central components of Windows 2000

TOUR OF WINDOWS 2000

Take a brief tour of Windows 2000 now. The remaining sections in this chapter, listed next, look at the five User Mode components plus deploying Windows 2000 and making the most of Windows 2000 Professional:

▼ Deploying Windows 2000

■ Networking Windows 2000

■ Communications and the Internet with Windows 2000

■ Administering Windows 2000

▲ Using Windows 2000 Professional

The sections used here are the same as the major sections of this book, so you can easily jump from this overview to the detail later in the book.

Deploying Windows 2000

The objective of bringing Windows 2000 into an organization *successfully* is accomplished by optimizing its performance while also making it look and work the way you want it to. To meet this objective throughout an organization, you must plan and then carry out the deployment, both for servers and for workstations.

Preparing for Windows 2000

To prepare for Windows 2000, you must make sure of the following:

▼ Your computers meet the requirements of Windows 2000

■ Windows 2000 supports all the hardware in your computers

■ You know the choice that provides your best operating environment for each of the installation decisions

■ Your computers have been prepared for an operating system installation

▲ You have a solid plan for carrying out the installation

Chapter 3 helps you to prepare for installation by looking at each of these areas for both Windows 2000 Server and Windows 2000 Professional, and discusses what you need to know to make the installation as smooth as possible.

Setting Up Windows 2000 Server

Windows 2000 Server can be installed in a variety of ways, but they fall into three categories:

▼ **Manually** Someone sits in front of the computer to be installed and, in real time, does the installation on that machine.

■ **Automated** A script or answer file is used to carry out the installation, so a person does not have stay in front of the computer being installed.

▲ **Remotely** A person sits in front of a server and performs the installation on a computer across the network. The installation can be manual or automated.

Chapter 4 describes in detail the manual approach for installing Windows 2000 Server with many variations, two of which are shown in Figure 1-2. Chapter 5 describes the automated approach for installing Windows 2000 Server, along with the manual and automated approaches for installing Windows 2000 Professional. The remote approach requires remotely bootable network interface cards and motherboards that support them, as well as a dedicated server or volume on a server. As a result, remote installation will not be covered here.

Networking Windows 2000

Windows 2000 is a network operating system, and it exists for its networking capability. This allows it to connect with other computers for the purpose of doing the following:

▼ Exchanging information, such as sending a file from one computer to another

■ Communicating by, for example, sending e-mail among network users

■ Sharing information by having common files accessed by multiple network users

▲ Sharing resources on the network, such as printers and backup tape drives

Figure 1-2. Windows 2000 Setup primary choices

Networking is important to almost every organization of two or more people who communicate and share information. It is a primary ingredient in the computer's contribution to improved productivity and, from the viewpoint of this book, is the single most important facility in Windows 2000.

Networking is a system that includes the physical connection between computers that facilitates the transfer of information, as well as the scheme for controlling that transfer. The scheme makes sure that the information is transferred correctly and accurately while many other transfers are occurring simultaneously. Thus, a networking system has these components:

▼ A networking scheme that handles the transfer

■ Networking hardware that handles the physical connection

▲ A networking standard or protocol that handles the identification and addressing

Chapter 6 describes the networking schemes that are available in Windows 2000, the hardware that can be used, and the protocols that are common in the industry. Chapter 6 then reviews the wide spectrum of networking alternatives that are available to provide the networking environment best suited to your needs. Chapter 7 provides a detailed description of setting up basic networking in either Server or Professional, and then looks at setting up Server to support the rest of the network. Chapter 8 reviews how NetWare compares to Windows 2000 networking, how to use it within Windows 2000, and how to migrate from NetWare to Windows 2000. Chapter 9 explores domains and how Active Directory provides a single directory for many different network-related functions, as you can see in Figure 1-3.

Communications and the Internet with Windows 2000

"Networking" in the previous section referred to using a LAN. In this age of the Internet, Windows 2000 networking has taken on a much broader meaning that includes all the types of connections that you make outside of your LAN using what was classically called "communications." Windows 2000 offers a single dialog box, Network and Dial-up Connections, from which you can set up both LAN and external connections.

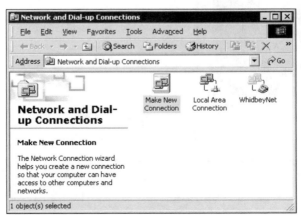

Figure 1-3.   Active Directory is a single source for network information

The types of external connections include the following:

▼ Leased-line and private-line WAN

■ Dial-up line computer-to-computer communications using a modem

■ Direct computer-to-computer using serial, parallel, or infrared ports

■ Remote Access Service (RAS) for accessing a LAN over a dial-up, leased, or private line

■ Dial-up, leased, and private line connections to the Internet

▲ Virtual private networking (VPN) to access a LAN over the Internet using one of several security procedures, including Point-to-Point Tunneling Protocol (PPTP), Internet Protocol Security (IPSec), or Layer 2 Tunneling Protocol (L2TP)

Windows 2000 communications capability includes the following possible ways to interchange information:

▼ Computer to computer

■ Computer to LAN

■ LAN to LAN

- ■ Computer or LAN to WAN
- ▲ Computer or LAN to the Internet

Communication may include a modem or other device to connect a single computer to a method of transmission, or it may use a router or other device to connect a network to the method of transmission. Communications can be over copper wires, fiber-optic cable, microwave, ground wireless, or satellite transmission.

Windows 2000 includes a number of programs that control or utilize communications, among which are Internet Explorer for web browsing; Outlook Express for e-mail; Fax; HyperTerminal for computer-to-computer communications; NetMeeting for multimedia communications; Phone Dialer; and both the Internet Connection Wizard and the Network and Dial-up Connections dialog box to establish connections. In addition, Windows 2000 networking includes programs to set up and manage RAS and VPN forms of networking over communications lines. Finally, Internet Information Services (IIS) can be used to publish web pages on either the Internet or an intranet.

Chapter 10 provides an overview of communications and how to set up the various Windows 2000 communications features. It then discusses establishing an Internet connection, using Internet Explorer, and setting up and using e-mail over the Internet. Chapter 11 looks at IIS, how it's set up, and how it's managed, including its administrative window, shown in Figure 1-4.

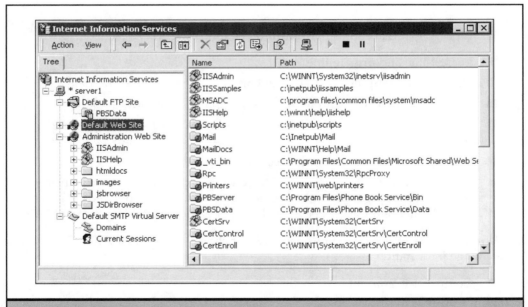

Figure 1-4. Internet Information Services administrative window

Administering Windows 2000

The job of administering a Windows 2000 network, even one as small as a single server and a dozen workstations, is a significant task. To assist in this, Windows 2000 has a number of system management tools that can be used to monitor and tune the system's performance, both locally and remotely. These tools can be broken into the following areas:

▼ File system management

■ Printing management

■ General system management

▲ Security management

File System Management

Windows 2000 is designed to work in a wide range of computing environments and with several other operating systems. As a result, the structure of its file storage has to be flexible. This is manifest in the types of storage that are available, and in the file systems that Windows 2000 can utilize.

Prior to Windows 2000, there was only one type of storage, called *basic storage*, which allowed a drive to be divided into partitions. Windows 2000 adds *dynamic storage*, which allows the dynamic creation of volumes. You must choose which type of storage you want for a given drive, but you can have both types in a computer with two or more drives.

The Windows 2000 file system extends well beyond a single drive, or even the drives in a single machine, to all the drives in a network, and even includes volumes stored offline on tape or disk. The management of this system is significant, and Windows 2000 thus has a very significant set of tools to handle system management, which are described in Chapter 12. Among these tools are the following:

▼ Disk Management

■ Dynamic Volume Management

■ Distributed File System

■ Removable Storage Manager

■ Remote Storage Service

▲ Disk Backup and Restore

Figure 1-5 shows the Disk Management window.

Printing Management

The ability to transfer computer information to paper or other media is still very important, and the ability to share printers is a major network function, as you can see in Figure 1-6. Both Windows 2000 Server and Windows 2000 Professional can serve as print servers.

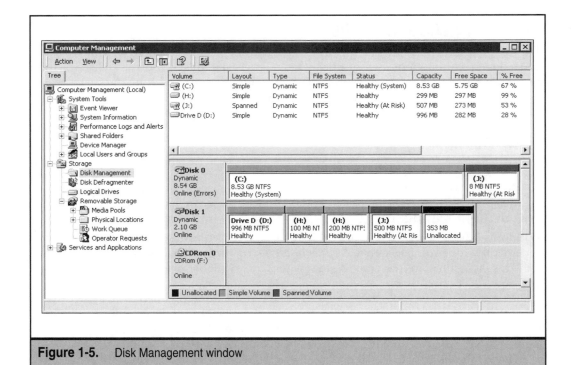

Figure 1-5.   Disk Management window

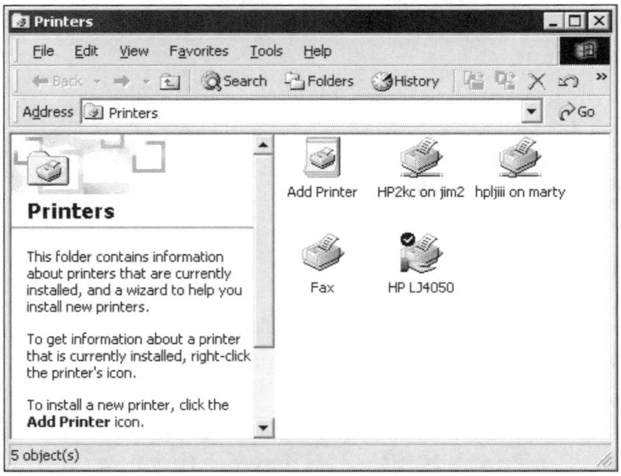

Figure 1-6.   Printers window with two network printers and one local printer

Chapter 13 describes what constitutes Windows 2000 printing, how to set it up, how to manage it, and how to manage the fonts that are required for printing.

General System Management

Windows 2000 has a variety of general system management tools to control many facets of the operating system. Chapter 14 looks at the system management tools and user management tools that are not part of setting up, networking, managing files, or printing.

System management tools are those that facilitate running parts of the operating system that are not discussed elsewhere. These tools include the following:

▼ The Control Panel

■ The Task Manager

■ The Microsoft Management Console

■ The Registry

▲ The Boot Process

Managing computer users with their varying needs and peculiarities, both in groups and individually, is a task to which Windows 2000 has committed considerable resources. These are addressed in terms of group policies and user profiles. Figure 1-7 shows Active Directory's Users and Computers window, in which you can manage users and groups.

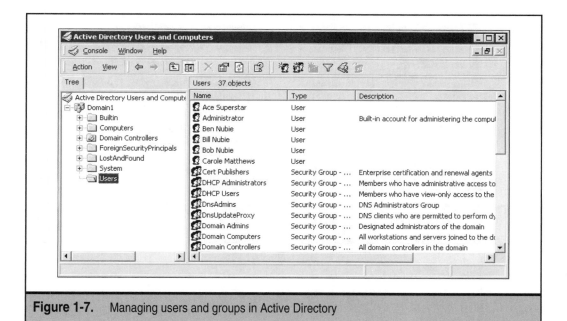

Figure 1-7.   Managing users and groups in Active Directory

Security Management

The demands for security in a computer network include:

▼ **Authenticating the user**   Knowing who is trying to use a computer or network connection.

■ **Controlling access**   Placing and maintaining limits on what a user can do.

■ **Securing stored data**   Keeping stored data from being used even with access.

■ **Securing data transmission**   Keeping data in a network from being misused.

▲ **Managing security**   Establishing security policies and auditing their compliance.

Windows 2000 uses a multilayered approach to implementing security and provides a number of facilities that are used to handle security demands, such as authentication certificates, as shown in Figure 1-8. Central to Windows 2000's security strategy is the use of Active Directory to store user accounts and provide authentication services, although other security features are available without Active Directory. Active Directory, though, provides a centralization of security management that is very beneficial to strong security.

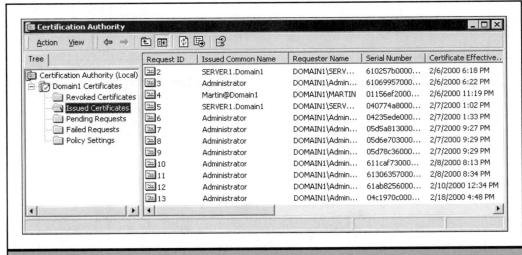

Figure 1-8.   Certificates are used to authenticate computers and individuals

Chapter 15 describes each of the security demands and the Windows 2000 facilities that address each demand, as well as the ways to implement those facilities.

Using Windows 2000 Professional

Windows 2000 Professional is a combination of the best parts of Windows NT Workstation and Windows 98. The ease of use and user friendliness of Windows 98 is joined with the robustness, reliability, and security of Windows NT. Windows 2000 Professional is aimed at giving business users a computing platform to handle their applications, communications, and processing needs. Whether the user is doing data entry, creating documents or images, communicating over the Internet, searching the Web, programming, or doing scientific research, Windows 2000 provides a powerful, reliable, and secure operating system to accomplish it. (For games, entertainment, and general home use, Windows 98 remains the recommended operating system.)

Getting the Most out of Professional

Windows 2000 Professional goes a long way toward allowing you to set up the computing environment that is right for you, as described in Chapter 16. Windows 2000 has added Personalized Menus, which you may have seen already in Office 2000. This feature automatically displays only the menus that you have recently used, unless you hold the mouse on the menu, in which case the whole menu will open. All of the desktop, Start menu, and taskbar customization features in Windows 98 are also available in Windows 2000. And once you get your system the way you want it, your preferences, as well as files and applications, will follow you from computer to computer.

Windows 2000 has an enhanced search capability that allows you to search over local files, network shares, and the Internet, as you can see in Figure 1-9. Also, you can speed up the searching process by allowing the Windows 2000 Indexing Service to keep a running index of your files, similar to Office's Find Fast. If this takes too much of your processing time, you can turn it off.

In addition to operating in client/server mode, Windows 2000 Professional can operate in peer-to-peer mode, so that it can be used in smaller networks.

Using Applications

Windows 2000 has done several things to improve the installation, maintenance, and use of applications, as explained in Chapter 17. The primary factor in these improvements is the introduction of Windows Installer, which manages not only the installation of applications, but also the repair of any bad files and the removal of applications. Applications can be installed and run from a floppy, across a LAN, and across the Internet or an intranet. Applications can be maintained using updates obtained online and through Microsoft Direct Access. Finally, applications can be started from a document file, an icon on the desktop or in the Quick Launch toolbar, the Program menu, or the Run command.

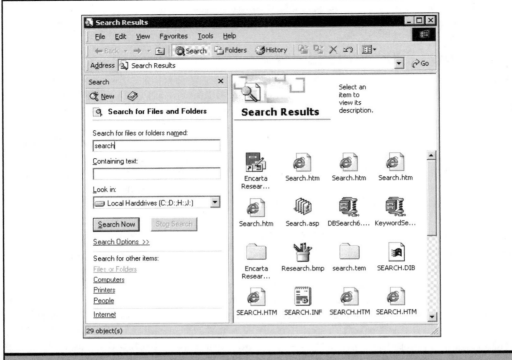

Figure 1-9. Searching can include local and network drives as well as the Internet

You can identify a primary language and several other languages that can be used in applications, as shown in Figure 1-10. Windows 2000 also has excellent multimedia capability to enhance the use of applications.

Windows 2000 Mobile

One of Windows 2000's strongest suites is its use in mobile computers. If you have a laptop or a notebook computer of a recent vintage with enough memory, I strongly recommend that you upgrade it to Windows 2000 (unless you are primarily using the computer for gaming). Chapter 18 looks at all the reasons behind this recommendation, but among them are the following:

▼ Secure infrared data exchange between two computers or a computer and a printer

■ Enhanced power management with an improved hibernate mode and improved power meter

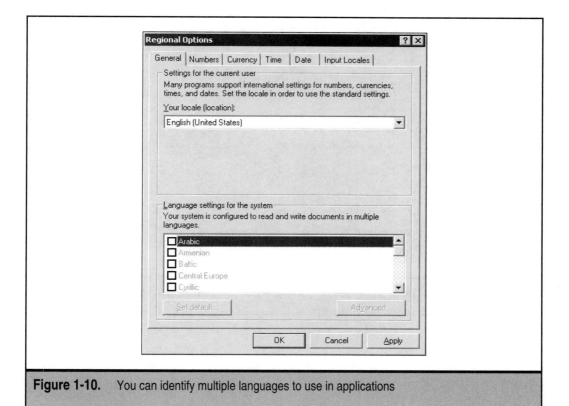

Figure 1-10. You can identify multiple languages to use in applications

■ Offline Folders and Synchronization Manager to take a file off the network, edit it on the laptop, and then automatically synchronize it with the original the next time you connect to the network

■ Encrypting File System (EFS) to encrypt individual files and folders

■ Built-in support for docking stations

■ Local network connections over RAS or VPN

▲ Inline file compression to compress single files or a single folder

You can both compress and encrypt individual files and folders in the Advanced Attributes dialog box, shown in Figure 1-11, which is accessed from the Properties dialog box of the individual file or folder.

Windows 2000 has a significant number of benefits that will be helpful to many people and organizations, but not to everyone. Chapter 2 will help you to determine whether migrating from your existing operating systems is the correct choice for you.

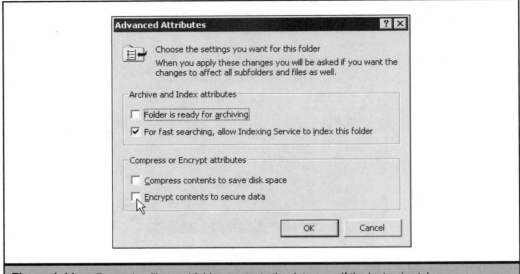

Figure 1-11.   Encrypting files and folders protects the data even if the laptop is stolen

CHAPTER 2

Migrating to Windows 2000

You most likely are wondering whether you and/or your organization should migrate to Windows 2000. There are, of course, many answers to that question depending on various factors. The purpose of this chapter is to look at those factors and discuss how to evaluate them so that you can make the right decision. Part II of this book will then describe how to do the actual migration.

The following factors are reviewed here:

▼   Organization size

■   Hardware and software

■   Networking environment

■   Security demands

▲   Support for the Internet

Each of the following sections will discuss one of these factors and look at how you should evaluate it with regard to your situation.

ORGANIZATION SIZE

As a general statement, the bigger the organization, the more obvious the decision is to migrate to Windows 2000. And, conversely, if you have a home office or a small office, it is less likely that you should migrate. Of course, these generalizations have many exceptions. The pros and cons of each statement are discussed next.

Larger Organizations May Favor Migration

Many features in Windows 2000 are aimed at larger organizations and therefore will encourage them to migrate. Among these features are the following:

▼   The scalability of Windows 2000 Server enables it to go from 1 computer with 1 processor to a cluster of 32 computers each with 32 processors, which can be a major plus for a large organization.

■   The ability of Windows 2000 to handle large data storage volumes better than Windows NT handles them can prove more valuable to larger organizations. The Windows 2000 facilities for large data storage include Dynamic Volume Management, Remote Storage Service, Removable Storage, and Quota Management. See Chapter 12 for a discussion of these facilities.

■   Windows 2000's Active Directory is more useful for a large organization because it can provide a central reference to shares and other services,

such as printers, on a number of servers and clients. Chapter 9 explores
Active Directory.

■ The Windows 2000 management features, such as the Computer Management
windows shown in Figure 2-1, are more valuable to larger organizations
because they make handling a large number of users, large storage volumes,
and multiple servers easier. Also, the addition of organizational units (OUs)
to the domain's hierarchical structure allows the system administration
to be more broadly distributed, which would benefit a large organization.
Windows 2000 management features are discussed in Chapter 14, while
domains are covered in Chapter 9.

▼ Windows 2000's significant security enhancements, including Kerberos
authentication, full implementation of a public key infrastructure (PKI), and
file encryption, may be of more interest to larger organizations, which tend to
be more security conscience. "Security Demands," later in this chapter, provides
an overview of these features, and Chapter 15 discusses security in depth.

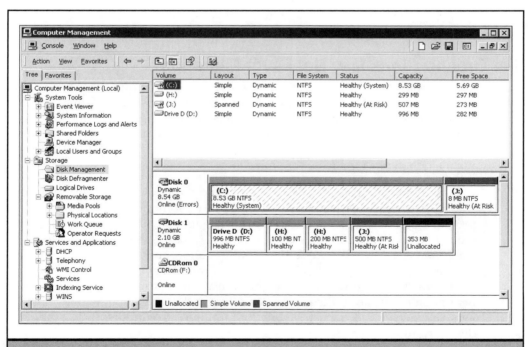

Figure 2-1.   Computer Management window with local Disk Management open

After considering the preceding features that favor migration, you must also consider the following roadblocks that may discourage a large organization's implementation of Windows 2000:

▼ The size of the migration task in a large organization requires lengthy planning, considerable staff training, and a lengthy transition period, all of which equates to a significant expenditure. This, at a minimum, means that a large organization must go slow in its migration. Part II of this book describes the deployment process.

■ A heterogeneous environment of mainframe, UNIX, and other non-Windows systems will reduce the benefits available from Windows 2000, especially Active Directory. This could mean that the return on investment (ROI) of a migration is not acceptable. The considerations needed in a heterogeneous environment are discussed primarily in Part III.

▲ Organizations heavily using Novell NetWare and Novell Directory Services (NDS) may not see enough advantage in Windows 2000 and Active Directory to warrant the migration. NDS is more mature and can handle a more heterogeneous environment. Using Novell NetWare with Windows 2000 is discussed in Chapter 8.

Smaller Organizations May Not Favor Migration

The size and complexity of Windows 2000 along with the effort required to set it up and maintain it are major stumbling blocks for smaller organizations (although this book will go a long way toward alleviating that problem). Also, scalability, the ability to handle large amounts of data, Active Directory, and improved security may or may not be very important to smaller companies. There are, though, two areas where Windows 2000 provides some major benefits for smaller organizations:

▼ If your organization is using laptop or notebook computers, you will probably want to run Windows 2000 Professional on those computers. Windows 2000 provides significantly enhanced power management with a true hibernate mode that allows you to simply close the cover, have the entire state of the computer saved to disk, and reduce power to almost nil. Then, when you open the cover, you can quickly be back to where you were without rebooting. Additionally, Windows 2000 has significantly improved the ability to use network files offline and then automatically synchronize them with the online version when you reconnect. Mobile computing with Windows 2000 is described in Chapter 18.

▲ If you share or want to share an Internet connection line, such as a digital subscriber line (DSL) or other high-speed line, Windows 2000 provides several features to facilitate this. Windows 2000 includes a built-in router that enables you to install a line termination (a modem, or an ISDN or DSL adapter) in a server and allow anyone on the network to access the Internet over that line.

Also, in Windows 2000, a modem can be set up to automatically dial an Internet service provider (ISP) whenever the modem is accessed. Finally, Internet Connection Sharing using network address translation (NAT) allows multiple people to share an Internet connection by mapping multiple LAN addresses to one IP address, which is what the ISP sees. Chapter 10 discusses communications and the Internet.

HARDWARE AND SOFTWARE

Windows 2000 is much more hardware-friendly than Windows NT 4, and is even a little better than Windows 98. Unfortunately, the same cannot be said about software. The following discussion looks at each of these statements in more detail.

Windows 2000 Hardware Friendliness

Windows NT 4 was a constant headache when it came to dealing with hardware components. Windows 2000 has added a number of features aimed at relieving that headache. Among these are the following:

▼ Full implementation of Plug and Play, which allows for virtually pain-free installation of Plug and Play–compliant hardware. (Older, non–Plug and Play hardware can still be a problem, but the following points mitigate that a bit.)

■ An extensive set of hardware drivers that are stored in compressed form on the computer, so you don't need the Windows 2000 CD-ROM to install a new device.

■ Online access to the latest drivers at the Microsoft site, and a program to check whether you need them. This is accessed by choosing Windows Update from the Start menu.

■ Online access to what hardware is and isn't compatible with Windows 2000, at http://www.microsoft.com/windows2000/upgrade/compat/default.asp. From this site, you also can download the Readiness Analyzer, which will list the compatibility issues on a particular computer.

■ Built-in support for recent hardware developments, including universal serial bus (USB) and Institute of Electrical and Electronics Engineers (IEEE) 1394 (FireWire) ports. USB ports can be used with keyboards, mice, and many other devices, whereas FireWire is a high-speed port used by video cameras and other video devices.

■ Efficient use of memory, but demands for a fair amount of it. Although you can run Windows 2000 Professional on 32MB, running it on 64MB provides a comfortable system, and 128MB makes a significant difference. Windows 2000 Server will run on 64MB, but 128MB is really the minimum practical system, and with any significant load, you will need 256MB. In all cases, the operating system makes good use of added memory.

- Excellent power management, including a hibernate mode, discussed earlier under "Smaller Organizations May Not Favor Migration."

▲ Ability to use the FAT 32 file system, which was not available in Windows NT 4, although Windows 2000 loses a lot of capability if NTFS (NT file system) is not used. Chapter 12 discusses FAT 32 and NTFS file systems.

Windows 2000 Software Considerations

Windows 2000 provides a 32-bit software environment with a lot of protection for the operating system from programs that "misbehave." This means that the first priority is to protect the operating system and keep it running, so a number of applications that step outside the proscribed "box" will not operate. These tend to be hardware-related programs, such as faxing, scanning, CD writing, and gaming software. Initially, at least, a number of these types of programs, especially from the Windows 98 environment, do not work under Windows 2000. Hopefully, there will be new versions of these programs, or at least new drivers that do work. Older 16-bit programs, especially DOS-based games, will not run on Windows 2000 unless they are rewritten.

At the same Microsoft web site referenced in the preceding bulleted list, you can check the compatibility of software. Also, the Readiness Analyzer at this site will check the compatibility of software on a computer, as well as the hardware. The compatibility results, an example of which is shown in Figure 2-2, will tell you at which of the following levels the software is classified:

▼ **Certified** A third party has tested and certified that the software is compatible with Windows 2000.

- **Ready** The software publisher has tested it with Windows 2000 and is willing to support it.

▲ **Planned** The current version of the software is not compatible, but a future version may be compatible.

NETWORKING ENVIRONMENT

Windows 2000 is a client/server network operating system, so how well it performs that function is one of the primary measures in the migration decision. A lot of emphasis has been placed on networking in Windows 2000, and many powerful features are included to support it. Primary among these are Active Directory and network management. In comparison to Windows NT 4 and its domain services, Windows 2000 and Active Directory is a substantial improvement and a big plus for migration.

In comparison to Novell NetWare and NDS, Windows 2000 and Active Directory do not look as attractive, and you might want to keep what you have, especially if you are using NetWare 5. NDS is a mature product in NetWare 5 and supports a heterogeneous

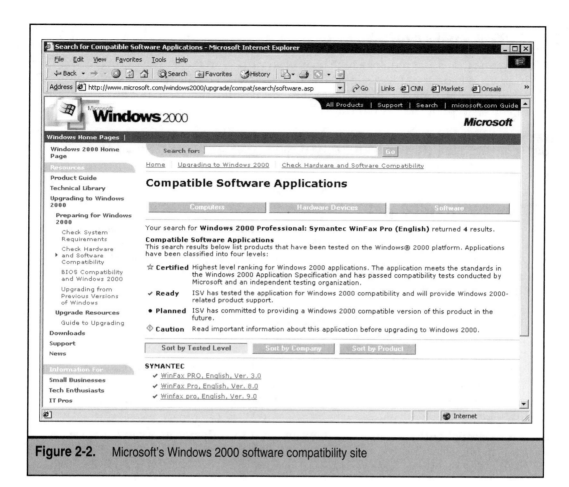

Figure 2-2.   Microsoft's Windows 2000 software compatibility site

environment, neither of which is true in Windows 2000 Active Directory. Also, Novell's ZENworks gives you a mature set of management features that is just appearing in Active Directory.

Windows 2000 and Active Directory depend heavily on the Domain Name Service (DNS), and Windows 2000 wants to be the DNS server on the network. If you have UNIX, Linux, or Solaris servers, they also want to be the DNS server, and the conflict will be difficult to resolve.

You can mix Windows 2000 and NetWare (Chapter 8 discusses several of the ways), but you want to think through that first to make sure that you'll get the benefits that you want.

SECURITY DEMANDS

For organizations that require a high level of security (and that is a fast-growing number), Windows 2000 offers a lot of support, and it could even be the reason for migrating. The big security pluses in Windows 2000 are Kerberos authentication, public key infrastructure, file encryption, and smart cards.

NOTE: Many of the security benefits in Windows 2000 require that NTFS 5 and Active Directory be used.

Kerberos Authentication

Kerberos, which was developed at Massachusetts Institute of Technology (MIT), provides the means to transmit secure data across unsecure networks and is the primary means of authentication on the Internet. As a result, the same authentication routines in Windows 2000 can validate both a local Windows 2000 client and an Internet-connected UNIX client. Other benefits of Kerberos are listed here:

▼ **Transitive trusts**   If computer A has a trust relationship with computer B, and computer B has a trust relationship with computer C, then computer A has a trust relationship with computer C.

■ **Kerberos tickets**   Once authenticated, these tickets stay with the user throughout a computer session and allow the user to be quickly authenticated anywhere they want to go, without having to query an authentication server each time.

▲ **Mutual authentication**   Allows the user to authenticate a service or server, while also allowing the service or server to authenticate the user. This prevents impersonation, which was possible in Windows NT 4, and is done using the Kerberos ticket.

Public Key Infrastructure

PKI incorporates all the facilities necessary to create, distribute, authenticate, and manage public key encryption. Chapter 15 provides a complete description of how this works. Briefly, the steps are as follows:

1. A user who is known to the security system is given a certificate.

2. Either the certificate contains a public and private key that are unique to the user, or, based upon the certificate, the user is given the keys.

3. When the user wants to exchange information with either a service or another user, they exchange public keys.

4. The public keys are used to encrypt information to be sent to the owner of the key.

5. Upon receipt of the encrypted information, the private key is used to decrypt it.

This is the process (and it is greatly simplified here) handled by PKI, and Windows 2000 is the only Windows operating system in which it has been fully implemented.

File Encryption

File encryption allows you to encrypt individual files so that if someone gets access to your disk, they will not be able to read the file. This is particularly important for laptop or notebook computers, which are frequently stolen. Once taken, the thief can use a variety of techniques to access the hard disk, but if critical files are encrypted, they will be unavailable to the thief.

To encrypt a file, the user, who must be the registered owner of the file, simply selects the encryption attribute in the file's or folder's Properties dialog box. The file will be encrypted with a symmetric key (the same key is used for both encryption and decryption). The symmetric key is itself encrypted with the public keys of both the creator and a recovery agent administrator and is then stored with the file. In the normal process of opening the file, the file system will see that it is encrypted and then check to see if the Kerberos ticket of the user has a private key that will open the file. If so, the file is opened. The only other person to be able to do this is the recovery agent administrator. When the file is resaved, it is again encrypted. The entire process of encryption and decryption of a file or folder is done in the background, and the user is only aware of it if the file cannot be decrypted.

Smart Cards

Smart cards are credit cards with an electronic circuit embedded in them that stores an ID and an encryption key. Smart cards are particularly valuable for remote entry to a network over the Internet using virtual private networking (VPN). Smart cards are also frequently used in the issuance of certificates of authenticity for documents.

Windows 2000 fully supports smart cards and lets them be used to log on to a computer or network or to enable certificate-based authentication for opening documents or performing some function like a calculation. Smart cards require a reader attached to the computer through either a serial port or a Personal Computer Memory Card International Association (PCMCIA) slot. With a smart card reader, users only need to insert their card, at which point they are prompted for their PIN. With a valid card and PIN, users are authenticated and allowed on the system in the same way they would be by entering a valid username and password.

Windows 2000 supports several Plug and Play–compliant smart card readers, and the drivers are included on the Windows 2000 CD. Windows NT 4 required third-party software and support for smart cards.

SUPPORT FOR THE INTERNET

Windows 2000 continues the trend to ever-greater support for the Internet or an intranet within the operating system, although most of the change is incremental to existing capabilities in Windows NT 4. This is seen in three areas:

▼ Built-in communications infrastructure

■ Internet Explorer and Outlook Express

▲ Internet Information Services (IIS)

Built-In Communications Infrastructure

Support for a modem has been included in operating systems for a long time, but Windows 2000 has gone beyond that traditional support with the following features (Chapter 10 discusses communications and the Internet):

▼ A built-in router that provides Internet access for an entire network over a single ISDN or DSL line

■ Automatic dialing of a modem whenever the modem is accessed over the network

▲ Network address translation that allows multiple people to share an Internet connection by mapping multiple LAN addresses to one IP address

Accessing the Internet

Accessing the Internet has become a high priority for most organizations, as an increasing number of business-to-business as well as business-to-consumer functions are handled there. To support this, Windows 2000 has fully integrated web browsing, e-mail, and a way to set them up with the following tools, all described in detail in Chapter 10:

▼ **Internet Connection Wizard**   Leads you through all the steps necessary to set up a modem, obtain an Internet service provider (ISP), and configure a connection to that ISP for regular service, e-mail service, and news service.

■ **Internet Explorer**   Allows you to search for and go to a web site, navigate within a web site, securely send to and receive information from a web site, store a web site's address in a list of favorites or in a links toolbar, print a web page, and maintain a history of the web sites you have visited.

▲ **Outlook Express**   Provides one-on-one communications through the sending, receiving, and storing of e-mail; participation in newsgroups through sending and receiving linked messages; and maintaining and using one or more address books.

Internet Information Services

IIS is the web server that has been included in Windows NT since Windows NT 3.51. IIS 5 is included in Windows 2000 and incorporates a number of performance, stability, and security enhancements. Among the enhancements in IIS 5 or in Windows 2000 to support web hosting are the following:

▼ Certificate and Permissions Wizards to greatly simplify the process of issuing security certificates and assigning the appropriate user permissions (the Certificate Wizard is shown in Figure 2-3).

■ Active Server Pages (ASP) that use scripts to efficiently generate a custom web page based on the request received by the server.

■ Distributed Authoring and Versioning (DAV) to allow greater and more direct control of web pages on a server from such tools as FrontPage and Netscape Composer.

Figure 2-3. Issuing and managing certificates to securely use web sites is easier in Windows 2000

■ Hypertext Transfer Protocol (HTTP) compression to speed up the transmission of a Hypertext Markup Language (HTML) document, which is the text part of a web page.

▲ Processor Accounting and Throttling allow you to monitor, control, and bill the processor time used by a particular web page. Prior to Windows 2000, there was no way that a Windows server could prevent a web page from taking over all processor time, or to bill for processor time.

CONCLUSION

So how do you sum all of this up? Everybody will do it differently, but there are some common denominators. Among these are the following:

▼ If your organization has laptop/notebook computers used primarily in a business environment, Windows 2000 Professional is definitely the operating system of choice.

■ If you are currently using Windows NT 4 domains, upgrading to Windows 2000 Active Directory will provide significant added benefits that will make the migration worthwhile.

■ If security is a major concern, then the addition of Kerberos authentication, PKI, file encryption, and the ability to use smart cards are powerful reasons to migrate.

■ If you are looking at significant network growth, then the scalability of Windows 2000 is a major asset, and when added to the ability to manage larger networks, these factors could be a reason to migrate.

■ System and network administration have taken significant strides in Windows 2000. Although it is not a reason in itself to migrate, it is strong support for such a decision.

■ Probably the biggest single strike against Windows 2000 is its newness. Any new system demands caution, but a new major network operating system demands it even more because so much depends on its smooth operation. It is probably prudent to wait for at least one if not two Service Packs to be released before migrating.

■ Migrating an organization to a new operating system is a very significant expenditure. Probably the smallest part of the cost is the new software. The major expenses are the people costs associated with training for, planning, and implementing the migration, as well as the costs associated with the disruption to the organization.

■   If you are currently using NetWare and NDS in a significant way and are satisfied with the results, you probably do not want to trade in that setup in the short term.

▲   If you have a heterogeneous mix of computers, especially one that uses UNIX, Linux, or Solaris in the network with Windows 2000, your benefits, especially from Active Directory, will be reduced substantially.

Only you can determine how to weigh these factors for your own situation. The balance of this book, though, will provide substantially more insight into Windows 2000, which will help you to make your migration decision.

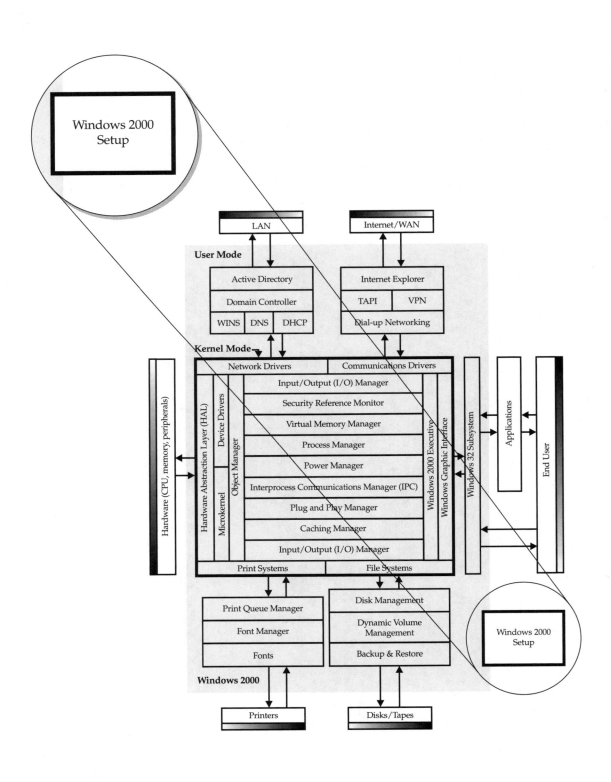

PART II

Deploying
Windows 2000

Deploying Windows 2000 is a significant undertaking that requires thorough planning and careful attention to details. The purpose of this part is to assist you in going through the planning process and then carrying out the detailed installation. Chapter 3 looks at all the steps that must be carried out prior to installing Windows 2000, including the possible pitfalls to steer clear of. Chapter 4 takes you through the various steps necessary to install the Server from different starting points or if you are upgrading or doing a clean install. Chapter 5 describes both the manual and automated approach to the installation of Professional.

CHAPTER 3

Getting Ready for Windows 2000

The installation of Windows 2000 is, on the surface, very simple: you put the CD-ROM in the drive or access the files over a network and follow the instructions on the screen. However, below the surface, the installation isn't necessarily that simple, because it assumes the following:

▼ Your computers meet the requirements of Windows 2000

■ Windows 2000 supports all the hardware in your computers

■ You know the choices that provide your best operating environment for each of the installation decisions

■ Your computers have been prepared for an operating system installation

▲ You have a solid plan for carrying out the installation

This chapter helps you prepare for installation by looking at each of these areas for both Windows 2000 Server and Windows 2000 Professional, and discusses what you need to know to make the installation as smooth as possible.

WINDOWS 2000 SYSTEM REQUIREMENTS

Windows 2000, especially Windows 2000 Server, has significant hardware requirements. Review Table 3-1 to make sure your systems meet the minimum requirements.

System Requirement Notes

The requirements in Table 3-1 are generalized, and special situations do exist where different requirements apply. These special situations are noted in the following paragraphs.

Processors

Windows 2000 Professional supports up to two processors in a single computer, known as *two-way symmetric multiprocessing* (SMP), while Windows 2000 Server supports up to four processors (four-way SMP). Windows 2000 Advanced Server supports up to 8 processors in a single computer, and Windows 2000 Datacenter Server supports up to 32 processors. This allows a wide range of scaling in a Windows 2000 installation, from a single computer with a single processor up to many computers each with a number of processors.

NOTE: Windows 2000 Advanced Server and Windows 2000 Datacenter Server are only discussed in comparison to Windows 2000 Professional and Windows 2000 Server, which are the primary topics of this book.

System Component	Windows 2000 Server	Windows 2000 Professional
Processor	166 MHz Pentium or higher	166 MHz Pentium or higher
RAM memory	64MB, 128MB recommended	32MB, 64MB recommended
Hard disk space	2GB with 850MB free	2GB with 650MB free
CD-ROM drive	12x or faster if CD installation	12x or faster if CD installation
Floppy disk drive	3.5-inch high density, optional if CD is bootable	3.5-inch high density, optional if CD is bootable
Video display system	VGA or higher resolution	VGA or higher resolution
Input devices	Keyboard and mouse (optional)	Keyboard and mouse (optional)
Network device	Compatible network card	Compatible network card

Table 3-1.   Windows 2000 Minimum Hardware

Windows 2000 runs only on Intel Pentium processors. Support for DEC (now Compaq) Alpha chips has been withdrawn.

RAM Memory

Windows 2000 Professional and Windows 2000 Server support up to 4GB (gigabytes) of memory, while Windows 2000 Advanced Server supports up to 8GB, and Windows 2000 Datacenter Server supports up to 64GB of memory.

System Bus

Windows 2000 will not support the Micro Channel system bus. Only ISA (Industry Standard Architecture), EISA (Extended ISA), and PCI (Peripheral Component Interconnect) can be used for a general-purpose system bus.

Hard Disk Space

The amount of free hard disk space required is dependent on a number of factors, especially in Windows 2000 Server. Among these factors are the following:

▼   The amount of memory in the system. Each 1MB of memory above 64MB requires 1MB of additional free disk space.

- The type of file system used. NT file system (NTFS) and FAT32 (file allocation table) are more efficient and are assumed in the minimum requirement. An additional 100 to 200MB of free disk space is required to use FAT.

- A network-based installation requires 100 to 200MB of additional free disk space to store additional files.

- An upgrade requires more space than a new installation to expand an existing user accounts database into *Active Directory,* which consolidates the access to all the resources on a network into a single hierarchical view and a single point of administration.

- ▲ The minimum required disk space assumes a normal installation of system components. If additional components are selected, additional disk space is required.

CD-ROM and Floppy Disk

A CD and a floppy disk are not required if a network-based installation is used. Also, a floppy disk drive is not required if the system can be booted from the CD-ROM drive.

Networking

A network card is not required if networking is not desired and a network-based installation is not used. If a network-based installation is used, it requires a suitable server to deliver the files.

Checking Hardware Compatibility

After you have checked and determined that your systems meet the minimum requirements for Windows 2000, you need to check to see if the particular brand and model of computers and component devices are compatible with the operating system. You can do this with the Hardware Compatibility List (Hcl.txt), available in the \Support folder on the Windows 2000 CD, or at http://www.microsoft.com/hcl/. Also, two other files in the root folder of the Windows 2000 CD, Read1st.txt and Relnotes.doc, contain late-breaking information on hardware usage and other information you need before you install.

TIP: You can save a lot of problem-resolution time by checking the HCL and making any necessary adjustments *before* installing Windows 2000.

When you check your hardware compatibility, you need to know the make and model of all the devices in your systems, and when you do the actual installation, you may need to know the settings on those devices. Even if you are fairly certain you know this information, it is a good idea to take an inventory of your systems before you start the installation.

Taking a System Inventory

There are two types of system inventory: a physical look at the devices, and an online look at how the system sees them.

Physical Inventory   The physical inventory requires that you open the computer and identify the circuit boards, disk drives, and other components. There are a great many types of computers, circuit boards, and disk drives, so it is not possible to describe how to do a physical inventory. If you don't know how, skip it, and the online inventory will have to suffice. If you do a physical inventory, here are the topics you need to consider, along with sample responses in parentheses (see "Online Inventory," next in this chapter for a complete list of topics that you need to handle with the system inventory):

TIP: If you have all the manuals and brochures or flyers that came with your equipment, you may be able to answer many of the physical inventory questions without opening the computer.

- ▼ Type of adapter card (network interface card, sound card, video adapter)
- ■ Make and model of the adapter card (3Com Etherlink XL PCI Combo, Creative Labs CT3930 Sound Blaster 32, Matrox Millennium II)
- ■ Type and position of card slot (ISA, EISA, PCI, or AGP; 1st, 2nd, or 3rd slot)
- ■ Settings on the adapter cards (interrupt request line, or IRQ; I/O port address; direct memory address, or DMA)

NOTE: The newer Plug and Play cards may not have settings on the card, because they are all handled with software.

- ■ Type, make, model, and size, if applicable, of disk drive (hard drive, IBM, DGHS-39110, 9.1GB; CD-ROM, Yamaha, CDRW6416SZ; floppy, Teac, 1.44MB)
- ▲ Type and position of disk drive interface (Small Computer System Interface, or SCSI, position 0 through 7 or 15; primary or secondary Integrated Device Electronics, or IDE, master or slave)

Online Inventory   The online inventory is done by recording information about your system that can be displayed on the screen or printed using your old operating system. The type and completeness of information that is available to you depends on the operating system you are using. In most cases, you get an initial startup message generated by the BIOS (basic input/output system) that provides a lot of information.

In Windows 95 or 98, you can get further information by opening the Start menu, selecting Settings | Control Panel, double-clicking System, choosing the Device Manager tab (shown in Figure 3-1), clicking Print, selecting System Summary, and clicking OK. This gives you a comprehensive report of the devices in your system, the resources (IRQs, I/O ports, DMA, and so on) they use, and the types and sizes of your disk drives. The first page of this report for one of my computers is shown in Figure 3-2.

In Windows NT 4, you can get additional information by opening the Start menu, selecting Programs | Administrative Tools | Windows NT Diagnostics (shown in Figure 3-3), clicking Print, making sure All Tabs and Summary are selected, and clicking OK. This also gives you a comprehensive report, although not as clear and to the point as the Resource Summary report generated in Windows 95 or 98. The first page of this report for one of my computers is shown in Figure 3-4.

NOTE: In Windows 2000, you can print a Resource Summary report similar to, and possibly an improvement on, the Windows 98 Resource Summary report. This report is available by opening the Start menu and selecting Settings | Control Panel | System | Hardware | Device Manager | View | Print.

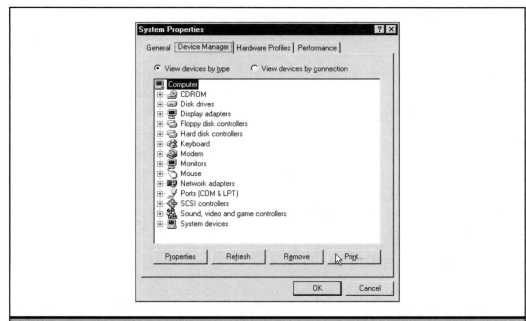

Figure 3-1. The System Properties dialog box allows you to print the Resource Summary report

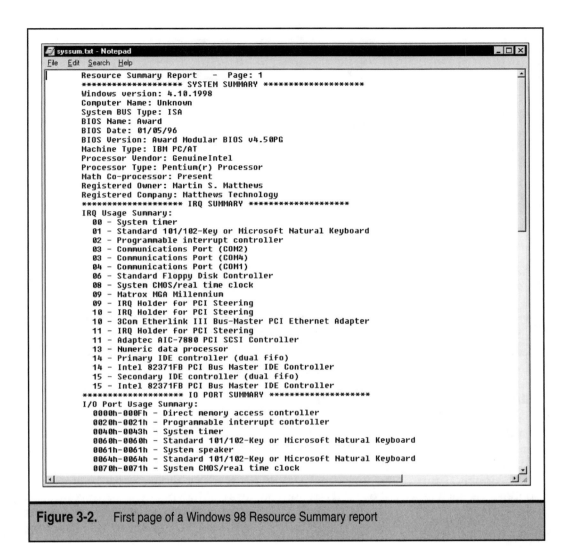

```
syssum.txt - Notepad
File  Edit  Search  Help
     Resource Summary Report   -   Page: 1
     ******************** SYSTEM SUMMARY ********************
     Windows version: 4.10.1998
     Computer Name: Unknown
     System BUS Type: ISA
     BIOS Name: Award
     BIOS Date: 01/05/96
     BIOS Version: Award Modular BIOS v4.50PG
     Machine Type: IBM PC/AT
     Processor Vendor: GenuineIntel
     Processor Type: Pentium(r) Processor
     Math Co-processor: Present
     Registered Owner: Martin S. Matthews
     Registered Company: Matthews Technology
     ******************** IRQ SUMMARY ********************
     IRQ Usage Summary:
       00 - System timer
       01 - Standard 101/102-Key or Microsoft Natural Keyboard
       02 - Programmable interrupt controller
       03 - Communications Port (COM2)
       03 - Communications Port (COM4)
       04 - Communications Port (COM1)
       06 - Standard Floppy Disk Controller
       08 - System CMOS/real time clock
       09 - Matrox MGA Millennium
       09 - IRQ Holder for PCI Steering
       10 - IRQ Holder for PCI Steering
       10 - 3Com Etherlink III Bus-Master PCI Ethernet Adapter
       11 - IRQ Holder for PCI Steering
       11 - Adaptec AIC-7880 PCI SCSI Controller
       13 - Numeric data processor
       14 - Primary IDE controller (dual fifo)
       14 - Intel 82371FB PCI Bus Master IDE Controller
       15 - Secondary IDE controller (dual fifo)
       15 - Intel 82371FB PCI Bus Master IDE Controller
     ******************** IO PORT SUMMARY ********************
     I/O Port Usage Summary:
       0000h-000Fh - Direct memory access controller
       0020h-0021h - Programmable interrupt controller
       0040h-0043h - System timer
       0060h-0060h - Standard 101/102-Key or Microsoft Natural Keyboard
       0061h-0061h - System speaker
       0064h-0064h - Standard 101/102-Key or Microsoft Natural Keyboard
       0070h-0071h - System CMOS/real time clock
```

Figure 3-2.   First page of a Windows 98 Resource Summary report

The end result of both the physical and online inventory should be a system inventory form containing the information in Table 3-2 (example answers are in italics).

For your systems, you may need to add or remove fields from those shown in Table 3-2, but creating and using such a form will help you prepare for the installation of Windows 2000.

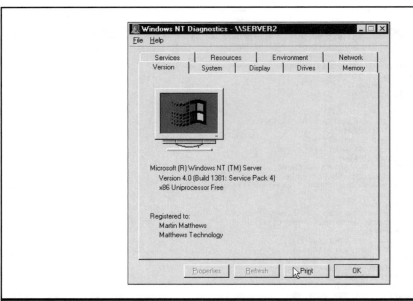

Figure 3-3.   The Windows NT Diagnostics dialog box allows you to print the Diagnostics report

Handling Incompatible Devices

If you find devices in your inventory that are not on the HCL and not mentioned in the Read1st.txt or Relnotes.doc files, it will often be the case that they will work fine using general-purpose drivers in Windows 2000. The only way to know for sure is to try to install Windows 2000 and see what happens. If there is a problem, you may be told about it while running Setup, or the device may simply not work when you are done. If this is a boot device, such as a SCSI or RAID (redundant array of independent disks) controller, you will not be able to finish the installation. The solution is to contact the manufacturer and obtain a Windows 2000 driver from them (you may be able to download it from the Internet).

If you have a third-party driver for hard drives that you want to use with Windows 2000, watch for a prompt early in the installation process that asks you to press F6. Then, follow the onscreen instructions to load the disk with the driver files and install the drivers. Chapter 5 will further discuss using third-party drivers.

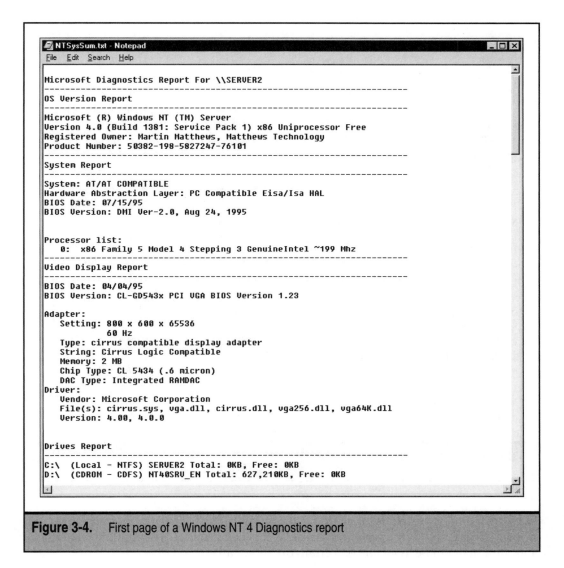

Figure 3-4.   First page of a Windows NT 4 Diagnostics report

MAKING THE CORRECT INSTALLATION CHOICES

During the installation process, Windows 2000 Setup gives you a number of choices on how you want it installed. If you consider these choices before you do the installation,

System Name: *Server1*	System Type: *Server/Workstation*	Domain Name: *Domain1*	Date: *12-23-2001*
Processor 1: *Pentium II 350*	Processor 2: *Model and speed*	BIOS & Date: *Award, 9-15-98*	Power Management: *Enabled*
Memory: *128MB*	Hard Disk 1: *SCSI-0, 10GB*	Hard Disk 2: *Interface and size*	Hard Disk 3: *Interface and size*
CD-ROM Drive: *SCSI-1, 32x*	Floppy Drive: *1.44MB*	Tape Drive: *SCSI-3, 8GB*	Other Drive: *DVD, CD-RW*
Mouse: *PS/2 or Serial*	Keyboard: *PS/2 or Serial*	SCSI Controller: *Adaptec AHA-2940*	RAID Controller: *Make and model*
Modem Card: *U.S. Robotics 56K Fax* *ISA, COM 2, IRQ 3* *I/O Port 3E8-3EF* *DMA – no*	Network Card: *3Com Etherlink III* *PCI, IRQ 9* *I/O Port B800-B81F* *DMA – no*	Sound Card: *Creative PCI128* *PCI, IRQ 5* *I/O Port B400-B43F* *DMA – 1*	Video Card: *Matrox G200* *AGP, IRQ 10* *I/O Port 3B0-3DF* *DMA – no*
External Modem: *Make and model* *Com 1-3, USB*	PCMCIA Slot 1: *Device, make and* *model*	PCMCIA Slot 2: *Device, make and* *model*	Parallel Port: *Device, make and* *model, ECP?*
COM1: *Device, make and* *model, IRQ*	COM2: *Device, make and* *model, IRQ*	COM3: *Device, make and* *model, IRQ*	COM4: *Device, make and* *model, IRQ*
USB Port 1: *Device, make and* *model*	USB Port 2: *Device, make and* *model*	Infrared Port: *Yes/No*	Video In/Out: *Yes/No*

Table 3-2.   System Inventory Information

and take the time to determine which choices will be best for your operation, you will probably end up better satisfying your needs. Some of the choices depend on earlier decisions and may not be available on certain decision paths.

Deciding to Upgrade or Install

Upgrading, in this case, is replacing a currently installed operating system with Windows 2000 in the same disk partition. *Installing*, on the other hand, is loading Windows 2000 in a separate disk partition without an operating system, where either the OS has been removed or the partition has never had one (also called a "clean install").

You can upgrade to the various versions of Windows 2000 only from the following operating systems:

▼ **Windows 2000 Professional:**
Windows 95
Windows 98
Windows NT 3.51 Workstation
Windows NT 4 Workstation

▲ **Windows 2000 Server:**
Windows NT 3.51 Server
Windows NT 4 Server or Terminal Server

If you are not currently running one of the identified upgradable products, you can either upgrade to one of those products and then upgrade to Windows 2000, or you can do a clean install.

The major reasons to upgrade, if you can, are the following:

▼ To preserve all the current settings (such as users, rights, and permissions), applications, and data on your computer. Your current environment is preserved intact while upgrading to a new operating system.

▲ To make the installation of Windows 2000 simpler. Most of the installation decisions are made for you, using the settings in the current operating system.

The major reasons to do a clean install are the following:

▼ To get around an operating system that cannot be upgraded.

■ To dual boot into both the old operating system and Windows 2000. This allows you to use either operating system.

▲ To really clean up your hard disks, which makes them more efficient, gets rid of unused files, and gives you back a lot of disk space.

If you can either upgrade or do a clean install (setting aside dual booting for a moment; see the next section), this decision is between preserving your current system with all of its settings, applications, and inefficient and wasted space, and doing a really clean install. The clean install gives your new operating system an environment not hampered by all that has been done on the computer in the past, *but* it is a *lot* more work. With a clean install, you have to reinstall all of your applications and reestablish all of your settings. This is not an easy decision. It may seem like it is a "no-brainer" to keep your current environment and forgo all the extra work, but are you really that happy with your current environment? Installing a new operating system is an excellent time to clean house and set up your system the way it should be, even if it takes a fair amount of extra time. Consider this decision carefully.

Deciding Whether to Dual Boot

Dual booting allows you to choose from among several operating systems each time you start your computer. If you are unsure if you want to switch to Windows 2000, or if you have an application that runs only on another operating system, then dual booting gives you a good solution. For example, if you want to keep Windows NT 4 Server and be able to use it after installing Windows 2000 Server, or if you have an application that runs under Windows 98 but not Windows 2000 Professional, then in both of these circumstances, dual booting provides the means to do what you want. If you are thinking of dual booting as a disaster recovery strategy for those instances in which you can't boot Windows 2000, that is not a good solution, because Windows 2000 has a number of built-in disaster recovery tools, such as Safe Mode, that assist in repairing the problem that caused the disaster. Safe Mode and other disaster recovery tools are discussed in Chapter 14.

You can dual boot Windows 2000 with MS-DOS, OS/2, Windows 3.*x*, Windows 95, Windows 98, and Windows NT 4. In all cases but Windows 98, you must have installed the other operating system before Windows 2000. If you are installing Windows 2000 on a computer that already has a dual-boot environment with OS/2 and any other product, Windows 2000 Setup will create a dual-boot environment with the *last operating system used*. So if you currently dual boot between OS/2 and MS-DOS, and MS-DOS was the last operating system used, Windows 2000 Setup will install dual booting between Windows 2000 and MS-DOS.

Dual booting also has significant drawbacks, such as these:

▼ You must install Windows 2000 in a separate partition so that it doesn't overwrite any of the files belonging to the original operating system. This means that you must reinstall all of your applications you want to run under Windows 2000 and you must reestablish all of your settings.

■ You have to handle some complex file-system compatibility issues and you can't share files that use the latest features of Windows 2000. See the discussion following this list of bulleted items.

■ Windows NT 4's Defrag and Chkdsk won't work on Windows 2000's NTFS partition.

■ The Plug and Play features of Windows 95, Windows 98, and Windows 2000, in a dual-booting situation, could cause a device to not work properly in one operating system because the other operating system reconfigured it.

■ Windows NT 4's Emergency Repair Disk won't work after installing Windows 2000.

■ Dual booting takes up a lot of disk space with two complete operating systems.

▲ Dual booting makes the operating environment much more complex than it would be otherwise.

When you dual boot, both operating systems must be able to read the files that you want to share between them. This means that the shared files must be stored in a file system that both operating systems can use. When you install Windows 2000, you have a choice of NTFS, FAT, and FAT32 files systems (see the next section, "Choosing the File System"). NTFS has significant new features in Windows 2000, such as Active Directory, improved security, and file encryption, but these features are not usable by Windows NT. Also, Windows NT 4 can only access the latest NTFS (NTFS 5) files if you have installed Service Pack 4 or later, and you still cannot use all the features of NTFS 5. Therefore, if you choose NTFS as your common operating system, you run the risk of Windows NT not being able to access the files. On the other hand, if you choose FAT, the lowest common denominator, you give up many of the benefits of a more powerful file system, such as file-level security and large disks, and FAT32 cannot be used by Windows NT.

NOTE: Windows 2000 can't be installed on, or directly access files on, a volume that has been compressed with DoubleSpace or DriveSpace.

One possible file system solution when dual booting Windows NT and Windows 2000 is to use FAT for the Windows NT partition where all shared files are stored and use NTFS for the Windows 2000 partition, knowing that Windows NT may not be able to access the files in the NTFS partition.

Dual booting is a compromise and doesn't give you all that you can get out of Windows 2000. It is therefore not recommended unless you have a need that is not handled any other way, such as an application that does not run under Windows 2000, and even there, you might leave it on a dedicated server and move most of your work to another server with Windows 2000.

NOTE: Although Windows NT may not be able to access some NTFS files on the same computer in a dual-boot situation, it, along with all other operating systems, can access those same files if the access is over a network (the server translates the files as they are passed to the network).

Choosing the File System

If you just read the preceding section on dual booting, you might think that choosing the file system to use with Windows 2000 is complex. In fact, it is not. In all but the dual-booting circumstance just described, you want to use NTFS. NTFS provides many significant advantages that far outweigh any consideration for FAT or FAT32. Among the reasons to use NTFS are that it does the following:

▼　Allows and fully supports the use of disk volumes up to 2TB (terabytes), and files can be as large as the total disk volume. Files on FAT are limited to 2GB, and files on FAT32 are limited to 4GB.

- Provides much more efficient large file and volume handling than does FAT or FAT32.

- Allows the use of file-level security, wherein you can identify how individual files are shared. In FAT and FAT32, this cannot be done below the folder level.

- Supports Active Directory and domains, which is not available with FAT and FAT32, for improved security, flexibility, and manageability.

- Allows the encryption of individual files, which is not available with FAT and FAT32, for a very high level of security.

- Provides for *sparse files,* which are very large files that only take up the disk space needed for the portion of the file that has been written.

▲ Supports disk quotas that control how much space an individual user can consume.

Unless you have to dual boot a system, you want to choose to use the NTFS file system. You can convert existing files to it during installation, or do it afterward by using the Convert.exe file located in the \Winnt\System32 folder.

Deciding on Partitioning

Partitioning divides a single hard disk into two or more partitions, or *volumes.* These partitions are given drive letters, such as *D, E,* or *F,* and so are called *logical drives.* When you do a clean install of Windows 2000, you are shown the current partitioning of the boot disk and asked if you want to add or remove partitions. When you have the partitions the way you want, you can determine on which partition you want to install Windows 2000. There are two main reasons for partitioning: to have two different file systems on the same drive, and to provide a logical separation of information or files. If you dual boot, you need to use at least two different partitions to keep the two operating systems separate so that the Windows 2000 installation does not replace any of the original operating system's files. Another reason for a separate partition is if you want to use the Remote Installation Service to remotely install Windows 2000 Professional on workstations.

When you are considering the partitioning you want, you also need to consider the size of each partition. For Windows 2000 Server by itself, you should probably allocate at least 2GB. While it could be smaller, it is wise to leave yourself some extra space. If you are working on a large, active server, you could allocate as much as 10GB for such things as Active Directory information, user accounts, RAM swap files, optional components, and future Service Packs.

Under many circumstances, you want only a single partition on a hard disk, to give yourself the maximum flexibility to use up to the entire disk. There are also many ways to manage your partitioning after you complete installation (see Chapter 12).

Choosing the Type of License

When you install Windows 2000 Server, you are asked if you want to use Per Seat or Per Server licensing, and if you choose Per Server, you must specify the number of Client Access Licenses (CALs) you want assigned to the server.

Per Server Licensing

Per Server licensing is licensing the *concurrent connections* to the server. Any workstation can use one of the connections, but you can have only so many connections at any one time. Each connection requires one CAL. The individual workstations do not need their own CAL; they can share several so long as they are not all connected at the same time, but they do need a license for their own operating system, such as Windows 2000 Professional or Windows 98. Per Server licensing usually is used for smaller businesses that have only one server, and it should be used if you don't know which licensing option to use. You can switch from Per Server to Per Seat without penalty, but you can't go the other way. You should also use Per Server licensing for Internet or remote access servers where the users are probably not licensed as Windows 2000 clients.

Per Seat Licensing

Per Seat licensing is licensing each *individual computer* that accesses the server. This means that each workstation has its own CAL in addition to its own operating system license and can use the CAL to access any number of servers. The servers can have any number of concurrent connections, so long as each connection has its own CAL. Larger companies with more than one server normally use Per Seat licensing. If you are going to install Terminal Services, you want to use Per Seat licensing unless you are going to use the Terminal Services Internet Connector.

The licensing decision is purely based on what you will be doing. If you have only one server or are primarily going to use the server being installed for Internet services, then you want to use Per Server licensing. If you have multiple servers or are going to use Terminal Services, you want Per Seat licensing.

Choosing Optional Components

There are a large number of optional components that you can choose to install while you are installing Windows 2000 Server. A simple expedient is to just accept the default selections, but there are so many possible things you might want to do with the server that it is a good idea to go through the options ahead of time and figure out what you need. In Windows 2000 Professional, you are not given a choice of selecting the components you want to install outside of networking, but in both Professional and Server, you can install additional components after you have completed the initial installation using Add/Remove Programs in the Control Panel. Although additional components add capability to your system, they also take up disk space and possibly utilize resources such as memory and CPU cycles if they are running. It is therefore important to install only the components that you are certain you will need.

The first step is to look at the major services that are available within Windows 2000 Server, as shown in Table 3-3, and determine which are required on the server you are installing.

The second step is to look at the details of the major services that you selected and determine which of the detail components fit the needs of the system you are installing. Following is a hierarchical list of all the options in Windows 2000 Server. Where the item is not self-explanatory, a brief explanation is provided.

Service	Function
Certificate Services	Provides the means to authenticate e-mail and Internet web transactions
Indexing Service	Provides the means to index the text in documents on a hard disk so that full text searches can be done very quickly
Internet Information Services (IIS)	Allows the distribution of web pages over the Internet or an intranet; it is a web or FTP server
Message Queuing Services	Provides the messaging services needed by applications that are distributed over a network, even when part of the network is down
Networking Services	Allows the transfer of information among both local and remote computers
Remote Installation Services	Provides for the remote installation of Windows 2000 Professional on clients that support remote booting
Terminal Services	Allows the use of minimal workstations or "thin clients" that run their applications on the server, similar to a time-sharing system

Table 3-3.   Major Optional Services Available in Windows 2000 Server

Accessories and Utilities   Tools and small applications that make use of the computer easier.

▼   **Accessibility Wizard**   Sets up the system for special vision, hearing, and mobility needs.

■   **Accessories**

 ■   *Calculator*

 ■   *Character Map*   Provides special characters and symbols that can be inserted in documents.

 ■   *Clipboard Viewer*   Allows looking at the information on the Clipboard.

 ■   *Desktop Wallpaper*   Provides background images that can be used for the desktop.

 ■   *Document Templates*   Provides document templates for the most common programs.

 ■   *Mouse Pointers*   Provides alternative mouse pointers.

 ■   *Object Packager*   Allows a linked or embedded object to be inserted in a document that is not OLE (object linking and embedding) compliant.

 ■   *Paint*   Provides the means to create and edit simple bitmapped pictures.

 ■   *WordPad*   Provides the means to create and edit short documents.

■   **Communications**

 ■   *Chat*   Allows text communications with other Windows users over a network.

 ■   *HyperTerminal*   Allows direct connection with other computers using a modem and phone line.

 ■   *Phone Dialer*   Allows dialing a phone using a modem connected to the phone line.

■   **Games**

 ■   *FreeCell*   Provides a logical form of the solitaire card game.

 ■   *Minesweeper*   Provides a strategy game.

 ■   *Pinball*

 ■   *Solitaire*

▲   **Multimedia**

 ■   *CD Player*   Allows playing music CDs on a properly equipped computer.

 ■   *DVD Player*   Allows playing movie DVDs on a properly equipped computer.

- *Media Player*   Allows playing audio and video files on a properly equipped computer.
- *Sample Sounds*   Provides sounds that can be played back on a properly equipped computer.
- *Sound Recorder*   Allows the recording of sound on a properly equipped computer.
- *Utopia Sound Scheme*   Provides a set of sounds that can replace the default sounds used by Windows 2000.
- *Volume Control*

Certificate Services   Provides the means to authenticate e-mail and Internet web transactions.

- ▼ **Certificate Services CA**   Creates a certification authority (CA) that can issue digital certificates for use with public key encryption of files sent over a network.
- ▲ **Certificate Services Web Enrollment Support**   Provides the means to request, receive, and authenticate digital certificates from others.

Indexing Service   Provides the means to index the text in documents on a hard disk or web site so that full text searches can be done very quickly.

Internet Information Services (IIS)   Allows the distribution of web pages over the Internet or an intranet—a web server.

- ▼ **Common Files**   Provides files required by other IIS components.
- ■ **Documentation**   Provides information on IIS.
- ■ **File Transfer Protocol (FTP) Server**   Allows the transfer of files over the Internet or an intranet using FTP.
- ■ **FrontPage 2000 Server Extensions**   Provides server support for many of FrontPage's features.
- ■ **Internet Information Services Snap-In**   Allows the management of IIS from the Microsoft Management Console (MMC).
- ■ **Internet Services Manager (HTML)**   Allows the management of IIS from a web browser such as Internet Explorer.
- ■ **NNTP Service**   Allows the use of the Network News Transfer Protocol (NNTP) in IIS to handle Internet or intranet newsgroups.
- ■ **SMTP Service**   Allows the use of the Simple Mail Transfer Protocol (SMTP) in IIS to handle Internet or intranet mail service.

- **Visual InterDev RAD Remote Deployment Support**   Provides for remote application deployment (RAD) using IIS.
- ▲ **World Wide Web Server**   Provides for the publishing of web pages on the Internet or an intranet.

Management and Monitoring Tools   Allows network performance monitoring and improvement.

- ▼ **Connection Manager Component**   Provides support for client dialing and the updating of client phone books.
- **Network Monitor Tools**   Allows the analysis of information transferred over a network.
- ▲ **Simple Network Management Protocol**   Allows the monitoring and reporting of activity in network devices.

Message Queuing Services   Provides the messaging services needed by applications that are distributed over a network, even when part of the network is down.

Networking Services   Allows the transfer of information among both local and remote computers.

- ▼ **COM Internet Services Proxy**   Allows applications that are widely distributed to communicate using HTTP (Hypertext Transfer Protocol) and IIS.
- **Domain Name System (DNS)**   Allows the use of server names instead of IP (Internet Protocol) addresses.
- **Dynamic Host Configuration Protocol (DHCP)**   Provides the dynamic assignment of IP addresses as they are needed so that clients do not need a permanent assigned IP address.
- **Internet Authentication Service (IAS)**   Provides the accounting and authentication service needed for dial-up networking and virtual private networking (VPN).
- **QoS Admission Control Service**   Allows the allocation and control of network bandwidth to applications, thus determining their quality of service (QoS).
- **Simple TCP/IP Services**   Provides the Character Generator, Daytime Discard, Echo, and Quote of the Day services used in TCP/IP.
- **Site Server ILS Services**   Maintains current user information based on the contents of TCP/IP stacks.

▲ **Windows Internet Naming Service (WINS)** Allows the use of names in place of IP addresses for older versions of Windows networking.

Other Network File and Print Services Allows Macintosh and UNIX users to access a Windows 2000 Server.

▼ File Services for Macintosh
■ Print Services for Macintosh
▲ Print Services for UNIX

Remote Installation Services Provides for the remote installation of Windows 2000 Professional on clients that support remote booting.

Remote Storage Provides for the automatic transfer of infrequently used files to removable media such as tape, as well as the automatic retrieval of those files when needed.

Script Debugger Provides for the development support and debugging of VBScript and JScript programs.

Terminal Services Allows the use of minimal workstations or "thin clients" that run their applications on the server, similar to a time-sharing system.

▼ **Client Creator Files** Creates installation disks for the Terminal Services clients.
▲ **Enable Terminal Services** Loads Terminal Services on the computer.

Terminal Services Licensing Allows the registration and tracking of Terminal Services clients and is required with Terminal Services.

Windows Media Services Provides streaming of multimedia (audio and video) to users on a network.

▼ **Windows Media Services** Creates a Windows Media server.
▲ **Widows Media Services Administrator** The means to manage Windows Media server.

Choosing Network Naming Conventions

In a network, each server and workstation requires a name with which to address each other. With TCP/IP, which is used in many local area networks (LANs), on the Internet, and is strongly recommended with Windows 2000, each server and workstation has a numeric IP address as well as an alphabetic name. When you set up Windows 2000 Server, you can choose how to assign IP addresses and how to translate a name into an IP address (called *name resolution*).

Assigning IP Addresses

IP addresses can be either automatically and dynamically assigned by the server identified as the domain controller or manually assigned by an administrator. In the Network and Dial-up Connections control panel, the Properties dialog box for TCP/IP allows you to specify the automatic assignment of an IP address or the entry of a static number. If you want to use the automatic assignment, then the server has to have the generation of IP numbers enabled. To do this, you must install and configure DHCP, which then will provide an IP address to each server and workstation on the network each time they log on. The domain controller itself, though, needs a static IP address, which is assigned during installation.

If you have a small network, the manual assignment of IP addresses is not a problem. You can either get a series of IP addresses from an Internet service provider (ISP) or use a series of IP addresses not used on the Internet, such as 10.0.0.1 to 10.255.255.255. So, if you have a five-member network, they could be assigned 10.0.0.1 through 10.0.0.5.

For a network of any size, especially one that is growing, it makes a great deal of sense to install and enable DHCP and allow it to dynamically assign IP addresses. This greatly simplifies adding and removing workstations and servers, from an IP address standpoint.

Resolving Network Names

Name resolution allows easily remembered names to be used to refer to workstations and servers and automatically translates the name into an IP address that is used by TCP/IP. This is particularly important when IP addresses are dynamically assigned, and thus changed, every time the computer logs on to the network. In Windows 2000, name resolution can be done using the Domain Name System (DNS) or Windows Internet Naming Service (WINS).

WINS is an older technology, and if you have clients using Windows NT or an earlier Microsoft operating system, then WINS should be included in a domain controller. WINS is installed as an optional networking component (see "Choosing Optional Components," earlier in the chapter). The server on which WINS is installed must have a static IP address. WINS is not required for Windows 2000 clients.

DNS is needed for Windows 2000 clients, Active Directory, Internet web browsing, and e-mail. DNS is automatically installed when a domain controller is created, and can be installed as an optional component. DNS also requires the server it is on to have a static IP address.

Deciding to Use Domains or Workgroups

During the installation of networking, which is part of Windows 2000 Server Setup, you are asked if you want to use domains or workgroups. A *workgroup* is a simple networking structure used to share folders and printers with a minimum of security. In a workgroup, there is no server structure and little difference between servers and clients. Workgroups are used only in the smallest networks.

A *domain* has a much more sophisticated structure that groups networking resources and user accounts under a domain name, provides for three levels of servers that can keep automatically replicated copies of the same information, and generally provides a high level of security. Windows 2000's Active Directory requires one or more domains.

Unless you have a very small network, under ten users, and very little potential for growth, choosing to use a domain is strongly recommended.

PREPARING SYSTEMS FOR INSTALLATION

Installing an operating system entails a moderate risk that you could lose some or all the information on the computer, which makes it a good idea to back up the hard disks before the installation. Installing an operating system is also a great opportunity to clean up and make the system more efficient. Additionally, you need to do certain things to the system to make sure that the installation runs smoothly. All of these tasks are included in the following steps to prepare for an operating system installation:

▼ Back up all hard disks

■ Inventory current software

■ Clean up current files

■ Upgrade hardware

▲ Disable conflicting hardware and software

Backing Up All Hard Disks

In a server environment, backing up is probably better disciplined than it is for a client workstation, unless the server also takes charge of backing up the workstation. Therefore, backing up may or may not be a routine task. In any case, it is important to perform a thorough backup prior to installing a new operating system. This should include all data files, including mail files, address books, templates, settings, My Documents, favorites, cookies, and history. Backing up application files not only is unnecessary (usually), because you should have copies on the distribution disks, but it is also very difficult, because the application files are in several folders.

The best technique for backing up data files if you don't already have a file list is to work down through a hard disk, folder by folder, looking at each of the files within each folder. This is definitely a tedious task, but very worthwhile not only for backing up, but also for the following cleanup and application inventory tasks. In many cases, you can back up entire folders if you know all the files are data files. In other cases, many of the files in a folder are application files, and you do not want to back them up, although a few files likely are custom templates, settings, or data files that you do want to preserve.

The tools (hardware and software) that you use to do a back up depends on what you have available. Backup within Windows NT 4 was fairly crude (Windows 2000 is better, but you need to back up before installing it); Windows 98 has a reasonable Backup program. The best choice is one of several third-party programs, such as VERITAS's (previously Seagate Software's) Backup Exec (http://www.veritas.com/). Backup media can include tape, removable hard disks, a Zip drive, writable or rewritable CDs, optical drives, or even a different hard disk on another system. Whatever you use, make sure that you can read it back in your Windows 2000 system.

TIP: With the very low cost of large hard disks, it might be worthwhile to get one just to hold the latest backup of one or more systems.

Another way to do a backup is to make a mirror copy of a hard disk onto another hard disk using products such as PowerQuest's Drive Copy for a one-to-one copy, or Drive Image for a compressed copy. This way, if you have a problem with the installation, you simply have to swap drives or restore a compressed image of the drive.

Another technique of keeping data handy and easy to back up is to put all of your data files in folders within My Documents. This is the default of Windows 2000 and makes it easy to determine which folders contain data. Similarly, if you create a separate partition on your hard drive in which you only store data, you not only can easily determine your data folders, but you also can reformat the partition with your operating system and application files without disturbing your data.

Inventorying Current Software

As you are going through the hard disks to back them up, you should also take an inventory of the applications on the disk, so that you know what was there in case you need to reinstall it. Separately from the disk review, note what is on the Desktop, the Start menu, the Programs menu, and on the taskbar if the system you are upgrading from is Windows 95 or 98. Additionally, open Add/Remove Programs from the Control Panel and note what programs it shows as being installed, as well as the Windows components that are being used. For each application, note the installed version, whether it is still used, what its supporting files are (such as templates and settings), and where the files are stored on the hard disk. (This latter information needs to be fed back to the backup process to make sure these files are included.) Finally, you need to make sure you have the distribution disks for each application and note where they are kept. These steps will assure that you have the knowledge, application files, and data files necessary to restore the applications that were running on the computer before Windows 2000 was installed.

Cleaning Up Current Files

Most of us mean to clean up the disks we are responsible for, to get rid of the files and applications that are no longer used, but few of us get around to it. It is a very difficult chore, and who is to say that an application or file will never be needed again.

Given that you have done a thorough job of backing up your data files and have a complete inventory of applications, then the question of whether a file will be needed again is moot, because you can always restore the file or application if you need it. That leaves only the objection that it is a long, arduous task—and it is.

The very best way to clean up a hard disk is also the easiest and the scariest because it is so final—reformatting the hard drive and reloading only the applications and files that you know will be immediately used. This puts a lot of pressure on backing up well and making sure you have a good application inventory, but given that you do, then reformatting the hard drive is a very good solution. Also, it is still a fair amount of work, because of the time to reload what you want on the hard drive.

Cleaning up a server adds another dimension covering the entire user- and permission-related information. Basically, the users and permissions database must be audited and unused and duplicate entries must be removed. Even harder is cleaning up the user and shared folders on the server. Again, these are tasks that get put off, but they are truly necessary if you are going to have a clean and efficient system. Explaining to users that you have a safe backup, and that if they really need a file you'll add it back, helps convince them that it is okay to remove from the server the lightly used (no one will admit it is never used) information.

Upgrading Hardware

Like cleaning up a hard disk, doing hardware upgrades gets put off because it can disrupt a system. So again, use the "new operating system" excuse to get it done. Use the inventory that you took earlier to determine what hardware you need or want to upgrade, and purchase and install the hardware before installing Windows 2000, so the new operating system has the benefit of the new hardware. In doing this, consider upgrading the BIOS on the motherboard by checking the manufacturer's web site to see whether an upgrade is available and, if so, whether it would benefit you.

Disabling Conflicting Hardware and Software

Certain hardware and software, if it is running, can cause Setup to fail. For that reason, you need to take the following steps on each computer to prepare for a Windows 2000 installation:

▼ Disable any UPS (uninterruptible power supply) device connected to the computer's serial port by removing the serial cable from the computer. The UPS can cause problems with Setup's device-detection process. You can reconnect the cable after Setup is complete.

■ If you are using disk mirroring, it needs to be disabled prior to starting Setup. You can restart disk mirroring when Setup completes.

■ Windows 2000 cannot reside on or access either DriveSpace or DoubleSpace volumes, so if you want to use such volumes with Windows 2000, they must be uncompressed. Make sure you have backed up and inventoried the volume first, because it is possible that uncompressing will lose information.

▲ Stop all programs that are running, especially any virus-detection programs, before starting Setup. These programs may give you spurious virus warning messages while Setup is writing to the disk. Sometimes these programs are automatically started when the system is booted, so you may have to go to some lengths to find and stop them (look in the \Windows\Start Menu\Programs\StartUp folder and in the Autoexec.bat file).

Preparing a Windows NT Domain

If your systems currently include a Windows NT domain, then, in addition to the preceding backup and other preparatory steps, you need to take two additional steps to insure the domain's integrity:

▼ You must upgrade the primary domain controller (PDC) first. So to protect the domain, select a backup domain controller (BDC) that can be promoted to PDC, and remove it from the system by disconnecting its network cable. If the upgrade to Windows 2000 fails, you can reconnect the BDC and promote it to PDC. If the upgrade succeeds, you reconnect the BDC and upgrade it as you do any other BDC.

▲ When a Windows NT domain is upgraded to a Windows 2000 domain, it will greatly expand the user accounts database to handle the requirements for Active Directory. For this reason, you want to leave plenty of extra disk space for this expansion. While the minimum free disk space for a Windows 2000 Server upgrade is roughly 1GB, having between 2 and 4GB or even more is not unreasonable, depending on the size of the network.

PLANNING A WINDOWS 2000 MIGRATION

Going through the tasks described so far in this chapter for a server and several workstations is a fair amount of work; doing it for a number of servers and many workstations is a major undertaking. In both cases, having a solid plan for how it will be accomplished is most helpful, and in the large installation case, it is mandatory.

A migration plan must reflect the organization it is designed for, but most plans should cover the following steps:

1. Identify what computers are to be upgraded or installed with Windows 2000 Server or Professional and the order in which they will be completed.

2. Identify the hardware that needs to be acquired and installed so that step 1 can be accomplished.

3. Develop a detailed list of tasks needed to complete steps 1 and 2.

4. Identify who will perform the tasks in step 3.

5. Develop a timeline for completing the tasks in step 3 given the labor identified in step 4.

6. Determine a set of dates on which to do the installation that will provide the minimum amount of disruption to the company's normal activities. A long weekend is often a good idea to everyone except those doing the changeover.

7. Develop a budget for the software, hardware, and labor specified in the preceding steps.

8. Identify realistically the possible disruptions to the company's business and the cost of such disruptions.

9. Identify the benefits of changing over to Windows 2000 and how those benefits translate into reduced costs and improved revenues.

Most organizations of any size require a plan such as this, and upper management will look long and hard at the results of steps 7 through 9. It is, of course, not a simple numerical comparison. The dollars in step 7 are hard, out-of-pocket funds, and the dollars in steps 8 and 9 may be hard to identify. The real question is whether the benefits of Windows 2000 are worth the costs, and how well could the company get along without the changeover. Every organization has to answer that question for itself.

Carrying out a changeover from one operating system to another is a very serious undertaking. Companies have been significantly harmed when it was poorly done, and have benefited greatly when it was done correctly. There are three key elements to success:

▼ Have a detailed knowledge of your current computers and networking system and what you want to achieve with Windows 2000.

■ Have a detailed plan of how you are going to carry out the conversion with minimal cost and disruption to the organization.

▲ Communicate continually and exhaustively with everyone involved.

It is my opinion that Windows 2000 provides very significant benefits to most organizations, as discussed in Chapters 1 and 2. Only you can determine if those benefits are worth the cost to your organization and then make sure that the conversion process does not erode the net value.

CHAPTER 4

Installing Windows 2000 Server

W ith the preparation described in Chapter 3 completed, you are ready to start the actual installation of Windows 2000 Server. If you have not read Chapter 3 or completed its preparatory steps, I strongly recommend you do that before continuing here.

There are a number of ways that Windows 2000 Server can be installed, but they fall into three categories:

▼ **Manually**   A person sits in front of the computer to be installed and, in real time, does the installation on that machine.

■ **Automated**   A script or answer file is used to carry out the installation, so a person does not have stay in front of the computer being installed.

▲ **Remotely**   A person sits in front of a server and performs the installation on a computer across the network. The installation can be manual or automated.

In this chapter, the manual approach, with many variations, is described in detail. In Chapter 5, the automated approach will be described along with the manual approach for Windows 2000 Professional. The remote approach requires remotely bootable network interface cards and motherboards that support them, as well as a dedicated server or volume on a server. Since this hardware is rare, remote installation will not be covered here.

The process of installing Windows 2000 Server, independent of the approach, has three distinct phases, each of which needs its own discussion:

1. Starting Setup
2. Running Setup
3. Configuring a server

STARTING SETUP

Setup can be started either over a network or locally, again independent of the approach. They both have a lot in common, but manually starting over a network is discussed first.

NOTE: Installing over a network is different than installing remotely. Installing over a network reverses the positions. You are in front of the machine being installed, accessing the network to get the installation files.

Starting over a Network

If you are active on a network where you can access a hard drive or CD-ROM drive on another computer, you can install Windows 2000 Server using files on that computer. Use these steps to do that:

1. On a server or any other computer on the network (I'll call this the "Setup server"), insert the Windows 2000 Server distribution CD in the CD-ROM drive.

2. Either copy the \I386 folder from the Windows 2000 Server distribution CD to the hard disk Setup server and then share that folder, or share the CD-ROM drive on that computer.

3. On the installation computer, using the tools available in its operating system, locate the other computer over the network and either the folder in which the I386 contents were placed or the CD-ROM drive.

4. If you are in DOS or Windows 3.*x* and in the correct directory or folder, run Winnt.exe.

5. If you are in Windows 95, Windows 98, Windows NT 3.51, Windows NT 4, or Windows 2000 and in the correct folder, double-click Winnt32.exe, as shown in Figure 4-1.

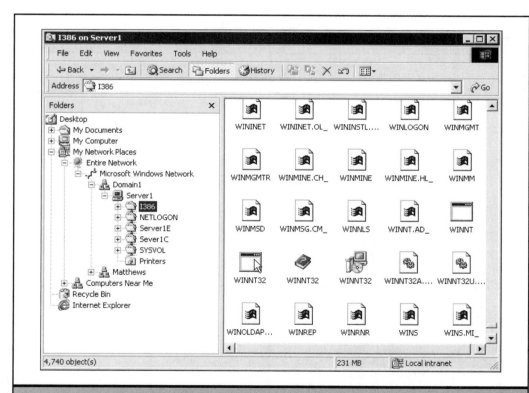

Figure 4-1.   Starting Setup using files on a computer across a network

NOTE: You can upgrade to Windows 2000 Server from Windows NT 3.51 Server, Windows NT 4 Server, and Windows NT 4 Terminal Server. Windows NT 4 Enterprise Server cannot be upgraded to Windows 2000 Server—you must use Windows 2000 Advanced Server. Windows 2000 Professional can be upgraded from Windows 95, 98, NT 3.51 Workstation, and NT 4 Workstation. You cannot upgrade from MS-DOS, Windows 3.x, or OS/2.

Starting Locally

There are a number of ways to start Setup locally, depending on whether:

▼ You want to boot Windows 2000 Setup directly or start it from an existing system

■ Your system can boot from a CD or requires that you use floppies

▲ You want to start from DOS, Windows 3.x, or a later version of Windows

These alternatives and their resultant starting steps are shown in Figure 4-2 and are further described in the next few sections.

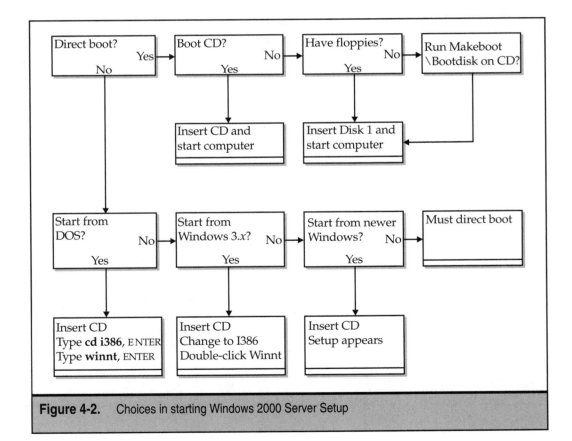

Figure 4-2. Choices in starting Windows 2000 Server Setup

NOTE: After starting by directly booting into Setup, you can only do a clean install. If you start Setup from an existing operating system, you can do either a clean install or upgrade from a compatible system (see the previous Note).

Starting by Directly Booting Setup

If you want to directly boot Setup, you can do so with a new unformatted hard drive or one that has any other OS on it. The only questions are whether you can boot from a CD, and, if not, whether you have the boot floppies to boot from. As you will see, you can create the boot floppies, if you don't have them already.

Booting from a CD   If the system on which you want to do the installation can boot from a CD instead of a floppy or hard disk, then you can start Setup simply by following these steps:

1. Insert the Windows 2000 Server CD in the CD-ROM drive.
2. Restart the computer.
3. If necessary, press ENTER or "any key," as suggested, to boot from the CD.
4. Windows 2000 Setup will begin to load.

If you can't boot from a CD, but believe you should be able to (most computers made after 1996 can boot from the CD), you may need to change one or more settings in the system BIOS (basic input/output system) at the very beginning of the boot process. Depending on the computer, the BIOS can be changed in several different ways. Recent BIOSs from the two most popular third-party BIOS manufacturers, Award and American Megatrends, Inc. (AMI), are changed as follows:

▼ **Award Version 4.51PG**   Press DEL right after memory check; select BIOS Features Setup; select Boot Sequence; press PGUP until "A, CDROM, C" is displayed; press ESC to quit; select Save & Exit Setup; press ENTER; press Y; and press ENTER.

▲ **AMI BIOS Version 2.4**   Press DEL right after the memory check; select Advanced Setup; select 1st Boot Device; choose CDROM; select 2nd Boot Device; choose Floppy; select 3rd Boot Device; choose IDE-0; press ESC twice; select Save Changes and Exit; press ENTER.

Booting from Floppies   If you can't boot from a CD, then you have to boot from floppies. A set of four boot floppies may have come with your Windows 2000 Server package, and you can use them to start Setup. If you do not have the floppies, but have the Windows 2000 Server CD, you can create the floppies with four blank formatted, high-density (1.44MB) floppy disks and these steps:

1. Start a system with a bootable OS, a CD-ROM drive, and a 1.44MB floppy drive.
2. Insert the Windows 2000 Server CD in the CD-ROM drive.

3. On the CD, browse to the Bootdisk folder and run either Makeboot.exe from DOS or Windows 3.*x*, or Makebt32.exe from a newer version of Windows, as shown in Figure 4-3.

4. Specify the drive to be used, and insert a formatted floppy in that drive.

5. When prompted, exchange the floppy in the drive for another floppy, and label the one removed. Repeat this three times.

6. Remove the last floppy and label it.

With a set of floppy boot disks, you can start Setup with these steps:

1. Insert the first Windows 2000 Server Setup Boot Disk in its drive.

2. Start or restart the computer.

3. Windows 2000 Setup will begin to load.

4. Insert the other floppy disks as requested, and press ENTER after each.

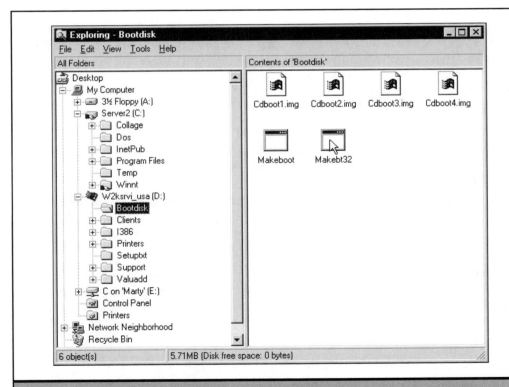

Figure 4-3.   Creating Windows 2000 Server boot floppies

If the system does not boot from the floppy, you may have to change the order in which the floppy, CD-ROM, and hard drives boot. See the discussion in the previous section, "Booting from a CD."

NOTE: The Windows 2000 Setup floppy disks only start Setup. You still need the CD to do the installation.

Starting from Another Operating System

You can start Windows 2000 Setup from these other operating systems:

▼ MS-DOS

■ Windows 3.1, Windows 3.11, or Windows for Workgroups

■ Windows 95 or 98, any version

▲ Windows NT 3.51, Windows NT 4 (any service packs), or Windows 2000 Server

Starting from DOS   With DOS running on the computer on which you want to install Windows 2000, use these steps to do the installation:

1. Insert the Windows 2000 Server CD in its drive.
2. At the DOS prompt, make the CD-ROM drive current by typing, for example, **d:** and pressing ENTER.
3. Type **cd\i386** and press ENTER. The directory will be changed to I386.
4. Type **winnt** and press ENTER. Windows 2000 Setup will begin to load.

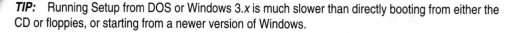

TIP: Running Setup from DOS or Windows 3.x is much slower than directly booting from either the CD or floppies, or starting from a newer version of Windows.

Starting from Windows 3.x   With Windows 3.x running on the computer on which you want to install Windows 2000, use these steps to do the installation:

1. Insert the Windows 2000 Server CD in its drive.
2. Start File Manager and open the CD-ROM drive.
3. Browse to and open the I386 folder.
4. Browse to and double-click Winnt.exe.
5. Windows 2000 Setup will begin to load.

Starting from a Newer Windows   With Windows 95/98 or Windows NT 3.51/4 running on the computer where you want to install Windows 2000, use these steps to do the installation:

1. Insert the Windows 2000 Server CD in its drive.

2. The Autorun feature, if active, will load the CD and a message window will pop up stating that the CD contains a newer version of Windows than what you are using and asking if you want to upgrade to the newer version.

3. Click No to close the message window, and click Close to close the Windows CD dialog box.

4. In any case, whether or not Autorun is active, use Windows Explorer to open the CD-ROM drive, browse to the I386 folder, and double-click Winnt32.exe. The Windows 2000 Setup Wizard will launch (as shown in Figure 4-4), asking whether you want to upgrade or install a new copy.

RUNNING SETUP

Setup has two distinct phases: a character-based phase called the Setup Program, and a GUI (graphical user interface) phase called the Setup Wizard. Also, if you start Setup from a newer Windows OS (Windows 95 or NT 3.51 and later), several GUI dialog boxes (beginning with the one shown in Figure 4-4) are used to gather some information that is otherwise done in the character-based process. Also, Setup is slightly different depending on whether you are doing an upgrade or a clean installation. All of these different aspects of running Setup are covered in the following sections:

▼ Running a Clean Install Started from a Newer Windows Version

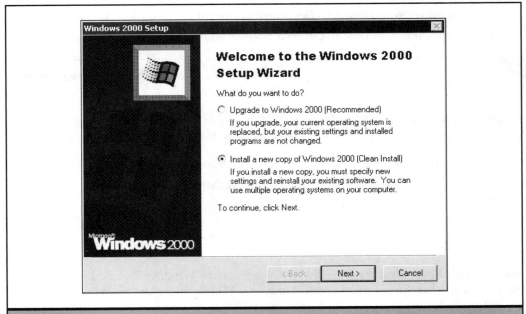

Figure 4-4.   You can upgrade or do a clean install after starting from a previous version of Windows

■ Running a Clean Install Started in Other Ways

▲ Running an Upgrade

Running a Clean Install Started from a Newer Windows Version

If you started Setup in a newer version of Windows, Setup has three phases:

▼ An initial GUI phase

■ An intermediate character-based Setup Program phase

▲ A final GUI-based Setup Wizard phase

CAUTION: By definition, a clean install means that anything that was previously on the hard disk partition or volume will be removed and therefore lost during a reformatting process, to give you a clean hard disk partition.

Initial GUI Phase

Having started from a newer version of Windows, you should have the dialog box previously shown in Figure 4-4 on the screen. The steps to continue from this point with Setup are as follows:

1. In the dialog box shown in Figure 4-4, choose Install a New Copy of Windows 2000 (see the discussion in Chapter 3) and click Next. The License Agreement dialog box opens.

2. Click I Accept This Agreement (or forget about installing Windows 2000) and then click Next. The Product Key dialog box opens.

3. Enter the product key located on the back of the Windows CD envelope or case, and click Next. The Select Special Options dialog box opens, shown in Figure 4-5. This allows you to change the language used by Windows 2000, select special accessibility options, and change the way files are copied. The specific choices you have are as follows:

    ■ **Language Options**   Allows you to select a primary language and one of the areas of the world that language is used. This determines not only the language to use, but also the formats for dates, times, currency, and numbers, as well as character sets, and keyboard layouts. You can also choose additional languages you want to use.

    ■ **Advanced Options**   Allows you to specify the location of the Windows 2000 Setup files and the folder in which you want Windows 2000 installed. You can also choose to copy all the Setup files from the CD to the hard drive, and choose the partition in which to install Windows.

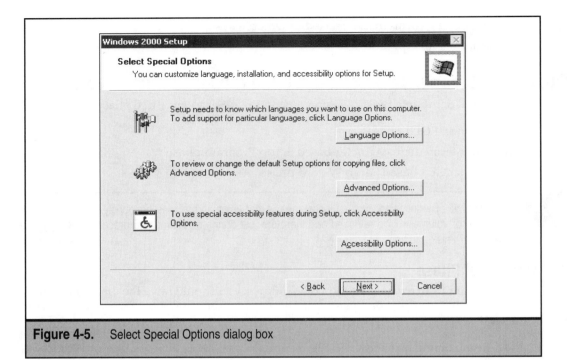

Figure 4-5. Select Special Options dialog box

NOTE: If you don't specify a partition and folder, the default is to install in the currently active partition and folder; in other words, to copy over the existing operating system.

- **Accessibility Options** Allows you to turn on a Magnifier to enlarge portions of the Setup screen for those with limited vision, and/or turn on a Narrator to read aloud the contents of the Setup screen for those who cannot see it (you must have a sound card and speakers).

4. Complete your selections and click Next. You are offered the opportunity to review the Directory of Applications on the Microsoft web site to see if the applications you want to use are compatible with Windows 2000. To do this, click Directory of Applications. You will be connected to the Microsoft web site (if you don't have an Internet connection, but have an attached modem connected to a phone line you will be lead through setting up an Internet connection). On the Microsoft web site, follow the directions for checking the compatibility of software you want to use. When you are done, close the Internet Explorer and the Internet connection, and then click Next.

5. Setup will begin copying files. This is fairly fast from a CD, but can take a while over a network, depending on the speed of the network and the traffic on it. When the copying process is complete, the computer is rebooted and the character-based Setup Program is started.

Intermediate Character-Based Setup Program Phase

The intermediate character-based Setup Program phase continues with these steps:

1. Upon restarting, you are given a choice of which operating system you want to start. Press ENTER to choose the default Windows 2000 Setup.

2. Setup inspects your hardware configuration and gives you a chance to press F6 to install a third-party Small Computer System Interface (SCSI) or redundant array of independent disks (RAID) mass-storage driver. If needed, press F6 and follow the instructions for installing the driver. Setup then loads the files that you need. Upon completion, you are asked whether you want to Set Up Windows 2000, Repair Windows 2000, or Quit Setup.

> **NOTE:** You need to press F6 rather quickly if you want to install a driver. You have only about ten seconds to make the decision and press the F6 key. If you are unsure about whether you need to make the decision, press F6. You can always exit without installing a SCSI or RAID driver.

3. Press ENTER to set up Windows 2000. (If you are installing over an existing copy of Windows 2000, you will be asked a second time if you want to repair the existing Windows 2000; if so press R, or to continue installing a fresh copy, press ESC.) You are next shown the existing partitions and asked which you want to use for the current installation.

4. Use the UP ARROW and DOWN ARROW keys to select the partition you want to use. You then can press ENTER to install in that partition, press C to create a new partition in unpartitioned space, or press D to delete an existing partition and create a new one in its place.

> **NOTE:** You will not be able to delete in this manner the partition from which you originally booted the computer. You should be able to do this if you boot into Windows 2000 Setup from the CD or floppy disks. If you can boot from the Windows 2000 CD or floppy disks, start Setup, follow the initial instructions through restarting of the computer, then choose Repair ("R") and Recovery Console ("C"). Here you have a DOS-like interface where you can get a list of commands by typing **help**. Use the Diskpart command to remove partitions (type **help diskpart** to learn how to do to this). Also, see "Using the Recovery Console" in Chapter 14. If that still doesn't work, boot from a DOS or Windows 3.x, 95, or 98 boot floppy disk and use Fdisk by typing **fdisk** and pressing ENTER. Follow the instructions to choose large disk support, treat NTFS (new technology file system) partitions as large, delete a partition, delete a non-DOS partition, and confirm that deletion. Press ESC twice to exit Fdisk.

5. If you truly want to do a clean install, press D. Confirm that you want to delete a system partition by pressing ENTER and then pressing L. You must then create a new partition in the unpartitioned space, by pressing C and then pressing ENTER to use the maximum size. To set up Windows 2000 in the new partition, select it and press ENTER.

6. Select whether you want the new partition formatted using NTFS or the FAT (file allocation table) file system and press ENTER. The new partition will be formatted as you directed. Setup then copies the necessary files to the computer. When this is completed, Windows 2000 restarts and the graphical Setup Wizard starts.

NOTE: Not using NTFS severely limits what a server can do. Most importantly, it cannot be a domain controller and cannot use Active Directory.

Final GUI-Based Setup Wizard Phase

When the Windows 2000 Setup Wizard starts, you see its Welcome dialog box. Continue through Setup with these steps:

1. Click Next (or if you wait a moment, this happens automatically). Setup tells you it is detecting and installing the hardware devices on the computer.

2. The Regional Settings dialog box appears. This allows you to choose a system or user locale that determines which language is the default, which other languages are available, and how numbers, currencies, time, and dates are displayed and used for the system in general, as well as for the current user. You can also choose which keyboard layout to use and several keyboard options.

3. Select the regional settings that you want, and click Next. The Personalize Your Software dialog box will appear.

4. Enter the person's name and organization to be associated with the computer, and click Next. The Licensing Modes dialog box appears.

5. Click either Per Server and enter the number of concurrent connections (5 is the default), where each *connection* must have its own Client Access License, or Per Seat, where each *computer* must have its own Client Access License. (See the discussion in Chapter 3.) After making the selection, click Next, and you'll see the Computer Name and Administrator Password dialog box.

6. Enter a unique name for the computer (it can be up to 63 characters long, but pre-Windows 2000 computers will only see the first 15 characters) and enter and confirm a password to be used by the system administrator. Click Next. The Windows 2000 Components dialog box appears, in which you select the optional components you want installed. The components are on a scrollable list, and you can select one by clicking in its checkbox. Many of the items have subitems. You can either choose the parent item and automatically select a default set of (often all) subitems, or individually select the subitems by clicking Details and selecting the items you want. If a parent item has all the subitems selected, it displays a black checkmark in a white checkbox. If only some of the items are selected, the checkbox is grayed. (Again, Chapter 3 provides a detailed discussion of the options available here.)

7. Select the components that you want to be installed, and click Next. If you have a modem, the Modem Dialing Information dialog box is displayed. This allows you to select the country or region you are in, your area or city code, the number that must be dialed to get an outside line, and whether the phone system uses tone or pulse dialing.

8. Enter the modem dialing information and then click Next. You'll see a dialog box for Date and Time Settings.

9. If necessary, set the current date and time, and click Next. The Networking Settings dialog box will appear and the Windows networking components will be installed. This allows you to connect to other computers, networks, and the Internet. When the networking software is installed, you are asked to choose either Typical settings, which creates network connections using the Client for Microsoft Networks, File and Print Sharing for Microsoft Networks, and the Transmission Control Protocol/Internet Protocol (TCP/IP) with automatic addressing, or Custom settings, which allows you to manually configure networking components. Choosing Custom allows you to add or remove clients, services, and protocols, such as the Gateway and Client Service for NetWare or the NetBEUI protocol.

10. Choose the network settings you want to use, and click Next. The Workgroup or Computer Domain dialog box appears, asking whether you want this computer to be a member of a domain.

11. If you click No and the computer is part of a workgroup, enter a workgroup name. If you click Yes, type the domain name. In the later case, you need to enter a username and password. Click Next when you are done with the domain settings. Setup will install the components that you have selected with the settings you specified.

12. You are told that you need to assign a static IP address (see Chapter 3) and that you now have the option to do that. Click OK. The Local Area Connection Properties dialog box will appear, from which you should do the following:

NOTE: If this server is not the Domain Name System (DNS) server, then you may not want it to have a static IP address. To get around assigning a static IP address you must go through the sequence *three* times of clicking OK to the original message, clicking OK to close the Local Area Connection Properties dialog box, and clicking OK to close a message confirming that you have chosen to continue using dynamically assigned IP addresses.

   a) Select Internet Protocol (TCP/IP) and click Properties. The Internet Protocol (TCP/IP) Properties dialog box will open.

   b) Click Use the Following IP Address and enter an IP address. Normally, a range of IP addresses is assigned to an organization by its Internet service provider (ISP). If you don't have an IP address, check with your ISP or make one up using the number range 10.0.0.0 through 10.255.255.255. For example, 10.0.0.9 is a legitimate number, and if it isn't used by another computer on your network, it will work fine. This range of numbers is not used on the Internet.

c) Press TAB to go to Subnet Mask. The subnet mask 255.0.0.0 should be filled in for you. Change the first 0 to **255** so that you have a subnet mask of 255.255.0.0.

d) Click OK twice. The installation of components will continue.

When component installation is done, Start menu items are installed, components are registered, settings are saved, and all temporary files are removed.

13. When the Setup Wizard is finished, you are told to remove the CD from its drive, if there is one, and to click Finish to restart the computer. Do that to finish Setup.

14. When the system is restarted, upon request, press CTRL-ALT-DEL, enter the Administrator's password you first entered in step 6, and click OK. If you installed the Client Service for NetWare, you will be asked to identify the NetWare server to which you want to connect. If you have none, leave None displayed and click OK.

When loading is complete, the Windows 2000 desktop will appear with its default icons and the Configure Your Server dialog box, shown in Figure 4-6. This dialog box and the steps to configure Windows 2000 Server are discussed later in this chapter under "Configuring A Server."

Running a Clean Install Started in Other Ways

When you boot from a CD or floppies, or start from DOS or Windows 3.*x*, you have only two phases: the character-based Setup Program and the GUI-based Setup Wizard. You see none of the startup GUI dialog boxes and go right into the character-based Setup Program.

Character-Based Setup Program

Having started Setup, begin the character-based Setup Program with the following steps:

1. If your boot device does not contain your Setup files, you need to confirm the drive and folder where those files exist. Often, the CD-ROM drive is drive D, in which case the correct response would be **D:\I386**. When the correct drive and folder are displayed, press ENTER.

2. If you are starting from an older version (5.*x* or 6.*x*) of DOS or Windows 3.*x* and don't have the DOS SmartDrive disk-caching system loaded, you will be reminded that having it will greatly improve the performance of Setup (although it is still slow compared to other ways of starting Setup). SmartDrive is started with the program Smartdrv.exe that was included with DOS 6.*x* and Windows 3.*x*. If you look at the original distribution diskettes for these products, you will

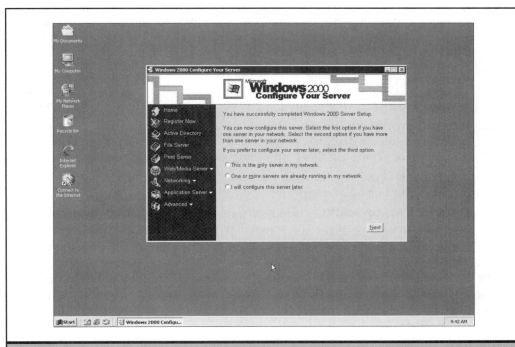

Figure 4-6.   The initial Windows 2000 desktop displayed the first time Windows 2000 is started

see the file Smartdrv.ex_. This is a compressed file that must be expanded with Expand.exe, also on the distribution diskettes (type **expand a:\smartdrv.ex_ c:\smartdrv.exe**, assuming that you are in the directory with Expand.exe). With Smartdrv.exe in the root directory of the hard disk, add the line **smartdrv.exe** to the Autoexec.bat file. After you have started DOS, you can check to see if SmartDrive is loaded by typing **smartdrv** and pressing ENTER. If loaded, you will see a report of the version, cache size, and status. An initial set of files is copied to the hard disk, which can be a very slow process if you started from DOS or Windows 3.*x*, and your system is rebooted.

3. Setup inspects your hardware configuration and gives you the opportunity to press F6 to install a third-party SCSI or RAID mass-storage driver. If needed, press F6 and follow the instructions for installing the driver. Setup then loads the files that you need.

NOTE: You need to press F6 rather quickly if you want to install a driver. You have only about ten seconds to make the decision and press the F6 key. If you are unsure about whether you need to press F6, press it. You can always exit that question without installing a SCSI or RAID driver.

4. If there is an existing Windows 2000 installation, Setup asks whether you want to repair the existing installation of Windows 2000 or set up a new Windows 2000 installation. Press ENTER for a new installation. If you started from floppy disks and do not have the Windows 2000 Server CD in the drive, you will be asked to insert it.

5. The Microsoft License Agreement is displayed and you are asked to press F8 if you agree to it or ESC if you don't. If you want to install Windows 2000, press F8.

6. If there is an existing Windows 2000 installation, you'll be asked again whether you want to repair that installation, which you can do by pressing R, or install a fresh copy of Windows 2000 by pressing ESC.

7. You are next shown the existing partitions and asked which you want to use for the current installation.

8. Use the UP ARROW and DOWN ARROW keys to select the partition you want to use. You then can press ENTER to install in that partition, press C to create a new partition in unpartitioned space, or press D to delete an existing partition and create a new one in its place.

9. If you truly want to do a clean install, press D. Confirm that you want to delete a system partition by pressing ENTER and then pressing L. To set up Windows 2000 in unpartitioned space, press ENTER (a partition will automatically be created for you).

10. Select whether you want the new partition formatted using NTFS (recommended) or the FAT file system, and then press ENTER. The new partition will be formatted as you directed.

11. If you only have an existing FAT or FAT32 partition, you will be asked whether you want to convert it to NTFS (recommended) or leave the current file system intact. Select Convert and press ENTER. Confirm that you want to convert the partition by pressing C. When the conversion or formatting is done, the remaining files are copied to the hard disk. Upon completion, the computer is restarted and the Windows 2000 Setup Wizard is started.

GUI-Based Setup Wizard

When the Windows 2000 Setup Wizard starts, you will see several dialog boxes telling you that Windows 2000 is loading files, and then the Welcome dialog box appears. Continue through Setup with these steps:

1. Click Next (if you wait a moment, this is done automatically). Setup then begins detecting and installing the hardware devices on the computer. When that is done, the Regional Settings dialog box appears. This allows you to choose a system or user locale that determines which language is the default, which other languages are available, and how numbers, currencies, time, and dates are displayed and used for the system in general, as well as for the current user. You can also choose which keyboard layout to use and several keyboard options.

2. Select the regional settings that you want, and click Next. The Personalize Your Software dialog box will appear.

3. Enter the person's name and organization to be associated with the computer, and click Next. The Product Key dialog box appears.

4. Enter the 25-character product key that appears on the back of the Windows 2000 envelope or case. When you are finished, click Next. The Licensing Modes dialog box appears.

5. Click either Per Server and enter the number of concurrent connections (5 is the default), where each *connection* must have its own Client Access License, or Per Seat, where each *computer* must have its own Client Access License. (See the discussion in Chapter 3.) After making the selection, click Next, and you'll see the Computer Name and Administrative Password dialog box.

6. Enter a unique name for the computer (it can be up to 63 characters long, but pre-Windows 2000 computers will only see the first 15 characters) and enter and confirm a password to be used by the system administrator. Click Next. The Windows 2000 Components dialog box appears, in which you select the optional components you want installed. The components are on a scrollable list, and you can select one by clicking in its checkbox. Many of the items have subitems. You can either choose the parent item and automatically select a default set of (often all) subitems, or individually select the subitems by clicking Details and selecting the items you want. If a parent item has all the subitems selected, it displays a black checkmark in a white checkbox. If only some of the items are selected, the checkbox is grayed. (Again, Chapter 3 provides a detailed discussion of the options available here.)

7. Select the components that you want to be installed, and click Next. If you have a modem, the Modem Dialing Information dialog box is displayed. This allows you to select the country or region you are in, your area or city code, the number that must be dialed to get an outside line, and whether the phone system uses tone or pulse dialing.

8. Enter the modem dialing information and then click Next. You'll see a dialog box for Date and Time Settings.

9. If necessary, set the current date and time, and click Next. The Windows networking components will be installed and the Networking Settings dialog box will appear. This allows you to connect to other computers, networks, and the Internet. When the networking software is installed, you are asked to choose either Typical settings, which creates network connections using the Client for Microsoft Networks, File and Print Sharing for Microsoft Networks, and the TCP/IP protocol with automatic addressing, or Custom settings, which allows you to manually configure networking components. Choosing Custom allows you to add or remove clients, services, and protocols, such as the Gateway and Client Service for NetWare or the NetBEUI protocol.

10. Choose the Network settings you want to use, and click Next. The Workgroup or Computer Domain dialog box appears, asking whether you want this computer to be a member of a domain.

11. If you answer No and the computer is part of a workgroup, enter a workgroup name. If you answer Yes, type the domain name. In the later case, you need to enter a username and password that has administrator privileges on the domain. Click Next when you are done with the domain settings. Setup will install the components that you have selected with the settings you specified.

12. You may be told that you need to assign a static IP address (refer to Chapter 3) and that you now have the option to do that. Click OK. The Local Area Connection Properties dialog box appears, from which you should do the following:

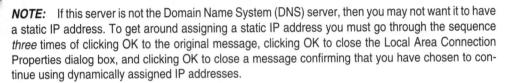

NOTE: If this server is not the Domain Name System (DNS) server, then you may not want it to have a static IP address. To get around assigning a static IP address you must go through the sequence *three* times of clicking OK to the original message, clicking OK to close the Local Area Connection Properties dialog box, and clicking OK to close a message confirming that you have chosen to continue using dynamically assigned IP addresses.

a) Select Internet Protocol (TCP/IP) and click Properties. The Internet Protocol (TCP/IP) Properties dialog box opens.

b) Click Use the Following IP Address and enter an IP address. If you don't have an IP address, you can make one up using the number range 10.0.0.0 through 10.255.255.255. For example, 10.0.0.9 is a legitimate number, and if it isn't used by another computer on your network, it will work fine. This range of numbers is not used on the Internet.

c) Press TAB to go to Subnet Mask. Subnet mask 255.0.0.0 should be filled in for you. Change the first 0 to **255** so that you have a subnet mask of 255.255.0.0.

d) Click OK twice. The installation of components will continue.

When component installation is done, Start menu items are installed, components are registered, settings are saved, and all temporary files are removed.

13. When the Setup Wizard is finished, you are told to remove the CD from its drive, if there is one, and to click Finish to restart the computer. Do that to finish Setup.

14. When the system is restarted, upon request, press CTRL-ALT-DEL, enter the Administrator's password you first entered in step 6, and click OK. If you installed the Client Service for NetWare, you will be asked to identify the NetWare Preferred Server to which you want to connect. If you have none, leave None displayed, and click OK. Otherwise, select the server and, if needed, enter the default tree and context and click OK.

When loading is complete, the Windows 2000 desktop will appear with its default icons and the Configure Your Server dialog box, shown earlier. This dialog box and the steps to configure Windows 2000 Server are discussed later in this chapter, under "Configuring A Server."

Running an Upgrade

An upgrade to Windows 2000 Server must be done from either Windows NT 3.51 Server or Windows NT 4 Server. That means that it must be started from one of those products. Also, many of the settings for Windows 2000 are taken from the earlier system. There are still three phases, but they are abbreviated.

Initial GUI Phase

Having started from a newer version of Windows, you should have on the screen the Upgrade vs. Install dialog box, which was shown earlier in Figure 4-4. The steps to continue from this point with Setup are as follows:

1. In the Upgrade vs. Install dialog box choose to upgrade and click Next. The License Agreement dialog box opens.

2. Click I Accept This Agreement (or forget about installing Windows 2000) and then click Next. The Product Key dialog box will open.

3. Enter the product key that is shown on the back of the Windows 2000 CD envelope or case and click Next. If there is a need, the Report System Compatibility dialog box opens, as shown in Figure 4-7. This tells you if any parts of the current system are not compatible with Windows 2000 and the consequences. You can save the incompatible items and get more information about them.

4. Handle any incompatible items, as necessary, and click Next. Setup will begin copying files. This is fairly fast from a CD, but can take a while over a network, depending on the speed of the network and the traffic on it. When the copying process is complete, the computer is rebooted and the character-based Setup Program is started.

Intermediate Character-Based Setup Program Phase

The intermediate character-based Setup Program phase continues with these steps:

1. Setup inspects your hardware configuration and then copies the files that you need. Upon completion, you are told that Setup will restart your computer.

2. Press ENTER to restart. You are given a choice of which operating system you want to start. Press ENTER to choose the default Windows 2000 Server.

3. Setup then begins installing the hardware devices on the computer. When this is completed, the Windows 2000 Setup Wizard is started.

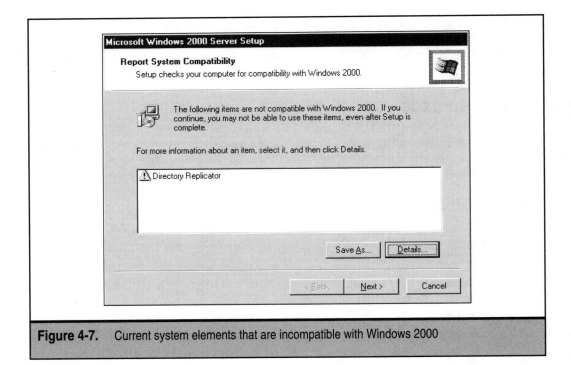

Figure 4-7. Current system elements that are incompatible with Windows 2000

Final GUI Phase

In a normal upgrade, the final GUI phase is just a series of dialog boxes telling you what is happening. No installer interaction is needed. Setup will load and install with their original settings the components that were in the previous system. When component installation is done, Start menu items are installed, components are registered, settings are saved, and all temporary files are removed.

When loading is complete, the Windows 2000 desktop will appear with its default icons and the Configure Your Server dialog box, which is discussed later in the chapter.

Upgrading a Domain Controller

If the server that is being upgraded is a domain controller, the Active Directory Installation Wizard will automatically start and display the dialog box shown in Figure 4-8. Use the following set of steps to complete the upgrading of the domain controller:

1. Click Next. Select whether you want to create a new domain or have the current domain be a child of an existing domain, as shown in Figure 4-9, and then click Next.

2. If you decide to create a new domain, choose if you want to create a new domain forest or a new domain tree in the existing forest. Click Next, enter the DNS name for the new domain, and click Next again.

Figure 4-8.   Upgrading a domain controller

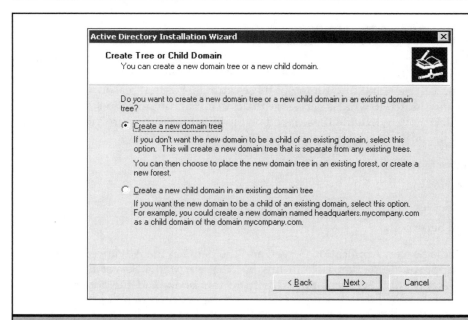

Figure 4-9.   Create a new tree or have the current domain be a child of an existing domain

3. If you choose the current server to be a child of an existing domain and if the current server is not a DNS server, clicking Configure DNS Client opens a Help window that tells you how to configure the server to be a DNS server. Also read the following section. Click Next when you are done.

4. If you chose the current server to be a child of an existing domain, enter the username, password, and domain name to access the parent domain, and click Next. Enter the parent domain name, the name of the new child domain, and click Next.

5. Accept the defaults or enter a location to store the Active Directory's database and log files, and click Next. Similarly, accept the default or enter the location to store the domain's Sysvol folder of public files, and click Next.

6. If you are installing a new domain, choose Yes Install and Configure DNS, and click Next.

7. Choose the type of permissions that you want—those compatible with older Windows, or only Windows 2000—and click Next. Enter and confirm the Password to be used with Directory Services Restore Mode, and click Next.

8. Review the summary of actions you have chosen for the new domain and Active Directory. If you want to change anything, use Back to go back and make the changes. When you are ready, click Next. The domain and active directory will be configured.

CONFIGURING A SERVER

The Configure Your Server dialog box, shown in Figure 4-10, provides access to the primary configuration tasks needed to get a usable server. Much of the rest of this book is spent on the discussion and fine-tuning of these settings. For that reason, the discussion here is brief and limited to what is necessary to do an initial configuration of a server. The areas that will be covered, out of those listed on the left of the Configure Your Server dialog box, and the order in which they will be discussed are as follows:

▼ Active Directory

■ Networking

■ File Server

▲ Print Server

Web/Media Server, Application Server, and the items in the Advanced category are left for the appropriate section later in this book (Web/Media Server is discussed in Chapter 11, Application Server is not covered in this book, and the advanced topics, which include message queuing, support tools, and optional components, are largely dis-

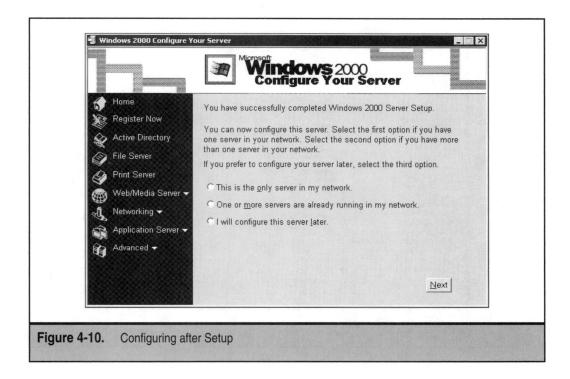

Figure 4-10.   Configuring after Setup

cussed in Chapters 12 and 14). Registration will be handled at the end of this chapter, after the modem is set up.

Before Configuring

You should do two tasks before you start configuring the server. The first is to take a quick look at how the server is configured coming out of the Setup. The second is to complete the opening page of the Configure Your Server dialog box.

Looking at the Current Configuration

The amount of initial configuration that you have to do will depend on whether you did a clean install or an upgrade. Since an upgrade maintains the previous settings, and even Active Directory is set up if the server is a domain controller, there may be very little for you to do in the next several sections. To check that out, take a quick look at the system before starting into the configuration, with the following steps:

1. Double-click My Computer. When it opens, click Folders in the toolbar for a view of your system similar to Figure 4-11.

Figure 4-11. Looking at a new installation

2. Open the hard drives and the folders on those drives by double-clicking them, to see what is on the disks.

3. Right-click your boot drive or volume and choose Properties to see how much room you have after installing Windows 2000 Server; an example for one of my servers is shown in Figure 4-12.

NOTE: If you have the default Enable Web Content in Folders selected (click Tools in the toolbar and choose Folder Options | General tab | Web View), you can see the used and free space by selecting a hard drive in My Computer or Windows Explorer without opening Properties.

4. Open My Network Places, the Entire Network, and Computers Near Me to see if you are connected to the network and you can see other computers to which you can link.

5. Open the Start menu, choose Programs, look at both Accessories and Administrative Tools, and note that you can restart Configure Your Server there, as shown in Figure 4-13. (Your Administrative Tools menu may be different than that shown in Figure 4-13, depending on the options you selected during installation.)

6. Again from the Start menu, choose Settings | Control Panel and double-click Administrative Tools. You'll see that it is the same as the Program menu option in the previous step. Click Back in the toolbar.

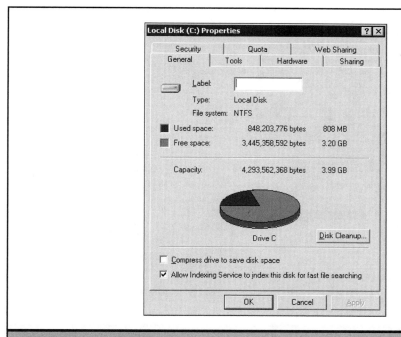

Figure 4-12.   Checking on free space after installing Windows 2000 Server

7. Double-click Printers in the Control Panel to see what is installed. Click Back and open any other Control Panel items, shown in Figure 14-14, that interest you. Close the Control Panel.

8. From the Start menu, choose Settings | Network and Dial-up Connections to see what is there.

9. Look around at anything else that you want to explore. When you are done, close all dialog boxes except Configure Your Server.

This gives you a very brief overview of your server, but it should give you an idea of what needs to be done to configure it.

Initial Page

On the initial (Home) page that is displayed in the Configure Your Server dialog box when you complete Setup (see Figure 4-10), there is a basic question that steers the rest of the network setup: Is this server the only one in the network? If you want Windows to set up the core networking services, such as DNS, Windows Internet Naming Service (WINS), and Active Directory on this server, then choose This Is the Only Server in My Network. If the core services are already set up on other servers, then choose One or More Servers Are Already Running in My Network. If you wanted Windows to set up these

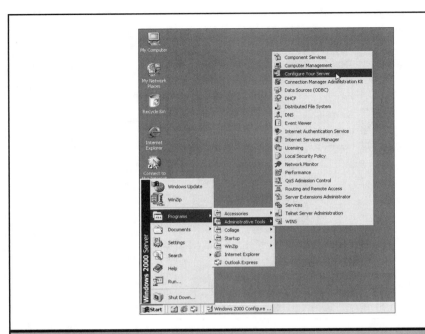

Figure 4-13. Seeing what is installed

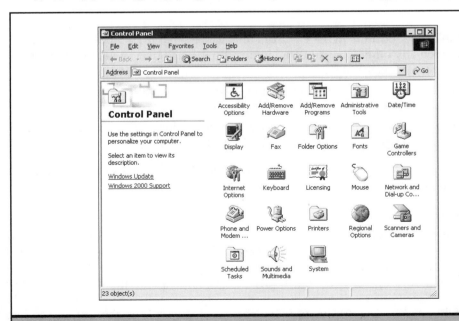

Figure 4-14. Looking through the Control Panel

services for you, you would make this choice now and click Next. For a more informative way of doing this, follow the next several sections of this chapter and see for yourself how these various services are set up.

> **NOTE:**   The first server you set up should have the core services on it, such as DNS, WINS, and Active Directory.

Setting Up Active Directory

Active Directory, which consolidates the access to all resources on a network into a single hierarchical view and a single point of administration, is a major focal point of Windows 2000 Server and a topic this book spends most of a chapter on (Chapter 9). Here, suffice it to say that if you have multiple servers, you will want to use Active Directory. Active Directory requires NTFS and must be resident on a domain controller. Part of configuring Active Directory will mean checking for these requirements and setting up the domain controller if necessary. Also, the Dynamic Host Configuration Protocol (DHCP), which provides the dynamic assignment of IP addresses as they are needed so that clients do not need a permanent assigned IP address, and DNS, which allows the use of server and client names instead of IP addresses, are so critical to networking that they also are created here. Configure Active Directory now with these steps:

1. Click Active Directory in the left portion of the dialog box, which then changes to look like Figure 4-15. This tells you that the Active Directory Installation Wizard will, if necessary, set up a domain controller and a DNS server, and requires an NTFS partition.

2. Scroll down and click Start. The Active Directory Installation Wizard opens, as you previously saw in Figure 4-8. Click Next. You are asked whether you want this server to be a domain controller for a new domain or a domain controller for an existing domain.

3. Make your choice, which probably is a domain controller for a new domain, if this is the first server to be set up in your network (what was called a *primary* domain controller in NT 4), and click Next. You are then asked, as you also saw in Figure 4-9, whether you want to create a new domain *tree* (a domain with its subsidiary servers and clients or *children*) or a child of an existing domain.

4. Make your choice, which again probably is a new domain, for the same reason as in step 3, and click Next. If you choose to be a child of an existing domain, you will need to enter a user name, password, and domain name for the domain you wish to be a child of, and then click Next. If you choose to create a new domain, you are asked whether you want to create a new *forest* (a group) of domains or a new domain in an existing forest.

5. Make your choice, which for a third time probably is a new forest, and click Next.

6. Enter the name of the new domain or the existing domain of which you want to be a child. This may be a simple name, such as Domain, or if you are on the

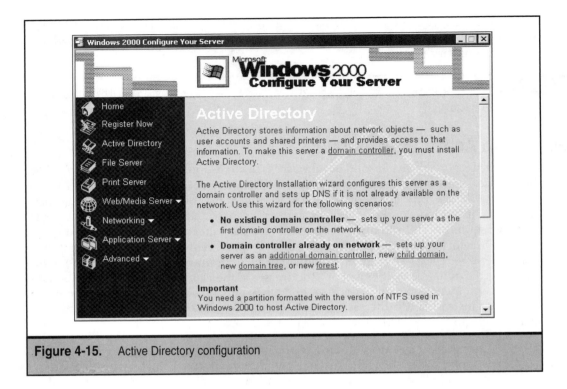

Figure 4-15. Active Directory configuration

Internet, a name such as Domain.Yourco.com. If you don't enter a name in the second format, you are prompted to do so, as you can see next, but there is no reason you need to do that if you are not on the Internet. When you have entered the name, click Next.

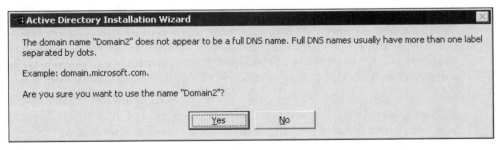

7. If you entered a name longer than 15 characters, it will be truncated and shown to you as the NetBIOS name. You can change it if you wish. If your name is already under 16 characters, it is left alone. Click Next when you are ready. The next dialog box asks where you want to store the Active Directory database and log, and cautions that they should be on separate hard disks.

8. Accept the default locations or enter new ones, and click Next. You are then asked where to store the Sysvol folder, the domain's public folders that are replicated on all domain controllers in the domain, and cautioned that the location must be on an NTFS 5 volume.

9. Enter the location or accept the default, and click Next. If you do not have a DNS server set up, you are told you need to do that. Click OK, and you are asked if you want the wizard to do it for you.

10. Click Yes and then Next. If you are setting up a new domain, the next dialog box asks if you want to allow NT 4 Remote Access Servers (RASs) to access this new domain, and informs you that if you do, permissions have to be weakened a bit. If you do that, you can strengthen the permissions in the future with the Netish.exe utility.

11. Make the choice that's correct for you and click Next.

12. Enter and confirm the Directory Services Restore Mode Administrator password. Finally, you are shown a list of actions that will be performed to install Active Directory and other necessary components and options, as shown in Figure 4-16 for a new domain.

13. Review the list, and if anything is not correct, click Back to go back and change the setting. When you are ready, click Next. You will see an animation indicating that Active Directory is being set up. When it finishes, you will get a final dialog box, as shown in Figure 4-17.

14. Click Finish to close the final dialog box and return to the Configure Your Server dialog box. You will be told that Windows must be restarted before the changes will take effect.

15. Click Restart Now. The computer is restarted and you are returned to the Configure Your Server dialog box. If you click Active Directory again, you see that it now says that Active Directory is already installed and that you can manage it here if you wish.

Managing Active Directory, as well as a lot more on how to configure it, will be covered in Chapter 9.

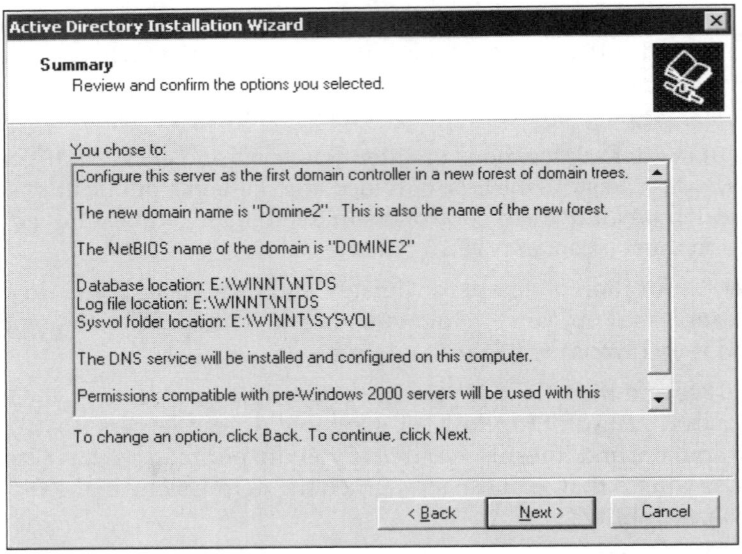

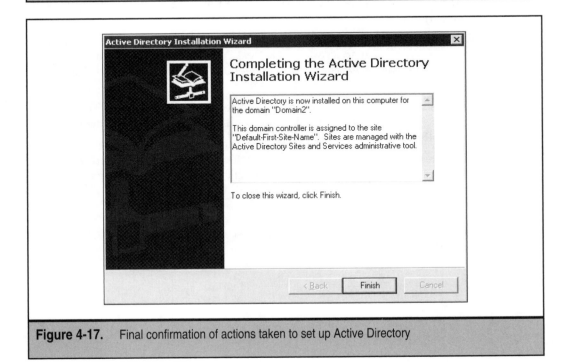

Figure 4-16. List of actions to be performed to set up Active Directory

Figure 4-17. Final confirmation of actions taken to set up Active Directory

Configuring Networking

Configuring networking on a server covers a number of topics, including the network adapter and TCP/IP settings, setting up network services such as DHCP and DNS, and properly identifying the installation server. The network settings and identification were handled during installation, and setting up DHCP and DNS was done with Active Directory, so there is little to do here. Chapter 7 also discusses these topics in some detail. (In the Configure Your Server dialog box, two other topics, Remote Access and Routing, are listed under Networking. These are discussed in Chapter 10.) Take a look at your network settings and identification first and then see what is left to be done with DHCP and DNS.

Network Settings and Identification

Review the network settings and identification with the following steps to make sure they are configured the way you want them.

1. In the Configure Your Server dialog box, click Networking in the left column. The network configuration instructions will be displayed on the right side of the dialog box, and a list of services will appear on the left side, as you can see in Figure 4-18.

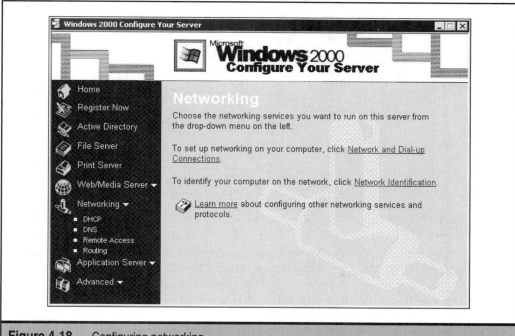

Figure 4-18.   Configuring networking

2. Click Network and Dial-up Connections on the right. A window with that name opens, showing at least two icons: Make New Connection and Local Area Connection.

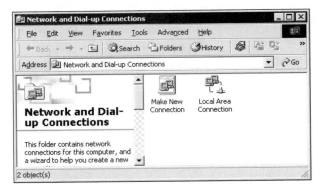

3. Double-click Local Area Connection. The status of the local area connection is displayed, including whether the computer is connected, the duration, and the speed. If this shows that you are connected and at the correct speed, you can skip the next four steps and continue with step 8.

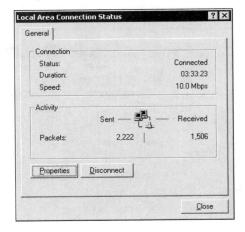

4. Click Properties to open the Local Area Connection Properties dialog box, shown in Figure 4-19.

5. Click Configure under the network adapter. This will tell you if the network adapter is working properly. If there is a problem, click the Resources tab and see if there are any conflicts. If that does not cure the problem, click Troubleshooter on the General tab. When you believe that the adapter is set up properly, click OK to close the adapter Properties dialog box.

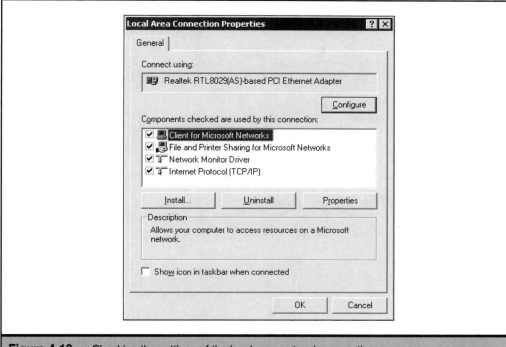

Figure 4-19.   Checking the settings of the local area network connection

6. Scroll the list of components in the Local Area Connection Properties dialog box until you see Internet Protocol (TCP/IP), and then double-click that component. The Internet Protocol (TCP/IP) Properties dialog box will open, as shown in Figure 4-20. If the server you are working on has both Active Directory and DNS resident on it, it must have a static IP address, as is shown in Figure 4-20. Also, the DNS server may have been assigned a static address.

7. If the IP addresses are not correct, see the discussion earlier in the chapter in step 11 under "Running a Clean Install Started from a Newer Windows Version/Final GUI-Based Setup Wizard Phase." When you are satisfied with the IP addresses, click OK twice to close both the IP and LAN Properties dialog boxes.

8. Click Close in the Local Area Connection Status dialog box, and close the Network and Dial-up Connections window.

9. Back in the Configure Your Server dialog box, click Network Identification. The System Properties dialog box opens, showing the Network Identification tab. This displays the full computer name and the domain name. Since this computer

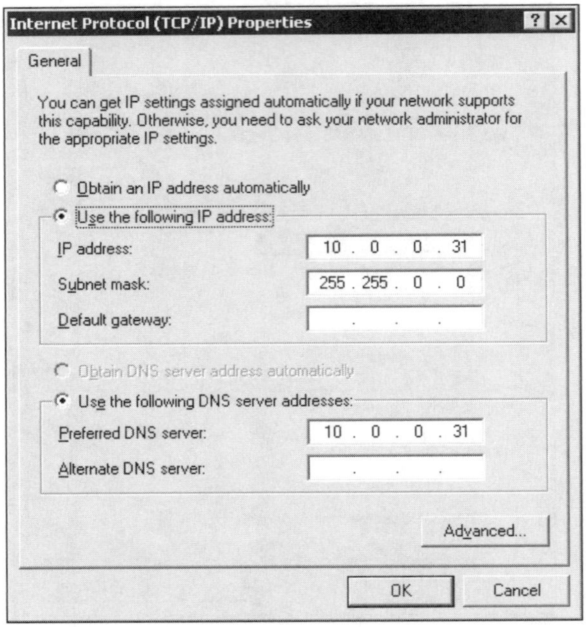

Figure 4-20. Setting static IP addresses

is the domain server, you cannot change the name. Close the System Properties dialog box. You are returned to the Configure Your Server dialog box.

Configuring DHCP

Although DHCP was installed in Active Directory, there are still several items that must be handled to configure it, as you'll see in the following steps:

1. Click DHCP under Networking on the left of the Configure Your Server dialog box. If DHCP was installed in the previous steps, the dialog box changes to tell you that DHCP is installed, but that you need to define a *scope* or range of IP addresses that DHCP will assign to clients. Skip to step 4.

2. If DHCP was not installed, click Start the Windows Component Wizard, which starts the wizard and shows you the list of components. Scroll to Network Services and click Detail. In the Networking Services list of subcomponents, click Dynamic Host Configuration Protocol (DHCP), and click OK. Back in the Windows Component Wizard, click Next. You will be told that Setup is making the requested configuration changes.

3. If you don't have a static IP address, you are told to assign one (see step 11 in "Running a Clean Install Started in Other Ways/GUI-Based Setup Wizard").

Click Finish to complete the Windows Component Wizard. Back in the Configure Your Server dialog box, click Networking in the left column to close it, and then click it again to reopen it. Click DHCP again and you should be told that it is installed.

NOTE: Chapter 7 will discuss the DHCP settings in detail. The purpose here is simply to get the operating system fully operational.

4. Click Open to start the DHCP Manager window, and click the server being installed in the tree on the left. A set of configuration instructions will appear, as shown in Figure 4-21.

5. Open the Action menu and click New Scope. The New Scope Wizard will open. Click Next.

6. Enter the name and description of the scope to identify the scope you are setting. Click Next.

7. Enter the starting and ending IP addresses for the scope or range that you want to define. As you enter the scope, you will see that the subnet mask is defined for you, as shown in Figure 4-22. Click Next. In the next dialog box, you can exclude one or more ranges within the range you just defined.

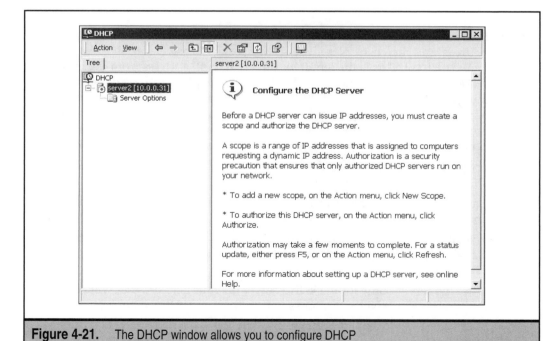

Figure 4-21.   The DHCP window allows you to configure DHCP

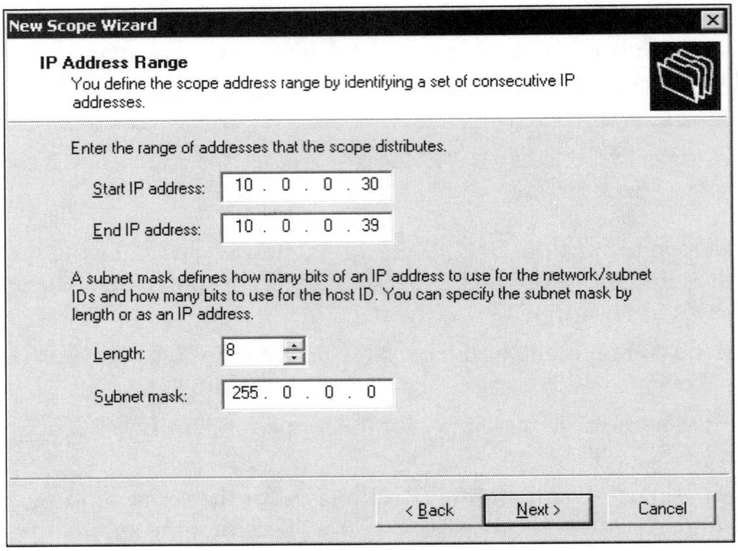

Figure 4-22.   Defining a DHCP range or scope

8. If desired, define one or more ranges to be excluded, such as the server's IP address, and then click Next. The setting for the Lease Duration is displayed and explained. This is the length of time that an IP address from the current scope is assigned to a client. As the dialog box explains, this is dependent on the type of clients on the network you are setting up, with the objective of having the duration equal to the average time a client is connected. If clients are generally permanently connected, you can set this for a long time. If most clients are getting on and off frequently, you'll want to set this for a short time.

9. Set the Lease Duration and click Next. You are asked if you want to configure DHCP options. Click Yes and Next.

10. Enter the IP Addresses for any routers or gateways that are on your network, and click Next.

11. Enter the Parent Domain to be used for DNS name resolution, enter the Server Name of the DNS server, click Resolve, and then click Add, as shown in Figure 4-23. Click Next.

12. Enter the server name for the WINS server on your network that will be used to convert or resolve NetBIOS names to IP addresses. If DNS is already installed

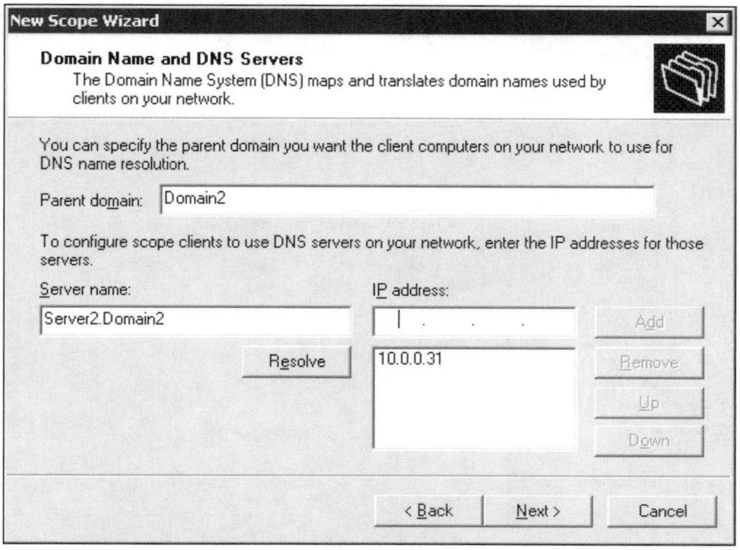

Figure 4-23. Identifying the DNS server

(and it should be), enter the server name and click Resolve. You should get an IP address. Enter the IP address if you don't get it, and click Next.

13. Click Yes to activate the scope you have just defined, click Next, and then click Finish.

14. Open the Action menu and choose Authorize. After a few moments, the window will be redrawn. Close the DHCP window.

Configuring DNS

Like DHCP, DNS is already defined, but you may need to create a names database, called a *zone*, as follows:

1. In the Configure Your Server dialog box, click DNS under Networking on the left. Information on DNS will be displayed, explaining how to create zones.

2. Click Manage. The DNS window will be displayed.

3. Open several levels of the tree on the left. You should see that your current domain is already designated as a forward lookup zone, as shown in Figure 4-24, which for current purposes is adequate. (Chapter 7 will go into this in more detail.)

4. Close the DNS window.

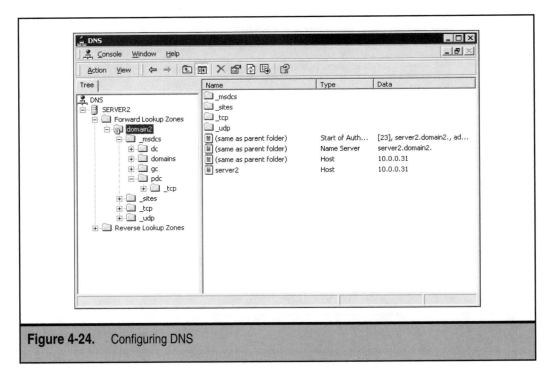

Figure 4-24. Configuring DNS

Setting Up a File Server

The primary file server functions are to identify and manage the shared folders on the server. You can create shared folders with the Create Shared Folder Wizard, as follows:

1. In the Configure Your Server dialog box, click File Server on the left and then click Start on the right. The Create Shared Folder Wizard will open.

2. Click Browse, select an existing folder to share, and click OK. Enter a share name and description, like this:

3. Click Next. Select the type of permission that you want to assign to the shared folder. Click Finish. You are asked if you want to share another folder. If so, click Yes (do that for these steps).

4. Back in the first Create Shared Folder dialog box, click Browse to create a new shared folder. Select a folder that you want to be a parent to the new shared folder.

5. Click New Folder, enter the name of the folder, and click OK. Enter the share name and description, click Next, enter permissions, and click Finish.

6. Repeat the preceding steps until you have shared all the folders you want to share. Then, click No to indicate that you do not want to share any more folders.

Setting Up a Print Server

For the Print Server, you need to set up one or more printers, which is done with the Add Printer Wizard.

1. In the Configure Your Server dialog box, click Print Server and then click Start to open the Add Printer Wizard.

2. Click Next, select either a local printer connected to the server you are working on or a network printer connected to another computer, and then click Next. If you select a local printer, Windows searches for a Plug and Play printer, and if it finds one, Windows asks you if that is the printer you want to install. If you answer Yes, it will be added to the system. If the wizard can't find a printer, it tells you that, and you have to install it manually. Follow that path for a moment and then the network path will be described.

3. To manually add a local printer, click Next in the dialog box that says it can't find a Plug and Play printer. Select an existing port or create a new port and again click Next.

4. Select the printer's manufacturer and model, as shown in Figure 4-25, and click Next.

5. Enter the name of the printer and indicate whether you want Windows-based programs to use this as the default printer. Click Next.

6. Select whether you want to share the printer and, if so, enter the shared as name. Click Next. Enter a location and comment, and click Next. Choose whether you want to print a test page, and click Next once more.

7. When you have completed all of your selections, they will be summarized for you. Click Finish to add the printer you have described. The printer files will be copied to your computer (you may be asked to insert the Windows 2000 Server Setup disk).

8. To add a network printer (assuming you made that choice in step 2 and clicked Next), select whether to find the printer in Active Directory, or to manually

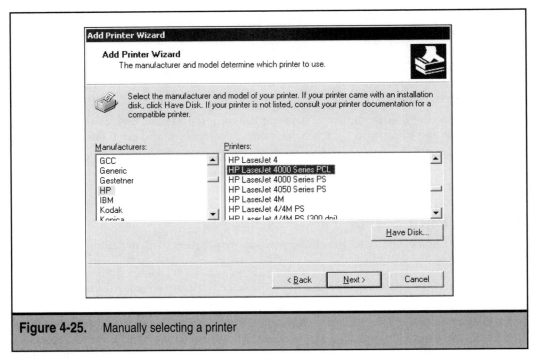

Figure 4-25. Manually selecting a printer

enter the printer's name or browse the network for it, or to connect to a printer on the Internet or intranet. Click Next.

9. If you browse the network, a list of computers on the network will be displayed, and if you open a computer, its printers will be listed, as you can see in Figure 4-26.

10. Select the printer you want to use, and click Next. Choose whether you want to use this printer as the system's default printer, and click Next.

11. Your printer selection will be displayed. Click Finish to add it to the printers available on this computer.

Getting on the Internet

In addition to the local area network, the other major connection that you probably need to make is with the Internet. Given that he computer you are installing is a domain controller, probably the most common connection is directly to the Internet over phone lines, not through another computer on the network. Here are the steps to make such a connection (Chapter 10 will describe connecting over the network):

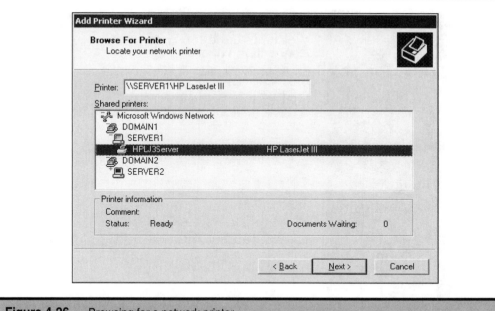

Figure 4-26. Browsing for a network printer

1. Double-click Connect to the Internet on the Windows 2000 Server desktop. The Internet Connection Wizard will start, as shown in Figure 4-27.

2. Select how you want to connect to the Internet: a new Internet account (Microsoft will suggest vendors) via modem, an existing account via modem, or a manually established account, which can be over a network or a modem. This exercise looks at manually establishing an account using a modem. Click Next after making your selection.

3. Choose whether to connect through a modem and phone line or over a network. Click Next.

4. Enter the area code, phone number, country, and whether the area code and country rules should be applied. If your ISP uses a protocol other than the Point To Point Protocol (PPP), requires you to enter a script at logon, or has permanently assigned you an IP address or DSN address, then you need to click the Advanced button and fill in that information.

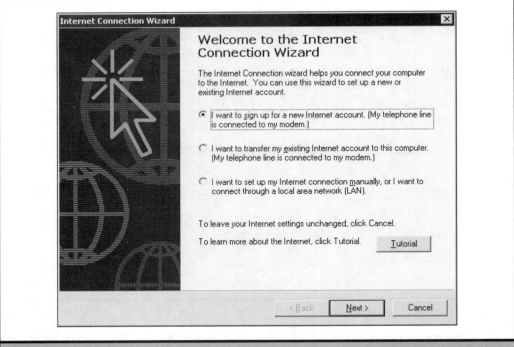

Figure 4-27. Setting up an Internet account

5. When you have completed the phone and connection-related information, click Next. Enter the username and password given to you by an ISP or an administrator and again click Next.

6. Enter the name of the connection that will allow you to recognize it, and click Next.

7. Decide if you want to set up an Internet mail account, and once more click Next.

8. If you do set up a mail account, you must also enter the name and e-mail address of the person who will receive the mail, select the type of incoming mail server, select the designation of the incoming and outgoing mail servers (the last two may be the same), and click Next.

9. Enter the mail account name and password, whether the system should remember the password, and whether the ISP requires Secure Password Authentication. Click Next.

10. If possible, leave the checkbox for an immediate Internet connection checked to test the system, and click Finish. The Dial-Up Connection dialog box should open. Click Connect. If the connection failed and you know that the modem is connected to a phone jack (check it), then the modem might not be Plug and

Play, and therefore did not get set up. Open the Control Panel (Start | Settings | Control Panel) and double-click Phone and Modem Options. If the list of modems just has Standard Modem, it means that Setup could not detect your modem. Select Standard Modem and click Remove. Then click Add. The Add/Remove Wizard will open and try again to detect both a Plug and Play and legacy modem. If that fails, click Next. Select the modem from the list of manufacturers and models, select the port to which it is attached, and click Finish when you see that the modem has been installed successfully.

11. When you connect, Internet Explorer will open and display its Home page, similar to Figure 4-28. The key is that you got on. Close Internet Explorer and choose Disconnect Now from the Auto Disconnect dialog box.

You can now attach to the Internet at any time by clicking the Internet Explorer icon on your desktop.

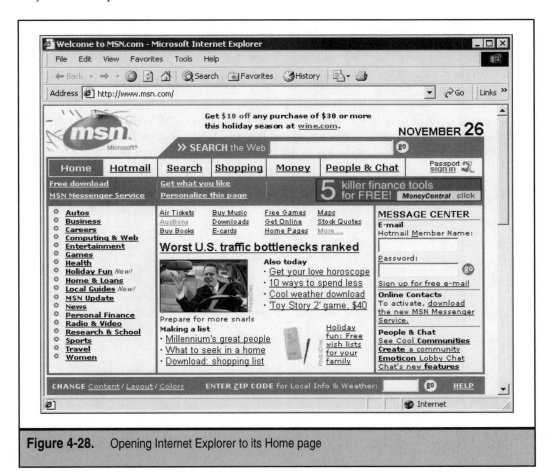

Figure 4-28.   Opening Internet Explorer to its Home page

Registering the Installation

Once you have the modem working, you can register your installation. This provides you with information on any new related products, so it is probably worth your while. To register, use these steps:

1. From the Configure Your Server dialog box, click Register Now on the left. The right side of the dialog box will change. Click Register Now on the right. The Registration Wizard will open. Click Next.

2. The wizard verifies the ability to connect to Microsoft, and then tells you how the information you give Microsoft will be used. Click Next.

3. Enter your name, your company name (if you have one), your e-mail address, your business address and phone number, the job category that best describes you, whether you want Microsoft to give away your name, whether you want Microsoft to have your system inventory, and your product ID. Click Next as necessary.

4. Finally, you are told that you are about to dial Microsoft on a toll-free line if you are in the United States. Click Connect.

5. When the registration is complete, you will be told that you have registered successfully.

Although several facilities within Windows 2000 Server still need to be configured, such as the web server, which is discussed in Chapter 11, this chapter has provided a fully operational network server connected to the Internet. A good starting position.

CHAPTER 5

Rolling Out Windows 2000 Professional

A client/server environment typically has a large number of clients and a small number of servers. As a result, the installation of the clients (Windows 2000 Professional) cries out for an automated way to do it. This chapter covers both manual and automated ways of installing Windows 2000 Professional. The automated approaches work equally well with Windows 2000 Server, if you have a number of servers to install.

MANUAL INSTALLATION OF WINDOWS 2000 PROFESSIONAL

The manual installation of Windows 2000 Professional is very similar to that for Windows 2000 Server. As a result, you need to read the "Starting Setup" section of Chapter 4 if you want to install Windows 2000 Professional manually, because starting Setup for Windows 2000 Professional is exactly the same as it is for Server 2000. You can start over a network or locally, you can boot from the installation CD-ROM or floppy disks (the latter of which can come from Microsoft or can be created from the CD), and you can start from MS-DOS or any version of Windows. All of this is described in Chapter 4's "Starting Setup."

Because running Setup for Windows 2000 Professional is sufficiently different from running it for Windows 2000 Server, the routine is presented again here, using the same section structure presented in Chapter 4:

▼   Running a Clean Install Started from a Newer Windows Version

■   Running a Clean Install Started in Other Ways

▲   Running an Upgrade

Running a Clean Install Started from a Newer Windows Version

If you start Setup in a newer version of Windows, Setup has three phases:

▼   An initial GUI phase

■   An intermediate character-based Setup Program phase

▲   A final GUI-based Setup Wizard phase

CAUTION: By definition, a clean install means that anything that was previously on the hard disk partition or volume will be removed and therefore lost during a reformatting process, to give you a clean hard disk.

Initial GUI Phase

Having started from a newer version of Windows, you should have the dialog box shown in Figure 5-1 on the screen. The steps to continue from this point with Setup are as follows:

1. In the dialog box shown in Figure 5-1, choose Install a New Copy of Windows 2000 (see the discussion in Chapter 3 under "Deciding to Upgrade or Install") and click Next. The License Agreement dialog box opens.

2. Click I Accept This Agreement (or forget about installing Windows 2000) and then click Next. The Product Key dialog box opens.

3. Enter the product key located on the back of the Windows CD envelope or case, and click Next. The Select Special Options dialog box opens, shown in Figure 5-2. This allows you to change the language used by Setup, select special accessibility options, and change the way files are copied. The specific choices you have are as follows:

   ■ **Language Options** Allows you to select a primary language and one of the areas of the world that language is used. This determines not only the

Figure 5-1.   You can upgrade or do a clean install after starting from a previous version of Windows

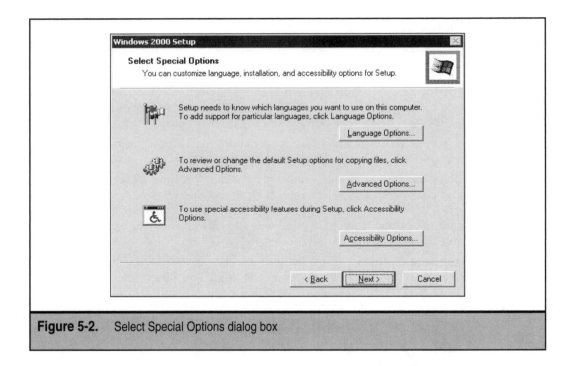

Figure 5-2. Select Special Options dialog box

language to use, but also the formats for dates, times, currency, and numbers, as well as character sets and keyboard layouts. You can also choose additional languages you want to use.

- **Advanced Options** Allows you to specify the location of the Windows 2000 Setup files and the folder in which you want Windows 2000 installed.

- **Accessibility Options** Allows you to turn on a Magnifier to enlarge portions of the Setup screen for those with limited vision, and/or turn on a Narrator to read aloud the contents of the Setup screen for those who cannot see it (you must have a sound card and speakers).

4. Complete your selections and click Next. Setup will begin copying files. From a CD, this is fairly fast, but over a network, it can take a while, depending on the speed of the network and the traffic on it. When the copying process is complete, the computer is rebooted and the character-based Setup Program is started.

Intermediate Character-Based Setup Program Phase

The intermediate character-based Setup Program phase continues with these steps:

1. Setup inspects your hardware configuration and gives you a chance to press F6 to install a third-party Small Computer System Interface (SCSI) or redundant

array of independent disks (RAID) mass-storage driver. If needed, press F6 and follow the instructions for installing the driver. Setup then loads the files that you need. Upon completion, you are told that Setup will restart your computer. (If you don't press F6, the computer doesn't restart at this point.)

NOTE: You need to press F6 rather quickly if you want to install a driver. You have only about ten seconds to make the decision and press the F6 key. If you are unsure about whether you need to press F6, press it. You can always exit without installing a SCSI or RAID driver.

---

2. If you pressed F6, press ENTER to restart. You are given a choice of which operating system you want to start. Press ENTER to choose the default Windows 2000 Professional Setup. You are asked whether you want to install a new Windows 2000 or repair the existing one.

3. Choose Install a New Windows 2000 and press ENTER. You are next shown the existing partitions and asked which you want to use for the current installation.

4. Use the UP ARROW and DOWN ARROW keys to select the partition you want to use. You then can press ENTER to install in that partition, press C to create a new partition in unpartitioned space, or press D to delete an existing partition and create a new one in its place.

NOTE: You will not be able to delete in this manner the partition from which you originally booted the computer. You should be able to do this if you boot into Setup from the Windows 2000 CD or floppy disks. If you can boot from the Windows 2000 CD or floppy disks, start Setup, follow the initial instructions through restarting of the computer, then choose Repair ("R") and Recovery Console ("C"). Here you have a DOS-like interface where you can get a list of commands by typing **help**. Use the Diskpart command to remove partitions (type **help diskpart** to learn how to do to this). Also, see "Using the Recovery Console" in Chapter 14. If that still doesn't work, boot from a DOS or Windows 3.x, 95, or 98 boot floppy disk and use Fdisk by typing **fdisk** and pressing ENTER. Follow the instructions to choose large disk support, treat NTFS (new technology file system) partitions as large, delete a partition, delete a non-DOS partition, and confirm that deletion. Press ESC twice to exit Fdisk.

---

5. If you have chosen to do a new installation and you are using an existing partition, you will get a message that you are going to copy over all the old operating system's files and settings, removing the old system and requiring reentry of all settings and applications. Press L to continue.

6. If you truly want to do a clean install, press D. Confirm that you want to delete a system partition by pressing ENTER and then pressing L. To set up Windows 2000 in the unpartitioned space, press ENTER (a partition will be created for you).

7. Select whether you want the new partition formatted using NTFS or the FAT (file allocation table) file system, and press ENTER. If you select NTFS, you are cautioned that you will not be able to read the older operating systems. Press C

to convert the drive. The new partition will be formatted as you directed, and if you choose NTFS, the computer will be restarted.

Setup then begins detecting and installing the hardware devices on the computer. When this is completed, the Windows 2000 Setup Wizard is started.

Final GUI-Based Setup Wizard Phase

When the Windows 2000 Setup Wizard starts, you see its Welcome dialog box. Continue through Setup with these steps:

1. Click Next (if you wait a moment, it is done for you). Setup begins installing devices, and you see a moving bar indicating the progress. When that is completed, the Regional Settings dialog box appears. This allows you to choose a system or user locale that determines which language is the default, which other languages are available, and how numbers, currencies, time, and dates are displayed and used for the system in general, as well as for the current user. You can also choose which keyboard layout to use and several keyboard options.

2. Select the regional settings that you want, and click Next. The Personalize Your Software dialog box appears.

3. Enter the person's name and organization to be associated with the computer, and click Next. The Computer Name and Administrator Password dialog box appears.

4. Enter a unique name for the computer (it can be up to 63 characters long, but pre-Windows 2000 computers will only see the first 15 characters) and enter and confirm a password to be used by the system administrator.

5. Click Next. The Modem Dialing Information dialog box is displayed. This allows you to select the country or region you are in, your area or city code, the number that must be dialed to get an outside line, and whether the phone system uses tone or pulse dialing.

6. Enter the modem dialing information and then click Next. You'll see a dialog box for Date and Time Settings.

7. If necessary, set the current date and time and click Next. The Networking Settings dialog box will appear and the Windows networking components will be installed. This allows you to connect to other computers, networks, and the Internet.

   When the networking software is installed, if you have a network card and Setup sees it, you are asked to choose either Typical settings, which creates network connections using the Client for Microsoft Networks, File and Print Sharing for Microsoft Networks, and the TCP/IP protocol with automatic addressing, or Custom settings, which allows you to manually configure networking components. Choosing Custom allows you to add or remove clients, services, and protocols, such as the Gateway and Client Service for NetWare or the NetBEUI protocol.

8. Choose the Network settings you want to use, and click Next. The Workgroup or Computer Domain dialog box appears, asking whether you want this computer to be a member of a domain.

9. If you click No and the computer is part of a workgroup, enter a workgroup name. If you click Yes, type the domain name. Click Next when you are done with the domain settings. If you selected Domain, you will need to enter a username and password and click OK. Setup will install the needed components with the settings you specified.

10. When component installation is done, Start menu items are installed, components are registered, settings are saved, and all temporary files are removed. You are asked to remove the CD from its drive, if there is one, and to click Finish to restart the computer. Do that to finish Setup.

11. When the system is restarted, the Network Identification Wizard will appear. Click Next. You are asked if you want to add a user to the computer.

12. If you want to add a user (you have already made Administrator a user), enter the username and the user's domain. If you do not want to add a user, click that option. In either case, click Next.

13. If you chose to add a user, you are asked to specify the level of access for that user: Standard, Restricted, or Other. Choose a level of access and click Next.

14. Whether or not you added a user, click Finish to complete Network Identification. Startup will continue.

15. Upon request, press CTRL-ALT-DEL, enter the user's name and password you first entered above in step 4, and click OK.

When loading is complete, the Windows 2000 desktop will appear with its default icons and the Getting Started with Windows 2000 dialog box, shown in Figure 5-3.

Running a Clean Install Started in Other Ways

When you boot from a CD or floppies, or start from DOS or Windows 3.*x*, you have only two phases: the character-based Setup Program and the GUI-based Setup Wizard. You see none of the startup GUI dialog boxes and go right into the character-based Setup Program.

Character-Based Setup Program

Having started Setup, begin the character-based Setup Program with the following steps:

1. If your boot device does not contain your Setup files, you need to confirm the drive and folder where those files exist. Often, the CD-ROM drive is drive D, in which case the correct response would be **D:\I386**. When the correct drive and folder are displayed, press ENTER.

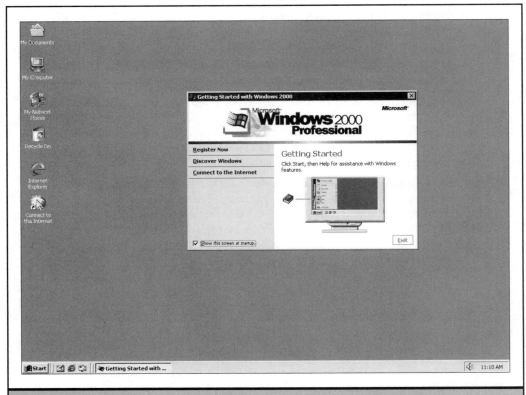

Figure 5-3.   Start up Windows 2000 desktop

2. If you are starting from an older version (5.*x* or 6.*x*) of DOS or Windows 3.*x* and don't have the DOS SmartDrive disk-caching system loaded, you will be reminded that having it will greatly improve the performance of Setup (although it is still slow compared to other ways of starting Setup).

SmartDrive is started with the program Smartdrv.exe that was included with DOS 6.*x* and Windows 3.*x*. If you look at the original distribution diskettes for these products, you will see the file Smartdrv.ex_. This is a compressed file that must be expanded with Expand.exe, also on the distribution diskettes (type **expand a:\smartdrv.ex_ c:\smartdrv.exe**, assuming that you are in the directory with Expand.exe). With Smartdrv.exe in the root directory of the hard disk, add the line **smartdrv.exe** to the Autoexec.bat file. After you have started DOS, you can check whether SmartDrive is loaded by typing **smartdrv** and pressing ENTER. If it's loaded, you will see a report of the version, cache size, and status. An initial set of files is copied to the hard disk, which can be a very slow process if you started from DOS or Windows 3.*x*, and your system is rebooted.

3. Setup inspects your hardware configuration and gives you the opportunity to press F6 to install a third-party SCSI or RAID mass-storage driver. If needed, press F6 and follow the instructions for installing the driver. Setup then loads the files that you need.

NOTE: You need to press F6 rather quickly if you want to install a driver. You have only about ten seconds to make the decision and press the F6 key. If you are unsure about whether you need to press F6, press it. You can always exit that question without installing a SCSI or RAID driver.

4. If there is an existing operating system, Setup asks whether you want to repair an existing installation of Windows 2000 or set up a new Windows 2000 installation. Press ENTER for a new installation.

5. If you started from floppy disks and do not have the Windows 2000 Professional CD in the drive, you will be asked to insert it.

6. The Microsoft License Agreement is displayed, and you are asked to press F8 if you agree to it or ESC if you don't. If you want to install Windows 2000, press F8.

7. If there is an existing Windows 2000 installation, you'll be asked again whether you want to repair that installation, which you can do by pressing R, or install a fresh copy of Windows 2000 by pressing ESC.

8. You are next shown the existing partitions and asked which you want to use for the current installation.

9. Use the UP ARROW and DOWN ARROW keys to select the partition you want to use. You then can press ENTER to install in that partition, press C to create a new partition in unpartitioned space, or press D to delete an existing partition and create a new one in its place.

10. If you truly want to do a clean install, press D. Confirm that you want to delete a system partition by pressing ENTER and then pressing L. To set up Windows 2000 in unpartitioned space, press ENTER (a partition will automatically be created for you).

11. Select whether you want the new partition formatted using NTFS (recommended) or the FAT file system, and then press ENTER. The new partition will be formatted as you directed.

12. If you only have an existing FAT or FAT32 partition, you will be asked whether you want to convert it NTFS (recommended) or leave the current file system intact. Select Convert and press ENTER. Confirm that you want to convert the partition by pressing C.

When the conversions or formatting is done, the remaining files are copied to the hard disk. Upon completion, the Windows 2000 Setup Wizard is started.

GUI-Based Setup Wizard

When the Windows 2000 Setup Wizard starts, you see several dialog boxes telling you that Windows 2000 is loading files, and then the Welcome dialog box appears. Continue through Setup with these steps:

1. Click Next (if you wait a moment, it is done for you). Setup then begins detecting and installing the hardware devices on the computer. When that is done, the Regional Settings dialog box appears. This allows you to choose a system or user locale that determines which language is the default, which other languages are available, and how numbers, currencies, time, and dates are displayed and used for the system in general, as well as for the current user. You can also choose which keyboard layout to use and several keyboard options.

2. Select the regional settings that you want, and click Next. The Personalize Your Software dialog box will appear.

3. Enter the person's name and organization to be associated with the computer, and click Next. The Product Key dialog box opens.

4. Enter the Product Key that is on the back of the Windows 2000 CD envelope or case. The Computer Name and Administrative Password dialog box appears.

5. Enter a unique name for the computer (it can be up to 63 characters long, but pre-Windows 2000 computers will only see the first 15 characters) and enter and confirm a password to be used by the system administrator.

6. Click Next. The Modem Dialing Information dialog box is displayed. This allows you to select the country or region you are in, your area or city code, the number that must be dialed to get an outside line, and whether the phone system uses tone or pulse dialing.

7. Enter the modem dialing information and then click Next. You'll see a dialog box for Date and Time Settings.

8. If necessary, set the current date and time, and click Next. The Windows networking components will be installed and, if you have a network card and Setup sees it, the Networking Settings dialog box will appear. This allows you to connect to other computers, networks, and the Internet.

   When the networking software is installed, you are asked to choose either Typical settings, which creates network connections using the Client for Microsoft Networks, File and Print Sharing for Microsoft Networks, and the TCP/IP protocol with automatic addressing, or Custom settings, which allows you to manually configure networking components. Choosing Custom allows you to add or remove clients, services, and protocols, such as the Gateway and Client Service for NetWare or the NetBEUI protocol.

9. Choose the Network settings you want to use, and click Next. The Workgroup or Computer Domain dialog box appears, asking whether you want this computer to be a member of a domain.

10. If you answer No and the computer is part of a workgroup, enter a workgroup name. If you answer Yes, type the domain name. Click Next when you are done with the domain settings. If you entered a domain name, you need to enter a username and password, and then click OK. Setup will install the necessary components and the settings you specified.

11. When component installation is done, Start menu items are installed, components are registered, settings are saved, and all temporary files are removed. You are asked to remove the CD from its drive, if there is one, and to click Finish to restart the computer. Do that to finish Setup.

12. When the system is restarted, the Network Identification Wizard will appear. Click Next.

13. Select whether the computer being installed is part of a network, and click Next. Then, choose whether the computer is part of a domain, and click Next. You are told that to be part of a domain, you need a username, password, and user account domain. Get this information from your network administrator, if you do not already have it.

14. Enter your username, password, and domain name, and click Next. If necessary, enter the computer name and domain name, and click Next. Click Finish to complete the network identification. Windows 2000 will restart. Upon request, press CTRL-ALT-DEL, enter the Administrator password you first entered in step 5, and click OK.

When loading is complete, the Windows 2000 desktop will appear with its default icons and the Getting Started with Windows 2000 dialog box, shown earlier.

Running an Upgrade

An upgrade to Windows 2000 Professional may be done from Windows 95, Windows 98, Windows NT 3.51 Workstation, or Windows NT 4 Workstation. (MS-DOS, Windows 3.1x, and OS/2 require a clean install.) It therefore can be started from any of the upgradable products. Many of the settings for Windows 2000 are taken from the earlier system, so there are fewer steps, although there are still three phases.

Initial GUI Phase

Having started from a newer version of Windows, you should have displayed onscreen the Upgrade vs. Install dialog box shown earlier in Figure 5-1. The steps to continue from this point with Setup are as follows:

1. In the dialog box shown in Figure 5-1, choose to upgrade and click Next. The License Agreement dialog box opens.

2. Click I Accept This Agreement (or forget about installing Windows 2000) and then click Next. The Product Key dialog box will appear.

3. Enter the product key that is shown on the back of the Windows 2000 CD envelope or case and click Next.

   You are told that Setup will check your hardware and software for compatibility with Windows 2000 Professional. If you have any upgrade files, you can use them when you are prompted. You can also connect to the Microsoft Windows 2000 web site and get the latest information on upgrades to various programs. If Setup finds something that is not compatible, you will be notified of it and given a chance to provide upgrade files. In Windows NT upgrades, you may see a Report System Compatibility dialog box, like the one in Figure 5-4.

   In Windows 95 and 98, the Preparing to Upgrade to Windows 2000 dialog box is opened, as shown in Figure 5-5. This asks you for any hardware or software upgrade files (most people don't have any) and tells you whether any parts of the current system are not compatible with Windows 2000 (and, if so, the consequences). You can save the incompatible items and get more information about them.

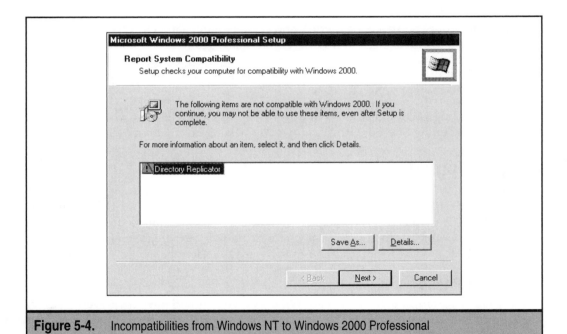

Figure 5-4. Incompatibilities from Windows NT to Windows 2000 Professional

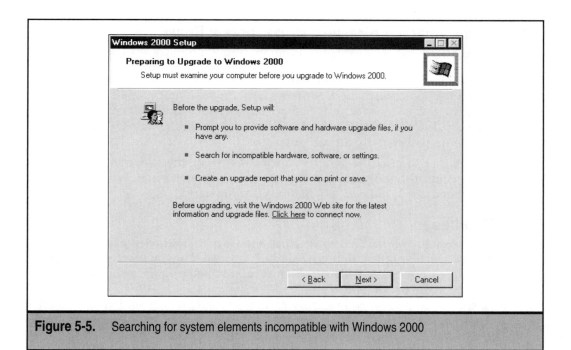

Figure 5-5.   Searching for system elements incompatible with Windows 2000

4. Click Next, handle any incompatible items, as necessary (for example, you may be told that a piece of hardware needs an upgraded driver), and click Next again. If you are upgrading from Windows 95 or 98, you are asked whether you want to upgrade to NTFS the hard drive on which you are installing Windows 2000. If you are going to dual-boot MS-DOS, Windows 95, or Windows 98, you should not do this. Otherwise, it is strongly recommended, to give you increased efficiency and security.

5. Choose whether to upgrade to NTFS, and click Next. If there is a problem, an upgrade report will be produced and displayed. Read through this and handle any outstanding issues. If necessary, restart Setup.

6. After you have handled all the issues on the Upgrade Report, click Next. You are told that Setup has all the necessary information and is ready to install Windows 2000. Your system will be restarted four times and the process can take up to an hour, during which time you do not need to do anything.

7. Click Next to begin installation. Setup will begin copying files. From a CD, this is fairly fast, but over a network, it can take a while, depending on the speed of the network and the traffic on it. When the copying process is complete, the computer is rebooted and the character-based Setup Program is started.

Intermediate Character-Based Setup Program Phase

The intermediate character-based Setup Program phase continues with these steps:

1. You are given a choice of which operating system you want to start. Press ENTER to choose the default Windows 2000 Professional Setup (if you wait a moment, this is done for you). Setup inspects your hardware configuration and then copies and loads the files that you need. Upon completion, you are told that Setup will restart your computer.

2. Press ENTER to restart (again, if you wait a moment, this is done for you). Setup then begins installing the hardware devices on the computer. When this is completed, the Windows 2000 Setup Wizard is started.

Final GUI Phase

In a normal upgrade, the final GUI phase is just a series of dialog boxes telling you what is happening. No installer interaction is needed. If you said that you wanted to convert to NTFS, this will be done. Setup will load and install with their original settings the components that were in the previous system.

If the computer was not previously part of a domain, and a domain is detected, you'll be asked if you want the computer to be a client of the domain. If you see this question, answer it and click Next. When component installation is done, Start menu items are installed, components are registered, settings are saved, and all temporary files are removed.

When loading is complete, the Windows 2000 desktop will appear with the Getting Started with Windows 2000 dialog box.

AUTOMATING WINDOWS 2000 INSTALLATION

Automating installation means to run Setup without intervention, to execute a command on a computer and walk away while setup installs or upgrades to Windows 2000. The end objective is to run Setup on a number of machines with a minimum of effort. Microsoft has developed two major ways of handling this:

▼ Command-line parameters

▲ Disk imaging

NOTE: When you perform an unattended Setup, there is a legal assumption that you and the organization for whom you are installing Windows 2000 have read and accepted Microsoft's End User License Agreement (EULA).

Command-Line Parameters

Setup is started by one of two commands, depending on from where you start it. From MS-DOS or Windows 3.1*x*, Setup is started with the command **winnt**, and from more recent versions of Windows and Windows NT, Setup is started with **winnt32**. Both Winnt and Winnt32 have a series of parameters and switches that allow them to be run with little intervention, as described in the next two sections.

Winnt Parameters and Switches

Winnt.exe can be run from any 16-bit OS running on an Intel-based computer that meets the minimum requirements for installing Windows 2000 Professional (see "Windows 2000 System Requirements" in Chapter 3). You can simply type **winnt** at a command prompt (DOS prompt or in the Windows Run command), but if you do, you must stay in front of the system for an hour or more and answer questions as Setup presents them. To remove the need for you to answer questions, you can use Winnt's parameters and switches to answer the questions. The full Winnt command has the following syntax, with the parameters described in Table 5-1:

winnt [/s:*sourcepath*] [/t:*tempdrive*] [/u:*answer file*][/udf:*id* [,*UDF_file*]]
   [/r:*folder*][/rx:*folder*][/e:*command*][/a]

Parameter or Switch	Description
/s:*sourcepath*	*Sourcepath* is the full path to the location of the Windows 2000 Setup files. You can have multiple /s:*sourcepath* parameters, but Setup will stop if the first one is not available. For example: /s:d:\i386 or /s:\\server\c:\win2kpro\.
/t:*tempdrive*	*Tempdrive* is the drive on which Setup will store temporary files during installation. If this isn't specified, Setup will use the drive where Windows 2000 is being installed. For example: /t:e:.
/u:*answer file*	*Answer file* provides some or all of the answers needed by Setup for an unattended operation. This requires /s. For example: /u:answers.txt.
/udf:*id* [,*UDF_file*]	*Id* identifies the value in an answer file (see the preceding description) that Setup is to override with a value in a Uniqueness Database File (UDF). If *UDF_file* is not specified, you are prompted to insert a disk with the $Unique$.udb file. For example, /udf:ComputerName,unique.udb overrides the ComputerName value in the answer file with the ComputerName value in Unique.udb.

Table 5-1.   Winnt Command Parameters and Switches

/r:*folder*	*Folder* is an optional folder to be installed and kept on the installation drive after Setup finishes. For example: **/r:c:\foldername**.
/rx:*folder*	*Folder* is an optional folder to be copied to the installation drive and then deleted when Setup finishes. For example: **/rx:c:\foldername**.
/e:*command*	*Command* is executed at the end of the final GUI-mode Setup. For example, **/e:c:\path\program** to launch a program named "program."
/a	Turns on the accessibility options.

Table 5-1.   Winnt Command Parameters and Switches *(continued)*

NOTE: Windows 2000 Winnt does not create floppy disks as Windows NT did, so the **/x** and **/b** switches for not creating floppies and for floppyless operation, respectively, are now gone.

Each of the Winnt parameters eliminates a possible user input during the running of Setup. **/t** is also used if there are multiple partitions on the hard disk or multiple hard disks. The answer file and UDF file are discussed further under "Creating Answer Files," later in the chapter.

Winnt32 Parameters and Switches

Winnt32.exe can be run from any 32-bit version of Windows (Windows 95/98 or Windows NT 3.51/4) running on an Intel-based computer that meets the minimum requirements for installing Windows 2000 Professional (see "Windows 2000 System Requirements" in Chapter 3). You can simply double-click Winnt32 in Windows Explorer or type **winnt32** in the Windows Run command, but, like Winnt, you must then stay in front of the system for an hour or more and answer questions as Setup presents them. To remove the need for you to answer questions, you can use Winnt32's parameters and switches to answer the questions. The full Winnt32 command has the following syntax, with the parameters (which are different from those for Winnt) described in Table 5-2:

winnt32 [/s:*sourcepath*] [/tempdrive:*drive*] [/unattend[*num*]:[*answer file*]]
    [/udf:*id*[,*UDF_file*]] [/copydir:*folder*] [/copysource:*folder*] [/cmd:*command*]
    [/debug[*level*]:[*filename*]] [/syspart:*drive*] [/checkupgradeonly] [/cmdcons]
    [/m:*folder*] [/makelocalsource] [/noreboot]

You can use Winnt32 parameters **/syspart** and **/tempdrive** to refer to the same secondary hard drive (not the boot drive in the current computer), and then use **/noreboot** to

Parameter or Switch	Description
/s:_sourcepath_	_Sourcepath_ is the full path to the location of the Windows 2000 Setup files. You can have multiple **/s:**_sourcepath_ parameters, but Setup will stop if the first one is not available. For example: **/s:d:\i386** or **/s:\\server\c:\win2kpro**.
/tempdrive:_drive_	_Drive_ is the drive on which Setup will store temporary files during installation. If this isn't specified, Setup will use the drive where Windows 2000 is being installed. For example: **/tempdrive:e:**.
/unattend	Used only with upgrades from a previous version of Windows 2000 in which all answers to Setup questions are taken from the previous installation.
/unattend[_num_**]:[**_answer file_**]**	_Answer file_ provides some or all of the answers needed by Setup for an unattended operation. If you are upgrading from Windows NT or Windows 2000, you can use _num_ to indicate the number of seconds between Setup finishing copying files and restarting the computer. For example: **/u30:answers.txt**.
/udf:_id_**[,**_UDF_file_**]**	_Id_ identifies the value in an answer file (see the preceding description) that Setup is to override with a value in a UDF file. If **_UDF_file_** is not specified, you will be prompted to insert a disk with the $Unique$.udb file. For example: **/udf:ComputerName,unique.udb** overrides the **ComputerName** value in the answer file with the **ComputerName** value in Unique.udb.
/copydir:_folder_	_Folder_ is copied to the folder in which Windows 2000 is installed, normally Winnt. You can have multiple copies of **/copydir:**_folder_. For example, **/copydir:Newdrivers** copies the folder Newdrivers to the Windows 2000 folder, probably C:\Winnt\.

Table 5-2.   Winnt32 Command Parameters and Switches

Parameter or Switch	Description
/copysource:*folder*	*Folder* is temporarily copied to the folder in which Windows 2000 is installed, normally Winnt, and then deleted when Setup is finished. You can have multiple copies of **/copysource:folder**. For example, **/copysource:Newdrivers** temporarily copies the folder Newdrivers to the Windows 2000 folder, probably C:\Winnt\. When Setup is finished, the folder is deleted.
/cmd:*command*	*Command* is executed at the end of the final GUI-mode Setup. For example, **/cmd:c:\path\program** to launch a program named "program."
/debug[*level***]:[***filename***]**	*Filename* is the name of a debug log created by Setup at the *level* specified. The levels are: 0-severe errors; 1-errors; 2-warnings; 3-information; and 4-detailed information. Each level includes lower levels. The default is C:\Winnt\Winnt32.log, at level 2. For example: **/debug3:C:\MySetup.log**.
/syspart:*drive*	*Drive* is a secondary hard drive onto which Setup is to copy the boot or startup files and mark the drive as active. When the drive is installed in another computer and that computer is started, Setup automatically starts at the next Setup phase. This requires **/tempdrive**. For example: **/syspart:e:**.
/checkupgradeonly	Produces the Compatibility Report after checking the upgrade compatibility with Windows 2000. The report is named Upgrade.txt in the Windows installation folder for Windows 95 and 98 upgrades, and is named Winnt32.log in the installation folder for Windows NT3.51 and 4 upgrades.

Table 5-2. Winnt32 Command Parameters and Switches *(continued)*

Parameter or Switch	Description
/cmdcons	Adds a Recovery Console option to the operating system selection screen to repair a failed installation after exiting Setup.
/m:_folder_	_Folder_ contains replacement files that Setup will use instead of the default files if the replacement files are present. For example: **/m:\\server\c:**.
/makelocalsource	Copies the installation source files to the hard drive on which Windows 2000 is being installed from either a CD or over a network, so that the files are available when the CD or network is not available.
/noreboot	Prevents restarting the computer after Setup's file-copy phase, so that another command can be executed.

Table 5-2.   Winnt32 Command Parameters and Switches _(continued)_

stop Setup after the file-copy phase. If you then remove the drive, place it in a different computer, and start that computer, Setup will continue with the Setup Wizard in the GUI phase. In this way, Setup can be started for a number of different types of machines by creating a disk image that can be customized after being restarted in the final machines.

CAUTION: In the just-described process of preparing a drive for another computer, don't reboot the original computer with the prepared secondary drive still installed. The computer will not boot and will hang because two boot devices are at the same level.

Creating Answer Files

Answer files are obviously the key to running Setup unattended. They are, by their nature, complex files with many parameters. To help you understand and create answer files, Microsoft has included five tools on the Windows 2000 Professional CD:

▼   A sample answer file named Unattend.txt in the \i386 folder

■   A guide to all the possible parameters in an answer file, along with more sample files in an over 160-page document named Unattend.doc in the \Support\Tools\Deploy.cab file

- A last-minute update to Unattend.doc in Readme.txt in the \Support\Tools\ Deploy.cab file

- A GUI program called Setup Manager Wizard to create answer files based on answering questions in Setupmgr.exe in the \Support\Tools\Deploy.cab file

▲ A help file for usage of Setup Manager in Deptool.chm in the \Support\Tools\ Deploy.cab file

NOTE: Deploy.cab is a compressed file that contains the preceding items, as well as other items. You can simply double-click on this file to unpack and see the files it contains, which you can then drag to another folder. You use the Setup.exe and 2000rkst.msi programs in the \Support\Tools folder to unpack and install the tools in Support.cab.

You can see that Microsoft takes this area seriously, as it should and as is needed due to its complexity. The best measure of this complexity is the 160-plus pages needed in Unattend.doc to document all the parameters and their options that can be in an answer file. This should not discourage you, because the vast majority of all answer files only use a small percentage of these parameters. Take a look at Unattend.txt, the sample answer file in the \i386 folder on the Windows 2000 Professional CD. Figure 5-6 shows it, but open it on your own screen where you can see it better. At the same time, open Unattend.doc so that you can switch back and forth between Unattend.txt and Unattend.doc. You'll want to look up the meaning of parameters and their possible values.

From the sample file, you can see a number of conventions, among which are the following:

▼ Comments begin with a semicolon (;). Even if you don't need to be reminded about what you were doing, it is a good idea to use lots of comments so that someone else can clearly understand what you were doing.

- The file is broken up into sections, each with a heading in square brackets.

- Within each section is a list of parameters that relate to that section.

- Parameters are assigned values by placing an equal sign (=), which may or may not be surrounded by spaces, after the parameter and before the value. For example:
Parameter = value

▲ If a value includes spaces, it must be enclosed in quotation marks ("), and other literal values may or may not have quotation marks.

NOTE: The [Unattended] section is required for the answer file to be used by Setup.

One way to create an answer file is to copy and modify Unattend.txt. In many instances, the parameters, and even some of the values, will be the same. Listing 5-1 is an

```
UNATTEND.TXT - Notepad                                                    _ □ ×
File   Edit   Format   Help
; Microsoft windows 2000 Professional, Server, Advanced Server and Datacenter
; (c) 1994 - 1999 Microsoft Corporation. All rights reserved.
;
; Sample unattended Setup Answer File
;
; This file contains information about how to automate the installation
; or upgrade of windows 2000 Professional and windows 2000 Server so the
; setup program runs without requiring user input.
;
[Unattended]
Unattendmode = FullUnattended
OemPreinstall = NO
TargetPath = WINNT
Filesystem = LeaveAlone

[UserData]
FullName = "Your User Name"
OrgName = "Your Organization Name"
ComputerName = "COMPUTER_NAME"

[GuiUnattended]
; Sets the Timezone to the Pacific Northwest
; Sets the Admin Password to NULL
; Turn AutoLogon ON and login once
TimeZone = "004"
AdminPassword = *
AutoLogon = Yes
AutoLogonCount = 1

;For Server installs
[LicenseFilePrintData]
AutoMode = "PerServer"
AutoUsers = "5"

[GuiRunOnce]
; List the programs that you want to lauch when the machine is logged into for the first
time

[Display]
BitsPerPel = 8
XResolution = 800
YResolution = 600
VRefresh = 70

[Networking]
; When set to YES, setup will install default networking components. The components to
be set are
; TCP/IP, File and Print Sharing, and the Client for Microsoft Networks.
InstallDefaultComponents = YES

[Identification]
JoinWorkgroup = Workgroup
```

Figure 5-6.   A sample answer file, Unattend.txt, in \i386 on the Windows 2000 CD

example answer file created by copying and modifying Unattend.txt. The purpose of this example answer file is to do a clean install to a new hard disk. You can see that very little modification was needed to make this file work. The primary changes were to repartition the hard drive with NTFS, personalize the file, and adjust it for my monitor. In "Using Setup Command Lines," later in the chapter, you see how this answer file can be used.

Listing 5-1:
Modified Sample Answer File

```
[Unattended]
; Delete all partitions on the boot drive, create one new partition,
; and reformat it with NTFS
Unattendmode = FullUnattended
OemPreinstall = NO
TargetPath = WINNT
Repartition = Yes

[UserData]
FullName = "Martin Matthews"
OrgName = "Matthews Technology"
ComputerName = "MTech1"

[GuiUnattended]
; Sets the Timezone to the Pacific Northwest
; Sets the Admin Password to NULL
; Turn AutoLogon ON and login once
TimeZone = "004"
AdminPassword = *
AutoLogon = Yes
AutoLogonCount = 1

[Display]
BitsPerPel = 16
XResolution = 1024
YResolution = 768
VRefresh = 60

[Networking]
; When set to YES, setup will install default networking components.
InstallDefaultComponents = YES

[Identification]
JoinWorkgroup = Matthews
```

Using the Setup Manager Wizard

If you want to do more with an answer file than what is done with the sample Unattend.txt, it becomes very laborious, both from having to look up in Unattend.doc the many parameters and the values that are allowed, and from having to manually enter everything while not making a typing and/or spelling mistake. The answer for this is to use the Setup Manager Wizard, which, in a GUI environment, creates an answer file for you based on your responses in its dialog boxes.

The Setup Manager Wizard prompts you to enter the information needed for the type of setup you are automating and the degree of user interaction you want. If you specify a fully unattended installation, the Setup Manager Wizard prompts you to enter all the necessary information. If you select a higher level of user interaction (there are five levels), the Setup Manager Wizard prompts you accordingly, and you can leave more questions unanswered in the answer file, forcing the end user to answer them in Setup.

Start the Setup Manager Wizard and create an answer file with the following steps:

1. If you haven't done so already, create a new folder called **Deployment** on your hard drive. Then, open the \Support\Tools folder on the Windows 2000 Professional CD, double-click Deploy.cab to open it, and drag its contents to your new Deployment folder.

2. In the Deployment folder, double-click Setupmgr.exe. The Setup Manager Wizard's welcome message will appear.

3. Click Next. You are asked whether you want to create a new answer file, modify an existing one, or create one that duplicates the current computer's configuration, as shown in Figure 5-7.

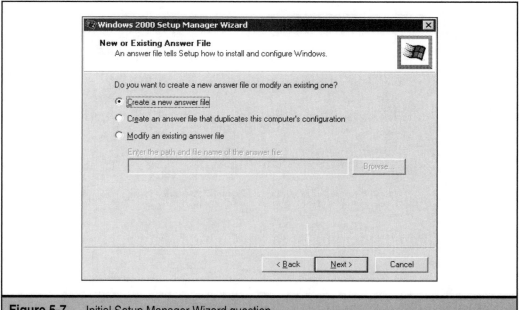

Figure 5-7. Initial Setup Manager Wizard question

4. Leave the default Create a New Answer File selected (or click it if it's not selected) and click Next. You are asked what the answer file will be used for: a Windows 2000 installation; Sysprep install, which is explained later in the chapter, under "Creating and Using Disk Images"; or Remote Installation Service (RIS).

5. Again, leave the default Windows 2000 Unattended Installation selected and click Next. Select the platform, Professional or Server, to which the answer file will install, and click Next. You are presented with a series of questions that goes through all the questions in Setup to give you a comprehensive answer file.

6. Provide the answers to the Setup Manager Wizard that are correct for the installation you want to perform, clicking Next at the bottom of each dialog box. In the fifth dialog box, shown in Figure 5-8, you must choose one of the five levels of user interaction. Click each of these levels and look at the description at the bottom of the dialog box. Table 5-3 provides another description of them.

NOTE: If you choose a fully automated installation, you must accept Microsoft's End User License Agreement before you can continue with the Setup Manager Wizard.

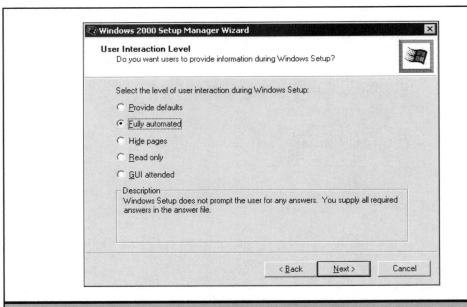

Figure 5-8.   Choosing the level of user interaction

Level of Interaction	Description
Provide Defaults	Defaults are provided to the end user, but he or she must make their own choice
Fully Automated	All answers to Setup's questions are provided in the answer file
Hide Pages	The Setup pages are hidden if you have provided all the answers
Read Only	The end user can see but not change questions that are answered in the answer file
GUI Attended	The final GUI Setup Wizard questions are left for the end user

Table 5-3.   Levels of User Interaction

7. When you are told that you have created a basic answer file, select Yes to edit additional settings, so that you can see the additional options that are available. Continue answering the questions, clicking Next in each dialog box.

8. When asked if you want to create or modify a distribution folder, click Yes (in the second related dialog box), you want to create a new one in the root directory or in another directory you have set up for that purpose, so you can look at it in the next section.

9. Save the answer file with the name **Answer1.txt** so that it does not copy over the Unattend.txt file.

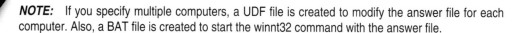

NOTE: If you specify multiple computers, a UDF file is created to modify the answer file for each computer. Also, a BAT file is created to start the winnt32 command with the answer file.

10. Specify the location of the Setup files, possibly D:\i386, that will be copied to the distributed folder. When the Setup Manager Wizard is done copying the Setup files, you are shown a summary of what it has done for you, as shown in Figure 5-9.

These steps should have created three or four objects in locations that you specified:

▼ **Answer1.txt**   The answer file that was your original objective

■ **Win2000dist**   A distribution folder with all the Setup files in i386 among other files

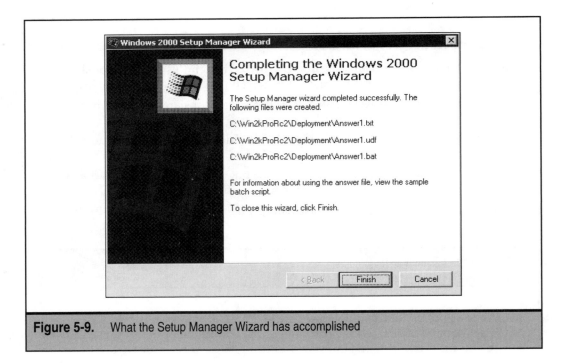

Figure 5-9. What the Setup Manager Wizard has accomplished

- ■ **Answer1.bat** A sample batch file that implements both the answer file and the distribution folder
- ▲ **Answer1.udf** If you have multiple computers, this file is included to supply the names of the computers

Each of these objects is discussed next, in turn.

Answer1.txt Answer File The answer file that is produced by the Setup Manager Wizard (shown in Figure 5-10) has some sections, parameters, and values not seen earlier:

- ▼ The [Data] section is used when booting from a CD, and contains the **AutoPartition** parameter, which with the value 1 tells Setup to eliminate all current partitions and reformat the hard drive with NTFS.
- ■ The parameters **OemSkipRegional** and **OemSkipWelcome** customize how Setup looks to the user.
- ■ The **ComputerName** parameter has a value of *, which will be substituted for the names in the UDF file.
- ■ The [TapiLocation] section provides the home area code.

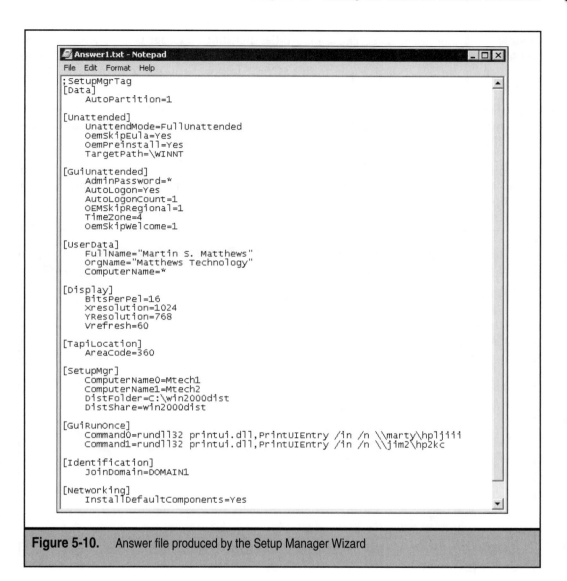

Figure 5-10.   Answer file produced by the Setup Manager Wizard

- ■ The [SetupMgr] section contains the two options for the computer name and the location of the distribution folder.
- ■ The [GuiRunOnce] section contains two commands to install different printers.
- ▲ The [Identification] section contains a parameter and value to join a domain.

Win200dist Distribution Folder   The Win2000dist distribution folder is a copy of the \i386 folder on the Windows 2000 Professional CD with the addition of the OEM folder, as shown in Figure 5-11. Possible uses for the OEM folder and its subfolders are described in Table 5-4.

NOTE:` OEM\$1\ and OEM\C\ are the same if drive C is the system drive on which Windows 2000 is installed. OEM\$1\ just gives you the flexibility of installing on any drive.

You can extend the OEM folder structure to include other folders, as necessary, for both Windows 2000 and other applications, to mirror the drive(s) in the computer being installed.

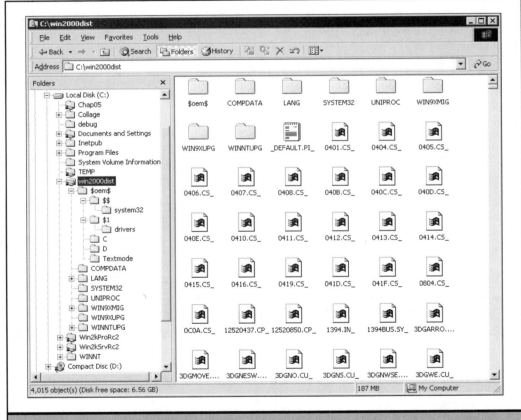

Figure 5-11.   Win2000dist distribution folder with its OEM subfolder

Folder	Description
OEM\	Holds files, folders, and applications that you want placed on a newly installed hard disk. A Cmdlines.txt file in the OEM folder can contain a list of commands, such as application-setup and .inf commands, that will be run at the end of the final GUI phase of Windows 2000 Setup.
OEM\$$\	Holds files and folders that you want copied into the Windows 2000 folder (normally named Winnt) on the computer being installed. You must follow the structure of the Windows folder, so fonts must be in OEM\$$\Fonts.
OEM\$$\System32\	Holds files, such as DLLs, that you want copied to what is normally named \Winnt\System32.
OEM\$1\	Holds files and folders that you want copied to the root directory of the system drive on which Windows 2000 is installed. The actual drive letter is assigned by Setup during installation, providing flexibility over multiple systems.
OEM\$1\Drivers\	Holds additional device drivers not included in Windows 2000.
OEM\C\	Holds files and folders that you want copied to the root directory of drive C.
OEM\D\	Holds files and folders that you want copied to the root directory of drive D.
OEM\Textmode\	Holds hardware-related files, such as SCSI and fiber channel device drivers, that are used in the early character-based or text mode of Windows 2000 Setup.

Table 5-4.   Purpose and Contents of the OEM Folder Tree

Answer1.bat Batch File   The Answer1.bat batch file, shown in Figure 5-12, is used to implement the answer file, UDF alternative file, and distribution folder created by the Setup Manager Wizard. It provides a basic command line that starts Winnt32 from the distribution folder using the answer and UDF files. The batch file is started by typing its name at a command prompt followed by the name of the computer on which the installation is being performed. For example, answer1 mtech1, if the computer name is Mtech1. The Winnt32 command line included in Answer1.bat has only a few of the many parameters and switches that are available, so any of the others may be added as you wish.

The contents of Answer1.bat follow the standard syntax for batch programs dating back to DOS. This syntax is briefly reviewed in Table 5-5.

Answer1.udf Alternative File   The Answer1.udf alternative file, shown next, is a simple file that supplies the computer name to the answer file. Since both the index and the data for the Answer1.udf file are the same, and there are only two alternatives, there seems to be little reason for it. If you were to have several variable fields, like the addition of FullName and OrgName, it might make more sense.

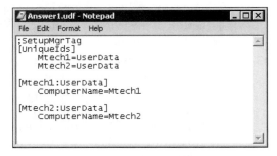

You can easily add a FullName field since it is in the [UserData] section, as shown next. It will replace the value that is in the answer file.

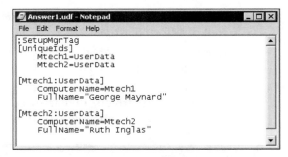

Using Setup Command Lines and Answer Files

The Setup command lines and answer files can be implemented in a number of ways, among which are the following:

▼   Type a setup command with appropriate parameters and switches at a command prompt (a DOS prompt or Windows Run command).

■   Create a batch file with a Setup command in it and execute the batch file by typing its name at a command prompt or double-clicking it from Windows.

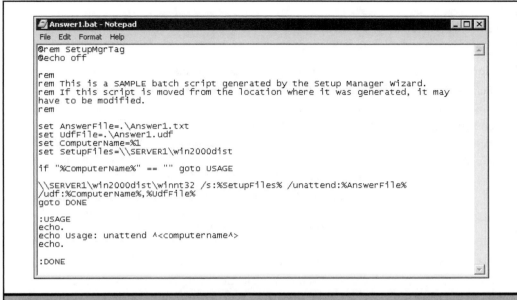

```
Answer1.bat - Notepad
File  Edit  Format  Help
@rem SetupMgrTag
@echo off

rem
rem This is a SAMPLE batch script generated by the Setup Manager wizard.
rem If this script is moved from the location where it was generated, it may
have to be modified.
rem

set AnswerFile=.\Answer1.txt
set UdfFile=.\Answer1.udf
set ComputerName=%1
set SetupFiles=\\SERVER1\win2000dist

if "%ComputerName%" == "" goto USAGE

\\SERVER1\win2000dist\winnt32 /s:%SetupFiles% /unattend:%AnswerFile%
/udf:%ComputerName%,%UdfFile%
goto DONE

:USAGE
echo.
echo Usage: unattend ^<computername^>
echo.

:DONE
```

Figure 5-12.   Answer1.bat batch file implements the answer and UDF files, as well as the distribution folder

- Copy a batch file with a Setup command in it to another computer and execute it from that computer. You may refer to Setup's files either in a distribution folder or on the Windows 2000 CD, and either on a server or on a local drive.

- Copy a batch file with a Setup command in it to a floppy disk. If the floppy is bootable, the Setup batch file can be started from the Autoexec.bat file on the floppy. Alternatively, the batch file on the floppy can be executed at a command prompt or by double-clicking it on the computer to be installed.

▲ If you can create a CD, especially a bootable one, you can include the batch file, answer and UDF files, and the complete distribution folder. The batch file then can be started from the Autorun.inf file on the CD.

You can probably think of other ways to use these files and folder. The batch file just mentioned, in all but the last scenario, can be very simple, or it can be even more complex than what you saw with the Setup Manager in Figure 5-13. You can decide whether or not the Setup command (Winnt32 or Winnt) refers to answer and UDF files, and whether or not you want to use the distribution folder. Look at a couple of examples that follow.

Simple Typed Command   The simplest situation is to upgrade Windows 2000. Suppose you have one of the prerelease versions of Windows 2000 and want to upgrade it for the final re-

Batch Command	Description
@	Prevents the current line from being displayed.
Rem	Treats the following text as a remark.
Echo off	Prevents following lines from being displayed.
Set (DOS command)	Defines environment variables, such as AnswerFile to be the string on the right of the equal sign.
%1 (one of nine input variables)	Stands in for the first string typed on the command line following the batch filename and a space. Additional spaces are used to separate additional strings.
If	Performs a test of a condition and executes a command if the condition is true, to implement branching in a batch command. The command is ignored if the condition is false.
%*string*%	Defines *string* to be an environment variable.
==	Generates a true condition if the strings on either side are the same. The strings can be variables or literal strings.
Goto	Transfers execution to the label that follows the **Goto** command.
:*string*	Defines *string* to be a label, which can contain up to eight characters, but no spaces or separators.
Echo	Displays onscreen the message that follows it.

Table 5-5. Batch Command Syntax

lease. To do that, unattended (meaning that all the current settings would come from the current installation), with the CD in drive D and the current installation in C:\Winnt, you would use these steps:

1. Place the Windows 2000 Professional CD in its drive. Click No in answer to the question "Would you like to upgrade…" and close the Windows 2000 CD install menu.

2. Open the Start menu and choose Run.

3. In the Open command line, type:
   D:\i386\winnt32.exe /s:d:\i386 /unattend

4. Press ENTER. Setup will start. You'll see the Upgrade vs. CleanInstall dialog box flash by, and you'll be asked to enter the product key and press ENTER. The

dialog boxes stating that files are being loaded will briefly appear, and then the computer will automatically restart in character mode. The file copying takes place, the previous configuration is used to create a new configuration, and the computer is again restarted with the GUI-based Setup Wizard. You see several dialog boxes onscreen giving you status information, and then Setup completes and, for a third time, reboots your system. The new version of Windows 2000 will appear.

5. Remove the CD, because you're done.

Okay, so that was too simple, but it indicates how simple Setup can be when done unattended.

Batch Command on a Floppy   One of the most common forms of distributing Windows within a company is to accompany the Windows CD with a company floppy that installs and configures Windows for the company's environment. Suppose you want to install Windows 2000 Professional on a number of workstations, and you are going to use the Setup Manager Wizard to prepare the answer file and batch file. Here are the steps:

1. On a server, start the Setup Manager Wizard and choose Fully Automated and the other choices that support Fully Automated and the installation you want to do. Edit the additional settings, but do not create a distribution folder. Name the answer file something other than Unattend.txt (use **Answer2.txt** for purposes of this example) and finish the Setup Manager Wizard with the answer file, shown in Figure 5-13, and a batch file, Answer2.bat, shown here:

```
Answer2.bat - Notepad
File  Edit  Format  Help
@rem SetupMgrTag
@echo off

rem
rem This is a SAMPLE batch script generated by the Setup Manager Wizard.
rem If this script is moved from the location where it was generated, it may
have to be modified.
rem

set AnswerFile=.\Answer2.txt
set SetupFiles=D:\i386

D:\i386\winnt32 /s:%SetupFiles% /unattend:%AnswerFile%
```

2. Double-click the Answer2.txt answer file and, under [UserData], remove the value after FullName and ComputerName. This will force the user to enter it. Save and close the Answer2.txt file.

NOTE: Deleting the answer file values for UserName and FullName is done here only to show what happens when you do this, but it is *not* the recommended way of handling custom name entry; see the note at the end of this section.

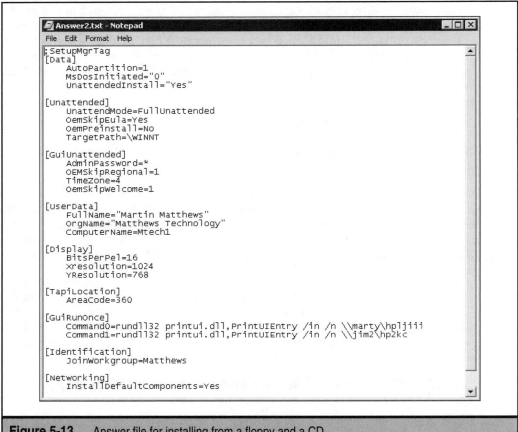

```
Answer2.txt - Notepad
File  Edit  Format  Help

;SetupMgrTag
[Data]
    AutoPartition=1
    MsDosInitiated="0"
    UnattendedInstall="Yes"

[Unattended]
    UnattendMode=FullUnattended
    OemSkipEula=Yes
    OemPreinstall=No
    TargetPath=\WINNT

[GuiUnattended]
    AdminPassword=*
    OEMSkipRegional=1
    TimeZone=4
    OemSkipWelcome=1

[UserData]
    FullName="Martin Matthews"
    OrgName="Matthews Technology"
    ComputerName=Mtech1

[Display]
    BitsPerPel=16
    Xresolution=1024
    YResolution=768

[TapiLocation]
    AreaCode=360

[GuiRunOnce]
    Command0=rundll32 printui.dll,PrintUIEntry /in /n \\marty\hpljiii
    Command1=rundll32 printui.dll,PrintUIEntry /in /n \\jim2\hp2kc

[Identification]
    JoinWorkgroup=Matthews

[Networking]
    InstallDefaultComponents=Yes
```

Figure 5-13.   Answer file for installing from a floppy and a CD

3. Right-click the Answer2.bat batch file, choose Edit, and delete "32" after "winnt" (in the bottom line) so that Answer2.bat can be started from DOS. Save and close Answer2.bat.

4. Format a floppy disk, copy the system files to it so it will boot, and then copy the answer and setup batch files to it.

5. Place the floppy you just created and the Windows 2000 Professional CD in their respective drives in the computer to be installed, and start the computer, making sure it is booting from the floppy, not the CD or hard disk. You'll see the initial character mode screen telling you that files are being copied to the hard disk.

6. While the copying is underway, remove the floppy so the computer does not reboot from it.

Upon completion of the initial copying from the CD to the hard disk, the computer will automatically restart and continue copying, really installing the files from their compressed image to their final working image. When the second phase of copying is complete, the computer will restart a second time with the GUI-based Setup Wizard. You will see several dialog boxes flash onscreen, but the personalization dialog box will stop and wait for the user to enter their name, organization, computer name, and administrator password. Next, the computer stops and asks for verification of the time and date and the network setup. Finally, you must click Finish. Then, Setup will complete and for a third time reboot the system. Windows 2000 Professional will appear.

7. Remove the CD, because you are done.

NOTE: Removing the value for the FullName and ComputerName caused Setup to ask for all information after that point. If you select Hide Pages and fill in everything but the FullName and ComputerName, then only those two pages (which also ask for the organization and administrator password) will be displayed.

Custom Bootable CD   Creating custom bootable CDs is very handy if you have a "CD burner" available to you. You can use the full set of objects produced by the Setup Manager Wizard, including the distribution folder. To make this work, you need to copy the contents of the distribution folder to a new folder named **I386** on the CD, change the batch and answer files for the new locations, and copy both of them and the UDF file to the root directory in the CD. There are several different types of CD creation tools, so my comments will be generic in that regard, although I assume your CD creation tool has a Windows Explorer–like capability in which you can create folders. Here are the steps to create a custom bootable CD:

1. Create the answer, batch, and UDF files and the distribution folder, as you did previously.

2. Open the answer file and, under the [SetupMgr] section, change DistFolder to point to where the files will be on the CD (probably **D:\i386**). Also change DistShare to be **i386**. Save and close the answer file.

3. Edit the batch file: change the value for SetupFiles to **D:\i386**, and change the path and program for Setup to **D:\i386\winnt**. Save and close the batch file.

4. In Notepad, create a small, two-line file that looks like the one shown next. Save the file with the name **Autorun.inf**.

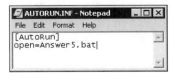

5. Make any changes you want to the OEM folder structure and then copy the files you want into that structure.

6. Insert a blank CD-R disk in its drive and start your CD creation program. Specify the disk is to be bootable, and point to where the program can find the system files necessary for booting. Name the CD something like **Win2kSetup**. (In Adaptec's Easy CD Creator, you open the File menu, choose CD Layout Properties, click the Data Settings tab, select ISO9660 in the File Settings drop-down list, click Bootable, and then click OK. Insert a bootable floppy in its drive and click OK.)

7. Copy the batch file, the answer file, the UDF file, and the Autorun.inf file to the root directory of the CD, and copy the contents of the distribution folder to the I386 folder on the CD. At this point in Easy CD Creator, the Explorer-like window looks like Figure 5-14.

8. Write the CD.

9. Place the CD in a computer on which you want to install Windows 2000 Professional, and restart the machine. Setup will start and run as you have seen before when booting from a CD.

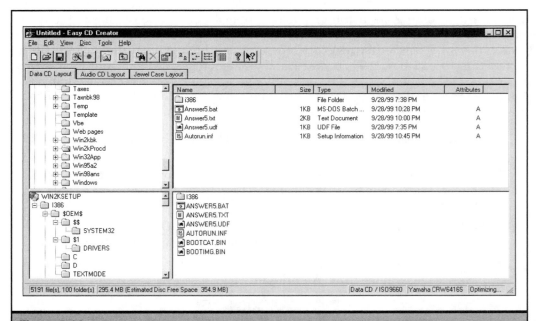

Figure 5-14. Files and folders ready for CD creation in Adaptec's Easy CD Creator

Creating and Using Disk Images

Another major way of distributing Windows 2000 is *disk imaging,* the process of creating and duplicating a standardized disk image or set of contents that is to be placed on the hard disks of multiple computers. This image can include—in addition to the OS—applications, data sets, and custom settings. Windows 2000 has a special tool, called the System Preparation tool, or SysPrep, for preparing the master image that will be cloned. In the master image, SysPrep places another program, Setupcl.exe, which, when a clone of the master image is first started, assigns a unique security ID (SID) to that computer and runs a five to ten minute GUI-mode Setup to personalize the computer with such information as the user, company, and computer names.

NOTE: For disk imaging to work, the systems must be nearly identical. The following items must be identical: the hardware abstraction layer (HAL), which is where the programming code is turned into machine language at the processor level; the Advanced Configuration and Power Interface (ACPI) for power management; the type of disk controller; the number of processors; and the platform (Intel vs. DEC). These items can differ: the processor model (Intel Pentium 200, PII-350, or PIII-500), RAM size, and Plug and Play devices, such as network interface cards, video cards, modems, and sounds cards.

The process of creating and using disk images involves five steps:

1. Create the master image of the operating system and applications that you want to replicate.
2. Prepare a special answer file and distribution folder for creating a disk image, using the Setup Manager Wizard.
3. Prepare the master image for copying, using the SysPrep tool.
4. Copy the master image onto other disks using a third-party product, either hardware or software, such as PowerQuest's Drive Image or Symantec's Ghost.
5. Start the clone for the first time and run through it in mini-Setup.

Look at each of these steps and the part they play in creating and using a disk image to deploy Windows 2000 Professional.

NOTE: Sysprep.exe and Setupcl.exe together replace Rollback.exe, which was used in Windows NT 4 to perform a similar function.

Creating a Master Image

Disk image duplication begins by installing Windows 2000 Professional on the hard disk that will serve as the master image. This is a normal installation, except that it should be done using a distribution folder, answer file, and command line (batch file) so that the master image has a consistent look and feel, and you can purposefully leave such things as the username, computer name, and so on blank. Once you have the OS installed the way you want to replicate it, install the applications, such as Office 2000, that you want to replicate. Finally, go through the settings, shortcuts, Start menu, and desktop and make them the way you want the system replicated.

When the master image is configured the way you want it, create or copy a Deployment folder on the master disk, as you did in step 1 of "Using the Setup Manager Wizard." This folder should contain at least Setupcl.exe, Setupmgr.exe, Setupmgx.dll, and Sysprep.exe.

Preparing Control Files for Drive Image Creation

The Setup Manager Wizard has a special set of features that prepares a unique answer file and distribution folder for use in image file creation. The following steps show how this works:

1. From the Deployment folder on the master image disk, double-click the Setup Manager Wizard and click Next on the welcome message.

2. Select Create an Answer File That Duplicates This Computer's Configuration and click Next to display the list of alternative end uses: Unattended Installation, Sysprep Install, and Remote Installation Services.

3. Select Sysprep Install and then click Next. This generates an answer file that can be used with the System Preparation tool. Continue on and answer the remaining Setup Manager Wizard questions as required to create the disk image you need, clicking Next as necessary.

4. Select Yes, Edit the Additional Settings, and continue for five or six dialog boxes until you see the one asking whether you want to create or modify a Sysprep folder.

5. Select Yes, Create or Modify the Sysprep Folder, and then click Next. A couple of dialog boxes later you are asked for the location of Sysprep.exe. This should be in the Deployment folder that you created from Deploy.cab earlier in this chapter, in the "Using the Setup Manager Wizard" section.

6. Supply the location of Sysprep.exe and click Open. Identify the location of the Windows 2000 Setup files (normally D:\i386 if D is the CD-ROM drive) and click Open. You are next asked for an OEM Duplicator String that will be placed in the Registry of all systems to identify this particular installation.

7. Enter the Sysprep information you want (location and filename) and click Next. You are told that an answer file has been created with the name Sysprep.inf (mine is shown in Figure 5-15). Click Finish.

8. If necessary, edit Sysprep.inf for the correct location of the files on the hard disk on the computer you are using. For example, you might want to change the DistShare reference from win2000dist to D:\i386 so that the CD is used for Setup files in place of the distribution folder.

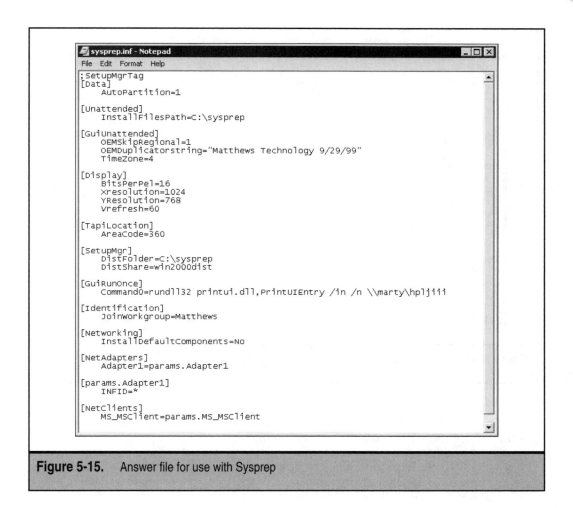

Figure 5-15.   Answer file for use with Sysprep

On your computer, you should find the new Sysprep folder, like the one shown in Figure 5-16. This has the OEM folder structure that you saw earlier in the normal Windows 2000 distribution folder, as well as the Sysprep.inf answer file, the Sysprep.exe and Setupcl.exe program files, and the Sysprep.bat file to start Sysprep. Note that Setup itself (the I386 folder normally) is not in this folder, but the answer file points to the original distribution folder (Win2000dist) for access to the Setup programs.

Preparing a Disk Image

Preparing a disk image is accomplished by running Sysprep.exe. Before doing that, make sure that Sysprep.exe, Setupcl.exe, and Sysprep.inf are together in the root of the Sysprep

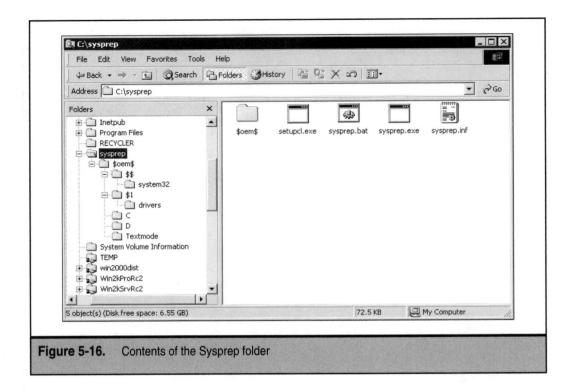

Figure 5-16.   Contents of the Sysprep folder

folder and that it is that copy of Sysprep.exe you use to begin the preparation. Once you are sure of the correct location, use the following steps to run Sysprep:

1. In Windows Explorer, open the Sysprep folder and double-click Sysprep.exe. A message appears stating that some of the security parameters may change and that the computer will be shut down when Sysprep is finished.

2. Click OK. Very quickly, Windows will shut down and, depending on your computer it will either shut itself off or you'll see a message saying it is now safe to do so.

3. If necessary, shut off your computer, and then remove the master image hard disk.

CAUTION: It is very important that you do not restart the original or another computer by booting off the master image hard disk. This is set up to be replicated, and when it or one of its clones is booted, a one-time setup process is run and then the Sysprep folder and its contents are deleted.

Copying a Disk Image

Once you have a master image disk, it can be duplicated in several ways. Hardware duplicators are available that copy a disk image to many disks at the same time. In addition, at least two software products, PowerQuest's Drive Image and Symantec's Ghost, can copy a disk image from one disk to another. In any case, the master hard drive must be removed from its former position as a boot device and its image (not just files) must be copied to another device. One way around having to remove the master image disk is to boot from a floppy. PowerQuest's Drive Image has the capability to make a set of floppies that you can use in this way.

The process of actually copying in PowerQuest's Drive Image is very simple. Once started, it tells you that it needs to run in DOS and asks whether that is OK. If you agree, Windows will be shut down and Drive Image will appear in its own GUI screen with mouse support. You will be asked whether you want to create a drive image, restore a drive image, or copy an image from one disk to another. After choosing the disk-to-disk copy, you'll need to select the From disk and which or all of its partitions, and then select the To disk and its partitions, which can be resized. If the To disk is formatted, you'll be asked if it is OK to remove the existing formatting. With your agreement, the process begins by checking the integrity of the data and the quality of the To drive, which is followed by the copying, and finally by verification. When it's done, you have an exact, bootable clone of the master image.

Starting Up a Clone for the First Time

When the end user first starts a computer in which one of the clone disks is installed, Windows goes through a miniature version of Setup that takes 5 to 10 minutes (versus 40 to 60 minutes for the full Setup). The mini-Setup goes through the following steps after loading the GUI environment:

1. A full hardware and Plug and Play detection is carried out.
2. The Setup Welcome message appears.
3. The End User License Agreement is displayed and the end user must accept it.
4. The end user must enter their name and organization.
5. The computer name and administrator's password must be entered.
6. Networking is set up based on how the answer file was established.
7. Windows is restarted.

The process is very straightforward and much less annoying than the full Setup. If you use My Computer or Windows Explorer to look at the hard disk, you'll see that the Sysprep folder and its contents are gone.

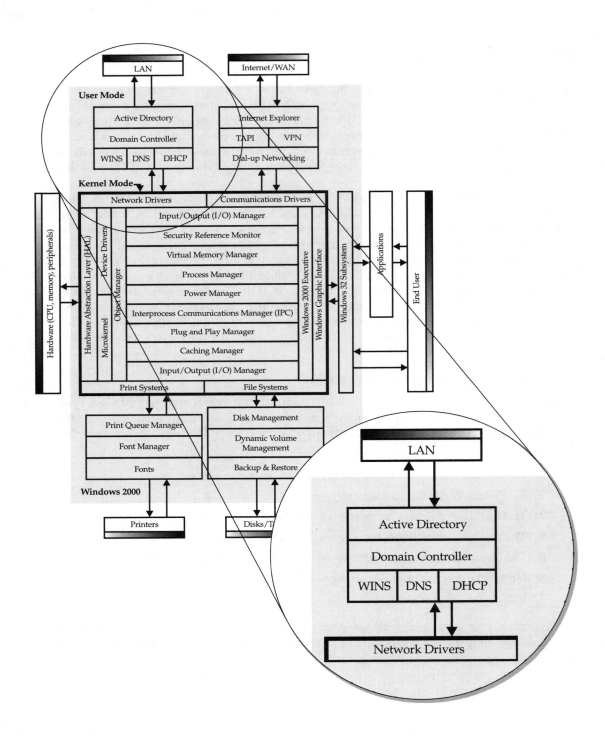

PART III

Networking
Windows 2000

Networking is the single most important function within Windows 2000. It is its reason for being. The ability to connect computers and allow them to share information and resources is at the forefront of today's push for improved productivity. In line with that importance, this part devotes four chapters to networking. Chapter 6 provides a comprehensive foundation on networking by describing the schemes, hardware, and protocols or standards that are used to make it function. Chapter 7 describes how networking is set up and managed in Windows 2000. Chapter 8 discusses how Novell NetWare works with Windows

2000 and how to migrate from NetWare to Windows 2000. Chapter 9 looks at how domains are used in Windows 2000 and the central role that Active Directory plays in managing networking.

CHAPTER 6

Windows 2000 Networking Environment

Windows 2000 is a *network operating system.* This allows the interconnection of multiple computers for the purpose of:

▼ Exchanging information, such as sending a file from one computer to another

■ Communicating by, for example, sending e-mail among network users

■ Sharing information by having common files accessed by network users

▲ Sharing resources on the network, such as printers and backup tape drives

Networking is important to almost every organization of two or more people who communicate and share information. Exchanging information allows multiple people to easily work from and utilize the same data and prevent errors caused by not having the latest information. E-mail communications facilitate the fast and easy coordination among people of current information, such as meeting arrangements. Sharing information allows multiple people to update and maintain a large database. Sharing resources allows an organization to purchase better (more capable and expensive) devices (for example, a color laser printer) than if they purchased one for each user. Networking is a primary ingredient in the computer's contribution to improved productivity, and from the viewpoint of this book, networking is the single most important facility in Windows 2000.

Networking is a system that includes the physical connection between computers that facilitates the transfer of information, as well as the scheme for controlling that transfer. The scheme makes sure that the information is transferred correctly (to the correct recipient) and accurately (the data is exactly the same on both the receiving and sending ends) while many other transfers are occurring simultaneously. To accomplish these objectives while other information is being transferred—generally, a lot of other information—there must be a standard way to correctly identify and address each transfer, and to stop one transfer while another is taking place. A networking system then has these components:

▼ A networking scheme that handles the transfer

■ Networking hardware that handles the physical connection

▲ A networking standard or protocol that handles the identification and addressing

Windows 2000 supports several different networking schemes, works with a variety of hardware, and handles several protocols. The purpose of this chapter is to look at the possible networking options provided for in Windows 2000 in enough detail for you to choose which of these options is best for your installation. Chapter 7 will then look at how to set up and manage networking with Windows 2000, and Chapters 8 and 9 will look at specific aspects of networking in greater depth.

NOTE: While this section of the book provides a great deal of networking information, it pales in comparison with Tom Sheldon's *Encyclopedia of Networking: Electronic Edition* (Osborne/McGraw-Hill). If you find you need more information than is presented here, see Tom's book. He also maintains an active web site at http://www.tec-ref.com.

NETWORKING SCHEMES

The schemes used to transfer information in a network substantially determine the hardware that is used, are integral to the software, and must implement the standards or protocols desired. It is therefore difficult to talk about just the schemes, just the hardware, or just the protocols. They are very interrelated. This is further complicated by the networking scheme being a function of both the type of networking and the technology it employs.

Network Types

The network type is determined by whether the network is confined to a single location or is spread over a wide geographic area.

A network that is spread over a wide geographic area is called a *wide area network* (*WAN*). WANs can use telephone lines, both shared and private, satellite links, microwave links, and dedicated fiber-optic or copper cabling to connect nodes across a street or on the other side of the world. WANs with reasonable amounts of bandwidth (100 Kbps and above) are very expensive, in the order of several thousand to many thousands of dollars per month, and demand sophisticated technology. They are therefore a major undertaking for a larger organization. A simpler and less expensive, although still not cheap, use of WANs is to interconnect smaller networks within a building or within a campus of closely located buildings. This use of intracampus WANs is discussed in several other places in this chapter.

NOTE: Many companies are using the Internet to do what WANs once handled, such as e-mail and private information exchange, so the growth in WANs is very modest.

A network that is confined to a single location is called a *local area network* (*LAN*). LANs use dedicated cabling or wireless channels and generally do not go outside of a single building, and may be limited to a single floor of a building or a department within a company. LANs are much more common than WANs and are the type of network primarily discussed in this and the next three chapters. LANs have two subcategories, peer-to-peer LANs and client/server LANs, which are distinguished based on how they distribute networking tasks.

Peer-to-Peer LANs

All computers in a peer-to-peer LAN are both servers and clients and therefore share in both the providing and using of resources. Any computer in the network may store information and provide resources, such as a printer, for the use of any other computer in the network. Peer-to-peer networking is an easy first step to networking, accomplished simply by joining existing computers together, as shown in Figure 6-1. It does not require the purchase of new computers or significant changes to the way an organization is using computers, yet resources can be shared (as is the printer in Figure 6-1), files and communications can be transferred, and common information can be accessed by all.

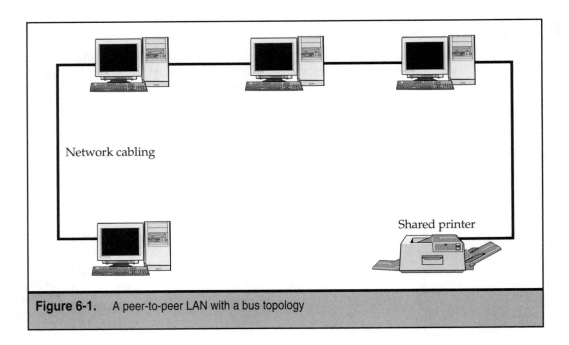

Figure 6-1. A peer-to-peer LAN with a bus topology

Peer-to-peer LANs tend to be used in smaller organizations that neither need to share a large central resource, such as a database, nor need a high degree of security or central control. Each computer in a peer-to-peer LAN is autonomous and often is joined together with other computers simply to transfer files and share expensive equipment. As you'll read later in the chapter, under "Networking Hardware," putting together a peer-to-peer LAN with existing computers is fairly easy and can be inexpensive (less than $50 per station).

Client/Server LANs

The computers in a client/server LAN perform one of two functions: they are either servers or clients. *Servers* manage the network, centrally store information that is to be shared on the network, and provide the shared resources to the network. *Clients,* or workstations, are the users of the network and are normal desktop or laptop computers. To create a network, the clients and server(s) are connected together, possibly with stand-alone network resources such as printers, as shown in Figure 6-2.

NOTE: The difference in network cabling between Figures 6-1 and 6-2 is *not* a function of one network being peer-to-peer and the other client/server, but rather is a function of the cabling topology used. See "Network Topologies" later in this chapter.

The management functions provided by the server include network security and managing the permissions needed to implement security, communications among net-

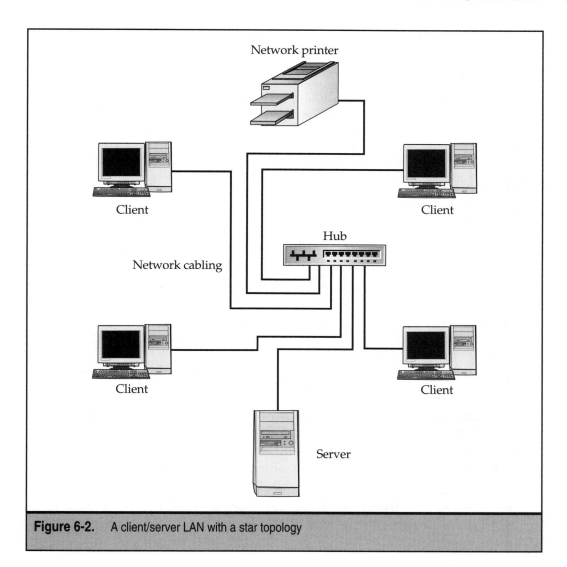

Figure 6-2.   A client/server LAN with a star topology

work users, and management of shared files on the network. Servers generally are more capable than clients in terms of having more memory, faster (and possibly more) processors, larger (and maybe more) disks, and more special peripherals, such as large, high-speed tape drives. Servers generally are dedicated to their function and are infrequently used for normal computer tasks, such as word processing.

Clients generally are less capable than servers and, infrequently, may not even have a disk. Clients usually are normal desktop and laptop computers that perform the normal functions for those types of machines, in addition to being part of a network. Clients can also be "miniservers," by sharing out some or all of their disk drives or other resources. Therefore, the principle difference between peer-to-peer networks and client/server networks is the addition of a dedicated server.

Windows 2000 is a client/server network operating system, with the Windows 2000 Server performing its function and Windows 2000 Professional being the client. Several Windows 2000 Professional workstations can operate in a peer-to-peer network, but the general assumption throughout this book is that you are principally interested in client/server networking using both Windows 2000 Server and Windows 2000 Professional.

The Networking Task

The task performed by the networking system is substantial and complex. At a minimum, the task includes these elements:

▼ Identifying each of the computers in a network

■ Identifying the information to be transferred as an individual *message*

■ Adding to each message a unique identification and the address of the sending and receiving computers

■ Enclosing the message in one or more moderate-size *packets,* similar to envelopes, with the sending and receiving address and where the packet belongs within a message

■ Encapsulating packets into *frames* that are transferred over the network

■ Monitoring network traffic to know when to send a frame

■ Transmitting a frame over the network (depending on the interconnection devices that are used, the frame may be opened and the packets put in new frames while en route)

■ Providing the physical means, including cabling and electronic parts, to carry the frame between computers

■ Monitoring network traffic to know when a frame is to be received

■ Receiving a frame that is on the network

■ Extracting the packets in one or more frames and combining the packets into the original message

▲ Determining whether the message belongs to the receiving computer and then either sending the message into the computer for further processing if it belongs to the computer, or ignoring the message if doesn't belong to the computer

NOTE: Names for pieces of information, such as messages, packets, and frames, are discussed further under "TCP (Transmission Control Protocol)" later in this chapter; Figure 6-21 in that section shows these pieces of information pictorially.

To better describe the networking task, the International Organization for Standardization, or ISO (a U.N. organization incorrectly referred to as the International Standards Organization; the acronym ISO comes from the Greek word "ISOS," meaning equal), developed a reference model for networking. This model is called the Open Systems Interconnection (OSI) model.

NOTE: The OSI model is useful for describing networking and for relating its various components. It does not necessarily represent Windows 2000 or any other networking implementation, but it is a widely known and accepted reference.

The OSI Model

The OSI model describes how information in one computer moves through a network to another computer. It defines networking in terms of seven layers, each of which performs a particular set of functions within the networking task, breaking the networking task into seven smaller tasks. Each layer can communicate with the layers above and below it and with its peer layer in another networked computer, as shown in Figure 6-3. The communication between peers goes down through the lower layers, across the physical connection, and back up the layers in the other machine.

In the OSI model, the lower two layers are implemented in a combination of hardware and software, while the upper five layers are all implemented in software. The software in the lower layers is dedicated to networking and may be burned into silicon. The software in upper layers is a part of the operating system or an application to which networking is only one of its tasks. For example, an e-mail client application wishing to get its mail off the server passes its request to the Application layer of the network system in its computer. This information is passed down through the layers until it reaches the Physical layer, where the information is placed on the physical network. The Physical layer in the server takes the information off the physical network and passes it up through the layers until it reaches the Application layer, which passes the request to the e-mail server application.

Each of the OSI layers can add, if necessary, specific control information to information being transferred over the network. The control information can be for other layers in its own stack or for its peer layer in the other computer and can be either requests or instructions. The control information can be added either as a header at the beginning of information being transferred or as a trailer at the end. The header or trailer added at one

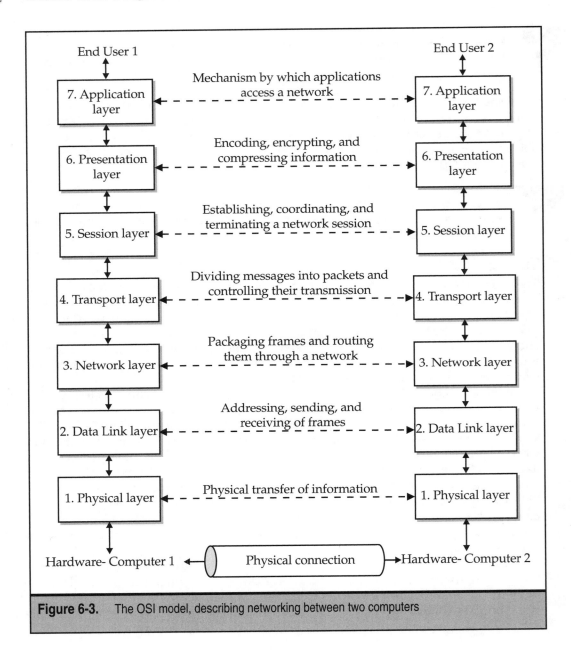

Figure 6-3. The OSI model, describing networking between two computers

layer becomes part of the basic information being transferred at another layer. The next layer may add another header or trailer or, if an existing header or trailer is intended for that layer, remove the header or trailer. The following lists the type of control information and function defined for each layer:

▼   **Physical layer**   Defines the physical specifications, such as voltages and timing, to make the network interface function as intended. These specifications are implemented in networking hardware.

■   **Data Link layer**   Defines the addressing of frames and the sending and receiving of frames between two linked computers. After passing a frame to the Physical layer to be sent, the Data Link layer waits for acknowledgment that the frame has been received, before it sends another frame; if the acknowledgment is not received, the Data Link layer resends the first frame. The Data Link layer provides point-to-point linkage between itself and the receiving computer by using physical addresses. The physical address at the Data Link layer is called the *media access control* (*MAC*) address. The Data Link specifications are implemented in a combination of hardware and dedicated networking software.

■   **Network layer**   Defines the packaging of packets into frames and the logical addressing (as opposed to the physical addressing used in the Data Link layer) necessary to provide internetwork routing through multiple, connected networks. Packets, which may be larger or smaller than frames, are broken up or combined to create a frame in the sending computer, and are reassembled or disassembled in the receiving computer to reproduce the original packets. The Network layer specifications are implemented in dedicated networking software.

■   **Transport layer**   Defines the division of a message into packets, the identification of the packets, and the control of the packet transmission to know whether the packets are being sent and received correctly, and, if not, to pause and resend a transmission. The Transport layer creates, regulates, and terminates a flow of packets by using a *virtual circuit* between the sending and receiving computers (the flow is still down through the other layers, across the physical connection, and up the other side, but it occurs as if the two Transport layers were directly talking to each other). The Transport layer specifications are implemented in networking-related OS software using networking protocols.

■   **Session layer**   Defines the dialog between computers so that they know both when to start and stop transmission, creating a *session*, and when to repeat a session if it is not correctly received. The Session layer also handles security-related issues and has its roots in the mainframe/terminal timesharing environment. The Session layer specifications are implemented in network-related OS software.

■   **Presentation layer**   Defines the encoding of information so that it is easily and securely transmitted and read by the receiving computer. This includes the conversion of character, graphic, audio, and video information into common data representation, the encryption and compression of information, and the return of the information to its native form upon receipt. The Presentation layer specifications are implemented in OS software.

▲ **Application layer**   Defines the mechanism by which applications access the network to send and receive information. This includes the two-way handling of information, as well as the identifying, locating, and determining of the availability of the partner for an information exchange. The Application layer specifications are implemented in OS and application software.

Keep the OSI model in mind as you read the remainder of this and the next several chapters. It will help you relate the various components used in networking. Later in this chapter, under "Interconnection Device Summary," you'll see how the OSI model relates to hardware devices such as hubs and switches, and under "Networking Protocols," you'll see how the OSI model relates to networking protocols and data-naming conventions.

LAN Technologies

LAN technologies are standards that span hardware and software, to handle a large part of the dedicated networking task. LAN technologies handle the entire Data Link layer and some of both the Physical and Network layers. In Windows 2000 LANs, you have a choice of three technologies: Ethernet, Token Ring, and Fiber Distributed Data Interface (FDDI).

Ethernet

Ethernet was developed in the early 1970s at Xerox PARC (Palo Alto Research Center) by Bob Metcalfe and was made into a standard (called the DIX standard) by Digital Equipment, Intel, and Xerox about ten years later. The Institute of Electrical and Electronics Engineers (IEEE, pronounced "eye, triple e") made slight modifications to the DIX standard and came out with its IEEE 802.3 standard for Ethernet. This is often referred to as Ethernet 802.3. Since Ethernet 802.3 has been adopted by ISO, making it a worldwide standard, and has become what most people and vendors mean when they say "Ethernet," it is what this book means by the term. There are now three IEEE 802.3 Ethernet standards: *IEEE 802.3*, the original Ethernet standard operating at 10 Mbps; IEEE 802.3u Fast Ethernet, operating at 100 Mbps; and IEEE 302.3z Gigabit Ethernet, operating at 1,000 Mbps. These will be referred to as "Ethernet," "Fast Ethernet," and "Gigabit Ethernet," respectively.

Ethernet is relatively inexpensive, works well interconnecting many different computer systems, and is easy to expand to very large networks. It therefore has become the dominant LAN technology by a wide margin, completely eclipsing some other early technologies, such as ARCnet, and significantly overshadowing Token Ring. As a result, Ethernet-related equipment and Ethernet support in software, such as Windows 2000, has become pervasive. This brought many vendors into the market to supply equipment, causing the pricing to become most reasonable. As a result, Ethernet (and, more recently, Fast Ethernet) has become the technology of choice for almost all new networks.

Ethernet technology covers three specifications:

▼ A media-access method that describes how multiple computers share a single Ethernet channel without getting in each other's way

■ An Ethernet frame that describes a standardized bit structure for transferring information over an Ethernet network

▲ A hardware specification that describes the cabling and electronics used with Ethernet

Ethernet Media Access Method   The objective of Ethernet is to have multiple computers operate independently of each other over a single connecting channel without interference. This is accomplished using a media-access method called Carrier Sense Multiple Access with Collision Detection (CSMA/CD). CSMA/CD works like this:

1. A networked computer wishing to transmit information listens to the network to determine when it is idle.

2. When the computer determines the network is idle, it puts its information on the network with the destination address, making it available to all other computers on the network.

3. Each computer on the network checks whether the address is its own, and if it is, that computer pulls the information off the network.

4. When the network is again idle, all other computers have an equal chance of being the next one to transmit information.

5. If two computers simultaneously begin transmission, a *collision* will occur and be detected. All information on the network is ignored, and the network will be returned to its idle status. The two sending computers then choose a random time to wait before resending their information, thereby minimizing the chance of repeated collisions.

Collisions are a normal and expected part of network transmission, even repeated collisions that result in data errors, which is why the higher levels of the OSI networking model put such emphasis on error detection and correction.

Ethernet Frame   The Ethernet *frame* is the standard format used for transferring data over an Ethernet network. The frame defines a specific layout that positions header information, source and destination addressing, data, and trailer information, as shown next. The specific definition and use of each field is as follows:

Preamble	SFD	Destination	Source	Length	Data	Padding	CRC
62 bits	2 bits	6 bytes	6 bytes	2 bytes	0-1500 bytes	46-0 bytes	4 bytes

▼ **Preamble**   A series of alternating 1's and 0's that is used by the receiving computer to synchronize the information in the frame.

■ **SFD (start of frame delimiter)**   A pair of 1's that is used to mark the start of the frame.

- **Destination and Source addresses** Two 48-bit numbers representing the receiving and sending computers. These numbers are assigned by the IEEE to manufacturers and contain a 24-bit unique manufacturer number and a 24-bit number unique to a specific network interface card (NIC). This means that every NIC comes with a unique address, and the end user does not have to worry about it. If a message is to be broadcast to all stations on a network, the destination address must contain all 1's.

- **Length** The number of bytes in the data field. In earlier Ethernet standards, this was a type code, which were all greater than 1,500 to avoid getting in the way of the length, which is 0 to 1,500.

- **Data** The data being transmitted, which can be from 0 to 1,500 bytes long.

- **Padding** Required if the data is less than 46 bytes, so if the data field contained 38 bytes, 8 bytes of padding would be included.

- ▲ **CRC (cyclical redundancy check)** Also called a Frame Check Sequence (FCS), it is a 32-bit (4-bytes) number derived from all the bits in the transmission by using a complex formula. The sending computer calculates this number and stores it in the frame sent to the other computer. The receiving computer also calculates the number and compares it to the number in the frame. If the numbers are the same, it is assumed that the transmission was received without error. If the numbers are different, the transmission will be repeated.

The principle difference between the original DIX Ethernet standard (called Ethernet II—Ethernet I was the original specification prior to DIX) and Ethernet 802.3 is that Ethernet II has a type code in place of the length in the frame. The type code is used to adapt Ethernet to different computer environments, which is done outside of the frame in 802.3. In the Internet protocol TCP/IP (see "Networking Protocols" later in this chapter), the Ethernet frame is used with a type code that identifies the Internet protocol.

Ethernet Hardware Ethernet LAN technology defines six alternative hardware standards, with a seventh just coming into play that can be used with Ethernet. Each hardware standard uses a specific type of cable and cable layout, or *topology*, and provides a rated speed on the network in Mbps, a maximum segment length, and a maximum number of computers on a single segment. The hardware standards are as follows:

> **NOTE:** In the IEEE names for the Ethernet hardware standards, such as 10Base5, the "10" is the speed in Mbps, the "Base" is for baseband, a type of transmission, and the "5" is the maximum segment length in hundreds of meters. In more recent standards, such as 10BaseT, the "T" stands for the type of cabling (twisted-pair in this case).

- ▼ **10Base5 (also called Thicknet)** The original hardware specification in the DIX standard. It uses a thick coaxial cable in a bus topology (see Figure 6-1) with a fairly complex connection at each computer to produce a 10 Mbps speed over a 500 meter (1,640 feet) maximum segment with up to 100 computers per segment and three segments. 10Base5 is expensive and cumbersome to use.

■ **10Base2 (also called Thinnet or Cheapernet)** Uses RG-58 A/U thin coaxial cable in a bus topology (see Figure 6-1) with a simple BNC barrel type of connector to produce a 10 Mbps speed over a 185 meter (606 feet) maximum segment with up to 30 computers per segment and three segments. Until only recently, Thinnet was the least expensive form of Ethernet networking for small (30 and under) organizations.

■ **10BaseT (also called Twisted-Pair)** Uses unshielded twisted-pair (UTP) telephone-like cable in a star topology (see Figure 6-2) with a very simple RJ-45 telephone-like connector to produce a 10 Mbps speed over a 100 meter (328 feet) segment with one computer per segment and 1,024 segments. Recently, 10BaseT has come down in price to that of 10Base2, and with its exceptional expandability, it has become very attractive for organizations on a tight budget.

■ **10BaseF** Uses fiber-optic cable in a star topology running at 10 Mbps to connect two networks up to 4,000 meters (13,120 feet, or about 2.5 miles) apart. This is often used to connect two or more buildings on a business campus.

■ **100BaseT (also called Fast Ethernet)** Has the same specifications as 10BaseT except that the cabling requirements are a little more demanding (requires Category 5 cable in place of Category 3) and it goes ten times as fast. 100BaseT is not a whole lot more expensive than 10BaseT, and with its significant added speed, it has become the Ethernet hardware standard of choice. With the appropriate connecting hardware (see "Networking Hardware," later in the chapter), you can mix 10BaseT and 100BaseT hardware in the same network to slowly upgrade a 10BaseT network. There are two subspecifications to 100BaseT: 100BaseTX, the most common, which runs over Category 5 UTP using two twisted pairs, and 100BaseT4, which runs over Category 3 UTP using four twisted pairs.

■ **100BaseF** Uses fiber-optic cable running at 100 Mbps to connect two networks up to 412 meters (1,351 feet) apart. Like 10BaseF, 100BaseF is primarily used to join two networks.

▲ **1000BaseT and F (also called Gigabit Ethernet)** Uses standard Category 5 or fiber-optic cable to run at 1,000 Mbps. The earliest installations of Gigabit Ethernet are just going in as this is written. The initial distance standards are 25 meters (82 feet) for copper UTP, and 550 meters (1,800 feet) for fiber. It is expected that the UTP distance will grow to as much as 100 meters (328 feet) in the near future. Category 5E (enhanced) and proposed Category 6 (shielded) cabling will improve the distance. In fall of 1999, the first Gigabit Ethernet equipment was coming on the market at about three times the price of high-quality, name-brand 100BaseT equipment for ten times the speed. If this follows the pattern of 100BaseT, these prices will drop by 40 to 50 percent in the next few years.

"Networking Hardware," later in this chapter, goes into more detail about the Ethernet hardware standards and the options that are available to connect Ethernet networks.

Token Ring

As Digital Equipment, Intel, and Xerox were promoting their DIX Ethernet standard in the mid 1980s, IBM was promoting Token Ring, which became the IEEE 802.5 standard. Although Token Ring started out at 4 Mbps (called Type 3), it very quickly jumped ahead of Ethernet's 10 Mbps with its 16 Mbps (called Type 1). For an eight to ten year period ending in 1997, Token Ring was held in high esteem as the Rolls Royce of networking. It was fast, it was reliable, it could connect personal computers, minicomputers, and mainframes, and it had the backing and nametag of IBM. It was also very expensive, as much as three to five times the cost of high-quality name-brand Ethernet equipment. Then, in 1997, 100BaseT became widely available and Token Ring became an also-ran. There is fiber-optic 16 Mbps Token Ring and some talk about a 100 Mbps Token Ring, but it is lost in the shouting about Gigabit Ethernet.

Token Ring Media Access Method   The Token Ring LAN technology is based on a media-access method that uses an electronic token to carry information and to tell the networked computers when the network is free. It works like this:

1. A networked computer with data to transmit watches the network for a free token.

2. When a free token is acquired, it is *burdened* with the destination address and the information to be transmitted, and sent on to the next computer in the ring.

3. Each computer that is not the destination receives and passes on the burdened token.

4. When the destination is reached, the computer removes the information and returns an acknowledgment to the sending computer.

5. Upon receipt of the acknowledgment, the original sending computer places a free token on the network.

One computer on the network (generally the first computer to come up) is designated the *active monitor,* which watches the network for abnormal conditions such as multiple tokens, missing tokens, and broken tokens. When these conditions are found, the active monitor removes all information on the network and places a free token back on.

Token Ring Frame   The Token Ring frame provides a standard format for transferring data over a Token Ring network. The frame layout, shown next, uses the following field definitions:

Starting Delimiter 1 byte	Access Control 1 byte	Frame Control 1 byte	Destination Address 6 bytes	Source Address 6 bytes	Data variable	CRC 4 bytes	Ending Delimiter 1 byte	Frame Status 1 byte

▼   **Starting Delimiter**   Uses a unique code to indicate the beginning of a frame

■   **Access Control**   Identifies whether the frame is a token and what its priority is

- **Frame Control**   Indicates the type of frame and how it is to be processed
- **Destination Address**   Identifies the address of the intended recipient
- **Source Address**   Identifies the address of the sender
- **Data**   Contains the information being transmitted
- **CRC (frame check sequence)**   Contains a calculated number used for checking the integrity of the frame (see "CRC" in the bulleted list under "Ethernet Frame")
- **Ending Delimiter**   Uses a unique code to indicate the end of the frame
- ▲ **Frame Status**   Indicates to the sending computer that the frame has been received

The frame for a free token has only three fields: Starting Delimiter, Access Control with the token identifier, and Ending Delimiter.

Token Ring Hardware   In Token Ring technology, information travels only one direction in a cable, requiring that the ends of the cable be connected together to form a ring. It also means that every computer must have two cables and connections to it, one incoming and the other outgoing. To make this easier, the cables, each a twisted-pair cable, are bundled together and use a single connector. Unlike Ethernet's 10BaseT UTP cable, Token Ring's cable is shielded twisted-pair (STP), and the connector is more complex, both of which add to Token Ring's cost. (The newer Token Ring NICs and other equipment have gone to the same Category 5 cable and RJ-45 connectors used by 10BaseT Ethernet.) To make the ring concept easier, Token Ring uses a *multistation access unit*, or MAU (also called MSAU, by purists, but MAU is the common usage), from which computers can be connected in a star fashion similar to an Ethernet hub, although a MAU is several times more expensive than an Ethernet hub. A MAU can function as a ring itself in a small network or be part of a larger ring as shown in Figure 6-4.

As shown pictorially in Figure 6-4, a MAU contains relays on each port that open when a computer or inter-MAU connection is live, but close when they are not powered. This allows the ring to maintain its integrity when a line is broken or a computer is disconnected.

Token Ring Type-1 cabling uses STP cable in a star-configured ring topology (see Figure 6-4) with an expensive connector to produce a 16 Mbps speed over a 100 meter (328 feet) segment with 1 computer per segment and a total of 260 computers in a ring.

Fiber Distributed Data Interface

FDDI is a token-passing, dual-ring LAN technology that operates at 100 Mbps. Originally, FDDI was designed to be used with fiber-optic cable, but newer implementations, called CDDI, use copper Category-5 UTP, although at much shorter distances and with more interference. FDDI has several similarities to Token Ring, in that both pass a token and use a ring topology.

FDDI, unlike Token Ring, has two complete rings, called Primary ring and Secondary ring, that operate in opposite directions, as shown in Figure 6-5. There are two types of

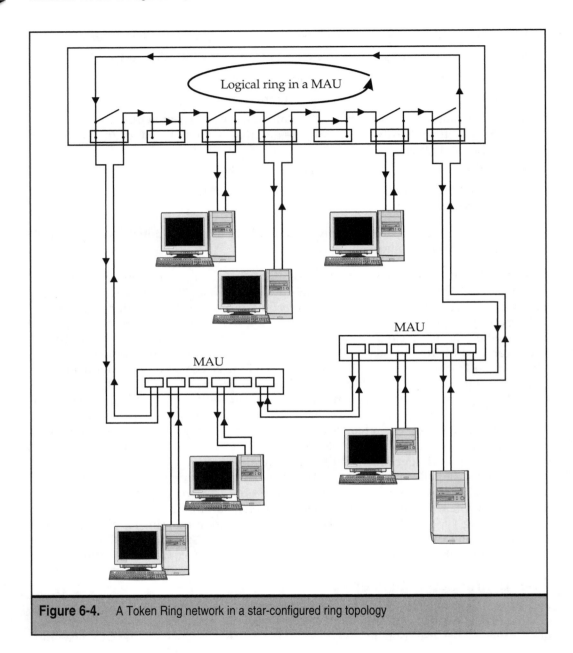

Figure 6-4. A Token Ring network in a star-configured ring topology

FDDI devices, both of which are used to connect to other networks. The FDDI device types are the *single attached station (SAS)*, which attaches to only one ring, and the *dual attached station (DAS)*, which attaches to both rings. The pair of rings provides substantial

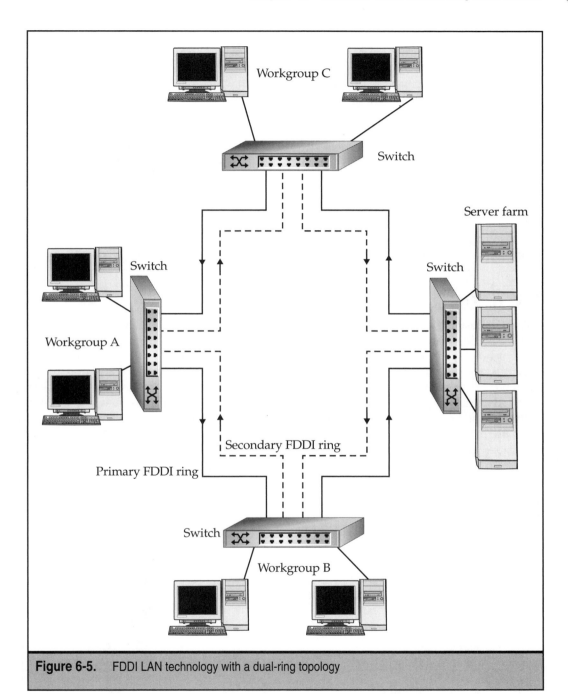

Figure 6-5.   FDDI LAN technology with a dual-ring topology

fault tolerance. If one ring is broken, the other can take over, and if one segment of both rings is broken, or one device is not working or removed, the two rings can join to reestablish the integrity of the ring.

FDDI is primarily used to link other networks in what is called a *backbone*, both within a building and between buildings. FDDI, using fiber-optic cabling in a ring topology (see Figure 6-5), can run at 100 Mbps over a total distance of 100 kilometers (60 miles) with no one segment longer than 2 kilometers (1.24 miles). In this configuration, FDDI can connect up to 500 network devices. CDDI is limited to 100 meters (328 feet). Fiber offers several advantages over copper: fiber is not susceptible to electromagnetic interference, is more difficult to tap and therefore more secure, does not attract lightening, and, most importantly, has a higher quality of transmission.

FDDI has another similarity to Token Ring in that it's a "Rolls Royce technology." It is fast and reliable, but it is also expensive in comparison to 100BaseF. Since 100BaseF shares the Ethernet technology with the very popular 10/100BaseT and is cheaper, 100BaseF is getting the lion's share of the business that FDDI might otherwise have received.

NETWORKING HARDWARE

In its simplest form, computer networking needs only a cable to join two computers, and two NICs that plug into the computer and onto which the cable connects, as shown in Figure 6-6.

For both the NICs and the network cable, there are several choices in the types and features, and when you go beyond two computers, there are additional components for which there are multiple choices. The first and major decision in making these choices is the LAN technology you are going to use, because that, in many cases, will determine your cabling and NIC, or at least put you in a certain category of cabling and NIC. Therefore, begin this look at hardware with a summary, shown in Table 6-1, of what has been described earlier in this chapter regarding the alternative LAN technologies.

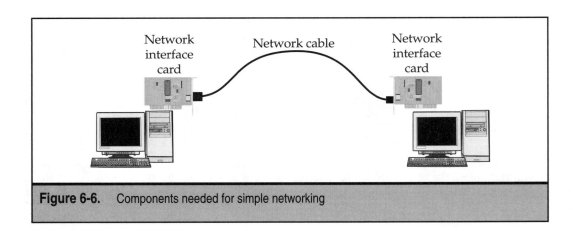

Figure 6-6.   Components needed for simple networking

Technology	Max. Speed Mbps	Type of Cabling	Max. Network Nodes	Max. Nodes/ Segment	Max. Segment Length	Min. Segment Length	Max. Network Length
Ethernet							
10Base5	10	Thick coax	300	100	1,640 ft	8.5 ft	8,200 ft
10Base2	10	Thin coax	90	30	606 ft	2 ft	3,035 ft
10BaseT	10	UTP-Cat 3	1,024	2	328 ft		
10BaseF	10	Fiber-optic		2	2.5 mi		
100BaseT	100	UTP-Cat 5	1,024	2	328 ft		
100BaseF	100	Fiber-optic		2	1,351 ft		
1000BaseT	1,000	UTP-Cat5		2	328 ft		
1000BaseF	1,000	Fiber-optic		2	1,800 ft		
Token Ring		STP or					
Type 1	16	UTP-Cat5		260	328 ft		
Type 3	4	UTP-Cat3		72	148		
Fiber	16	Fiber-optic			2.5 mi		
FDDI							
Fiber	100	Fiber-optic	500		1.24 mi		60 mi
Copper	100	UTP-Cat5			328 ft		

Table 6-1.   LAN Technology Specification Summary

NOTE: A *node* is a workstation, a server, or a stand-alone network printer.

In choosing a LAN technology, Ethernet 10BaseT and 100BaseT are the predominant choices. Probably well over 90 percent choose it, with 100BaseT getting the lion's share of new installations and many upgrades. A few 10Base2 are still going in for the smallest and most cost-conscience installations (although the cost difference between 10Base2 and 10BaseT is small; see the example in Table 6-2). Also, a lot of used 10Base2 equipment is available that costs next to nothing and is being used by small offices to get started. The decision between 10BaseT and 100BaseT is really based on what you think are the future needs of your organization. If you will never have the network traffic to cause congestion at 10 Mbps, then 10BaseT is still cheap enough to pull you that way. If you can't confidently say that you'll "never" have that much traffic, then the cost differential may not look that attractive; see Table 6-3. Also, you can always get 10/100 NICs and use them with 10 Mbps hubs and upgrade those at a later time when their price comes down.

Prices 10/99*	4 Node 10Base2	4 Node 10BaseT	6 Node 10Base2	6 Node 10BaseT	8 Node 10Base2	8 Node 10BaseT
SMC NIC $25/$20	$100	$80	$150	$120	$200	$160
SMC HUB 4/8 port	-	$40	-	$55	-	$55
10' cables $12/$9	$36	$36	$60	$54	$84	$72
Total	$136	$156	$210	$229	$284	$287

*10Base2/10BaseT, from Data Comm Warehouse catalog 55p, 10/99, page 23

Table 6-2. 10Base2 vs. 10BaseT Cost Comparison for Small Networks

100BaseF increasingly is being used to interconnect networks, buildings, and floors within a building. The following hardware alternatives focus on the needs of these technologies.

NOTE: Wireless networking and cable sharing are two new emerging technologies for networking that are worth keeping an eye on, although they aren't yet standardized and aren't used widely enough for you to consider them. Wireless networking uses a transceiver at each client and a base station at the server. With cable sharing, the computer network uses either the telephone cabling or the power cabling in a building. Both of these technologies are relatively slow and more expensive, but save the cost of installing network cabling.

Prices 10/99*	8 Node 10BaseT	8 Node 100BaseT	16 Node 10BaseT	16 Node 100BaseT	24 Node 10BaseT	24 Node 100BaseT
SMC NIC $20/$25	$160	$200	$320	$400	$480	$600
SMC HUB 8/16/24port	$55	$160	$130	$470	$200	$650
Total	$215	$360	$450	$870	$680	$1250
Extra/port		$18.12		$26.25		$23.75

*10BaseT/100BaseT, from Data Comm Warehouse catalog 55p, 10/99, page 23

Table 6-3. 10BaseT vs. 100BaseT Cost Comparison

Network Interface Cards

Even though you have decided on Ethernet over Token Ring and from among 10Base2, 10BaseT, and 100BaseT, the decision on which NIC to buy still has several considerations:

▼   Which bus will the card use

■   What type of card to use

■   Do you want it to be able to wake up the computer

▲   Which brand should you buy

Which Card Bus

Many NIC manufacturers provide NICs that plug into ISA (Industry Standard Architecture), EISA (Extended Industry Standard Architecture), and PCI (Peripheral Component Interface) card slots. (Figure 6-7 shows a 3Com EtherLink III Combo card that can be used with 10Base2, 10Base5, or 10BaseT and that plugs into the ISA bus. Figure 6-8 shows a 3Com Fast EtherLink XL that is used with either 10BaseT or 100BaseT and that plugs into the PCI bus.) You may not have a choice on the bus you can use in the computers you are adding to the network, but if you do (most computers built in the last three or four years have both ISA and PCI slots), you want to choose PCI. ISA slots are either 8 or 16 bits wide (NICs generally use 16 bits), whereas EISA and PCI slots are 32 bits wide and thus have a wider data path and are noticeably faster. EISA is an older technology and lacks one of PCI's major benefits—you don't have to worry about the IRQ (interrupt request line), because it is uniquely handled in PCI slots. In ISA and EISA slots, you have to figure out what IRQs other cards are using, and hopefully have one left over for the NIC. So if it is available, you want to choose PCI-bus NICs.

What Type of Card to Use

Most manufacturers, especially the larger name brands, make several different types of 10/100BaseT NICs in addition to cards for different buses and special features. These differences include whether a NIC is full-duplex or half-duplex, whether it is made for a server, and whether it is multiport. All of these features add to the speed and efficiency of the board, but they also add to the cost, so you need to give them some consideration.

Half-Duplex vs. Full-Duplex   *Half-duplex* means that when a card is receiving it can't transmit, and visa versa. *Full-duplex* allows the card to transmit and receive at the same time. Obviously, full-duplex is faster, but it does not double the speed as you might expect; rather, it offers between 30- and 50-percent improvement over half-duplex. Currently, most name-brand 10/100 NICS are full-duplex, but it wouldn't hurt to check this factor when you are researching which ones to buy.

Using Server NICs   Server NICs are developed for use in servers, and they supply several features to support that role. Among these features are higher reliability and more intelligence. The higher reliability is usually a combination of better parts and higher quality control. The more intelligence means that there is a processor and even memory on the

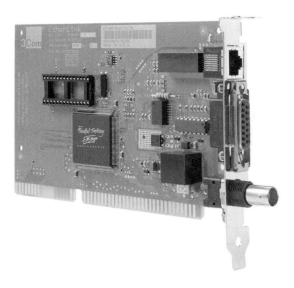

*Photo courtesy of 3Com Corporation, http://www.3com.com

Figure 6-7. 3Com EtherLink III Combo for 10Base2, 10Base5, or 10BaseT and the ISA bus*

*Photo courtesy of 3Com Corporation, http://www.3com.com

Figure 6-8. 3Com Fast EtherLink XL for 10BaseT or 100BaseT and the PCI bus*

NIC so that it doesn't have to go out to the computer's CPU and memory to handle its processes. This makes the card faster, allowing it to handle a higher volume of information. These features, of course, cost money, so you need to determine whether they are worthwhile. The higher-reliability cards cost about 30 to 50 percent more than a normal name-brand NIC. The intelligent NICs cost three to four times the cost of a normal name-brand NIC. While that sounds like a lot, it translates to at most $250 additional per card, and you do not have to buy very many of them. When you compare this to the cost of upgrading a CPU, it's reasonable. My recommendation is that an intelligent NIC made for a server is worth the price.

Multiport NICs   NICs are available for servers that have two or four ports, the equivalent of two or four NICs in the server. Given that PCI card slots are generally at a premium in most servers, these multiport boards may be attractive. The problem is that a dual-port NIC costs about two and a half times the cost of a name-brand server NIC, and a four-port NIC costs about five and a half times the cost of a name-brand server NIC. If you don't have the PCI slots, then this might be a solution, but another solution is to use an interconnection device in front of the NIC (see "Interconnection Devices," later in this chapter). This is one of those situations in which there is no one right answer. It depends on the network design you are trying to construct.

Wake on LAN and Other Special Features

Several manufacturers, 3Com and Intel among them, have NICs with a "Wake on LAN" feature that will power up a computer to full operating status after they have been turned off. This allows a network administrator or support person to update a computer after hours. Wake on LAN requires a *motherboard* (the main system circuit board in a computer where a NIC plugs in) that implements the PCI bus standard 2.2 or later. Most computers produced in the last two to three years use this standard.

There are at least two other special features that are in some NICs and may prove useful: remote management and remote booting. Remote management allows a network administrator or a server with the appropriate software to monitor the activity and do remote management on a computer across a network. Remote booting allows a server to start a computer without depending on the operating system in the computer. This is important for diagnosing problems in the computer and for the remote installation of Windows 2000. Remote booting also requires PCI bus standard 2.2 or later.

If these features are of interest to you, look carefully before buying a NIC and make sure the motherboard you are intending to use it with supports the feature(s) you are getting on the NIC. Remote booting in particular may require special support on the motherboard that is *not* included on most motherboards.

Which Brand

If you look at most catalogs (such as the Data Comm Warehouse catalog used in the previous pricing examples) and online, you will see that there are at least three pricing levels of NICs:

▼   Name brand (3Com, Intel) with the special features previously mentioned: $75 through $120

- ■ Name-brand basic boards (without the special features): $35 through $75
- ▲ Generic basic boards (without the special features): $15 through $35

Although some of the price range in each of the three levels is caused by differences in features, much of the differential is caused by differences in what suppliers charge for the same board. You can see that by looking at PriceWatch (http://www.pricewatch.com), which compares the prices of the same item from different suppliers. In any case, make sure you know what you are buying and what the handling and freight charges are.

The pertinent question is whether the name-brand boards are worth the $20 to $40 differential. From my viewpoint, the answer is clearly yes. In the ten years I have been working with PC networking, I have worked with approximately an equal number of generic and name-brand NICs. I have had troubles with both, but I have had to throw away several of the generic boards, while I have always gotten the name-brand boards fixed or replaced. The backing and support of a name brand is comforting (3Com's lifetime warranty in particular) and sometimes they have added features such as diagnostics that may be valuable. Granted, the lower prices of the generic boards are also attractive, but when a network goes down, that price may not look so good. If you buy a generic from a better supplier to get the supplier's support, your price is very close to the name brand. My recommendation is to choose the name-brand board with the thought that it is going to be more easily recognized in software, such as Windows 2000, and provide better support should it be needed.

Cabling

The primary networking technologies use one of three types of cabling, each of which has several considerations:

- ▼ Thin coax for 10Base2
- ■ Unshielded twisted-pair for 10BaseT and 100BaseT
- ▲ Fiber-optic for 10BaseF and 100BaseF

Thin Coax

The cable used for 10Base2 networking is a coaxial type and is smaller in diameter than the cable used for 10Base5, 10Base2's predecessor, which was thick and hard to handle. Coaxial cable has an inner wire, surrounded by a plastic insulator, covered by a braided metal outer conductor, and finally a plastic outer jacket, as shown next. There are several types of coaxial cable, or "coax." Among these are the following:

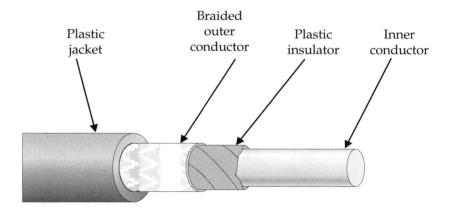

Plastic jacket · Braided outer conductor · Plastic insulator · Inner conductor

▼ RG-8A/U and RG-11A/U is the "thick" coax used with 10Base5 and has a 50 ohm impedance

■ RG-58A/U is the "thin" coax used with 10Base2 and has a 50 ohm impedance

■ RG-59/U is used with cable TV systems and has a 75 ohm impedance

▲ RG-62/U is used with ARCnet networking and has a 93 ohm impedance

It is very important to use the correct cable for an intended function. Even though TV coax cable looks almost identical to thin coax, it will not work, because its impedance is different.

Thin coax uses twist-to-lock barrel connectors on each end of the cable and connects to a NIC using a T connector, as shown in Figure 6-9. Stringing computers together in this manner forms a long line called a *bus topology*. At each end of this network is a 50-ohm terminator, and *one* of these terminators, and only one, needs to be grounded by connecting it to a screw on the case of the computer to which it is connected.

Thin coax and its connectors are slightly more expensive (see the upcoming "Cabling Cost Comparison" section) and a little harder to handle than the UTP used with 10/100BaseT, but thin coax is less susceptible to radio-frequency and electrical interference. Cabling is probably not the reason to make the decision, but it adds weight to 10BaseT.

Unshielded Twisted-Pair

UTP cable used in 10/100BaseT is similar to, but generally not the same as, telephone wiring. For 10BaseT, this cable contains two pairs of wires, or four wires, first twisted in pairs, and then the pairs are twisted together. An RJ-45 modular connector is placed on each end. Although only two pairs are used, the actual cable in both Category 3 and Cate-

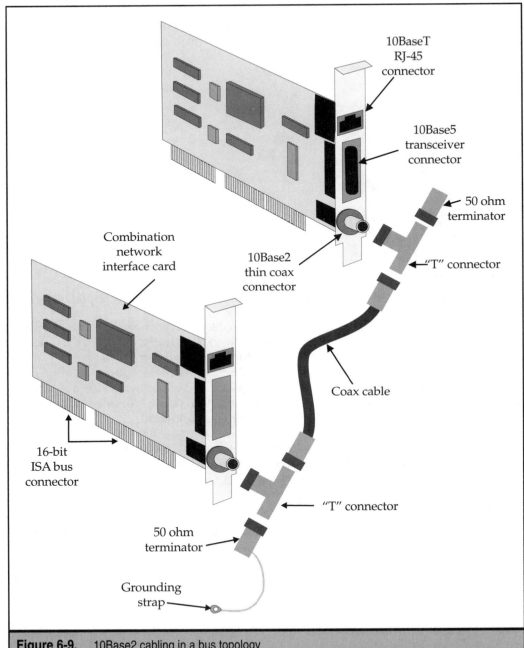

Figure 6-9.   10Base2 cabling in a bus topology

gory 4 cabling has four pairs, as shown in Figure 6-10. The RJ-45 connector, which can handle four twisted-pairs of wires, is similar to but slightly larger than the RJ-11 connector, which can handle two pairs of wires and is used in a normal phone connection. 100BaseT and 1000BaseT use four pairs or all eight wires in Category 5 cable and the same RJ-45 connector.

The pairs of wires in a UTP cable are twisted because that reduces the electrical interference that is picked up in the cable. The number of twists per foot has become a very exact science, and it is important to keep the cable properly twisted up close to the connector. An alternative to UTP is STP, with various degrees of shielding: shielding around each pair, around both pairs, or shielding around both the individual pairs and around the combination. STP is considerably more expensive than UDP and is more difficult to handle. To handle the interference problem, there are several rules to follow when running the cable:

▼ Don't run the cable near a florescent light fixture

■ Don't run the cable near an electrical motor, such as those in fans, water coolers, and copiers

■ Don't run the cable alongside a power cable

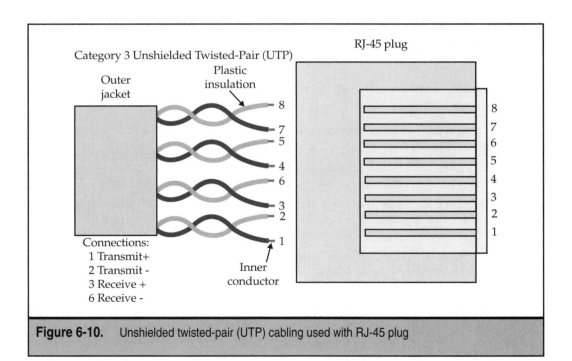

Figure 6-10. Unshielded twisted-pair (UTP) cabling used with RJ-45 plug

- ■ Don't make tight turns that can crimp the cable
- ▲ Don't use a staple gun, which can crimp the cable

NOTE: Crimping network cabling can change the spacing between individual wires and therefore change its electrical characteristics and performance.

Between voice and data (phone and network), a number of different types of UTP cable exist. These differences are in the degree of fire resistance, in the type of inner core, and in the grade or category of cable, which also specifies the number of twisted pairs.

Degree of Fire Resistance   UTP cables come in two degrees of fire resistance: *plenum* cable, marked "CMP," and *PVC* or *riser* cable, marked "CMR." Plenum cable doesn't give off dangerous fumes if it does burn and is more fire resistant. PVC or riser cable, while reasonably fire resistant, is made with polyvinyl chloride (PVC), which gives off potentially dangerous fumes if it does burn. Plenum cable costs between two and two and a half times what PVC cable costs, but it can be used in air passages such as raised floors and suspended ceilings, while PVC cable can be used only in walls and out in the open (check your own local codes for the type of cable you should use).

Type of Inner Core   The inner core of UTP cable can be stranded or solid. Stranded wire is more flexible and less prone to breaking when bent a number of times. It is used in situations where it is frequently moved, such as in a patch panel and between a wall outlet and a computer. Solid wire has lower signal loss and therefore is better for longer runs where it won't be moved frequently, such as in walls and ceilings.

UTP Categories   The following are the seven categories of UTP cable that are used with voice and data communications:

- ▼ **Category 1**   Used in telephone installations prior to 1983 and has two twisted pairs.
- ■ **Category 2**   Used in telephone installations after 1982 and has four twisted pairs; used in some early data networks with speeds up to 4 Mbps.
- ■ **Category 3**   Used in many data networks and most current phone systems, has four twisted pairs, generally has three twists per foot (not in the specs), and easily handles speeds of 10 Mbps.
- ■ **Category 4**   Used in Token Ring networks, has four twisted pairs, and can handle speeds up to 16 Mbps.
- ■ **Category 5**   Used in most current networks, has four twisted pairs, has eight twists per foot, can handle 100 Mbps, and in bulk (1,000 feet) is approximately 10 cents per foot for solid PVC and 25 cents a foot for solid Plenum.
- ■ **Category 5e (enhanced Category 5)**   Used in premium installations, has the same physical characteristics as Category 5 but with a lower error rate, and in bulk (1,000 feet) is approximately 15 cents per foot for solid PVC and 35 cents a foot for solid Plenum.

▲ **Category 6 (really STP)** Used where electrical interference is a problem, and has four twisted pairs with a foil wrap around each pair and another foil wrap around all pairs. It is planned to handle Gigabit Ethernet, and in bulk (1,000 feet) is approximately 24 cents per foot for solid PVC and 54 cents a foot for solid Plenum.

Connecting UTP UTP cabling simply plugs into a NIC and then into a wall outlet or hub, making 10/100BaseT installation very simple, as you can see in Figure 6-11. For UTP to work between two computers, the wires must be *crossed over*—the transmitting wires on one computer must become the receiving wires on the other computer. This is one of the functions of a hub, so the wires connecting a computer to a hub must be the same on both ends. When two computers are directly connected to each other, a special cable must be used that has the end connections reversed.

TIP: To stay within the 100 meter (328 foot) limit for a 10BaseT segment, keep the cable run from the wiring closet to the wall outlet at less than 300 feet, the run from the wall outlet to the computer at less than 20 feet, and the patch panel at less than 8 feet.

Fiber-Optic Cable

Fiber-optic cable transmits light over a very pure strand, or *fiber,* of glass less than the thickness of a human hair. The glass is so pure that there is very little loss of light in a very long cable. The light source is either a light-emitting diode (LED) or a laser. Information is transmitted by turning the light source on and off to produce digital ones and zeros. At the other end of the cable is a light detector that converts the light back to electrical pulses. Fiber-optic cable is immune to electrical and electromagnetic interference and does not radiate energy itself. This means that it is very hard for someone to tap undetected a fiber-optic cable and get the information it is carrying. The result is that fiber-optic cable is a very secure and efficient means of quickly carrying information over a long distance.

Fiber-optic cable, shown below, has a central core of transparent glass (or for short distances of a few meters, it can be plastic). This is surrounded by a reflecting glass called *cladding* that redirects any light coming out of the core back into it. The cladding is covered by one or more layers of plastic and other strengthening materials to make a sheath or jacket. There are two kinds of fiber-optic cable:

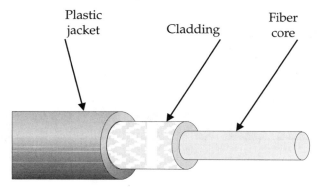

Plastic jacket Cladding Fiber core

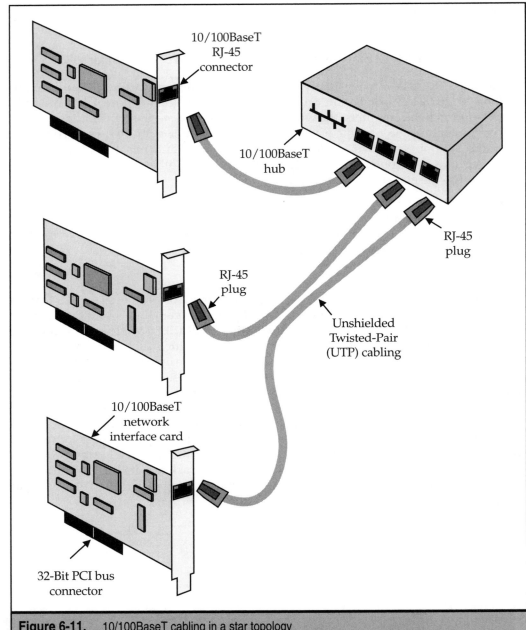

Figure 6-11. 10/100BaseT cabling in a star topology

▼ **Single-mode or monomode fiber** Uses a laser with a very small inner glass core (4 to 10 microns for the core and 75 to 125 microns for the core and cladding combined, written 4/75 to 10/125). Single-mode fiber carries the light, in essence, straight down the fiber. This has a high efficiency, allowing for longer distances—as much as ten times the distance of multimode fiber—but it is also the most expensive, costing up to twice the cost of multimode fiber. Single-mode fiber is used in long-distance WANs, in wiring campus networks, and less frequently in building backbones.

▲ **Multimode fiber** Generally used with a LED and has a much larger glass core (the FDDI standard is 62.5 microns for the core and 125 microns for the core and cladding). Multimode fiber allows the light to bounce off the walls, thus giving it a lower efficiency but at a substantially lower cost. Multimode fiber is used in *premise* wiring, wiring within a building.

The most common fiber-optic cable is multimode fiber with the FDDI dimensions of 62.5/125. It comes with a single fiber (*simplex*), with two fibers (*duplex* or *zipcord*), or with 4, 6, 12, and more fibers. Like UTP cable, fiber-optic cable comes with PVC (riser) and plenum outer jackets. Since most systems require two fibers, one for transmitting and one for receiving, the two-fiber zipcord is encountered most often. At this time, FDDI PVC zipcord costs about 33 cents a foot, while plenum zipcord is about 35 cents, both in 1,000-foot spools.

Gigabit over fiber (1000BaseF) requires the use of lasers (LEDs are not fast enough), and as a result has a longer maximum distance than 100BaseF (1,800 feet vs. 1,351 feet), which standard is based on LEDs. The standards for 1000BaseF are still in the proposal stage, but the current proposal is as follows:

Type of Fiber	Core Size	Maximum Distance
Multimode	50 or 62.5 microns	1,800 feet
Single-mode	10 microns	16,000 feet or 3 miles

A number of connectors are used with fiber-optic cables, as shown in Figure 6-12. Among the more common are the following:

▼ **ST connectors** Used for a single fiber and have a spring-loaded metal outer ring that you twist to lock (fourth from the bottom in Figure 6-12)

▲ **SC connectors** Used for a single fiber and have a square plastic housing that snaps into its mate (third from the bottom in Figure 6-12)

The cost of fiber-optic cabling is coming down significantly and, as a result, is being used more and more frequently for the backbone and even some of the horizontal wiring in a building (see the following section). Up to a few years ago, all of the backbone wiring was 10Base5, but that has mostly been replaced by fiber-optic, which is faster and cheaper.

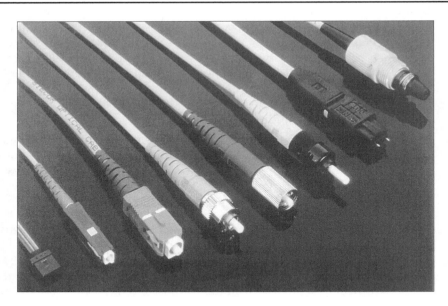

*Photo courtesy of Siecor Corporation, Hickory, NC, http://www.siecor.com

Figure 6-12. Fiber-optic connectors*

TIA/EIA Cabling Standards

The Telecommunications Industry Association (TIA) and the Electronic Industries Association (EIA) together have defined a set of wiring standards for telecommunications and computer networking in a commercial building. The purpose of the standards is to provide a common set of specifications for cabling data, voice, and video in a building that provides the users and owners of the building quality, flexibility, value, and function in their telecommunications infrastructure while allowing diverse manufacturers to build equipment that will interoperate. The most applicable of these standards are the following:

▼ **TIA/EIA-586-A**   For data, voice, and video cabling in a commercial building

■ **TIA/EIA-569**   For the areas and pathways that hold telecommunications media in a building

■ **TIA/EIA-606**   For the design and management of a telecommunications infrastructure

▲ **TIA/EIA-607**   For the grounding and bonding requirements in telecommunications equipment and cabling

These standards define the rules and limitations for each part of the telecommunications and networking infrastructure in a building. The standards break this infrastructure into a defined set of areas and wiring types within a building, as shown on the last page of the Blueprints section of this book, and defined as follows:

▼ **Entrance Facilities**   Where the telecommunications services and/or a campus backbone enters a building

■ **Main Cross-Connects**   The central facility within a building to which all the equipment rooms are connected with backbone wiring; there may also be a main cross-connect for a campus that ties together all the building main cross-connects

■ **Backbone Wiring**   The fast, heavy-duty wiring that runs, generally vertically, from the main cross-connects to the equipment rooms in a building or between main cross-connects on a campus

■ **Equipment Rooms**   The areas located on each floor of a building that provide the connection between the backbone wiring going to the main cross-connect and the horizontal wiring going to the telecommunications closets

■ **Horizontal Wiring**   The second-level wiring that runs, generally across a drop ceiling, from the equipment rooms to the telecommunications closets, as well as the third-level wiring that runs across a ceiling and down a wall from the telecommunications closets to the wall outlets

■ **Telecommunications Closets**   The areas located in several places on a floor of a building that serve a contiguous group of offices and provide a connection between the horizontal wiring running to the equipment rooms and the horizontal wiring running to individual wall outlets

▲ **Work Area Wiring**   The external (not in a wall or ceiling) devices and wiring that provide a connection between the termination of the horizontal wiring in a wall outlet and the computer or other device connected to the network

NOTE: The TIA/EIA standards discuss both telecommunications and computer networking, and in reading them, you need to make sure what a given topic is discussing. For example, UTP for voice can run up to 800 meters or 2,624 feet, whereas UTP for data can only run up to 100 meters or 328 feet.

You can get more information on the TIA/EIA standards from the TIA web site at http://www.tiaonline.org or from Hubbell (a connector manufacturer) at http://www.hubbell-premise.com/EIA568A.asp.

Cabling Cost Comparison

Table 6-4 provides a comparison of the cost of various types of network cables. This should be used only as a relative comparison between types and not as an indication of the current cost, which changes frequently. Also, there are significant differences in suppliers and quantity discounts.

Cable Type (1,000-foot prices 10/99*)	Cost/Foot for PVC	Cost/Foot for Plenum
Thin coax	15 cents	43 cents
Category 5	10 cents	25 cents
Category 5e	15 cents	35 cents
Category 6	24 cents	54 cents
Fiber-optic FDDI zipcord	33 cents	35 cents

*Data Comm Warehouse catalog 55p, 10/99

Table 6-4.   Cabling Cost Comparison

Interconnection Devices

If you have more than two computers in a 10/100BaseT network, you need some device to which you connect the additional computers. The simplest of these devices is a hub, but you might also use a switch, a router, or a bridge, depending on what you want to do. Each of these devices has a particular use, although there is overlap, and each has several variations. These devices act as building blocks that allow you to expand a network segment and interconnect multiple segments. While reading about these interconnection devices, look at the network configurations in the Blueprints section of this book to see how the various devices can be used.

Hubs

Hubs are used to connect other devices on the network. Normally these are workstations, but they can also be servers, printers, other hubs, and other interconnection devices. A hub is a repeater device that takes whatever comes in on one line and puts it out on all other lines without any filtering or intelligence applied to the information stream or where it is going. This means that every station can hear what every other station has put on the network. As the traffic grows, the number of collisions between frames will increase, causing significant degradation in the network throughput. Hubs operate at the Physical layer of the OSI model, simply repeating the information they receive. There are three types of hubs: stand-alone hubs, stackable hubs, and modular hubs.

Stand-Alone Hubs   Stand-alone hubs, shown in Figure 6-13, are used in smaller networks and the final workgroup segment of larger networks. Stand-alone hubs come in 4-, 8-, 12-, 16-, and 24-port models for 10BaseT, 100BaseT, and auto-switching 10/100BaseT. 10BaseT hubs are $8 to $10 per port, 100BaseT hubs are $10 to $20 per port, and 10/100BaseT hubs are $26 to $34 per port. There is a lot of variability in this pricing, but generally speaking, the price per port goes down with more ports in the hub.

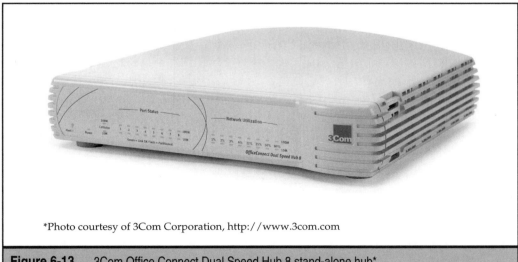

*Photo courtesy of 3Com Corporation, http://www.3com.com

Figure 6-13.   3Com Office Connect Dual Speed Hub 8 stand-alone hub*

Most stand-alone hubs are simple devices into which you plug in the 4 to 24 other devices and that's it. If you want to make a change in the configuration, you have to physically unplug and replug in the devices as needed to make the change. You can get smart stand-alone hubs with a management capability that is most often found in stackable and modular hubs. This allows a hub to be monitored and configured remotely using a software package that normally comes with the hub and either SNMP (Simple Network Management Protocol) or RMON (Remote Monitoring). The software generally works with only one brand of hub, so it might be worthwhile to standardize on one brand if you are getting the additional management capability. Stand-alone hubs that can be managed cost $5 to $10 more per port, and then have a separate charge for the management capability of $250 to $450.

Stackable Hubs   As you build a network with 10/100BaseT's star topology, you do so with a hierarchical structure, as shown in Figure 6-14. Such a structure has a limit of a maximum of four hubs (called "repeaters" in the literature) or levels and five cable lengths between any workstation and the server for 10BaseT, and a maximum of two hubs and three cable lengths for 100BaseT. When you daisy chain one stand-alone hub to another at any level to simply attach more workstations at that level, each hub counts as an additional level, and you can't exceed four. To get around this limitation, stackable hubs were developed, which add ports at the same level by joining the backplane of the hubs as if they were one hub. Therefore, any two devices connected anywhere in the stack have only a single hub between them.

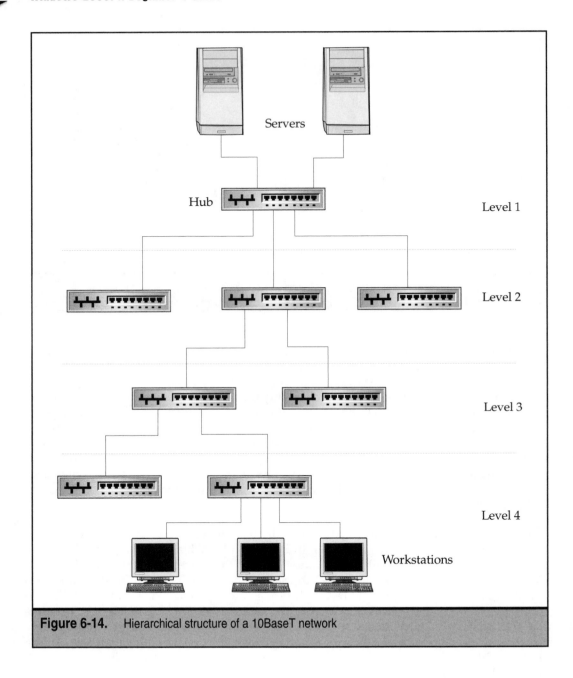

Figure 6-14. Hierarchical structure of a 10BaseT network

Stackable hubs, shown in Figure 6-15, are similar in appearance to stand-alone hubs, and the only real difference is that the backplanes of stackable hubs can be connected.

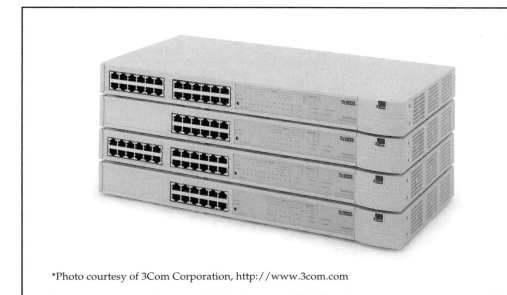

*Photo courtesy of 3Com Corporation, http://www.3com.com

Figure 6-15.   3Com Super Stack II Dual Speed Hub 500 stackable hubs*

Stackable hubs can be stacked six to eight hubs high and cost from $30 to $50 per port. These hubs include the option to be managed with the additional management capability, which costs $300 to $1,050 for the stack.

Modular Hubs   A modular hub, also called an *enterprise hub*, a *modular switch*, or an *enterprise switch*, is really a large chassis or cabinet with a power supply and backplane into which you can plug many different boards, including hubs, switches, bridges, and routers, as shown in Figure 6-16. By using a single backplane, modular hubs get around the four-layer limit, as do stackable hubs. Modular hubs actually preceded stackable hubs, and in the lesser-demanding roles (where all you need are the hub functions), stackable hubs are now being used where modular hubs once were, because a stackable hub is much cheaper.

There are many forms of modular hubs, because you can buy the modules you want to use (hubs, switches, bridges, or routers) and plug them in to a modular backplane that can span one network segment, multiple network segments, or multiple networks. Basically, you buy a chassis with power supply and then buy the modules you need to build the device that fits your network requirements. Modular hubs provide a lot of flexibility, but at a steep price.

In addition to flexibility, modular switches provide another very significant benefit, called a *collapsed backbone.* If the modules were separate devices, you would connect them

*Photo courtesy of 3Com Corporation, http://www.3com.com

Figure 6-16.   3Com CoreBuilder 9000 chassis populated with hubs and switches*

with a high-speed backbone running at, at least, 100 Mbps or 1 Gbps, and maybe double those figures if you run at full-duplex. If you move all of these devices into a single modular hub where they are connected by the backplane, what in a stackable switch is a backbone connection is now collapsed onto the backplane and runs at between 100 Gbps and 600 Gbps (that's a "G" not an "M").

Bridges

A bridge is used to either segment a network or join two networks, as you can see in Figure 6-17. A bridge looks at the physical or MAC address in a frame on one side of the bridge and if the frame has an address on the other side of the bridge, the frame is passed on to the other side. If the frame has an address on the originating side of the bridge, the bridge ignores the frame, because all devices on the originating side already can see the frame. Since a bridge looks at a frame's physical address, it is operating at the Data Link layer of the OSI model, one layer above where a hub operates.

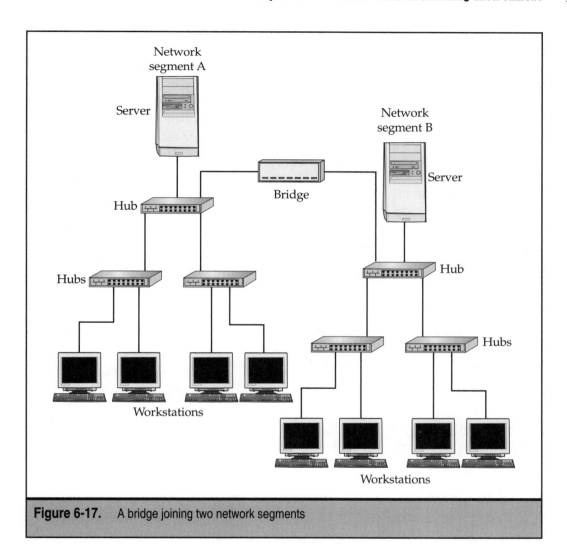

Figure 6-17. A bridge joining two network segments

The purpose of the bridge is to reduce the traffic in a network by segmenting it, although it is still one network. If a hub replaced the bridge, the entire network would have all the traffic on both sides of what was the bridge, increasing the collisions and decreasing the throughput.

When you join two networks with a bridge, the result is one network with two segments, but only the traffic that is addressed to the other segment gets through the bridge. Traffic that is addressed within the originating segment stays within its segment. A bridge also lets you have additional hub layers above the four-hub limit in a simple Ethernet network. A frame can travel through four hubs, cross a bridge, and then travel through four more hubs. The bridge, in essence, takes a frame from one side and, if it is properly addressed, re-creates it on the other side.

The bridging discussed so far has described local bridging within a single facility. Bridges can also be used to connect a local network with a remote one and, in so doing, produce a single network with two segments where the traffic between them is limited to that destined for the other network. In this remote scenario, there would be a bridge on either side of the line connecting the two segments so that the local traffic in each segment stays in that segment.

Bridges are basically simple devices and are limited to a single network (both the source and destination address must be in the same network) and to a single cabling or media type. Theoretically, a 10BaseT network cannot be joined to a 10BaseF network with a bridge, but by building converters into the bridge, you can join them. Bridges range in price from around $300 to over $1,500, depending on their capabilities and brand.

NOTE: Bridges are becoming hard to find because you can generally perform the same function with a router or a switch for close to the same price.

Routers

Routers can perform the same segmenting and joining functions as a bridge, but do so at a higher level of sophistication, using the logical address of the OSI model's Network layer. The resulting added abilities of a router are significant:

▼ Routers connect separate networks, leaving them independent with their own addressing

■ Routers connect different types of networks; for example, 10Base2 and 10BaseT

■ Routers select from among alternative routes a path through a complex network in order to get to an end destination

▲ Routers clean up network traffic by checking if a frame is corrupted and if it is lost (traveling endlessly in the network), and if it is corrupted or lost, the frame is removed from the network

For these reasons, routers are routinely used to connect to the Internet and within the Internet, and to connect a WAN to a LAN. Routers generally are intelligent devices with a processor and memory. With this capability, a router unpacks every frame that comes to it, looks at each packet within the frame, recalculates its CRC, checks to see how many times the packets have been around the network, looks at the logical destination address, determines the best path to get there, repackages the packets into a new frame with the new physical address, and sends the frame on its way. In addition, routers talk to other routers to determine the best path and to keep track of routes that have failed. Routers do all of this at amazing speeds. At the low end, routers process over 250,000 packets per second, and go above several million packets a second on the upper end. Routers begin at around $400 and go up to many thousands, depending on what they do.

Switches

A switch, like a hub, has a number of ports, from 2 to 24, and takes information that comes into one port and sends it out to one or more other ports. Unlike a hub, which does no filtering or processing on the information that flows through it, a switch is an intelligent device that looks at the physical destination address of the frame flowing into it and directs the frame to the correct port for that destination. This removes that frame from the rest of the network, since the frame goes over only the part of the network that connects the sending and receiving devices. This is similar to the maturing of the telephone system from the original party-line system to the modern direct-dial system.

Switches, like bridges and routers, segment a network to reduce the traffic and collisions, and ultimately improve the throughput. Switch segmentation can be done at any level where you would otherwise have a hub, a bridge, or a router. Such a switch functions as a multiport bridge and is therefore operating at the Data Link layer of the OSI model. Further intelligence can be added to some switches so that they become multiport switching routers that unpack frames and operate on the logical address in the packets. Such switching routers operate at the Network layer of the OSI mode. For this reason, they are called *Level 3 switches*.

NOTE: If the top two hubs in Figure 6-17 were switches, you could join the two network segments without a bridge simply by running a cable between the two switches, getting the same segmentation.

Switches, like hubs, come in stand-alone and stackable models with and without management capability. The simplest switches cost about $40 a port and go as high as $200 a port.

Interconnection Device Summary

When you are building a network, you have many choices regarding interconnection devices. You not only have the choice between hubs, bridges, routers, and switches, but you also have a number of choices within each of those devices. You can get some insight into an answer by looking at where in the OSI model each of the devices operates, as shown in Figure 6-18. Another aspect is the cost of each of the devices, shown in Table 6-5.

Network Topologies

Topology is the design of a network, the way it is laid out. In the figures in this chapter, you have seen several different topologies. 10Base2 and 10Base5 both use a *bus* topology, wherein all the network devices are attached to a single long cable, as you saw in Figures 6-1 and 6-9. 10BaseT and 100BaseT both use a *star* topology, where the network devices fan out on separate cables from a central hub, as you saw in Figures 6-2, 6-11, and 6-14. FDDI uses a *dual-ring* topology, like the one shown in Figure 6-5, and Token Ring uses a *star-configured ring* topology, shown in Figure 6-4. Finally, when the backbone cabling is added to a 10/100BaseT network, you have a *star/bus* topology, shown in the Blueprints section of this book.

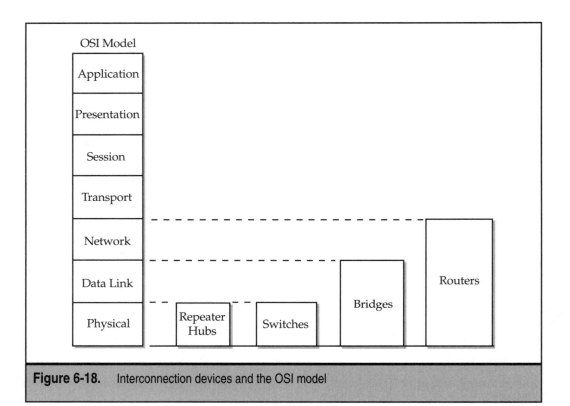

Figure 6-18. Interconnection devices and the OSI model

Interconnection Device	Cost 10/99 (various sources)
10BaseT hubs	$8 to $10 per port
100BaseT hubs	$10 to $20 per port
10/100BaseT hubs	$18 to $30 per port
Management capability	$5 to $10 per port plus $250 to $450
10/100 stackable hubs	$30 to $50 per port
Bridges	$300 and up
Routers	$400 and up
10/100 switches	$40 to $200 per port

Table 6-5. Cost Comparison of Interconnection Devices

The bus topology was the original Ethernet topology, but it has the major disadvantage that a break in any part of the network brings the entire network down. In a star topology, a break in a line takes out only those parts of the network connected to the line, potentially only one station. In a self-correcting topology, such as the star-configured ring of Token Ring, if a station is disabled or removed or if a line is broken, the system re-forms a ring and continues operating.

There are disagreements as to whether a bus or a star is easier to cable, but although a star takes more cable, it is cheaper cable, and it is easier to manage. You can put the cable for a star topology in the wall and not connect it to a hub or switch if it is not being used. Also, it is easy to move a station from one network segment to another simply by changing a jumper cable that connects the station from one hub to another.

Laying Out a Network

Once you have decided on the network technology, type of NIC, cabling, and interconnection devices that you want to use, you still have to figure out how to lay out the network. This includes a lot of questions, such as:

▼ Which workstations are grouped into which hubs?

■ Do you stack several hubs, or immediately use a switch?

■ Should the servers be centralized in one location or decentralized in each department?

■ When do you need a switch, a router, or a bridge?

▲ How do you connect two buildings separated by 1,500 feet or more?

There is no one right answer to any of these questions and there is a lot of difference in the impact between the first question and the last questions. You can easily alter the connections to change how workstations are grouped, but setting up a wide area network is a job for professionals because you are talking about serious money to purchase the equipment and install it, and significant expense if you want to change it. The Blueprints section of this book, called "Network Designs," provides simplified schematic diagrams of how small- to medium-sized networks might be wired.

In an Ethernet 10BaseT or 100BaseT network there are several rules that should be followed in a layout. These vary slightly with different manufacturers, but the general rules of thumb are shown in the following table:

Rule of Thumb	Ethernet 10BaseT	Fast Ethernet 100BaseT
Maximum cable length between hub and workstation	100 meters or 328 feet	100 meters or 328 feet
Minimum cable type	Category 3	Category 5
Maximum number of hubs between two workstations or a switch and a workstation	Four hubs	Two hubs

Rule of Thumb	Ethernet 10BaseT	Fast Ethernet 100BaseT
Maximum number of cable segments between two workstations or a switch and a workstation	Five cable segments	Three cable segments with a maximum total distance of 205 meters or 672 feet

There is a wonderful tool for both planning the layout of a network as you are building it and maintaining the network after it is installed. This tool is Visio 2000, either the Professional or Enterprise Editions. With Visio 2000 you can easily design the network layout that you want to use, quickly communicate that design to others, create a bill of material, and have a ready reference during installation. After a network is completed, Visio 2000 will search the network and automatically discover and document all of the network devices at the Data Link (layer 2) and Network (layer 3) layers. Visio is now owned by Microsoft and can be reached at http://www.microsoft.com/office/visio/.

NETWORKING PROTOCOLS

Protocols are the standards or rules that allow many different systems and devices to interconnect and operate on a network, be it a small office network or the worldwide Internet. Protocols specify *how* and *when* it should happen, and *what* it is that should happen.

Protocols are developed in many different ways, but for one to become widely used, it must be accepted by a number of organizations, most importantly those building networking software and networking devices. To gain this acceptance, protocols are initially circulated as draft protocols, using documents called Requests for Comments (RFCs). If someone or some organization wants to change a protocol, a new RFC gets circulated with a higher number than the original RFC. The Information Sciences Institute (ISI) of the University of Southern California classifies RFCs as being approved Internet standards, proposed Internet standards, Internet best practices, and For Your Information (FYI). ISI also maintains a web site that lists RFCs and their classification (http://www.rfc-editor.org/) from which you can get copies of the RFCs. You can determine how a piece of software has implemented a protocol by looking at which RFCs are supported. For example, in Windows 2000, you can look up the topic "TCP/IP RFCs" in Help and see a list of RFCs that are supported.

Numerous protocols deal with computer networking, but "networking protocols" normally refers to the logical addressing and transfer of information. These protocols deal with the Transport and Network layers of the OSI networking model, as shown in Figure 6-19. In this area, Windows 2000 supports five protocols:

▼ **AppleTalk**   For communicating with earlier Apple Macintosh systems

■ **DLC**   For communicating with earlier IBM mainframes

■ **IPX/SPX**   For communicating with Novell NetWare

■ **NetBEUI**   For communicating with earlier Microsoft networking systems

▲ **TCP/IP**   For communicating with the Internet and most newer systems

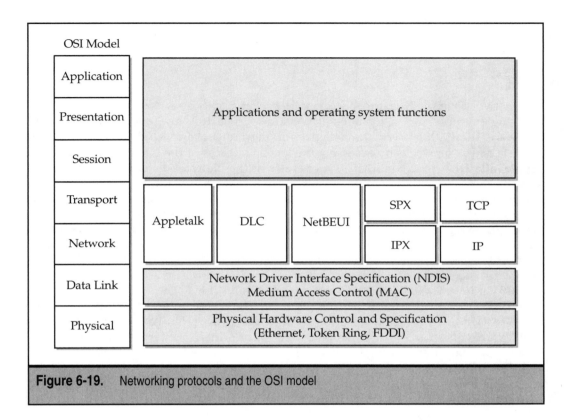

Figure 6-19. Networking protocols and the OSI model

AppleTalk

AppleTalk is a networking protocol that appeared early in the history of the Macintosh. It originally worked with the Macintosh's LocalTalk network, but was subsequently enhanced to work with Ethernet, Token Ring, and FDDI. AppleTalk was designed for small local workgroups, not for large complex networks. With AppleTalk installed in Windows 2000 and the appropriate permissions established, a Mac can browse a Windows 2000 network. While Apple and newer operating systems such as Windows 2000 still support AppleTalk, newer Macintosh systems now can also use TCP/IP (see the upcoming section "TCP/IP").

DLC

Data Link Control is a networking protocol developed by IBM for use with its earlier mainframes, and is a part of its System Network Architecture (SNA). More recent IBM mainframes can also use TCP/IP. Also, some older Hewlett-Packard (HP) laser printers that had stand-alone network interfaces (the network attached directly to the printer, not to a computer that attached to the printer) required that the DLC protocol be installed and used by the computer addressing the printer. More recent HP laser printers with stand-alone network interfaces use TCP/IP.

IPX/SPX

Internetwork Packet Exchange/Sequenced Packet Exchange is Novell NetWare's networking protocol and is included in Windows 2000 to allow internetworking with NetWare. IPX/SPX is a very capable networking protocol and is fully routable (able to operate across networks by accessing the logical address of the Network layer), unlike AppleTalk, DLC, and NetBEUI. IPX operates at the Network layer of the OSI model, thereby controlling the assembly of packets and providing the routing services. SPX operates at the Transport layer, which establishes and maintain a connection with another network node. Once this connection is established, SPX tells IPX to begin assembling and transmitting packets. The packet that IPX assembles has a data area of up to 64KB and a header with the source and destination address and other control information of 30 bytes. In most instances, the network at the Data Link and Physical layers will limit the packet size to around 1.5KB.

In Windows 2000, IPX/SPX is implemented in NWLink. Through NWLink, a Windows 2000 computer using Client Services for NetWare can access information on a NetWare server or print on a NetWare-controlled printer. Similarly, with NWLink, a NetWare client can access information on servers or print to printers connected to a Windows 2000 computer running File and Print Services for NetWare. NWLink can directly use IPX, called *direct hosting,* or it can use NetBIOS over IPX, which is the default. Either technique works for all combinations of clients (MS-DOS, Windows for Workgroups, Windows 95, Windows 98, and Windows 2000) and for the same list of servers *except* that a Windows 2000 client cannot access a Windows 2000 server using direct hosting.

NOTE: Chapter 8 discusses in depth using NetWare with Windows 2000.

NetBEUI

NetBIOS Extended User Interface (where NetBIOS is Network Basic Input Output System) is a networking protocol designed by Microsoft and IBM for earlier and smaller networks. While Microsoft is still fully supporting NetBEUI, the recommended networking protocol on Microsoft systems is TCP/IP, unless a legacy system requires NetBEUI. NetBEUI does not have a separate Network layer and therefore lacks routing capability. It is limited to a single network and a moderate number of workstations.

TCP/IP

Transmission Control Protocol/Internet Protocol is a set of networking protocols that grew out of the Internet and has been refined over 15 years to be an excellent tool for transmitting large amounts of information reliably and quickly over a complex network.

The two components, TCP and IP, were originally combined and later were separated to improve the efficiency of the system.

IP

The Internet Protocol, like IPX, operates at the Network layer of the OSI model controlling the assembly and routing of packets (called *datagrams* in IP). To send a datagram to a remote node across a complex network, such as the Internet, these are the steps that take place:

1. The datagram is assembled at the Network layer, and the IP address of the destination (which is a logical address, not a physical address) is added.

2. The datagram is passed to the Data Link layer, which packages the datagram in a frame and adds the physical address of the first router that starts the datagram on its way to its destination.

3. The datagram is passed to the closest router, which unpacks the frame, looks at the logical address on the datagram, repackages the datagram in a frame, and adds the physical address of the next router that continues the datagram on its way to its destination.

4. Repeat step 3 for each router along the path.

5. At the last router before the destination, the destination physical address is added to the frame and the frame is sent to its destination.

This technique allows the information to follow any path through the network, with the decision on which path to take made by the local router based on its knowledge of the local situation. IP is a connectionless service. It sends the datagram on its way not knowing whether it is received or what route it took. Determining whether it is received and replacing the packet if it isn't is the function of TCP at the Transport layer. The route that the datagram takes is a function of the routers at the Data Link layer. The datagram that IP assembles has a maximum of up to 64K, including a variable header with the source and destination address and other control information. The header, which is always a multiple of 4 bytes, is shown in Figure 6-20 and has these fields:

▼ **Version**   Protocol version number

■ **IHL**   Header length in 4-byte words (five-word minimum)

■ **Type of Service**   The speed and reliability of service requested

■ **Total Length**   Total datagram length in bytes or "octets"

■ **Identification**   Fragment identification, so it can be reconstructed

■ **Flags**   Fragmentation indicator (DF: 0 = may fragment, 1 = don't fragment, MF: 0 = last fragments, 1 = more fragments)

■ **Fragment Offset**   Number in a set of fragments; the first is 0

■ **Time to Live**   The remaining number of times through a router before the datagram is discarded

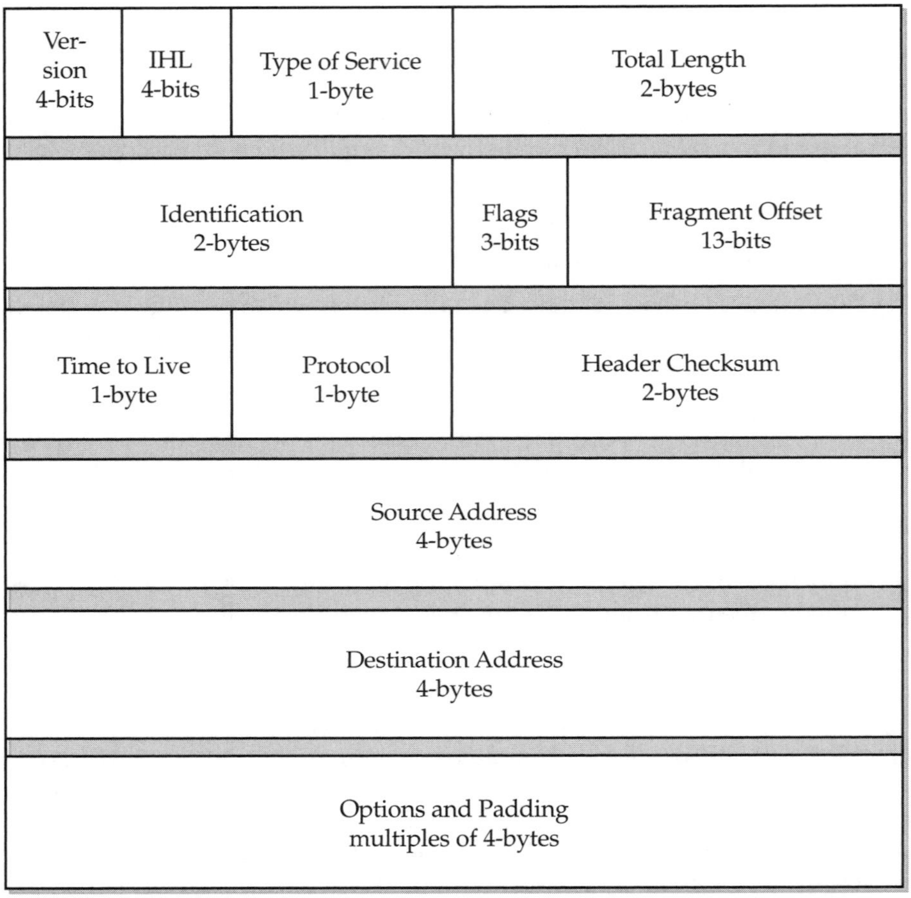

Ver-sion 4-bits	IHL 4-bits	Type of Service 1-byte	Total Length 2-bytes	
Identification 2-bytes			Flags 3-bits	Fragment Offset 13-bits
Time to Live 1-byte		Protocol 1-byte	Header Checksum 2-bytes	
Source Address 4-bytes				
Destination Address 4-bytes				
Options and Padding multiples of 4-bytes				

Figure 6-20.   IP datagram header

- ■ **Protocol**   The protocol to use at the Transport layer
- ■ **Header Checksum**   Number to check the integrity of the header only
- ■ **Source Address**   The source computer's IP address
- ■ **Destination Address**   The destination computer's IP address
- ■ **Options**   Security, routing, and other optional information
- ▲ **Padding**   Ensure that header is in multiples of 4 bytes

IP Addressing

The source and destination addresses in the IP header are the logical addresses assigned to particular computers, as compared to the physical address on a network card. These 32-bit or 4-byte numbers, called *IP addresses,* can have one of three formats, which vary the sizes of the network and host segments of the address. The leftmost ("high order") bits identify the particular format or "class." All of these classes have a network segment and a host segment that allow for locating a particular computer or router (*host*) within a particular network, as described here:

- ▼ Class A can identify up to 16,777,214 hosts in each of 126 networks
- ■ Class B can identify up to 65,534 hosts in each of 16,382 networks
- ▲ Class C can identify up to 254 hosts in each of 2,097,150 networks

NOTE: The general IP specification is in RFC 791, while addressing is additionally discussed in RFCs 790 and 796. All of these RFCs are available from http://www.ietf.org/rfc.html.

The IP address is commonly represented as four decimal numbers separated by periods. For example: 127.168.105.204. Each number is 1 byte in the address. To assist in identifying how to parse (or divide) an IP address into a network segment and a host segment, you must specify a *subnet mask* that serves as a template for this purpose. The subnet mask for class A is 255.0.0.0, for class B it is 255.255.0.0, and for class C it is 255.255.255.0. The subnet mask focuses the attention on local hosts within the current network. If you are working within the current network, the subnet mask can speed up the processing of the IP address.

The majority of IP addresses have been assigned and there is much discussion on how to handle the growth caused by public acceptance of the Internet. A number of temporary measures have been taken that fit within the current version (version 4) of IP. The long-term solution is a major revision of IP, as proposed in RFCs 1883 and 1887, for IP version 6 (IPv6) that lengthens the address space from 4 bytes to 16 bytes. This allows enough room for every person on earth and every device, including VCRs and cars, to have an IP address!

NOTE: IPv6 is just on the verge of implementation and includes many other changes besides lengthening the address field. Among the other changes are the following: cleaning up the header fields to reduce the processor cost; special labeling of real-time audio and video to improve their flow; and adding more capability for authentication and privacy.

TCP

The Transmission Control Protocol, like SPX, operates at the Transport layer, which handles connections. Its purpose is to assure the reliable delivery to a specific destination. TCP (and SPX) is a connection-oriented service, in contrast with IP (and IPX), which is connectionless. TCP makes the connection with the final destination and maintains contact with the destination to make sure that the information is correctly received. Once a connection is established, though, TCP depends on IP to handle the actual transfer. And, because IP is connectionless, IP depends on TCP to assure delivery.

The sending and receiving TCPs maintain an ongoing, full-duplex (both can be talking at the same time) dialog throughout a transmission to assure a reliable delivery. This begins by the sending TCP making sure that the destination is ready to receive information. Once an affirmative answer is received, the sending TCP packages a data message into a *segment* containing a header with control information and the first part of the data. This is then sent to IP, and TCP creates the remaining segments while watching for an acknowledgement that the segments have been received. If an acknowledgment is not received for a particular segment, it is re-created and handed off. This process continues until the final segment is sent and acknowledged, at which point the sender tells the receiver that it's done. In the process of transmission, the two Transport layers are constantly talking to make sure that everything is going smoothly.

NOTE: Different and sometimes confusing names are used to refer to pieces of data being transferred through a network, depending on where you are in the OSI model and the protocol you are using. Assuming the TCP/IP protocol and Ethernet, as shown in Figure 6-21, at the top of the OSI model, applications create messages to be sent over a network. The message is handed down to the Transport level, which puts the message into *segments* that include a segment header with port addresses. The segments are passed down to the Network layer, where IP packages the segments into *datagrams* with logical IP addresses. The datagrams are sent down to the Data Link layer, where Ethernet encapsulates them into a *frame* with a physical address. The frames are passed to the Physical layer, which sends them over the network to the physical address, where the reverse process takes place. Alternatively, in the Transport and Network layers, a piece of information is generically called a *packet* of information.

The communication between the sending and receiving TCPs takes place in the segment header, which is shown in Figure 6-22 and explained in the following list. The two protocols use the sequence number, the acknowledgment number, codes, sliding window size, urgent pointer, and options to carry on a very complex conversation about how a transmission is progressing. And all of it is happening in very small fractions of a second.

▼ **Source Port** The port number in the Session layer, called a *socket*, that is sending the data

■ **Destination Port** The port number in the Session layer, or socket, that is receiving the data

■ **Sequence Number** A number sent to the receiver to tell it where the segment fits in the data stream

■ **Acknowledgment Number** A number sent to the sender to tell it that a segment was received; the sequence number increments by one

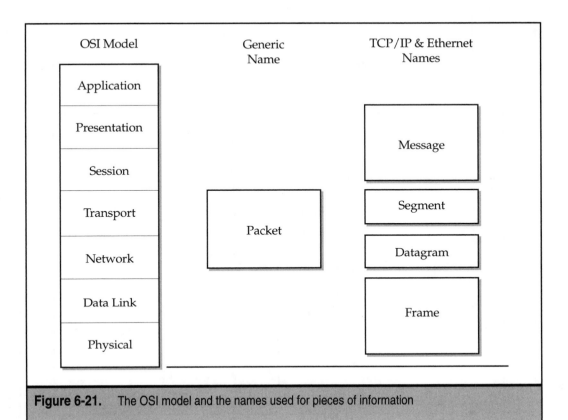

Figure 6-21.   The OSI model and the names used for pieces of information

- **Header Length**   The length of the header and therefore the offset from the start of the header to the data
- **URG**   The Urgent field; if 1, the Urgent Pointer is valid
- **ACK**   The Acknowledgment field; if 1, the Acknowledgment Number is valid
- **PSH**   The Push field; if 1, the receiver is to not buffer data, but instead send it directly to the application, as with real-time audio and video
- **RST**   The Reset field; if 1, the communication must be interrupted and the connection reset
- **SYN**   The Synchronize field; if 1, a connection is requested by the sender; if accepted, the receiver leaves SYN = 1 and makes ACK = 1
- **FIN**   The Finish field; if 1, the transmission is to be terminated
- **Window Size**   The number of bytes that the receiver can accept in the next transmission

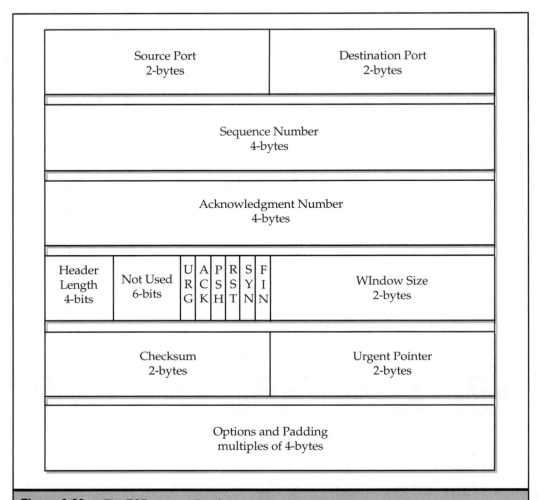

Figure 6-22.   The TCP segment header

- ■ **Checksum**   A number with which to check the integrity of the segment
- ■ **Urgent Pointer**   If URG =1, this is a number used as an offset to point to an urgent piece of information the receiver should look at
- ■ **Options**   Used for special circumstances; normally absent
- ▲ **Padding**   Used to ensure that the header is in multiples of 4 bytes

NOTE: The general TCP specification is in RFC 793, which is available from http://www.ietf.org/rfc.html.

The functions performed by TCP and IP: the packaging, addressing, routing, transmission, and control of the networking process in a very complex environment is mind boggling. When you add to that the ease and reliability of networking, it is truly stunning. Now that you know all the networking ingredients presented in this chapter, isn't it amazing that networking works even in a small workgroup, let alone the Internet? That the Internet is such a worldwide success has to be one of the great wonders of the modern world.

At the beginning of this chapter, I stated that networking is the single most important facility in Windows 2000. Having read this chapter, I think you can see that the job of networking is a very complex task with many demands, and for Windows 2000 to handle it well is a tall order. In the next chapter, you'll see how Windows 2000 tackles these demands, and how to control what Windows 2000 does. I think you'll conclude that Windows 2000 is well suited to this most important function.

CHAPTER 7

Setting Up and Managing a Windows 2000 Network

W hen you installed Windows 2000, a basic set of networking services was installed and configured using your input and system defaults. This setup may, but often doesn't, provide an operable networking system. In any case, there is a wide spectrum of networking alternatives that should be reviewed and set to provide the networking environment best suited to your needs. The purpose of this chapter is to do just that, first by looking at how to set up basic networking in either Windows 2000 Server or Windows 2000 Professional, and then by looking at how to set up Windows 2000 Server to support the rest of the network.

SETTING UP BASIC NETWORKING

Basic networking means that the computer can communicate with other computers in the network. To do that, you must do the following:

1.   Assure the network interface card (NIC) is properly set up

2.   Install the networking functions that you want to perform

3.   Choose and configure a networking protocol

Setting Up Network Interface Cards

In a perfect world, the computer you are setting up has a NIC that is both on Microsoft's Hardware Compatibility List (HCL) and fully Plug and Play–compatible. If this describes your computer, then your NIC was installed by Setup without incident and you don't need to read this section. As is known by anyone who has installed an operating system on more than two computers, it is an imperfect world. Therefore, this section looks at how the NIC was installed and what you need to do to make it fully operational.

If you installed Windows 2000 Server using the instructions in Chapter 4, and went through the section "Configuring Networking," then you can skip this section if you believe your NIC is operating correctly. If you had problems with that section of Chapter 4 or did not go through it, then this section will be worthwhile to you.

Assuming that a NIC *is* properly plugged into the computer, any of these three things could be causing it to not operate:

▼   The NIC driver is either missing or not properly installed

■   The required resources are not available

▲   The NIC is not functioning properly

Look at each of these possibilities in turn in the next several sections.

Checking on the NIC Driver

During installation, you may have gotten a message stating that a driver could not be found (although Setup often completes without telling you it skipped network setup because of the lack of a driver). Use the following steps to check whether you have a driver installed and, if you don't, to try to install one:

1. Open the Start menu and choose Settings | Network and Dial-up Connections. The Network and Dial-Up Connections window opens. If you have at least two icons in the window, including Local Area Connection, you probably have the NIC driver properly installed and you can go on to the next major section, "Installing Network Functions."

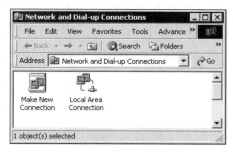

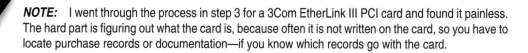

TIP: You can change the name Local Area Connection (for example, if you install two NIC cards, you can give each of them a descriptive name), so it may be named something else in step 1; you cannot rename Make New Connection.

2. If you do not have a Local Area Connection icon, you cannot create one by clicking Make New Connection. You must first install the NIC using Add/Remove Hardware.

3. At this point, it is highly likely that you will need a Windows 2000 driver for the NIC, so it is best to get it before proceeding. If one did not come with the NIC, then you need to get onto another computer, bring up the manufacturer's web site, locate and download the driver (you need to know the make and model of the NIC), and then copy it onto a floppy disk.

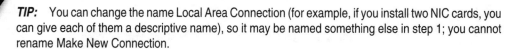

NOTE: I went through the process in step 3 for a 3Com EtherLink III PCI card and found it painless. The hard part is figuring out what the card is, because often it is not written on the card, so you have to locate purchase records or documentation—if you know which records go with the card.

4. Again open the Start menu and click Settings | Control Panel | Add/Remove Hardware. The Add/Remove Hardware Wizard opens.

5. Click Next. Accept the default Add/Troubleshoot a Device and click Next again. A list of devices will appear. You may or may not see Ethernet Controller on the list (with a problem icon), shown in Figure 7-1.

6. If you don't see Ethernet Controller, double-click Add a New Device. Choose No, you don't want Windows to search for new hardware (if it was going to find it, it would have), and click Next. Skip to step 8.

7. If you see Ethernet Controller, as shown in Figure 7-1, double-click it and you will most likely get a Device Status telling you that a driver was not installed. Click Finish to close the Add/Remove Hardware Wizard and start a troubleshooter. The Upgrade Device Driver Wizard opens. Click Next. Choose Display a List of Known Drivers, and click Next.

8. Independent of whether you saw the Ethernet Controller, double-click Network Adapters. A list of network adapters appears. If your NIC had been on the list, Setup would have found it, so you need to insert and use the floppy disk you made in step 3.

9. Click Have Disk. Accept the default of the A drive (assuming that is the floppy drive) and click OK. When it is displayed, select the driver for your adapter, and click Next. When told that the device will be installed, click Next again.

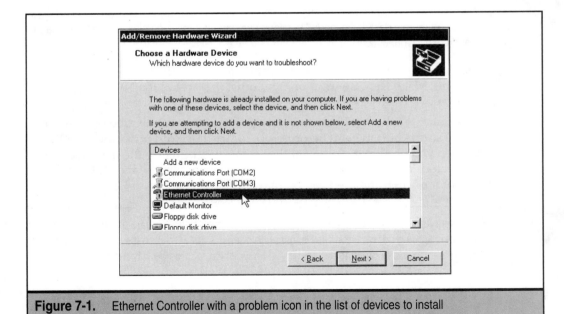

Figure 7-1. Ethernet Controller with a problem icon in the list of devices to install

10. You may get a message stating that the driver you are about to install does not have a Microsoft digital signature. Click Yes to go ahead and install it anyway. The driver and its necessary supporting software will be installed.

11. Click Finish. The Network and Dial-Up Connections window should now show the Local Area Connection icon. If you see the Local Area Connection icon, go to the next major section, "Installing Network Functions."

If you still do not have a Local Area Connection, or some other problem occurred in the preceding process that does not point to an obvious solution, continue through the next two sections to see if a solution is presented.

Checking NIC Resources

Most interface or adapter cards in a PC require dedicated resources in order to operate. The resources include interrupt request (IRQ) lines, I/O ports, and direct memory access (DMA) lines. Generally, two devices cannot share the same resources, except that PCI devices can share IRQs. Therefore, if two devices are assigned the same resource, a conflict occurs and the device will not operate properly. This will cause a NIC to not function and the Local Area Connection icon to not appear in the Network and Dial-Up Connections window. Check the resources used by the NIC, with these steps:

1. Open the Start menu and click Settings | Control Panel | System. The System Properties dialog box opens.

2. Click the Hardware tab and then click Device Manager on the right of the middle section. The Device Manager window opens. If you see a problem icon (an exclamation point) on your network adapter, as shown on the Communications Port in Figure 7-2, then there is probably a problem with the resource allocation.

3. Open the Network Adapters category and double-click the particular network adapter that is being researched. The Properties dialog box for that device will open and give you a device status. If there is a resource problem, then it should show up here.

4. Click the Resources tab. In the Conflicting Device List at the bottom of the dialog box, you will see the specifics of any resource conflicts.

5. If you have a conflict, click Use Automatic Settings to turn that setting off, and then go through each of the configurations in the Setting Based On drop-down list to see if any of them cure the problem.

6. If none of the canned configurations cures the problem, click the problem resource and click Change Setting. Click the up or down arrow to change the setting, and then click OK to see if that fixes the problem. Try several settings.

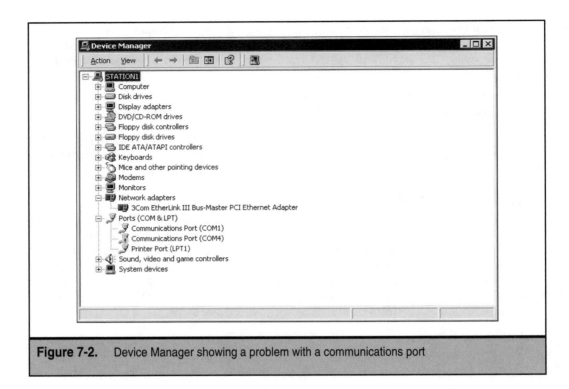

Figure 7-2.   Device Manager showing a problem with a communications port

7. If you are having a hard time finding a solution, go back to the Device Manager (you can leave the NIC Properties dialog box open), open the View menu, and choose Resources By Type. Here, you can see all of the assignments for a given resource and find an empty resource to assign to the NIC.

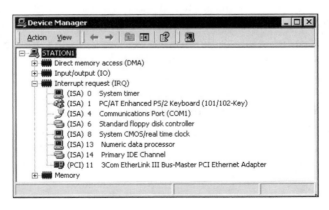

8. If you find an unassigned resource, go back to the NIC Properties dialog box and assign it to the NIC. If you cannot find an unassigned resource, you may have to make a tough choice between the NIC and a conflicting device. Networking is a pretty important service, and if it is conflicting with a sound card, for example, you may have to remove the sound card to get networking. If both of the cards are ISA cards and you have PCI slots available, you may be able to get a new PCI card and remove the conflict.

9. If none of the previous suggestions works, return to the NIC Properties dialog box, click the General tab, and then click Troubleshooter. Windows 2000 Help will open and lead you through a series of steps to try to resolve the problem.

10. When you have solved the resource problem as best you can, close the NIC Properties dialog box and close the Device Manager. If you made changes in the resources, you will be told that you need to restart your computer and asked whether you want to do it now. Click Yes, and the computer will restart.

11. If you successfully made a change to the resources, you should now see a Local Area Connection icon in the Network and Dial-Up Connections window. If you do, go to the next major section, "Installing Network Functions." If you don't see a Local Area Connection icon, continue with the following section.

NIC Not Functioning

If neither installing a NIC driver nor changing its resource allocation caused the Local Area Connection icon to appear, it is very likely that the NIC itself is not functioning properly. The easiest way to test that is to replace the NIC with a known good one, ideally one that is both on Microsoft's HCL and Plug and Play–compatible. It is wise to have several spare NICs; they are not terribly expensive (see "Network Interface Cards" in Chapter 6), and switching out a suspected bad one can quickly solve problems.

NOTE: The HCL is on the Windows 2000 CD-ROM as Hcl.txt in the Support folder; for the very latest update, contact Microsoft's web site at http://www.microsoft.com/hcl/default.asp.

Installing Networking Functions

Networking functions provide the software for a computer to access other computers, and, separately, for other computers to access the computer you are working on. In other words, the two primary functions allow the computer to be a client (access other computers) and to be a server (other computers access it). Make sure that these two services are installed by following these steps:

1. In the Network and Dial-Up Connections window, double-click Local Area Connection. The Local Area Connection Status dialog box opens, as shown in Figure 7-3. In the particular case shown in Figure 7-3, the computer thinks it is connected to the network and it is sending out packets, but it is not receiving them, so all is not well. In this and the next section, we'll try to fix that.

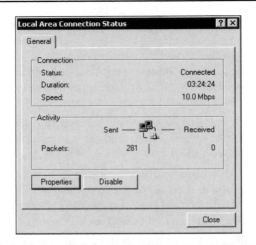

Figure 7-3.   Local Area Connection Status dialog box

2. Click Properties. The Local Area Connection Properties dialog box, shown in Figure 7-4, opens and displays the services and protocols that have automatically been installed. Under the default circumstances, this includes two functions—Client for Microsoft Networks, and File and Printer Sharing for Microsoft Networks—and one protocol—Internet Protocol (TCP/IP). If you have the two functions installed, you have achieved the objective of this section, but in any case, continue and explore the alternatives.

3. Click Install. The Select Network Component Type dialog box opens, in which you can add clients, services, and protocols.

4. Double-click Client. If you already have Client for Microsoft Networks installed, you will only have Client Service for NetWare (or Gateway [and Client] Services for NetWare in a domain server) in the list.

5. If Client for Microsoft Networks is not installed, select it and click OK. If you also need to access a NetWare server, select Client Service for NetWare and click OK.

6. Back in the Select Network Component Type dialog box, double-click Service. If you already have File and Printer Sharing for Microsoft Networks installed, you have QoS (quality of service) Packet Scheduler and SAP Agent available to be installed.

7. If File and Printer Sharing for Microsoft Networks is not installed, select it and click OK. If you need either of the other two services, select the one(s) you need, and click OK.

This should assure that you have the two primary functions installed.

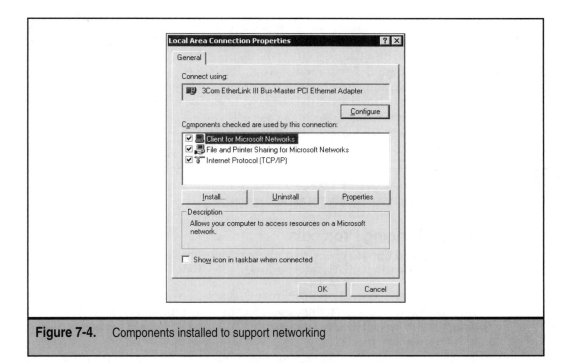

Figure 7-4.   Components installed to support networking

Choosing and Configuring a Networking Protocol

As you read in Chapter 6, networking protocols are a set of standards used to package and transmit information over a network. The protocol determines how the information is divided into packets, how it is addressed, and what is done to assure it is reliably transferred. The protocol is therefore very important to the success of networking, and its choice is a major one. Windows 2000 offers five protocols:

▼   **AppleTalk**   For use with earlier Apple computers

■   **Data Link Control (DCL)**   For use with earlier IBM mainframes and earlier HP printers

■   **Internetwork Packet Exchange/Sequenced Packet Exchange (IPX/SPX)** For use with networks running Novell NetWare

■   **Network Basic Input Output System (NetBIOS) Extended User Interface (NetBEUI)**   For use with computers running earlier Microsoft operating systems

▲   **TCP/IP**   For use with the Internet and most newer systems

NOTE: IPX/SPX is implemented in Windows 2000 with the NWLink IPX/SPX/NetBIOS Compatible Transport Protocol.

You can see that AppleTalk, DCL, and NetBEUI are all for *earlier* systems. All Apple, IBM, and Microsoft computers and operating systems, as well as HP printers produced in the last several years can also use TCP/IP. If the computer you are working on is or will be connected to the Internet, it will require TCP/IP. TCP/IP is a very robust protocol that's suitable for a demanding environment (is there a network environment more demanding than the Internet?) and accepted worldwide. Because of this, it is recommended that TCP/IP be installed as your protocol of choice. If you also need one of the other protocols, because you need to network with an older system or a Novell system, then you can additionally install that protocol.

TIP: Each protocol that you install uses CPU, memory, and disk resources and slows startup, so it is important to only install the protocols that are truly needed.

Checking and Changing Protocols

Use the following instructions to check on and potentially change the protocols that have been installed and the settings that are being used.

1. In the Local Area Connection Properties dialog box, you should see at least one protocol installed, as shown previously in Figure 7-4. In most cases, TCP/IP should already be installed, and possibly NWLink IPX/SPX if that need was identified during setup.

2. Click Install and then double-click Protocol. The Select Network Protocol dialog box opens, shown next. This lists the protocols that are not currently installed; since TCP/IP is currently installed, all the others are listed here. If you want to install another protocol, do so now by double-clicking that protocol. Otherwise, click OK to close the Select Network Protocol dialog box.

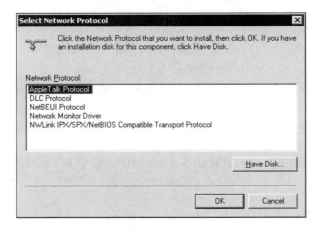

3. Select the TCP/IP protocol in the Local Area Connection Properties dialog box and click Properties. The Internet Protocol (TCP/IP) Properties dialog box opens, shown in Figure 7-5, in which you can choose to use either a dynamic

IP address automatically assigned by a server running the Dynamic Host Configuration Protocol (DHCP), or a static IP address that you enter in this dialog box.

A server that is a DHCP and/or a Domain Name Service (DNS) server must have a static IP address; otherwise, all computers in a network can be automatically assigned an IP address from a DHCP server. If the DHCP server is down or nonexistent, Automatic Private IP Addressing (APIPA) assigns an IP address from the block of 65,000 numbers 169.254.0.0 through 169.254.255.255. It also generates a subnet mask of 255.255.0.0. APIPA is limited insofar as a computer using APIPA can talk only to other computers in the same subnet with an address in the same range of numbers. If all computers in a small network are using either Windows 98 (which also uses APIPA) or Windows 2000 and have Obtain an IP Address Automatically selected, without a DHCP server, they will automatically use the 169.254.0.0 through 169.254.255.255 range of IP numbers.

4. If you are working on a server that will be the DHCP server, the DNS server, or both, or if you know you must assign a static IP address to this computer, then do so by clicking Use the Following IP Address and entering an IP address. The IP address that you use should be from the block of IP addresses that your organization has been assigned by its Internet service provider (ISP) or other

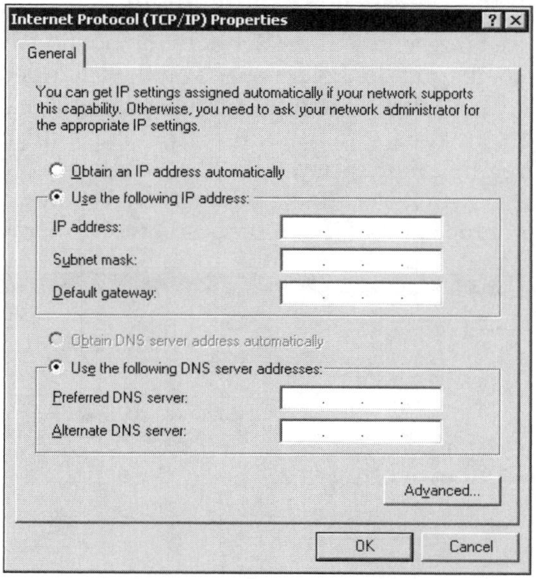

Figure 7-5.   Choosing the method of setting the IP address

authority (see the discussion under "Getting Blocks of IP Addresses," later in this chapter). If your organization is small and doesn't plan to access an outside network, then the static IP address can be from the block of APIPA numbers (but manually entered; refer to the limitations in step 3) or from several other blocks of private IP addresses (see "Getting Blocks of IP Addresses").

5. If you entered a static IP address, you must also enter a subnet mask. This mask tells the IP which part of an IP address to consider a network address and which part to consider a computer or *host* address. If your organization was assigned a block of IP numbers, it was also given a subnet mask. If you used the APIPA range of addresses, then use 255.255.0.0 as the subnet mask.

6. If you don't have a specific reason to use a static IP address, don't click Obtain an IP Address Automatically, and use the addresses from either the DHCP server or APIPA.

7. Click OK to close the Internet Protocol (TCP/IP) Properties dialog box, click OK to close the Local Area Connection Properties dialog box, and click Close to close the Local Area Connection Status dialog box.

8. Open the Start menu, choose Shut Down, select Restart from the drop-down list that appears, and click OK.

9. When the computer restarts, the Network and Dial-Up Connections windows should still be open. Double-click Local Area Connection to open the Local Area Connection Status dialog box. You should now see activity on both the Sent and Received sides, as shown in Figure 7-6.

10. If you do not see both send and receive activity, open My Computer and click Folders in the toolbar. In the Folders pane on the left, open My Network Places, click Entire Network, click Search for Computers, enter a computer name in your same subnet that uses an IP address from the APIPA range (if the current computer is from that range), and then click Search Now. You should see the computer appear with its location on the right, as shown next. If it does appear, then the computer is networking. If it doesn't work, then you have a problem.

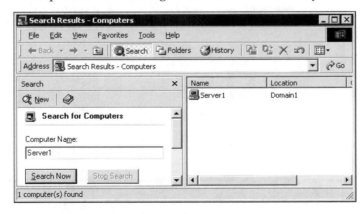

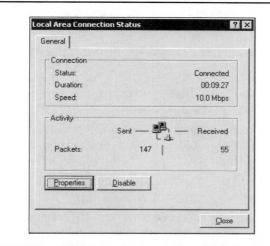

Figure 7-6.   The result of setting up both the networking functions and the networking protocol should be both send and receive activity

11. If you think you have a problem, double-check all the possible settings previously described. If you are using APIPA, make sure that the computer you are trying to contact is also using that range of numbers either as a static assigned address or with automatic assignment. If all the settings are correct, then check the cabling by making a simple connection of just several computers (if you do a direct UTP connection between two computers, remember that you need a special *crossover* cable with the transmit and receive wires reversed) and, finally, replace the NIC. With a good NIC, good cabling, and the correct settings, you'll be able to network.

Testing a Network Setup and Connection

There are several command-line utilities that can be used to test a TCP/IP installation. The more useful of these commands are the following:

▼ **Ipconfig**   Used to determine if a network configuration has been initialized and an IP address assigned. If an IP address and valid subnet mask are returned, then the configuration is initialized and there are no duplicates for the IP address. If a subnet mask of 0.0.0.0 is returned, then the IP address is a duplicate.

■ **Hostname**   Used to determine the computer name of the local computer.

▲ **Ping**   Used to query either the local computer or another computer on the network to see whether they respond. If the local computer responds, you know that TCP/IP is bound to the local NIC and that both are operating correctly. If the other computer responds, you know that TCP/IP and the

NICs in both computers are operating correctly and that the connection between the computers is operable.

Use the following steps to test a network setup with these utilities. Figure 7-7 shows the results on my system.

1. Open the Start menu and choose Programs | Accessories | Command Prompt. The Command Prompt window opens.

2. Type **ipconfig** and press ENTER. The IP address and subnet mask of the current computer should be returned. If this did not happen, there is a problem with the current configuration.

3. Type **hostname** and press ENTER. The computer name of the local computer should be returned.

4. Type **ping** *computer name* and press ENTER, where *computer name* is the name of another computer on your network. You should get four replies from the other computer.

5. If Ping did not work with a remote computer, try it on the current computer by typing **ping 127.0.0.1** and pressing ENTER. Again, you should get four replies, this time from the current computer. If you didn't get a reply here, then you have a problem with either the network setup or the NIC. If you did get a reply here, but not in step 4, then there is a problem either in the other computer or in the line connecting them.

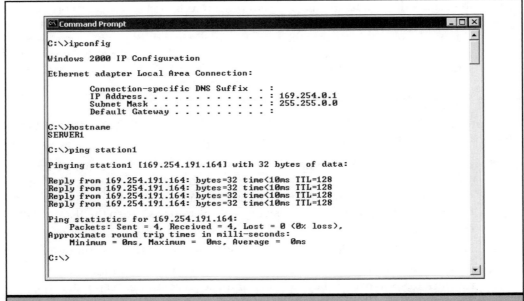

Figure 7-7. Testing a network with TCP/IP utilities

NOTE: The 127.0.0.1 IP address is a special address set aside to refer to the computer on which it is entered.

If you do find a problem here, use the steps in "Checking and Changing Protocols" to isolate and fix the problem.

SETTING UP WINDOWS 2000 SERVER TO SUPPORT NETWORKING

To set up Windows 2000 Server to support the rest of the network, the following services and facilities must be installed and configured:

▼ Dynamic Host Configuration Protocol (DHCP)

■ Windows Internet Name Service (WINS)

■ Domain Name System (DNS)

■ User accounts and group permissions

▲ Domains and Active Directory

In the process of determining the best settings for all of these elements, we'll also explore the elements themselves in greater depth. Domains and Active Directory are the subject of a separate chapter, Chapter 9, but the remaining elements are discussed here.

Network Addressing

For networking to function, one computer must know how to address another. To do this, every computer has at least two, and probably three, addresses:

▼ **Physical address**   Address that the manufacturer builds onto each network device or NIC (also called the *machine address*). In Ethernet cards, this is the Media Access Control (MAC) address.

■ **Logical address**   Address assigned to a computer by a network administrator or a server and ultimately by an addressing authority. In TCP/IP, the IP address is the logical address and the Internet Assigned Numbers Authority (IANA) is the addressing authority that assigns a block of addresses, distributed as needed by a server or, less frequently, by an administrator.

▲ **Computer name**   Address used in most applications and in My Network Places. In earlier Microsoft Windows networking, this is the *NetBIOS name*. In TCP/IP, this can be a two-part name. The first and required part is for the current computer and is the *host name*; an example is server1. The second part is the *domain name* for the domain that contains the computer; for example, domain1.com, making the complete name server1.domain1.com.

These three addresses operate at different layers of the OSI networking model (see the Chapter 6 section "The OSI Model"), as shown in Figure 7-8. The physical address operates at the Physical layer, the logical address operates at the Network layer, and the computer name is used above the Network layer.

For all three of these addresses to work together, there must be a method of converting one to another. Given a computer name, it must be *resolved* to a logical address, and the logical address must be resolved to a physical address. The task of resolving a computer name into a logical address is the job of DNS or WINS, and resolving a logical address into a physical one is done by the networking protocol (for example, in TCP/IP, this is the Address Resolution Protocol, or ARP). In addition, with an ever-shorter supply of IP addresses, these addresses generally are distributed as needed by a server using DHCP. Choosing and setting up a networking protocol, as well as setting up DNS and DHCP, are major topics in this chapter, so the many tasks surrounding addressing are a connecting thread throughout the chapter.

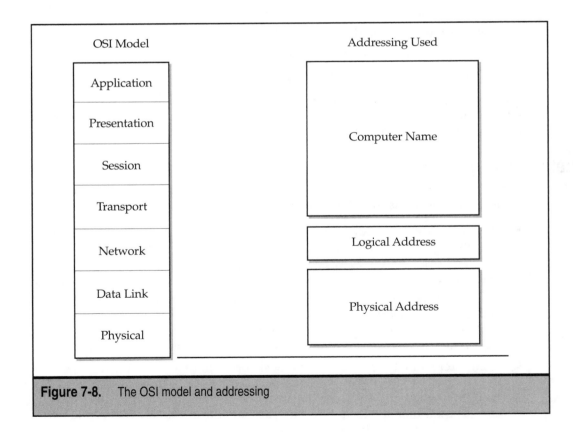

Figure 7-8. The OSI model and addressing

Setting Up the Dynamic Host Configuration Protocol

DHCP, which runs on one or more servers, has the job of assigning and managing IP addresses in a network. A *scope,* or range, of IP addresses is given to DHCP, which in turn *leases* (or assigns for a certain period) an IP address to a client. DHCP removes the possibility of errors inherent in manually assigning and entering IP addresses and also removes the management task of keeping track of who has what IP address. In an environment with very many mobile users, the management task becomes all but impossible, and even in a fairly stable environment, this task is not easy.

For DHCP to perform its function, three steps must be taken:

▼ DHCP must be enabled on the server

■ DHCP must have a scope of IP addresses and a lease term

▲ Clients must have Obtain an IP Address Automatically selected in the Internet Protocol (TCP/IP) Properties dialog box, as discussed earlier in "Choosing and Configuring a Networking Protocol"

How DHCP Works

The first time a client is restarted after Obtain an IP Address Automatically has been selected, it goes through the following process to get an IP address:

1. The client broadcasts on the network a request for a DHCP server and an IP address. It uses 0.0.0.0 as the source address, 255.255.255.255 as the destination address, and includes its physical (MAC) address.

2. All DHCP servers that receive the request broadcast a message that includes the MAC address, an offered IP address, a subnet mask, a length of lease, and the server's IP address.

3. The client accepts the first offer that reaches it, and broadcasts that acceptance, including its new IP address and the IP of the server that offered it.

4. This acceptance is acknowledged by the offering server.

Each time the client is started after receiving an IP address, it attempts to use the same IP address from the same server. The server can accept this or not, but during the lease term, it normally is accepted. Halfway through the lease term, the client will automatically ask for the lease to be extended, and under most circumstances, it is extended. If the lease isn't extended, the client will continue to use the IP address and broadcast a request for any other server to renew the current IP address. If this is refused, the client will broadcast a request for any IP address, as it did at the start.

Installing DHCP

If you followed the instructions in Chapter 4, DHCP should be installed and properly configured. If you know this to be the case and are comfortable adding and tailoring scopes, then you can skip the rest of this section. Since DHCP is an optional networking component, we'll look at how to install it, and then look at how to add and tailor scopes.

If DHCP is not installed or you are not sure whether it is, use the following instructions to check and, if necessary, install it:

NOTE: The following instructions also make sure that DNS and WINS are installed.

1. To install DHCP, you need to insert the Windows 2000 Server CD in its drive and click Exit to close the Autorun window that opens.

2. Open the Start menu, choose Settings | Control Panel, and double-click Add/Remove Programs. The Add/Remove Programs dialog box opens.

3. Click Add/Remove Windows Components and then click Components in the upper-right corner of the dialog box. The Windows Components Wizard opens.

4. Select Networking Services (click the item, not the checkbox, which is probably grayed) and click Details. The Networking Services dialog box appears, in which you should see Dynamic Host Configuration Protocol (DHCP) on the list, as shown in Figure 7-9.

5. If the DHCP checkbox is not checked, check it. Check the boxes for both Domain Name System (DNS) and Windows Internet Name Service (WINS) (if either or both are not checked) and then click OK.

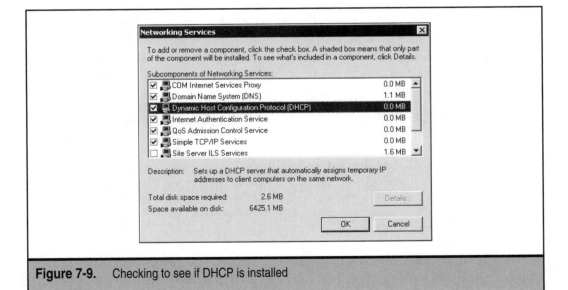

Figure 7-9. Checking to see if DHCP is installed

6. Back in the Windows Component Wizard, click Next and then, when it is displayed, click Finish to complete the installation. Click Close to remove the Add/Remove Programs dialog box, and, finally, click the Close button on the Control Panel to remove it.

Configuring DHCP

Configuring DHCP is the process of defining IP address scopes, which include the following elements:

▼ Scope name

■ Starting IP address in the scope range

■ Ending IP address in the scope range

■ Subnet mask to be used with this range of IP addresses

■ Starting and ending addresses of the ranges to exclude from the scope

■ DHCP client lease duration

▲ Server, scope, and client options

Getting Blocks of IP Addresses   Which block of IP addresses is used in a scope depends on whether the computers to be assigned the addresses will be public or private. If the computers will be interfacing directly with the Internet, they are *public* and thus need a globally unique IP number. If the computers will be operating only on an internal network, they are *private* and need only organizational uniqueness. IANA has set aside three blocks of IP addresses that can be used by any organization for its private, internal needs without any coordination with any other organization, but these blocks should not be used for connecting to the Internet. These private-use blocks of IP addresses are as follows:

▼ 10.0.0.0 through 10.255.255.255

■ 172.16.0.0 through 172.31.255.255

▲ 192.168.0.0 through 192.168.255.255

In addition is the APIPA range from 169.254.0.0 through 169.254.255.255, discussed earlier in this chapter. Remember, though, that APIPA works only with computers within its own subnet and with IP addresses from the same range. In a small network, though, you can mix DHCP and APIPA addressing and always be assured that an IP number will be available independent of DHCP.

If you want a block of public IP addresses, you must request it from one of several organizations, depending on the size of the block that you want. At the local level for a moderate-sized block of IP addresses, your local ISP can assign it to you. For a larger block, a regional ISP may be able to handle the request. If not, you have to go to one of three regional Internet registries:

▼ American Registry for Internet Numbers (ARIN), at http://www.arin.net/, which covers North and South America, the Caribbean, and sub-Saharan Africa

■ Réseaux IP Européens (RIPE), at http://www.ripe.net/, which covers Europe, Middle East, and northern Africa

▲ Asia Pacific Network Information Center (APNIC), at http://www.apnic.net/, which covers Asia and the Pacific

The coordination of these three organizations is performed by IANA, at http://www.iana.com/. In December 1997, IP addressing authority for the Americas was transferred from Network Solutions, Inc. (InterNIC) to ARIN. ARIN, RIPE, APNIC, and IANA are all nonprofit organizations representing a broad membership of ISPs, communications companies, manufacturers, other organizations, and individuals. The smallest block that ARIN will allocate (to ISPs for reassignment) or assign (to organizations and individuals) is 4,096 addresses, for which they currently charge $2,500 per year. Larger blocks can cost up to $20,000 per year. ISPs will allocate smaller blocks using their own fees. The ARIN minimum block size and fee apply to the current Internet Protocol version 4 (IPv4), which has been referred to as "IP addressing" so far in the book. IPv6 is just beginning to be assigned, is a much larger number, and has its own rules for allocation and assignment, but it has a similar current fee structure that ranges from $2,500 to $20,000 per year.

Enabling and Defining a DHCP Scope   With an IP address range to use, you are ready to enable and define a DHCP scope, using the following instructions:

1. Open the Start menu and choose Programs | Administrative Tools | DHCP. The DHCP window appears, as shown in Figure 7-10.

2. Open the Action menu and choose New Scope. The New Scope Wizard opens.

3. Click Next. Enter a name and description for the scope, and click Next again.

4. Enter the starting and ending IP addresses for the range to be included in the scope.

5. Enter either a length of a subnet mask or the subnet mask itself. The purpose of a subnet mask is to divide an address into a network address and a host address. When you are working on a local network, only the host portion is searched, so it will speed up the process if only a portion of the address is searched. An IP address is 32 bits long, so if you say that half of it (16 bits) is a network address, you will help the local network. The 16-bit subnet mask is 255.255.0.0, as shown in Figure 7-11.

6. Click Next. Enter the IP addresses to exclude from the scope you are working on. These can be either a range, by entering a starting and ending address, or a single address, by entering it in just the Start IP Address position, as shown

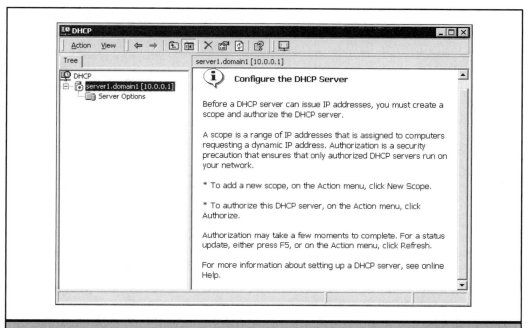

Figure 7-10. Setting up DHCP in the DHCP window

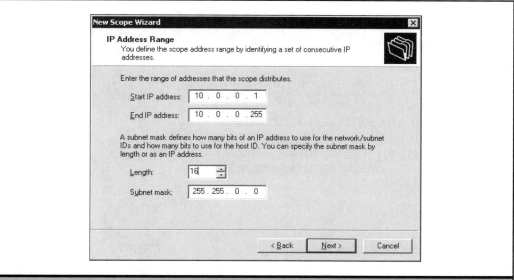

Figure 7-11. Entering a scope and its subnet mask

in Figure 7-12. You should enter an exclusion for each static address that has been assigned to a server, workstation, or router.

7. Click Add after entering each exclusion address or range. When you have entered all exclusions, click Next.

8. Enter the lease duration, which is the length of time that a client can use an IP address that has been assigned to it. The default is 8 days, but the correct time for your operation could be any where from 1 hour for clients mainly jumping on and off a mail server, to 4 days for clients who are mainly traveling mobile computer users, to 90 days for clients in a stable desktop environment.

9. Click Next. Choose Yes to configure DHCP options, and click Next again. Enter the IP address of each router directly addressed by the network, clicking Add after each.

10. Click Next. If there is a parent domain that you want to use for DNS name resolution, enter that name. Otherwise, enter the server name in the current network that is or will be your DNS server. If you have entered a server name, click Resolve to generate its IP address and then click Add.

11. Click Next. Enter the server name for the WINS NetBIOS name resolution, click Resolve, and click Add.

12. Click Next. Select Yes, you want to activate the scope now, click Next, and then click Finish. Your new scope should appear on the left of the DHCP window.

13. Open the Action menu and choose Authorize. After a few moments, the window will be redrawn.

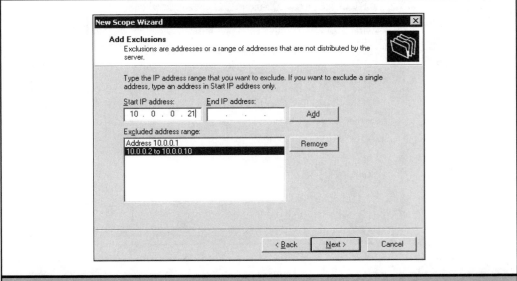

Figure 7-12.   Entering the exclusions for a scope

14. After the DHCP window is redrawn, click Address Pool, and you should see the details of the scope you defined. Click Address Leases, and you see a list of the clients that are leasing IP addresses from this server.

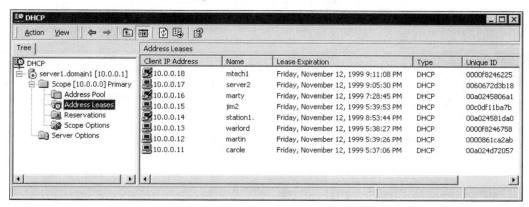

Creating DHCP Reservations Suppose that you want a client to have a particular and permanent IP address. You can configure that by creating a *client reservation* that specifies an IP address to be assigned to the client. In this way, the IP address will not expire until the reservation is removed. To do that, follow these steps:

1. In the scope tree in the DHCP window, select Reservations and click Add Reservations in the toolbar. The New Reservation dialog box opens.

2. Enter a name, IP address, and associated MAC physical address (you can get the MAC address from the Unique ID column shown on the list of Address Leases). Do not include the hyphens that are often used to display a MAC address (although they are not shown in the Unique ID column of the list of Address Leases). Enter a Description, if you want one, and leave the Supported Types as the default, Both. Click Add and repeat the process for

each reservation you want to make. Close the New Reservation dialog box when you're through.

3. Click Refresh in the toolbar. If Reservations is selected in the left pane of the DHCP window, your new reservation will appear on the right. Also, if you select Address Leases, you'll see the reservation in the list of leases.

NOTE: Another way to get the physical or MAC address needed in step 2 is to open the Command Prompt window and type **ping *ipaddress***, where *ipaddress* is the numeric IP address of the computer for which you need the MAC address, and then press ENTER. Then, at the command prompt, type **arp –a** and press ENTER. The physical address will be displayed, as shown here:

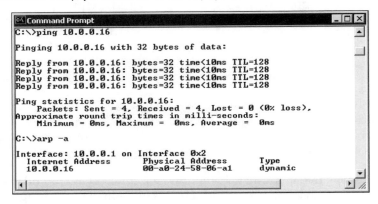

Setting DHCP Options   When you went through the steps for the New Scope Wizard a few pages back, there was a group of settings related to the scope's options (steps 9, 10, and 11). You can add to and change those scope options in the DHCP window, but that is only one of three levels of options that you can set. The three option levels are as follows:

▼ **Server level options**   Apply to all DHCP clients

■ **Scope level options**   Apply only to clients who lease an address from the scope

▲ **Client level options**   Apply to a client with a reservation

Try setting and/or changing the options with the following steps:

1. In the DHCP window, right-click Server Options and choose Configure Options. The Server Options dialog box opens. Here, you can make a number of settings that apply to all DHCP clients. For example, you can keep a list of DNS servers, as shown in Figure 7-13.

2. Click OK to close the Server Options dialog box, right-click Scope Options, and choose Configure Options. You'll see a similar dialog box, called Scope Options, with a similar list of available options.

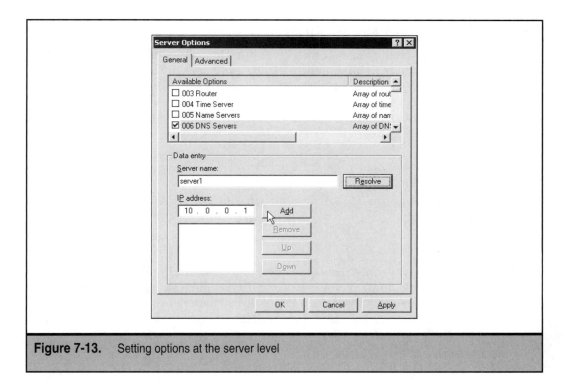

Figure 7-13. Setting options at the server level

3. Click OK to close the Scope Options dialog box. If you previously created a reservation, open the Reservation object in the scope tree, right-click your reservation in either the left or the right pane of the window, and choose Configure Options, to get a third similar list of options.

4. Click OK to close the Reservation Options dialog box. Your DHCP window now looks much different than it did initially.

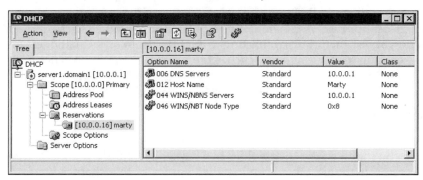

5. Close the DHCP window.

Setting Up the Domain Name System

DNS has the job of resolving or converting an easy-to-remember user-friendly name into an IP address. It does this by maintaining a database of name-IP address pairs. DNS is an application in the TCP/IP protocol suite and was developed to handle the name resolution needed on the Internet. As a result, it uses a hierarchical *domain name space* that you use on the Internet. For example, the name server1.editorial.osborne.com has the following structure:

Root domain	.
Top-level domain	com
Second-level domain	osborne
Third-level domain	editorial
Host name	server1

A host name is always the leftmost portion of a name and refers to a specific computer. Within a specific domain, you need only to use the host name. It is only as you move outside of a domain that you need to use the domain names.

TIP: When creating a domain name space, keep it simple. Use short, simple, unique names and keep the number of levels to a minimum.

To make a domain name space easier to manage, it can be broken into *zones,* or discrete segments. A separate name database is kept for each zone, giving a network administrator a more manageable task. A DNS server, or a *name server,* can contain one or more zones, and multiple servers may contain the database for the same zone. In the latter case, one server is designated as the *primary server,* and the other name servers within that zone periodically query the primary server for a *zone transfer* to update the database. As a result, all zone maintenance must be performed on the primary server.

DNS can resolve a name to an IP address, called a *forward lookup,* as well as resolve an IP address into a name, called a *reverse lookup.* In the process of name resolution, if a local name server cannot resolve a name, it passes it on to the other name servers the local server knows about, including connecting to the Internet to query name servers there. As a name server queries for a name, it caches the results, so that it does not have to do the query again in the near future. This caching is done for a finite period of time, called the *time to live* (TTL), which you can set, and has a default of 60 minutes.

Setting Up DNS

Setting up DNS assumes that DNS has been installed on the server from which you want it to run. If you followed the instructions in Chapter 4, DNS should have been installed, and if it wasn't, it should have been installed earlier in this chapter, under "Installing DHCP." Use the following instructions to set up DNS:

1. Open the Start menu and choose Programs | Administrative Tools | DNS. The DNS window opens.

2. Open Forward Lookup Zones and then open one of the zones within it, so you see the host names that are contained there, as shown in Figure 7-14.

3. Add a host name to the open zone by right-clicking the zone and choosing New Host. The New Host dialog box opens.

4. Enter the host name and IP address and then click Add Host. Repeat this for as many hosts as you want to enter. When you are finished adding hosts, click Done.

5. Add a zone to the current name server by opening the Action menu and choosing New Zone. The New Zone Wizard opens. Click Next. Leave the default of Standard Primary to store the zone in a text file. Chapter 9 will explore storing the zone in Active Directory.

6. Click Next. Again, accept the default of Forward Lookup Zone and click Next. Enter a name for the zone.

7. Click Next. Accept the default filename, click Next, and then click Finish.

8. Add new host names to this zone, as you did in step 3. When you are finished adding hosts, click Done to close the New Host dialog box.

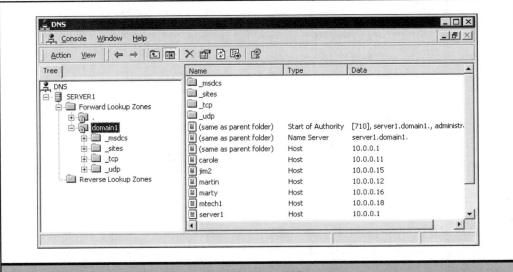

Figure 7-14.   DNS window showing the host names within a zone

Setting Up Reverse Lookup Zones

Reverse lookup zones, which allow the resolution of an IP number into a name, are only used in problem solving and by Internet Information Services (IIS) to add a name instead of an IP address in log files. To implement a reverse lookup capability, a special domain named In-addr.arpa is automatically created when DNS is set up. Within this domain, subdomains are defined for each *octet* or portion of an IP address between periods for the network portion of the address, and then *pointer* records are created for the final host portion of the address giving the host name and IP address. See how a reverse lookup zone is set up with these steps:

1. Right-click Reverse Lookup Zones and choose New Zone. The New Zone Wizard appears. Click Next.

2. Accept the default of Standard Primary zone type and click Next.

3. In the Network ID, enter the network portion of your IP address. For example, if your IP address range is 10.0.0.1 through 10.0.0.255 with a subnet mask of 255.255.255, then your network ID is 10.0.0.

4. Click Next. Accept the default of creating a file with the name that begins with the reverse of your network ID (with 10.0.0. as your network ID, the filename is 0.0.10.in-addr.arpa.dns), click Next, and then click Finish.

5. Right-click the new zone that was just created and choose New Pointer. The New Resource Record dialog box opens with the Pointer (PTR) tab active.

6. Enter the host portion of an IP number and the host name that corresponds with this.

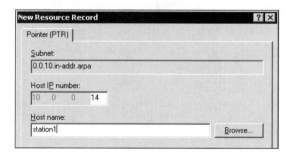

7. Click OK. Repeat steps 5 and 6 as necessary to add additional pointers.

NOTE: You can automatically create pointer records every time you create a new host record by clicking Create Associated Pointer (PTR) Record in the New Host dialog box.

Setting Up Dynamic DNS

The process of adding hosts to a zone, while not terrible, is not something you want to do every time DHCP changes an address assignment. The purpose of dynamic DNS (DDNS) is to automatically update a zone host record every time DHCP makes a change. DDNS ties DHCP and DNS together so that when DHCP makes a change, it sends the information to the appropriate zone in DNS, which then reflects the change. Both DNS and DHCP must be correctly set for this to work. Use the following steps to do that:

1. In the DNS window, right-click the zone to which you want to add DDNS, and choose Properties.

2. In the General tab, opposite Allow Dynamic Updates, open the drop-down list and click Yes. (If the DNS server has been integrated with Active Directory, see Chapter 9, which explains how you can choose to allow only secure updates.)

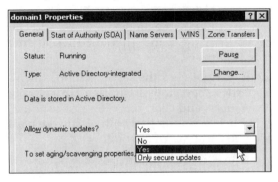

3. Click OK to close the zone's Properties dialog box.

4. Open the Start menu and choose Programs | Administrative Tools | DHCP.

5. Right-click the scope that you want to tie to the DNS zone you have been working on, and choose Properties.

6. In the DNS tab, make sure Automatically Update DHCP Client Information in DHS is checked and then click Always Update DNS.

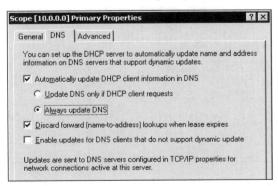

7. Click OK to close the Scope Primary Properties dialog box. Close the DHCP window.

Testing DNS

You can test to see whether DNS is working by doing the following:

▼ Trying to use it

■ Using a test facility in DNS

▲ Using Nslookup in the Command Prompt window, if you created a reverse lookup zone

Quickly try all three of these with the following steps:

1. Open My Computer, click Search in the toolbar, click Computers in the Search Options, enter a computer name on the network, and click Search Now. If DNS and DHCP are working, the search should be successful and the computer found. Close My Computer.

2. In the DNS window, right-click the server within which you created a scope, and choose Properties. Open the Monitoring tab, select both A Simple Query and A Recursive Query, and click Test Now. You should get test results at the bottom of the dialog box stating that both tests were passed. Close the server's Properties dialog box and the DNS window.

3. Open the Start menu, choose Programs | Accessories | Command Prompt, type **nslookup**, and press ENTER. If you created a reverse lookup zone that included the server, you get the name of the server and its IP address. Type a host name, press ENTER, and you get the full host name with its domain and its IP address. Type an IP address, and you get the full host name with its domain. After typing these three items, your Command Prompt window should look like this:

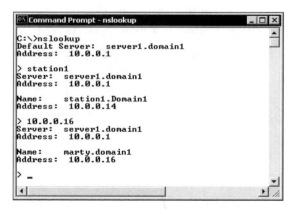

4. Type **Exit** to get out of Nslookup, and type **Exit** again to close the Command Prompt window.

NOTE: Nslookup requires that you have a reverse lookup zone, which is one of the reasons for creating one.

Setting Up Windows Internet Name Service

WINS has the same job as DNS: resolving or converting an easy-to-remember user-friendly name into an IP address. WINS utilizes the NetBIOS naming convention developed by IBM and Microsoft as part of an early networking scheme. NetBIOS, which operates at the Session (fifth) layer of the OSI networking model, normally interacts with NetBEUI at the Transport and Network layers of the OSI model (see Figure 7-15) and does so by converting a user-friendly name directly to a physical (MAC) address. WINS, which like DNS is an application, maintains a database of NetBIOS names and their IP address equivalents. NetBIOS names using NetBIOS over TCP/IP, which calls on WINS, can then be used with TCP/IP in place of NetBEUI.

WINS requires very little maintenance, initially building itself, and maintaining itself as changes occur. You only need to turn it on and specify the server IP address in the cli-

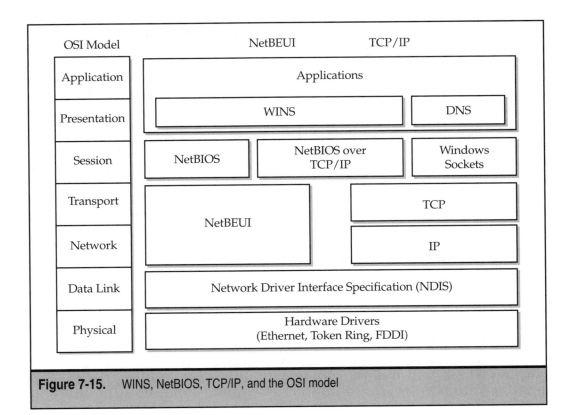

Figure 7-15. WINS, NetBIOS, TCP/IP, and the OSI model

ents. WINS, while still available in Windows 2000, has had its function largely usurped by DDNS, because DDNS is integrated into Active Directory (see Chapter 9), and because DNS offers security features that are not available in WINS. If your network has only Windows 2000 servers and clients, you do not need WINS, because NetBIOS names are not used. If you have computers with earlier Windows operating systems (Windows 95, 98, or NT 4) in your network, then WINS may be beneficial.

WINS can safely and advantageously coexist with DNS, *if* you don't have security concerns about the WINS database being automatically created and updated, and if the integration with Active Directory is not important to you. In a shared environment, WINS handles the 16-character-maximum (the user can enter 15) single-part NetBIOS name used in all Microsoft operating systems up through Windows 98 and NT 4, while DNS handles the multipart, 255-character-maximum domain name used in Windows 2000.

NOTE: In smaller networks (having a practical maximum in the range of 35 to 50 computers, and an absolute maximum of about 70), you do not need to use either WINS or DNS. Each computer in the network periodically broadcasts to the other computers in the network for their NetBIOS names and their IP addresses and then stores this information in a working file on the computer making the initial request. This generates a lot of network traffic, and as the network grows, that traffic can be overpowering. You can reduce this traffic by manually creating and maintaining a static text file named Lmhosts (LM for *Lan Manager*, the original Microsoft networking system) that is checked before broadcasting on the network (search for Lmhosts, open it with Notepad, and follow the instructions at the beginning of the file to create it). Maintaining this file on a number of computers becomes a major chore and is the reason that WINS was developed. A similar static file, Hosts, can be used with DNS, but both of these text files are practical for only the smallest networks.

WINS, like DNS, resides on a server. To use it, a client queries the server with a NetBIOS name, and the server replies with an IP number for that name. When you set up a WINS server and start a client by giving it the server's address, the client automatically registers its name and IP address with the server. The server responds with the TTL, the amount of time it will maintain the registration. From then on, each time the client starts it will repeat this process, or if it is on for half of its TTL, it will automatically re-register its name.

Setting Up WINS on a Server

Set up WINS on the server with these steps:

1. Open the Start menu, choose Settings | Network and Dial-Up Connections, right-click Local Area Connection, and choose Properties. The Local Area Connection Properties dialog box opens.

2. Select Internet Protocol (TCP/IP) and click Properties. The Internet Protocol (TCP/IP) Properties dialog box opens.

3. Click Advanced, select the WINS tab, and click Add. Enter the IP address of the WINS primary server and click Add. If you have a secondary (or more) WINS server, enter it in the same way.

4. When you are done entering WINS servers, click OK three times to close all the open dialog boxes.

5. Open the Start menu and choose Programs | Administrative Tools | WINS. The WINS window should open with your WINS server listed.

6. Open the server, right-click Active Registrations, choose Find by Owner, and then click Find Now. A list of NetBIOS names and IP addresses should be displayed, as shown in Figure 7-16.

7. If you have non-WINS clients, you can add static registrations for them by right-clicking Active Registrations and choosing New Static Mapping. The New Static Mapping dialog box opens.

8. Enter the computer name and the NetBIOS scope, if desired (the scope is an extension to the name used to group computers). Then, choose a type (see Table 7-1) and enter one or more IP addresses, as needed. When done, click OK to close the dialog box, and then close the WINS window.

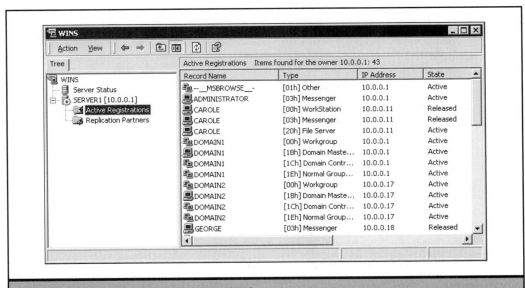

Figure 7-16. Active registrations within WINS

Type	Explanation
Unique	A single computer with a single IP address
Group	A group name with only one IP address for the group
Domain Name	A domain name with up to 25 IP addresses for its members
Internet Group	A group name with up to 25 IP addresses for its members
Multihomed	A computer with up to 25 IP addresses for multiple NICs

Table 7-1.   Types of Static WINS Registrations

Setting Up WINS on Clients

Setting up a WINS client often is done on computers running something other than Windows 2000. The steps for doing that in Windows 2000 are very similar to the first several steps previously given for setting up the server. They are repeated here, with notes on how to do it in Windows 98:

1. Open the Start menu, choose Settings | Network and Dial-Up Connections, right-click Local Area Connection, and choose Properties. The Local Area Connection Properties dialog box opens. (In Windows 98, use Start | Settings | Control Panel | Network to open the Network Control Panel.)

2. Select Internet Protocol (TCP/IP) and click Properties. The Internet Protocol (TCP/IP) Properties dialog box opens. (In Windows 98, double-click TCP/IP for the NIC to open the TCP/IP Properties dialog box.)

3. Click Advanced, select the WINS tab, and click Add. Enter the IP address of the WINS primary server and click Add. If you have a secondary (or more) WINS server, enter it in the same way. (In Windows 98, click the WINS Configuration tab and click Enable WINS Resolution. Enter the WINS server IP address and click Add.)

4. When you are done entering WINS servers, click OK three times to close all the open dialog boxes. (In Windows 98, click OK twice.)

5. Repeat steps 1 through 4 for each client on the network.

Setting Up User Accounts and Group Permissions

To gain access to another computer or to other resources (such as a printer) on the network, a user must have been given permission to do so. Such permission begins with the user being a known entity, by having a user account. You can have *local user* accounts, which provide access to one computer, and *domain user* accounts, which provide access to all the resources in the domain. Domain user accounts, which can be very valuable and can provide the way to structure a network in many cases, are discussed in Chapters 9 and 15.

Instead of assigning permissions to individuals, you assign individuals to groups that have certain permissions. This section looks at setting up local user accounts, setting up groups, and assigning users to groups.

User accounts, groups, and permissions are an important part of network security, and the security aspects of these elements, such as password strategies, are discussed in Chapter 15. This section focuses on setting up the elements, not on how they should be used for security purposes.

NOTE: If you are using or are going to use a domain, it is important to set up domain user accounts rather than local user accounts on computers within the domain. Local user accounts are not recognized by the domain, so a local user cannot use domain resources and a domain administrator cannot administer the local accounts.

Planning for Usernames and Passwords

Before setting up either domain or local user accounts, your organization should have a plan for the usernames and passwords that the company will use. The objectives are to be consistent and to use prudent practices. Here are some considerations:

▼ Are you going to use first name and last initial, first initial and last name, or full first and last names?

■ How, if at all, are you going to separate the first and last name? Many organizations don't use any separation, whereas others use either periods or the underscore.

■ How are you going to handle two people with the same first and last name? Adding a number after the name is a common answer.

■ Do you need a special class of names for, for example, subcontractors in your organization? If so, how, if at all, do you want to differentiate them from other users? One method is to precede their names with one or more characters to indicate their position, such as "SC" for subcontractor.

■ Names must be unique, cannot be over 20 characters, and are not case-sensitive.

▲ Passwords must be unique, cannot be over 128 characters, can use both upper- and lowercase letters, should use a mixture of letters, numbers, and symbols, and should be at least 8 characters long.

NOTE: If your password is over 14 characters, you will not be able to log on to the network from a Windows 95/98 computer.

Setting Up Local User Accounts

Windows 2000, both Server and Professional, creates several user accounts when installed, among which are two that initially are named Administrator and Guest. You can change the name and password of these accounts, but you cannot delete them. When you go through the installation of Windows 2000, as described in Chapters 3 and 4, you establish the initial password for the Administrator account, but all other account creation and maintenance is done outside Setup.

NOTE: If your server is a domain controller, you'll only be able to set up domain user accounts. Local user accounts can be created only on servers that are not DCs or on clients.

Follow these steps to see how local user accounts are set up:

1. Open the Start menu and choose Programs I Administrative Tools I Computer Management. The Computer Management window opens.

2. Open System Tools and then open Local Users and Groups. Right-click Users and choose New User. The New User dialog box opens.

3. Enter a User Name, Full Name, Description, and Password, as shown in Figure 7-17. Select how you want to handle passwords, and click Create.

4. Repeat step 3 for as many local users as you have.

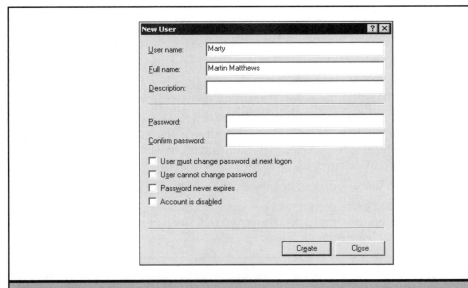

Figure 7-17. Entering a new user

Setting Up Groups and Their Members

Groups allow you to define what a particular type of user is allowed to do on the computer. Once you have done that, the users you have defined can be made members of these groups and they will then have the same permissions as the groups to which they belong. Windows 2000 comes with a number of groups already defined, so the first step is to understand what those are. Then, you can add one or more of your own groups.

1. In the Computer Management window, open Groups in the System Tools | Local Users and Groups tree. The list of currently defined groups appears.

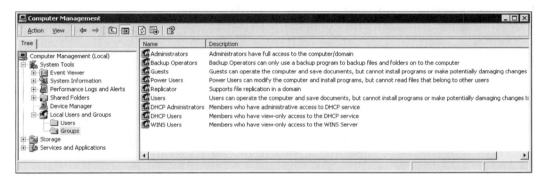

The standard set of groups provides a good spectrum of permissions, as you can see by reading the Description column in the preceding Computer Management window.

2. Create a new group by right-clicking Groups in the left pane and choosing New Group. The New Group dialog box opens.

3. Enter the group name and a description, which should list the permissions the group has.

4. Click Add, and the Select Users or Groups dialog box opens. Either select the users or groups you want in your new group from the upper list or type them in the lower text box, clicking Add after each selection or entry.

5. When you are done, click OK, click Create to create the new group, and click Close to close the New Group dialog box.

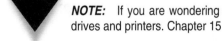

NOTE: If you are wondering how permissions get assigned, it is done with objects such as disk drives and printers. Chapter 15 discusses in detail how to set permissions.

Adding Users to Groups

Although you can add users to groups when you create the groups, you most often will add users to groups independently of creating groups, as follows (you should still have the Computer Management window open):

1. Click Users in the left pane, locate and right-click a user whose group memberships you want to change in the right pane, and choose Properties. The user's Properties dialog box opens.

2. Click the Member Of tab, and click Add. The Select Groups dialog box opens, as shown in Figure 7-18.

3. Select one or more groups in the list and click Add. When you have selected all the groups you want, click OK.

4. When you are done with the user account, click OK to close the Properties dialog box, and then click Close to close the Computer Management window.

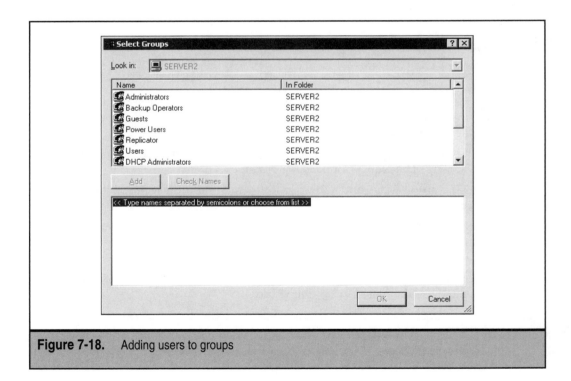

Figure 7-18. Adding users to groups

The user's Properties dialog box contains two tabs not previously mentioned: Profile and Dial-In. Profile allows you to define a profile for a user so that when that user logs in to a computer, the profile automatically sets up the desktop, menus, and other features for that user. Profiles are discussed in Chapter 14. Dial-In sets up how a user will work with remote access and virtual private networking, which is the subject of Chapter 10.

Remember that local user accounts are limited to a single computer and cannot be centrally managed. The broader and more easily managed way to implement user accounts is with domains, which are discussed in Chapter 9.

CHAPTER 8

Working with NetWare

For many years before Windows NT became the predominant network operating system (NOS) for local area networks, Novell NetWare was the market leader. While substantially different from Windows NT and Windows 2000 Server in its architecture and operation, NetWare provides many of the same basic functions and services. NetWare was originally designed to provide the basic file and print services that are the mainstay of a NOS, but now it includes a full-featured enterprise directory service as well as an application and Internet server platform.

Although NetWare's popularity has been eclipsed by Windows NT/2000 in recent years, it still has a large installed user base, and interoperability between the two operating systems is a major concern for both Microsoft and Novell. Windows 2000 includes NetWare client capabilities that can function simultaneously with its Windows network client, and Novell NetWare includes its own client packages for the Windows operating systems.

To explain how network administrators running both Windows 2000 and Novell NetWare handle that environment, this chapter:

▼   Compares the NetWare and Windows 2000 operating systems

■   Examines the NetWare client capabilities included with Windows 2000 and available from Novell

■   Describes the procedures for running NetWare and Windows 2000 on the same network

▲   Explores migration from NetWare to Windows 2000

COMPARING NETWARE WITH WINDOWS 2000

In Chapter 6, you learned about the differences between peer-to-peer and client/server operating systems. Windows 2000 can be said to fit both definitions, because while every 2000 system, Server or Professional, is capable of both sharing its own resources and accessing other system's shared resources, many networks run it using the client/server model. Novell NetWare, however, is strictly a client/server product, which consists of a dedicated server operating system and client software packages for various workstation operating systems. A NetWare server is an Intel-based PC that functions exclusively as a server running its own dedicated NOS. The system can share its file and print resources with clients and run applications that provide services to those clients, but it cannot function as a client itself, nor does the NetWare client software enable workstations to share their resources.

Novell NetWare has been on the market since the mid 1980s, and while its fundamental architecture remains largely unchanged, the functions it performs and the way it looks and behaves to the end user have changed significantly from NetWare 3.x to 4.x and from Novell 4.x to 5.x. NetWare 5.x includes additional services and support for additional protocols, but the product's original functionality is still intact. Throughout its history, NetWare has most commonly been used for its file and print services, tasks for which it excels. When Windows NT was introduced, its capabilities as an application server were a major reason for its rapid growth in popularity. Although Windows NT and 2000 provide file and print services that are equivalent to those of NetWare, and although NetWare can function as an application server, many networks continue to run both operating systems in their traditional roles.

The NetWare Server

The NetWare server operating system is proprietary and launches from a DOS prompt. Once loaded, however, NetWare takes over all aspects of the system, and you can remove the DOS code from memory. Windows 2000 systems use the same interface whether they're functioning as clients, servers, or both. NetWare servers, however, use a proprietary interface that is character-based and that provides access to server monitoring and configuration functions only. Most server commands run from a command prompt, but there are also character-based menuing utilities, such as that shown in Figure 8-1, that provide the same functions. NetWare 5 and higher also include a Java-based graphical interface for the server, but the use of this interface is optional. While it may seem anachronistic for NetWare to rely so heavily on character-based menus and the command prompt in this age of graphical displays, remember that the server's only function is to service clients and that system resources devoted to graphical displays and other cosmetic elements can detract from that functionality.

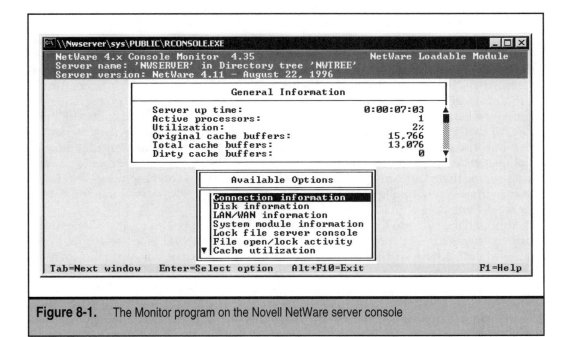

Figure 8-1.   The Monitor program on the Novell NetWare server console

NetWare Loadable Modules

NetWare servers run programs that take the form of executables called NetWare Loadable Modules (NLMs). NLMs are completely different from the EXE files used by Windows 2000, and require an independent development effort. The various applications and services that run on NetWare consist of one or more NLMs that you execute using the LOAD command at the server prompt and that may or may not add additional screens to the server console. As with Windows 2000, you can configure a NetWare server to load a series of applications whenever it starts, so that the services required by clients are always available. Compared to Windows NT/2000, relatively few NetWare applications are available. Many of the software developers that focused on NetWare at one time are now devoting most of their resources to NT/2000 versions of the products.

NetWare Protocols

One of the other anachronisms about NetWare is its long-standing reliance on a proprietary collection of networking protocols, usually referred to as the IPX protocol suite. The Internetworking Packet Exchange (IPX) protocols were developed by Novell specifically for use with NetWare, and unlike other manufacturers, it refused to allow the protocols to be published as open standards like those defining the Transmission Control Protocol/Internet Protocol (TCP/IP) protocols.

NOTE: IPX was developed at a time when TCP/IP was under development by the Department of Defense and not available for public use. For Novell to have a product to release, it had to develop its own protocol.

The IPX protocols are intended exclusively for use on *local* area networks (LANs), whereas TCP/IP was aimed at wide area networks (WANs), such as the Internet. Unlike IP, IPX protocols do not include their own address space, relying instead on the hardware address (called a media access control, or MAC, address) coded into the network interface card (NIC) in each computer. Because NetWare operates only in client/server mode, there is also no need for each computer on the network to have a name, as is the case with Windows systems. Only NetWare servers need names, because NetWare clients communicate only with servers, and not with each other. The net result of these differences is that IPX is a simpler networking protocol than IP and therefore IPX is easier to administer if you are dealing only with LANs.

Although the rights to the IPX protocols are still retained by Novell, the Windows operating systems include support for IPX, as well as TCP/IP and other protocols. When Microsoft entered the NOS market, NetWare was the industry standard, and for Windows to succeed on networks, it had to be interoperable with NetWare. Microsoft therefore developed its own implementation of the IPX protocols, which enables Windows systems to access NetWare resources, whether or not they have a Novell Client installed. You can run a Windows 2000 network using only the Microsoft version of IPX, if you wish, but in most cases, IPX is used only for interoperability with NetWare.

Despite the fact that virtually all other NOSs, including Windows NT/2000, came to rely on TCP/IP as their primary protocols, Novell steadfastly stood by IPX until long after it was prudent to do so. IPX relies more heavily on broadcast transmissions than TCP/IP, and as a result generates more extraneous network traffic. On a heavily trafficked network, this can be one of the major drawbacks of running Windows 2000 and NetWare servers simultaneously.

Later NetWare versions supported the use of the TCP/IP protocols for Internet services (such as web and FTP servers), and a product called NetWare/IP could carry standard file and print traffic by encapsulating IPX data within IP packets, but it was not until the release of NetWare 5 in 1998 that the operating system could use TCP/IP as its native protocol, eliminating the need for IPX on NetWare networks entirely. For many network administrators, one of the primary reasons for upgrading an existing NetWare network to version 5 is to eliminate IPX from the network and use TCP/IP for all communications.

NetWare Versions

The various versions of NetWare differ primarily in the server OS. You can use the NetWare client included in Windows 2000 or the latest Novell Client to connect to a server running any version of NetWare. At this time, three versions of NetWare are on the market:

▼ **NetWare 3.2** The ultimate version of the bindery-based NetWare OS, version 3.2 does not include Novell Directory Services (NDS), the enterprise directory service used by all later versions. Designed for use on relatively small networks, many administrators continue to use NetWare 3.2 because of its relative simplicity and modest server hardware requirements, or simply out of inertia. A NetWare 3.2 server can run on a 386 PC with as little as 6MB of RAM.

■ **NetWare 4.2** The primary advantage of NetWare 4.2 is the inclusion of NDS, as well as a large number of additional programs and services. NDS unifies the NetWare resources on the network and provides users with the ability to access all the resources they need with a single login. A NetWare 4.2 server can run on a 386 system with as little as 16MB of RAM.

▲ **NetWare 5.1** The most current version of NetWare requires a Pentium system with at least 128MB of RAM, and includes NDS, native TCP/IP support, a Java-based administrative console, and a large suite of applications, including Internet services and Oracle database server software.

All of these NetWare versions include support for all the major client platforms, including all versions of DOS and Windows, as well as UNIX and Macintosh (although additional software may be needed). A great many networks are also running older versions of the NetWare server, virtually all of which are interoperable with Windows 2000. Many administrators have clung to their older NetWare installations, despite the addition of Windows NT or 2000 systems, mostly out of adherence to the "if it ain't broke, don't fix it" rule. The fact that many networks include NetWare servers up to ten years old that continue to coexist with cutting-edge Windows systems demonstrates how compatible these two operating systems are.

Directory Services

NetWare versions 3.2 and earlier are bindery-based. The *bindery* is a basic directory of users and groups that a NetWare server uses to authenticate users. Each NetWare server has its own bindery, which means that a user wanting to access multiple servers must have an account in each server's bindery and must perform separate logins. In 1993, Novell released NetWare 4, which introduced NetWare Directory Services (later known as Novell Directory Services). NDS is an enterprise directory service that is shared by all the NetWare servers on a network. With NDS, a user can log in to the network once and gain access to resources hosted by servers anywhere on the network.

NDS is composed of objects arranged in a hierarchical tree that represent the hardware, software, and human resources on a network. Each object is composed of a collection of attributes that define the properties of that object. *Leaf objects* represent physical elements, such as users and computers, whereas organizational objects, called *containers*, are used to build the tree structure. For example, Figure 8-2 shows a simple NDS tree that consists of container objects, including corpnet, which contains both user objects, such as

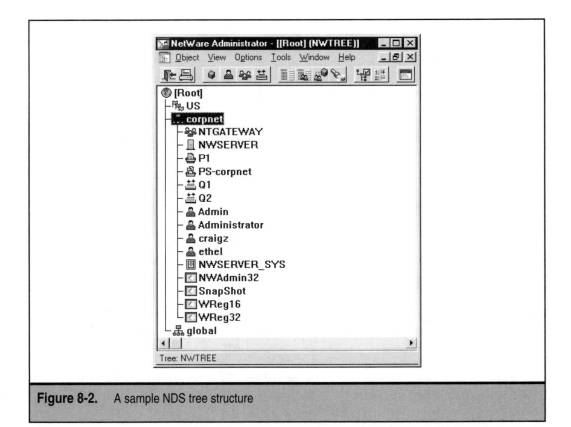

Figure 8-2.   A sample NDS tree structure

Administrator, and server objects, such as NWSERVER. The container in which a particular leaf object is located is called its *context.* The NDS database can be partitioned and replicated, so that multiple copies of the directory are stored on various servers all over the network. NDS is also extendable. Applications can create new object types or new attributes for existing objects, thus enabling them to use NDS for their own purposes.

If all of this sounds rather similar to Active Directory (AD) included with Windows 2000, it should. NDS and AD are both largely based on the X.500 standard published by the International Telecommunications Union (ITU), and AD is certainly designed to be competitive with NDS. However, Novell has had seven years to refine and develop its directory service, whereas AD is just getting off the ground, so although these two directory services undoubtedly will be comparable in their capabilities and reliability, NDS clearly has a head start over AD.

Security

Windows 2000 and NetWare are similar in the methods that they use to protect their resources from unauthorized access, even if the underlying security mechanisms are quite different. The file systems on both platforms use a series of permissions, assigned by administrators to directories or individual files, that provide users with specific types of access, such as Read and Write. The basic file permissions for the NetWare and NTFS file systems are shown in Table 8-1. By combining these permissions, you can exercise precise control over the access granted to specific users and groups. The primary difference between the way that the two operating systems treat permissions is that NetWare uses an additive model and Windows 2000 a subtractive model. In other words, Windows 2000 grants users full access to a resource by default and relies on administrators to revoke them as needed. NetWare, on the other hand, provides no rights by default and expects administrators to grant them (actually, all new users become members of the Everyone group, whose permissions are preset by an administrator). From the viewpoint of many administrators, the NetWare approach is both safer and easier to administer.

NOTE: The file permissions shown in the table for NTFS are called *individual permissions.* Although you can work with individual permissions directly, they are most often assigned in preconfigured combinations called *standard permissions,* of which there are five: Read, Write, Read & Execute, Modify, and Full Control. Because NTFS provides more individual permissions to work with, its access control capabilities are far more precise than those of the NetWare file system. For more information on Windows 2000 security and NTFS permissions, see Chapter 15.

In addition to file system permissions, both NetWare and Windows 2000 maintain a separate system of permissions to control access to the objects in their respective directory services. The user and group objects in AD and NDS are the primary mechanisms used by Windows 2000 and NetWare to control access to network resources, so it is essential for the properties of the objects themselves to be secure.

Windows 2000 NTFS File Permissions	NetWare File System Permissions
Traverse Folder/Execute File	Read
List Folder/Read Data	Write
Read Attributes	Create
Read Extended Attributes	Erase
Create Files/Write Data	Access Control
Create Folders/Append Data	Modify
Write Attributes	File Scan
Write Extended Attributes	Supervisor
Delete Subfolders and Files	
Delete	
Read Permissions	
Change Permissions	
Take Ownership	
Synchronize	

Table 8-1. Windows 2000 NTFS and NetWare File System Permissions

In summation, the security capabilities of Windows 2000 and NetWare are comparable, as far as basic LAN communications are concerned. When it comes to more stringent security requirements, however, Windows 2000 has a distinct edge over NetWare with its support for features like file system encryption, virtual private networking, and the IPSec security protocol (although it can be argued that IPX is a natural firewall to the Internet).

NetWare Clients

To access the resources provided by a NetWare server, a computer must be running an appropriate client. The Novell NetWare product itself includes clients for most of the common workstation operating systems, although some platforms, such as Macintosh or UNIX, may require the purchase of additional products from either Novell or a third party. Clients for the Windows 95/98 and NT/2000 operating systems are included with NetWare, but the Windows OSs themselves also include NetWare clients created by Microsoft. One of the main issues of running a combined Windows 2000/NetWare network is which client you will use on your workstations.

As a general rule, the clients supplied by Novell provide more functionality than the Microsoft clients, but they also utilize a greater amount of system resources and may be slower in performance. For Windows 2000 users who require basic access to NetWare file and print services, either client will do, but for network support personnel who have to administer NetWare servers and the NDS database, only the Novell NetWare 4.*x* and 5.*x* clients include the dynamic link libraries (DLLs) needed to run support applications such as NetWare Administrator.

Redirectors

In many cases, networks run both Windows 2000 and NetWare servers, either as a temporary measure during migration from one platform to the other or as a permanent solution. In order for workstations to access both Windows 2000 and NetWare resources at the same time, they have to be running a client for each platform. The basic function of a Windows 2000 client is to determine whether a file or other resource requested by an application is located on the local system or on the network. When you open a network file in an application, the request is passed to a module called a *redirector*. The redirector, instead of passing the request to the I/O Manager on the local system, passes it down through the appropriate networking stack, enabling the system to transmit it to the network server where the file is stored.

Every system on a Windows 2000 network has a redirector for the Windows network client installed. When you run more than one client on a Windows 2000 workstation, there is a separate redirector for each client. Each redirector is associated with the protocols and other modules needed to communicate with the respective servers. Thus, when you install a NetWare client on a workstation, a second redirector is added. In most cases, the redirector for a NetWare client is associated with the IPX protocol stack, while the Windows network redirector uses TCP/IP or NetBEUI. If you are running NetWare 5, however, it's possible for you to use TCP/IP for both clients, but there are still two separate redirectors.

Multiple UNC Provider

In order for a multiclient Windows 2000 system to effectively access both networks, the workstation has to be able to determine which network hosts each requested resource, so that it can pass the request to the proper redirector. When you open a file in an application, the file can be located on a local drive or on a server associated with either one of the networks. Once the I/O Manager determines that the requested resource is not located on the local machine, it passes the request to a module called the *multiple UNC provider* (*MUP*). No matter whether the resource is located on a Windows 2000 or a NetWare server, the request is formatted using standard Windows Universal Naming Convention (UNC) names. The function of the MUP is to determine whether a given UNC name refers to a Windows network share or a NetWare volume.

The MUP uses what is essentially a trial and error process to determine which redirector should receive the request for a particular resource. The MUP module checks each of the following resources in turn to determine whether the requested resource exists there:

▼ Distributed file system (Dfs)

■ MUP cache

■ First client redirector

▲ Second client redirector

If the system is configured to use the Dfs (see Chapter 12), the MUP first tries to locate the requested UNC name there. Failing that, the MUP checks the cache of UNC information that it maintains for all of the resources accessed by the system during the most recent 15 minutes of operation. If the requested UNC name is not in the cache, the MUP checks each of the redirectors installed on the system, in turn, to see if the requested resource exists there. If the MUP finds the requested name on more than one network, the MUP sends the request to the redirector with the highest priority (typically, the one that was installed first).

Windows 2000 or NetWare?

The question of whether Windows NT/2000 or NetWare is the better NOS is one that has been—and certainly will be—argued for a long time, but the bottom line is that both are capable of providing the basic file and print services needed by most network clients, and both can run a large variety of third-party applications that provide additional services, as well. In most cases, the selection of Windows 2000 or NetWare is based either on the investment already made by an organization in one operating system or the other, or on the need to run a particular software application.

If you have invested a significant amount of time and resources on a NetWare/NDS network, it is probably not worthwhile to junk that investment in order to run Windows 2000 and Active Directory, just because it is the newest kid on the block. In the same way, replacing a large fleet of Windows servers with NetWare is rarely a practical move. If you have to run an application that requires a different operating system from what you already have installed, you can easily add new servers and run both platforms for the time being. The Windows operating systems are designed to run multiple clients effectively, and the following sections examine the various NetWare client capabilities that are available to Windows 2000 users.

However, administrators for a large number of networks currently running NetWare have decided to migrate to Windows 2000. Later in this chapter, you will learn about the various procedures needed to perform a migration of this type, and the strategies that you can use to deploy Windows 2000 Server in a manner that is suitable to your users and your environment.

USING THE MICROSOFT CLIENTS FOR NETWARE

Whether you choose to run Windows NT/2000, NetWare, or a combination of the two on your network, your workstations will probably run one of the Windows OSs, and Windows 2000 contains the same client alternatives as Windows NT 4. Windows 2000 Professional and all of the Windows 2000 Server variants include a NetWare client that was developed by Microsoft.

When Microsoft was first developing Windows NT in the early 1990s, it struck an arrangement with Novell that called for Novell to supply the requester that Windows NT systems would use to access NetWare resources. When Novell failed to provide a satisfactory client, Microsoft set about developing its own NetWare client. These delays resulted in the first Windows NT version (3.1) shipping without a NetWare client, but Microsoft soon released the NetWare Workstation Compatible Service (NWCS) as a free add-on, and incorporated it into Windows NT 3.5. Eventually, Novell released its own NetWare client for Windows NT, and ever since, both Microsoft and Novell clients have been available that enable Windows NT and 2000 systems to access NetWare servers.

Starting with the Windows NT 4 release in 1996, the Microsoft client for Novell NetWare has taken two forms. Windows NT Workstation 4 and Windows 2000 Professional both include Client Service for NetWare (CSNW), a client that provides basic access to NetWare resources using either an NDS or bindery login. Windows NT Server 4 and Windows 2000 Server, Advanced Server, and DataCenter Server all include Gateway Service for NetWare (GSNW), a service that provides the same client access to NetWare resources, and also enables Windows network clients to use the NT/2000 Server as a gateway to NetWare (the choice on the server actually reads "Gateway (and Client) Services for NetWare").

You can use either CSNW or GSNW to provide the workstations on your network with access to NetWare resources, depending on whether you are looking for a permanent solution or a temporary one. The following sections examine each of these client services and how it fits into a heterogeneous networking strategy.

Using Client Service for NetWare

CSNW is the latest development of the client that began as the NetWare Workstation Compatible Service. Even though the first release of Windows NT did not include a NetWare client, it did include Microsoft's version of the IPX protocols used to communicate with NetWare servers. The CSNW implementation in Windows 2000 Professional continues to use this protocol. While the protocol appears in the NT/2000 interface as the NWLink IPX/SPX/NetBIOS Compatible Transport Protocol, it's more commonly known by the internal name NWLink.

NWLink enables the Windows 2000 system to exchange messages with NetWare servers using the NetWare Core Protocol (NCP), which is the NetWare equivalent of the Server Message Block (SMB) protocol used to provide file and print services on Windows networks. Although NetWare 5 can use TCP/IP as its native protocol instead of IPX, and some previous versions of NetWare support a product called NetWare/IP that encapsulates IPX messages within IP datagrams, CSNW supports neither of these features. To use CSNW (or GSNW) on your network, your NetWare servers must be configured to use the IPX protocol in its standard form.

NDS Support

The other NetWare client function that has a history of problems with Windows NT is support for NDS. When you run NetWare version 4 or higher servers using NDS, workstations log in to the NDS tree instead of to individual servers. This single login grants the user access to NetWare resources anywhere on the network. Before the release of Windows NT 4 in 1996, users could only log in to an NDS tree with the Novell Client for Windows NT, and even then the client provided only limited NDS capabilities. The CSNW service included with Windows NT 4 Workstation and Windows 2000 Professional, however, has both NDS and bindery login capabilities, although they are not equal to those of Novell's client.

With CSNW installed, a Windows 2000 workstation can log in to an NDS tree and navigate to objects representing NetWare server volumes and printers. However, CSNW's NDS capabilities do not support the use of more advanced NetWare features, such as Novell Distributed Print Services, Novell Storage Management Services, and ZENworks (Zero Effort Networks). In addition, you cannot run the applications needed to manage the NDS tree with CSNW, such as NetWare Administrator and NDS Manager. To use any of these applications or services, you must run the Novell Client for Windows NT/Windows 2000. The inability to run the NetWare Administrator utility is of primary importance to the network support personnel who maintain the NDS database, and ensures that at least some of the workstations on the network will be running a Novell client.

Installing CSNW

By default, when you install Windows 2000 Professional on a system with a network interface adapter, the system installs the Client for Microsoft Networks and the TCP/IP protocol, along with the appropriate driver for the network adapter. This provides the computer with access to resources on other Windows 2000 systems, either servers or other workstations. To install CSNW, you can use the following steps:

1. Open the Start menu and choose Settings | Network and Dial-up Connections to open the Network and Dial-up Connections window.

2. Right-click the Local Area Connection and choose Properties to open the Local Area Connection Properties dialog box.

3. Click Install, select Client, click Add, select Client Service for NetWare from the Select Network Component Type dialog box, and click OK.

4. Select either the preferred NetWare server for bindery-based NetWare or the default tree and context for NDS, and click OK.

5. Click Yes to shut down and restart your computer. Upon restarting, the system will add the following modules to the network components list (see Figure 8-3):

■ Client Service for NetWare

■ NWLink NetBIOS

■ NWLink IPX/SPX/NetBIOS Compatible Transport Protocol

Because NWLink is required by CSNW, the service installs it automatically, if it is not already present on the system. As mentioned earlier, CSNW can coexist with the Client for Microsoft Networks, but not with the Novell Client for Windows NT/2000.

Configuring CSNW

Installing CSNW creates a new CSNW icon in the Control Panel that provides access to the Client Service for NetWare dialog box shown in Figure 8-4. This dialog box also appeared in step 4 in the preceding section just after you installed CSNW, and also appears when you start the system without having previously specified values. Here, you specify either the default NetWare server that the client should use when performing a bindery login, or the default tree and context for an NDS login.

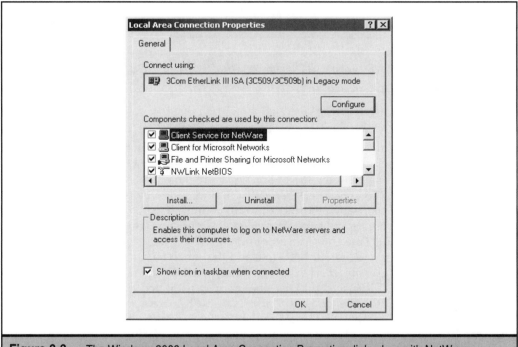

Figure 8-3.   The Windows 2000 Local Area Connection Properties dialog box with NetWare components

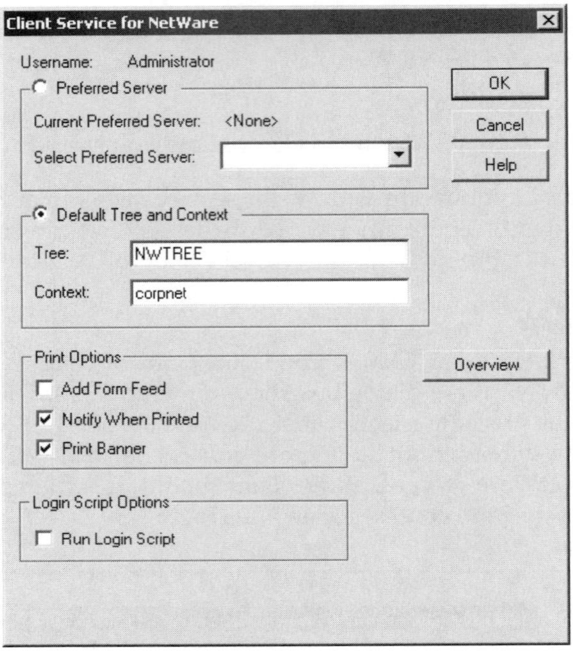

Figure 8-4. The Client Service for NetWare dialog box

A bindery login is a connection to a specific NetWare server, or to a specific container object (called the *bindery context*) in an NDS tree. If you are running NetWare 3.*x* or earlier on your servers, you select the Preferred Server option in the Client Service for NetWare dialog box and select the name of the server that you want the workstation to attach to during the login sequence. NetWare servers broadcast Service Advertising Protocol (SAP) messages at regular intervals, which the client uses to compile a list of the available servers.

If your NetWare servers are running version 4.*x* or higher, you perform an NDS login by choosing the Default Tree and Context option in the Client Service for NetWare dialog box and filling in the name of your NDS tree and the context (that is, the name of the container) in which your user object is located. In the sample NDS tree shown earlier, the name of the NDS tree is NWTREE and the user object craigz is located in the corpnet container. Thus, to log in to NDS, the user craigz specifies NWTREE and corpnet as his tree name and context. In this case, the context is located in the top level of the NDS tree hierarchy, so only the simple name corpnet is required. If your context is located farther down in the tree, you must supply its full name, which consists of all the containers running back to the root of the tree. For example, the Marketing container object in Figure 8-5 is located in the NY container, which in turn is located in the global container. The context for a user object located in Marketing would therefore consist of all of these container names, separated by periods, as follows:

```
Marketing.NY.global
```

Also the NWSERVER object, which is in the same context, the Marketing container, is a NetWare server that the user wants to access. Because the user and the server objects are in the same container, it is easy for the user to access that server's resources, but NDS also enables users to access resources located anywhere else in the tree, as long as the user has the appropriate permissions.

In addition to enabling you to specify the server, tree, and context fields, the Client Service for NetWare dialog box also enables you to specify whether or not the client should execute the login scripts associated with the user and configure the following print options:

▼ **Add Form Feed**   Causes the printer to eject an extra page at the end of each print job

■ **Notify When Printed**   Causes the print server to send a message to the client, informing it when each print job is completed

▲ **Print Banner**   Generates a separator page before each print job, identifying the user that generated it and the document being printed

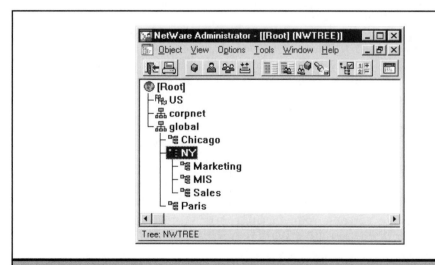

Figure 8-5.   A sample NDS tree hierarchy containing multiple layers of container objects

Although you don't need to use them, NetWare supports login scripts, just as Windows 2000 does, and you can choose to run them in the Client Services for NetWare dialog box. Various types of scripts are available for the different types of logins. Bindery accounts support two types of scripts: system login scripts, which are applied to all of the users in the bindery, and individual login scripts, which are associated with single users. NDS has four different types of scripts:

▼ **Container login scripts**   Apply to all the user objects in a particular container

■ **Profile login scripts**   Apply to users associated with a particular profile object

■ **User login scripts**   Associated with individual user objects

▲ **Default login script**   Runs when no user login script is present

You can use any combination of the scripts permitted for each login type, and CSNW will execute all of the commands in those scripts in turn.

Configuring IPX

In most cases, the NWLink IPX/SPX/NetBIOS Compatible Transport Protocol module requires no configuration for use with NetWare, but it does have a Properties dialog box (shown in Figure 8-6) that you access by double-clicking the protocol module in the Local Area Connection Properties dialog box.

The Internal Network Number field needs to be modified from its default value of zero only in rare cases in which the system is running an application that requires IPX routing services. The Frame Type field specifies the format of the Data Link layer protocol frame used on the NetWare network. NetWare supports four different Ethernet frame types (Ethernet_802.2, Ethernet_802.3, Ethernet_II, and Ethernet_SNAP), and two frames each for Token Ring and FDDI. These various frame types are reflected as slight differences in the header fields applied by the protocol. When you install your NetWare servers, you select the frame type (or types) that it will use, and your workstations must use one of the same types in order to communicate with the servers.

By default, CSNW automatically detects the frame type used by the NetWare servers on the network by trying each one in turn. When the client receives a response from a NetWare server using one of the frame types, it configures the client to use that frame type and sets the Network Number using the value received in the response message. However, it is possible for a system on the network to respond with incorrect information, and you can override the automatic detection mechanism by specifying a Frame Type and Network Number value in the NWLink IPX/SPX/NetBIOS Compatible Transport Protocol dialog box. You determine the appropriate values for these fields by examining the configuration files on a NetWare server or by asking the NetWare server administrator.

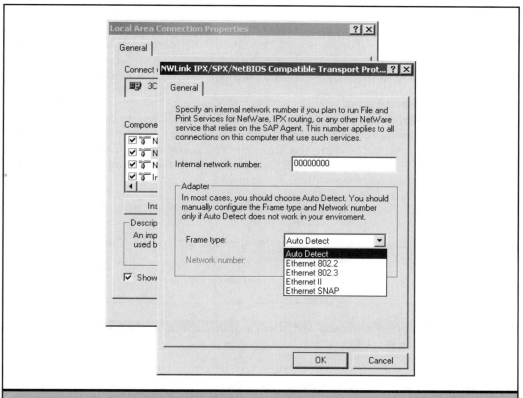

Figure 8-6.   The NWLink IPX/SPX/NetBIOS Compatible Transport Protocol Properties dialog box

Logging In

When CSNW and the Client for Microsoft Networks are both installed on a Windows 2000 Professional system, the system uses for the NetWare login the same name and password that you supply for the Windows network logon. This means that there must be a user account of the same name and with the same password in both the Windows 2000 domain and the NetWare resource specified in the Client Service for NetWare dialog box (either the bindery of the preferred server or the specified context of the NDS tree).

NOTE: For reasons that remain obscure, Windows clients are said to log *on* to a network, while NetWare clients log *in* to a network.

If the account name used to log on to the Active Directory domain does not exist in NetWare, then no NetWare login occurs. This is in contrast to the behavior of the Novell Client for Windows NT/2000, which prompts you for separate login credentials when necessary. If the account name exists in NetWare but uses a different password, then CSNW prompts you to supply an alternate password during the login process.

Logging In Other Than at Startup   When a NetWare login is not performed during the system startup sequence, either because the required NetWare account does not exist or because you have supplied an incorrect password, no NetWare connectivity exists initially. However, the client adds NetWare-specific menu commands to Windows Explorer, such as those shown in Figure 8-7, that enable you to connect to and disconnect from NetWare servers as needed. These commands are as follows:

▼ **Who Am I**   Displays the account name used to log in to the highlighted resource, and indicates whether a bindery or NDS login was performed

■ **Log Out**   Disconnects the user from the highlighted NetWare server

▲ **Attach As**   Logs in to the highlighted NetWare server after generating a dialog box in which you specify a username and password

Figure 8-7.   CSNW adds NetWare commands to the File and context menus of Windows Explorer

Using Attach As   The server connections resulting from the use of the Attach As command are, in most instances, bindery connections only. It is not possible to perform an NDS login, except as part of the initial system login sequence. If, however, you perform an NDS login during the initial sequence, you can disconnect from the NDS tree by using the Log Out command, and then reconnect to NDS at a later time by using Attach As, as long as you supply the same credentials used for the original NDS login. For example, if you log in to NDS as jdoe during the initial sequence, you can log out and then log back in to NDS later as jdoe, but you can't log back in to NDS as Administrator, even if you have the correct password. The Administrator login will, in this case, provide a bindery connection only.

Bindery Emulation   If you use Attach As to connect to a NetWare 4 or 5 server using different credentials from the initial connection, the client still logs in to NDS, but it does so using *bindery emulation.* A bindery emulation login is a connection to a specific NDS context that provides access only to the resources located in that context. NetWare version 4.*x* and higher include bindery emulation capabilities in order to support non-NDS clients.

Multiple Bindery Logins   If your initial NetWare connection is a bindery login, you are granted access to the server specified in the Preferred Server field of the Client Service for NetWare dialog box. To access other NetWare servers on the network, you must perform individual bindery logins for each one, using the Attach As command. You can use a different username and password for each bindery connection, if needed; Windows Explorer provides unified access to all of the connected servers, using the proper credentials for each one.

Accessing NetWare Resources

NetWare has its own command-line utilities for performing standard network access operations, such as Login.exe and Logout.exe for connecting to and disconnecting from the network, and Map.exe for mapping drive letters to NetWare volumes. However, Windows 2000 does not support these utilities. Once you've logged in to an NDS tree or NetWare bindery server, you can proceed to access NetWare file and print resources by using the standard Windows 2000 tools.

Installing CSNW adds to My Network Places an icon called NetWare or Compatible Network, from which you can browse through the NDS tree or the NetWare servers on your network, as shown in Figure 8-8. Expanding a server icon displays the volumes on that server, and you can then browse through the directory structure of individual volumes. Expanding the NDS tree icon displays the container objects in the tree, which in turn contain server and volume objects.

Accessing the directories and files on NetWare volumes using CSNW is no different from working with Windows network drives. You can manage files directly in My Network Places, either in a separate window or in Windows Explorer, or you can associate a drive letter with a NetWare volume using the standard Explorer Map Network Drive function. In the Printers Control Panel, you can create a printer definition that points to a NetWare printer just as you would install a Windows network printer.

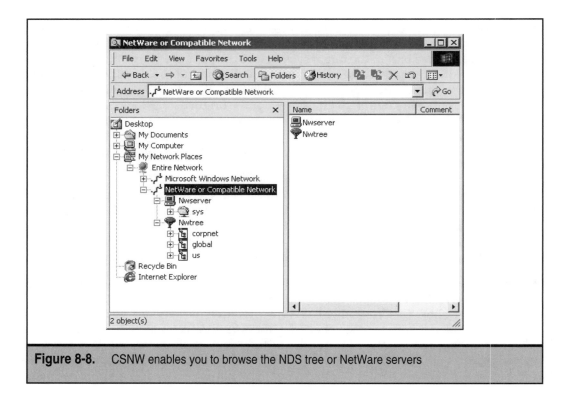

Figure 8-8. CSNW enables you to browse the NDS tree or NetWare servers

In addition to Windows 2000's GUI tools, you can access NetWare resources from the command prompt by using NET commands, the same way in which you can access Windows network resources from the command prompt. You can notate NetWare volume names on the command line using standard Windows UNC names, NetWare server/volume notation, or NDS names. For example, to map a drive letter to a NetWare volume, you can use any one of the following commands:

```
net use g: \\nwserver\sys
net use g: nwserver/sys:
net use g: \\nwtree\nwserver_sys.corpnet
```

The first example uses UNC notation in the form *server**volume*. The second example expresses the same information in NetWare's own format. The third example is a UNC name, but it identifies the volume using the NDS name of the volume object, which is nwserver_sys, located in the corpnet container, both of which are found in the NWTREE tree.

Using Gateway Services for NetWare

The Gateway Service for NetWare included in Windows 2000 Server is a superset of Windows 2000 Professional's Client Service for NetWare. The NetWare client capabilities of GSNW are identical to those of CSNW, and everything discussed in the previous sections on CSNW applies to GSNW as well. The difference between the two is that GSNW adds a gateway capability that enables you to provide NetWare access to Windows network clients without installing a NetWare client on each workstation.

A *gateway* is a system that provides access to a particular resource by accessing that resource itself and relaying it to other systems. The client capabilities of GSNW enable a Windows 2000 Server system to access NetWare resources, just as CSNW does. The gateway feature enables the system to publish NetWare volumes as Windows network shares, so that other Windows clients on the network can access them. GSNW is therefore an alternative method you can use to provide NetWare connectivity to your network workstations.

GSNW Versus CSNW

The primary advantage of GSNW as a NetWare access solution is that you don't have to install a new client on all of your workstations. If you have an existing Windows network and want to add a NetWare server, deploying CSNW (or the Novell Client) means that you have to visit every workstation to perform a separate client installation. With GSNW, you have to perform an installation on only one server, and all of your workstations can access the NetWare volumes through that server.

Another advantage of using GSNW is that you might be able to limit the use of IPX on your network. With CSNW, every client must use IPX to communicate with the NetWare servers. With GSNW, only the server functioning as the gateway has to use IPX; the communications between the Windows workstations and the gateway server can use TCP/IP or NetBEUI instead. If the Windows 2000 server and the NetWare servers are located on the same network segment, then the broadcast traffic generated by IPX can be limited to that segment.

GSNW also minimizes the number of accounts needed in NDS or on the NetWare servers to support the network clients. When you use GSNW, only the gateway server accesses the NetWare servers directly, so only a single account is needed. All of the Windows clients accessing the NetWare volumes through the gateway are, in essence, sharing that one account. CSNW, however, requires the user of each workstation to have an individual NetWare access account.

The use of a single NetWare account by GSNW can be both an advantage and a disadvantage. While using one account obviously reduces the burden on the NetWare administrators, it also limits the ability to control access to the NetWare volumes. When you use CSNW, each user's NetWare account is individually managed, and administrators can use NetWare's security permissions to grant users varying degrees of access to NetWare resources. A gateway server, on the other hand, has only one NetWare user account and one set of NetWare permissions. The only way to limit the access of the Windows clients to NetWare resources is by using share permissions. You can grant individual Windows network users full control, read-only, change-only, or no access at all to the shares created by the gateway, but you cannot control their access to the individual NetWare files and directories that make up the share.

Another possible disadvantage to using GSNW is that it concentrates all of the NetWare traffic generated by the workstations onto the gateway server, which can cause a bottleneck that slows down the performance of the network. If you elect to use a Windows 2000 Server as a gateway to NetWare, be sure that system is equipped with the hardware needed to support the traffic that will result.

Generally speaking, GSNW is preferable as a short-term NetWare access solution, such as during an interim period while NetWare servers are being migrated to Windows 2000. The gateway provides users with NetWare access with a minimum of installation and administrative overhead. If a long-term solution is needed, CSNW is more difficult to deploy, but provides more administrative control over the clients.

Configuring the Gateway

To install GSNW, you use exactly the same procedure as with CSNW, except that you select Gateway (and Client) Services for NetWare from the Select Network Component Type dialog box. Once the service is installed, you can access NetWare resources on the gateway system just as you would with Windows 2000 Professional and CSNW. In order for other Windows network clients to access NetWare resources, however, you must first configure the gateway. To do this, you open the GSNW Control Panel and click the Gateway button to display the Configure Gateway dialog box, as shown in Figure 8-9.

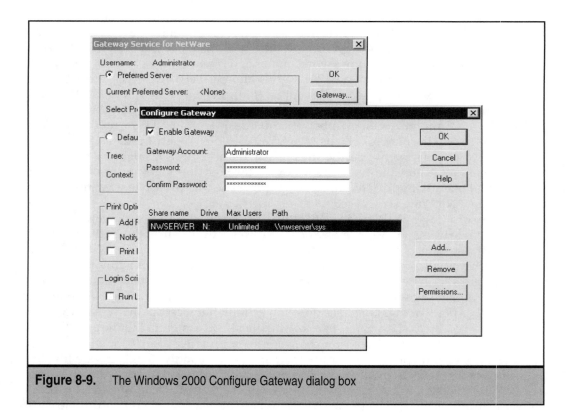

Figure 8-9. The Windows 2000 Configure Gateway dialog box

In the Configure Gateway dialog box, you can enable the gateway service, specify the name and password of the account that the gateway will use to access the NetWare servers, and create the shares that will be associated with the NetWare volumes. To use a particular NetWare account with the gateway, you must first create a group called NTGATEWAY, in either the NDS tree or the NetWare bindery, and make the user account a member of that group. Then, you assign the appropriate permissions to the NTGATEWAY group for the NetWare resources you want the Windows network clients to access.

To create a Windows network share out of a NetWare volume, you click the Add button in the Configure Gateway dialog box to display the New Share dialog box, shown in Figure 8-10. Here, you specify the parameters that the system will use to create the share, including the Share Name, the Network Path to the NetWare volume or directory that will be the root of the share, and the drive letter on the gateway system that the share will use. You can also limit the number of users that can access the share at any one time. After you create a gateway share, it's listed in the Configure Gateway dialog box, and you can click the Permissions button to specify what access your Windows 2000 clients should be granted to the share.

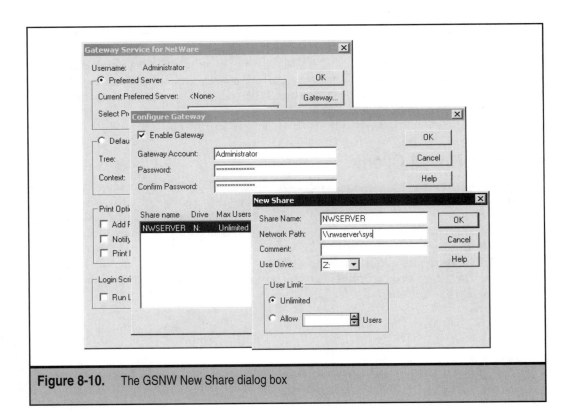

Figure 8-10. The GSNW New Share dialog box

USING THE NOVELL CLIENT FOR WINDOWS NT/2000

The alternative to using the Microsoft clients included with Windows 2000 to access NetWare servers is to use the Novell Client for Windows NT/2000, which you can install on either a Windows 2000 Server or Professional system. When Novell failed to produce a suitable NetWare client for the first Windows NT release, it continued its own development project, despite Microsoft's substitution of its own client software. Eventually, Novell released its own client for Windows NT, which supported NDS, unlike the first Microsoft client versions, but it also suffered from a number of performance issues and installation constraints that made deployment of the client difficult. Today, however, the Novell Client for Windows NT/2000 is an excellent NetWare access solution that provides many more features than Microsoft's own client.

All versions of NetWare include Novell clients for the various Windows OSs, which have gone by slightly different names throughout the years, such as intraNetWare Client and Client32. Today, the names have been standardized as the Novell Client for *specific operating system*, and they can be used with any version of NetWare. Interim releases of the clients are far more frequent than NetWare releases, though, so you should generally obtain the latest client version from the Novell web site or by ordering it on a CD-ROM.

NOTE: As of this writing, the latest version of the Novell Client for Windows NT/2000 is 4.7, available for download at www.novell.com/download. Although the download is free, the current client version totals over 75MB. You can avoid performing these large downloads by ordering the Novell Client CD, which includes the Windows NT/2000, Windows 95/98, and DOS/Windows 3.1 clients, for $29.00 at http://www.novell.com/products/clientscd.

Installing the Novell Client

The distribution files for the Novell Client for Windows NT/2000 are arranged in a complex directory structure on the CD that is compressed into archive files for downloading from Novell's web site. A single shell program, called Winsetup.exe, enables you to install the various components included with the client (see Figure 8-11). In addition to the client itself, the package includes the ZENworks Starter Kit, the client documentation, and the Adobe Acrobat Reader and Netscape Navigator programs used to view the documentation. These last two components (which most people already possess) account for more than 15MB of the client's size.

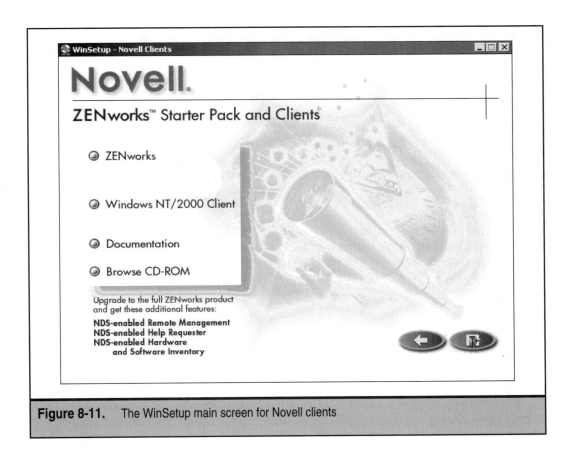

Figure 8-11.   The WinSetup main screen for Novell clients

When you select Windows NT/2000 Client from WinSetup's main screen, the program launches the client installation program (Setupnw.exe), which enables you to select from the following client components:

▼ **Novell Client for Windows 2000**   Installs the core client software that enables the workstation to access NetWare resources

■ **Novell Distributed Print Services**   Enables bidirectional communication between the workstation and network printers

■ **Novell IP Gateway**   Enables IPX-only workstations or workstations on private IP networks to access the Internet through NetWare servers that have been configured to operate as IP/IPX gateways

■ **Novell Target Service Agent**   Enables NetWare-based backup programs to automatically back up the drives on the client workstation

■ **Novell Workstation Manager**   Enables network administrators to manage and configure workstations using specialized objects created in the NDS database

▲ **ZENworks Application Launcher NT Service**   Enables the ZENworks Application Launcher to install applications on Windows NT/2000 workstations, as needed

Only the core Novell Client for Windows 2000 files are required for a client installation. All of the additional components are optional, and require you to install NetWare server components to support them. Once you've made your selections, the installation program prompts you to select the protocols that the client should use, using the following options:

▼ **IP Only**   Enables client workstations to communicate only with NetWare 5 server running the IP protocol.

■ **IP with IPX Compatibility**   Enables client workstations to use the IPX protocol on IP-only networks by converting IPX packets into IP. NetWare's Service Location Protocol is required to locate NetWare services using IP.

■ **IP and IPX**   Enables client workstations to communicate with NetWare 5 servers running IP or any version of NetWare server running IPX. This is the default option.

▲ **IPX**   Enables client workstations to communicate only with NetWare servers running the IPX protocol.

Finally, the installation program prompts you to specify whether you want the client to perform NDS or bindery logins. If the workstation has either CSNW or GSNW already installed on it, the installation program notifies you that it will remove the Microsoft client for NetWare before installing the Novell Client. If you already have the NWLink and TCP/IP protocol modules installed on your system, the Novell Client uses them. If the selected protocols are not installed, the client program installs them. Once installed, you can manage the client functions from the Novell Client Configuration dialog box (see Figure 8-12), which provides a large number of adjustable parameters.

NOTE: While earlier versions of the Novell Clients supplied their own IPX implementation, version 4.7 uses the Windows 2000 protocol modules.

The Novell Client package also includes the ZENworks Starter Pack, which is a subset of the Novell ZENworks package, available as a separate product. The Starter Pack includes the latest version of the NetWare Administrator utility, as well as functions that enable you to deliver network applications to workstation desktops and manage workstations using NDS objects. Because the Starter Pack is not an essential element of the Novell Client, its installation is performed as a separate procedure.

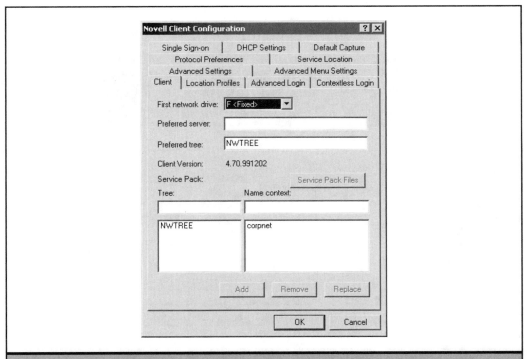

Figure 8-12.   The Novell Client Configuration dialog box

Logging In

The Novell Client replaces the Windows 2000 logon dialog box with one of its own (see Figure 8-13) and provides numerous login options that the Microsoft client lacks, such as the ability to select a tree and a context for the login by browsing NDS. The Microsoft client enables you to browse for a preferred server, but not for NDS resources. In addition, with the Novell Client, you can specify different usernames and passwords for the Windows and NetWare network logins. The Novell Client also provides more flexibility when it comes to running login scripts. You can choose the login and profile scripts that you want to run during the login process and also specify custom values for up to four variables used in the scripts. The Novell Client also includes a mechanism that enables you to synchronize the passwords of your NetWare and Windows network accounts during the login sequence.

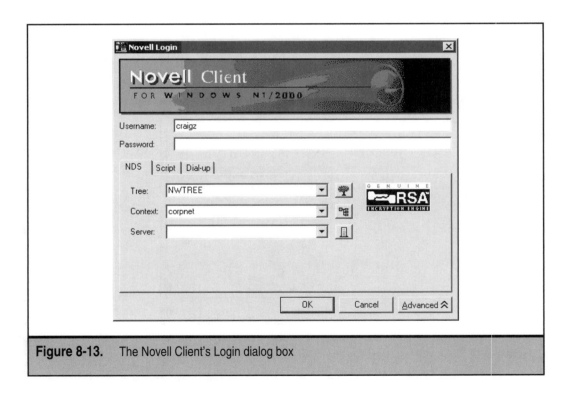

Figure 8-13.   The Novell Client's Login dialog box

Accessing NetWare Resources

Like CSNW and GSNW, the Novell Client adds its own NetWare-specific commands to the Windows 2000 interface, but quite a few more of them, as shown in Figure 8-14. The context menus for NDS objects and NetWare servers contain some different commands, and all the NetWare commands are flagged with a red N icon. A similar N icon appears in the taskbar tray, providing access to a large number of NetWare utilities, as well.

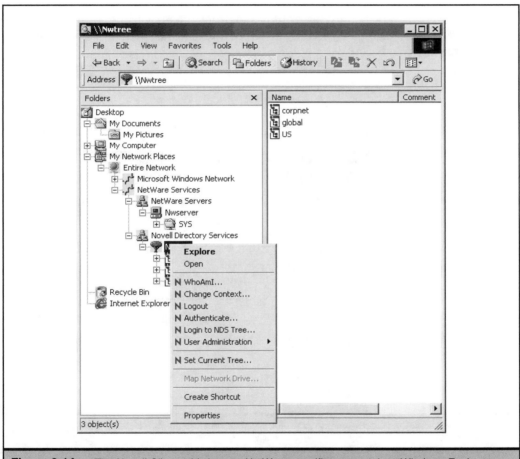

Figure 8-14.   The Novell Client adds its own NetWare-specific commands to Windows Explorer context menus

In addition to offering commands similar to those provided by CSNW and GSNW, the Novell Client enables users to exercise more control over NDS. With this client, the Windows 2000 system can run any of NetWare's utilities, including the NetWare Administrator program, which is essential for network support personnel. The Novell Client itself, however, includes utilities that enable users to modify their own NDS account attributes, as shown in Figure 8-15.

The Novell Client integrates NetWare resources into Windows Explorer, just like the Microsoft clients integrate NetWare resources, enabling you to perform standard file management functions using either Novell's utilities or those built into Windows 2000. For example, you can map NetWare volumes to drive letters by using the standard Windows 2000 tool or by using the Novell Map Drive utility, which provides additional functionality, as shown in Figure 8-16.

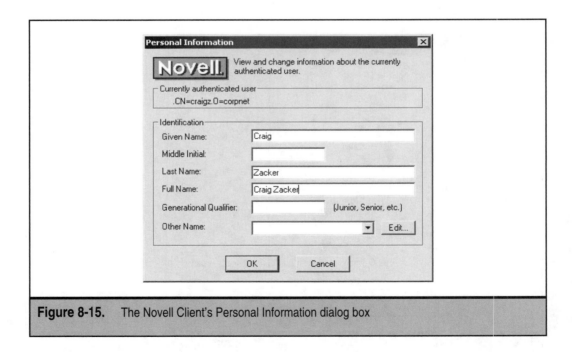

Figure 8-15. The Novell Client's Personal Information dialog box

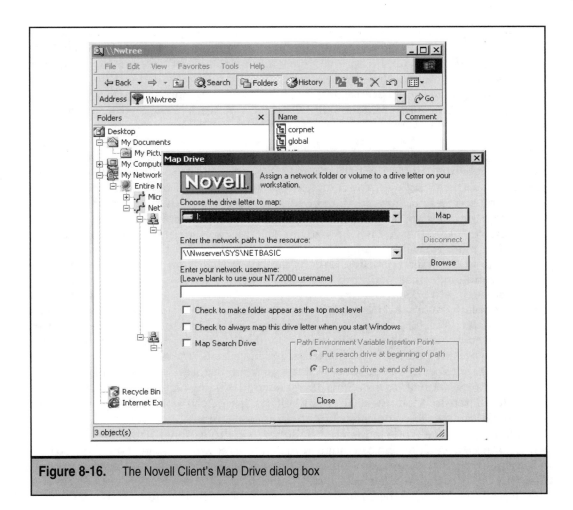

Figure 8-16. The Novell Client's Map Drive dialog box

MIGRATING FROM NETWARE TO WINDOWS 2000

The NetWare clients available from Microsoft and Novell make it possible for Windows 2000 and NetWare servers to coexist on the same network, and for Windows 2000 clients to access both of them simultaneously. Either one of these clients can function as a permanent NetWare access solution, or as an interim measure during a migration from one server platform to the other.

Deploying Windows 2000 and Active Directory on a network is a complex process that requires careful planning. However, migrating a network from NetWare to Windows 2000 can be even more difficult, because you have a functioning NetWare infrastructure that you must duplicate as closely as possible using the new tools provided by Windows 2000. On a large corporate network consisting of many hundreds or thousands of PCs, the migration process can be a massive undertaking. On smaller networks, ranging from a handful of systems to one or two hundred, the process is simpler, but no less critical.

In most cases, the object of the migration process is for users to have as little awareness of the process as possible. This means keeping all usernames and passwords intact, as well as retaining all the permissions used to control access to file systems, directory services, and other resources. The complexity of the migration is dependent on the applications and services you run on your network. If you're currently running e-mail, group scheduling, or other applications that maintain their own directories of users and passwords on NetWare, then you will have to find suitable replacements that run on the Windows 2000 platform, and arrange to carry over the data and the directory from one application to the other. Some applications can export their data and directory information in a common format, while others cannot.

On smaller networks, you may have to deal only with the migration of data files from one server platform to the other, and the migration of directory service information from NDS to Active Directory. While the file migration may seem to be simply a matter of copying from one system to another, remember that the process may be complicated by the need to preserve the access permissions you have set on the NetWare file system.

In addition to servers, remember that the migration process will most likely also involve reconfiguration of workstations. If you have an existing NetWare network that you intend to migrate to Windows 2000, your workstations are probably running some earlier version of Windows that you can configure to access your new 2000 servers, or you may want to upgrade the workstations to Windows 2000 Professional. Thus, the amount of work required at each system can range from a simple reconfiguration of the client so that it logs on to an Active Directory domain instead of NDS, to a complete OS upgrade that may even involve the installation of additional memory or other hardware needed to run Windows 2000. Multiply the amount of work needed for each system by the number of workstations on the network, and you'll have an idea of how big the project is that you're undertaking.

Rapid Migration Versus Gradual Migration

The first couple of decisions that you must make when planning a migration of this type is when it will occur, and how long it will take. This is obviously a question that depends on the size of your network and the amount of work to be done. For a modest ten-node network, you may be able to perform the entire migration, server and workstations, in a weekend. This is called a *direct migration*, in which all of your users log out from their NetWare servers on Friday and log on to Windows 2000 servers on Monday.

The problem with this method is that if you encounter any problems that delay the migration process, you must have a fallback so that your users can still work on Monday morning. As a result, it is usually not a good idea to perform in-place server migrations, in which you take down your NetWare servers, back up their data, and install Windows 2000 on the same machines. Whenever possible, install the new operating system on a different computer, so that even if you don't complete the entire migration on time, your users can still work. This also applies if you get your servers migrated on time, but fail to complete all of the workstation modifications. If your old servers are still intact, the unmodified workstations will still be operational.

This type of fallback planning is very important, because the type of major computer modifications you will be performing rarely go completely as planned. You may find that your servers need some special drivers, or you may encounter a hardware incompatibility, or half of your staff may call in sick, but something always seems to happen that throws off the timetable. A good rule of thumb to use if you're planning a direct migration is to estimate the amount of time you think you'll need and then double it.

Gradual migrations are generally much less stressful, because you can stretch them out over a longer period of time. In most cases, you perform a gradual migration by installing new Windows 2000 servers while the existing NetWare servers remain operational. You can then split the three basic migration tasks—directory service migration, file migration, and workstation modifications—into segments by department or geographic location and move them one at a time from NetWare to Windows 2000.

For example, you can spend one weekend installing your Windows 2000 servers and building your basic Active Directory domain structure. During the work week, you create the Active Directory objects for the users in the Sales department, and over the following weekend, you migrate the files belonging to the Sales users to the Windows 2000 servers and modify the workstations in the Sales department to log on to the Windows 2000 domain instead of NDS. On Monday, the Sales users begin using the Windows 2000 servers, but can fall back to NetWare in the event that a serious problem occurs. During the rest of the week, you prepare for the migration of another department, to be performed over the following weekend.

This way, you can gradually move all of your users to the new environment without the entire business grinding to a halt if something goes wrong. If you have limited time or personnel, or if your environment is more complex, you can migrate the users in smaller groups or stretch the timetable out to every other weekend. If the migrated users are faced with major changes to their working habits, for example, working with a smaller group makes it possible for you to spend more time supporting them and helping them adjust. Once the entire migration process is complete, you can take down the NetWare servers and redeploy them as Active Directory domain replicas or use them for other purposes.

Automated Versus Manual Migration

Another important decision to make is how you are actually going to perform the migration. Third-party tools are available that can automate parts of the migration process by re-creating NDS objects in Active Directory and by migrating files from NetWare to

Windows 2000 servers with their permissions intact, but in some cases, spending additional money on these tools and devoting time to learning how to use them may not be worthwhile. For small networks, the simplest solution may be to manually build the new network infrastructure from scratch. This means building a new domain tree in Active Directory and manually creating and configuring the objects needed to represent your users and other network resources. In addition, you'll have to copy your users' data files from the NetWare servers to your new Windows 2000 servers and manually set the permissions that restrict user access. Finally, you'll have to modify each workstation to log on to Active Directory and access the Windows 2000 servers instead of the NetWare ones.

Naturally, if you have hundreds of directory service objects to create or hundreds of workstations to convert, or if you've built up a complex system of access permissions over the years, performing a manual migration is not a practical alternative. In such cases, automating the installation in any way possible is preferable. As this is written, Microsoft is just getting ready to release a product called Services for NetWare v.5 that contains tools that can help you to perform migrations from NetWare to Windows 2000. The product contains three components:

▼ Microsoft Directory Synchronization Services (MSDSS)

■ File Migration Utility

▲ File and Print Services for NetWare

Microsoft Directory Synchronization Services

MSDSS is a service that can replicate objects between Active Directory and NDS in several different ways, converting the information found in one directory service into the format used by the other. The service runs on a Windows 2000 domain controller on which you've installed a NetWare client. By accessing the information in the NDS database or in a NetWare bindery, the service can create new objects in an Active Directory domain. You can use MSDSS in a variety of migration scenarios, including the following:

▼ **One-time migration** If you plan to perform a direct migration, you can use MSDSS to perform a single copy of an NDS container object to an AD container, which includes all of the user, group, and container objects found in the source container. This enables you to replicate the same tree structure from NDS to an AD domain in a single step.

■ **One-way synchronization** For a more gradual migration plan, you can establish sessions between NDS and AD containers that perform replications at regular intervals. This enables you to modify information in one of the directory services and have the changes propagated to the other automatically. You can, for example, migrate all of your NDS information to AD using a one-time migration, and then set up a synchronization that copies your directory service data from NDS to AD again, on a daily basis. This way, you can continue to maintain the directory in NDS during the migration process, without having to keep track of which users are using which directory service.

▲ **Two-way synchronization**   During longer-term migration plans, or for permanent coexistence of the two directory services, you can create a two-way synchronization that enables you to modify object properties in either NDS or AD and have the changes in each directory replicated to the other.

In any of these scenarios, you may find that your Active Directory tree uses a design that is substantially different from that of your NDS tree. When this is the case, you can create multiple sessions between the two directory services, to associate specific pairs of containers and copy data between them. Another important concern is the treatment of the passwords that are part of the user objects. MSDSS enables you to specify how passwords should be treated during the replication process, so that sensitive information need not be transmitted over the network.

File Migration Utility

The File Migration utility is a console that you can use to migrate files from NetWare servers to Windows 2000 servers, either gradually or in a single pass. More than just a file-copying utility, the most important feature of the program is that it preserves the permissions associated with the NetWare files and translates them into the equivalent NTFS permissions on your Windows 2000 server drives. When you use MSDSS to migrate NDS information to Active Directory, the service creates an ACL-mapping table that the File Migration utility uses to retain the permissions while copying files.

File and Print Services for NetWare

The File and Print Services for NetWare product enables a Windows 2000 server to emulate a NetWare 3.12 server on the network, enabling NetWare clients to log on and access resources on the Windows 2000 machine as if they were on a NetWare server. This capability makes it possible for you to continue to support NetWare client workstations that have not yet been configured to log on to the Windows network using an Active Directory domain account, even after your NetWare servers are no longer operational.

Once you install the service on a Windows 2000 system, the computer begins to generate Service Advertising Protocol messages on the network that advertise it to clients as a NetWare 3.12 server. The service also emulates the NetWare bindery using the Windows 2000 user accounts and creates a virtual NetWare volume out of a directory you specify. A workstation running a NetWare client can log on to the server in the normal way, and users can access the server's printers and the files in the volume without knowing that they are actually connected to a Windows 2000 system.

CHAPTER 9

Using Active Directory and Domains

Probably the single biggest change in Windows 2000 over Windows NT is the addition of Active Directory (AD), which provides a single reference, called a *directory service*, to all the objects on a network, including users, computers, printers, policies, and permissions. For a user or an administrator, AD provides a single hierarchical view from which to access or manage all of the network's resources. AD utilizes Internet protocols and standards, including Kerberos, Secure Sockets Layer (SSL), and Transport Layer Security (TLS) authentication; the Lightweight Directory Access Protocol (LDAP); and the Domain Name System (DNS). AD requires one or more domains in which to operate.

A *domain*, as used within Windows NT and Windows 2000, is a collection of computers that share a common set of policies, a name, and a database of their members. A domain must have one or more servers that serve as *domain controllers* and store the database, maintain the policies, and provide the authentication of domain logons. A *domain*, as used within the Internet, is the highest segment of an Internet domain name and identifies the type of organization; for example, .gov for government agencies, and .net for Internet service providers (ISPs). A *domain name* is the full Internet address used to reach one entity registered on the Internet. For example, www.osborne.com or www.mit.edu.

ACTIVE DIRECTORY ENVIRONMENT

AD plays two basic functions within a network: that of a directory service containing a hierarchical listing of all the objects within the network, and that of an authentication and security service that controls and provides access to network resources. These two roles are very different in nature and focus, but combine together to provide increased user capabilities while decreasing administrative overhead. At its core, Windows 2000 AD is a directory service that is integrated into DNS, plus a user authentication service for the Windows 2000 operating system. This explanation, however, introduces a few new terms and involves a number of complex concepts.

While AD is both a directory and a directory service, the terms are not interchangeable. In Windows 2000 networking, a *directory* is a listing of the objects within a network. A hierarchical directory has a structure with a top-to-bottom configuration that allows for the logical grouping of objects, such that lower-level objects are logically grouped and contained in higher-level objects for as many levels as you want. This grouping can be based on a number of different criteria, but the criteria should be logical and consistent throughout the directory structure.

Two of the more common directory structures in use within networks are based on object function (such as printers, servers, and storage devices) and organizational responsibility (such as marketing, accounting, and manufacturing). The organizational model allows you to store objects in groups, or *containers*, based on where they are in an organization, which might have its own structure, such as departments within divisions. A particular department would be the first organizational point within an organization. A container holding all the objects in a department is called an *organizational unit* (OU) and is itself grouped into higher-level OUs based on the logical structure.

After you create a group of OUs, you may find that the structure causes your directory to be cluttered and/or awkward to navigate. As a result, you may need to change your network to have more high-level OUs or more low-level OUs. At the top of all directories is the master OU that contains all the other OUs. This directory is referred to as the *root* and is normally designated by a single period. Such a hierarchical structure might look like this:

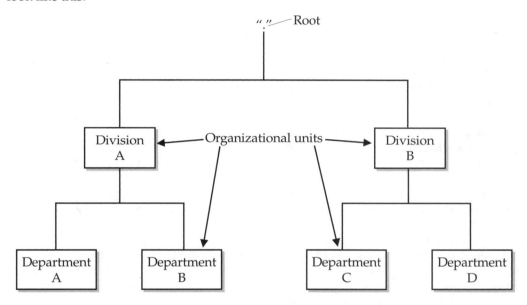

AD is just as basic as the organization just displayed. However, much of AD's core structure has already been mapped out by Microsoft and is consistent throughout all Windows 2000 implementations. For this reason, some of the containers, which are just OUs, have been assigned specific names and roles within AD. As this preconfigured directory structure is explained in the rest of the chapter, don't let the terms and names confuse you. Everything is still simply a collection of objects within OUs.

The "service" in "directory service" adds to a server features that are not otherwise available. Primarily, a directory service provides access to the directory of information, as well as to services that provide information about the location, access methods, and access rights for the objects within the directory service tree. This means that users can access a single directory and then be directly connected to a variety of other servers and services that appear to all be coming from the original directory. Much of this chapter discusses the different kinds of objects and methods of access that AD can provide to both users and administrators.

NOTE: X.500 is an internationally recognized standard used to create a directory structure. AD, Exchange 5.x, and Novell's NDS are all based on the X.500 standard. Specifically, AD is based on the newer X.509 version of the X.500 family.

Integration with DNS

Much of AD's structure and services, as well as the namespace that it uses are based on DNS. (*Namespace* is the addressing scheme that is used to locate objects on the network. Both AD and the Internet use a hierarchical namespace separated by periods, as described earlier in this chapter.) How AD uses DNS will be discussed in a moment, but it is necessary to first look at the structure and workings of DNS and how it is used to build the AD foundation.

All servers and services on the Internet are given an Internet Protocol (IP) numerical address, and all Internet traffic uses this IP number to reach its destination. IP numbers change, and may host multiple services at the same time. In addition, most people have a hard time remembering large arbitrary numbers such as IP addresses. IP addresses are decimal-based descriptions of binary numbers without a discernable pattern. DNS services were created to solve these problems by allowing servers and other objects on the network to be given a user-friendly name, which DNS translates to an IP number. For example, a user-friendly name such as mail.osborne.com might be translated, or *resolved*, in a DNS server to an IP address such as 168.143.56.34, which the network can then use to locate the desired resource.

DNS servers use hierarchical directory structures, just like the example described at the beginning of the chapter. At the core of DNS servers are root domains with a root directory, which is described by a single period. The first groups of OUs below the root are the various types of domains that can exist. For example, COM, NET, ORG, US, GOV, and EDU. Over 250 of these top-level domains are controlled by an Internet agency called InterNIC, which owns and controls a number of root servers that contain a listing of all the entries within each subdomain.

The next group of OUs following the ".COMs" consists of domain names, such as coke.com, microsoft.com, and osborne.com. These domains are registered and administered by the organizations or individuals who own them. Eight companies are contracted with InterNIC to sell and configure new domain names added to the Internet, with Network Solutions (www.networksolutions.com) being the most dominant of those companies.

A domain name, such as osborne.com, can contain both additional OUs, called *subdomains,* and actual server objects. In the example previously given, mail.osborne.com, the mail server, is an object in the osborne.com domain. A server name such as mail.osborne.com that contains all OUs between itself and the root is called a *fully qualified domain name* (FQDN). Figure 9-1 shows the actual name resolution process required when a client requests a DNS server to resolve an FQDN to an IP address.

Active Directory and Domains

AD and DNS share the same central OU, called a *domain.* For those familiar with Windows NT 4, the domain concept should be a familiar one. A domain is a central authentication and directory service that contains all the information for a group of computers. NT 4 had a number of significant limitations in the utilization of domains. Primarily, domains were not actual directory servers, because they contained only users, groups, and computers in a

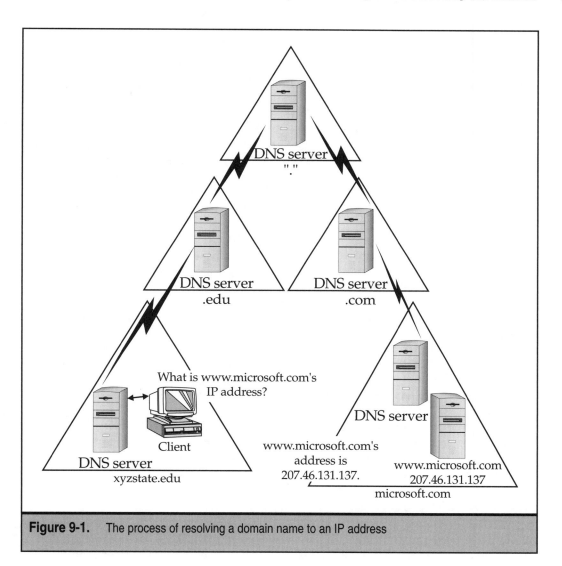

Figure 9-1. The process of resolving a domain name to an IP address

nonhierarchical structure. Although all computers were able to use the central repository of information for authentication issues, the directory was not available for object location or resource management. In AD, the core features and look of legacy NT domains are still present, but they have been greatly extended. Among the many enhancements, which will be discussed over the course of this chapter, is the ability of AD domains to scale to virtually any size, as opposed to the 40,000-object limit placed on NT domain structures. Another enhancement is AD's ability to form transitive two-way trusts with other domains in the network (this will be discussed further, later in the chapter).

The close integration between AD and DNS can, at first, be a little confusing. Looking at AD and DNS, it is easy to think they are actually the same thing, because they use the same names and naming scheme. However, this is not true. In actuality, DNS and AD are separate directory services that are using the same names for different namespaces. Each directory contains different objects, and different information about the objects in its own database. However, those object names, as well as the directory structure, often are identical.

Every Windows 2000 domain has an FQDN. This domain name is a combination of its own computer name and the domain name of the domain in which it currently resides. For example, Windows 2000 computers in the Osborne domain may very well have a computer name equal to *computername*.osborne.com. However, that same computer may in fact be a member of the subdomain of editorial.osborne.com. In this case, the computer's FQDN would actually be computername.editorial.osborne.com.

DNS Directories

A DNS directory doesn't really store objects in its database. Rather, DNS stores domains, the access information for each domain, and the access information for the objects (such as servers and printers) within the domain. The access information is normally just the FQDN and the related IP address. All queries for an object's IP address will match the FQDN in the request to the FQDN index in the DNS directory and return (*resolve to*) the IP address. In some cases, the access information (or *resource reference*) simply points to another object (or *resource*) within the same or a different DNS domain.

A standard DNS domain is not capable of reversing this process by returning an FQDN when provided with an IP address. To make this kind of resolution possible, a reverse lookup domain is required. These domains are referenced as "in-addr-arpa" domains within the DNS hierarchy.

Among the other special functions of DNS that add features to a network is the Mail Exchanger reference that can be added to a DNS domain name. A Mail Exchanger reference (referred to as MX) enables mail servers to locate the mail servers of other domains to allow for the transferring of e-mail across the Internet.

Active Directory Services

AD services contain a lot more information than what is available in DNS directories, even though the names and structure are nearly identical. AD resolves all information requests for objects within its database using LDAP queries. The AD server is able to provide a varied amount of information about each object within its database. The information that AD can provide includes, but isn't limited to, the following:

▼ Username

■ Contact information, such as physical address, phone numbers, and e-mail address

- Administrative contacts
- Access permissions
- Ownerships
▲ Object attributes, such as object name features; for example, Color Laser Jet Printer, 20 sheets per minute, duplex printing

Although DNS does not require AD, AD requires a DNS server to be in place and functioning correctly on the network before a user will be able to find the AD server. With Windows 2000 moving entirely to Internet standards for its network operating system, a method of locating network services had to be found other than using the NetBIOS broadcasts used in Windows NT. This was done through the use of a new DNS domain type known as *dynamic DNS (DDNS)* domains. A DDNS domain, which is integrated into AD, allows all domain controllers to use the same database, which is automatically updated as new Windows 2000 computers are added and removed from the network. The DDNS domain also allows DNS to function with networks based on DHCP (Dynamic Host Configuration Protocol), where the IP addresses of the network objects are constantly changing. Besides providing the name resolution for the network, the DDNS domains also contain a listing of all the domains and domain controllers throughout the network. This means that as new Windows 2000 systems are added to a network, they will query the DDNS servers to get the name and connection information, including IP address, of the domain controllers they are closest to.

NOTE: In Windows NT installations, Windows Internet Naming Service (WINS) servers provided new workstations with the location of the domain controllers. To allow for compatibility with Windows 3.11, Windows 95, and Windows 98 workstations not running the AD client, WINS servers are still required on the network. Both Windows 2000 and legacy NT servers have the ability to host WINS services and integrate them with DNS.

Active Directory and the Global DNS Namespace

AD domains are designed and intended to exist within the naming scheme of the global DNS domain operated through the Internet. This means that, by design, the DNS domain of your network would also match the AD domain-naming scheme. In some organizations, migration from a legacy NT local area network (LAN) is difficult, because independent LAN and Internet domains are already in place and entrenched. In this case, DDNS servers can be used for the LAN AD domain and hosted on internal DNS servers. The external servers providing Internet web hosting services, such as the Simple Mail Transfer Protocol (SMTP) and the Hypertext Transfer Protocol (HTTP), would still use the Internet DNS structure and provide the necessary resource mapping in each domain to allow for coexistence, as shown here:

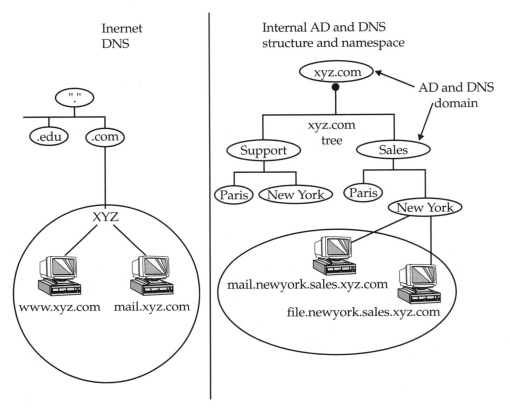

 NOTE: The functions provided by the DDNS domain that are required for AD are the listing of the domain information and the location of the domain servers. These functions are provided by a resource object called a *Service Location Resource (SRV)*. SRVs are not unique to Windows DDNS domains and therefore some third-party DNS server products work with AD. However, configuring these third-party DNS servers to integrate with AD can be a significant undertaking.

INSTALLING ACTIVE DIRECTORY

There are two ways to install AD: into an existing domain, or to form a new domain. (For those a little more familiar with AD, some issues regarding forests and trees are affected here, as well, but those will be discussed later in the chapter.) Installing AD on a server turns the server into a *domain controller*, a server that hosts a central database of all users and groups within the domain and manages all domain-related functions, such as user logon authentication and trust relationships. This process can be done on existing NT servers or on newly installed Windows 2000 AD servers. Windows 2000 is the first Windows platform that allows for the promotion of member servers to domain controllers. If a domain contains multiple AD servers, then the AD services can be removed from a domain controller and the server can be returned to a standard member server within the domain.

When installing AD into an existing legacy NT-based domain, the primary domain controller (PDC) of the domain has to be a Windows 2000 Server running AD. This is obviously only an issue in cases in which both Windows 2000 and legacy NT domain controllers exist in the domain (called a mixed-mode network). In cases where you are installing the first AD server in an existing legacy domain, the existing PDC will have to be upgraded to Windows 2000, and then AD can be added. A Windows 2000 Server can exist without AD in an NT legacy domain, but before AD can be added, the PDC has to be upgraded to Windows 2000.

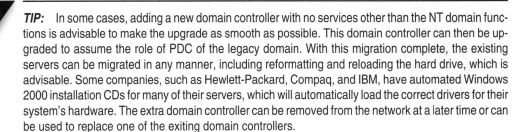

TIP: In some cases, adding a new domain controller with no services other than the NT domain functions is advisable to make the upgrade as smooth as possible. This domain controller can then be upgraded to assume the role of PDC of the legacy domain. With this migration complete, the existing servers can be migrated in any manner, including reformatting and reloading the hard drive, which is advisable. Some companies, such as Hewlett-Packard, Compaq, and IBM, have automated Windows 2000 installation CDs for many of their servers, which will automatically load the correct drivers for their system's hardware. The extra domain controller can be removed from the network at a later time or can be used to replace one of the exiting domain controllers.

To install AD on a Windows 2000 Server, use the AD Installation Wizard, accessed through the Configure Your Server dialog box (see "Setting Up Active Directory" in Chapter 4). When using the AD Installation Wizard, you are prompted to install into an existing domain or create your own. This is done at two points:

▼   First, in the initial Configure Your Server dialog box, shown in Figure 9-2, in which you specify whether the new server is the only server

▲   Second, in the AD Installation Wizard, in which you specify whether this is a new domain or an additional controller on an existing domain, as you can see in Figure 9-3

When installing into an existing domain, your administrative rights on the domain will be checked. It is possible to have administrative rights on the server being upgraded but to not have sufficient rights on the domain and domain controllers to do the installation. After you install the AD service, you do the remaining configuration through the AD Domains and Trusts, AD Users and Computers, and AD Sites and Services snap-ins for the Microsoft Management Console (MMC), see Figure 9-4.

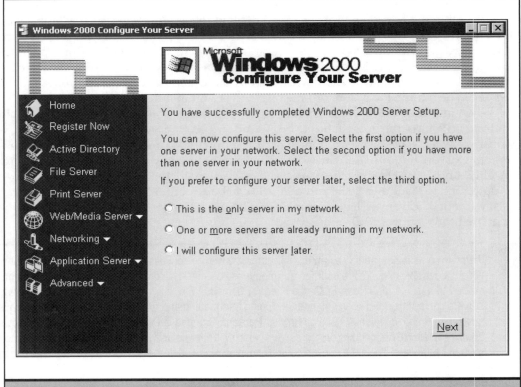

Figure 9-2. Specifying that a new server is the only server in a network

Replacing Existing Domain Controllers

Windows 2000 servers functioning in native domains (domains that contain only Windows 2000 domain controllers) act as peers with all members containing the AD services database with equal read-write privileges. In legacy NT domains, only the PDC contains the master, read-write copy of the domain's directory store. All the other domain controllers, referred to as *backup domain controllers* (*BDCs*), contain read-only copies of the domain directory information store. BDCs are able to authenticate users and provide domain information, but all additions and modifications to the existing data has to be made to the PDC. When installed in mixed mode, an AD server will still respond to remote procedure calls (RPCs) as if it were a PDC and then replicate directory changes to the legacy BDCs. This means that all remaining legacy domain controllers do not recognize that there has been any major modifications to the network.

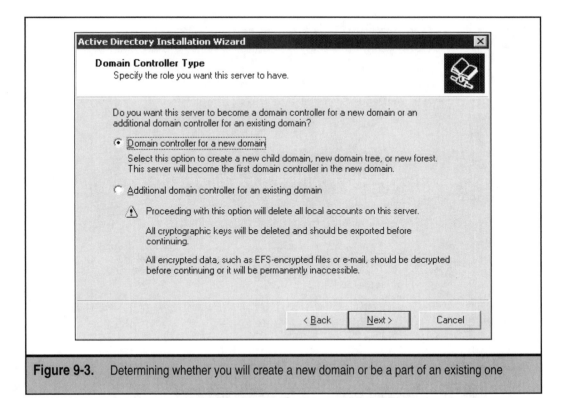

Figure 9-3.   Determining whether you will create a new domain or be a part of an existing one

The method of operation used by AD is that of *multimaster replication,* which means that changes can be made to any AD server and those changes will be replicated to other servers throughout the network. Within this multimaster replication scheme are a couple of important concepts that involve the first AD server installed in the domain, which is automatically configured to be the following:

▼   A global catalog server

▲   The operations master

Global Catalog Server

The global catalog is a new database type that is at the core of the directory services. The *global catalog* contains a listing of the services that can be accessed within the network, and not just the local domain. The global catalog can be kept on multiple domain controllers, but always has to be installed on at least one, and by default is always created on the first AD server installed in a new forest. (The forest concept is explained later in the chapter.)

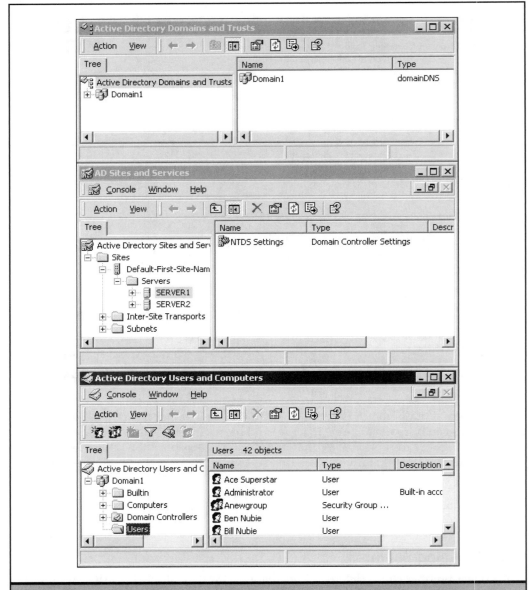

Figure 9-4.   Configuring AD in one of three MMC snap-ins

The configuration of the global catalog and its placement on various servers throughout the network is done through the AD Sites and Services MMC snap-in.

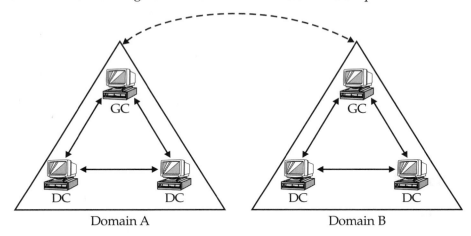

Domain A   Domain B

DC = Domain controller
—— = Domain directory replication
– – = Global catalog replication
GC = Global catalog

TIP: When operating in mixed mode, all domain controllers can perform user logins independently. However, when operating in native mode, a query to a global catalog server is required (because it determines a user's global group memberships). Therefore, the rules for installing multiple global catalogs within a network are very similar to those for installing additional BDCs to an NT 4 domain. When installing multiple distant sites, having a global catalog server in each site will decrease the network load of the WAN links otherwise used to provide user authentication. Additionally, having multiple global catalog servers to distribute the network load of authentication traffic evenly across multiple servers, instead of stacking this load onto a single server to handle, is much more efficient. Of course, the need for additional global catalog servers increases the network bandwidth consumed for directory synchronization.

In general, two main features are provided by the global catalog servers within a network: logon and querying. When operating a domain in native mode, universal groups are allowed to exist within the forest. Because universal groups can contain users and groups from multiple domains, the universal group cannot exist within an individual domain. Therefore, the global catalog maintains the universal groups within the network as well as each group's memberships. This means that whenever operating a network in native mode, the AD server logging a user into the network has to query a global catalog server to determine the universal group memberships that the user may be a part of. In cases in which a user logs in and a global catalog server is not available, they will be granted access only to the local computer. This avoids any potential security issues in which a global group based in the domain granted a user access to a resource that the universal group excluded the user from gaining access to. In case of an emergency, however, any user account that is a member of the local domain's Domain Admin group will be allowed to log in to the network.

The second major feature provided by the global catalog, querying, is a little more obvious. A large network may have numerous domains that all exist together. In this case, the global catalog provides a single place for all of the network's users to reference whenever searching for specific resources. The alternative to the global catalog in this instance would be the requirement for each user either to know the exact location of the resources they want to use, or to search each domain independently. The querying feature of AD provides another main reason to have multiple global catalog servers throughout a network.

Operations Master

The second main service added to the first AD server within a network is the operations master. Within Windows 2000 domains, there is a need to centralize some changes to the directory services. Even though AD is based on the multimaster replication model, and all domain controllers are peers within Windows 2000, there are still some changes that can cause too many issues if configured from multiple locations. For this reason, only one Windows 2000 domain controller within any forest and within any domain is assigned to become the operations master for that domain or forest. For domain operations, three roles are assigned to the domain's operations master:

▼ **PDC emulator**   Looks like a PDC to legacy network members in a mixed-mode network

■ **Relative ID master**   Assigns blocks of security IDs to the other domain controllers in a network

▲ **Infrastructure master**   Updates the other domain controllers for changes in usernames and group-to-user references

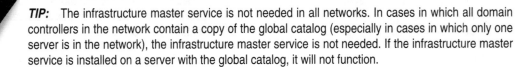

TIP: The infrastructure master service is not needed in all networks. In cases in which all domain controllers in the network contain a copy of the global catalog (especially in cases in which only one server is in the network), the infrastructure master service is not needed. If the infrastructure master service is installed on a server with the global catalog, it will not function.

A forest has only two roles that are assigned to the forest's operations master:

▼ **Domain naming master**   Adds and removes domains in a forest

▲ **Schema master**   Updates the directory schema and replicates that to the other domain controllers in a forest

ACTIVE DIRECTORY STRUCTURE AND CONFIGURATION

An AD network contains a number of objects in a fairly complex structure and can be configured in several ways. This section focuses on some of the main objects in Active Directory, as well as some of the basic configuration involved with each of these objects. This covers the following:

▼ AD objects and what they do

■ Domains, trees, forests, and the other OUs within AD

▲ Sites and site-based replication

Active Directory Objects

An *object* within AD is a set of attributes (name, address, and ID) that represents something concrete, such as a user, printer, or application. Like DNS, AD groups and lists these objects in OUs, which are then grouped into other OUs until you reach the root. Also, like DNS, AD then provides access to and information about each of these different objects. As a directory service, AD maintains a list of all objects within the domain and provides access to these objects either directly or through redirection. The focus of this section is the foundation and structure of the objects in AD. By recalling the differences between AD and DNS and the objects that they contain, you can appreciate the wide variety of objects allowed in directory services. In the case of AD and the other X.500-based directory services, the creation and use of this variety of objects is governed by the schema used in the directory.

Schema

The *schema* defines the information stored and subsequently provided by AD for each of its objects. Whenever an object is created in AD, the object is assigned a globally unique identifier, or GUID, which is a hexadecimal number unique to the object. A GUID allows an object's name to be changed without affecting the security and permissions assigned to the object, because the GUID is still the same. Once the object is created, AD uses the schema to create the fields defined for the object, such as phone number, owner, address, description, and so forth. The information for each of these fields is supplied by the administrator or a third-party application pulling the information from a database or preexisting directory structure, such as Microsoft Exchange.

NOTE: For reverse-compatibility reasons, support for security identifiers (SIDs), NT 4's version of GUIDs, is also maintained within AD.

Adding to the Base Schema

Because the schema provides the rules for all objects within AD, you'll eventually need to extend the default object classes that come standard within AD. One of the first times this will happen is when a mail server is added to the network, which will require that mail-specific attributes be added to the AD schema. This addition may also require that new object classes be created. The process of adding classes and attributes is done by modifying or adding to the AD schema. The modification of the schema takes place using an automated installation function that affects the schema for the entire network. Schema updates cannot be reversed, so always exercise caution when updating the schema.

TIP: It is possible to modify the schema through the Active Directory Service Interface (ADSI) and by using the LDAP Data Interchange Format utility. It is also possible to modify the schema directly by using the AD Schema tool. These programs should be used only by AD experts and should always be tested in a lab environment before being implemented on production servers.

Publishing Items to the Directory

At face value, Windows 2000 functions very much like legacy NT-based products, especially in its sharing and security functions. When an item is shared or a new resource is added to Windows 2000, such as a printer, the object is shared and secured using nearly the same process as with legacy NT servers. Additionally, not all Windows NT–based servers may become AD servers. With these two facts in mind, some method is needed to distribute information about objects hosted on Windows 2000 servers throughout the network into AD. This process is called *publishing*. When an object is published in AD, information about the resource is added to AD, and users are then able to access that resource through AD. The main benefit provided by publishing is that it allows large networks with resources hosted by servers throughout their various sites to all share their information from a central point on the network. Users within the network can access the AD servers and search for, locate, and access the resources they need through the single entry point of AD.

Some objects are added to AD automatically, such as user, group, and server objects. However, some objects have to be published in AD by an administrator. The two most common items that most administrators will find themselves adding to AD are directories and printers.

Directory Publishing   To add a directory to AD, a share or folder for the directory must first be created and secured using standard security practices (see the Sharing tab of the Application Data Properties dialog box). This security has to include both share-level security and the NTFS permission associated with the directory and all of the files and subdirectories within that share.

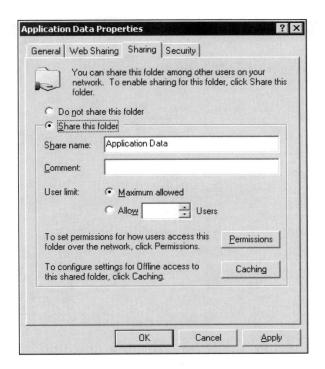

TIP: With the advent of AD, new methods of organizing and providing access to network resources have been added to the network administrator's tools. However, the methods for administering network security that were used with Windows NT are still very much in effect.

Printer Publishing   Publishing a printer in AD is a simple process that provides several new features that were not available with previous versions of NT. Primarily, when a number of printers exist within an AD network, users within that network can search for printers based on specific features, such as color, resolution, or duplexing.

To publish a printer in AD, the printer must first be installed and configured to function on the print server in question. (The print server in this case is simply any Windows 2000–based computer, and can include Windows 2000 Professional.) After a printer is configured, shared, and has the proper security set (see Chapter 13 for details on how to do this), it is ready to be published in AD. In fact, the default action taken by Windows 2000 servers is to publish any printer automatically after it has been installed and shared. Once published, the printer can then be managed and accessed through all AD servers within the domain, and is automatically included in the global catalog for the other domains within the forest.

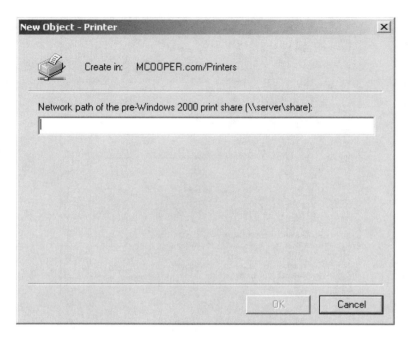

In some cases, especially domains still running in mixed mode, non-Windows 2000 servers may be hosting printers that are of significant importance to the domain. In this case, an object can be added to the AD domain by using the URL of the printer share. This can be accomplished using the AD Users and Computers snap-in, or through the use of a Visual Basic script (Pubprn.vbs) included with Windows 2000 and located in the System32 folder. Although a little more difficult to set up, using Pubprn.vbs enables you to add numerous printers to AD at one time.

NOTE: Resources shared on the network should not always be published in AD. Only objects used by a large part of the network or that need to be available for possible searches should be published. Objects published in AD increase the domain's replication traffic that is necessary to ensure all AD servers have the most recent information. In large networks with multiple domains, the replication traffic to synchronize the global catalog servers for each domain can be overwhelming if poorly planned.

The Structure of Active Directory

There are various OUs within AD that have very specific roles within the network. These roles are established via the schema. To administer and configure an AD network, you need to understand what each of these OUs are, and the role that each plays within the network.

Active Directories are made up of one or more domains. When the first AD server is installed, the initial domain is created. All AD domains map themselves to DNS domains, and DNS servers play a crucial role within any AD domain.

Domains

Domains are at the core of all Windows NT–based network operating systems, and Windows 2000 isn't an exception. This section looks at the structure of domains within AD, as well as the various factors involved in creating multiple domains within a network.

Domains in AD delineate a partition within the AD network. The primary reason for creating multiple domains is the need to partition network information. Smaller networks have very little need for more than one domain, even with a network spread across multiple physical sites, since domains can span multiple Windows 2000 sites. (The site concept is covered in more detail later in this chapter.) However, there are still reasons to use multiple domains within a network:

▼ **Provide network structure**   Unlike legacy NT domains, there is no real limit to the number of objects that can be added to an AD domain running in native mode. For this reason, most networks do not need to establish separate domains for each business unit. However, in some very large networks, various political factors may necessitate multiple domains. For example, one company may own several subsidiary companies that are completely autonomous from the parent company. A central AD shared between the companies provides numerous benefits; a shared domain may not make as much sense. In this case, a separate domain can be set up for each company.

■ **Replication**   AD servers contain information only about their own domain. Global catalog servers are required to publish information between domains for user access. This means that all objects within a domain are replicated to all the other domain controllers, but external resources are replicated only between global catalog servers. In large networks spread across multiple slow WAN links, each physical site should be its own domain, to ensure that unnecessary replication traffic does not consume the limited bandwidth of the WAN links.

■ **Security and administration**   Although AD provides the appearance of a central network infrastructure to the users of the network, administrative abilities and user permissions will not cross domain partitions. This is overcome through the use of global and universal groups and trust relationships, but domains are truly separate administrative groups that may or may not be linked together.

▲ **Delegation of administration**   Although the delegation of administrative authority throughout the network makes multiple domains easy to handle, and Windows 2000 provides a number of new administrative tools, there still may be benefits for some networks in splitting domains along the lines of administrative authority and responsibility.

Forests

Besides domains, AD is composed of forests, trees, and other custom OUs. Each of these OUs exists on a specific level of AD's hierarchy, beginning with the uppermost container, forests. A *forest* is the highest OU within the network and can contain any number of trees and domains. All domains within a forest share the same schema and global catalog. In essence, forests are similar to DNS's root container. A vast majority of organizations implementing AD will have only one forest; in fact, smaller organizations that have only one domain may not even realize the existence of the forest, because all functions appear to exist on the domain level only. In effect, the forest is used as the main directory for the entire network. The forest encompasses all the domains as well as all the published information for each domain.

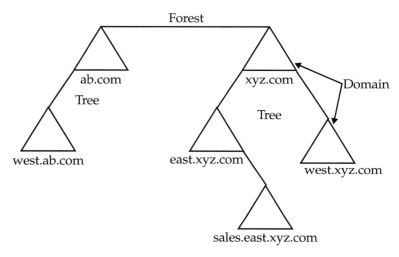

Domains within a forest are automatically configured with two-way transitive trusts. A trust relationship allows two domains to share user and group resources so that users authenticated by a "trusted" domain can access resources on the "trusting" domain. *Transitive trusts,* shown in Figure 9-5, allow user accounts within a domain to use a second domain's trust relationships to access resources in a third domain. Legacy NT domains did not support transitive trust relationships. In Figure 9-5, a user account from Domain A is able to access resources in Domain C because both Domain A and Domain C have established transitive trust relationships with Domain B. If Figure 9-5 were illustrating a legacy NT domain, a trust relationship would have to be directly established between Domains A and C before the resources could be accessed.

Creating additional forests in a network should be undertaken with great care. The additional forests can cause a tremendous amount of administrative overhead, especially

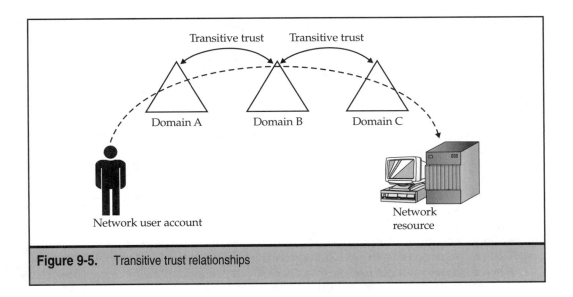

Figure 9-5.   Transitive trust relationships

when adding AD-aware messaging platforms, such as Exchange 2000. Other than the obvious political issues, there are very few reasons for any one network to have multiple forests.

Trees

Within AD, trees are used more for administrative grouping and namespace issues than anything else. Basically, a *tree* is a collection of domains that share a contiguous namespace and form a hierarchical environment. For example, it is possible for an organization such as Microsoft to split its DNS structure so that the Microsoft.com domain name is not the primary name used in e-mails and resource references. For example, assume that Microsoft is split geographically first, so that there is a West Coast OU and an East Coast OU within the Microsoft domain, and that these OUs (or child domains) contain a tree of further divisions, such as Sales and Tech Support, which could be further split into Operating Systems and Applications. In this example, so far, Microsoft would have two trees within its DNS structure, West Coast and East Coast. Both of these domains are then split further still, creating a potential FQDN of a server within the technical support department as follows:

```
ServerName.OperatingSystems.TechSupport.WestCoast.Microsoft.Com
```

The entire discussion of trees within AD so far has focused entirely on DNS, since AD has to match the DNS domain structure in the network, although the directory services contained by the two services are independent. In cases in which an organization has decided to implement multiple domains, and those multiple domains exist within a contiguous DNS naming scheme, as previously outlined, the network will have formed itself a tree connecting the multiple domains. Because the DNS requirements to host such a domain are very large, most organizations implementing trees host the DNS services for the tree internal to the network only, and maintain a separate DNS substructure for Internet hosting services.

All domains within a tree are linked by two-way transitive trust relationships, although the domains are independent. Domains within a tree, just like domains within a forest, share a trust relationship and a namespace (in the case of a tree, it's a contiguous namespace), but the independence and the integrity of each domain remain unchanged. Administration of each domain, as well as directory replication of each domain, is conducted independently, and all information shared between the domains is done through the trust relationships and the global directory.

When there are multiple trees within a forest, it is possible for each tree to maintain its own independent naming scheme. Looking at the Microsoft example, if you move up the DNS hierarchy, the Microsoft forest may very well include both MSN.com and Microsoft.com. In this case, there is no clear upper layer to the AD domain structure.

The first domain created in the forest is called the *forest root domain*. Two default groups exist within the entire forest, and they exist within the forest root domain:

▼ Enterprise Administrators

▲ Schema Administrators

Additionally, the root domain for each tree automatically establishes a transitive trust relationship with the forest's root domain. This relationship is highlighted in Figure 9-6, which is based on the hypothetical Microsoft AD structure. In this example, a third domain is added, MSNBC.com, to further highlight the transitive trusts that are formed throughout the network. Microsoft.com is the forest root domain in this example.

TIP: Domains cannot be moved between forests and cannot be removed if they contain child domains underneath them. Therefore, it is best to plan the entire AD network from top to bottom, before the first AD is installed. A little time spent planning can save a lot of time improvising.

Shortcut Trusts

The transitive trust relationships that exist between domains in AD forests can be a very tricky subject. Specifically, the overhead and time involved using the transitive trust rela-

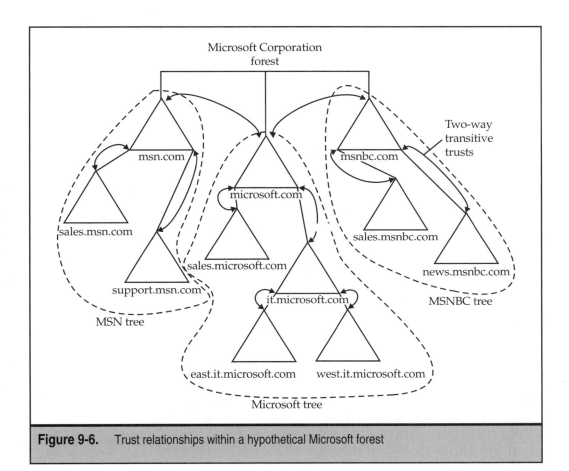

Figure 9-6.   Trust relationships within a hypothetical Microsoft forest

tionships to pass all authentication requests throughout a network can sometimes be tremendous. Looking back to the Microsoft example and Figure 9-6, assume that the users who exist in the Microsoft IT group are always logging in to the News.MSNBC.com domain to fix some problems. This means that all login traffic is first passed up the MSNBC.com tree, and then down the Microsoft.com tree, before being authenticated by the IT domain. In cases like these, a *shortcut domain* can be created to pass the information directly between the two domains in question. Shortcut domains are one-way transitive domains that are used for authentication in large networks with diverse tree structures. A modified version of the domain from Figure 9-6 is shown in Figure 9-7, with the necessary shortcut trusts added.

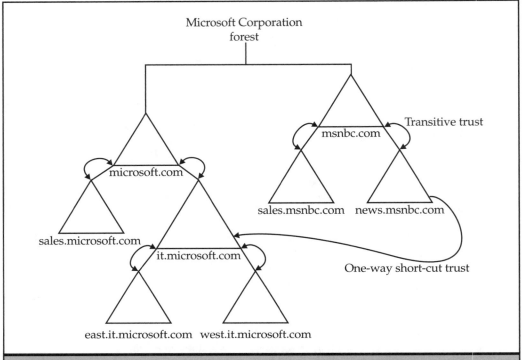

Microsoft Corporation
forest

Transitive trust

msnbc.com

microsoft.com

sales.msnbc.com   news.msnbc.com

sales.microsoft.com

it.microsoft.com

One-way short-cut trust

east.it.microsoft.com   west.it.microsoft.com

Figure 9-7.   A shortcut trust short-circuits trust relationships between domains in a forest

Other OUs

OUs are simply containers in which multiple objects and additional OUs can be stored. Within AD, some of these OUs are predefined and serve specific roles within the network, such as creating domains. Other OUs revolve around the needs and interests of the administrator, and not those of AD. Within AD, administrators have the ability to create their own AD structure below the OUs that are predefined or serve a specific role. These other OUs can be used to group users, printers, or servers together for ease of administration.

There aren't a lot of rules on the creation of OUs within AD, so instead you must rely on general guidelines and practical uses. Initially, recall that users have the ability to search AD for the resources they need to use. This searching function allows users to specify the specific resource or the type of resource they want to locate, so this should be considered the primary means by which most users will operate with AD. Therefore, administrative needs rather than user needs can determine the creation of OUs. Group policies can be set on OUs that allow the administrator to customize the desktop and permissions of the users and resources within that container. Likewise, giving permission to an entire OU allows an administrator to easily delegate to others administrative rights to specific objects within the domain without compromising the security of the overall network.

Sites

Domains are at the root of the directory services in Windows 2000. Everything within AD is simply a collection of one or more domains. Even with the fundamental role of domains defined, many issues still need to be addressed. For example, how is interdomain synchronization handled within small and large domains? How is a large domain split between multiple physical networks? How is intersite replication traffic controlled? For the answers to all of these questions, a new concept needs to be introduced. Windows 2000 domains can be divided into units called *sites*. Sites can be used to regulate replication traffic across slower WAN links and connections, and can use various connection methods and replication schedules to ensure a minimal network bandwidth. In general, sites provide a number of basic services for Windows 2000 networks, including:

▼ Minimizing the bandwidth used for intersite replication

■ Directing clients to domain controllers in the same site, where possible

■ Minimizing replication latency for intrasite replication

▲ Allowing the scheduling of intersite replication

In general, sites are not related to domains, even though they provide a solution to many of the issues faced by domains previously listed. A site maps to the physical layout of the network, such as offices, floors, and buildings, whereas a domain's layout can be affected by everything from the physical structure to the political structure of a network. Organizations should split a domain into multiple sites whenever the network will span a connection that is less than LAN speed (10MB). Because most WAN connections will be routed, a separate IP subnet should exist on both sides of the WAN connection. For this reason, Microsoft has mapped most site discrimination to IP subnets. Officially, a site is a collection of "well-connected" (meaning LAN speed or better) Windows 2000 systems on the same IP subnet. Sites are managed and created using the AD Sites and Services MMC snap-in.

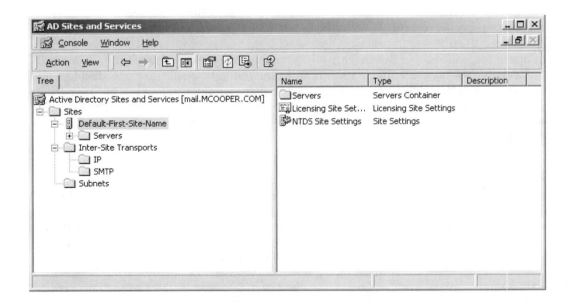

REPLICATION

In AD, *replication* means the copying of directory information among domain controllers so that they all have the same information and any of the domain controllers can be queried with the same results. Within an AD domain, four main categories of information require replication: configuration, schema, domain, and global catalog information. Each of these categories is stored in separate directory partitions. These partitions are what each AD server replicates and are used by different servers throughout the forest depending on their role within the network. The following three partitions are held by all the AD servers in a forest:

▼ **Configuration data partition**   Holds information stored and used by AD-aware applications and is replicated across all domains in the forest.

■ **Schema data partition**   Holds the definitions of the different types of objects, as well as their allowable attributes, and is replicated across all domains in the forest.

▲ **Domain data partition**   Holds information unique to the domain in which the server resides. It contains all the objects in the directory for the domain, and is replicated only within the domain. The data in this partition is not replicated between domains, and will differ greatly from domain to domain.

The fourth type of partition is used by global catalog servers to allow directory information to be shared between domains:

▼   **Global domain data partition**   Holds information about all the objects in the global catalog, but includes details on only a few of the objects' attributes, to allow quick searches for and access to resources in external domains, and to reduce the bandwidth used in replications. This information is replicated to all the other global catalog servers within the network. When a client in a foreign domain actually needs access to the resources or the nonreplicated attributes of a resource, the client is directed to that resource's native domain.

Internal Site Replication

There will always be at least one site within every AD implementation. When the first Windows 2000 domain controller is installed, it creates a site called the Default-First-Site-Name. The new domain controller then adds itself to that site. Whenever new domain controllers are added to the network, they are automatically added to this new site first, and can be moved at a later time. There is, however, an exception to this statement. When a new site is created, one or more IP subnets are assigned to that site. After there are two or more sites, all new domain controllers added to the forest will have their IP addresses checked and will be added to the site with a matching IP address.

Directory information within a site is replicated automatically to ensure all domain controllers within the site have the same information. Additionally, all intersite replication occurs in an uncompressed format, which consumes more network traffic but less system resources. For these reasons, a site should always be a LAN network of high-speed connections (10MB or higher). When multiple domains exist within a single site, replication occurs only between domain controllers for their respective domain. However, replication traffic between each global catalog server occurs across the site on an as-needed/uncompressed basis, as well. Figure 9-8 shows the single-site replication traffic between two domains.

Site-to-Site Replication

When deciding to split a network into multiple sites, a number of new issues arise. These issues, and the configuration needed to make multiple sites work, are the subject of the remainder of this section.

Two main rules should be adhered to whenever planning a multisite design, to minimize the potential problems:

▼   Sites always should be split by geographic regions. When two or more LANs are connected by WAN links, each LAN should represent its own site.

▲   Whenever possible, each site should have its own AD and global catalog server. In some smaller networks, this server may be the only server in the site, in which case it should also serve as the DNS and DHCP server. This will increase fault tolerance as well as client performance, while decreasing WAN bandwidth utilization.

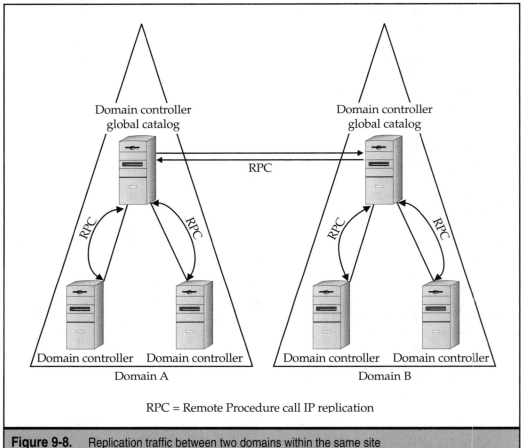

RPC = Remote Procedure call IP replication

Figure 9-8.   Replication traffic between two domains within the same site

Site Connectivity

Sites are connected using *site links,* which are domain controllers configured to serve as a connection to a particular site. Site links have to be manually configured using the AD Sites and Services MMC plug-in. When creating a site link, the administrator has a number of configuration options.

The first of these configuration options is the replication schedule. An administrator can determine when replication should occur across a particular site link. When setting the replication schedule, an administrator will set the replication cost, replication availability, and replication frequency associated with the site link. When the site link is created and configured, AD automatically creates a connection object, which will use the information provided by the site link to actually transfer the information between the domains.

By default and design, all site links are transitive, which allows sites to be used in the same manner transitive trusts are used. This means that a site can replicate its changes to another site, via a site connector to a third site, as long as the third site has a valid connection to both sites. In some organizations in which multiple field offices all connect to central corporate offices, this kind of replication allows for the greatest efficiency. All sites replicate their information to the central office site, which in turn replicates the information back out to the other field offices.

Protocols

There are two protocol options within any network for connecting sites together. Both options, though, are protocols within the TCP/IP protocol stack. There is no way to connect two sites using anything other than IP.

▼ **RPC (IP replication)**   RPC (remote procedure calls) is an IP-based, connection-oriented protocol that is at the base of legacy Exchange installations. RPC is fast and reliable when used on connection-friendly networks (networks that allow packets to travel the same path and arrive in sequence at the destination). However, RPC is less than reliable in large mesh networks, such as the Internet. RPC communication is still the default replication method for servers within the same site as well as intrasite communication for other Microsoft services such as Exchange 5.*x*.

▲ **SMTP**   A new feature in Windows 2000 and Exchange 2000 is the ability to connect sites using SMTP connectors. SMTP is just beginning to be used and cannot be used for replication between servers in the same site (although it will be the default for Exchange 2000). SMTP is not capable of replicating the domain partition, and therefore is suitable only for linking two sites that are also separate domains. SMTP can pass the schema, configuration, and global catalog partitions very efficiently. The use of SMTP connection methods should increase as the Windows 2000 technology matures.

NOTE: SMTP is, by nature, very insecure. All SMTP messages are sent in formats that can be easily interpreted by the most basic of sniffing tools. For this reason, using the SMTP protocol to connect two sites requires that an enterprise certification authority be installed and configured on the network. This allows for all SMTP traffic generated by AD to be encrypted using at least 56-bit encryption.

Collision Detecting and Resolution

What happens when the same object is modified from two different spots in the network at the same time, or two objects with the same name are created at the same time within the network? Even in the most basic networks, if two domain controllers exist, the two directories that exist on each domain controller will not be exactly the same at all times, because replication takes time. Legacy versions of NT dealt with this issue by allowing only one read-write copy of the directory to exist on the network at any one time. This meant that all changes could be made only by one server, and those changes were then propagated to the read-only copies of the directories that the remaining domain controllers maintained.

When a change to an object occurs before a previous change to that object has been completely replicated, a replication *collision* occurs. AD can track the version of objects by looking at each object's version number. When an object is changed, its version number is increased, so that when a server receives an update, it can compare the version number of the incoming object with the version number of the existing object. When the existing object's version number is less than the version number coming in, the replication continues and all is considered well. A collision occurs when the version number of the existing item is equal to or greater than the version number of the incoming item. In this case, AD compares the timestamp of the incoming object to the timestamp of the existing object to determine which one it's going to keep. This is the only instance in which time is used in replication. If the timestamps don't settle the issue, the item with the highest GUID is kept. In situations in which the incoming version number is actually lower than the existing version number, the replication object is considered to be stale and is discarded.

ACTIVE DIRECTORY SUMMARY

One of most important new features of Windows 2000 is the Active Directory service. AD is really just a simple directory service based on the X.500 directory scheme that contains a variety of predefined and preconfigured objects and OUs. A large part of any Windows 2000 administrator's job will be the administration and configuration of the special objects and OUs within the AD forest. Additionally, the namespace of AD has to match that of a DNS domain, and in cases in which the AD domain and the Internet DNS domain for the company don't match, separate DNS domains have to be maintained, because AD requires DNS to allow for client connectivity.

If used correctly, AD can add tremendous value and reliability to a network, as well as decrease the administrative overhead involved in the network's daily maintenance. However, if configured incorrectly or ill-planned, AD can drastically increase the administrator's workload, and decrease the network customer's satisfaction. When dealing with AD, a little bit of forethought and planning can save a huge amount of work and heartache.

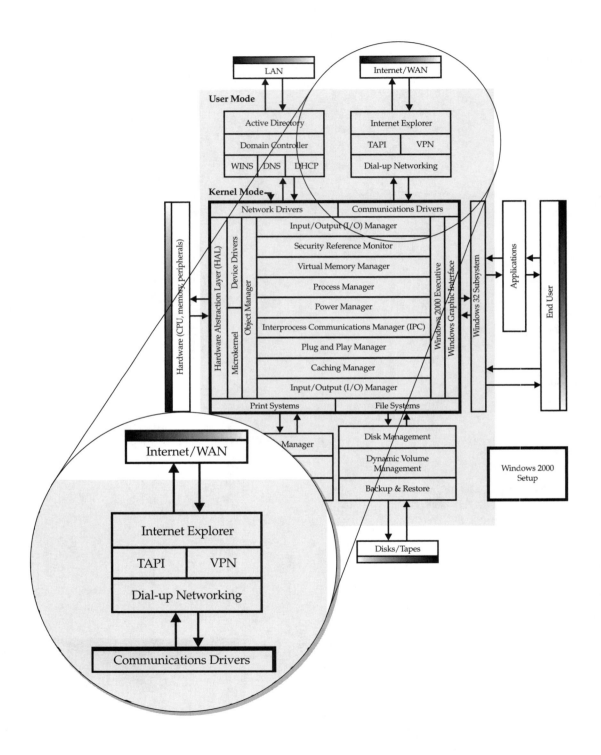

PART IV

Communications and the Internet

Networking today definitely extends beyond the local area network (LAN) to include the Internet itself, as well as using the Internet and other forms of communication to access your LAN or other computers. This part of the book covers the ways that you and your organization can reach out from your LAN to connect to others, or allow others to connect to you. This chapter provides an overview of communications and how to set up the various Windows 2000 communications features. It then discusses establishing a dial-up connection and using it with the Remote Access Service (RAS). This chapter concludes by explaining how to set up and use an Internet connection with Internet Explorer and Outlook Express for accessing the Web and exchanging e-mail, respectively. Chapter 11 looks at Internet Information Services (IIS), how it's set up, and how it's managed.

CHAPTER 10

Communications and Internet Services

Networking in the previous part of this book referred to using a LAN. In this age of the Internet, Windows 2000 networking has taken on a much broader meaning that includes all the types of connections that you make outside of your LAN using what was classically called "communications." Windows 2000 offers a single dialog box, Network and Dial-up Connections, from which you can set up both LAN and external connections.

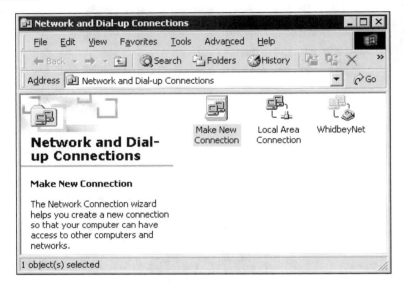

Communication may include a modem or other device to connect a single computer to a method of transmission, or it may use a router or other device to connect a network to the method of transmission. Communications can be over copper wires, fiber-optic cable, microwave, ground wireless, or satellite transmission.

Windows 2000 includes a number of programs that control or utilize communications, among which are Internet Explorer for web browsing; Outlook Express, for e-mail; HyperTerminal, for computer-to-computer communications; NetMeeting, for multimedia communications; Phone Dialer; and both the Internet Connection Wizard and the Network and Dial-up Connections dialog box to establish connections. In addition, Windows 2000 includes programs to set up and manage RAS networking over communications lines. HyperTerminal, NetMeeting, and Phone Dialer are discussed in Chapter 16. The remaining programs are discussed here.

Communications can be broken into three areas:

▼ Direct connections between computers other than a LAN

■ Telephony connections between computers other than the Internet

▲ Connections to and through the Internet

DIRECT CONNECTION BETWEEN COMPUTERS

If you want to transfer information between two computers, at least one of which is not connected your LAN, you can do so by using a direct connection between the computers. Such a connection can connect to a network if the other computer is connected to it, and it can be used to connect a handheld Windows CE computer. Two computers can be directly connected in either of two ways:

▼ A special parallel or serial cable

▲ An infrared port

Using a Parallel or Serial Cable

The most common way to directly connect two computers, other than through a LAN, is by using either a special serial cable, called a *null modem cable,* or a special parallel cable, both of which are made just for PC-to-PC file transfer. These cables are sometimes called *LapLink* cables, after an early program of that name that was used to transfer information between laptop and desktop computers. The cables have the same connectors on both ends (DB9 female connectors on the serial cable, and DB25 male connectors on the parallel cable), but the wires are crossed in the cable so that the wire connected to the transmit pin on one end is connected to the receive pin on the other end.

TIP: Often, the nine-pin serial port on a computer is used by a mouse, and the parallel port is used by a printer. The mouse normally is more important than the printer when using Windows, and parallel ports are faster than the serial ports, because you are sending 8 bits at a time instead of 1 bit. Therefore, if you have a choice, the parallel cable is a better one.

To set up a direct connection between two computers, you need to do the following:

▼ Purchase and install a parallel or serial PC-to-PC direct connect cable

■ Set up a computer to be the host in a direct connection

▲ Set up another computer to be the guest in a direct connection

Purchasing and Installing a Cable

You can purchase a direct connect serial or parallel cable at most computer stores (including catalogs and Internet sites). Be sure you order a PC-to-PC file transfer cable, also called a *direct cable connection* cable, a LapLink cable, or a *null modem* cable. Both ends should be the same, and the wires need to be "crossed over," not "straight through." Belkin, a brand of cables carried by many stores, has a serial PC-to-PC file transfer cable, part number F3B207, and a similar parallel cable, part number F3D508. Several catalogs and web sites have these cables, namely PCZone (http://www.zones.com), MicroWarehouse (http://www.warehouse.com), CDW (http://www.cdw.com), and PCConnection (http://www.pcconnection.com).

NOTE: Parallel and serial extension and switchbox cables will not work for PC-to-PC file transfer, because the wires are straight through and often the ends are a different gender.

To install the cables, simply locate the parallel or serial connectors on the back of the computers that are opposite in gender to the cables (the parallel connection on the computer would be a 25-pin female connector and the serial connection would be a 9-pin male connector). Insert the cables and screw them down tightly.

Setting Up the Host Computer

To set up the host computer, which can be running either Windows 2000 Server or Windows 2000 Professional, you should be signed on as the Administrator or a member of the Administrators group and then use the following steps:

NOTE: If the host computer to which you want a direct connection is a domain controller, you must follow a different procedure. See the next section, "Using a Domain Controller to Host a Direct Connection."

1. Open the Start menu, choose Settings | Network and Dial-up Connections, and then double-click Make New Connection. The Network Connection Wizard will open.

2. Click Next. In the Network Connection Type dialog box, select Connect Directly to Another Computer, as shown in Figure 10-1, and then click Next.

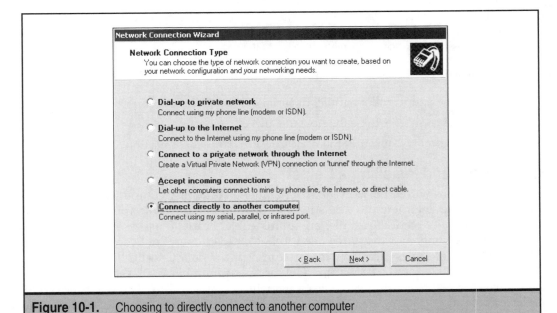

Figure 10-1. Choosing to directly connect to another computer

3. Choose the role of Host, and click Next. The Connection Device dialog box opens, enabling you to choose from the parallel (Direct Parallel), serial (Communications Port), and infrared ports that the computer has available.

4. Choose the connection device that you want to use. If that device is a serial port and has not been used for this purpose in the past, you will be told that the port is not enabled for a direct connection and that the Network Connection Wizard will do that for you. Then, after the connection is established, you can right-click the connection icon in the Network and Dial-up Connection dialog box and set the properties, such as speed, for this port.

5. Click Next. Select the users that you want to be allowed to use this connection. If you are the administrator, this should include you. If you want others to be able to use the port, then select Guest. If you want to add a new user, click Add, enter the username, full name, and password, confirm the password, and then click OK.

6. Select Administrator and click Properties. In the user's Properties dialog box's General tab, you can add or change the same information that you could add for a new user. The Callback tab is not meaningful for a direct cable connection and will be discussed later in this chapter.

7. Change any other user properties that need to be changed, and then click Next. You will be told that the name of the connection you are creating is Incoming Connections. Accept that and click Finish. A new icon will appear in your Network and Dial-up Connections window.

Incoming
Connections

NOTE: You can create several direct connections for different ports and computers by copying the first direct connection, renaming the copy, and changing the settings.

Using a Domain Controller to Host a Direct Connection

If you are setting up a direct connection host site on a domain controller, you must use Routing and Remote Access to be the incoming host. Do that by turning to the "Setting Up Remote Access Service" section later in this chapter. Once you have set up the RAS server, you need to perform an extra step of enabling incoming connections:

1. Open the Start menu and choose Programs | Administrative Tools | Routing and Remote Access. The Routing and Remote Access console will appear.

2. Open the local server, right-click Ports, and choose Properties. In the Ports Properties dialog box, select Direct Parallel and click Configure.

3. Select Remote Access Connection (Inbound Only), and click OK. When you are done, the top portion of your Ports Properties dialog box should look similar to this:

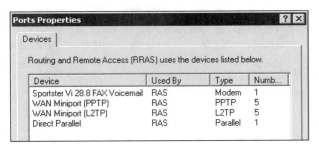

4. Click Apply and then OK to close the dialog box. The Direct Parallel port should appear in the list of ports on the right of the Routing and Remote Access console.

Setting Up the Guest Computer

The guest computer can be either a server or a workstation, but it is most likely a workstation. You do not have to be signed on as an administrator, but if you want to use a serial port that is not currently configured for a direct connection (a null modem), you need an administrator to do that. Here are the steps for setting up a guest computer in a direct cable connection:

1. Open the Start menu, choose Settings | Network and Dial-up Connections, and then double-click Make New Connection. The Network Connection Wizard will open.

2. Click Next. In the Network Connection Type dialog box, select Connect Directly to Another Computer and then click Next.

3. Choose the role of Guest, and click Next. The Select a Device dialog box opens, enabling you to choose the type of connection.

4. Choose your connection device and click Next. Choose whether you want this connection only for yourself or for all users, and then click Next. You will be told that the name of the connection you are creating is Direct Connection. Accept that and click Finish. A new icon will appear in your Network and Dial-up Connections window.

Direct
Connection

Transferring Information over a Direct Connection

Once you have set up a direct cable connection, you can use it with these steps:

1. Open the Start menu, choose Settings | Network and Dial-up Connections, and double-click the Direct Connection icon. The Connect Direct Connection dialog box will open.

2. Enter the appropriate username and password and click Connect. You will see messages stating that the connection is being made, that the username and password are being checked, that the computer is being registered on the network, and then that the connection is complete. Click OK. The connection icon will appear on the right of the taskbar.

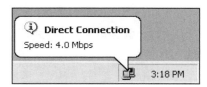

3. Utilize the connection by opening Windows Explorer, My Network Places | Entire Network | Microsoft Windows Network, and finally the domains or workgroups, computers, and shares that you want to access.

4. Transfer information across the direct cable connection in the same way as you transfer any information in Windows Explorer, by locating the destination folder in the left pane, selecting the files or folders to be transferred in the right pane, and then dragging the information from the right pane to the folder in the left pane, as you can see in Figure 10-2.

5. When you are done using the direct cable connection, you can terminate it by double-clicking the connection icon in the taskbar or the Direct Connection icon in the Network and Dial-up Connections window, and then clicking Disconnect in the dialog box that opens.

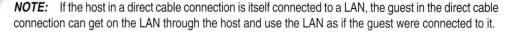

NOTE: If the host in a direct cable connection is itself connected to a LAN, the guest in the direct cable connection can get on the LAN through the host and use the LAN as if the guest were connected to it.

While a direct cable connection is operational, the host can look at the status of the connection, see who is connected to it, see how much information has been transferred, and disconnect them if desired. This is done in two slightly different ways, depending on whether or not the host is using the RAS server.

Host Status on a RAS Server   If RAS is being used to provide incoming services for a direct cable connection, status and control of the connection can be obtained with these steps:

1. Open the Start menu and choose Programs | Administrative Tools | Routing and Remote Access.

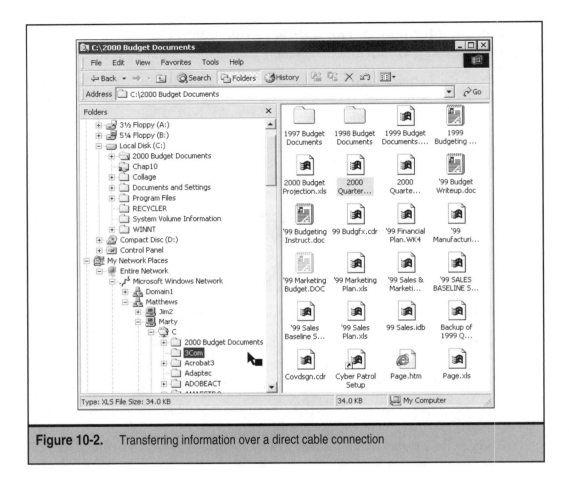

Figure 10-2.   Transferring information over a direct cable connection

2. Open the local server and select Ports. The right pane should show a list of ports, including a direct connection, either parallel or serial.

3. Right-click the direct connection port and choose Status. The Port Status dialog box will open, as shown in Figure 10-3.

4. If you wish to disconnect the guest, click Disconnect; in any case, when you are done, click Close and then close the Routing and Remote Access console.

Host Status on Incoming Connections   If Network and Dial-up Connections is being used to provide an incoming connection, status and control of the connection can be obtained with these steps:

1. Open the Start menu and choose Settings | Network and Dial-up Connections. You will see that the Incoming Connections icon is shown as active and has been retitled with either the name of the user or Unauthenticated User.

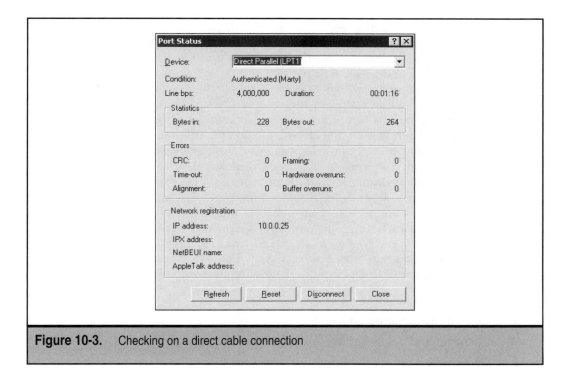

Figure 10-3. Checking on a direct cable connection

2. Right-click the connection icon and choose Status. The connection's Status dialog box will open.

3. If you wish to disconnect the guest, click Disconnect; in any case, when you are done, click Close and then close the Network and Dial-up Connections window.

Using an Infrared Port

If you have two infrared ports, such as one on your laptop and one on your desktop, you may create a direct connection between the computers by following the preceding steps for a parallel or serial cable, but instead selecting the infrared port in place of a parallel or serial port.

TELEPHONY CONNECTIONS

Using telephony (telephone lines, their switches, and their terminations) to connect computers has been done for some time. The most common approach is to use a *modem* (short for "modulator-demodulator") to convert a digital signal (patterns of ones and zeros) in a computer to an analog signal (current fluctuations) in a phone line and then use a second modem on the other end to convert the analog signal back to digital for use in the connecting computer. Modems can be inside a computer (called an "internal" modem), in which case the phone line connects to the computer, or external, whereby the phone line plugs in to the modem and the modem plugs in to a serial port in the computer. The fastest modems today receive data at up to 56 Kbps (thousand bits per second) and send data at up to 33.6 Kbps.

In recent years, telephone companies have started to offer several forms of digital signals over phone lines, so that a modem isn't necessary—all you need is a connection between the digital line and the computer. Two common forms of digital telephone service are ISDN (Integrated Services Digital Network) and DSL (digital subscriber line). ISDN was the first digital service and is both expensive and relatively slow (a maximum speed of up to 128 Kbps) when compared to DSL. There are several forms of DSL, the most common of which is ADSL (asymmetric digital subscriber line), over which data is received at up to 1.5 Mbps and sent at up to 512 Kbps. Most often, an ISDN or DSL line is terminated in a router that directly connects to your network and not to a computer. Later in this chapter, though, you'll see how a computer with Windows 2000 Server can act as a router for lines terminated in it through an ISDN or DSL adapter.

Communications is a very broad subject, on which entire books have been written. Thus, this chapter narrows the focus to the following four subjects:

▼   Installing a modem

■   Establishing a dial-up connection

■   Setting up and using Remote Access Service

▲   Setting up and using the Windows 2000 router

Installing a Modem

There are several ways to install modem support within Windows 2000. The first time you attempt to connect to the Internet, support for a modem will be installed for you. If you set up a dial-up connection and you don't have modem support installed, it will be installed for you. Here, though, we'll look at installing a modem by itself. Later, we'll also look at installing it with a dial-up connection, and then with an Internet connection.

To install a modem, of course, you must have one plugged in or attached to your computer. There are two type of modems, internal and external. An *internal* modem is a card that plugs in to an expansion slot on the main or "mother" board inside your computer. An *external* modem is a small box that plugs in to a serial or communications (COM) port on the outside of your computer. Also, both external and internal modems may have switches or jumpers that need to be set, or they may be *Plug and Play*, which means that they do not have switches or jumpers—software sets them up. Whichever kind of modem you have, the instructions that came with it tell you whether it is internal or external, how to plug it in, and how to set it up.

With a modem physically attached to your computer (and, if external, turned on), use the following instructions to install it in Windows 2000:

1. Open the Start menu, choose Settings | Control Panel, and double-click Phone and Modem Options. The Phone and Modem Options dialog box will open.

2. Open the Modems tab. If it shows Unknown Modem, select that and click Remove. If it shows a likely modem, such as U.S. Robotics 56K FAX INT, you already have a modem installed and you can skip to the next section.

3. Click Add. You are told that Windows will try to detect your modem, and are reminded to turn on the modem and to quit any programs that may be using it. Click Next. A list of possible modems is shown to you. If only the correct modem is displayed, skip the next step. If several modems are shown and one is correct and the rest are not, uncheck the incorrect ones and skip the next step. If an incorrect modem or Unknown Modem is shown, select it and click Change.

4. Select the correct manufacturer from the list on the left and the correct model from the list on the right and click OK. If your modem is not on the list, but you have a disk, click Have Disk, insert the disk, select the drive, click OK, select the manufacturer and model, and click OK.

5. Click Next. Windows starts to install your modem. If you are using an older modem, you may be told that the driver does not have a digital signature. If so, click Yes to continue. Finally, you are told that your modem has been installed successfully. Click Finish.

6. Back in the Phone and Modem Options dialog box, select your newly installed modem, and click Properties. In the Properties dialog box, click the Diagnostics tab, and then click Query Modem. You will be told that the query process will take a few minutes. If your modem is properly installed, you'll see a set of commands and responses, as shown in Figure 10-4. Not all of the responses have to be positive. The point is that Windows 2000 is talking to the modem. If you do not get the set of commands and responses, you will probably get some sort of error message, such as Modem Not Found, which has three possible causes: the modem is not operating correctly, the wrong driver is installed, or the wrong COM port is being used. You generally can tell whether the COM port is correct by looking at what Windows detected. It may not detect the type of modem correctly, but it generally detects the port that has a modem attached to it. To find the correct manufacturer and model for the driver, you may need to look at the actual modem by physically opening the computer. To get a driver that is not in the Windows 2000 driver database, use another computer to connect to the Internet, browse the modem manufacturer's web site, and download the correct driver. Put that driver on a floppy disk and take it to the computer you are installing. If you are certain that both the port and driver are correct, then the modem may be malfunctioning.

7. Click OK to close the Properties dialog box, and then click OK to close the Phone and Modem Options dialog box.

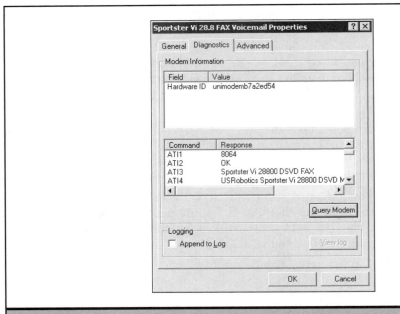

Figure 10-4. Commands/responses showing communication with a modem

Establishing a Dial-up Connection

Establishing a dial-up connection identifies a particular destination to which you want to dial—a phone number that is dialed and a connection that is made to your modem. The following steps, which assume that a modem has already been set up (as done in the previous section), show how to establish a dial-up connection:

1. Open the Start menu, choose Settings | Network and Dial-up Connections, and double-click Make New Connection. The Network Connection Wizard will open. Click Next.

2. Select Dial-up to Private Network and click Next. Enter the phone number that will be the destination of the connection. If you want to use area/city/country codes, click Use Dialing Rules. Click Next when the phone number has been entered.

3. Choose whether you want all users or only yourself to have access to the new connection, and then click Next. Enter the Name for the new connection and

NETWORK DESIGNS

Network Designs provides simplified schematic diagrams of how small-to-medium–sized networks might be wired. This is not the only way the wiring could be accomplished, just a typical way.

Small Office 10/100BaseT Network

In a small office, you begin by joining several workstations with a hub, and you can join several hubs with another hub. As the network grows, you will want to join the hubs with a switch, as explained on the subsequent blueprint, "Joining Networks and Network Segments."

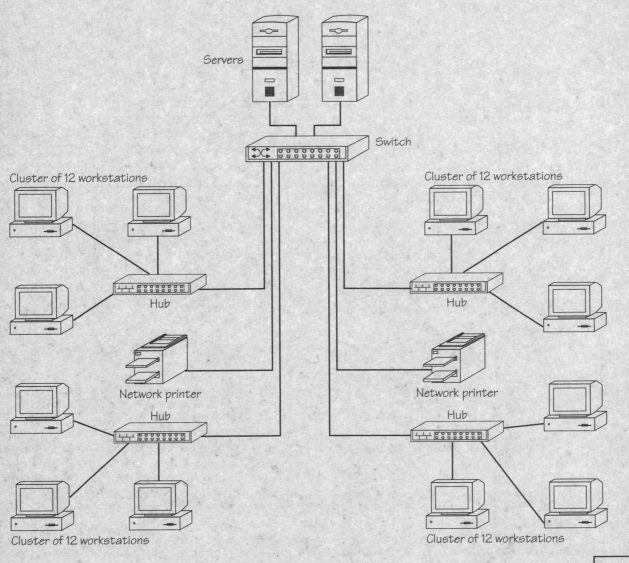

Servers

Switch

Cluster of 12 workstations

Hub

Network printer

Hub

Cluster of 12 workstations

Cluster of 12 workstations

Hub

Network printer

Hub

Cluster of 12 workstations

Centralized Network

Centralization provides for central control of the servers, their content, and their use. It also provides better load sharing and backup if one should fail. Finally, a server is available for the Web.

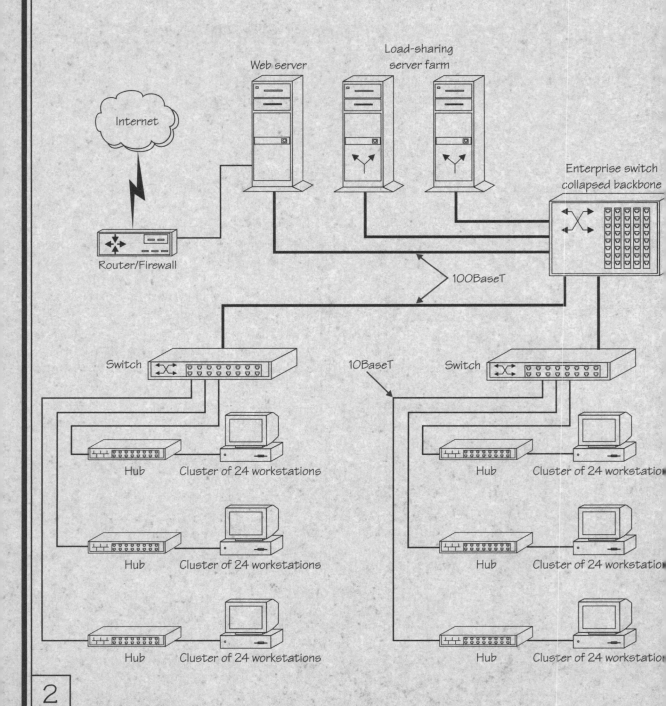

Internet

Router/Firewall

Web server

Load-sharing server farm

Enterprise switch collapsed backbone

100BaseT

Switch

10BaseT

Switch

Hub   Cluster of 24 workstations

Hub   Cluster of 24 workstations

Hub   Cluster of 24 workstations

Hub   Cluster of 24 workstations

Hub   Cluster of 24 workstations

Hub   Cluster of 24 workstations

Distributing the network provides local workgroup control of the server and possibly more immediate response to local problems. There may also be less network congestion.

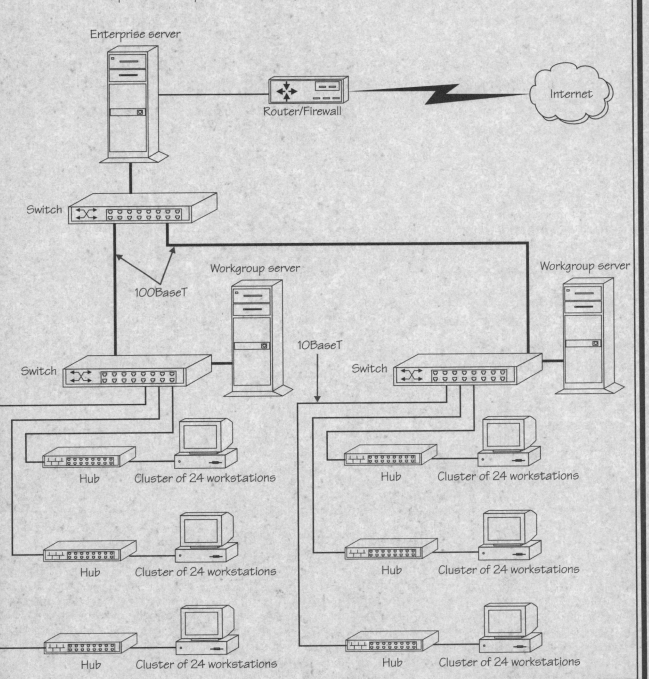

Enterprise server

Router/Firewall

Internet

Switch

100BaseT

Workgroup server

Workgroup server

10BaseT

Switch

Switch

Hub   Cluster of 24 workstations

Hub   Cluster of 24 workstations

Hub   Cluster of 24 workstations

Hub   Cluster of 24 workstations

Hub   Cluster of 24 workstations

Hub   Cluster of 24 workstations

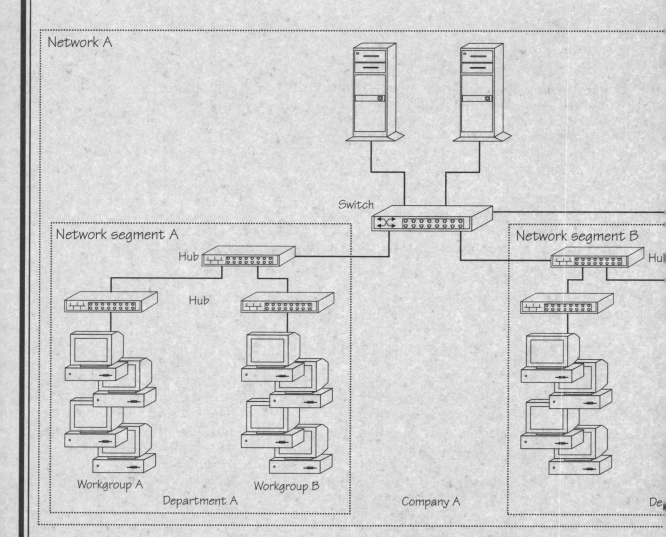

Network A

Switch

Network segment A

Hub

Hub

Workgroup A

Workgroup B

Department A

Company A

Network segment B

Hub

De

Party Line

Workgroups A and B are joined by a hub. Hubs operate at the Physical, or first, layer using only the hardware addresses. As a result, all packets within these workgroups, which form a network segment, are seen by every device it contains. The traffic on any link in the segment is the sum of all traffic in the segment.

Switched Independence

Departments A and B are joined by a switch. Switches operate at the Data link, or second, layer using the host portion of the IP addresses. As a result, packets whose from and to address are in the same department or network segment stay in that segment and are not seen by the other segments. Both segments, though, must be in the same network.

4

Joining Networks and Network Segments

There are a number of different devices that can be used to join networks and network segments. The circumstances under which you would use three common devices are described here. The major criterion is the degree of isolation you want.

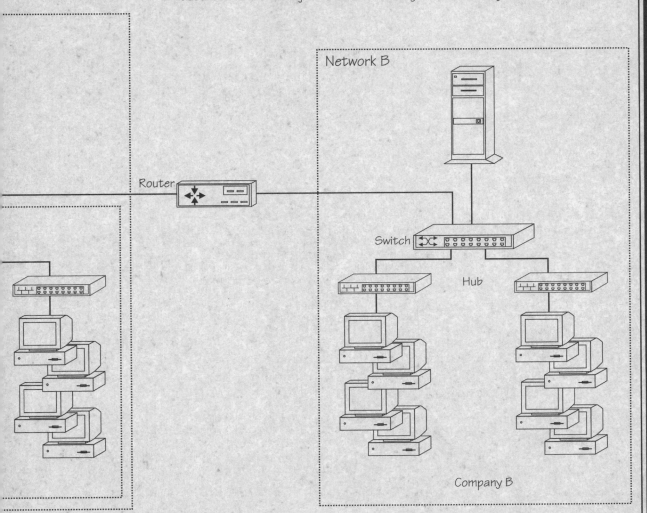

Isolation

Companies A and B are joined by a router. Routers operate at the Network, or third, layer using full IP addresses. As a result, the companies are considered separate networks and only packets with the full IP address (both network and host portions) are exchanged between the networks.

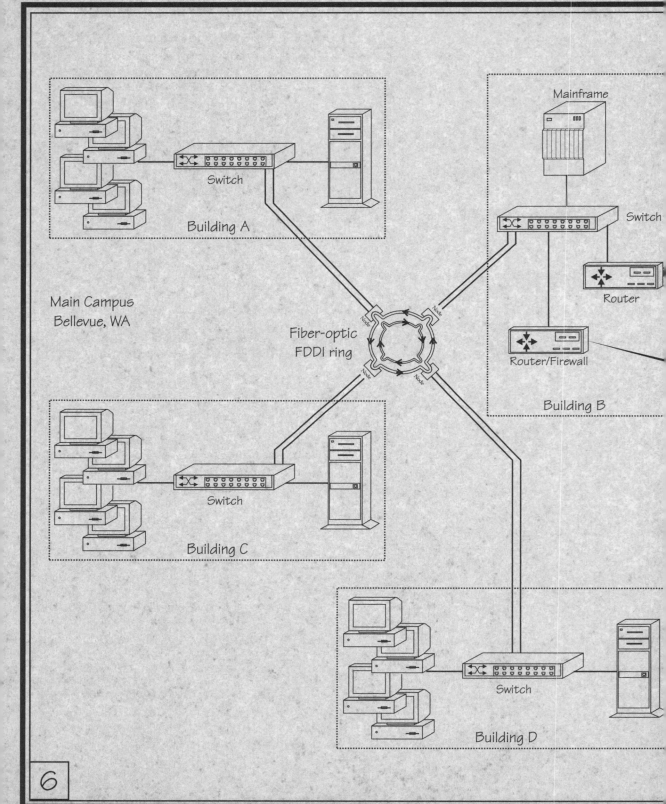

Main Campus
Bellevue, WA

Building A

Switch

Fiber-optic
FDDI ring

Node

Building C

Switch

Mainframe

Switch

Router

Router/Firewall

Building B

Switch

Building D

6

Extending a network beyond a moderate building, be it across a campus or across the country, becomes more complex and generally requires professional assistance. Some of the techniques used, though, are shown here.

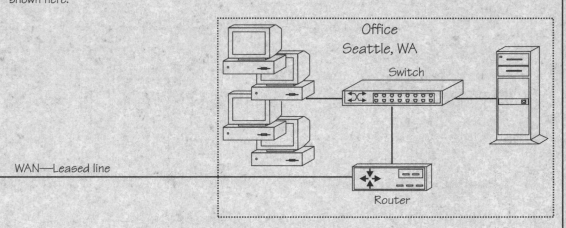

Office
Seattle, WA

Switch

Router

WAN—Leased line

WAN—VPN (Virtual Private Network)
over the Internet

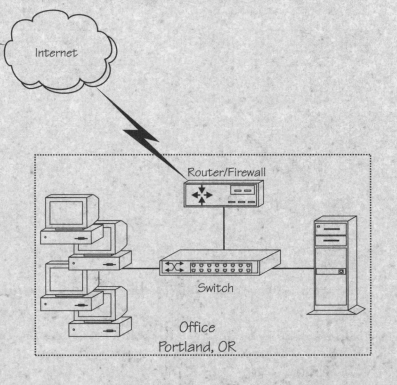

Internet

Router/Firewall

Switch

Office
Portland, OR

TIA/EIA Standard Areas and Wiring Types

The Telecommunications Industry Association/Electronic Industries Association (TIA/EIA) has developed a standard set of terminology used to describe network wiring and the building areas that contain it, as shown here.

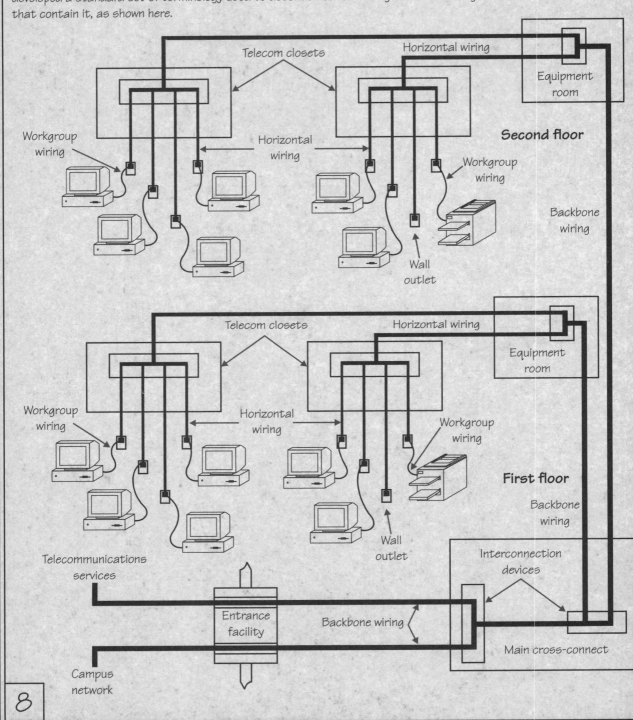

specify whether you want a shortcut on the desktop. Click Finish when you are done. An icon will appear in the Network and Dial-up Connections window.

MatTech

NOTE: If you set up this connection on a domain controller, you get an additional dialog box after the Connection Availability dialog box (users) and before the final one, called Internet Connection Sharing, that asks whether you want to enable Internet connection sharing for this connection. This allows other computers on a network to share a connection to an ISP. In that case, click Yes, select Enable On-Demand Dialing, and click Next.

4. To dial the connection, double-click its icon. You should hear the modem dialing, the ring at the other end, and the answering tone.

A dial-up connection can be used with RAS, discussed next.

Setting Up Remote Access Service

RAS provides access to a LAN from a dial-up line, a leased line, or a direct connection. RAS acts as a host or server to a dial-up or direct connection guest or client. RAS commonly is used by travelers whose laptops have a dial-up connection that can be used from a remote location to connect through RAS to the home office LAN. The next set of steps shows how RAS is set up and then used:

1. Open the Start menu and choose Programs | Administrative Tools | Routing and Remote Access. The Routing and Remote Access console will open.

2. Select the local server (the computer you are working on), open the Action menu, and choose Configure and Enable Routing and Remote Access. The Routing and Remote Access Server Setup Wizard will open. Click Next.

3. Select Remote Access Server, as shown in Figure 10-5, and click Next. The Remote Client Protocols list will be shown with the default of TCP/IP, which is the recommended protocol for Internet, direct connect, and direct dial-up connections. If that is sufficient, leave Yes selected. If you want another protocol, such as IPX for NetWare, choose No. In any case, click Next.

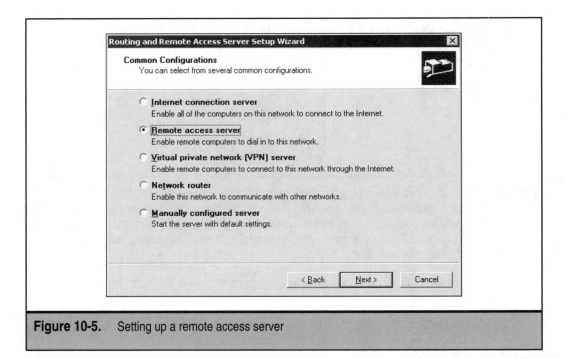

Figure 10-5.   Setting up a remote access server

4. If you have chosen No, you are shown a list of protocols from which you can choose. Make your choices and then click OK to return to the Routing and Remote Access Server Setup Wizard.

5. Determine how you want to assign IP addresses, with Automatically being the default and general preference, and click Next.

6. Choose whether to use Remote Authentication Dial-In User Service (RADIUS) authentication for several RASs. It provides another level of authentication that you may or may not need. Click Next.

7. Choose whether you want to see the Help pages on managing a remote access server, and then click Finish.

NOTE: If you are setting up RAS on a server in Active Directory that is not the primary domain controller and you are not a domain administrator, a domain administrator must add the server on which you are working to both the RAS and IAS Servers group in the Computers folder of the Active Directory Users and Computers console and to the list of servers in Routing and Remote Access on the primary domain controller. To support the relaying of DHCP messages from remote access clients, the domain administrator must configure the properties of the DHCP Relay Agent with the IP address of your DHCP server.

Using Remote Access Service

With a dial-up connection set up on the guest or client computer (for this example, a laptop in a remote city) and a remote access server set up and enabled on the host computer (for this example, a server in the home office), you can use RAS with these steps:

1. Log on to the dial-up client (laptop) with a username and password that can be authenticated by the RAS. Then, on the client, open the Start menu, choose Settings | Network and Dial-up Connections, and double-click the dial-up connection icon. The Connect dialog box opens.

2. Enter the appropriate username and password and click Dial. You will see messages stating that the number you entered is being dialed, that the username and password are being checked, that the computer is being registered on the network, and then that the connection is complete. Click OK. The connection icon will appear on the right of the taskbar.

3. Utilize the connection by opening Windows Explorer, My Network Places | Entire Network | Microsoft Windows Network, and finally the domains or workgroups, computers, and shares that you want to access.

4. Transfer information across the dial-up connection in the same way as you transfer any information in Windows Explorer, by locating the destination folder in the left pane, selecting the files or folders to be transferred in the right pane, and then dragging the information from the right pane to the folder in the left pane, as shown previously for a direct cable connection.

5. When you are done using the RAS connection, you can terminate it by double-clicking the connection icon in the taskbar or the dial-up connection icon in the Network and Dial-up Connections window, and then clicking Disconnect in the dialog box that opens.

While a dial-up connection is operational, you can see the connection in the Routing and Remote Access window and see who it is by opening the server and clicking Remote Access Clients in the left pane, as shown in Figure 10-6. If you right-click the user in the right pane and choose Status, you can see how much information has been transferred, and disconnect the user, if desired.

Setting Up the Windows 2000 Router

Routers are network devices that are used to join two separate, independent networks, such as a LAN and the Internet. Routers operate at the Network (third) layer of the OSI (Open Systems Interconnection) networking model and therefore use the full IP address, consisting of both network and host components (see Chapter 6 sections "The OSI Model" and "Routers," and page 5 in the Blueprints section of this book). A router looks at all the traffic on both networks, but transfers only those packets that are specifically addressed to the other network. Routers also provide a network address translation (NAT)

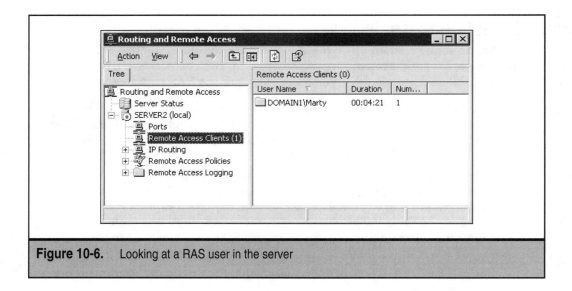

Figure 10-6. Looking at a RAS user in the server

function. NAT allows your LAN to use a set of non-Internet-usable IP addresses, such as 10.0.0.9, but when the LAN users access the Internet, they are assigned an Internet-usable IP address, with the router translating between the two. Finally a router can be used to connect two networks that use two different protocols, such as TCP/IP (Transmission Control Protocol/Internet Protocol) and IPX (Internetwork Packet Exchange).

Normally, a router is a stand-alone electronic device (or "box") separate from a computer, to which two networks are connected. One of the network connections may be a phone connection (DSL, ISDN, or T1 line) and the other may be a standard 10/100BaseT Ethernet connection, or both may be Ethernet connections, or some other combination. Windows 2000 Server can provide some of a router's capabilities, the most important of which are the functions of connecting a LAN to the Internet or WAN (wide area network), NAT, and connecting two networks with dissimilar protocols. To function, the Windows 2000 Server must be connected to both networks, for example the Internet and the LAN. The LAN connection is just the standard network interface card (NIC), while the Internet or WAN connection is some sort of telephone line termination in or directly connected to the computer, such as a modem, an ISDN adapter, or a DSL termination.

If you want to set up a server connection to the Internet that can be used by the entire network, then the server that you want to be the router must have both LAN and communications connections. Also, you must be an administrator or have Administrator privileges. You can then set up this router function through the Routing and Remote Access console and the following steps:

1. Open the Start menu and choose Programs | Administrative Tools | Routing and Remote Access. The Routing and Remote Access console will open.

2. Select the local server (the computer you are working on), open the Action menu, and choose Configure and Enable Routing and Remote Access. The Routing and Remote Access Server Setup Wizard will open. Click Next.

NOTE: If you have RAS running that was set up earlier in this chapter, you must disable it to install the Internet Connection Server. To do that, in the Routing and Remote Access Window, select the local server, open the Action menu, and choose Disable Routing and Remote Access. Then, open the Action menu again, choose Add Server, select This Computer, and click OK. Finally, go back and try step 2.

3. Select Internet Connection Server and click Next. If you have a small network and do not use DHCP, select Set Up Internet Connection Sharing (ICS). If you use DHCP, then you need to choose Set Up a Router With the Network Address Translation (NAT) Routing Protocol. In either case, click Next.

4. It you want to use an internal Internet connection, such as a modem, DSL, or ISDN adapter, select Create a New Demand Dial Internet Connection and click Next twice to open the Demand Dial Interface Wizard, where you need to click Next again.

5. Enter the name you want to use for the interface, and click Next. Choose to use a modem or other telephony connecting device and click Next. Choose the specific modem or adapter to use, and click Next. Enter the phone number and click Next.

6. Select the options that you want to use. In most cases, the default Route IP Packets is all you need. After selecting the needed options, click Next. Enter the username, domain name, and password, confirm the password, and click next. Click Finish twice.

Maintaining a Windows 2000 Router

You can see, test, and maintain the router you have just installed in the Routing and Remote Access console. In the next set of steps, you locate the new router, connect it to its destination, and see how to set up IP filters and the hours the router can be used:

1. In the Routing and Remote Access console, which should be open from the last exercise, open the local server and select Routing Interfaces. In the right pane, you should see your demand-dial interface, similar to mine (WhidbeyRemote) in Figure 10-7.

2. Right-click your demand-dial interface and choose Set Credentials. Here, you can change the username, domain, and password that are used to connect to the ISP. When you open this dialog box, the password is cleared and must be reentered. Also, you may not need to enter a domain. Click OK after you have completed the entry.

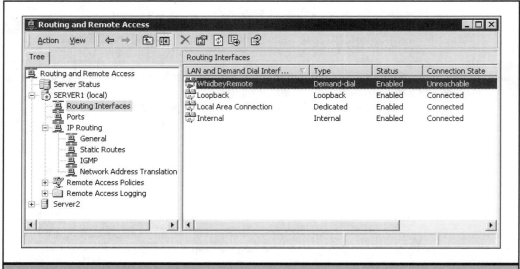

Figure 10-7. Locating the demand-dial connection in Routing and Remote Access

3. Right-click the demand-dial interface and choose Connect. You should hear the modem dialing and see a message with the status of "Connecting." When the actual connection is made, the Connection State in the Routing and Remote Access dialog box will change to Connected.

4. Right-click the demand-dial interface and choose Set IP Demand-Dial Filters. This enables you to specify either IP addresses that will be the only ones allowed into the network or, conversely, IP addresses that are not allowed into the network. The IP address can be within the LAN or in the remote network. After you have set the filters you want, click OK.

5. Right-click the demand-dial interface and choose Dial-out Hours. Here, you can specify the hours that the demand-dial connection will not be available by selecting a particular hour and clicking Denied. For example, if you want from 10 P.M. Saturday through 2 A.M. Sunday to be blocked out, the dialog box will look like Figure 10-8 after you have selected times. After you have set the times you want, click OK.

6. Right-click the demand-dial interface and choose Properties. This allows you to set the properties of the connection, including the phone number, the type of connection, several security options, and network properties. When you are done, click OK and then close the Routing and Remote Access console.

To use the router, you need to install an Internet connection in the client that connects through a LAN. See the upcoming section "Setting Up an Internet Connection."

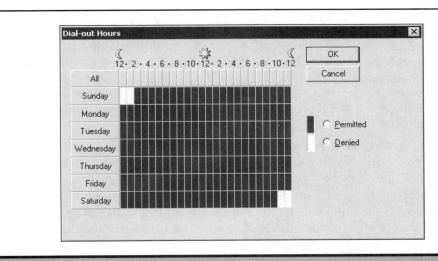

Figure 10-8.   Setting the times that a demand-dial interface is available

INTERNET CONNECTION

An Internet connection is one of the major reasons (and sometimes the only reason) to own a computer. In businesses, more and more work is being done through business-to-business transactions over the Internet. Making the most of the Internet connection is therefore of significant importance. This section looks at the following:

▼   Setting up an Internet connection

■   Finding information on the Internet

▲   Sending and receiving Internet mail

Setting Up an Internet Connection

Setting up an Internet connection begins by clicking the Connect to the Internet icon, and continues with the next set of steps. These steps assume that neither a modem nor a dial-up connection has been previously set up, although they do assume that the phone is connected to a modem and that the modem is installed in or connected to the computer being set up.

NOTE: If you have an existing Internet account or are getting your own new Internet account (and not using Microsoft's suggested providers), you need to know the phone number for your modem to dial (the ISP's modem phone number), and the username and password for your account. If you want to use Internet mail, you need to know your e-mail address, the type of mail server (POP3, IMAP, or HTTP), the names of the incoming and outgoing mail servers, and the name and password for the mail account.

1. Double-click the Connection to the Internet icon on the desktop. The Internet Connection Wizard opens. If you do not have an existing Internet account and want to let Microsoft steer you to an ISP, choose the first option. If you have an existing ISP account and want Windows to look for it from among the ISPs in its database, click the second option. If you have an existing ISP account and want to enter it yourself (recommended), or you connect to the Internet through your LAN, then choose the third option. After you make your choice, click Next.

2. If you want to use a modem to connect to the Internet and you don't have a modem installed, you will be asked to install one, in which case you should go to step 3; otherwise, go to step 6.

3. Click Next. Windows will try to detect a modem; click Next. A list of possible modems is shown to you. If only the correct modem is displayed, skip the next step. If several modems are shown and one is correct and the rest are not, uncheck the incorrect ones and skip the next step. If an incorrect modem or Unknown Modem is shown, select it and click Change.

4. Select the correct manufacturer from the list on the left and the correct model from the list on the right and click OK. If your modem is not on the list, but you have a disk, click Have Disk, insert the disk, select the drive, click OK, select the manufacturer and model, and click OK.

5. Click Next. Select the COM port to which your modem is attached, and click Next. Windows starts to install your modem. If you are using an older modem, you may be told that the driver does not have a digital signature. If so, click Yes to continue. Finally, you are told that your modem has been set up successfully. Click Finish.

6. If you selected either of the first two Internet connection choices in step 1, you will be connected to a Microsoft site, and a list of ISPs for your area will be downloaded and displayed. If your ISP or the one you want to be your ISP is on the list, click it, click Next, and go to step 8. If your ISP is not on the list, select that option, click Next, and go to step 7.

7. If you selected the third (manual) Internet connection choice in step 1 or your ISP was not on the list in step 6, enter the phone number to be used to connect to your ISP. If you do not need to use an area or city code, uncheck Use Area Code and Dialing Rules. Click Next, enter your username and password, and click Next again. Enter a name for this Internet connection, and click Next.

8. Choose whether you want to set up an Internet mail account, and click Next. If you do, go to step 9; otherwise, go to step 10.

9. For your Internet mail account, enter the name you want to be displayed when your account is referenced, and click Next. Enter your e-mail address, and click Next. Select the type of mail service that you have (POP3 is the most common) and the name of the incoming and outgoing mail service, and click Next. Enter

the mail account's name and password, choose whether you want Windows to remember the password, choose whether you need to use Secure Password Authentication, and click Next.

10. If you do not want to immediately connect to the Internet, clear that checkbox and click Finish to complete your Internet connection. Otherwise, Internet Explorer will open and the Dial-up Connection dialog box will appear.

11. Click Connect. Your modem dials the number, and you will be connected, which will be indicated by the icon on the right of the taskbar. By default, you will be connected to MSN's Home page, similar to the one shown in Figure 10-9. The next section shows you how to change this default.

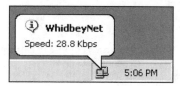

Finding Information on the Internet

Once you are connected to the Internet with Internet Explorer open, you most probably will want to go to pages other than the MSN Home page. There are a number of ways to do that, including the following:

▼ Navigating within a web site

■ Going directly to a web site

■ Searching for a web site

▲ Setting up a different default home page

Navigating Within a Web Site

A good web site gives you many ways to navigate within it. As you look at the MSN Home page in Figure 10-9, you see a number of terms or phrases that are underlined. These are *links* that, when clicked, take you to another part of the web site. The Home page is almost all links of several kinds. It has horizontal menus (Home, Hotmail, and so forth), vertical menus (Autos, Business, and so on), block menus (Air Tickets, Auctions, and so forth), headings, terms by themselves (Help), and article lists. Also, there is normally a text search capability, similar to the one at the top of the MSN Home page. Here, you can enter a term or a phrase and click Go.

TIP: Often, if you enter a phrase in a text search, the search will be done on each word, not on the complete phrase. To fix that, in many text searches, you can enclose the phrase in quotation marks and the search will be done on the entire phrase.

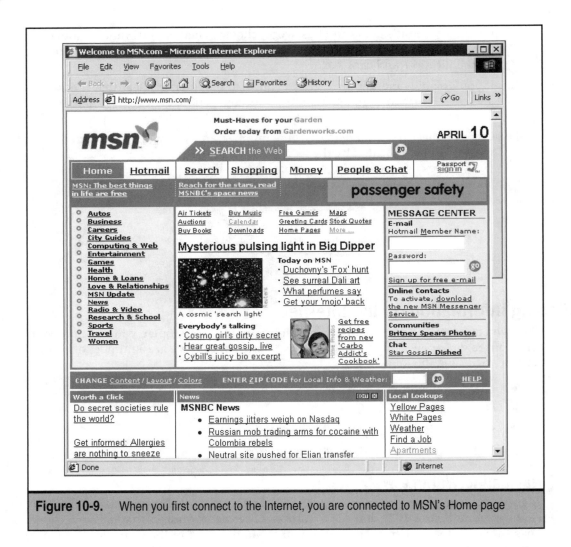

Figure 10-9. When you first connect to the Internet, you are connected to MSN's Home page

Internet Explorer also provides tools to navigate within a site: the Back and Forward arrows on the toolbar take you to the previous and next pages, respectively. Also, the down arrows on the right of the Back and Forward arrows will list the last several pages you have viewed in each direction.

Going Directly to a Web Site

To go directly to a site, you must know the address, or URL (Uniform Resource Locator), for that site. With increasing frequency in publications, letterheads, and advertising, you will find an organization's URL. When you have a site's URL, you can enter it into the address box under the toolbar in Internet Explorer, as shown next, and then press ENTER or click Go, which takes you directly to the site. URLs that you frequently use can be stored in the Favorites folder, on the desktop, and in the Links folder on the Address bar of Internet Explorer. If you select one of these addresses and you are not already connected to the Internet, you will be connected automatically (or you might have to click Dial in a connection dialog box), Internet Explorer will open, and the addressed site will be displayed.

Placing a URL in Favorites   You can store a URL in the Favorites folder by entering it or otherwise displaying it in the Address box of Internet Explorer, opening the Favorites menu, and choosing Add to Favorites. The Add Favorite dialog box will open, show you the name the site will have in the Favorites folder, and allow you to place the URL in a subfolder with the Create In option.

NOTE: The Favorites folder is in each user's area of the hard disk. By default, this is C:\Documents and Settings*User*\Favorites.

Placing a URL on the Desktop   You can place a URL on the desktop or in the Quick Launch toolbar by dragging the icon in the Address box of Internet Explorer to the desktop or Quick Launch toolbar. This creates a shortcut that, when double-clicked or clicked, connects to the Internet, opens Internet Explorer, and displays the site.

Placing a URL in the Links Folder   The Links folder is a subfolder of Favorites and is displayed on the right of the Address bar in the upper part of Internet Explorer windows. Drag the Links bar to the left to display more of it. You can add a URL to the Links folder and bar by dragging the icon in the Address box to the Links bar on the right. You can place it within the Links bar in the location you want. You can remove any unwanted links by right-clicking them and choosing Delete.

Searching for a Web Site

If you don't know a web site's URL, you can search for it in either of two ways. If it is a web site that you have been to recently, you likely can find it in your web site history. If you have not been to the site recently, you can do a full search of the Internet to find it.

Checking History   To check the history of your web site visits, click History in the Internet Explorer toolbar. A History pane will open and show you the sites you have visited by day for the current week, and then by week for the last several weeks. By opening a day or week, you can see and select a URL that you have previously visited and have it quickly displayed.

You can determine how many days to keep History and clear History by opening the Tools menu and choosing Internet Options. In the General tab of the dialog box that opens, in the bottom panel, you can set the Days to Keep Pages in History and clear History.

Searching the Internet   You can search for a web site on the Internet at three levels:

▼   Type in the Address box what you believe is part of the URL, and Internet Explorer will search for a site that has in its URL the text you entered. For example, if you enter 3Com and press ENTER, the Search pane appears on the left displaying a list of possible URLs, and the page representing the most likely URL will be opened and displayed on the right, as you can see in Figure 10-10.

■   Click Search in the toolbar, and the Search pane will open on the left of Internet Explorer. Here, you can enter a word or phrase and click Search. A list of web sites containing that word or phrase will be displayed. You can then click

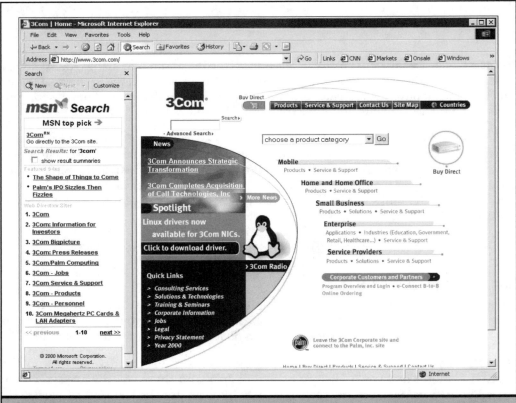

Figure 10-10.   Searching for 3Com

a site in the list and it will be displayed on the right. As described earlier in the tip under "Navigating Within a Web Site," if you want to search for a complete phrase, you need to place the phrase within quotation marks.

▲ Refine how and by whom the search is carried out, by clicking Customize at the top of the Search pane to open the Customize Search Settings dialog box, shown in Figure 10-11. Here, you can select the search engines that you want used in carrying out the search, as well as the order in which you want them used. You can do this not only when searching for web pages, but also when searching for a person's mailing address or e-mail address, finding a business, locating a map, looking up a word, finding a picture, finding a reference in a newsgroup, and searching your previous searches.

Setting Up a Different Default Home Page

The page that opens when you first start Internet Explorer or click the house icon in Internet Explorer's toolbar is called Home, your home page. By default, when you first in- stall Windows 2000 with Internet Explorer, this page is the MSN (Microsoft Network)

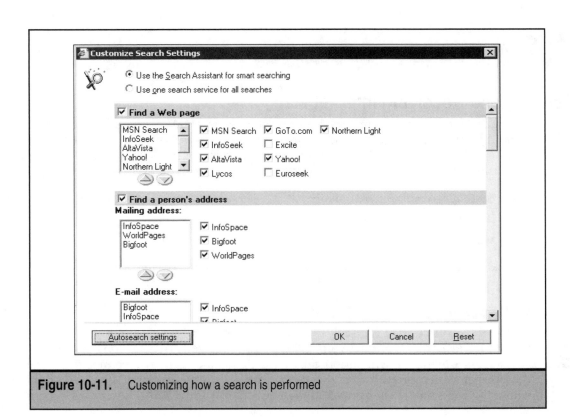

Figure 10-11. Customizing how a search is performed

Home page. If you want to change that to, say, the CNN home page, you can do so with these steps:

1. Open Internet Explorer and display the page that you want to be your home page, which is the CNN home page in this example.
2. Open the Tools menu and choose Internet Options.
3. In the General tab, Home Page section, click Use Current.

If you ever want to return to using MSN as your home page, reopen Internet Options and click Use Default.

TIP: If you don't have a particular site you want to go to every time you open Internet Explorer, and don't want to wait while one displays, click Use Blank.

Sending and Receiving Internet Mail

It is arguable which is the more important aspect of the Internet, the World Wide Web or Internet e-mail. E-mail provides one-on-one communications, which is vital to carrying out business functions as well as building and maintaining relationships. With Windows 2000, e-mail is handled with Outlook Express, which enables you to do the following:

▼ Send, receive, and store e-mail
■ Participate in newsgroups
▲ Maintain and use an address book

Clicking the Outlook Express icon in the Quick Launch area of the taskbar starts Outlook Express, which is shown in Figure 10-12.

Send, Receive, and Store E-Mail

When you first open Outlook Express, it automatically connects to the Internet and retrieves any mail that your ISP is holding for you. Then, as long as Outlook Express is loaded, it will periodically try to get your e-mail, by reconnecting to the Internet as necessary. You can change if and how often your mail is checked by opening the Tools menu, choosing Options, and looking under Send/Receive Messages

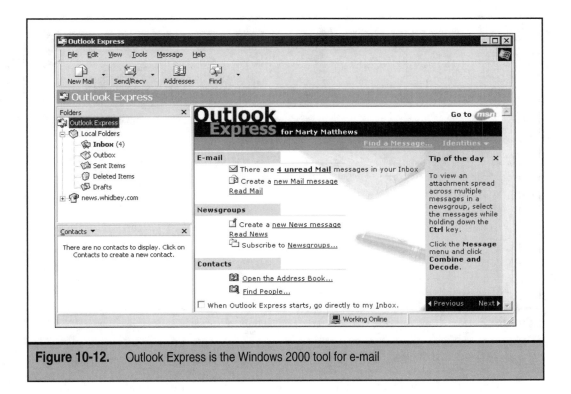

Figure 10-12.   Outlook Express is the Windows 2000 tool for e-mail

in the General tab. You can also manually retrieve your mail by clicking Send/Recv in the toolbar, or by clicking the down arrow on the right of Send/Recv to choose to either send or receive, and select the account to send to or receive from. By opening Local Folders and clicking Inbox in the left pane of the Outlook Express window, you will see in the upper-right pane a list of the messages you have received. If you click a message, some of the content of the message appears in the bottom-right pane. If you double-click a message, the message opens in its own window. Finally, if you do not delete the message, it stays in the Inbox for as long as you want.

You can create a new message to send by clicking New Mail in the toolbar. This opens a New Message window, shown in Figure 10-13, in which you enter the e-mail address(es) of the recipients (separated by semicolons), a subject, which is helpful for identifying and locating messages, and the body of the message. When you are done with the message, click Send, and it will be sent. You can also get a New Message window with the recipient(s) and subject already filled in by clicking Reply or Reply All in the toolbar of a message you have received. Reply will only fill in the address of the sender of the original message, whereas Reply All fills in the addresses of all the people, sender and recipients, in the original message. If you click Forward on a message you receive, the original message is copied to a New Message window, but the address fields are left blank for you to fill in.

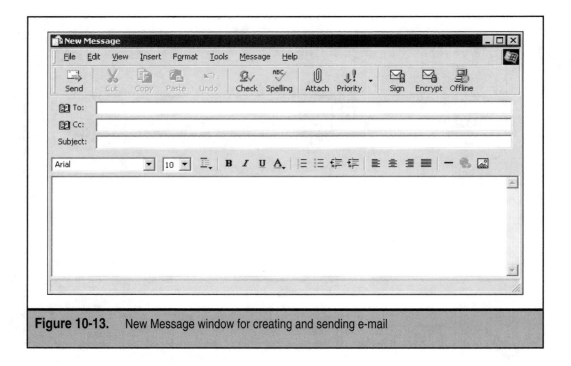

Figure 10-13.   New Message window for creating and sending e-mail

You can attach one or more computer files to an e-mail message either by dragging the file from Windows Explorer or the desktop to the New Message window, or by clicking Attach in the toolbar of a New Message window and entering the file path and name or browsing for the attachment.

Participate in Newsgroups

Newsgroups are an organized chain of messages on a particular subject. Newsgroups are sponsored by some organization, such as a company, university, or club, and allow people to enter new messages and respond to previous ones. To access a newsgroup, you need to set up a new account for the newsgroup, similar to the account you set up for your e-mail. To set up and use a newsgroup account, you need the name of the news server and possibly an account name and password. Then, use the following steps:

1.   In the Outlook Express window, open the Tools menu and choose Accounts. The Internet Accounts dialog box will open.

2.   Click Add | News. Enter the name you want displayed, and click Next. Enter your e-mail address so that people can directly reply to you, and click Next.

3. Enter the name of your news server. Your ISP or another sponsoring organization will give this to you. If you do not need to enter an account name and password, your ISP or sponsoring organization will tell you this, in which case you can skip to step 5.

4. If you need to enter an account name and password, click My News Server Requires Me to Log On, and click Next. Enter your account name and password, click Remember Password (if desired), and then, if necessary (your ISP or sponsor will tell you), click Log On Using Secure Password Authentication (SPA).

5. Click Next, click Finish, and then click Close. A new folder will appear in the Folders pane of Outlook Express.

6. You will see a message asking whether you want to download the newsgroups from the news account you just set up. Click Yes. If necessary, click Connect to connect to the Internet. If all of your entries are okay, you will be connected. If your account name and password are in error, you are told so and given a chance to fix them.

7. A list of newsgroups will be displayed. Double-click the ones to which you want to subscribe (meaning read and reply to messages it contains). After you have selected the newsgroups, click OK. You are returned to Outlook Express.

8. In the Folders pane on the left, click a newsgroup you want to open. A list of messages will be displayed. Click one to have it shown in the bottom pane, or double-click to have a message opened in its own window.

You can treat a newsgroup message like an e-mail message, but with two differences. You can choose to reply to the newsgroup or to the individual, and a new message is called a New Post. In newsgroups, a new message is "posted" like one would be on a bulletin board. If someone replies to this message, it gets added to the end of the original message, thereby creating a chain, or *thread*, of messages on a given subject. For example, Figure 10-14 shows a thread on the topic of brake fluid disappearing on the Jaguar automobile, in a newsgroup on that car.

Maintain and Use an Address Book

Outlook Express maintains an address book to help you keep track of your e-mail and snail-mail addresses and phone numbers. When you reply to a message that you have received, the addresses automatically go into the address book. When you create a new message, as you start typing a name, it will be looked up in the address book and completed for you, if it's already in the address book. You can also manually add a name to the address book, manually look up an address, and create a group of addresses that can be referred to by the group name and added to a message all at once.

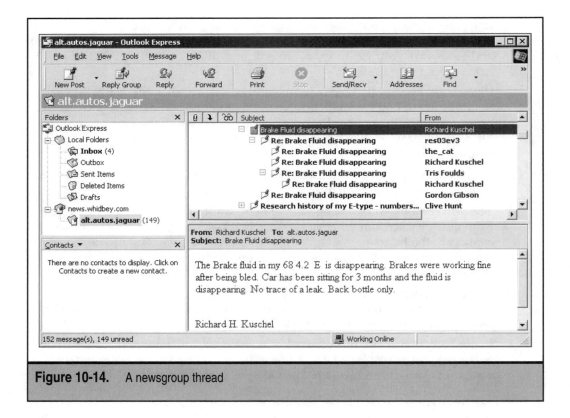

Figure 10-14. A newsgroup thread

Add a Name to the Address Book   The following are a few ways to add names to the address book:

▼ From the Outlook Express window, click Addresses in the toolbar to open the Address Book window, click New in its toolbar, select New Contact, and fill in the dialog box that opens.

■ From a New Message window, click the address book icon to open the Select Recipients dialog box, click New Contact, and fill in the dialog box that opens.

▲ From an existing message, right-click an address anywhere in the message and choose Add to Address Book.

Look Up an Address   You look up addresses in much the same way as you add them to the address book:

▼   From the Outlook Express window, click Addresses in the toolbar to open the Address Book window. Use the scroll bar or begin typing a name to locate it. When it is found, the e-mail address is shown in the Address Book windows. If you want the postal address or other information not shown in the windows, double-click the name to open the Properties dialog box, which shows all of the information on that individual.

▲   From a New Message window, click the address book icon to open the Select Recipients dialog box. Double-click all the entries you want to receive the message, and then click OK.

Create and Use a Group   To create a group of addresses that you can repeatedly use to send e-mail to a group of people, open the Address Book window, open the File menu, and choose New Group. Enter a name for the group, and click Select Members. Either type a name or use the scroll bar to find it, and then double-click the name to add it to the list of members. When you are done, click OK twice. An entry with a distinctive icon will appear in the address book. You use the group entry in the same way you use any other entry in the address book, but when you choose a group entry, all of the members are added to the list of recipients.

CHAPTER 11

Internet Information Services Version 5

This chapter introduces you to Internet Information Services Version 5 (IIS 5) and the indispensable role that IIS plays within Windows 2000. In addition, this chapter discusses the major changes from IIS 4 to IIS 5. The Windows 2000 operating system (OS) is designed to integrate with IIS, and future Microsoft BackOffice Products will be built directly into the core protocol support provided to Windows 2000 by IIS. This chapter looks at some of the new features included in IIS 5 as well as how to install, customize, and migrate IIS installations to meet various business and networking goals.

THE IIS 5 ENVIRONMENT

IIS is a collection of web-enabled services and protocols configured to run with and on the Windows NT OS. IIS 5, the latest in the line, is the first of the IIS products to be completely integrated into an NT OS, in this case Windows 2000. While IIS is primarily known for hosting web services, within Windows 2000, IIS also provides a number of services and protocols fundamental to a Windows 2000–based organization.

Based on the Transmission Control Protocol/Internet Protocol (TCP/IP) and common Internet and industry standards, mainstream IIS first appeared with IIS 2, which is an installation option of NT Server 4. Initially, IIS offered services based on the Hypertext Transfer Protocol (HTTP), File Transfer Protocol (FTP), Gopher, and Simple Mail Transfer Protocol (SMTP). IIS 3 and 4 were available via Service Pack upgrades to the NT platform and introduced a number of new services, most notably Active Server Pages (ASP). With the advent of IIS 4, Microsoft dropped support of the Gopher web service, but continued to add support for emerging web technologies, such as the Web Distributed Authoring and Versioning (WebDAV) protocol and the Extensible Markup Language (XML).

IIS has always been primarily a web server, which basically is a server that hosts web services, such as Hypertext Markup Language (HTML) web pages for use by external clients, normally via web browsers and HTTP connections, although IIS is a lot more than this. As previously mentioned, IIS can also host FTP and SMTP services.

Whenever you use a web browser to connect to a web site, such as www.microsoft.com, you connect to a web server, download the text, media, and images found there, and then look at this information on your local computer system. Obviously, the quality and complexity of each web site varies tremendously, as does the quality and stability of web servers. This chapter will spend some time talking about the unique features and functions offered by IIS 5 that support both higher quality web sites and improved server stability.

While it is easy to pigeonhole IIS for web use only, IIS is actually used in a variety of non-web-related areas. The following are some of the areas that represent the diversity of functions offered by IIS:

▼ **FTP** An industry-standard, file-exchange protocol that allows different systems to exchange files. A large number of organizations running both NT- and UNIX-based platforms are using FTP to exchange files. This is even possible with larger systems, such as Alpha and SUN. FTP allows systems to exchange files across the Internet in a quick and efficient manner. With FTP, data that's input and processed within a mainframe environment can be FTPed to an NT server and automatically input into an SQL database with no user interaction, through the use of a few simple scripts running on each server.

▲   **SMTP**   A TCP/IP-based protocol that allows for the formation and transfer of text messages between systems. In short, SMTP is e-mail. If you've ever used e-mail over the Internet, you've used SMTP. Within Windows 2000, SMTP is now a part of Active Directory and can be used to link Active Directory sites together across the Internet. With SMTP, Windows 2000 organizations can be integrated through the Internet using nothing but standard Internet technologies.

NOTE: Windows 2000 uses the IIS certificate server to keep the information exchanged between the two Active Directory sites encrypted and secure from prying eyes.

IIS 5 Enhancements

Because of strong integration with the OS, IIS 5 makes it easier to share documents and information across a company intranet or the Internet. With IIS, you can also deploy scalable and reliable web-based applications. In addition, bringing existing data and applications to the Web using Active Directory is much easier and provides a higher level of security and control. Technically, IIS 5 offers a variety of new features (which will be addressed in this chapter) that focus on the data collaboration and sharing that is at the core of the Windows 2000 BackOffice family. IIS 5's integration into the Windows 2000 OS leads to a number of other advantages, including drastically increased reliability and stability, compared to IIS 4/NT 4 systems. Besides integration with the OS, IIS 5 also provides a higher degree of integration with the other BackOffice Platforms, such as Exchange 2000 and SQL 2000. Some of these new features are based around the WebDAV protocol and emerging XML technologies, which allow for a higher degree of data sharing between dissimilar applications.

Reliability and Performance

IIS 4 installations within many organizations had some reliability and performance issues. While no application is perfect, IIS 4 occasionally suffered from memory leaks (system resources that are not returned to the system's control when an application or script ends). Although these issues were rare, they would occasionally cause a server to consistently have to be rebooted before the lost system resources would be returned to the system for use by other services or applications. These and other issues did not stop e-commerce-based companies from developing e-commerce sites on the IIS 4 platform, but they still caused extra network administration in already hectic situations.

One of the main technologies that IIS 4 did add is an HTML alternative called *Active Server Pages.* Originally introduced with IIS 3, ASP became native and stable within the IIS 4 platform. ASP is the cornerstone of a lot of very successful IIS deployments, including www.microsoft.com. Because of the success IIS 4 has achieved, Microsoft has been able to focus primarily on the reliability and performance of IIS 5 instead of on the addition of new features. In fact, in some instances, IIS 5 has increased performance up to 40 percent over like-configured IIS 4 installations, a number that can translate into millions of dollars in hardware to large e-commerce sights. In addition to the general integration changes made to IIS 5, the following specific changes have been made:

▼ **Reliable restart feature** Allows an administrator to restart web services without rebooting the computer.

■ **Application protection** Allows applications to run in their own environments, separate from the memory space of the web services and other applications running on the server. If an application environment fails, the OS will not fail and will not need to be restarted. Only the process that fails needs to be restarted, which the OS can do automatically.

■ **CPU throttling and socket pooling** Protect the OS and other users by placing limits on the resources any one user can consume.

▲ **Development tools** Provide features that benefit the web site developer by improving the ease and reliability in the development process. Among these features are the following:

■ Scriptless Microsoft ASP processing

■ ASP self-tuning

■ Performance-enhanced ASP objects

New Features in IIS 5

Many of the new features in IIS 5 are just new versions of, or enhancements to, existing services available in IIS 4. These new features make the product very easy to learn for those administrators already familiar with previous versions of IIS. The following sections describe a number of the more significant new features and enhancements within the IIS 5 product, separated by the subcategories to which they best relate.

Security In keeping with the increased emphasis on security in the rest of Windows 2000, a number of new or enhanced security features were added to IIS 5. These include the following:

▼ **Digest authentication** Adds user authentication across proxy servers and firewalls, which was not available in NT 4–based systems due to their inability to securely pass authentication credentials between servers. With the advent of Kerberos (which is explained later), a user can now authenticate to a single "front-end server" and then access network resources behind that server securely and without having to continually log in to each server via cleartext. With digest authentication, the server negotiates a kind of certificate exchange utilizing encryption in a way that the server and client can be sure of reliable authentication.

- **Server-Gated Cryptography (SGC)**   Allows 128-bit encryption between client and server using Secure Sockets Layer (SSL) and a special SGC type of certificate, assuming the client's browser supports 128-bit encryption.

- **Security wizards**   Make it easier to set up the more complicated encryption components, including the following:

    - **Web Server Certificate Wizard**   Assists in administering certificates

    - **Permissions Wizard**   Assists in setting up access permissions to virtual directories

    - **CTL Wizard**   Assists in setting up a list of certified authorities, also called and named after a certificate trust list (CTL), with Kerberos v5 compliance

- **Kerberos**   Provides Internet standards–based authentication for accessing Active Directory–managed objects. Kerberos lets a user request an encrypted "ticket" that is used for authentication so that the user's credentials, such as username and password, are no longer needed. Kerberos is based on public key/private key technologies and cannot be used by others to access secure network resources. Since Kerberos is an industry standard, Windows 2000 users can use it to interact with third-party products, as well as other OSs.

- **CryptoAPI**   Provides a single certificate management system for both IIS and Windows 2000 that allows you to store, back up, and configure server certificates.

- ▲ **Fortezza**   Allows use of a U.S. government security standard in IIS 5. This standard satisfies the Defense Message System security architecture with a family of cryptographic products, including smart cards, modems, and Ethernet cards that provide message confidentiality, integrity, authentication, nonrepudiation, and access control to messages, components, and systems.

Administration   Being able to control the web sites that are being hosted by an IIS server is extremely important. Windows 2000 has added several very important administrative tools to IIS that are described in the following points:

- ▼ **Reliable restarts**   Allows you to stop and restart all of your Internet services from within IIS, making it unnecessary to restart your computer when applications misbehave or become unavailable.

- **Process accounting**   Adds fields to the World Wide Web Consortium (W3C) extended log file to record information about how web sites use CPU resources on the server. With this information, CPU utilization can be analyzed in relation to IIS performance.

- ▲ **Process throttling**   Limits how much processor time a web site's out-of-process applications are permitted to utilize. This ensures that processor time is available to other web sites and non-web applications.

Programmability   Web sites are becoming increasingly sophisticated, and that sophistication is coming from programming. IIS 5 has added the following features in support of programming:

▼ **Application environment**   Expands the web server's application development environment by building on new technologies included in Windows 2000 Server. These include Active Directory and the expanded Component Object Model (COM+). In addition, enhancements to IIS ASP, such as scriptless ASP processing, as well as improved flow control and error handling, let developers write more efficient web-centric applications.

▲ **New ASP features**   Includes the following new improvements, which significantly reduce the time spent in troubleshooting web page problems:

   ■ New flow-control capabilities

   ■ Error handling

   ■ Scriptless ASP

   ■ Performance-enhanced objects

   ■ XML integration

   ■ Windows script components

   ■ ASP self-tuning

Application Protection   In IIS 4, applications can be set to run in the same process (memory space and virtual machine) as web services or in a process separate from web services. IIS 5 now offers a third option in which multiple applications can be run in a pooled process together, but still separate from the main IIS process and other applications. Other features in IIS 5 that provide application protection include the following:

▼ **ADSI 2 support**   Gives administrators and application developers the ability to add custom objects, properties, and methods to the existing Active Directory Service Interface (ADSI) provider, offering more flexibility in creating a site, as well as isolation from the actual data store and protocol being used.

■ **Web Distributed Authoring and Versioning (WebDAV)**   Extends the HTTP/1.1 protocol to allow clients to publish, lock, and manage resources on the Web. Most of the features supported by WebDAV are only supported by browsers that have fully adopted and integrated the HTTP/1.1 protocol standard. Presently, only Internet Explorer version 5 or later fully supports IIS 5's WebDAV features, but other supporting browser technology may have been released by the time you read this. Integrated into IIS 5, WebDAV allows clients to do the following:

   ■ Manipulate resources

   ■ Modify properties

- Lock and unlock resources

- Search

■ **FTP restart**   Resumes an FTP download if an Internet connection is lost. This feature resumes the download at the same spot it was interrupted.

▲ **HTTP compression**   Compresses web pages for download to a supporting browser. This feature should be balanced between processor utilization and network bandwidth consumption. Increasing compression decreases the bandwidth consumed by the request, but increases processor load during the compression.

NOTE: IIS 4 is the latest product available for use on NT 4, because IIS 5 is supported only by Windows 2000, due to its high degree of integration with the OS. However, in organizations not ready to switch to Windows 2000 completely, a new server running Windows 2000 and IIS 5 can be integrated into the security domains provided by NT 4 with very little configuration and effort.

Internet Services in IIS 5

IIS 5 publishes information using standard Internet services and protocols, including the World Wide Web (WWW), FTP, SMTP, and Network News Transfer Protocol (NNTP). A basic understanding of each of these services is required for a complete understanding of the IIS product.

▼ **WWW services**   Uses HTTP to allow users to publish content to the Web using HTML. Files are placed in folders or subdirectories connected to a web site. These documents can be viewed by using an Internet browser, such as Netscape Navigator or Internet Explorer. Because of the graphical nature of HTML, businesses can use this format to display and explain products and services, as well as create e-commerce applications to purchase these products and services.

■ **FTP services**   Used to transmit files over the Internet. This is an older protocol that provides a reliable and speedy transfer of files. FTP can be used with a web browser via web-FTP, to speed up downloading large files from normal web sites, as well as using an independent legacy FTP client connected to an FTP server, which can provide access to files that are independent of HTTP protocols. FTP.Microsoft.com is an example of an open FTP server. While some web browsers can be used to access FTP servers, separate FTP clients are normally used. Although all Microsoft clients contain an FTP client as part of the TCP/IP stack, this client is DOS and command-line driven (type **FTP** at the command prompt). Many third-party 32-bit FTP clients are available that can run within the Microsoft OS and that provide numerous additional features not provided by the built-in FTP clients. The classic example of such a client is WS_FTP, which is available from http://www.ipswitch.com/products/ws_ftp/. Many other FTP clients are available.

- ■ **SMTP services** Used for Internet e-mail, it is dependant on TCP/IP protocols and uses the Domain Name System (DNS) servers of the Internet to translate an e-mail name such as microsoft.com to an IP address like 192.168.3.4.

- ▲ **NNTP services** Allows a web site to host its own newsgroups, which provide for the exchange of threaded messages connected to a single topic. Messages are sent to the news server, which posts them to the appropriate newsgroup. A newsgroup is a community of people interested in a specific subject. The people in this community log on to the newsgroup to read and reply to messages on the subject of the newsgroup. (Refer to Chapter 10 for more details on newsgroups.)

WWW services and FTP services are installed with IIS by default. By utilizing the WWW services, graphical HTTP sites can be hosted. Using FTP services, files can be distributed quickly across the Internet. Both services allow multiple sites to be set up on one IIS server, such that the one web server can appear to be multiple WWW and/or FTP sites to a user on the Internet.

SMTP and NNTP services augment, and can be optionally installed with, IIS. These services allow multiple communication options. SMTP allows e-mail communication with users of the Internet, as well as an additional method of communication between servers. NNTP allows another form of one-on-one communication with users of the Internet and the organization sponsoring the newsgroup, providing feedback and communication directly to the organization.

INSTALLING AND MIGRATING IIS

As already mentioned, IIS is a collection of applications, services, and protocols. Consequently, no single method of installation applies in every case. However, as a whole, IIS is a web server. When you install IIS, Windows 2000 installs certain features and settings by default, not under the assumption that a web site (internal or external) will be installed on the server, but rather that some of the features included in the IIS subsystem will be needed by the server for use with other services. However, some features of IIS are necessary only if this server is going to be hosting specific web-based functions. Those features are the focus of the rest of this chapter.

Two ways exist to install web-hosting services in Windows 2000: installing from scratch with a default or custom installation of IIS 5 and Windows 2000, or migrating an existing site to IIS 5.

Installing IIS from Scratch

When setting up IIS for web-hosting purposes, you need to create one or more dedicated web servers. In some larger organizations, the potential load on the web servers can be dramatic. However, in smaller organizations, single-server installation of the entire BackOffice suite is possible. (In this situation, the Microsoft BackOffice Small Business Server product is advisable, because it comes with Exchange, IIS, SQL, and Proxy configured and ready to run on a single server. As of this printing, the Windows 2000 version of Small Business Server has not yet shipped, but it is expected to ship in the fourth quarter of 2000.) The design of any two networks is rarely going to be exactly the same, because various political and geographical factors affect even the most basic of network installations.

When designing and eventually installing a web server based on IIS 5 and Windows 2000, you need to consider a variety of factors, primary among which are what services the web site will host and what connection security the site will implement. For web sites hosting information that is free and available for everyone to see, anonymous access should be used. All users connecting to the web server will automatically be granted access to the server based on the Guest account and will not be prompted for a username or password. This situation then allows the user to pass secure information to the server (such as credit card data, to place an order) via technology such as SSL (discussed later in this chapter). When data is being hosted on the server that needs to be secure from unauthorized access, some form of authentication is required, such as Windows Authentication (Kerberos or the Challenge Handshake Authentication Protocol).

A default installation of IIS 5 includes the following:

▼ Web server

■ FTP server

■ IIS documentation

■ Internet Information Server Snap-In

■ Internet Services Manager

■ FrontPage 2000 Server Extensions

▲ Required IIS common files

The following are optional services that can be included in a custom installation:

▼ NNTP

■ SMTP

▲ Visual InterDev RAD (Remote Deployment Support)

As the web server is utilized more and functions expand, it may be necessary to add components. The optional components can be added at any time. It is not necessary to include everything in the initial install. Adding or removing components is very simple.

IIS 5 is installed with Windows 2000 Server by default. If you chose not to install it initially in the Windows 2000 setup, you can add it separately. You can also remove IIS if it is not needed. Additional components can be added at any time. To make changes to the IIS 5 services, use the Add/Remove Programs application in the Control Panel. Use the following steps to install IIS, if it was not done during the installation of Windows 2000:

1. Open the Start menu, choose Settings | Control Panel, and then double-click Add/Remove Programs.

2. Select Add/Remove Windows Components, click Components, and scroll down to Internet Information Services (IIS), as shown in Figure 11-1.

3. Click Internet Information Services (IIS) to select it and then click the Details button to install, remove, or add components to IIS, as shown in Figure 11-2.

NOTE: When upgrading existing NT 4 servers, the installation options chosen for Windows 2000 will match those of the current system. This means that IIS itself will install only if it is currently on an existing NT 4 server (most NT 4 servers do contain some form of IIS). While in-place upgrades work, it is very important to ensure that a full and complete backup of the server is made before any upgrade or migration is attempted.

Migrating to IIS

The migration process is dependent on what type of web server is being upgraded:

▼   **Current users of IIS**   Will be upgraded to version 5 by Windows 2000 Server Setup. Once installation is complete, IIS can be configured in the Windows 2000 Configure Your Server dialog box, shown in Figure 11-3. Setup and Configuration have been greatly improved over IIS 4

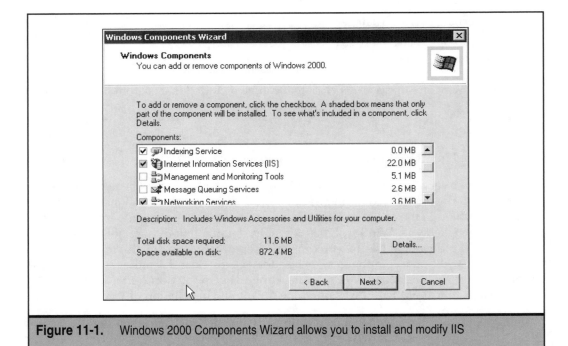

Figure 11-1.   Windows 2000 Components Wizard allows you to install and modify IIS

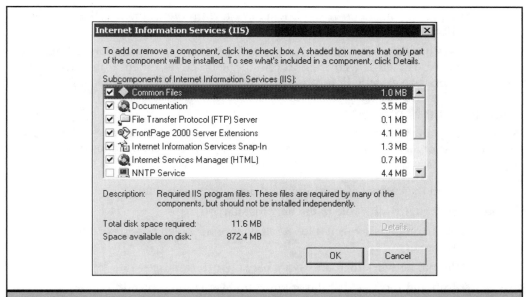

Figure 11-2. Windows 2000's IIS dialog box lists IIS components that may be installed

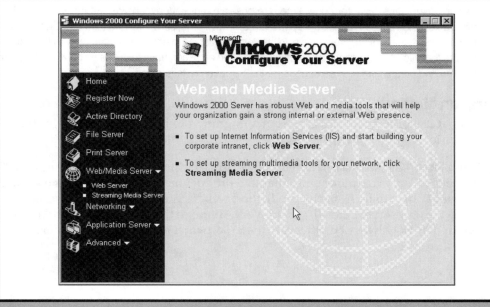

Figure 11-3. Configure Your Server dialog box with Web/Media Server options

Setup, and current users of IIS will have few problems making the transition to IIS 5.

▲ **Users of other web servers**   Will need to transfer configuration settings and content, as well as web applications, to the IIS environment from such web servers as Netscape Enterprise Server or Apache HTTP Server.

Planning the Migration

When an organization has a current Internet and/or intranet site or sites, planning is an essential part of any migration, to maintain that site's presence. In choosing a migration path, the primary considerations are as follows:

▼ Risk to the current system and total downtime acceptable

■ Existing hardware role in the new installation

■ Content changes expected to web data (are new web pages expected with the new servers?)

■ Potential network load and available network resources

▲ Additional services that the organization is planning on adding

TIP: In some organizations, a certain amount of downtime is acceptable and expected; however, in other organizations, such as e-commerce businesses, a web site is supposed to be available always. In-place migrations, with zero downtime, are possible, but very expensive and tricky to plan. Most managers, when asked to define acceptable system downtime, set a very low number. However, when those same managers are presented with the support costs to maintain that number, they normally set a more realistic goal. In general, you can expect to find an exponential relationship between downtime allowed and planning/resources needed for the migration to take place.

Migration Methods

There are at least three ways to carry out a migration to IIS 5, as described in the next several sections.

Migrate to a Clean Windows 2000 Installation   Perform a clean installation of Windows 2000 Server and IIS 5 on a computer other than the production web server. Migrate settings, content, and applications from the production web server to the new IIS 5 server. Test and debug the new server before it is deployed. Although this is the ideal solution in most any case, it may not always be practical, due to software, hardware, and cost factors.

Hardware Needed	Pros	Cons
A second computer is required, in addition to the existing production web server.	Downtime. You can opt to put new, updated hardware in place at the same time you perform the migration. You also avoid taking your production web server offline until the new server is tested and deployed. Following deployment, if problems arise with the new server that didn't appear during testing, you can use the original server as a backup.	Cost. You might need new hardware. However, the cost will be offset at least partly by the time saved conducting the migration as well as troubleshooting any problems that occur during the migration. If you are running an e-commerce site, the added revenue of leaving the site up may cover some or all of the cost of new equipment.

Migrate to a Mirror NT-based Web Server   If you are migrating from a computer running Microsoft Windows NT, you can use this approach. On a second computer, install the same software as exists on the production web server, and then use the Windows 2000 Server Setup to upgrade to Windows 2000 Server and IIS 5. Migrate the web configuration settings, content, and applications to the new web server. Test and debug the new server before deploying it. This option allows for the testing of third-party applications to be installed on the new, mirrored server, to test for compatibility with Windows 2000 and IIS 5.

Hardware Needed	Pros	Cons
A second computer is required, in addition to the existing production web server.	Downtime. You can opt to put new, updated hardware in place at the same time you perform the migration. You also avoid taking your production web server offline until the new server is tested and deployed. Following deployment, if problems arise with the new server that didn't appear during testing, you can use the original server as a backup.	Cost. You might need new hardware. However, the cost will be offset at least partly by the time saved conducting the migration as well as troubleshooting any problems that occur during the migration. If you are running an e-commerce site, the added revenue of leaving the site up may cover some or all of the cost of new equipment.

Migrate the Production Web Server   If your production web server is currently running Windows NT Server and IIS 4, you can take it offline long enough to upgrade it and get IIS 5 installed. Use the Windows 2000 Server Setup to upgrade it to Windows 2000 Server with IIS 5. For a new installation, install Windows 2000 on a primary disk partition, which may require reformatting and repartitioning of the hard disk, and migrate web configuration settings, content, and applications to IIS "in place" on the production web server. Test and debug the server before deploying it.

Hardware Needed	Pros	Cons
No new hardware is required.	There is no hardware cost.	Downtime. If the server installation does not go as planned, this could be one of those really long weekends that all administrators dread. However, in most IT shops where cost is a factor, this may be the only option where you do not need a second server.

Preinstallation Requirements

IIS requires or can benefit by the following software and protocols, which must be installed on the computer prior to installing IIS:

▼ **Windows TCP/IP protocol**   Provides the means to convert information into packets and the transmission and control of those packets over a network, which could be the Internet. TCP/IP, which is required by IIS, in turn requires the following IP addresses or mask, which are supplied by your Internet service provider (shown in Figure 11-4):

   ■ IP address

   ■ Subnet mask

   ■ Default gateway's IP address (the default gateway is the ISP computer through which your computer routes all Internet traffic)

■ **DNS service**   Provides a central index of computer names to their IP addresses. DNS is easily set up on a large or small network using the Windows 2000 Configure Your Server Wizard.

■ **NT File System (NTFS)**   Provides improved security, the use of Active Directory, and many other functions and features.

▲ **FrontPage**   Allows the creation and editing of HTML pages for generating web sites using a WYSIWYG (what you see is what you get) editor that provides a friendly, graphical interface for tasks such as inserting tables, graphics, and scripts.

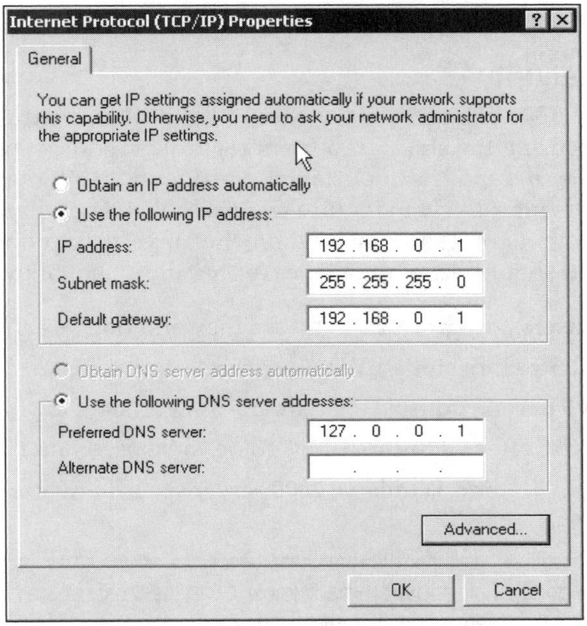

Figure 11-4.   IP address information

Implementing the Migration

Once the planning is complete, the physical migration is next. The main tool for migrating servers is the IIS Migration Wizard, which is included on the Windows 2000 Server Resource Kit Companion CD-ROM. The IIS Migration Wizard prompts you for the necessary information for the various types of migration. If you have prepared well for the migration, you should have all the information.

The Migration Wizard will accomplish the following processes:

▼   Migrating web and FTP sites

■   Replicating Windows-based files

■   Preserving permissions and audit settings

■   Preserving hyperlinks and web structure

■   Preserving share information

■   Replicating UNIX-based files (if applicable)

▲   Converting UNIX filenames and path names (if applicable)

Upon completion of these processes, the server should be thoroughly tested to verify a successful migration.

Implementing Security

Once the web server is running, security should be implemented. All sites need some level of security. Securing the site is important regardless of the size of the company or who will be using the site, and it is important to consider both internal and external users. Statistically, the users most likely to require security policies are those in your own organization. Laxity about internal security is where the majority of problems pop up. In setting up security, you should develop policies for handling the following issues:

▼ **Migrating users and groups**   Who are they and how are they aggregated?

■ **Setting NTFS permissions**   What are the assignments to various groups?

■ **Setting IIS 5 permissions**   What are the assignments to various groups?

■ **Security certificates**   How are they going to be used and managed?

▲ **Integrating UNIX and Windows 2000 server security** (if applicable)   How will it be done?

TIP: What most good administrators already know is that the most secure method of administering a server connected to the Internet is to assume anonymous/everyone access permission, regardless of what it's actually set to. Said another way, when it comes to the Internet, the best assumption is that everything that touches the Internet is going to be seen by everyone, and thus the only information to put on the Internet is information you don't mind everyone seeing. With Virtual Private Networking (VPN) technology taking hold, securing data on public web servers may become less of a problem, but in this arena, there is no such thing as being too paranoid.

CUSTOMIZING AND MAINTAINING IIS

After you have completed installing IIS, it then needs to be customized and maintained. In IIS 4, the tool for managing was called Internet Service Manager (ISM). Although the remote web service is still called ISM, Microsoft has renamed the non-web version of this service, calling it Internet Information Services Snap-In. ISM was one of the predecessors of the Microsoft Management Console (MMC) interface that Microsoft now uses to manage Windows 2000 (see Chapter 14 for a discussion of the MMC) and is the container for the IIS Snap-In. The IIS Snap-In can be configured to allow administration locally at the server or remotely from an administrator's workstation. It allows the administration of the IIS server components and services, either by snapping into the MMC or as a separate console or window. Figure 11-5 shows the IIS window.

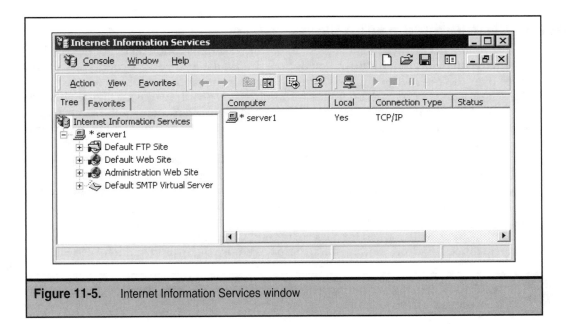

Figure 11-5.   Internet Information Services window

There are two ways to open the IIS window: one through the MMC, which opens the window shown in Figure 11-5, and the other through Computer Management. Start by looking at IIS through Computer Management and then in the MMC with the following steps:

1. Open the Start menu and choose Programs | Administrative Tools | Computer Management.

TIP: You can also open Computer Management by right-clicking My Computer and choosing Manage.

2. In the Tree tab on the left, open Services and Applications, and then expand IIS. This gives you IIS components (explained in the remaining sections of this chapter), which you can open for management purposes.

3. Open the Start menu and choose Programs | Administrative Tools | Internet Information Services.

4. In the Tree tab on the left, open the server under Internet Information Services. The windows should look like Figure 11-5. Once again, you have the IIS components available to manage.

Administering Sites Remotely

Because it may not always be convenient to perform administration tasks on the computer running IIS, two remote administration options are available. If you are connecting to your server over the Internet or through a proxy server, you can use the browser-based ISM (HTML) to change properties on your site. If you are on an intranet, you can use either the ISM (HTML) or the IIS Snap-In in the MMC. ISM (HTML) offers many of the same features as the snap-in, such as starting, stopping, and pausing services, as well as adjusting permissions. ISM (HTML) can't be used to create new web and FTP sites, or to make property changes that require coordination with Windows utilities, such as certificate mapping.

ISM (HTML) uses the Administration Web Site to access IIS properties. When IIS is installed, a port number between 2,000 and 9,999 is randomly selected and assigned to this web site. The site responds to web browser requests for all domain names installed on the computer, provided the port number is appended to the address. If Basic authentication is used, the administrator will be asked for a username and password when the site is reached. Only members of the Windows Administrators group can use the Administration Web Site.

NOTE: In ISM (HTML), right-clicking is not supported, and many of the familiar toolbar buttons and tab headings are displayed as links in the left frame.

To enable the browser-based ISM (HTML), follow these steps:

1.   In either the IIS Snap-In or Computer Management window on the local computer, open IIS for the server in question, right-click Administration Web Site, and choose Properties. Note the TCP port number on the Web Site tab, as shown in Figure 11-6.

2.   In the Directory Security tab, click Edit under IP Address and Domain Name Restrictions to set permissions for computers that will be used to administer IIS remotely, like this:

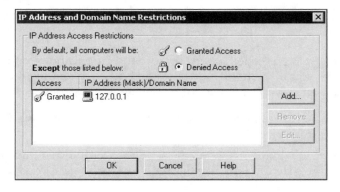

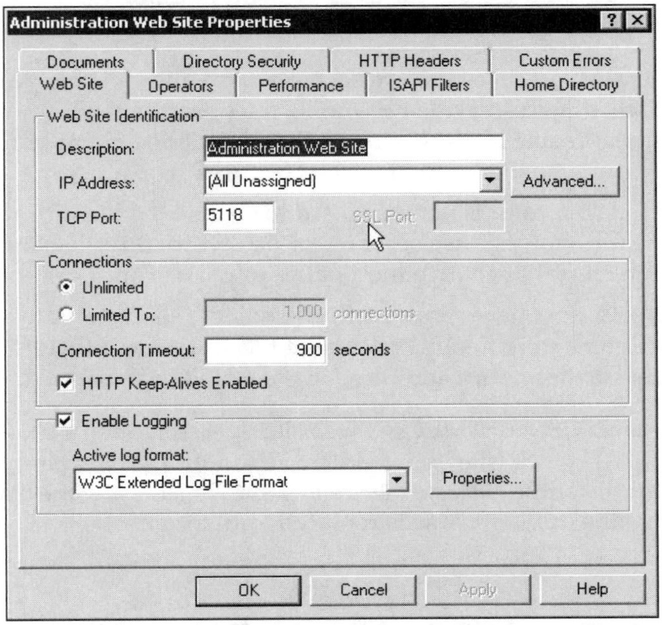

Figure 11-6.   The randomly assigned TCP port number is used for remote administration of IIS

3. After you make the settings you want, click OK twice to close the two dialog boxes.

To start the browser-based ISM (HTML), open a browser and type the domain name and the assigned port number for the Administration Web Site. For example, http://www. *companyname*.com:*port number*/.

Managing Web Site Operators

Management of specific web sites on IIS can be distributed to *web site operators*, a special group of users who have limited administrative privileges on individual web sites. Operators can administer properties that affect only their respective sites. They do not have access to properties that affect IIS, the Windows server computer hosting IIS, or the network. In this way, specific rights can be granted to a web site operator without giving rights to the entire IIS server.

Web site operators are possible because of the way Active Directory integrates between Windows 2000 and IIS 5. This gives system administrators several advantages with regard to web site operators:

▼ Each operator can act as the site administrator and can change or reconfigure the web site as necessary. For example, the operator can set web site access permissions, enable logging, change the default document or footer, set content expiration, and enable content ratings features.

■ The web site operator is not permitted to change the identification of web sites, configure the anonymous username or password, throttle bandwidth, create virtual directories or change their paths, or change application isolation.

▲ Because operators have more limited privileges than web site administrators, they are unable to remotely browse the file system and therefore cannot set properties on directories and files, unless a UNC path is used.

To remotely access ISM (HTML) as a web site operator, open a browser and type the domain name for the web site followed by **/iisadmin/**. For example, http://www.*companyname*.com/iisadmin/iis.asp. Figure 11-7 shows accessing the ISM (HTML) on the local computer, so the domain name is replaced with localhost.

Figure 11-7. Internet Services Manager (HTML)

Creating Web Sites and FTP Sites

Once the server is set up, web sites can be created using web services. IIS 5 can manage one site or multiple sites. Each site can appear as a separate location to Internet web surfers. When you install IIS 5, a default web site is set up for you. You can publish your content in the default web site immediately. Most organizations, though, start with a new site, so that the site can be customized to the needs of the organization. You can add new sites to a computer by launching the Web Site Creation Wizard with the following instructions:

1. In the IIS Snap-In (opened through Start | Programs | Administrative Tools | Internet Services Manager), select the local server and open the Action menu.

 NOTE: The following steps work in the IIS Snap-In, but not the IIS folder in Computer Management.

2. Click New | Web Site or FTP Site. The Web Site Creation Wizard will open. Click Next.

3. Enter a description for the site and click Next. Enter the IP address to use for the site, or open the drop-down box and select the IP address for the server. Accept the default port address of 80 and leave the Host Header blank. Click Next.

4. Enter or browse for the path on the server with the home directory containing the HTML files to be displayed when the web site is accessed. Click Next.

5. Enter the permissions that you want to assign. Click Next and then click Finish.

Hosting Multiple Sites

In the past, each domain name represented an individual computer. Today, multiple web or FTP sites can be hosted simultaneously on a single computer running IIS. This gives the appearance of separate and distinct sites to the web surfer. Each IIS server has the ability to host one or more domain names. For this reason, sites are sometimes referred to as *virtual servers*.

A web site has three identifiers it uses to identify itself on the Internet or an intranet. When queried, it must be able to respond with each of these settings:

▼ A port number

■ An IP address

▲ A host header name

By changing one of these three identifiers, you can host multiple sites on a single computer:

▼ **Port numbers**   By using appended port numbers, your site needs only one IP address to host many sites. To reach your site, clients would need to attach a port number (unless using the default port number, 80) at the end of the static IP address. Using this method of hosting multiple sites requires clients to type the actual numerical IP address followed by a port number. Host names or "friendly names" cannot be used.

- **Multiple IP addresses**   To use multiple IP addresses, you must add the host name and its corresponding IP address to your name resolution system, which is DNS with Windows 2000 Active Directory. Then, clients need only type the text name in a browser to reach your web site. Multiple IP addresses can be hosted on the same network card (however, instability has occurred in some cases when 60 or more IP addresses were assigned to any one card).

NOTE: If you are using this method of hosting multiple sites on the Internet, you will also need to register the text names with InterNIC. InterNIC has contracted eight third-party companies to host and sell these registrations, as well as their subsequent DNS listing, in InterNIC's DNS tables. The largest of these external companies is Network Solutions, which can be reached at www.networksolutions.com.

- ▲ **Host header names**   Sites can also use host header names with a single static IP address to host multiple sites. Like the previous method, you would still add the host name to your name resolution system. The difference is that once a request reaches the computer, IIS uses the host name passed in the HTTP header to determine which site clients are requesting. If you are using this method of hosting multiple sites on the Internet, you will also need to register the host header names with InterNIC.

NOTE: Sites cannot use host headers when using SSL. Host headers are part of the encrypted request and cannot be interpreted and routed to the correct site. Be aware that older browsers do not support host header names.

The majority of multiple web site hosting is done with multiple IP addresses.

Web Site Management

Whether your site is on an intranet or the Internet, the principles of publishing information are the same. Here are the steps:

1. Web files are placed in directories on the server.

2. The directories are identified to IIS as belonging to a web site.

3. When a user establishes an HTTP connection to that site, IIS sends the files to the user's browser.

While the process to store the files is simple, part of the web site manager's job must be to determine how the site is deployed, and how it and the storage will evolve. Most successful web administrators are kept busy accommodating ever-changing web content. Step back a minute from the content and look at the basics of managing a web site's infrastructure, from redirecting requests to dynamically altering web pages.

Defining Home Directories

Each web or FTP site must have a home directory, which is where the root site information is stored. As a user logs in to a specific site, IIS knows the home directory and the default first document that all users see when connecting, and provides that document to the requesting user's browser for translation and display. For example, if your site's Internet domain name is www.mycompany.com, your home directory is C:\website\mysite, and the default document is Default.htm, then browsers use the URL http://www.mycompany.com, which causes IIS to access your home directory C:\website\microsoft, and transmit the file Default.htm.

On an intranet, if your server name is Marketing, then browsers use the URL http://marketing to access files in your home directory. A default home directory is created when IIS is installed or when a new web site is created. The web site properties determine the location of the files.

Changing the Home Directory

When setting up both a web site and an FTP site on the same computer, a different home directory is specified for each service (WWW and FTP). The default home directory for the WWW service is C:\inetpub\wwwroot. The default home directory for the FTP service is C:\inetpub\ftproot. The home directory can be changed to any location on the network and can be listed as a URL or a path statement. Here is how to change the home directory:

1. In the IIS Snap-In, right-click a web or FTP site and open its Properties dialog box.

2. Click the Home Directory tab, and then specify where your home directory is located. You can select:

   ■ A directory located on a hard disk on your computer

   ■ A shared directory located on another computer

   ■ A redirection to a URL (although an FTP directory cannot be redirected this way)

3. In the text box, type in the path name, share name, or URL (WWW only) of your directory, as shown in Figure 11-8 for a web site.

Virtual Directories

Virtual directories allow access to files located on a directory not within the home directory. This is a big advantage when trying to access information to be published on an intranet that is located in multiple locations across the network. Using virtual directories is one way to link that information more easily. For the browser, everything seems to be

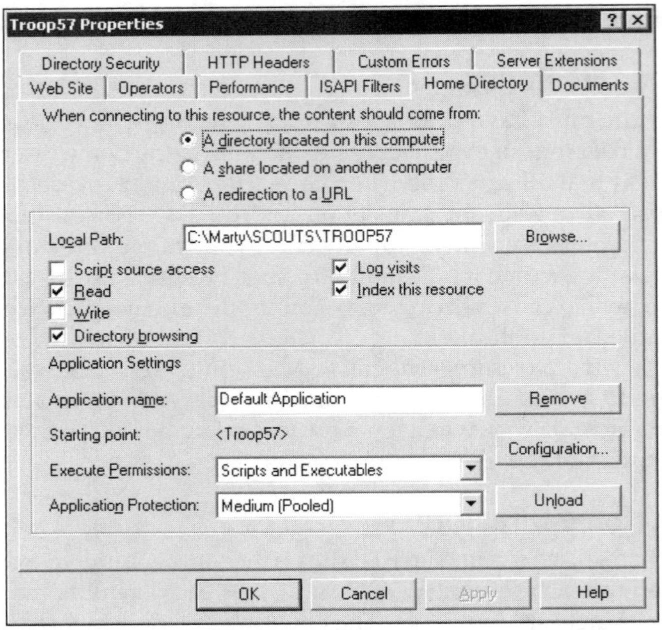

Figure 11-8. You can modify a web site's location from the Home Directory tab

in one location. For the administrator who has to collect everything, it can be easier to store each person's data in a separate virtual directory.

A virtual directory has an alias that the web browser uses to access that directory. As added benefits, using an alias often is more convenient than typing a long path and file-name, and the URL for a site does not have to change when the directory changes; only the mapping between the alias and the physical location needs to change.

Creating Virtual Directories   Create virtual directories to include those files in your web site located in directories other than the home directory. To use a directory on another computer, specify the directory's Universal Naming Convention (UNC) name in the form *servername**drive**path**filename*, and provide a username and password to use for access permission. Use the following steps to create a virtual directory:

1. In the IIS Snap-In, select the web site or FTP site to which you want to add a directory.

2. Open the Action menu (or right-click the site) and choose New | Virtual Directory, as shown in Figure 11-9. The Virtual Directory Creation Wizard will open. Click Next.

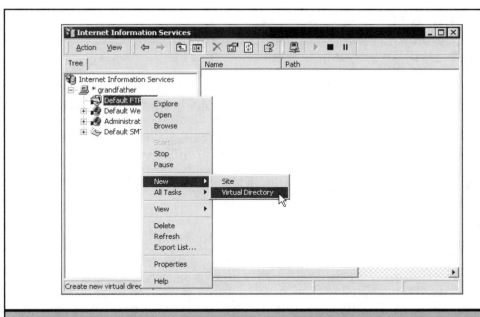

Figure 11-9.   Creating a new virtual directory

3. Enter the alias you want to use, and click Next. Enter or browse to the path that contains the desired files. Click Next.

4. Enter the username and password needed to access the files, and click Next. Enter the permissions that you want to give to the people who access these files. Click Next and then click Finish.

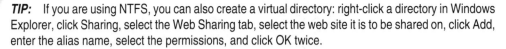

TIP: If you are using NTFS, you can also create a virtual directory: right-click a directory in Windows Explorer, click Sharing, select the Web Sharing tab, select the web site it is to be shared on, click Add, enter the alias name, select the permissions, and click OK twice.

Deleting Virtual Directories   To delete a virtual directory, use the following steps:

1. In the IIS Snap-In, select the virtual directory you want to delete.

2. Click the Action button (or right-click the site), select Delete, and click Yes when asked if you are sure you want to delete the item.

NOTE: Deleting a virtual directory does not delete the corresponding physical directory or files.

Troubleshooting IIS

A lot of issues affect the performance of IIS. Problems have three main causes: hardware issues, software issues, and site activity issues. Each of these causes is discussed in the following sections.

When troubleshooting IIS, it is important to have a baseline to compare problems against. To create a baseline for your IIS server, you apply a typical network load to the server, normally using simulation software, and log all of the server's performance characteristics. This provides a picture of how the server looks with respect to CPU, memory, hard drive performance, and utilization. Then, when performance is questionable, you can compare the baseline to the current situation to determine where the possible bottleneck is occurring. The issues in the following sections should be analyzed when baselining and later troubleshooting an IIS server.

Memory Allocation

On a Windows NT or Windows 2000 server running IIS, memory allocation must be balanced with all applications and other processes running on the server. Allocating too much memory to any one process or application may have consequences to overall system performance. The following is a list of some Performance Monitor counters to monitor and troubleshoot memory allocation issues (these should all have a baseline established for them). Figure 11-10 shows adding counters to the Performance Monitor.

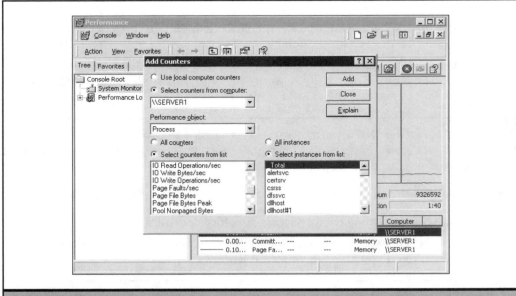

Figure 11-10.   Adding counters to Performance Monitor

Access Performance Monitor by opening the Start menu and choosing Programs | Administrative Tools | Performance. Then, right-click the right pane and choose Add Counters. In the Performance Object drop-down list, choose Memory. Select the counters listed below one at a time and click Add. You can get more information about each counter by selecting the counter and clicking Explain.

▼   **Memory: Available Bytes**   Measures the total physical memory available to the OS.

▲   **Memory: Committed Bytes**   Measures the memory required to run all the processes and applications on your server.

The comparison between Committed and Available bytes should be tracked over several days to cover several periods of peak activity. You should always have at least 4MB or 5 percent more available memory than committed memory.

▼   **Memory: Page Faults/sec**   Measures page faults that occur when an application attempts to read from a virtual memory location that is marked "not present." Zero is the optimum measurement. Any measurement higher than zero delays response time. This counter measures both *hard page faults*, which occur when a file has to be retrieved from a hard disk rather than virtual memory, and *soft page faults*, which occur when a resolved page fault, found elsewhere in physical memory, interrupts the processor; soft page faults have much less effect on performance than hard page faults.

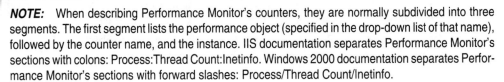

NOTE: When describing Performance Monitor's counters, they are normally subdivided into three segments. The first segment lists the performance object (specified in the drop-down list of that name), followed by the counter name, and the instance. IIS documentation separates Performance Monitor's sections with colons: Process:Thread Count:Inetinfo. Windows 2000 documentation separates Performance Monitor's sections with forward slashes: Process/Thread Count/Inetinfo.

Processor Threads

If you have web sites that use ASP or ISAPI applications, you will want to baseline and monitor the processor threads used by these applications. IIS 5 sets the default value of ASP worker threads per processor at 25. A quad-processor computer would, therefore, have 100 threads. In IIS 4 you can change the number of threads per processor value by changing ProcessorThreadMax in the Registry. In IIS 5 this is handled automatically.

Here are some Performance Monitor counters that will help you monitor threads:

▼   **Process: Thread Count: dllhost**   Counts the number of threads created by the pooled out-of-process application and displays the most recent value.

- **Process: Thread Count: dllhost#1, #2,U, #N**   Counts the number of threads created by the isolated out-of-process application and displays the most recent value.

- **Process: Thread Count: Inetinfo**   Counts the number of threads created by the process and displays the most recent value.

- **Thread: % Processor Time: Inetinfo =>Thread #**   Measures how much processor time each thread of the Inetinfo process is using.

- ▲ **Thread: Context Switches: sec: Inetinfo =>Thread#**   Measures the maximum number of threads per processor, or thread pool. You should monitor this counter to make sure you are not creating so many context switches that the memory being lost to context switches supercedes the benefit of added threads, at which point your performance will decrease rather than improve.

Load Testing

Load testing, or stress testing, allows you to test the stability of your environment under any given number of users. You can stress test your environment by using the Microsoft Web Application Stress Tool (WAST), a tool designed to simulate multiple browsers requesting pages from a web application (this tool is available on the Windows 2000 Server Resource Kit CD). With WAST, you can use the following Performance Monitor counters to help you measure and monitor your web site:

- ▼ **Web Service: Get Requests/sec**   Measures the rate at which HTTP requests using the GET method are made. GET requests generally are used for basic file retrievals or image maps, though they can be used with forms.

- **Web Service: Post Requests/sec**   Measures the rate at which HTTP requests using the POST method are made. POST requests generally are used for forms or gateway requests.

- **Processor: % Processor Time**   Measures the percentage of elapsed time that all of the threads of this process used the processor to execute instructions. An *instruction* is the basic unit of execution in a computer, a *thread* is the object that executes instructions, and a *process* is the object created when a program is run. Codes executed to handle some hardware interrupts and trap conditions are included in this count. On multiprocessor machines, the maximum value of the counter is 100 percent times the number of processors.

- ▲ **Active Server Pages: Requests/sec**   Measures the number of requests executed per second.

Remember that performance tuning is an ongoing process. As the contents of your environment evolve, your environment performance should be continuously monitored, making one adjustment at a time. Continue to tune and stress test until you find the right combination of settings that work best for the web site.

WINDOWS MEDIA SERVICES

Windows Media Services enables streaming of multimedia content over all types of networks. These networks can range from low-bandwidth, dial-up Internet connections to high-bandwidth, local area networks. Windows Media Services is installed from the Add/Remove Programs control panel, as previously described in "Installing IIS." The complete installation includes both Windows Media Services and Windows Media Administrator. There is also an installation that includes only Windows Media Administrator, but you must install Windows Media Administrator if you install Windows Media Services. Windows Media Administrator is used for directly or remotely administering one or more media servers. This discussion assumes that both Windows Media Services and Windows Media Administrator are installed.

NOTE: Streaming audio and video allows the media to be played on the receiving computer as it is being downloaded, instead of waiting for it to completely download before playing it. The Microsoft Windows Media Player, included in Windows 2000, can be used to play streaming audio and video.

Windows Media Services

Utilizing Windows Media Services, a media server can stream audio and video content over the Web. To understand why this is significant, it helps to understand the way a typical HTTP session works. First, a web browser logs on to the web server. The web server recognizes the URL and downloads the appropriate information to the local computer. Once downloaded, the browser displays the web pages that it received from the site. When the user clicks another link, the browser requests another download. This works great for small file sizes, such as a web page, but video and audio files are so large that waiting for files to download in this way is like waiting for paint to dry. Windows Media Services uses streaming technology to enable you to load and play the audio or video while it is still downloading. This greatly increases the satisfaction of the user who is downloading the file.

Streaming Methods

There are two ways to stream audio and video. One uses a web server alone, the other separates the web tasks from the streaming media tasks. This is done utilizing a media server to stream audio or video, in conjunction with a web server used to download the rest of the web information.

Streaming with a Web Server   The server sends the audio and video files in the same fashion as it would send any type of file. The streaming client stores, or *buffers*, a small amount of the audio or video stream and then starts playing it while continuing the download. Buffering theoretically allows the media to continue playing uninterrupted during periods of network congestion. In fact, it is normal for it to get interrupted on a 56 Kbps connection. The client retrieves data as fast as the web server, network, and client connection allow.

> **NOTE:** Only certain media file formats support this type of "progressive playback." Microsoft's Advanced Streaming Format (ASF) is one of them.

Streaming with a Media Server With a media server, the first step is to compress the media file and copy it to a specialized streaming media server (such as Microsoft Windows Media Services). Next, a reference is made on the web page so that IIS knows when and where to retrieve the streaming data for the page. Then, data is sent to the client such that the content is delivered at the same rate as the compressed audio and video streams. The server and the client stay in close touch during the delivery process, and the streaming media server can respond to any feedback from the client.

Streaming with Windows Media Services Designed specifically for the task of delivering live or on-demand streaming media rather than many small HTML and image files, a Windows Media Services server offers many advantages over standard web servers:

▼ More efficient network throughput

■ Better audio and video quality to the user

■ Support for advanced features

■ Cost-effective scalability to a large number of users

■ Protection of content copyright

▲ Multiple delivery options

Windows Media Services, diagrammatically shown in Figure 11-11, automatically switches to the appropriate protocol, so no client-side configuration is necessary.

Managing Windows Media Services

Once Windows Media Services is installed, you can configure and manage it on an ongoing basis through the Configure Your Server dialog box or directly through the Windows Media Administrator. Unless you do the configuration as you install Windows 2000 Server, which automatically opens Configure Your Server and in turn opens Windows Media Administrator, it saves you a step to directly open Windows Media Administrator.

Look at Windows Media Administrator by opening the Start menu and choosing Programs | Administrative Tools | Windows Media. The Windows Media Administrator will open, as shown in Figure 11-12. This provides lots of discussion as well as the tools to set up and manage one or more servers. Read the concepts and terms at the bottom and then go through the discussion of the steps to configure Windows Media Services.

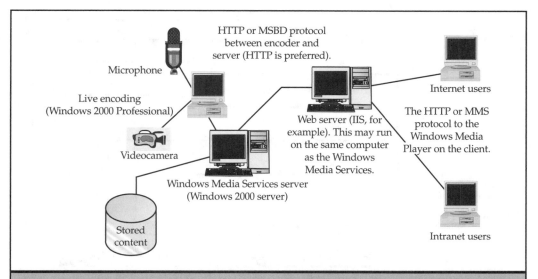

Figure 11-11.   Windows Media Services interacts with a web server to provide streaming content to a client's browser

Figure 11-12.   Windows Media Administrator is used to manage Windows Media Services servers

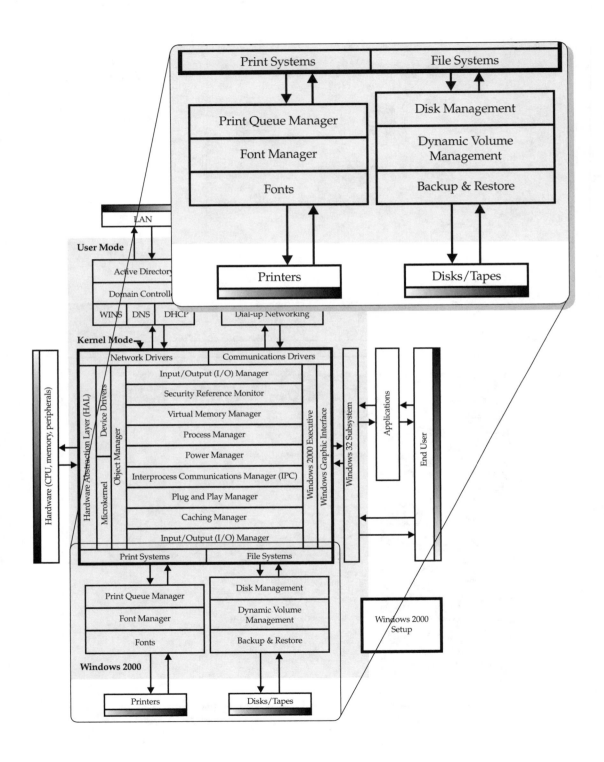

PART V

Administering Windows 2000 Server

The job of administering a Windows 2000 network, even one as small as a single server and a dozen workstations, is a significant task. To assist in this, Windows 2000 has a number of system management tools that can be used to monitor and tune the system's performance both locally and remotely. The purpose of Part V is to explore these tools and discuss how they can best be used. Chapter 12 looks at the extensive set of tools that are available in Windows 2000 to handle the various types of storage systems and the files and folders they contain. Chapter 13 describes what constitutes Windows 2000 printing, how to set it up, how to management it, and how to manage the fonts that are required for printing. Chapter 14 discusses the system management tools and user management tools that are not part of setting up, networking, file management, or printing. Chapter 15 describes each of the security demands and the Windows 2000 facilities that address that demand, as well as the ways to implement those facilities.

CHAPTER 12

Storage and File System Management

The foundation task of a server is to store, retrieve, and manage files. If that is not done easily and efficiently, there is not a lot of reason for the server. This chapter looks at how Windows 2000 handles this function. In the process, the chapter discusses the structure and systems used for file storage, and the management features that Windows 2000 makes available in this area.

WINDOWS 2000 FILE STORAGE STRUCTURE

Windows 2000 is meant to work in a wide range of computing environments and with several other operating systems. As a result, the structure of its file storage has to be flexible. This is manifest in the types of storage that are available, and in the file systems that Windows 2000 can utilize.

Types of Storage

Prior to Windows 2000, there was only one type of storage, called *basic storage,* which allowed a drive to be divided into partitions. Windows 2000 adds *dynamic storage,* which allows the dynamic creation of volumes. On a disk-by-disk basis, you must choose which type of storage you want to use, because you can use only one type on a drive. You can have both types in a computer that has two or more drives.

Basic Storage

Basic storage, which provides for the partitioning of a hard disk, is the default type of storage in Windows 2000 and is the type of storage used in earlier versions of Windows, Windows NT, and MS-DOS. Partitioning uses software to divide a single disk drive into *partitions* that act as if they were separate disk drives. There are primary partitions and extended partitions.

Primary partitions are given a drive letter, are separately formatted, and are used to boot or start the computer. There can be up to four primary partitions on a single drive. One partition at a time is made the *active* partition that is used to start the computer. You can put different operating systems on different partitions and start them independently. Since each partition is formatted separately, another use of partitions is to put data on one partition and the programs and operating system on another partition, allowing you to reformat the applications/OS partition without disturbing the data.

NOTE: There are some limitations and/or downsides to dual booting. See "Deciding Whether to Dual Boot" in Chapter 3.

One partition on a disk drive can be an *extended* partition in place of a primary partition, so there can only be three primary partitions if there is an extended partition. An extended partition does not have a drive letter and is not formatted; rather, you divide an extended partition into *logical drives,* each of which is given a drive letter and separately formatted. An extended partition with logical drives allows you to divide a disk into more than four segments. You do not need to have a primary partition to create an extended partition, but in that case, you must start the computer from another drive.

Partitions are usually created and changed while you are doing a clean install of an OS. In Windows 2000, though, you can use the Disk Management pane (see "Disk Management," later in this chapter) to create a new partition if there is enough unpartitioned space, or you can delete a partition to create more unpartitioned space. If you delete a partition, you lose all of its contents and must reformat any new partition that is created.

Dynamic Storage

Dynamic storage uses a single partition spanning an entire disk that has been upgraded from basic storage. This single partition can be divided into volumes. *Volumes,* which in their simplest form are the same as partitions, may also have additional features. The following are the five different types of volumes:

▼   **Simple volumes**   Identify disk space on a single drive, and are the same as partitions.

■   **Spanned volumes**   Identify disk space on 2 to 32 disk drives. The space is used sequentially, as it is on a single drive. When the first drive is filled, the second drive is used, and so on. If any disk in a spanned volume fails, the entire volume fails.

■   **Mirrored volumes**   A pair of simple volumes on two separate disk drives on which the exact same information is written simultaneously. If one disk fails, the other can be used.

■   **Striped volumes**   Identify disk space from 2 to 32 disk drives, where a portion of the data is written on each drive at the same time. This makes for very fast reading and writing, but if any disk fails, the entire volume fails.

▲   **RAID-5 volumes**   Striped volumes on at least three disks where error-correction information has been added such that if any disk fails, the information can be reconstructed. (RAID stands for *redundant array of independent disks* or, alternatively, *redundant array of inexpensive disks.*)

Unlike basic storage, dynamic storage can be changed in real time without rebooting the computer. Using Dynamic Volume Management (discussed later in the chapter), you can upgrade basic storage to dynamic storage and add, delete, and change the size of volumes, all without rebooting. You cannot upgrade to dynamic storage in either portable computers or on removable storage.

File Systems

File systems determine the way data is stored on a disk, and are the data structure or format of the data. When you format a disk, you must specify the file system that will be used. In Windows 2000, you have a choice of three file systems: FAT (file allocation table), FAT32, and NTFS (new technology file system).

FAT and FAT32 File Systems

FAT was the original file system used in MS-DOS and early versions of Windows through Windows 3.*x* and Windows for Workgroups. The initial releases of Windows 95 used VFAT (virtual FAT), and Windows 95 OSR2 (original equipment manufacturers, or OEMs, service release 2) and Windows 98 used FAT32. FAT is a 16-bit file system with a maximum disk partition size of 512MB, and uses a maximum eight-character filename with a three-character extension. VFAT is also a 16-bit file system, but it supports disk partitions up to 2GB and allows long filenames of up to 255 characters. FAT32 is a 32-bit file system, allows disk partitions of over 2TB (terabytes or trillion bytes), and allows long filenames. In Windows NT and 2000, FAT partitions can go up to 4GB.

FAT, VFAT, and FAT32 store information using a fixed-size increment of the disk, called a *cluster*. Clusters range in size from 512 bytes to 32KB, depending on the size of the disk partition, as shown in Table 12-1. Therefore, as the size of the partition increases, the minimum cluster size increases. A large cluster size can be very inefficient if you are storing a lot of small files. FAT32 made a big improvement in the minimum cluster size and is therefore a major benefit with today's large disks.

Since most files are substantially larger than the cluster size, a number of clusters are necessary to store a single file. The FAT has an entry for each file, containing the filename, the creation date, the total size, and the address on the disk of the first cluster used by the file. Each cluster has the address of the cluster after it, as well as the address of the preceding cluster. One cluster getting corrupted can break cluster chains, often making the file unreadable. Some utilities occasionally can restore the file by several techniques, including reading backward down the cluster chain. The common end result is orphaned clusters, which can only be deleted.

Disk Partition	FAT and VFAT Cluster	FAT32 Cluster
0 – 31MB	512 bytes	512 bytes
32 – 63MB	1KB	512 bytes
64 – 127MB	2KB	512 bytes
128 – 255MB	4KB	512 bytes
256 – 511MB	8KB	4KB
512 – 1,023MB	16KB	4KB
1,024 – 2,047MB	32KB	4KB
2 – 4GB	64KB	4KB
4 – 8GB		4KB
8 – 16GB		8KB
16 – 32GB		16KB
33GB and above		32KB

Table 12-1.   Cluster Sizes Resulting from Various Partition Sizes

Clusters can be written anywhere on a disk. If there is room, they are written sequentially, but if there isn't room, they can be spread all over the disk. This is called *fragmentation,* which can cause the load time for a file to be quite lengthy. Utilities are available, including one in Windows 2000, to defragment a partition by rearranging the clusters so that all the clusters for a file are contiguous (see "Drive Defragmentation," later in this chapter).

NTFS File System

NTFS was developed for Windows NT and contains features making it much more secure and less susceptible to disk errors than FAT or FAT32. NTFS is a 32-bit file system that can utilize very large (in excess of 2TB) volumes or partitions and can use filenames of up to 255 characters, including spaces and the preservation of case. Most importantly, NTFS is the only file system that fully utilizes all the features of Windows 2000, such as domains and Active Directories.

One of the most important features of NTFS is that it provides file- and folder-level security, whereas FAT and FAT32 do not. This means that with FAT or FAT32, if someone gets access to a disk, every file and folder is immediately available. With NTFS, each file and folder has an *access control list* (ACL), which contains the *security identifiers* (SIDs) of the users and groups that are permitted to access the file.

Other features that are available under NTFS and not under FAT or FAT32 are the following:

▼ File encryption

■ Disk compression

■ Remote storage management (in Windows 2000 Server only)

■ Disk quotas

▲ Improved performance with large drives

The first four items are discussed further later in this chapter. The improved performance with large drives occurs because NTFS does not have the problem of increasing cluster size as the disk size increases.

The sum of all this is that NTFS is strongly recommended. The only situation in which you would not want to use NTFS is if you want to dual boot with another operating system that cannot read NTFS.

Converting a FAT or FAT32 Drive to NTFS

Normally, you would convert a drive from FAT or FAT32 to NTFS while you are installing Windows 2000. Chapters 4 and 5 have instructions to do that. You can also convert a FAT or FAT32 partition, volume, or drive at any other time in either of two ways:

▼ By formatting the partition, volume, or drive

▲ By running the program Convert.exe

"Disk Management," later in the chapter, discusses formatting, which of course deletes everything on the partition, volume, or drive. Using Convert.exe preserves the partition, volume, or drive. Use the following instructions to use Convert.exe:

NOTE: Many of the steps in this chapter require that you be logged on either as the Administrator or as someone with Administrator permissions.

1. Open the Start menu and choose Programs | Accessories | Command Prompt. The Command Prompt window opens.

2. At the command prompt, type **convert** *drive:* **/fs:ntfs** and press ENTER, where *drive* is the drive letter of the partition, volume, or drive that you want converted. If you would like to see a list of the files that are being converted, you can add /v after /fs:ntfs and a space. The partition, volume, or drive will be converted.

3. When you see Conversion Complete, at the command prompt, type **Exit** and press ENTER.

Convert.exe has only three switches:

▼ **/fs:ntfs**   Specifies a file system conversion to NTFS

■ **/v**   Specifies verbose mode, which displays all the files being converted

▲ **/nametable:***filename*.**log**   Creates a log in the root directory of the filenames that are converted

The only way to return a partition, volume, or drive to FAT or FAT 32 after converting it to NTFS is to reformat it.

FILE SYSTEM MANAGEMENT

The Windows 2000 file system extends well beyond a single drive, or even all the drives in a single machine, to all the drives in a network and even includes volumes stored offline on tape or disk. The management of this system is significant, and Windows 2000 has a very significant set of tools to handle it. Among these are the following:

▼ Disk Management

■ Dynamic Volume Management

■ Distributed File System

■ Removable Storage Manager

■ Remote Storage Service

▲ Disk Backup and Restore

Disk Management

Disk Management provides a means for managing both local and remote network drives, which includes partitioning, disk compression, disk defragmentation, and disk quotas. Disk management is handled by the Disk Management pane of the Computer Management window. Use the following steps to open Disk Management:

1. Open the Start menu and choose Programs | Administrative Tools | Computer Management. The Computer Management window opens.

NOTE: In Windows 2000 Professional, Administrative Tools isn't on the Programs menu by default. To add it, open the Start menu and choose Settings | Taskbar & Start Menu. In the Advanced tab, click Display Administrative Tools and click OK.

2. Open Storage in the left pane and click Disk Management. The Disk Management pane appears, as shown in Figure 12-1.

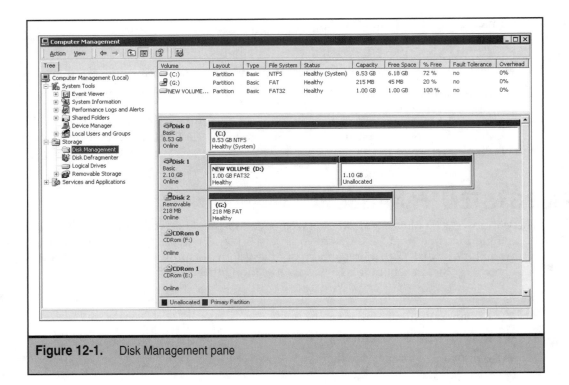

Figure 12-1. Disk Management pane

Disk Management Pane

The Disk Management pane has two main sections: a character-based listing of partitions, volumes, and drives at the top, and a graphic display of the same objects at the bottom. Explore the Disk Management pane with the next set of steps:

1. Right-click an object in the character-based listing to open its context menu. From this menu, you can look at the contents in either My Computer or Windows Explorer; mark the partition or volume as active, if it isn't already so; change the drive letter and path; format or delete the partition or volume if it isn't the active or system partition or volume; open the partition's or volume's Properties dialog box; and get help.

2. Right-click a partition or volume on the right of the graphic display at the bottom of the pane. You'll see a menu similar to that in step 1 (depending on the type of partition, you may see some differences).

3. Right-click a drive on the left of the graphic display. You will see a drive menu that allows you to upgrade to a dynamic disk, if you click a basic disk that is

not removable and you are in a desktop computer, not a laptop. This menu also allows you to open the drive's Properties dialog box, and open Help.

4. Click the Action menu to open it. Here, you can quickly refresh the current status of the storage objects; rescan all drives, which is usually only done when the computer is restarted, and is used to display a drive that has been added or removed without restarting the computer (*hot swapping*); restore a previous drive configuration; display the menu for the partition, volume, or drive that is currently selected (All Tasks); and access Help.

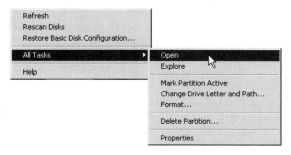

Customizing the Disk Management Pane

The Disk Management pane can be significantly customized through both the toolbar and the View menu. Disk Management is an important tool, so you should take the time to customize it by using these steps:

1. In the Computer Management window, open the View menu. The first two options let you determine what is in the top and bottom sections of the pane. The default is a list of partitions or volumes at the top and the graphical view at the bottom. The third alternative is a list of disk drives, which is the same information that is presented in the graphical view.

2. Try several changes to see if any suit you more than the default. Figure 12-2 shows a compact alternative with the Disk list on top and the Volume list on the bottom. Keep the layout you like best.

3. Either click Settings on the right of the toolbar or reopen the View menu and choose Settings. The View Settings dialog box opens. In the Appearance tab, you can choose the colors and patterns used to represent the various types of partitions and volumes.

4. Select the colors you want to use, and click the Scaling tab. Here, you can choose the way that disks and disk regions (partitions and volumes) are graphically displayed relative to each other. To show capacity logarithmically is probably the best choice if you have drives and regions of substantially different sizes.

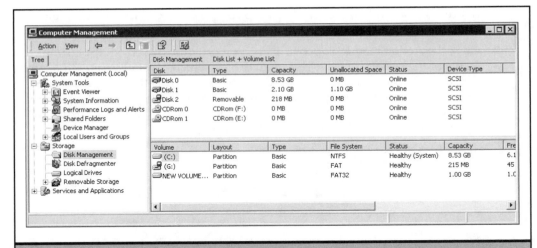

Figure 12-2.   An alternative layout for the Disk Management pane

5. Make the choices that are correct for you and click OK. Reopen the View menu and choose Customize. The Customize View dialog box opens. Here, you can customize the Computer Management window (called MMC in the dialog box, for Microsoft Management Console).

6. Try several changes to see if you like them, and configure the window the way that is best for you. When you are finished, click OK to close the Customize View dialog box.

NOTE: The All Drive Paths option of the View menu will be discussed in "Dynamic Volume Management," later in this chapter.

Drive and Partition Properties

There are separate Properties dialog boxes for drives and for partitions. What many people have thought of as the drive properties are really the partition or volume properties. See this for yourself next:

1. Right-click a drive on the left side of the graphic view and choose Properties. The Disk Properties dialog box, similar to Figure 12-3, opens. This is primarily an information dialog box, and the only function you can perform is to open the Properties dialog box for a partition or volume.

2. Right-click a partition or volume in the lower part of the Disk Properties dialog box and click Properties. The Properties dialog box for the partition or volume

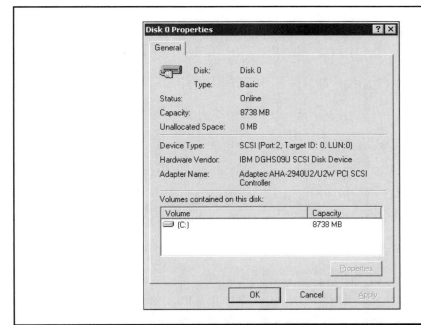

Figure 12-3.   Disk properties dialog box that contains primarily information

opens, as you can see in Figure 12-4. This dialog box also provides some information, but unlike the Disk Properties dialog box, it is primarily a place to perform tasks on partitions and volumes. Many of these functions are discussed elsewhere in this chapter, although sharing and security are discussed in Chapter 15, and web sharing is discussed in Chapter 11.

3. Click Disk Cleanup. You'll see a message telling you that Disk Cleanup is calculating how much space will be freed up by eliminating various types of files. When this is finished, the Disk Cleanup dialog box opens with a list of file types that can be deleted. When you click a file type in the list, the Description describes the files; in most cases, you can click View Files to see a list of the files that will be deleted.

4. Review the file types and select those to be deleted. Do not compress old files. That is discussed under "Data Compression," later in this chapter. When you have selected all the files to be deleted, click OK, and answer Yes, you are sure you want to delete files. You will be told what is happening. When Disk Cleanup is done, the Used Space value in the Properties dialog box for the partition or volume will decrease by the amount you recovered.

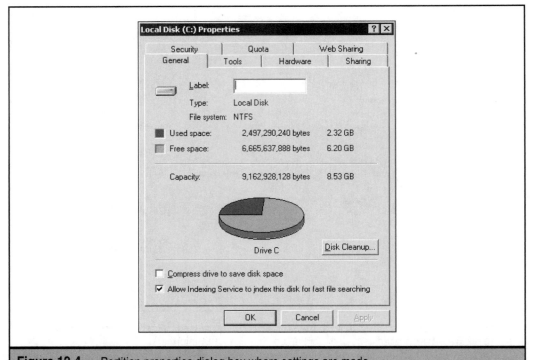

Figure 12-4.   Partition properties dialog box where settings are made

5. Click each of the tabs of the Properties dialog box to see the many features and tools that are available. Two features that are not discussed elsewhere are Error-Checking in the Tools tab and the Hardware tab.

6. Open the Tools tab and click Check Now in the Error-Checking section. The Check Disk dialog box opens and explains that you can, at your option, fix file system errors, such as lost clusters, and look for and attempt to recover data that is in a bad sector on the disk.

7. Select what disk checking you want to do, and click Start. If you are on an active server, you are told that exclusive access is not available and thus disk checking could not be done; you are asked whether you want to do the checking the next time you restart the computer. Choose what you want to do, by clicking Yes or No.

8. Open the Hardware tab. Here, you see a list of the drives in the computer. If you select a drive and click Properties, you'll see yet another drive Properties dialog box (the same Properties dialog box as in Device Manager). All other tabs are discussed elsewhere.

9. When you are done looking at the Properties dialog box for the partition or volume, click OK to close it.

NOTE: The Properties dialog box for a partition or volume can be opened by right-clicking a partition or volume and choosing Properties.

Adding and Removing a Disk Drive

If you have hardware that allows *hot swapping* (adding and removing standard, normally not removable disk drives while the computer is running), or you have a removable disk drive that is meant to be removed while the computer is running, Windows 2000 has several tools to support this that don't require restarting the computer. Normally, a computer scans its disk drives to determine what is available only when it is started or restarted. Windows 2000 makes this scan available while the computer is running, through the Rescan option in the Action menu. Also, if you just remove a disk drive, either hot-swappable or removable, without preparing for it, problems can result, such as losing data or causing your computer to crash, as described in Figure 12-5. To accommodate this, the Windows 2000 Hardware Wizard has an Unplug/Eject option, and you can even put an Unplug/Eject icon on the taskbar for this purpose, again as described in Figure 12-5.

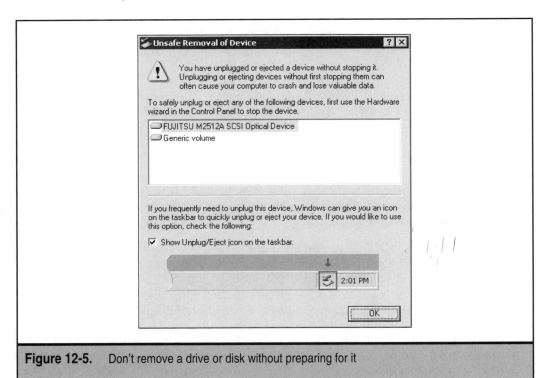

Figure 12-5.   Don't remove a drive or disk without preparing for it

CAUTION: Don't add or remove a disk drive while the computer is running unless you know for sure that the hardware supports hot swapping. Significant damage can occur to both the drive and the computer or to either one of them.

Adding a Drive   You can add a new drive or a drive that you have taken out of another computer. After physically adding a new drive—one that has never been used or has been newly formatted prior to installing it—open the Disk Management pane and choose Rescan from the Action menu. After rescanning, the drive should appear in Disk Management, and you can partition and format it as you wish (see the upcoming section "Partitioning and Formatting").

If you bring in a disk that has been used on, and contains data from, another computer, use Rescan as just described. After rescanning, the new disk may be marked "Foreign" if Windows 2000 detects that the disk is a dynamic disk from another Windows 2000 computer (which store their own configuration data). Right-click the foreign drive, choose Import Foreign Disks, and follow the directions that you see.

Removing a Drive   If you want to remove a drive that is either hot-swappable or removable, it is important to prepare the drive for that event by telling Windows 2000 that you are going to remove it, before you actually do so. Knowing this, Windows 2000 will prevent further writing to the drive and perform any hardware-specific tasks, such as spinning down the drive and/or ejecting the platter. Depending on your drive and how it has been implemented in Windows 2000, you'll have various ways to tell the operating system that you want to remove the drive.

The most general approach is to use the Control Panel Add/Remove Hardware Wizard, as follows:

1. Open the Start menu, choose Settings | Control Panel, and double-click Add/Remove Hardware. The Add/Remove Hardware Wizard opens.
2. Click Next. Choose Uninstall/Unplug a Device. Click Next again.
3. Click Unplug/Eject a Device and again click Next. A list of hardware devices that you can unplug or eject appears.
4. Select the device you want to unplug or eject, click Next, confirm you have the right device, and click Finish. The device will be made ready and, if appropriate, ejected.

As you saw in Figure 12-5, if you do the removal/ejection very often, you can shorten the preceding process by putting an icon on the taskbar. When you click this icon, the list of devices appears, and you have to do step 4 only.

On some devices, such as removable drives, you can right-click the drive on the left of the graphical part of the Disk Management pane and choose Eject. The disk will be prepared and ejected. Other devices have similar commands.

Partitioning and Formatting

The first step in preparing a disk for use is to partition it and then format it. Partitioning can be done only when there is unallocated space on the drive—space that is not currently used for an existing partition. If you have no unallocated space, then the only way to create a new partition is to delete an existing one. Therefore, start out looking at deleting partitions, then adding partitions, formatting them, adding logical drives, and changing drive letters.

TIP: *Free space* is the amount of space available to create logical drives from extended partitions. *Unallocated space* is space that is not allocated to anything.

CAUTION: Deleting a partition and then formatting it eliminates all information in the partition. Be very sure you want to do this before you execute the commands.

Deleting Partitions To delete a partition, as with the rest of the partitioning and formatting functions, you should have the Disk Management pane open in the Computer Management window. From that point, right-click the partition to be deleted and choose Delete Partition. You are warned that all data will be lost. Click Yes if you are sure you want to do that. The partition is deleted.

Adding Primary Partitions Adding a primary partition is a little more complex and has its own wizard. To add a partition:

1. Right-click an unallocated area of a disk and choose Create Partition. The Create Partition Wizard opens.

2. Click Next. Choose the type of partition you want, either a primary partition or an extended partition. You need to use a primary partition to start an operating system, but you can only have four partitions. If one of the four partitions is an extended partition, you can then divide it into 23 logical drives. After making the decision, click Next.

3. Select the size of the partition. The maximum is the size of the unallocated space; the minimum is 7MB, as you can see in Figure 12-6. When you have selected the size, click Next.

4. Assign a drive letter. The drop-down list shows you the options available, which is the alphabet less the other drives already in the computer. There are two other options: you can make this partition a folder on any other drive that supports drive paths (most do), and you can leave the drive letter unassigned. Make your choice and click Next.

5. Choose how you want the partition formatted (if at all), the label to use, and whether you want to use file and folder compression, as shown in Figure 12-7. Then, click Next.

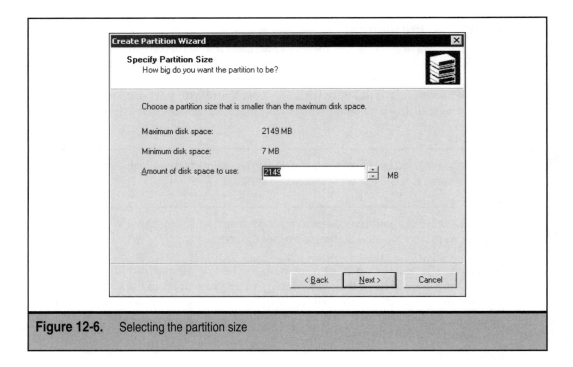

Figure 12-6.   Selecting the partition size

6. Review the options that you have chosen and use Back to correct any that are not what you want.

7. When all the choices are the way you want them, click Finish. The partition will be created and formatted as you instructed.

TIP: One good reason to attach a new partition to an existing drive and folder is to increase the space available in an existing shared folder ("a share") on a server, so the users can continue to use an existing path for storing or accessing files.

Formatting Partitions   Often, you'll format a partition when you create it, as described in the previous section, but you can also separately format the partition, if either it was not done when the partition was created or you want to replace an existing format. The following steps show you how.

NOTE: If you try to format a partition that contains Windows 2000, you'll get a message box that says you can't.

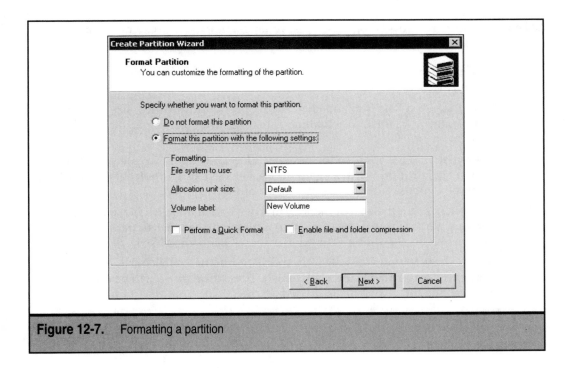

Figure 12-7. Formatting a partition

1. Right-click the partition that you want to format, and choose Format. A small Format dialog box opens, asking for the label, the file system, and the allocation unit size.

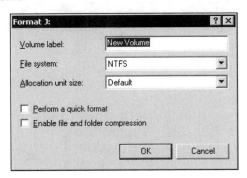

2. Make the choices that are correct for you and click OK. You will be warned that all data on the partition will be erased. Click OK. The drive will be formatted.

Adding Logical Drives   To add logical drives, you must first have an extended partition, so do that first. Then, add logical drives, as follows:

1. Right-click an unallocated area of a disk and choose Create Partition. The Create Partition Wizard opens. Click Next.

2. Select Extended Partition and click Next. Specify the partition size and again click Next. Click Finish to actually create the partition. The partition will be created.

3. Right-click the free space in the new partition and choose Create Logical Drive. The Create Partition Wizard again opens. Click Next. The Select Partition Type dialog box opens, with Logical Drive as your only option.

4. Click Next. Enter the size of the logical drive and again click Next. Assign a drive letter (see the discussion on assigning a drive letter or path in the previous section "Adding Primary Partitions") and click Next.

5. Choose the way you want the logical drive formatted, click Next, review the choices you have made, and click Finish. The logical drive will be created as you described it.

6. Repeat steps 3 through 6 for as many logical drives (up to 23) as you want.

Changing Drive Letters   Changing a drive letter is similar to the previous functions:

1. Right-click the partition or logical drive whose drive letter you want to change, and select Change Drive Letter and Path. The Change Drive Letter and Paths dialog box opens.

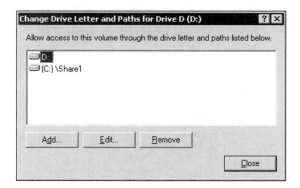

You can add additional drive letters and paths on existing drives, edit existing drive letters to change them, and remove (delete) existing drives and/or paths.

2. Click Add, Edit, or Remove, fill in the necessary information, click OK, and
    click Close.

NOTE: You can have several drive letters and/or paths for a single partition or logical drive.

Data Compression

Data compression allows you to store more information in a given amount of disk space.
Different types of file compress differently. For example, some graphics files can be compressed to under 10 percent of their original size, whereas a database file may not get under 90 percent. Compressed files, folders, and partitions or volumes can be used in the
same manner as you use uncompressed data. They are uncompressed as they are read,
and are recompressed when they are saved again. The negative side of compression is
that all file-related actions (reading, writing, copying, and so on) take a little longer.

Data compression in Windows 2000 is a lot different from the early compression
schemes, in which your only choice was to compress an entire partition. In Windows
2000, you can compress a partition or volume, a folder, or a file. You can also automatically compress files that have not been used for a given period of time, as a way to archive them.

NOTE: Data compression in Windows 2000 can be done only on or within NTFS-formatted partitions
or volumes, and the cluster size must be no larger than 4KB.

Compressing Partitions or Volumes   To use compression on a partition or volume, open
the Disk Management pane in the Computer Management window, and then follow
these steps:

1. Right-click the partition to be compressed and choose Properties. The drive's
    Properties dialog box opens, as previously shown in Figure 12-4.

2. Click the checkbox opposite Compress Drive to Save Disk Space and then
    click OK. You are asked whether you want to compress just the root folder
    (for example, D:/) or all the subfolders and files in the root folder.

NOTE: A folder can be compressed without its subfolders being compressed, and the subfolders
can be compressed without the containing folder being compressed.

3. Make the choice that is correct for you and click OK. You see a message box
    showing that the compression is taking place. When the message box goes
    away, the compression is complete.

NOTE: To uncompress data, reverse the steps used to compress it. For a partition, remove the checkmark in the Properties dialog box and confirm that you want to uncompress.

Compressing Files and Folders   You can compress individual files and folders. This is done from Windows Explorer or My Computer, as follows:

1. Right-click the file or folder and choose Properties. The file's or folder's Properties dialog box opens.

2. Click Advanced. The Advanced Attributes dialog box opens, as you can see in Figure 12-8.

3. Click Compress Contents to Save Disk Space and then click OK twice to close both the Advanced Attributes and the Properties dialog boxes. A Confirm Attributes Changes dialog box opens, giving you a choice between applying the changes to the current folder only or to include the subfolders and files it contains.

4. Make the choice that is correct for you and then click OK. The compression will be done. If the file or folder is large enough for the compression to take a minute or more, you'll see a message telling you the compression is taking place.

If you reopen the Properties dialog box for the file or folder, you will be shown both the actual size and the size on disk, as shown in Figure 12-9.

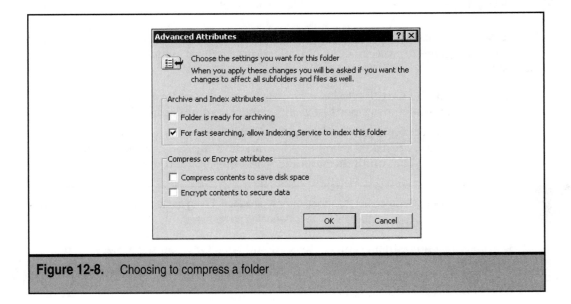

Figure 12-8.   Choosing to compress a folder

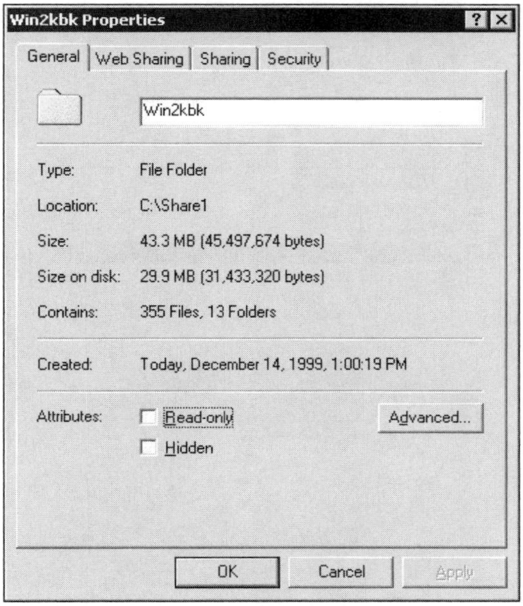

Figure 12-9.   The results of compressing a folder of many different files and folders

Automatic Archival Compression   Automatic archival compression is a routine that automatically compresses any file that goes unused for a period of time that you set. This gets around the worst problem of compression: if you are regularly using a file, it remains uncompressed and therefore faster to access. If a file is primarily just being stored, it can be compressed without much penalty.

As you read earlier in the chapter in "Drive and Partition Properties," automatic archival compression can be turned on as a part of Disk Cleanup. See how by following these steps:

1. In the Disk Management pane, right-click a partition or volume where you want to use archival compression, and choose Properties. The partition's Properties dialog box opens, as shown earlier in Figure 12-4.

2. Click Disk Cleanup to open the Disk Cleanup dialog box. In the Disk Cleanup tab, scroll the Files to Delete list until you see Compress Old Files, as you can see in Figure 12-10. This does not delete files, but rather compresses them when they have not been accessed for a certain number of days.

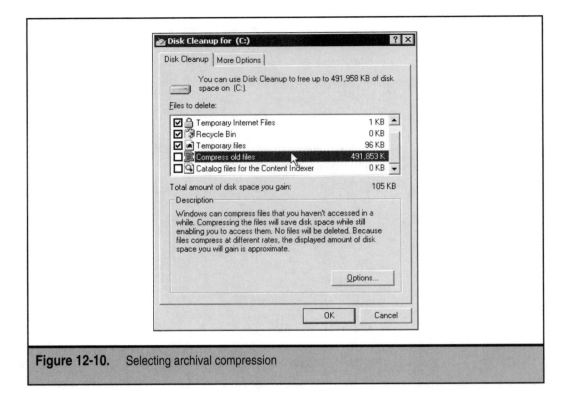

Figure 12-10. Selecting archival compression

3. Select Compress Old Files and click Options. The Compress Old Files dialog box opens and asks you to set the number of days a file must go unused before it is compressed.

4. Enter the shortest number of days that you think is realistic for you. Remember that you can still access the files even if they are compressed—it just takes a moment longer.

5. Click OK twice and answer Yes, you want to delete files (you won't be deleting the compressed files). You will see a message that the disk cleanup is taking place. When it is done, click OK to close the Properties dialog box.

Using NTFS-Compressed Files   If you compress just some of your files and folders, you'll want to know which are compressed and which aren't, and understand how the files behave when they are copied and moved. To know which files and folders are compressed and which aren't, you can change the color in which compressed files and folders (actually their labels) are displayed. To do that, open Windows Explorer's Tools menu, choose Folder Options, and in the View tab of the Folder Options dialog box that opens, click Display Compressed Files and Folders with Alternate Color.

When copying and moving compressed files and folders, they are a little slower to process and don't always end up the way they started out. Here are the rules for copying and moving:

▼ When you copy a compressed file or folder within its original partition or volume or between NTFS partitions or volumes, the file or folder inherits the compression of the folder to which it is copied.

■ When you copy a compressed file or folder to a FAT partition or a floppy disk, the file or folder decompresses.

■ When you move a compressed file or folder within its original partition or volume, the file or folder retains its original compression.

■ When you move a compressed file or folder between NTFS partitions or volumes, the file or folder inherits the compression of the folder to which it is moved.

▲ When you move a compressed file or folder to a FAT partition or a floppy disk, the file or folder decompresses.

Drive Defragmentation

As explained earlier under "File Systems," files are made up of smaller segments called clusters, and these clusters may not always be stored together in one contiguous region of a disk. The result is the fragmentation of files, causing an increased file-access time. Windows 2000 has a utility to defragment the files in a partition or volume, which can be formatted as FAT, FAT32, or NTFS. Defragment a partition or volume with these steps:

1. In the Disk Management pane, right-click the partition or volume to defragment, and choose Properties.

2. In the Properties dialog box, click the Tools tab, and click Defragment Now. The Disk Defragmenter dialog box opens.

3. Select a partition or volume and click Analyze. When the analysis is complete, you see a display of the fragmented and contiguous files in the partition, similar to that shown in Figure 12-11. You also get a recommendation of whether the partition should be defragmented, and an option to view a detailed report from which the recommendation is drawn.

4. If it is recommended, click Defragment. Depending on the amount of information in the partition, this will take some time, but you can watch as the partition slowly becomes defragmented.

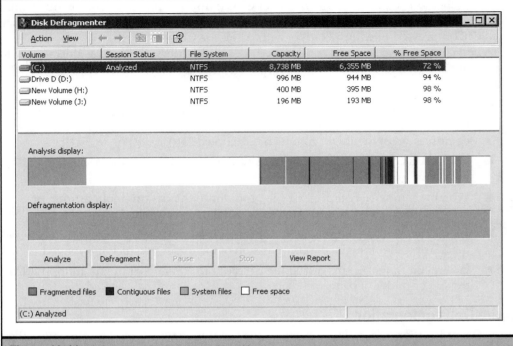

Figure 12-11. Analysis of a fragmented partition

5. When the defragmentation is complete, you can see the results, an example of which you can see in Figure 12-12. When you are done looking at the results, close the Disk Defragmenter and the partition Properties dialog boxes.

NOTE: The Disk Defragmenter can take a lot of processor resources and significantly slow down disk access. It is therefore important to do the defragmentation during a time when there is light usage of the computer.

Drive Quotas

With NTFS, you can monitor and set policies and limits on the disk space used in a partition or volume, and make sure that one user does not take up more of the disk than is desired. This is particularly important on Internet and intranet file servers. See how to set quotas next:

1. In the Disk Management pane, right-click the partition or volume in which the quotas are to be set, and choose Properties.

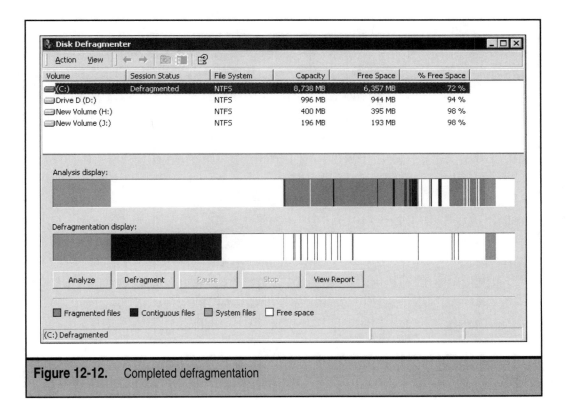

Figure 12-12. Completed defragmentation

2. In the Properties dialog box, click the Quota tab, and then click Enable Quota Management. Set the limits, warnings, and logging that you want to use. Figure 12-13 shows one possible group of settings.

3. When you have the settings that you want, click OK. After you have used the partition for a while, return to the Quota tab in the partition's Properties dialog box and click Quota Entries to open the Quota Entries window. This shows who is using the partition and how that usage relates to the quotas that have been set.

NOTE: Disk quotas are allocated by person within a partition or volume. Compression is ignored when calculating quota usage, and the free space reported to a user is the space remaining within their quota.

File and Folder Encryption

Windows 2000 NTFS allows the encryption of individual files and folders. With an encrypted file, if someone gets access to the computer, they still cannot access the file. The

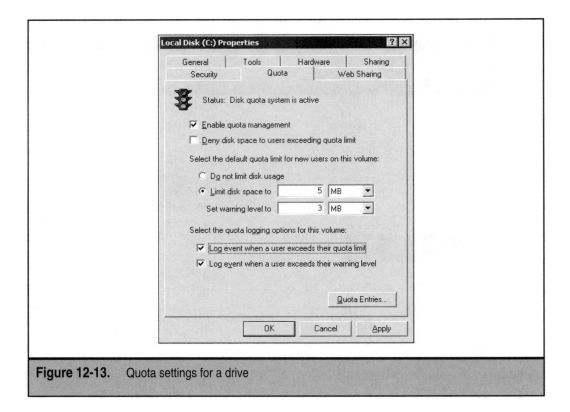

Figure 12-13. Quota settings for a drive

person who is logged on when the file is encrypted must be logged on to read the file. Any other person will find the file unreadable, although to all indications, the file is the same. (Chapter 15 discusses file and folder encryption further.) Here's how to encrypt a file or a folder:

1. Right-click the file or folder to be encrypted and choose Properties. The Properties dialog box opens.

2. Click Advanced. The Advanced Attributes dialog box opens, as shown earlier in Figure 12-8.

3. Click Encrypt Contents to Secure Data and click OK twice. Now, if you sign off the computer and someone else signs on, or if someone tries to access the file over the network, they will find the file unreadable.

NOTE: You cannot both encrypt and compress a file or folder. If you select one of these attributes, you cannot select the other.

Dynamic Volume Management

Dynamic Volume Management enables you to create, change, or mirror partitions or volumes without rebooting, by using dynamic storage and disks. A dynamic disk has a single partition within which you can create volumes. Simple volumes are the same as partitions except that they are dynamic (can be changed on the fly), can span disks, and include additional types for advanced hardware (stripped, mirrored, and RAID-5).

Upgrading to Dynamic Storage

Most basic disks can be upgraded to dynamic disks very easily. The exceptions are disks on portable computers and removable disks. Also, the disk must have 1MB of unallocated space. Here's how to upgrade:

1. In the Disk Management pane, right-click a disk on the left of the graphical display and select Upgrade to Dynamic Disk from the pop-up menu.

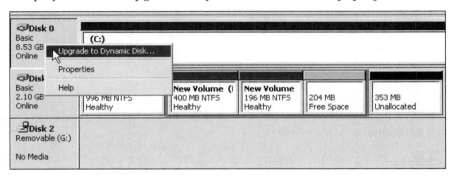

2. Confirm the disk that you want to upgrade, and click OK. The Disks to Upgrade (or Upgrade to Dynamic Disk, with a single disk) dialog box opens showing the disk(s) to be upgraded. If you click Details, you are shown the volumes that will be automatically created within the disk.

3. Click OK if you opened the Upgrade Details and then click Upgrade. You are warned that you will not be able to boot a previous version of Windows from a dynamic disk, and then are asked if you really want to upgrade.

4. If you in fact want to upgrade, click Yes. You are then told that the file systems on the disk(s) to be upgraded will be dismounted, meaning that the system will be restarted, and again you are asked if you want to continue.

5. If you do want to continue, click Yes and then click OK to reboot the computer. After rebooting, you get a message that Windows 2000 has "...finished installing new devices..." and are asked if you want to restart the computer a second time. Click Yes.

NOTE: The only way to change a dynamic disk back to a basic disk is to delete all dynamic volumes, and therefore all files, and then right-click the drive and choose Revert to Basic Disk.

Creating Volumes

You can create a new volume within the unallocated space of a dynamic drive. Do that with these steps:

1. Right-click the unallocated space of a dynamic drive and choose Create Volume. The Create Volume Wizard appears.

2. Click Next. The Select Volume Type dialog box is displayed. Choose Simple Volume and click Next.

3. Select the drive on which you want the volume (or accept the default), enter the size of the volume, and click Next.

4. Assign a drive letter, and click Next. Choose how you want the drive formatted, and again click Next.

5. Confirm the steps you want taken, going back and fixing those that are not correct if necessary, and then click Finish.

Extending Volumes

Volumes that are created on a dynamic disk, but not those that were upgraded from basic disks, can be extended. Here's how:

1. Right-click a volume you want to extend and choose Extend Volume. The Extend Volume Wizard opens.

2. Click Next. Select the drive on which you want to extend the volume (or accept the default), enter the size of the extended volume, and click Next.

3. Confirm the steps you want to perform, and click Finish.

In the graphical section of Disk Management, this looks like two separate volumes, as shown in Figure 12-14, but they have the same drive letter and appear as one volume in the Volume section.

Creating a Spanning Volume

A spanned volume can include disk space on 2 to 32 dynamic disks, and to the user it looks like a single volume. This is a way to get a large volume, but it is also risky, because

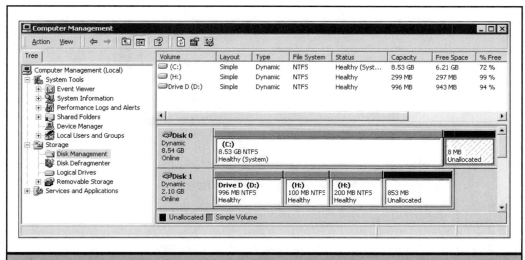

Figure 12-14. An extended volume looks separate, but it isn't

every disk that is added to the volume increases the chance the entire volume will fail. Create a spanned volume with the following steps:

1. In Disk Management, right-click an area of unallocated space on one of the disks to be included in the volume (all disks must be dynamic disks), and choose Create Volume. The Create Volume Wizard opens. Click Next.

2. Select Spanned Volume and click Next. Select the disks that you want to include in the spanned volume and the amount of space to use on each disk, as shown in Figure 12-15.

3. Click Next. Assign a drive letter or a folder at which to mount the volume, and again click Next.

4. Specify how you want the folder formatted, and click Next. Confirm the tasks you want performed, and click Finish. The volume will be created and formatted, with the final result displayed in both disks, similar to Figure 12-16.

NOTE: A spanned volume cannot be stripped or mirrored, is not fault-tolerant, and a failure on any one disk is a failure of the entire volume.

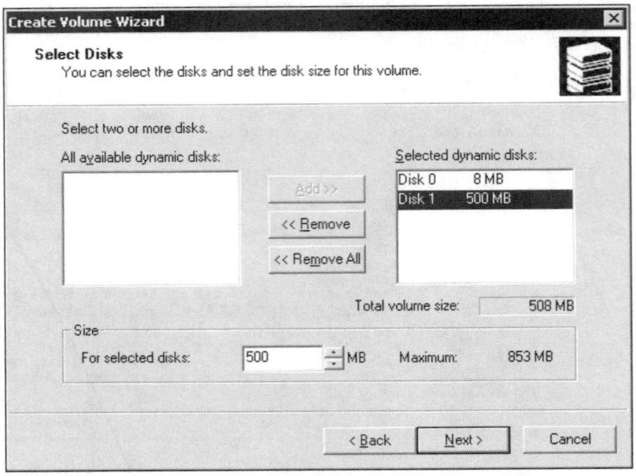

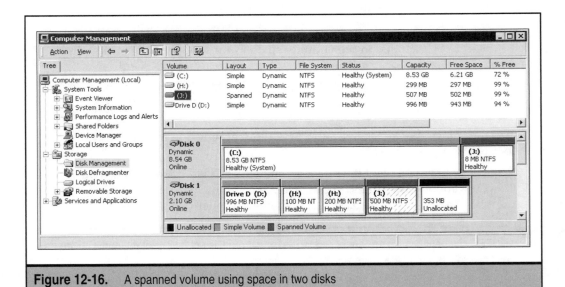

Figure 12-15.   Selecting disks to span

Figure 12-16.   A spanned volume using space in two disks

Distributed File System

The Distributed file system (Dfs) provides for the creation of a directory that spans several file servers and allows users to easily search and locate files or folders distributed over the network. To users of Dfs, files spread throughout a network can appear as though they are on a single server, which makes their use much easier than if they appear on their actual servers. Users need to go to only one place on the network to access files located in many different places. Dfs also assists in load balancing across several servers, by allowing the distribution of files over those servers without penalizing the end user. Dfs can be either stand-alone or domain-based with Active Directory, wherein spreading the information across several domain controllers provides a degree of fault tolerance.

Dfs has both server-based and client-based components. The Dfs client runs on Windows 95 and 98 as well as on Windows NT 4 (Service Pack 3 and above) and Windows 2000. The Dfs server-based components, Dfs roots and Dfs links, run on Windows NT 4 (Service Pack 3 and above) in stand-alone mode, and on Windows 2000 in both stand-alone and domain-based modes.

The *Dfs client* caches referrals for a period of time to Dfs roots and Dfs links. *Dfs roots* store shared files and *Dfs links*, which point to other Dfs roots, individual shared files, or domain volumes. In a domain-based Dfs, the Dfs client must be a member of the same domain as the Dfs root it is seeking. The stand-alone Dfs client is included in Windows 98, NT 4 (with Service Pack 3 and above), and Windows 2000, and is available for download for Windows 95 and domain-based versions at http://www.microsoft.com/NTServer/nts/downloads/winfeatures/NTSDistrFile/download.asp.

There are several important reasons to use domain-based Dfs. Domain-based Dfs uses Active Directory to store the Dfs *topology,* or configuration, providing a common interface for all server-based file handling. Also, by using Active Directory, there is automatic replication to the other domain controllers within the domain.

Creating a Distributed File System

The process of creating a Distributed file system includes creating a Dfs root and adding Dfs links to the Dfs root.

Creating a Dfs Root   A Dfs root can be on any server or domain controller in a network, and the server be formatted with FAT, FAT32, or NTFS, although NTFS offers better security and the use of domains. A server can have only one Dfs root. Dfs uses its own window to create and manage Dfs. Open that first and create a Dfs root with these steps:

1. Open the Start menu and choose Programs | Administrative Tools | Distributed File System. The Distributed File System window opens.

2. Open the Action menu and choose New Dfs Root. The New Dfs Root Wizard opens.

3. Click Next. Determine whether you want a domain-based Dfs (recommended) or a stand-alone Dfs and then click Next again.

4. If you choose a domain-based Dfs, select the host domain and click Next. Enter or browse for the host server. Again click Next.

5. Create a starting share or select an existing one and click Next. Enter a name for the Dfs root and any comments you want.

6. Click Next. Confirm your choices and click Finish. The new Dfs root will be created, like this:

Adding a Dfs Link With a Dfs root, you can add a Dfs link to additional shared folders. See how to do this next (the Dfs window should still be open on your screen):

1. With the Dfs root selected, open the Action menu and select New DFS Link. The Create a New DFS Link dialog box opens.

2. Enter the link name, the shared folder it will point to, and any comments.

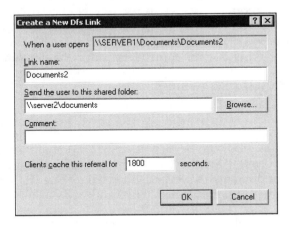

3. When the link is the way you want it, click OK. The Dfs link will appear under the Dfs root.

You can create as many links as you want in this manner. The following shows four Dfs links under a Dfs root. If you open Windows Explorer and open the Dfs root, you'll also see the new Dfs links you have added.

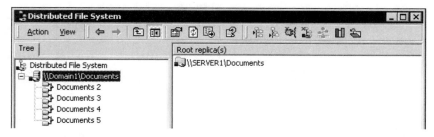

Managing a Distributed File System

There are several tools to facilitate managing the Distributed file system. These include replicating the Dfs tree, checking whether all the links are still valid, and controlling the display of Dfs root.

Replicating the Dfs Root   You can assure that the distributed file system is always available by making sure its structure and links are replicated on several other domain controllers:

1. In the Distributed File System window, right-click the Dfs root you want to replicate and choose New Root Replica.

2. Enter the name of the server that will host the replica, and click Next.

3. Select or create the Dfs root share for the replication and click Next. The replica will be placed on the new domain controller and appear in the Dfs window.

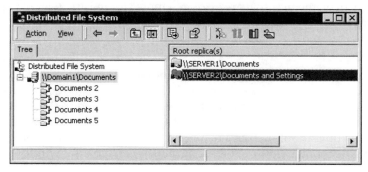

Checking Dfs Links   You can quickly check the links in a Dfs root or Dfs link by right-clicking the object you want to check and choosing Check Status. If the check did not find any problems, a green checkmark appears next to the object, but if a problem is found, an × appears in a red circle.

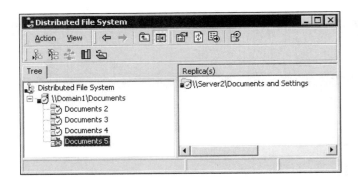

When you find a problem, it is often because a share is offline. Depending on how easy that is to check, it might be easier to just remove and re-create the link.

Controlling the Display of the Dfs Root   You can remove the display of the Dfs root by right-clicking it and choosing Remove Display of DFS Root. A message tells you what will happen and that client access is not affected. Click Yes to proceed.

If you want to turn the display back on, open the Action menu and choose Display an Existing DFS Root. Enter or select the domain and Dfs root you want to display, and click OK.

Handling Removable and Remote Storage

Removable Storage provides tracking for media, such as tapes and optical disks, stored both individually and in hardware libraries, such as jukeboxes. Remote Storage monitors disk space and which files have copies in Removable Storage. When free disk space drops below a certain level, the files that are also on remote storage are deleted to provide more room on the hard disk.

Using Removable Storage

Removable Storage manages media, such as tapes and disks, not the data on the media. Removable Storage works with programs such as Backup, which controls the data on the removable media, to organize and track the media that is used for the program. The media is placed into *media pools* in such a way that a media pool provides enough storage space for a given operation, such as a recurring backup. Removable Storage is controlled by the Removable Storage option in the Computer Management window.

Removable Storage Option   Open and look at the Removable Storage option by following these steps:

1. Open the Start menu and choose Programs | Administrative Tools | Computer Management. The Computer Management window opens.

2. Under Storage, open Removable Storage and then each of the objects it contains: Media Pools, Physical Locations, and each drive, similar to what is shown in Figure 12-17.

3. Left- and right-click each object under Removable Storage to get an understanding of what is there.

You can see that Removable Storage provides a way to control media and the drives that use it.

Working with Media Pools   The purpose of media pools is to differentiate among both types and uses of media, based on the properties that you assign to the media pools available to you. Media pools can hold other media pools or media, but they can't hold both. All media in a given media pool that contains media must be of the same type, such as tape cartridges, optical disks, or rewritable CDs (CDRW). A parent media pool can contain subordinate media pools with different media.

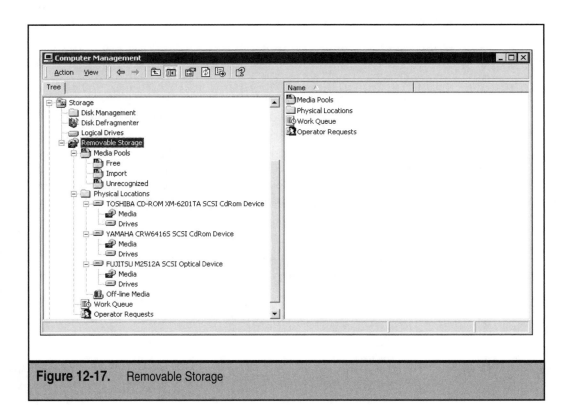

Figure 12-17.   Removable Storage

There are two classes of media pools: system and application. *System* media pools are created by Windows 2000 and are meant to hold media not used by an application. *Application* media pools are obviously created by applications, such as Remote Storage or Backup (both discussed later in this chapter), or by an administrator and contain media that is currently being used by that application.

The following are the three default system media pools:

▼ **Free** Contain media that can be drawn by an application and that does not contain useful information.

■ **Import** Contain media that has not been used in the current location but has recognizable data from, for example, a different office. It should be moved to either an application or free media pool.

▲ **Unrecognizable** Contain new media that does not have recognizable data on it. It should be moved to a free media pool.

The following steps show how to create a parent media pool for backing up, and then how to create two subordinate pools, one each for two different types of media (the Computer Management window should be open with Removable Storage open showing Media Pools in the left pane):

1. Right-click Media Pools and choose Create Media Pool. The Create a New Media Pool Properties dialog box opens, as you can see in Figure 12-18.

2. In the General tab, enter a Name and a Description and leave the default Contain Other Media Pools under Media Information. Click the Security tab, set the permissions as you need them, and click OK.

3. Right-click your new media pool, choose Create Media Pool, enter a Name and a Description, and click Contains Media of Type. Open the drop-down list and select the first media type you want to store. Choose the allocation/deallocation policy you want to use, set the permissions you need, and click OK.

4. Repeat step 3 for the second type of media you want to store. When you are done, you should have a hierarchical structure.

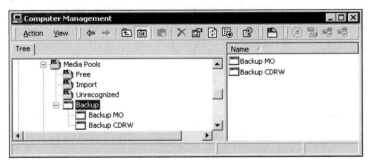

Create a New Media Pool Properties

General | Security

Name: [   ]

Description: [   ]

Type: Application-specific

Media information

○ Contains other media pools

○ Contains media of type:

[2.5" Avatar Floppy   ▼]

Allocation / Deallocation policy

☐ Draw media from Free media pool

☐ Return media to Free media pool

☐ Limit reallocations [100 ⬍] reallocations

[OK] [Cancel]

Figure 12-18. Creating a new media pool

Working with Removable Devices Under Physical Locations in the Removable Storage tree on the left of the Computer Management window, you should find all of your removable storage hardware devices.

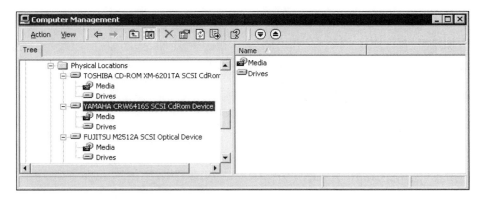

Removable storage devices are of two types: stand-alone devices, such as a tape drive or a rewritable CD-ROM drive, and storage libraries, such as tape and disk jukeboxes. Stand-alone devices have only one piece of media to work with at a time, whereas storage libraries have a number of pieces. There are a number of controls in Windows 2000 for libraries, and if you have such a device, you need to look into them; but, for the constraints of this book, we will only talk about stand-alone drives. The following procedure shows you how to enable a device, specify its media, and inject and eject that media:

1. Right-click a device you have under Physical Locations in the Computer Management window, and choose Properties. The device's Properties dialog box opens, as you can see in Figure 12-19.

2. Enable or disable the drive by selecting or deselecting Enable Library in the lower part of the dialog box.

3. Click the Media tab and click Change to open the Change Media Types dialog box. Scroll the Available Types list to select the appropriate media types for your drive, clicking Add for each one you select. When you have selected the types you want to use, click OK.

4. Look at the other tabs, and in the Security tab, set the permissions you need. When you are finished, click OK to close the Properties dialog box.

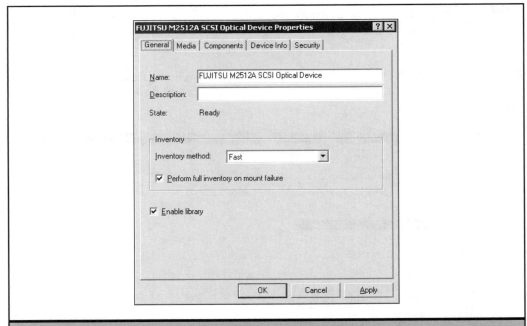

Figure 12-19.   Setting the properties for a removable storage device

5. Right-click the device you just set up, and choose Inject. The Media Inject Wizard appears. Click Next.

6. Place the media in the drive and click Next. You'll see a notice that the media is being injected, and then a notice that it is done. Click Finish.

7. Click Media under your drive and you see the media you just inserted.

8. Right-click the media entry and choose Properties. The media's Properties dialog box opens. Here, you can enter a name for the media. Note that it has been assigned to the Import media pool. If your media is double-sided, you can enter a name and description for each side. Click OK when you are done with the media's Properties dialog box.

9. Open the media type within the Import media pool and you should again see the media you inserted into the drive. (Notice how the media types that you use have been added to the media pools.) Drag this media from the Import folder to either the Free folder of that media type or an application folder you previously created (it must be the same media type and must be writable) depending on which folder is free (you get a message that all data on the media will be destroyed).

10. Select Media under the drive again and right-click the media in the right pane. Choose Eject. The Media Eject Wizard opens. Depending on the drive you have, the media may be automatically ejected. If it isn't, manually eject the media. Click Next and click Finish.

The particular piece of media is no longer displayed in Media under the drive, but if you look at where you dragged it, you'll see that it is still there.

The primary means of adding media to media pools is through the drives. The other media-related options that were not demonstrated are

▼   Prepare, which is used to prepare a piece of media to enter the Free media pool, normally to format the media;

▲   Mount and Dismount, which are applicable only to devices which, separately from loading, place the media online, as you would do in a jukebox device.

Using Remote Storage

Remote Storage is a way to extend hard disk space by monitoring disk usage and, as space gets tight, automatically copying seldom-used files to a remote storage tape device. If a need arises for one or more files that have been stored offline, and that need is requested in the same way it would be if the file were online, the file(s) will be requested automatically from the offline device. With Remote Storage, you can use SCSI 4mm, 8mm, and DLT tape devices, but you cannot use Exabyte 8200, QIC tape, or removable disk devices. Remote Storage uses Removable Storage to track the tapes it has used for offline storage. Backup, on the other hand, is an independent product that does not interact with or replace Remote Storage, nor is it replaced by Remote Storage.

Installing Remote Storage   Remote Storage is not part of the Typical Windows 2000 Server installation. If you did not specifically select it during installation, it was not installed. You can determine whether Remote Storage is installed on your computer by opening the Start menu, choosing Programs | Administrative Tools, and seeing whether Remote Storage is on the menu. If not, you need to install it, as follows:

1. Place the Windows 2000 Server CD-ROM in its drive. When the Autoload dialog box appears, click Install Add-on Components. The Windows Components Wizard dialog box opens.

2. Scroll the list of components until you see Remote Storage. Click it to select it (if it already has a checkmark, it already is installed, so you don't want to check it).

3. Click Next. The necessary file will be copied to the server. You will be told when that is done, at which point click Finish. You then are told that the computer needs to be restarted.

4. Click Yes to restart the computer.

Setting Up and Using Remote Storage   The process of setting up and using Remote Storage is basically one of establishing the parameters around which Remote Storage will work. This includes doing the following:

▼ Specifying the volumes or partitions that will be managed by Remote Storage

■ Setting the amount of free space that is to be kept on each volume or partition

■ Defining the criteria for selecting the files to be kept offline

▲ Specifying the tape devices to be used for the offline storage

Once the setup process is complete, Remote Storage makes an initial copy onto tape of all files on the selected volumes or partitions that fit the criteria. Then, Remote Storage begins its automatic space management functions by monitoring the free space on the specified volumes against the desired free space. When there is less free space than desired, designated files that have been copied to tape are removed from the volume or partition until there is enough free space. If there is a request for one of the removed files, Remote Storage automatically obtains the file from tape.

Backup and Restore

The Backup and Restore utility is used to blunt the impact of losing information on a volume or partition caused by a hardware failure of a drive or a computer, or the inadvertent erasure of one or more files for whatever reason. You can back up all files in a volume or partition, or just selected files. You can create an Emergency Repair Disk (ERD), back up Remote Storage files, and copy the computer's *system state,* the system files such as the Registry and Active Directory. You can back up files on another hard disk, on a tape, on a writable CD, or on a removable disk. Once you have created a backup of whatever data you want, you can restore the data either to the original computer and disk or to others.

Types of Backup

The following are the five types of backup:

▼   **Normal backup**   Copies all the files that have been selected to the backup media and marks the files as having been archived (the Archive bit is cleared).

■   **Differential**   Copies all the files that are new or changed since the last normal or incremental backup. The Archive bit is not cleared, so the files are continually backed up until the next normal or incremental backup.

■   **Incremental**   Copies all the files that are new or changed since the last normal or incremental backup. The Archive bit is cleared, so the files are not backed up again.

■   **Copy**   Copies all the files that have been selected, but does not clear the Archive bit, so it does not affect normal and incremental backups.

▲   **Daily**   Copies all the files that have changed on the day of the backup. The Archive bit is not cleared, so any of the other forms of backup will also copy the files.

If you use a combination of normal and differential backup, your backups will be slower and you will use more media, but restoration will be much faster. If you use a combination of normal and incremental backup, your backups will be faster and you will use less media, but your restoration will take the longest. You need to determine which resources—backup time, restore time, or media—are more important to you. Since you probably back up frequently and restore seldom, optimizing the backup time is often the choice.

Using Backup

Backup can be done manually or on an automatic, scheduled basis.

Manually Backing Up   Manually backing up means to select the files and folders that are to be backed up and then issue the command to do it:

1. Open the Start menu and choose Programs | Accessories | System Tools | Backup. The Backup window opens and gives you a choice of backing up, restoring, or creating an Emergency Repair Disk.

2. Click Backup Wizard. The Backup Wizard dialog box opens. Click Next.

3. Choose from among backing up everything on the computer, backing up just selected files, and backing up System State data (this includes Active Directory and the Registry). When you have made the choice, click Next. The Items to Back Up dialog box appears, as shown in Figure 12-20.

4. Select the folders, subfolders, and files that you want backed up. Selecting a folder selects everything in that folder, but if you want most of a folder, select it and then deselect what you don't want. When you have selected all the files you want to back up, click Next.

5. Select the drive you want to use for the backup, enter a filename, and click Next. You are shown the choices you have made. If you want to change them, click Back.

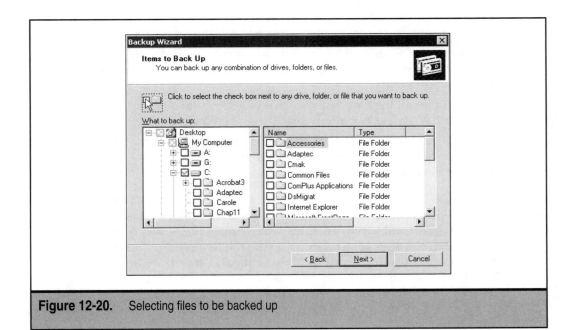

Figure 12-20.   Selecting files to be backed up

6. When everything is the way you want it, click Advanced. Here, you can select the type of backup from the types described in the preceding section. Normal backup is the default and is what is recommended for this first backup. Click Next.

7. Choose whether you want to verify what you have backed up. This gives you added assurance, but it takes about twice as long. The default is to not verify. After making the decision, click Next.

8. Choose whether to append the current backup to other data on the media or to replace that other data. Append is the default. Click Next. Accept or change the labels that will be used. Click Next.

9. Choose whether to run the backup now or at a later date. Leave the default to run it now. Click Next and then Finish. The backup will begin. You can watch the progress in the Backup Progress dialog box that appears, as you can see in Figure 12-21.

Doing Scheduled Backups   A scheduled backup goes through the same steps as a normal backup, but instead of running it now, you schedule it to be run in the future. This allows you to both run backup when there is light activity, and to set up a recurring backup. To

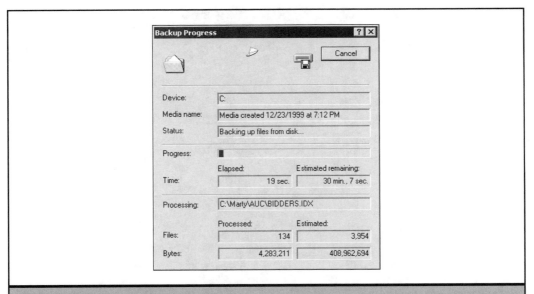

Figure 12-21.   The progress of a backup

see how this is done, repeat the first eight steps of the immediately preceding list, and then continue with these steps:

1. In the When to Back Up dialog box of the Advanced options, select Later. The Set Account Information dialog box opens.

2. Enter the ID and password, twice, of the person who will be responsible for maintaining this backup, and then click OK.

3. Enter the Job Name, and click Set Schedule. The Schedule Job dialog box opens. Here, you can enter the schedule you want to use, as shown in Figure 12-22.

4. Click Advanced. In the Advanced Schedule Options dialog box, you can enter a stop date and add variation to the repetition cycle. Enter the schedule you want to use, clicking OK twice to close the Advanced Schedule Options dialog box and then the Schedule Job dialog box.

5. In the Backup Wizard, click Next, and then click Finish.

6. In the Backup window, click Schedule Jobs. A monthly calendar opens showing the days on which your scheduled backup will run; in Figure 12-23, the scheduled backups will run on Saturdays. If you move the mouse over the

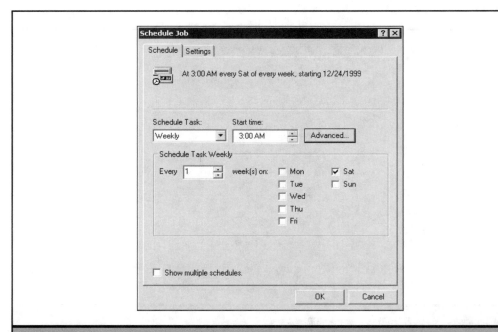

Figure 12-22.   Setting a backup schedule

backup icon, you see the job name; if you click the icon, the Scheduled Job Options dialog box opens, in which you can change the characteristics of, or delete, the job.

7. Close the Backup window.

Using Restore

The purpose of backing up is to be able to restore data that, for whatever reason, has been lost. There are many different circumstances in which data is lost, and the loss can affect a single file or folder, up to an entire disk. Therefore, you want to be able to restore data to fit the circumstance. Windows 2000 Backup can do that; see how with these steps:

1. Open the Start menu, choose Programs | Accessories | System Tools | Backup, and when the Backup window appears, click Restore Wizard. The Restore Wizard opens.

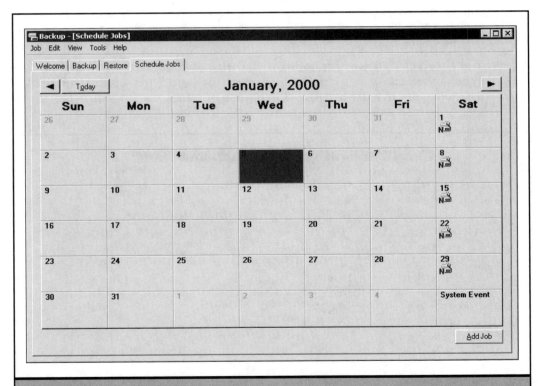

Figure 12-23.   Viewing a backup schedule

2. Click Next. The What to Restore dialog box appears. Open the hierarchical list in the left pane. If you drill down deep enough, you get a little dialog box that asks for the filename of the backup file for which a catalog will be opened. If you want to restore an entire backup, you do not need the catalog, but if you want to restore selected files and/or folders, you need to open the catalog.

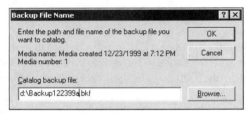

3. Enter a backup name and click OK. The complete details of all the files and folders that were backed up is displayed, as shown in Figure 12-24.

4. Select the folders and files that you want to restore, and click Next. You are shown the steps that will be taken to perform the restore. If these are all correct, you could click Finish and be done. For the sake of this exercise, look further by clicking Advanced.

5. You are given a choice of restoring to the original location (the default), an alternative location, or a single folder. If you choose anything but the original location, you can enter or select that location or folder. Click Next.

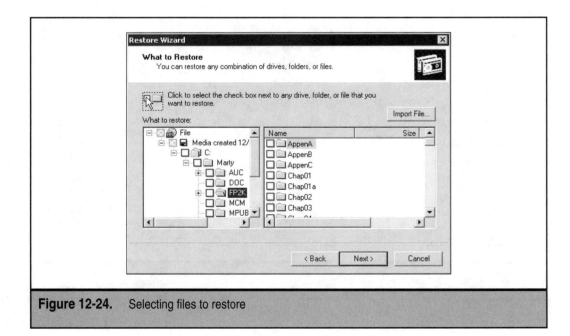

Figure 12-24. Selecting files to restore

6. You are asked whether and under what circumstances you want to replace existing folders with those that are backed up. Consider this carefully, because you might lose information with an answer that is incorrect for your situation. Click Next.

7. You can then choose to restore several specific storage elements if they exist. These are the original security components, such as permissions; the Removable Storage database; and the folder ("junction point") and the data on a drive mounted to a folder on another drive. When you are done, click Next.

8. You are again shown a summary of the steps to be taken in the restore. If they are not correct, use Back to change any of your selections. When you are ready, click Finish.

9. You are asked to confirm the source files for the restore. Either change it and click OK or simply click OK. The Restore Progress dialog box appears, similar to the Backup Progress dialog box previously shown in Figure 12-21. Finally, you are told the restore is complete.

Emergency Preparedness

The whole reason for backing up is to prepare for an emergency in which you would otherwise lose information. Besides the normal backup of information, Backup provides several tools to help you prepare for a computer emergency. Two of these tools are used to create an Emergency Repair Disk and to back up your system state.

Emergency Repair Disk   An Emergency Repair Disk does not back up any information, but it allows you to start the computer in DOS or character mode so that you can work on its repair. See how this is done by following these steps:

1. Open the Backup window (as you previously did), and in the Welcome tab, click Emergency Repair Disk.

2. When told to do so, insert a blank, formatted floppy disk in its drive. If desired, you can also make an extra copy on your hard drive of the Registry to help in system recovery.

3. When the disk has been inserted, click OK. You'll be shown the progress and told when the operation is complete. When you remove the disk, label it "Emergency Repair Disk" along with the current date. Store it safely.

Backing Up System State   While it is possible to make a mirror image copy of a disk to use as a replacement in case something should happen to the original, the system information on the copy is only as current as when it was last backed up. Since copying a large disk is a major undertaking, you don't want to do this frequently. A solution is to periodically, when convenient, back up the entire disk, and, more frequently, back up the system files, or what Backup calls the *system state*. Do that now:

1. With Backup running, click the Backup tab. At the bottom of the list of drives on the left, you should see System State, as you can see in Figure 12-25.

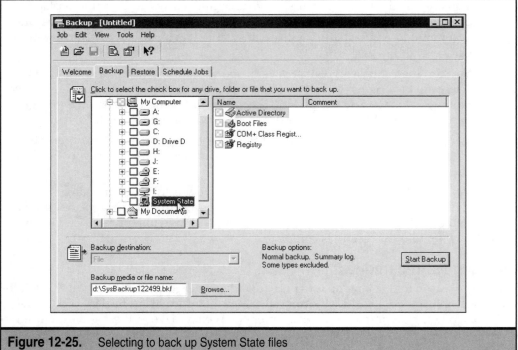

Figure 12-25. Selecting to back up System State files

2. Select System State, enter a path and filename, and click Start Backup. The Backup Job Information dialog box opens. You can change the description, choose to append or replace data, and choose to directly start the backup, schedule it, or review advanced options.

3. Click Advanced. The Advanced Backup Options dialog box opens. Here, you can choose to back up Remote Storage data, verify what has been backed up, automatically back up system-protected files when you do a System State backup, and choose a type of backup. The key here is the backup of the system-protected files. If that is selected, click OK.

4. Click Start Backup. The Backup Progress dialog box appears, as you saw previously.

Storage and file system management is a vital function in Windows 2000, and it is well worth any effort you put into it.

CHAPTER 13

Setting Up and Managing Printing

Although talk of a paperless society continues, it does not look like it will occur any time soon. As a result, the ability to transfer computer information to paper or other media is very important and a major function of Windows 2000. Both Windows 2000 Server and Windows 2000 Professional can serve as print servers, although Windows 2000 Professional is limited to ten concurrent users and cannot support Macintosh or Novell NetWare users, whereas Windows 2000 Server does not have a user limitation and can support Macintosh and NetWare users. Unless otherwise noted, comments in this chapter apply equally to Windows 2000 Server and Windows 2000 Professional.

In this chapter, you'll look at what constitutes Windows 2000 printing, how to set it up, how to management it, and how to manage the fonts that are required for printing.

WINDOWS 2000 PRINTING

Windows 2000 printing is very similar to both Windows NT 4 and Windows 98 printing, and many of the concepts are the same. Take a moment, though, and make sure you are familiar with the foundation printing concepts and understand the resource requirements.

Printing Concepts

It may seem obvious what a printer is, but when considering the term, you must remember to include "printing" to a file and "printing" to a fax. Also, although "printing" to a network printer does end up using a physical printing device, to the local computer, this form of "printing" is just a network address. So what does "printer" mean to Windows 2000?

▼ **Printer**   A name that refers to a set of specifications used for printing, primary among which are a hardware port, such as LPT1 or COM1, a software port, such as FILE or FAX, or a network address.

■ **Printer driver**   Software that tells the computer how to accomplish the printing task desired; also part of the printer specifications.

■ **Printing device**   The actual piece of hardware that does the printing. *Local printing devices* are connected to a hardware port on the computer requesting the printing; *network printing devices* are connected either to another computer or directly to the network.

▲ **Print server**   The computer controlling the printing, and to which the printing device is connected.

Printing Requirements

Windows 2000 printing has the following requirements that must be satisfied:

▼ One or more computers on the network must be set up as print servers with one or more local printing devices connected to them.

- The print server must be running either Windows 2000 Server or Windows 2000 Professional, but if Windows 2000 Professional is used, there is a limit of ten concurrent users, and neither Macintosh nor NetWare users on the network can use the printer.

- The print server must have enough disk space to handle the expected print load. This varies greatly from organization to organization, so there is no good rule of thumb. Look at the size of documents that your organization normally prints and at the worst-case number of these documents that might be printed at the same time. If ten people in an office are sharing a printer and their largest print jobs are around 2MB, then 20MB is probably enough, but to be conservative, provide 50 to 100MB.

▲ Enough memory must be available to handle the printing load. This is a minimum of 128MB, and for a serious print load, 256MB would not be too much. Providing a fair amount of memory will insure the best performance.

SETTING UP PRINTING

Setting up printing is done through the Printers folder and window shown in Figure 13-1. This folder, which is opened by opening the Start menu and choosing Settings | Printers, contains an Add Printer icon that opens the Add Printer Wizard. This wizard leads you through the process of setting up printers that will be available to the computer on which you are working.

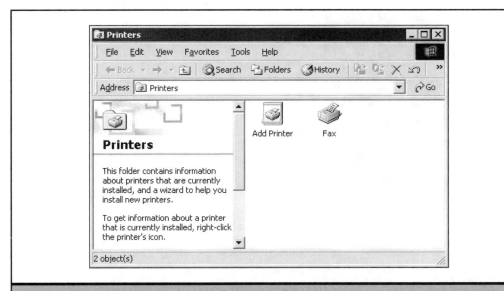

Figure 13-1. All setup and management of printing is done through the Printers folder

After clicking Next on the opening dialog box, the very first question asked by the Add Printer Wizard is whether you want to set up a local printer or a network printer:

▼ **Local printer**   Directly connected to the computer you are sitting at.

▲ **Network printer**   Connected either to another computer on the network or directly to the network, and has been *shared* or set up so that others can use it.

Setting Up Local Printers

To set up a printer connected to the computer you are at, use these steps:

1. Choose Local Printer. If you believe that the printer is Plug and Play–compatible (most printers made since 1997 are), click that checkbox and then click Next. The Add Printer Wizard will try to detect the printer. If it is successful, you are told which printer has been found and it is installed. You then are asked if you want to test the printer by printing a page.

2. Choose Yes and click Next. The printer name, the port it is connected to, and other information is presented, as shown in Figure 13-2. Click Finish. If you chose to print a test page, it will be printed. If the page printed satisfactorily, click OK to that question; otherwise, click Troubleshoot and follow the suggestions you are given.

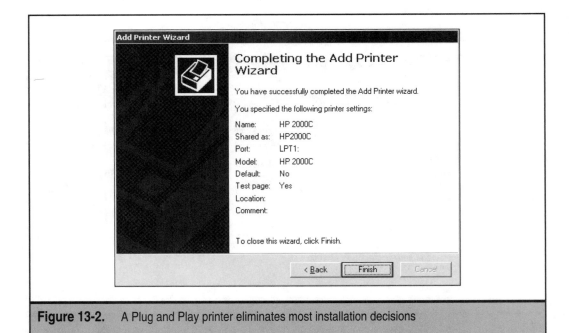

Figure 13-2.   A Plug and Play printer eliminates most installation decisions

3. If the local printer you want to set up is not Plug and Play–compatible and you tried to have the wizard detect it, you will be told you need to click Next to manually install it. Do so. Otherwise, choose to install a local printer without trying Plug and Play. In either case, the Select the Printer Port dialog box appears.

4. Select a printer port to which the printer is attached. This is most commonly LPT1, the first parallel port. If it is a serial printer, you might use COM2, because a mouse is often on COM1. After choosing a port, click Next. A list of manufacturers and their printer models are presented.

5. Click the printer manufacturer's name in the left list and then select the printer model in the right list, as shown in Figure 13-3. If your printer is not listed, but you have a disk with a Windows 2000 driver on it, click Have Disk. If your printer is not listed and you don't have a driver, click Windows Update to connect to the Microsoft site over the Internet to see if a recent driver is available for your printer.

6. When you have selected your printer's manufacturer and model, click Next. Enter a printer name and click Next; choose whether to share the printer and the share name and click Next; if you have chosen to share the printer, enter the printer's location and any comments and click Next; choose whether to print a test page, and click Next one final time.

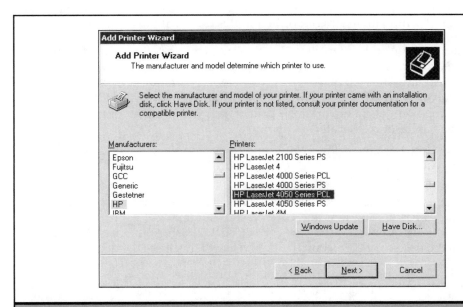

Figure 13-3.   In a manual install you need to choose a printer's manufacturer and model

7. A final summary of your decisions is displayed, as previously shown in Figure 13-2. If it is all correct, click Finish. If it is not correct, click Back until you get to the dialog box in which you can change the offending selection. When the summary is the way you want it, click Finish.

8. If you choose to print a test page, it should be printed now. If it was printed successfully, click OK. Otherwise, click Troubleshoot and follow the suggestions that are presented.

When the last Add Printer Wizard dialog box closes, you should see the printer that you added represented as an icon in the Printers folder.

Setting Up Network Printers

Setting up network printers refers to setting up a client computer so that it can utilize printers elsewhere on a network. The following are the two types of network printers:

▼ Those connected to another computer

▲ Those directly connected to the network

The process of setting up each of these is quite different.

Setting Up Printers Connected to Other Computers

The process of setting up access to printers connected to other computers is what is normally considered setting up a network printer and is done with these steps:

1. In the second Add Printer Wizard dialog box, choose Network Printer and click Next. The Locate Your Printer dialog box opens, in which you can search for a printer in the Active Directory, by entering a unique printer name using the Universal Naming Conventions (for example, \\Server1\HPLJ4000), by searching your local network for a printer, or by entering an Internet URL (Universal Resource Locator) to a printer.

2. If you select Type the Printer Name and then click Next without entering a name, you can browse for a printer, as Figure 13-4 shows. When you have selected a printer, click Next.

3. Choose whether the printer you are installing is the default printer for Windows-based programs and click Next. A summary of your printer decisions is presented. If they are correct, click Finish; otherwise, click Back, make the necessary corrections, and then click Finish.

Again, when you return to the Printers folder, you will see an icon for the network printer. It will have a cable running beneath it to indicate that it is a network printer.

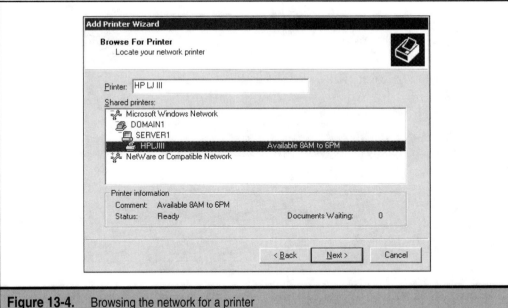

Figure 13-4. Browsing the network for a printer

NOTE: Computers running Windows 2000 and NT 4 check to see whether they have the latest printer drivers whenever they go to print, and if they don't, they seek a new driver. In Windows 2000, a drivers database is installed on each machine.

Setting Up Printers Directly Connected to the Network

A printer directly connected to the network has built in to it a network protocol that it uses to communicate on the network. This protocol, for most recent printers, is TCP/IP. If the printer is using TCP/IP, it may be assigned an IP address by the DHCP server (see Chapter 7 for a discussion of TCP/IP and DHCP), or an IP address may be directly assigned when the printer is setup. Before beginning the process of setting up this type of printer, you must know the protocol it uses and how it is addressed. Here are the steps to set up a printer directly connected to the network using TCP/IP and a known IP address:

1. From the Printers folder, double-click Add Printer and click Next on the Welcome message.

2. Select Local Printer, clear the Automatically Detect and Install My Plug and Play Printer checkbox, and click Next. The Select the Printer Port dialog box opens.

3. Click Create a New Port and select Standard TCP/IP Port from the drop-down list, as shown in Figure 13-5. Click Next. The Add Standard TCP/IP Printer Port Wizard opens.

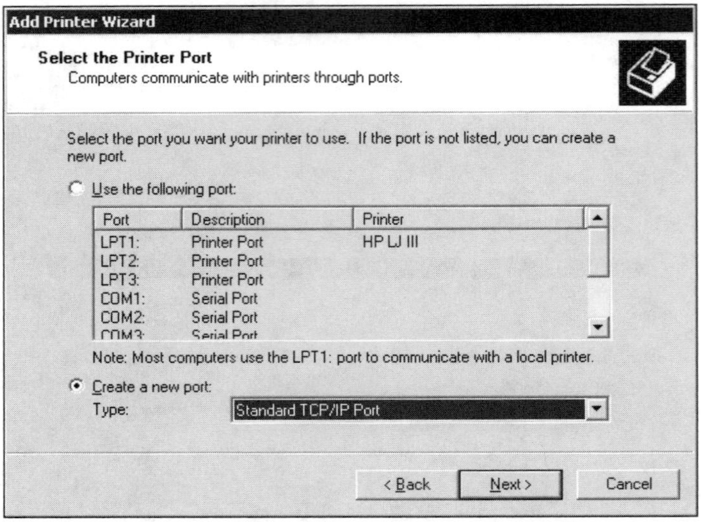

Add Printer Wizard

Select the Printer Port
Computers communicate with printers through ports.

Select the port you want your printer to use. If the port is not listed, you can create a new port.

○ Use the following port:

Port	Description	Printer
LPT1:	Printer Port	HP LJ III
LPT2:	Printer Port	
LPT3:	Printer Port	
COM1:	Serial Port	
COM2:	Serial Port	
COM3:	Serial Port	

Note: Most computers use the LPT1: port to communicate with a local printer.

● Create a new port:

Type: Standard TCP/IP Port

[< Back] [Next >] [Cancel]

Figure 13-5. Setting up a TCP/IP port for a printer directly connected to the network

4. Make sure the printer is turned on and connected to the network, and then click Next. The Add Port dialog box opens and asks for the Domain Name Service (DNS) name of the printer or its IP address.

5. Enter the name or IP address. As you do so, you see the Port name automatically filled in. Click Next. The Printer Port Wizard will go out and try to identify and set up the printer. If it is successful, you are told which printer network card was found; otherwise, you are told that the device could not be identified and are asked to select the device type. Click Next.

6. A summary of your responses is displayed. If they are not correct, use Back to correct them. When all are correct, click Finish. You are returned to the Add Printer Wizard, where you must identify the manufacturer and model of printer, enter a name, and supply other information, as you did when manually setting up a local printer. Click Finish when the settings are the way you want them.

7. If you printed a test page and it printed satisfactorily, click OK when asked that question; otherwise, click Troubleshoot and follow the suggestions that are presented.

If a printer directly connected to the network uses a networking protocol other than TCP/IP, you must install that protocol by using the steps for installing a networking protocol described in Chapter 7. With the protocol installed, you will be able to create a new port that uses that protocol. Identifying the printer will vary depending on the protocol.

MANAGING PRINTING

Managing printing involves two aspects: tuning a printer's configuration to get the most out of the printer, and controlling a printer's queue.

Tuning a Printer's Configuration

As a general rule, the default configuration for a printer works well in most situations, so unless you have a unique situation, it is recommended that you keep the default settings. That said, it is also wise to know what your alternatives are, so look at the settings you can use to control your printer (these settings vary depending on the printer that you are configuring, so look at your printer during this discussion).

A printer's settings are contained in its Properties dialog box, shown in Figure 13-6. This is accessed by opening the Printers folder (Start menu | Settings | Printers), right-clicking the icon of the printer you want to configure, and choosing Properties. For purposes of this discussion, the six tabs in the printer Properties dialog box can be grouped into printer configuration, printing configuration, and user configuration.

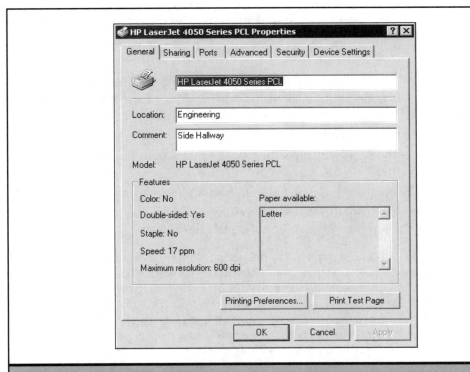

Figure 13-6. Configuring a printer

Printer Configuration

Printer configuration has to do with controlling the printer itself. On the General tab (shown in Figure 13-6), you can change the name of the printer, identify its location, and enter a comment about it. In the Ports tab, you can change the port used by the printer; add, delete, and configure ports; turn on and off bidirectional communication with the printer; and set up printer pooling. In the Device Settings tab, you can set what is loaded in each paper tray, how to handle font substitution, and what printer options are available. Your particular printer may have different or additional options, so review these tabs for your printer. Most of the printer configuration settings are self-explanatory, such as the name and location, and others are rarely changed from their initial setup, such as the port and bidirectional communication, which speeds using the printer. Several items, though, are worthy of further discussion: printer pooling, printer priority, and assigning paper trays.

Printer Pooling   Printer pooling allows you to have two or more physical printing devices assigned to one printer. The printing devices can be local or directly connected to the network, but they must share the same print driver. When print jobs are sent to the printer, Windows determines which of the physical devices is available, and routes the job to that device. This eliminates the need for the user to determine which printing device is available, provides for better load sharing among printing devices, and allows the management of several devices through one printer definition.

You can set up printer pooling with these steps:

1. Install all printers as described previously in "Setting Up Printing."

2. In the Printers folder, right-click the printer to which all work will be directed, and choose Properties. The printer's Properties dialog box opens.

3. Click the Ports tab and click Enable Printer Pooling.

4. Click each of the ports with a printing device that is to be in the pool, as you can see in Figure 13-7.

5. When all the ports are selected, click OK to close the Properties dialog box.

6. If the printer that contains the pool isn't already selected as the default printer, right-click the printer and choose Set As Default Printer.

Printer Priority   You can do the opposite of printer pooling by assigning several printers to one printing device. The primary reason that you would want to do this is to have two or more settings used with one device. For example, if you want to have two or more priorities automatically assigned to jobs going to a printing device, you could create two or more printers, all pointing to the same printer port and physical device, but with different priorities. Then, have high-priority print jobs printed to a printer with a priority of 99, and low-priority jobs printed to a printer with a priority of 1.

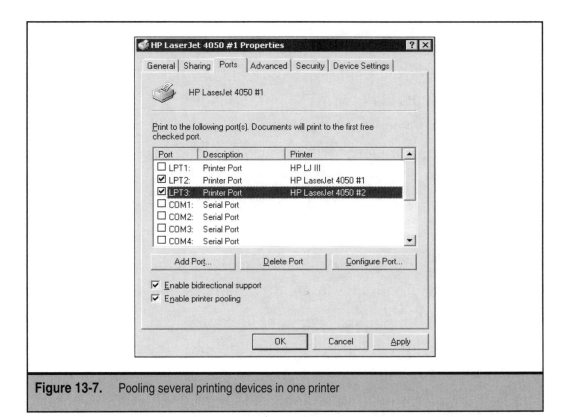

Figure 13-7. Pooling several printing devices in one printer

Create several printers with one print device using the following steps:

1. Install all printers as previously described in "Setting Up Printing." Name each of the printers to indicate its priority. For example, "High Priority Printer" and "Low Priority Printer."

2. In the Printers folder, right-click the high-priority printer and choose Properties. The printer's Properties dialog box will open.

3. Select the Advanced tab and enter a Priority of 99, as shown in Figure 13-8, and click OK.

4. Similarly, right-click the other printers, open their Properties dialog box, select the Advanced tab, and set the priority from 1 for the lowest priority to 98 for the highest priority.

Jobs that are printed with the highest priority will print before jobs with a lower priority if they are in the queue at the same time.

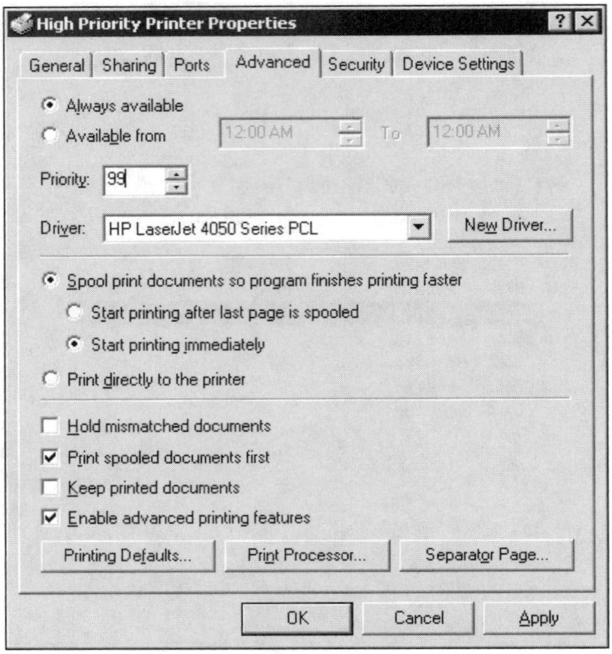

Figure 13-8. Setting one of several priorities for a single device

Assigning Paper Trays   Depending on your printer, it may have more than one paper tray and, as a result, you may want to put different types or sizes of paper in each tray. If you assign types and sizes of paper to trays in the printer's Properties dialog box, and a user requests a type and size of paper when printing, Windows 2000 automatically designates the correct paper tray for the print job. Here's how to assign types and sizes of paper to trays:

1. In the Printers folder, right-click the printer whose trays you want to assign and choose Properties. The printer's Properties dialog box opens.

2. Select the Device Settings tab. Open each tray and select the type and size of paper in that tray, similar to what you see in Figure 13-9.

3. When you have set the paper type and size in each tray, click OK.

Printing Configuration

Printing configuration has to do with controlling the process of printing, not the printer itself or particular print jobs. Printing configuration is handled in the Advanced tab of a printer's Properties dialog box, such as the one shown previously in Figure 13-8. As

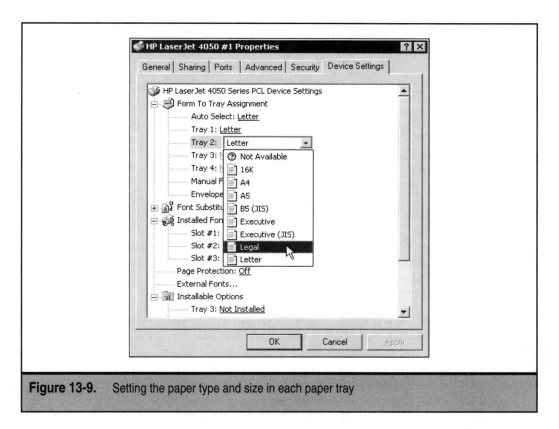

Figure 13-9.   Setting the paper type and size in each paper tray

stated earlier, in most cases, the default settings are appropriate and should be changed only in unique situations. Two exceptions to this are the spooling settings and using separator pages, discussed next.

Spooling Settings   In most instances, the time it takes to print a document is considerably longer than the time it takes to transfer the information from an application to the printer. The information is therefore stored on disk in a special preprint format, and then the OS, as a background task, feeds the printer as much information as it can handle. This temporary storage on disk is called *printer spooling*. Under the majority of cases, you want to use printer spooling and not tie up the application waiting for the printer. However, an alternative pair of settings is available:

▼   **Start Printing After Last Page Is Spooled**   By waiting to print until the last page is spooled, the application finishes faster and the user gets back to the application faster, but it takes longer to finish printing.

▲   **Start Printing Immediately**   The printing will be done sooner, but the application will be tied up a little longer.

There is no one correct choice for this. Normally, the default Start Printing Immediately provides a happy medium between getting the printing and getting back to the application. But if you want to get back to the application in the shortest possible time, then choose to wait until the last page is spooled.

Using Separator Pages   If you have a number of different jobs on a printer, it might be worthwhile to have a separator page between them, to more easily identify where one job ends and another begins. You can also use a separator page to switch a printer between PostScript (a printer language) and PCL (Printer Control Language) on Hewlett-Packard (HP) and compatible printers. Four sample SEP separation files come with Windows 2000:

▼ **Pcl.sep**   Prints a separation page before the start of each print job on PCL-compatible printers. If the printer handles both Postscript and PCL, it will be switched to PCL.

■ **Pscript.sep**   Does *not* print a separation page, but printers with both PostScript and PCL will be switched to PostScript.

■ **Sysprint.sep**   Prints a separation page before the start of each print job on PostScript-compatible printers.

▲ **Sysprtj.sep**   The same as Sysprint.sep, but in the Japanese language.

NOTE: The separation files work with HP and PostScript or compatible printers. They will not work with all printers.

If you know or have a guide to either the PCL or PostScript language (or both), you can open and modify these files (or copies of them) with any text editor, such as Notepad, to suite your particular purpose.

User Configuration

User configuration has to do with controlling the users of a printer. This is the one area where you may want to change the default, which is to share the printer and allow anyone on the network to print on it. User configuration is controlled in the Sharing tab of the printer's Properties dialog box, which turns sharing on and off, and in the Security tab of the same dialog box.

If a printer is shared, then the Security tab determines who has permission to use, control, and make changes to the printer, as you can see in Figure 13-10. The three levels of permissions and the functions that they allow are as follows:

▼ **Print**   Allows the user to connect to a printer; print; and cancel, pause, resume, and restart the user's own documents.

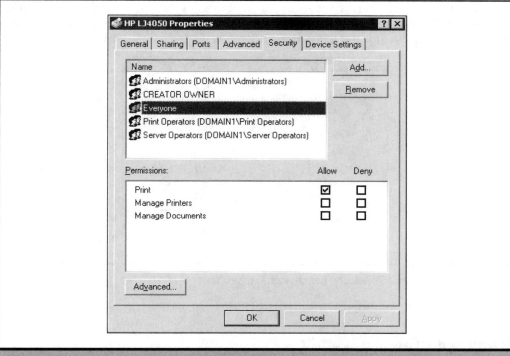

Figure 13-10.   Setting permission to use, control, and make changes to a printer

- ■ **Manage Documents**   Allows the user to perform all Print functions, plus control job functions for all documents, including canceling, pausing, resuming, and restarting other users' documents.
- ▲ **Manage Printers**   Allows the user to perform all Print and Manage Documents functions, plus control printer properties, including setting permissions, sharing a printer, changing printer properties, deleting a printer, and deleting all documents.

For each person or group in the Name list, you can select the permissions that you want to give that person or group. The permission can be set in terms of allowing or denying a certain set of functions. Denying takes precedence over allowing, so if a function is denied in one place and allowed in another, it will be denied.

CAUTION: If you deny a set of functions for the Everyone group, then literally everyone will be prevented from performing those functions, even if they have been allowed elsewhere.

If you want a more detailed level of permission, click Advanced at the bottom of the Security tab. Select a particular permission and click View/Edit. This lets you select what the permission applies to, and lets you further refine the permission itself, as shown here:

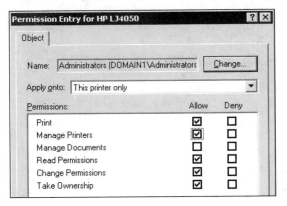

NOTE: Chapter 15 discusses permissions in more detail.

Controlling a Printer's Queue

As jobs are printed by applications, they are spooled onto a disk and then fed out to the printer at whatever rate the printer can handle. If several print jobs are spooled at close to the same time, they form a queue, waiting for earlier jobs to finish. Controlling this queue is an important administrative function and covers pausing and resuming printing, canceling printing, redirecting documents, and changing a document's properties. These tasks are handled in the printer's window that is similar to Figure 13-11, which is opened by double-clicking the appropriate printer in the Printers folder.

Pausing, Resuming, and Restarting Printing

As printing is taking place, a situation may occur in which you want to pause the printing. This may be caused by the printer—the need to change paper, for example—in which case you would want to pause all printing. The situation may also be caused by a document, in which case you would want to pause only the printing of that document—for example, for some problem in the document, such as characters that cause the printer to behave erratically. In Windows 2000, you can pause and resume printing of all documents, and pause and resume or restart printing of a single document.

Pausing and Resuming Printing for All Documents   Pausing and resuming printing of all documents is in essence pausing and resuming the printer. See how that is done with these steps:

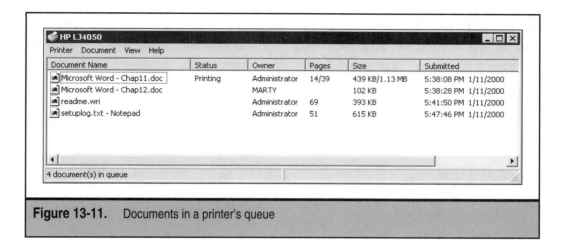

Figure 13-11. Documents in a printer's queue

1. In the printer's window, such as the one shown in Figure 13-11, open the Printer menu and choose Pause Printing. "Paused" will appear in the title bar, and if you look in the Printer menu, you will see a checkmark in front of Pause Printing.

2. To resume printing, again open the Printer menu and choose the checked Pause Printing. "Paused" disappears from the title bar and the checkmark disappears in the Pause Printing option in the Printer menu.

Pausing, Resuming, and Restarting Printing for a Single Document   When you want to interrupt the printing of one or more, but not all, the documents in the queue, you can do so and then either resume printing where it left off or restart from the beginning of the document. Here are the steps to do that:

1. In the printer's window, select the documents or document that you want to pause, open the Document menu, and choose Pause. "Paused" will appear in the Status column opposite the document(s) you selected.

2. To resume printing where the document was paused, select the document and choose Resume. "Printing" will appear in the Status column opposite the document selected.

3. To restart printing at the beginning of the document, select the document and choose Restart. "Restarting" and then "Printing" will appear in the Status column.

NOTE: If you want to change the order in which documents are being printed, you cannot pause the current document that is printing and have that happen. You must either complete the document that is printing or cancel it. You can use Pause to get around intermediate documents that are not currently printing. For example, suppose you want to immediately print the third document in the queue, but the first document is currently printing. You must either let the first document finish printing or cancel it. You can then pause the second document before it starts printing, and the third document will begin printing when the first document is out of the way.

Canceling Printing

Canceling printing can be done either at the printer level, which cancels all the jobs in the printer queue, or at the document level, which cancels selected documents. A canceled job is deleted from the print queue and must be restarted by the original application if that is desired. Here's how to cancel first one job and then all the jobs in the queue:

1. In the printer's window, select the job or jobs that you want to cancel. Open the Document menu and choose Cancel. The job or jobs will disappear from the windows and no longer be in the queue.

2. To cancel all the jobs in the queue, open the Printer menu and choose Cancel All Documents. You are asked whether you are sure you want to cancel all documents. Click Yes. All jobs will disappear from the queue and the printer window.

Redirecting Documents

If you have two printers with the same print driver, you can redirect the print jobs that are in the queue for one printer to the other printer, where they will be printed without the user having to resubmit them. You do this by changing the port to which the printer is directed:

1. In the printer's window, open the Printer menu, choose Properties, and select the Ports tab.

2. If the second printer is in the list of ports, select it. Otherwise, click Add Port, which opens the Printer Ports dialog box. Choose Local Port, and click New Port, which opens the Port Name dialog box.

3. Enter the UNC name for the printer (for example, \\Server1\HPLJ4050) and click OK.

4. Click Close and then click Close again. The print queue will be redirected to the other printer.

Changing a Document's Properties

A document in the print queue has a Properties dialog box, shown in Figure 13-12, which is opened by right-clicking the document and selecting Properties. This allows you to set the relative priority to use in printing the document from 1, the lowest, to 99, the highest; which logged on user to notify when the document is printed; and the time of day to print the document.

Setting Priority   A document printed to a printer with a default priority setting (see "Printer Priority," earlier in the chapter) is given a priority of 1, the lowest priority. If you want another document to be printed before the first one, and the "first one" hasn't started printing yet, then set the second document priority to anything higher than 1 by dragging the Priority slider to the right.

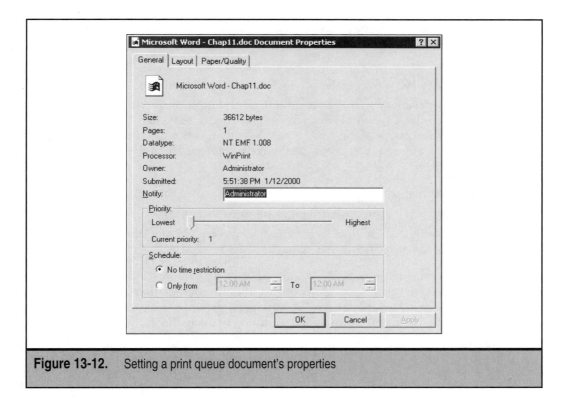

Figure 13-12.   Setting a print queue document's properties

Who to Notify   Normally, the printer notifies the owner of a document of any special situations with the printing and when the document is finished printing. The owner is the logged-on user who sent the document to the printer. Sometimes it is beneficial to notify another logged-on user. You can do that by putting the logon name of the other user in the Notify text box of the document's Properties dialog box.

Open Printers folder | File menu | Server Properties | Advanced tab and see whether Notify when Remote Documents Are Printed is selected; this doesn't seem to be on by default.

Setting Print Time   Normally, a job is printed as soon as it reaches the top of the print queue. You can change this to a particular time frame in the document's Properties dialog box General tab (see Figure 13-12), by selecting Only From at the bottom under Schedule and then entering the time range within which you want the job printed.

This allows you to take large jobs that might clog the print queue and print them at a time when there is little or no load.

MANAGING FONTS

A *font* is a set of characters with the same design, size, weight, and style. A font is a member of a *typeface* family, all members of which have the same design. The font 12-point Arial bold italic is a member of the Arial typeface with a 12-point size, bold weight, and italic style. Systems running Windows 2000 have numerous fonts that you can choose from, including these:

▼ **Resident fonts**   Built in to printers

■ **Cartridge fonts**   Stored in cartridges plugged into printers

▲ **Soft fonts**   Stored on disks in the computer to which the printer is attached and downloaded to the printer when they are needed

A number of soft fonts come with Windows 2000, and there are many, many more that you can add from other sources, including the Internet, or that are automatically added when you install an application. The font management job is to minimize the time taken downloading fonts, while having the fonts you want available. Minimizing download time means that resident and cartridge fonts are used when possible, which is automatically done by the print driver whenever a font that is both resident and available for download is requested. Font availability means that the fonts you want are on the print server's disk and fonts you don't want are not on the disk wasting space and handling time. In this section, you'll look at the fonts in Windows 2000, how to add and remove fonts, and how to use fonts.

Fonts in Windows 2000

There are three types of soft fonts in Windows 2000:

▼ **Outline fonts**   Stored as a set of commands that is used to draw a particular character. As a result, the fonts can be scaled to any size (and are therefore called *scalable* fonts) and can be rotated. Outline fonts are the primary fonts used both onscreen and downloaded to printers. Windows 2000 supports three types of outline fonts: TrueType fonts developed by Microsoft for Windows 95; OpenType fonts, also developed by Microsoft and an extension of TrueType; and Type 1 fonts, developed by Adobe Systems, Inc. All the outline fonts in Windows 2000 are OpenType fonts.

■ **Bitmapped fonts**   Also called *raster fonts*, these are stored as a bitmapped image for a specific size and weight, and a specific printer. They cannot be scaled and rotated. They are included for legacy purposes and are not used in most cases.

▲   **Vector fonts**   Created with line segments and can be scaled and rotated. Primarily used with plotters and not onscreen or with printers.

You can view and work with the fonts in Windows 2000 by opening the Fonts folder to display the Fonts window shown in Figure 13-13. The Fonts folder is opened by opening the Start menu, choosing Settings | Control Panel, and then double-clicking Fonts.

TIP: If you have chosen to expand your Control Panel on the Start menu (Start | Settings | Taskbar & Start Menu | Advanced tab) when you point to or click Fonts, you are shown a list of the fonts on your machine, and you won't see an option to open the Fonts windows. To open the Fonts window, double-click Fonts.

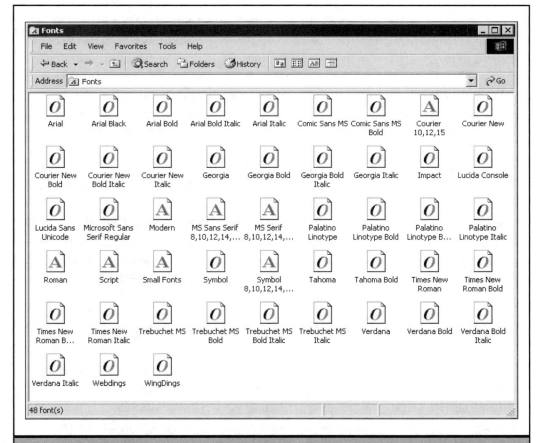

Figure 13-13.   Fonts installed with Windows 2000

If you haven't installed any other fonts or had them installed by an application, you will see the 48 fonts that are installed by Windows 2000, which are described in Table 13-1. Fonts with the *O* in the icon are OpenType fonts, and those with an *A* are either bitmapped or vector.

Font	Type	File Name	Type Sample
Arial	Outline	Arial.ttf	AbcklmtwABCKLMTW10
Arial Black	Outline	Ariblk.ttf	**AbcklmtwABCKLMTW10**
Arial Bold	Outline	Arialbd.ttf	**AbcklmtwABCKLMTW10**
Arial Bold Italic	Outline	Arialbi.ttf	***AbcklmtwABCKLMTW10***
Arial Italic	Outline	Ariali.ttf	*AbcklmtwABCKLMTW10*
Comic Sans MS	Outline	Comic.ttf	AbcklmtwABCKLMTW10
Comic Sans MS Bold	Outline	Comicbd.ttf	**AbcklmtwABCKLMTW10**
Courier 10,12,15	Bitmap	Coure.fon	AbcklmtwABCKLMTW10
Courier New	Outline	Cour.ttf	AbcklmtwABCKLMTW10
Courier New Bold	Outline	Courbd.ttf	**AbcklmtwABCKLMTW10**
Courier New Bold Italic	Outline	Courbi.ttf	***AbcklmtwABCKLMTW10***
Courier New Italic	Outline	Couri.ttf	*AbcklmtwABCKLMTW10*
Georgia	Outline	Georgia.ttf	AbcklmtwABCKLMTW10
Georgia Bold	Outline	Georgiab.ttf	**AbcklmtwABCKLMTW10**
Georgia Bold Italic	Outline	Georgiaz.ttf	***AbcklmtwABCKLMTW10***
Georgia Italic	Outline	Georgiai.ttf	*AbcklmtwABCKLMTW10*
Impact	Outline	Impact.ttf	**AbcklmtwABCKLMTW10**
Lucida Console	Outline	Lucon.ttf	AbcklmtwABCKLMTW10
Lucida Sans Unicode	Outline	L_10646.ttf	AbcklmtwABCKLMTW10
Microsoft Sans Serif Regular	Outline	Micross.ttf	AbcklmtwABCKLMTW10
Modern	Vector	Modern.fon	AbcklmtwABCKLMTW10
MS Sans Serif 8,10,12,14,18,24	Bitmap	Sserife.fon	AbcklmtwABCKLMTW10
MS Serif 8,10,12,14,18,24	Bitmap	Serife.fon	AbcklmtwABCKLMTW10
Palatino Linotype	Outline	Pala.ttf	AbcklmtwABCKLMTW10
Palatino Linotype Bold	Outline	Palab.ttf	**AbcklmtwABCKLMTW10**
Palatino Linotype Bold Italic	Outline	Palabi.ttf	***AbcklmtwABCKLMTW10***
Palatino Linotype Italic	Outline	Palai.ttf	*AbcklmtwABCKLMTW10*
Roman	Vector	Roman.fon	AbcklmtwABCKLMTW10

Table 13-1.   Fonts Included with Windows 2000

Font	Type	File Name	Type Sample
Script	Vector	Script.fon	*AbcklmtwABCKLMTW10*
Small Fonts	Bitmap	Smalle.fon	AbcklmtwABCKLMTW10
Symbol	Outline	Symbol.ttf	Αβχκλμτω ΑΒΧΚΛΜΤΩ10
Symbol 8,10,12,14,18,24	Bitmap	Symbole.fon	Αβχκλμτω ΑΒΧΚΛΜΤΩ10
Tahoma	Outline	Tahoma.ttf	AbcklmtwABCKLMTW10
Tahoma Bold	Outline	Tahomabd.ttf	**AbcklmtwABCKLMTW10**
Times New Roman	Outline	Times.ttf	AbcklmtwABCKLMTW10
Times New Roman Bold	Outline	Timesbd.ttf	**AbcklmtwABCKLMTW10**
Times New Roman Bold Italic	Outline	Timesbi.ttf	***AbcklmtwABCKLMTW10***
Times New Roman Italic	Outline	Timesi.ttf	*AbcklmtwABCKLMTW10*
Trebuchet MS	Outline	Trebuc.ttf	AbcklmtwABCKLMTW10
Trebuchet MS Bold	Outline	Trebucbd.ttf	**AbcklmtwABCKLMTW10**
Trebuchet MS Bold Italic	Outline	Trebucbi.ttf	***AbcklmtwABCKLMTW10***
Trebuchet MS Italic	Outline	Trebucit.ttf	*AbcklmtwABCKLMTW10*
Verdana	Outline	Verdana.ttf	AbcklmtwABCKLMTW10
Verdana Bold	Outline	Verdanab.ttf	**AbcklmtwABCKLMTW10**
Verdana Bold Italic	Outline	Verdanaz.ttf	***AbcklmtwABCKLMTW10***
Verdana Italic	Outline	Verdani.ttf	*AbcklmtwABCKLMTW10*
Webdings	Outline	Webdings.ttf	(Webdings sample)
WingDings	Outline	Wingding.ttf	(Wingdings sample)

Table 13-1. Fonts Included with Windows 2000 *(continued)*

In the Fonts folder, you can look at a font by double-clicking its icon. This opens a window for the font showing it in various sizes and giving some information about it, as shown in Figure 13-14. From this window, you can print the font by clicking Print. It is sometimes handy to keep a notebook with printed samples of all the fonts on a print server.

Adding and Removing Fonts

You can add fonts to those that are installed by Windows 2000 with the following steps:

1. Open the Start menu, choose Settings | Control Panel, and double-click Fonts. The Fonts window opens, similar to the one previously shown in Figure 13-13.

2. Open the File menu and choose Install New Font. The Add Fonts dialog box opens, like the one in Figure 13-15.

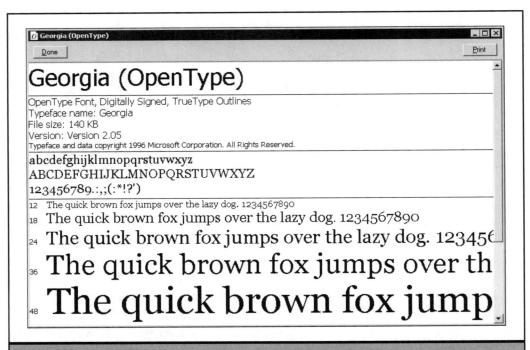

Figure 13-14. Double-clicking a font file opens a window that displays the font

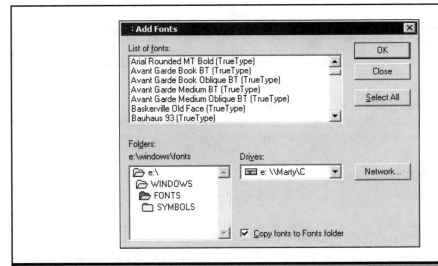

Figure 13-15. Selecting fonts to install

3. Open a drive and folder that contains the fonts you want to install (this can be a floppy disk, a CD-ROM, or another hard drive on the network, such as the one shown in Figure 13-15).

4. Select the fonts you want to install from the list (hold down SHIFT to select several contiguous fonts, or hold down CTRL to select several fonts that are not contiguous) and then click OK. The new fonts appear in the Fonts window.

You can remove fonts simply by selecting them and pressing DELETE. Alternatively, you can right-click the font(s) and choose DELETE. In either case, you are asked whether you are sure. Click Yes if you are. The fonts will be placed in the Recycle Bin, in case you made a mistake and want to retrieve one. If you haven't mistakenly deleted any, you can empty the Recycle Bin.

Using Fonts

Fonts are normally used or applied from within an application. For example, in Microsoft Word, you can select a line of text and then open the font drop-down list, as shown in Figure 13-16. Every application is a little different, but they all have a similar function. One nice feature of Word 2000 and several other recent applications is that they show what the font looks like in the list, as you can see in Figure 13-16.

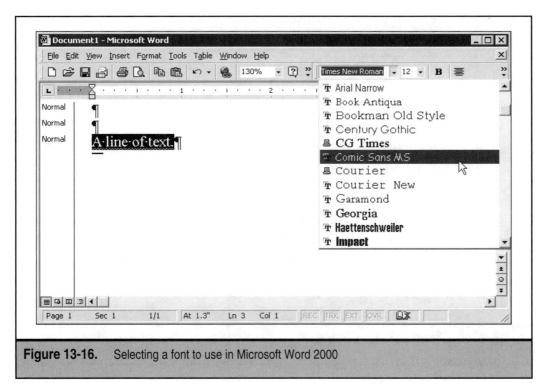

Figure 13-16.   Selecting a font to use in Microsoft Word 2000

Fonts used correctly can be a major asset in getting a message across, but they also can detract from a message if improperly used. Two primary rules are to not use too many fonts, and to use complementary fonts together. In a one-page document, two typefaces should be enough (you can use bold and italic to have as many as eight fonts), and in a longer document, three—and at most four—typefaces is appropriate. Complementary fonts are more subjective. Arial and Times Roman are generally considered complementary, as are Futura and Garamond, and Palatino and Optima. In each of these pairs, one typeface (for example, Arial) is *sans serif* (without the little tails on the ends of a character) and is used for titles and headings, while the other typeface (for example, Times Roman) is *serif* (it has the tails) and is used for the body text. There are of course many other options and considerations in the sophisticated use of fonts.

The Fonts window View menu has two options that help you look at similar fonts. The List Fonts By Similarity option re-sorts your fonts according to similarity to a selected font, and the Hide Variations option hides the bold and italic variations of a font, making it easier for you to look at just the typefaces (see Figure 13-17).

Figure 13-17. Fonts ordered by their similarity to Arial, with font variations hidden

CHAPTER 14

Windows 2000 Management Tools

Oration one of Windows 2000's greatest strengths is the variety of management tools that are available to control the many facets of the operating system. The purpose of this chapter is to look at the general-purpose tools, those that are not part of setting up, networking, file management, or printing. The discussion of these tools is broken into system management tools and user management tools.

SYSTEM MANAGEMENT

System management tools are those tools that facilitate running the parts of the operating system and the computer that are not discussed elsewhere. These tools include the following:

▼ The Control Panel

■ The Task Manager

■ The Microsoft Management Console

■ The Registry

▲ The Boot Process

The Control Panel

The Control Panel, which is shown in Figure 14-1, has been a part of Windows for a long time. It is a folder that holds a number of tools that control and maintain configuration information, mainly for system hardware. Here, we'll look at the following Control Panel tools:

▼ Accessibility Options

■ Folder Options

■ Keyboard

■ Mouse

■ Regional Options

■ Scheduled Tasks

■ Sounds and Multimedia

▲ System

Many of the other Control Panel tools are discussed in other places in this book. Add/Remove Hardware, Add/Remove Programs, some Administrative Tools, Date/Time, Display, and Licensing features are discussed in Part II. Other Administrative Tools features are discussed in Part III, while still others are discussed in Chapter 12. Fax, Game Controllers, and Scanners and Cameras deal with applications outside the scope of this book. Fonts and Printers are discussed in Chapter 13. Internet Options and Phone and Modem Options are discussed in Chapter 10. Network and Dial-up Connections is discussed in Parts III and IV; Power Options is discussed in Chapter 18.

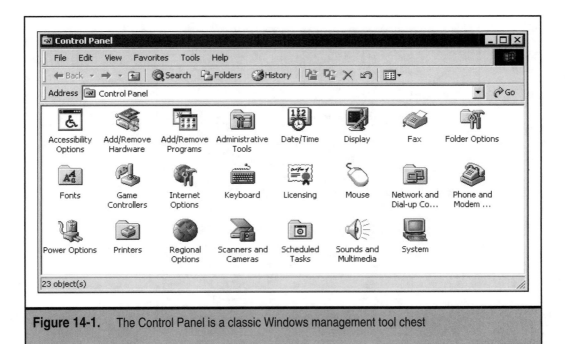

Figure 14-1. The Control Panel is a classic Windows management tool chest

Before looking at any of the specific tools, open your Control Panel and look at the tools you have available. You may have slightly different tools than those shown in Figure 14-1, depending on the hardware and software you have and the components of Windows 2000 that you have installed. Open the Control Panel by opening the Start menu and choosing Settings | Control Panel.

Accessibility Options

Accessibility Options allows a user with physical limitations to more easily use Windows 2000. The Accessibility Options dialog box, shown in Figure 14-2 and opened by double-clicking Accessibility Options in the Control Panel, provides four tabs (Keyboard, Sound, Display, and Mouse) in which you can enable and configure options to improve accessibility. A description of each of the options in each area is provided in Table 14-1.

The General tab of the Accessibility Options dialog box provides settings for managing the options, including when to automatically turn off the options and whether to give a warning when turning on an option.

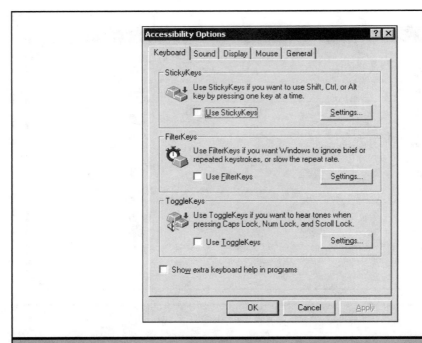

Figure 14-2. Accessibility Options provide ways to make the use of Windows 2000 easier

Area	Option	Description	Turn On or Off
Keyboard	StickyKeys	Enables the user to simulate the effect of pressing a pair of keys, such as CTRL-A, by pressing one key at a time. The keys SHIFT, CTRL, and ALT "stick" down until a second key is pressed, which Windows 2000 then interprets as the two keys pressed together.	Press either SHIFT key five times in succession

Table 14-1. Accessibility Options

Area	Option	Description	Turn On or Off
Keyboard	FilterKeys	Enables a user to press a key twice in rapid succession and have it interpreted as a single keystroke, and also slows down the rate at which the key is repeated if the user holds it down.	Hold down the right SHIFT key for eight seconds
Keyboard	ToggleKeys	Plays a tone when CAPS LOCK, NUM LOCK, and SCROLL LOCK are pressed.	Hold down NUM LOCK for five seconds
Sound	SoundSentry	Displays a visual indicator when the computer makes a sound. The indicator can be a flashing active caption bar, a flashing active window, or a flashing desktop.	Open Accessibility Options and click Use SoundSentry in the Sound tab
Sound	ShowSounds	Tells compatible programs to display captions when sound and speech are used.	Open Accessibility Options and click Use ShowSounds in the Sound tab
Display	HighContrast	Uses high-contrast colors and special fonts to make the screen easy to use.	Press together: left SHIFT, left ALT, and PRINT SCREEN
Mouse	MouseKeys	Enables the user to use the numeric keypad instead of the mouse to move the pointer on the screen.	Press together: left SHIFT, left ALT, and NUM LOCK

Table 14-1. Accessibility Options *(continued)*

Folder Options

Folder Options in the Control Panel allows you to customize the way folders and files are displayed and handled in various Windows 2000 windows, including My Computer and Windows Explorer. The Folder Options dialog box, shown in Figure 14-3 and opened by double-clicking Folder Options in the Control Panel, can also be accessed by opening

Tools menu and choosing Folder Options in either Windows Explorer or My Computer. The Folder Options dialog box has four tabs: General, View, File Types, and Offline Files.

NOTE: There is one important difference between opening Folder Options from the Control Panel and opening it from My Computer or Windows Explorer. From the Control Panel, it sets the default for all folders; from My Computer or Windows Explorer, it sets the properties for the current open folder unless you click Like Current Folder in the View tab.

General   The General tab allows you to choose how you want to handle four different questions.

The first two questions, Active Desktop and Web View, ask whether you want to use web content on the desktop and in file folders or, alternatively, use the classic displays.

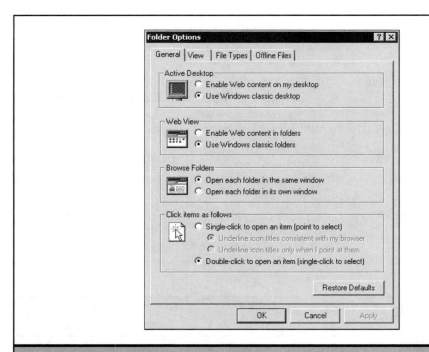

Figure 14-3.   Determining how folders are displayed and handled

This is a matter of personal choice. Web content generally gives you more information, such as the amount of free disk space on a drive, but it also takes up more room.

The third question, Browse Folders, asks whether you want to open a new window each time a new folder is opened, or repeatedly use the same window. Opening a new window with each folder is convenient if you want to compare two folders, but it also clutters the screen. The default and most popular choice is to use the same window.

The fourth question, Click Items, asks whether you want to single-click, as you do in a web browser, or double-click, as you do classically in Windows, to open a folder or a file. If you choose single-click, then simply pointing on the item selects it. If you choose double-click, then single-clicking selects the item. If you are a newer user, single-clicking saves you time and the confusion between single- and double-clicking. If you have been double-clicking for very many years, it is hard to stop, and so trying to single-click can be confusing.

View   The View tab, shown in Figure 14-4, determines how files and folders and their at-tributes are displayed in Windows Explorer and My Computer. The Advanced Settings list has a number of settings that you can turn on or off and that are a matter of personal preference. I like to see everything, so I turn on the display of the full path in either the ad-dress bar or title bar; I show hidden files; I turn off both the hiding of file extensions and the hiding of protected files. You may have other preferences. It is easy to try the different settings to see what you like by opening Folder Options in Windows Explorer. You can always return to the default settings by clicking Restore Defaults.

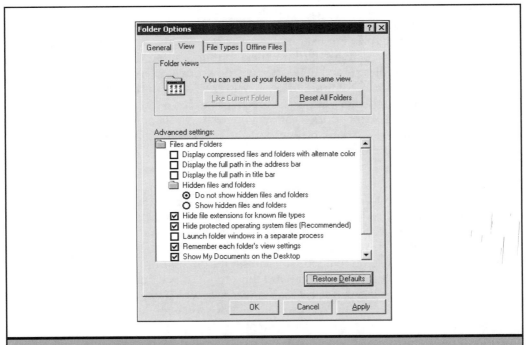

Figure 14-4.   Setting specific attributes for displaying files and folders

File Types   The File Types tab allows you to specify which application is associated with, and will open, a particular type of file, as identified by the file extension. When Windows 2000 is installed, a number of file associations are registered, and each time you add an application, more file associations are added. You can register additional file types or change existing associations in the File Types tab. By clicking New, you can enter a new file extension. If you click OK, the file extension will be registered as that extension's file type. For example, if you were to register the extension MSM, the file type would be "MSM file." In the Create New Extension dialog box, you can click Advanced and select from a long list of file types. Neither of these steps associate the file with an application that can open the file. To do that, you must select the file and click Change. This opens the Open With dialog box, which allows you to select an existing application to open the file, or you can enter a new application by clicking Other and browsing for it.

In the File Types tab, you can select an extension and then click Advanced to open the Edit File Type dialog box. Here, you can change the icon and specify the actions, such as Open, Print, and Preview, that you want to set up for a type of file. For each action, you can specify an application to be used for that action.

TIP: A fast way to associate a file type with an application is to double-click a file of that type in Windows Explorer. If no application is associated with the file, the Open With dialog box opens, in which you can select the application.

Offline Files   The Offline Files tab, shown in Figure 14-5, is new to Windows 2000 and sets up how you want to handle working with network files when you are offline or disconnected from the network. For example, if you are working on a document stored on the server and you have enabled Offline Files, the file will be temporarily stored in a folder named Offline Files. If the network goes down or you intentionally disconnect from the network, you can continue to work with the copy in the Offline Files folder. When you reconnect to the network, you can choose to have the file synchronized with the copy on the network. Other options allow you to choose if and how often you want to be reminded that you are working offline, and choose how much of your disk space you want to allocate to offline files.

Keyboard

Keyboard in the Control Panel allows you to set the configuration of your keyboard. As Figure 14-6 shows, the Speed tab allows you to set both how long to wait before repeating a key and how fast to do the repeating once it is started. You can click in the text box on that tab and try out your settings. Also on that tab, you can set the cursor blink rate (although the relationship between that and the keyboard is tenuous).

Keyboard

The Input Locales tab lets you select the languages in which you will be typing and how you want to switch among them. You can also set how you want to turn off the CAPS LOCK key. The Hardware tab shows the description of the device, allows you to troubleshoot it, and, through Properties, gives you access to the drivers that are being used with it.

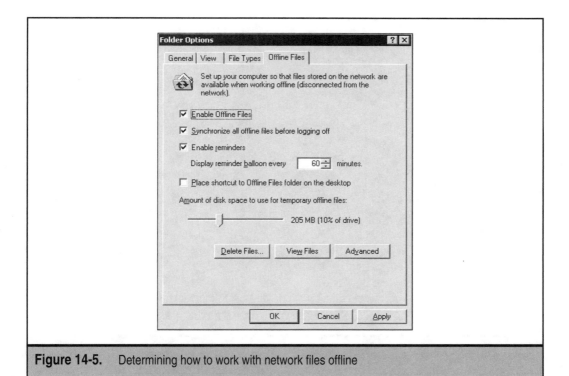

Figure 14-5.   Determining how to work with network files offline

NOTE: Besides selecting languages in the Input Locales tab, you can select the keyboard layout, not only to match other languages you might choose, but also to use variations of the U.S. keyboard, such as Dvorak.

Mouse

Mouse in the Control Panel allows you to set the configuration of the mouse, as shown in Figure 14-7. The Buttons tab lets you choose whether you want to use the mouse with your left or right hand. This reverses the effect of the two primary buttons on a mouse. As you also saw in the Folder Options dialog box, you can select whether to single-click or double-click to open a file, and choose the speed at which a double-click is interpreted as a double-click.

Mouse

The Pointers tab lets you choose or create a scheme for how the mouse pointer looks in various situations. The Motion tab lets you set how fast you want the pointer to move and accelerate, and whether you want the pointer to automatically go to the default button when a dialog box opens. I find this last option very handy. Like the Hardware tab in the Keyboard dialog box, the Mouse Hardware tab shows the description of the device, allows you to troubleshoot it, and, by clicking Properties, gives you access to the drivers that are being used with it.

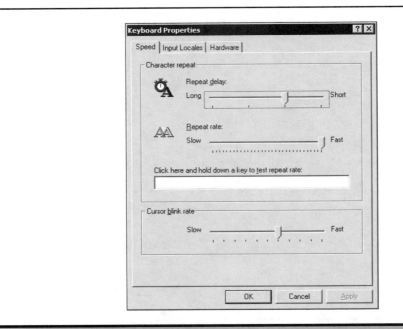

Figure 14-6. Configuring the keyboard (and the cursor)

Regional Options

Regional Options in the Control Panel lets you determine how numbers, dates, currency, and time are displayed and used on your computer, as well as the languages that will be used. By choosing the primary locale, such as French (France), all the other settings, including those for formatting numbers, currency, times, and dates, are automatically changed to

Regional Options

the standard for that locale. You can then go into the individual tabs for currency, time, and so on and customize how you want items displayed. The Input Locales tab is the same as you saw in the Keyboard dialog box and lets you select the languages in which you will be typing and how you want to switch among them.

NOTE: The custom settings for numbers, currency, time, and dates will remain set only as long as you maintain the same locale. When you change to a new locale and then change back to the original one, your custom settings will be gone, although you can use a separate profile to prevent this from occurring. See "Employing User Profiles," later in the chapter.

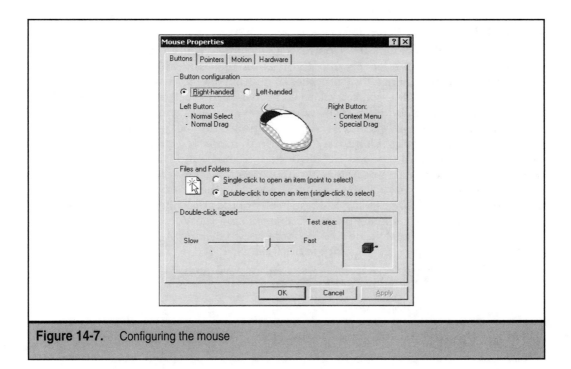

Figure 14-7. Configuring the mouse

Scheduled Tasks

Scheduled Tasks allows you to set up certain tasks, such as performing a backup or disk defragmentation, on a periodic basis and have those tasks carried out automatically. Double-clicking Scheduled Tasks in the Control Panel opens the Scheduled Tasks windows where, after they are identified, you see the scheduled tasks. Double-clicking Add Scheduled Task in the Scheduled Tasks window opens the Scheduled Task Wizard, with which you can select the program you want to run from among all the installed programs that are either part of the operating system, such as Backup, or independent, such as Veritas's Backup Exec. Then, you select the frequency with which you want to do the backup, the time of day and day of the week to do it, and finally the username and password of the person authorizing the running of this program. You then are shown what you have scheduled. If you made an error, click Back and make the correction; otherwise, click Finish to establish the scheduled task. An icon for the newly scheduled task will appear in the Scheduled Tasks window. If you want to make a change in the task, double-click its icon, which opens a dialog box that allows you to change everything from the program that is run to the schedule, date, and time.

Scheduled
Tasks

Sounds and Multimedia

Sounds and Multimedia in the Control Panel allows you to assign sounds to various computer events, configure audio recording and playback, and look at and change the properties of multimedia hardware. As you can see in Figure 14-8, you can take a computer event, such as Critical Stop, and assign a sound file, such as Chord.wav, to that event. When the event occurs, the sound is played. After assigning a number of sounds to events, you can save that scheme by clicking Save As, entering a name, and clicking OK. You can also select one of the default schemes. At the bottom of the Sounds tab, you can control the sound volume and whether or not the volume control is shown on the taskbar.

The Audio tab allows you to assign audio devices to the recording and playback capabilities in Windows 2000. Clicking Volume in any of the areas opens the Volume Control dialog box, which also is available by double-clicking the Volume Control icon in the taskbar or choosing the Volume Control accessory. Clicking Advanced allows you to make some performance settings for the devices.

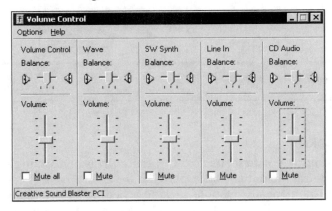

The Hardware tab allows you to select from a list of multimedia devices, see a description of the selected device, troubleshoot it, and, by clicking Properties, gain access to the drivers that are being used with that device.

System

Double-clicking System in the Control Panel opens the System Properties dialog box, the central place to establish, view, and change hardware settings. The System Properties dialog box can also be opened by right-clicking My Computer and choosing Properties. The first two tabs provide general and network identification. If the computer is not a domain controller, you can change the network name and join a domain from the Network Identification tab.

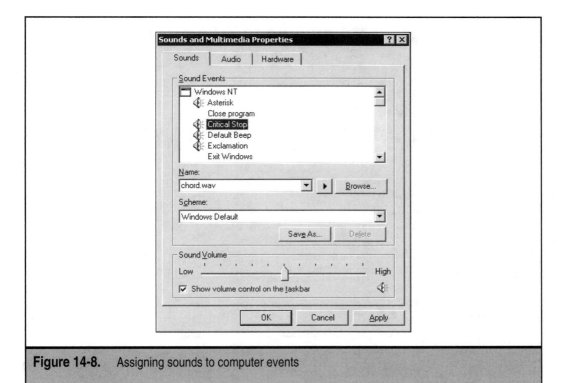

Figure 14-8. Assigning sounds to computer events

Hardware The Hardware tab enables you to start the Hardware Wizard, which also can be started by double-clicking Add/Remove Hardware in the Control Panel. You can also open the Hardware Profiles dialog box, in which you can set up and manage multiple hardware profiles, such as those used with laptops and their docking stations. Hardware profiles are discussed further in Chapter 18, which covers mobile computing. Driver digital signing gives you assurance of who created the driver and other installation files, and that they have not been changed. The Driver Signing option opens a dialog box where you can determine whether you want to be prevented from using, be warned about, or ignore files that are not digitally signed.

Device Manager The Device Manager, shown in Figure 14-9, is the most important facility in System, enabling you to look at and configure all of your hardware in one place. You can immediately see whether you have a hardware problem; for example, the Audio Adapter in Figure 14-9 has a problem, as indicated by the exclamation mark icon. You can then directly open that device by double-clicking it, and attempt to cure the problem. In most cases, a Troubleshooter will lead you through a problem search. Two common problems that often can be cured with a Troubleshooter are a wrong or missing driver (the case in Figure 14-9), or incorrect resources being used, often because the correct ones

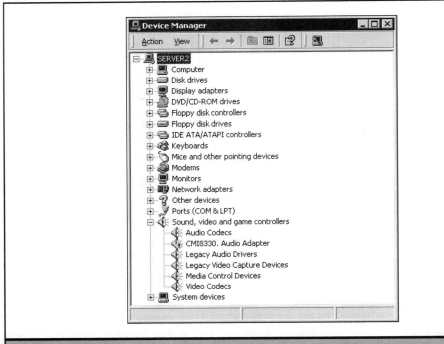

Figure 14-9.   Scanning all hardware devices in the Device Manager

weren't available. If you open the Properties dialog box for a device and look at the General tab, you will get a quick device status. The Driver tab will then allow you to reinstall or update the driver, and the Resources tab will show you where the problem is and allow you to select different resources (resources include interrupt request lines, or IRQs, and input/output ports).

NOTE: You can print a System Resource Summary that shows all the resource assignments (IRQs, DMAs, and I/O ports) on the computer by opening the View menu and choosing Print in Device Manager.

Advanced Tab   The System Properties dialog box's Advanced tab provides access to the settings for three operating system features:

NOTE: If you have installed multiple user profiles, you will also have a Users Profiles tab, which is discussed later in this chapter under "Employing User Profiles."

▼ **Performance Options**   Optimize performance between running applications or running background services, as are required in a file or print server; you also can determine the amount of disk space you want to set aside for temporary page files, the storing of memory on disk.

- **Environment Variables** Add and change both user and system variables, such as Temp, that tell the OS where items are stored on disk.

▲ **Startup and Recovery** Select the default OS to use on startup, how long to wait for a manual selection of that OS, and what to do on a system failure.

TIP: The Startup area is where you can change the amount of time the computer sits idle during startup waiting for you to pick an OS. You might want to change it to something shorter, such as five seconds.

Task Manager

Windows Task Manager allows you to look at and control what is running in Windows 2000. You can start Task Manager, shown in Figure 14-10, either by right-clicking a blank area of the taskbar and choosing Task Manager or by pressing CTRL-ALT-DEL and choosing Task Manager. The Applications tab shows you the application tasks that are currently running and allows you to terminate a task, switch to a task, or start a new task by using the Run command.

The Processes tab shows the processes that are currently loaded. These include the programs needed for the applications that are running, as well as the OS processes that are active. You can display a large amount of information for each of the processes, and you can select what you want to display by choosing View | Select Columns, as shown

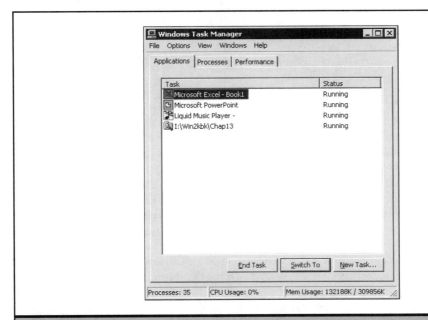

Figure 14-10. Looking at the applications that are currently running

next. After you choose the columns you want to display, you can arrange the columns by dragging the column headers, and you can sort the list by clicking the column you want sorted. You can end any process by selecting it and clicking End Process.

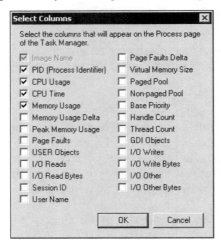

The Performance tab, shown in Figure 14-11, shows you how the tasks being performed by the computer are using the CPU and memory, and what are the components of that usage. This information is particularly important in heavily used servers. You can see if either or both the CPU and memory are reaching their limit and what the system is doing to handle it. If you have multiple CPUs, you can see how each is being used, and assign processes to particular processors by right-clicking the processes in the Processes tab. You can also set the priority of a process by right-clicking it in the Processes tab.

The Microsoft Management Console

The Microsoft Management Console, or MMC, is a shell to which you can add, and then customize, management tools that you want to use. You can create several different *consoles* containing different tools for different administrative purposes and save these consoles as MSC files. There are two types of management tools that you can add to an MMC: standalone tools that are called *snap-ins,* and add-on functions that are called *extensions.* Extensions work with and are available for particular snap-ins. Extensions are automatically added with some snap-ins, whereas other snap-ins require you to select the extensions. An example of a snap-in with automatic extensions is Computer Management, and one of its many extensions is the Disk Defragmenter. There are two modes in which you can create consoles: *Author* mode, in which the consoles can be added to and revised, and *User* mode, in which the console is frozen and cannot be changed. User mode also has full-access and two limited-access options.

Windows 2000 Server comes with a number of consoles already created that you have used in earlier chapters. These consoles, which I have called "windows" (because that is

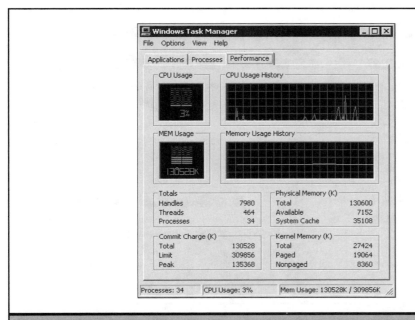

Figure 14-11. Looking at how CPU and memory are being used

what they are), are located in the Administrative Tools folder (Start | Programs | Administrative Tools) and include Computer Management, DHCP, and Distributed Files System. All of the built-in consoles are in User mode and cannot be changed or added to.

NOTE: You can only set up an MMC for NT machines. Trying to do so with Windows 98 will not work.

Creating an MMC Console

A console that I have found to be handy is one to manage several remote computers on my network. In this one console, I have added Computer Management for these computers. Therefore, as the administrator on the server, I can remotely look at most of the administrative information on these computers, as you can see in Figure 14-12. Use the following instructions to create a similar console:

NOTE: Most sets of steps in this chapter require that you be logged on as an Administrator.

1. Open the Start menu and click Run. In the Run dialog box, type **mmc** and click OK. The MMC will open showing only a console root, the window in which you add snap-ins.

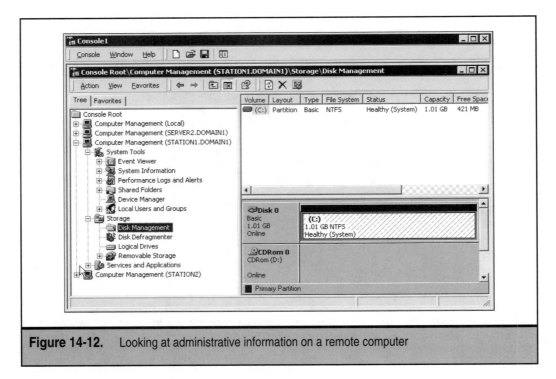

Figure 14-12.   Looking at administrative information on a remote computer

2. Open the Console menu and choose Add/Remove Snap-In. In the
   Add/Remove Snap-In dialog box that opens, click Add. The Add
   Standalone Snap-In dialog box will open.

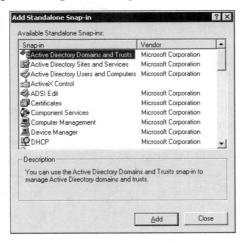

3. Click any of the snap-ins that are not familiar to you and look at the description
   in the lower part of the dialog box.

4. After you look at all the snap-ins that you want to, double-click Computer Management. The Computer Management dialog box opens, asking you to choose between the local computer you are on and another computer. You may or may not want to include the local computer in this console. Assume you do for these instructions, and click Finish. Computer Management (Local) will appear in the Add/Remove Snap-In dialog box.

5. Double-click Computer Management a second time, click Another Computer, browse for the other computer, and, after it is found, click Finish. Computer Management for the second computer will appear in the Add/Remove Snap-In dialog box.

6. Repeat step 5 for as many computers as you want to manage in one console. After you add all the snap-ins that you want, click Close in the Add Standalone Snap-In dialog box.

7. In the Add/Remove Snap-In dialog box, click Extensions. The list of extensions is displayed, as shown in Figure 14-13. You can see that the default is to add all the extensions, which has been done. If you want to remove some of the extensions, uncheck the Add All Extensions checkbox and then uncheck the extensions you don't want (doing this once will apply to all Computer Management snap-ins).

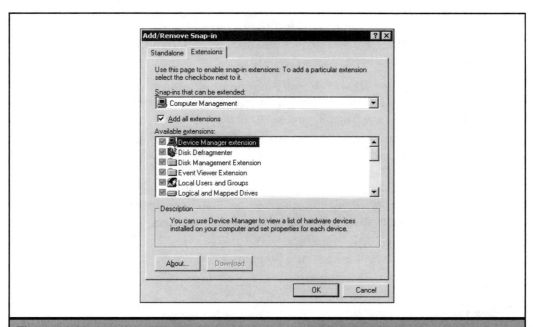

Figure 14-13.   Selecting the extensions for the Computer Management snap-in

8. After you complete all the changes you want to make to the extensions, click OK. You are returned to the MMC and your snap-ins appear in the left pane. Open several of the snap-ins and their extensions to get a view, similar to Figure 14-12.

9. In the MMC, open the Console menu and choose Options to open the Options dialog box. Here, you can choose either Author or User mode. Look at the description of what each mode means and what each of the User mode's options means.

10. When you have chosen the mode you want to use, click OK to close the Options dialog box and return to the MMC.

11. Again open the Console menu and choose Save As. Enter a name that is meaningful to you and click Save. Finally, close the MMC.

Using an MMC Console

Your custom consoles are kept in the Administrative Tools folder in the shared Administrator area of your hard disk (C:\Documents and Settings\Administrator\Start Menu\Programs\Administrative Tools). If you haven't created one or more custom consoles, you won't have an Administrative Tools folder here, but after you create your first custom console, that folder is created and the console is automatically placed in it. This is not the same as the Administrator Tools folder containing all the built-in consoles, which is in the shared All Users area of your hard disk (C:\Documents and Settings\All Users\Start Menu\Programs\Administrative Tools), but when you log on as Administrator, both Administrative Tools folders will open as one from the Start menu. See how that works by following these steps:

1. Open the Start menu and choose Programs | Administrative Tools. If necessary, expand the menu so that you can see all the options. On it, you should see the new console you have created.

2. Click your new console to open it. Open one of your remote computers and then continue to open the extensions to see, for example, a particular hardware resource, such as IRQs, as shown in Figure 14-14.

3. Continue to open the various extensions within the Computer Management console and see the capabilities that are available; note that some features are read-only, and that to do remote disk defragmentation, you must buy an add-on package from Executive Software International.

4. After you finish looking at what you can see and do within your new console, close it.

The Registry

The Registry is the central repository of all configuration information in Windows 2000. It contains the settings that you make in the Control Panel, in most Properties dialog boxes, and in the Administrative Tools. Almost all programs get information about the local com-

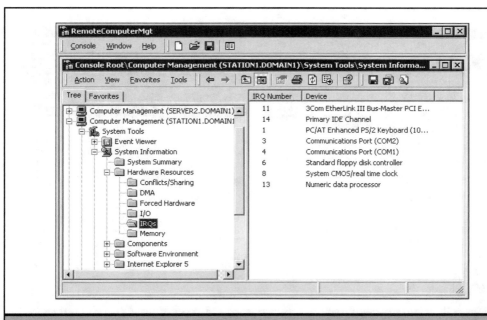

Figure 14-14. Looking at the hardware resources on a remote computer

puter and current user from the Registry and write information to the Registry for the OS and other programs to use. The Registry is a complex hierarchical database that in most circumstances should not be directly changed. The majority of the settings in the Registry can be changed in the Control Panel, Properties dialog boxes, or Administrative Tools.

CAUTION: If you directly edit the Registry, it is very easy to make an erroneous change that will bring down the system, so you are strongly advised to directly edit the Registry only as the last alternative used in trying to change a setting.

With the preceding caution firmly in mind, it is still worthwhile understanding and looking at the Registry. Windows 2000's Registry Editor enables you to view the Registry, as well as make changes to it if you have to.

TIP: If you make a change to the Registry that doesn't work, you can restore the Registry to the way it was the last time the computer was started by restarting the computer and pressing F8 when you see the message Select An Operating System. Select Last Known Good Condition and press ENTER. The most recent backup of the Registry will be used to start the computer.

Start the Registry Editor by opening the Start menu, choosing Run, typing **regedt32**, and clicking OK. The Registry Editor will appear, as shown in Figure 14-15.

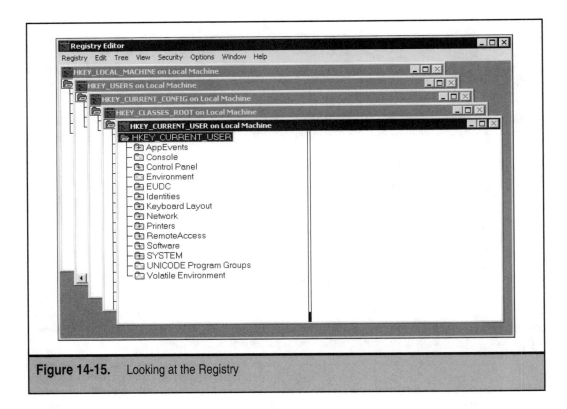

Figure 14-15. Looking at the Registry

Keys and Subtrees

The Registry consists of two primary keys, or *subtrees* (HKEY_USERS and HKEY_
LOCAL_MACHINE), and three subordinate keys, also called subtrees (HKEY_
CURRENT_USER, HKEY_CURRENT_CONFIG, and HKEY_CLASSES_ROOT). HKEY_
CURRENT_USER is subordinate to HKEY_USERS, and HKEY_CURRENT_CONFIG
and HKEY_CLASSES_ROOT are subordinate to HKEY_LOCAL_MACHINE. Each of the
five subtrees is a folder and a window in the Registry Editor, and they all are shown at the
same level for ease of use. The purpose of each subtree is as follows:

HKEY_USERS Contains the default information common to all users and is used until a
user logs on.

▼ **HKEY_CURRENT_USER** Contains the preferences, or *profile*, of the user
currently logged on to the computer. This includes the desktop contents, the
screen colors, Control Panel settings, and Start menu contents. The settings
here take precedence over those in HKEY_LOCAL_MACHINE, where they
are duplicated. Later in this chapter, under "Employing User Profiles," you'll
see how to set up and manage user profiles.

HKEY_LOCAL_MACHINE   Contains all the computer and OS settings that are not user-re-lated. This includes the type and model of CPU; the amount of memory; the keyboard, mouse, and ports available on the hardware side; and the drivers, fonts, and settings for individual programs on the software side.

▼   **HKEY_CURRENT_CONFIG**   Contains the hardware profile for the current computer configuration. This includes the drives, ports, and drivers needed for the currently installed hardware. This is important with mobile computers and their docking stations.

▲   **HKEY_CLASSES_ROOT**   Contains the file type registration information that relates file extensions to the programs that can open them.

Keys, Subkeys, and Hives

Within each of the primary keys or subtrees are lower-level keys, and within those keys are subkeys, and within the subkeys are lower-level subkeys, and so on for many levels. For example, Figure 14-16 shows a subkey nine levels below HKEY_LOCAL_MACHINE. You can think of keys and subkeys as folders that have folders within them and folders within those folders.

Several of the keys immediately beneath the two primary keys (HKEY_LOCAL_MACHINE and HKEY_USERS) are deep groupings of keys and subkeys. These keys (De-fault, SAM, Security, Software, and System) are called *hives* and are stored as separate files in the C:\Winnt\System32\Config folder (assuming the default installation). Each hive has

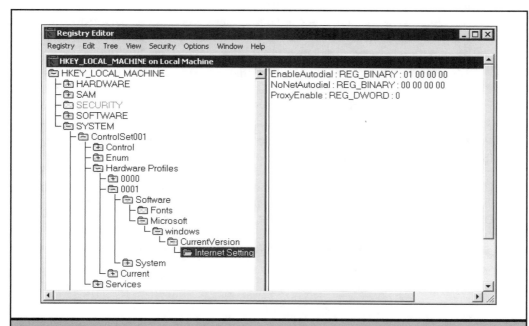

Figure 14-16.   There are often many subkeys within each key in the Registry

at least two files, and most often three or more. The first file, without an extension, is the Registry file that contains the current Registry information. The second file, with the .log extension, is a log of changes that have been made to the Registry file. The third file, with the .sav extension, is the Last Known Good backup of the Registry (known to be good because the system was successfully started with it).

NOTE: The SAM key stands for Security Account Manager. It is used for storing the username and password in stand-alone computers.

You can work with the hives to save a particular group of settings, make changes to the settings, and then either restore the original settings or add the original settings to the new ones. Here are the Registry Editor's Registry menu commands to do that:

▼ **Save Key**   Used to save a selected hive to your disk or a floppy. To use this command, select the hive, open the Registry menu, choose Save Key, select a folder, enter a name, and click Save. A saved hive can be either restored or loaded.

■ **Restore**   Used to replace an existing hive in the Registry. To use this command, select the hive to be replaced, open the Registry menu, choose Restore, select a drive and folder, enter or select a name, and click Open. The restored hive will overwrite the current one.

■ **Load Hive**   Used to add a saved hive to an existing one. To use this command, select either HKEY_LOCAL_MACHINE or HKEY_USERS, open the Registry menu, choose Load Hive, select a drive and folder, enter or select a name, and click Open. When asked, enter the name that you want to give the additional hive, and click OK. A new subkey is created with the name you have given it. This can then be used by software that knows about the new name.

▲ **Unload Hive**   Used to remove a hive that has been loaded (this cannot be done if the hive was restored). Unload a loaded hive by selecting it, opening the Registry menu, and choosing Unload Hive.

NOTE: You can make additional copies of the Registry files in two ways using the Backup utility (Start | Programs | Accessories | System Tools | Backup). One way is to back up to an external media—tape, CD-R (recordable CD), or removable disk—by starting the Backup Wizard and backing up the System State data. The other way is to create an Emergency Repair Disk and choose to back up the Registry to the Repair folder. This complete backup of the Registry is stored by default in C:\Winnt\Repair\RegBack and is used automatically by the Emergency Repair Process (see discussion under "Running Emergency Repair," later in the chapter), but can also be used manually to replace the current Registry folders in C:\Winnt\System32\Config. I recommend that you do both the external and internal backup.

Entries and Data Types

At the lowest level of the Registry tree, you will see a *value entry* in the right pane opposite the key it applies to. All value entries have three elements, separated by colons: a name on the left, a data type in the middle, and the value on the right. You can see three value entries on the right of Figure 14-16. The data type determines how to look at and use the value. Also, the Registry Editor has a value editor for each data type. Table 14-2 provides the name of each data type, its editor, and its description.

TIP: You can automatically open the correct editor for a particular data type by double-clicking the value entry that contains the data type.

Data Type	Editor	Description
REG_BINARY	Binary	A single value that is expressed in the Registry Editor as a hexadecimal number, generally a complex number that is parsed and used to set switches
REG_DWORD	Dword	A single value that is a hexadecimal number of up to eight digits, generally a simple number such as decimal 16, or 60, or 1024
REG_SZ	String	A single string of characters, such as a filename; it can include spaces
REG_EXPAND_SZ	String	A single string of characters that contains a variable that the OS replaces with its current value when the value is requested; an example is the environment variable *Systemroot* that is replaced with the root directory of Windows 2000 (by default, C:\Winnt)
REG_MULTI_SZ	Multi-String	Multiple strings of characters separated by spaces, so each string cannot contain spaces

Table 14-2.   Data Types Used with Value Entries

The Boot Process

The Windows 2000 startup or *boot* process is reasonably complex and can have problems. Therefore, it is worthwhile for you to understand what is taking place during booting, what you see on the screen, and what files are being used. Armed with this information, hopefully you'll be able to correct or work around any problems that occur.

Boot Files

Booting uses nine primary files, two optional files, and however many driver files that are needed. Table 14-3 describes these files, shows in which stage of the boot process each file is used, and lists the default location in which each file is stored.

Filename	Description	Where Used	Stored In
Ntldr	Basic operating system loader	Preboot	C:\
Boot.ini	Identifies the optional OSs into which you can boot, as well as the timeout seconds; this file is directly editable	Boot	C:\
Ntdetect.com	Detects and prepares a list of currently installed hardware components	Boot	C:\
Ntoskrnl.exe	The operating system kernel; creates the current hardware Registry key, loads device drivers, and starts Session Manager	Load	C:\Winnt\System32
Hal.dll	Hardware abstraction layer; provides the interface between the operating system and the specific set of hardware in the computer	Load	C:\Winnt\System32
Smss.exe	Session Manager; loads basic services, creates the pagefile, starts the Win32 I/O subsystem, and begins the logon process	Initialization	C:\Winnt\System32
System	Registry file providing the primary operating system parameters	Initialization	C:\Winnt\System32\Config

Table 14-3.   Files Used in the Startup/Boot Process

Filename	Description	Where Used	Stored In
Winlogon.exe	Handles the logon process and starts the Local Security Authority	Logon	C:\Winnt\ System32
Lsass.exe	Local Security Authority; provides the security-checking mechanisms	Logon	C:\Winnt\ System32
Optional Files			
Bootsect.dos	Optional boot sector used to dual boot into MS-DOS, Windows 95, or Windows 98	Boot	C:\
Ntbootdd.sys	Optionally used to boot from SCSI (Small Computer System Interface) disks	Boot	C:\

Table 14-3. Files Used in the Startup/Boot Process *(continued)*

TIP: To see the preceding system files in Windows Explorer or My Computer, you need to set the appropriate options in the Tools | Folder Options | View tab (Show Hidden Files should be selected, and Hide Protected Operating System Files should not be checked).

The optional files are placed on the computer by Setup only if it detects the need for them. If you don't have SCSI disks, you won't find Ntbootdd.sys, and if you have not set up dual booting, you won't find Bootsect.dos.

Steps in the Booting Process

As you can see from Table 14-3, the boot process has five major stages: preboot, boot, load, initialization, and logon. Within each of these stages are several steps that take place that load and use the files in Table 14-3. In each of these stages, look at the process that is taking place, how the particular files are used, and what you see on the screen.

Preboot Preboot is the hardware-dependent, BIOS-enabled startup process. It is started either by power coming on or the system being reset. The first step is to see what hardware is available and its condition by using the power-on self test (POST) routines. Next, the boot device is located and the master boot record (MBR) is read. From it, the active partition is found on the partition table and its boot sector is read. Because Windows 2000 Setup has written it there, the active partition's boot sector specifies that the Ntldr file should be loaded and run. On the screen, you see the memory check, the identification of hardware, and the search for a boot device.

Boot   Boot is OS-dependent. For Windows 2000, it is controlled by Ntldr (the NT loader), which begins by loading the Ntdetect.com file, which in turn determines what hardware and drivers are available. Ntldr then switches from real mode to 32-bit mode and loads a miniature file system that can operate with either FAT- or NTFS-formatted disks. If a SCSI file system was detected, the Ntbootdd.sys file is loaded to implement the SCSI drivers.

Next, the Boot.ini file is read and, if applicable, the user is asked to choose the OS they want to use. If a choice is not made before the timeout, the default in Boot.ini is loaded. If a Boot.ini file is not found, Ntldr uses the first disk, first partition, and /Winnt folder from which to load the operating system.

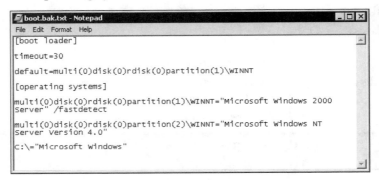

If the MS-DOS or Windows 95/98 operating system is chosen, the Bootsect.dos file is used to return the boot sector on the active partition to its state prior to installing Windows 2000. This boot sector is then used to boot into the prior operating system.

If you are booting Windows 2000 and have set up two or more hardware profiles, you are given the option of pressing the SPACEBAR to select a hardware profile you want to use; for example, if you have a laptop that you sometimes use with a docking station. If you press the SPACEBAR, you can choose the hardware profile you want; otherwise, the default profile is used.

Load   Following the operating system and hardware profile selection, the screen is cleared and black and white vertical bars at the bottom of the screen are slowly filled in to be solid white. While this is happening, Ntldr loads the following:

▼ **Ntoskrnl.exe**   The operating system kernel

■ **Hal.dll**   The hardware abstraction layer that provides the interface between the operating system and a particular set of hardware

■ **System**   Registry file from HKEY_LOCAL_MACHINE

▲ **Device drivers**   Drivers for basic hardware devices, such as the monitor, as specified in System

Initialization   Ntoskrnl.exe is initialized and takes over from Ntldr, bringing up a graphical display with a status bar. Ntoskrnl.exe then writes the HKEY_LOCAL_MACHINE\HARDWARE key and HKEY_LOCAL_MACHINE\SYSTEM\SELECT subkey (called the "Clone Control Set") and loads the remainder of the device drivers. Finally, Smss.exe, the Session Manager, is started. Smss.exe executes any boot-time command files, creates a paging file for the Virtual Memory Manager, creates links to the file system that can be used by DOS commands, and finally starts the Win32 subsystem to handle all I/O for Windows 2000.

> **NOTE:**   Figure 1-1, the Central Components of Windows 2000, shows and relates the kernel, Win32 Subsystem, and HAL.

Logon   The Win32 subsystem starts the final Windows 2000 GUI and then Winlogon.exe, which displays the logon dialog box. After a successful logon, the necessary services are started and the Last Known Good control set is written based upon the Clone Control Set.

Correcting Booting Problems
Numerous situations can cause a computer to not boot. To counter this fact, Windows 2000 has several features to help you work around the problem and to help you fix it. Among these features are the following:

▼ Returning to the Last Known Good Registry files

■ Running Emergency Repair

■ Using Safe Mode and other Advanced Options

■ Using the Recovery Console

■ Repairing the boot sector

▲ Creating boot floppy disks (Emergency Repair Disks)

Returning to the Last Known Good Registry Files   If a computer doesn't successfully complete the boot process, and you have just tried to install a new piece of hardware or software or have otherwise changed the Registry, the problem often is due to the Registry trying to load a device driver that doesn't work properly, or the result of some other Registry problem. You would normally learn of this problem late in the boot process, probably in either the Initialization or Logon stages. The fastest cure for a Registry problem is to return to the Last Known Good Registry files, by following these steps:

1. Restart the computer, and press F8 when you see the message For Troubleshooting and Advanced Startup Options for Windows 2000, Press F8.

2. Use the arrow keys to select Last Known Good Configuration, and press ENTER. The Last Known Good Registry files will be used to start up Windows 2000.

The Last Known Good Registry files were saved the last time you successfully completed booting and logged on to Windows 2000.

Running Emergency Repair   The second easiest way to try to repair a problem starting the operating system is to use the automated option of Emergency Repair, which is located on the Windows 2000 Setup CD-ROM. To do this, though, you need an Emergency Repair Disk (ERD) and a Repair folder on the computer's hard disk. The ERD, discussed in Chapter 12, and the Repair folder are created in the Backup utility. Create the ERD and Repair folder here so that you have it ready. First you need to format a floppy disk:

1. Insert a floppy disk whose contents are of no value, and then open My Computer.

2. Right-click the floppy disk icon, choose Format in the context menu, click Start, and click OK when warned that formatting will erase all data on the disk. Finally, click OK when told that formatting is complete, and then click Close.

3. Leave the floppy disk in its drive and start the Backup utility by opening the Start menu and choosing Programs | Accessories | System Tools | Backup.

4. In the Welcome tab of the Backup window, click the button opposite Emergency Repair Disk.

5. Click the checkbox to back up the Registry in the Repair folder and click OK to create the Repair folder and write the ERD.

6. Click OK when you are told that the ERD was saved successfully. Remove the floppy, label it, and store it in a safe place that you can easily find and get to in an emergency.

Emergency Repair is started from the Windows 2000 Setup disks (either CD or floppy) used for installing Windows 2000:

1. Restart the computer and boot from either the Setup floppies or the CD. You will see the normal Setup file loading take place onscreen.

2. When asked whether you want to set up Windows 2000 or repair Windows 2000, press R to repair it.

3. When asked whether you want to use the Recovery Console or the Emergency Repair Process, again press R for the Emergency Repair Process (you'll find a discussion of the Recovery Console later in this chapter).

4. Choose Fast Repair by pressing F to automatically run through all the repair options.

5. Since you already have the ERD in its drive, press ENTER twice. Press ENTER again to examine the disk drives, or press ESC if the drives are not a potential problem. After examining your hard drives, the system will want to restart. Remove the ERD in the floppy drive before doing that. Windows 2000 will start and hopefully come up normally.

Using the Last Known Good Configuration and the Emergency Repair Process are the only automated means to try to repair a problem starting Windows 2000. All other techniques require that you manually work on the files that are required to start Windows 2000.

Using Safe Mode and Other Advanced Options   Safe Mode uses only minimal default drivers to start the basic Windows 2000 services, with the idea that, in that mode, you can fix the problem that's preventing the full startup. You start Safe Mode with the same steps used to start Last Known Good Configuration, except that you choose one of three Safe Modes: Safe Mode, Safe Mode With Networking, and Safe Mode With Command Prompt. Basic Safe Mode does not include networking and comes up with a minimal Windows graphics interface. The second Safe Mode option adds networking capability, and the third option places you at a command prompt; otherwise, these two options are the same as Safe Mode.

As you start Safe Mode, you see a listing of the drivers as they are loaded. If the boot fails at that point, you are left looking at the last drivers that were loaded. Once you get into Windows, you might not have a mouse available, so you'll need to remember the shortcut keys for important functions, as shown in Table 14-4.

While working in Safe Mode, the System Information window is very handy, as shown in Figure 14-17. Start the System Information window by opening the Start menu and choosing Programs | Accessories | System Tools | System Information. Within System Information, Hardware Resources | Conflicts/Sharing, Components | Problem Devices, and Software Environment | Running Tasks are particularly of value.

Function	Shortcut Key
Open Start menu	CTRL-ESC
Open context menu	SHIFT-F10
Close active windows	ALT-F4
Open Help	F1
Open Properties	ALT-ENTER
Search for files or folders	F3
Switch tasks	ALT-ESC
Switch programs	ALT-TAB
Switch tabs	CTRL-TAB
Turn on MouseKeys	Left-SHIFT-left-ALT-NUM LOCK
Undo last operation	CTRL-Z

Table 14-4.   Windows 2000 Shortcut Keys

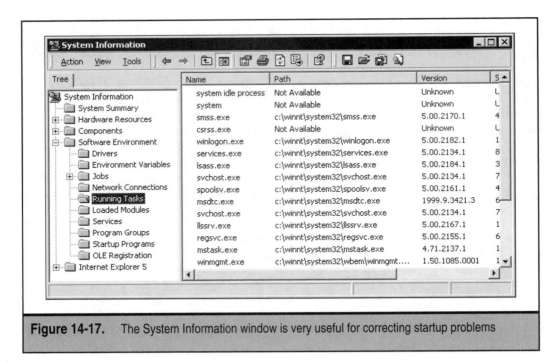

Figure 14-17. The System Information window is very useful for correcting startup problems

In addition to Safe Mode and Last Known Good Configuration, the Advanced Options menu has the following options. These are in addition to the options, Boot Normally and Return To OS Choices Menu (where you can select the Recovery Console, see the next section), which do not need explanation:

▼ **Enable Boot Logging** Logs all the events that take place during startup in the file Ntbtlog.txt, located by default in the C:\Winnt folder. The loading of all system files and drivers is logged, as shown next, so that you can see if one failed while it was being loaded. Boot logging is done in all advanced startup options except Last Known Good Configuration.

```
ntbtlog.txt - Notepad
File  Edit  Format  Help
Microsoft (R) windows 2000 (R) version 5.0 (Build 2195)
 1 27 2000 12:13:22.500
Loaded driver \WINNT\System32\ntoskrnl.exe
Loaded driver \WINNT\System32\hal.dll
Loaded driver \WINNT\System32\BOOTVID.DLL
Loaded driver pci.sys
Loaded driver isapnp.sys
Loaded driver pciide.sys
Loaded driver \WINNT\System32\DRIVERS\PCIIDEX.SYS
Loaded driver ftdisk.sys
Loaded driver MountMgr.sys
Loaded driver Diskperf.sys
Loaded driver \WINNT\System32\Drivers\WMILIB.SYS
Loaded driver dmload.sys
Loaded driver dmio.sys
Loaded driver PartMgr.sys
Loaded driver atapi.sys
Loaded driver disk.sys
Loaded driver \WINNT\System32\DRIVERS\CLASSPNP.SYS
Loaded driver Dfs.sys
Loaded driver KSecDD.sys
Loaded driver Ntfs.sys
Loaded driver NDIS.sys
```

▼ **Enable VGA Mode**   Sets the display for a minimal video graphic adapter (VGA) with 640 × 480 resolution using a known good default driver. All other drivers and capabilities are loaded normally. The VGA mode is also used in Safe Mode.

■ **Directory Services Restore Mode**   Restores Active Directory in domain controllers and then goes into Safe Mode, except that the mouse is available and normal video display mode is used (not VGA mode). In computers that are not domain controllers, this option is the same as Safe Mode.

▲ **Debugging Mode**   Turns on the debugger and then boots up into the normal configuration for the computer. This allows you to work on scripts that might be getting in the way of a proper startup.

Using the Recovery Console   The Recovery Console is a DOS-like command-line interface that allows you to read, write, format, and partition or delete partitions on both FAT and NTFS disks, as well as repair the boot and master boot records on a disk. Like the Emergency Repair Process, the Recovery Console is started from the Windows 2000 Setup disks (either CD or floppy) used for installing Windows 2000. Boot from either the floppy disk or the CD and follow the instructions to repair a Windows 2000 installation using the Recovery Console. If you have several partitions with different operating systems in them, you are asked to choose which you want to log on to by typing a number of the drive (the drive numbers are listed for you) and pressing ENTER. You then must enter the Administrator's password and press ENTER. The command prompt will appear, such as C:\Winnt.

TIP: If you have copied the Windows 2000 Setup CD's I386 folder, either Server or Professional, onto your hard disk, you can install the Recovery Console as a startup option by typing the Run command **c:\i386\winnt32/cmdcons**, given that C:\i386 is the folder in which you placed your Setup files. You can then select Windows 2000 Recovery Console from the OS Choices menu.

At the Recovery Console's command prompt, you can type many familiar DOS commands, such as Attrib, Cd, Chkdsk, Cls, Copy, Del, Dir, Format, Md, More, Rd, and Ren. You can get a complete list of commands by typing **Help** and pressing ENTER. You can also get an explanation of any of the commands by typing the command followed by /?, or you can type **Help** and a command name, and pressing ENTER after any entry.

You can also use commands that are unique to the Recovery Console, some of which are quite powerful. Among these commands are the following:

▼ **Batch**   Executes a set of commands in a text file.

■ **Disable** and **Enable**   Stops and restarts, respectively, a device driver or Windows system service. (You use Listsvc to get the drivers and services that are available.)

■ **Diskpart**   Adds and deletes disk partitions.

■ **Expand**   Decompresses a compressed file.

- ■ **Fixboot** and **Fixmbr**   Correct problems with the boot and master boot records, respectively. (See the next section for more details.)

- ■ **Listsvc**   Lists the device drivers and system services available on the computer.

- ■ **Logon**   Logs on to a different Windows 2000 installation.

- ■ **Map**   Shows the drives (and their drive letters) that are available on the computer.

- ▲ **Systemroot**   Changes the directory to the system variable Systemroot, which by default is C:\Winnt.

TIP: The Recovery Console's Diskpart is Windows 2000's answer to Fdisk that was available in MS-DOS and Windows 95/98.

When you are done with the Recovery Console, type **Exit** and press ENTER.

Repairing the Master Boot and Boot Sectors   Two commands in the Recovery Console are particularly significant to fixing problems when booting:

- ▼ Typing **fixboot** *drive id* and pressing ENTER at the command prompt in the Recovery Console writes a new boot sector in the identified drive. The *drive id* is optional, and if not stated, the first partition or system partition of the boot device is assumed.

- ▲ Typing **fixmbr** *device name* and pressing ENTER at the command prompt in the Recovery Console repairs the master boot record in the boot partition of the named device. The *device name* is optional, and if not stated, the boot device is assumed. If the partition table is not usable, you will be prompted for further information.

Creating a Boot Disk   If you cannot boot onto your hard disk due to errors in the boot sectors or root directory, and you cannot boot from a CD, then your last alternative is to boot from a floppy disk. This will allow you to work around the boot sectors and root directory, but it does require all the files and subfolders in what is by default C:\Winnt. If that is still good, a boot disk will allow you to start Windows 2000 in normal mode and potentially fix whatever is wrong with the boot sectors and root directory. To do this, you must have created in advance a boot disk for the particular computer that you want to start. You can create a boot disk with the following instructions:

1. Insert a newly formatted (see the earlier section "Running Emergency Repair") floppy disk in its drive and open My Computer.

2. Open the root directory of the hard drive from which Windows 2000 boots. In most instances, this is C:\.

3. Press and hold CTRL while clicking the following files to select them together: Boot.ini, Bootsect.dos (if not on the disk, you do not need it), Ntbootdd.sys (if not on the disk, you do not need it), Ntdetect.com, Ntldr

4. Right-click one of the selected files and choose Send To | 3½ Floppy (A). A Copying dialog box will appear, showing you the status.

5. When the copying process is complete, remove the floppy disk, label it **Boot Disk** along with the current date and computer name, and store it in a safe place where you won't forget it.

To use the boot disk, simply restart the computer with the disk in the floppy drive. This assumes that your BIOS setup allows you to boot from your floppy drive. The system will be booted off the floppy and then, after the OS selection, will use the files on the hard disk located in (by default) the C:\Winnt folder.

NOTE: The ERD discussed earlier in the chapter and created in the Backup utility is not the same thing as the boot disk described here. The boot disk starts the computer and then passes control to Windows 2000 on the hard disk. The ERD is used with the Emergency Repair Process on the Setup CD, using the R option as described previously under "Running Emergency Repair."

USER MANAGEMENT

Managing computer users with their varying needs and peculiarities, both in groups and individually, is a major task and one to which Windows 2000 has committed considerable resources. The key areas for this are the following:

▼   Using group policies

▲   Employing user profiles

Using Group Policies

Group policies provide the means to establish the standards and guidelines that an organization wants to apply to the use of its computers. Group policies are meant to reflect the general policies of an organization and can be established hierarchically from a local computer at the lowest end, to a particular site, to a domain, and to several levels of organizational units (OUs) at the upper end. Normally, lower-level units inherit the policies of the upper-level units, although it is possible to block higher-level policies, as well as to force inheritance if desired. Group polices are divided into *user policies* that prescribe what a user can do, and *computer policies* that determine what is available on a computer. User policies are independent of the computer on which the user is working, and follow the user from computer to computer. When a computer is started (booted), the applicable computer group policies are downloaded to it and stored in the Registry HKEY_LOCAL_MACHINE. When a user logs on to a computer, the applicable user group policies are downloaded to the computer and stored in the Registry HKEY_CURRENT_USER.

Group policies can be very beneficial to both an organization and the individuals in it. All the computers in an organization can automatically adjust to whichever user is currently logged on. This can include a custom desktop with a custom Start menu and a unique set of applications. Group policies can control the access to files, folders, and applications, as well as the ability to change system and application settings, and the ability to delete files and folders. Group policies can automate tasks when a computer starts up or shuts down, and when a user logs on or logs off. Group policies can also automatically store files and shortcuts in specific folders.

Creating and Changing Group Policies

Group policies can exist at the local computer level, the site level, the domain level, and the OU level. Although the process to create or change group policies is the same at the site, domain, and OU levels, it is sufficiently different at the local computer level to merit discussing this level separately.

Changing Group Policies at the Local Computer Level   Every Windows 2000 computer has a single local group policy created by Setup during installation and stored by default in C:\Winnt\System32\GroupPolicy. Since there can be only one local group policy, you cannot create another, although you can edit the existing one by following these instructions:

1. Open the Start menu, choose Run, type **gpedit.msc**, and press ENTER or click OK. The Group Policy window will open.

2. Open several levels of the tree on the left so that you can get down to a level that shows policies and their settings on the right, as shown in Figure 14-18.

3. Double-click a policy to open its dialog box. Here, as shown in Figure 14-19, you can change the local policy settings. You are also shown the effective policy setting based on domain-level policies, which override local policies.

4. Add additional users or groups to a policy by clicking Add and selecting one or more user and/or groups that you want to add.

5. Expand User Configuration | Administrative Templates | Windows Components and look at Internet Explorer, Windows Explorer, Start Menu & Taskbar, and Desktop. Note how they are all "Not Configured" and the variety of functions and features that you can control.

6. When you are done making the changes that you want to make to the local computer group policies, close the open dialog boxes and the Group Policy window.

Although group policies can be implemented at the local computer level, and are by default for the computer, they are expected to be overridden at the site, domain, or OU levels.

Creating and Changing Group Policies at the Site, Domain, and OU Levels   Group policies above the local computer level are Active Directory objects and are therefore called *group policy objects* (*GPOs*). They are created as one object, but they are stored in two pieces: a group policy

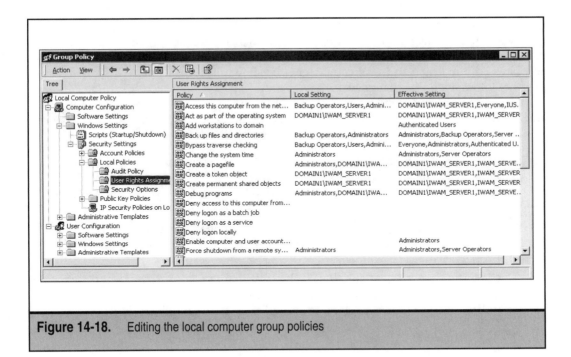

Figure 14-18. Editing the local computer group policies

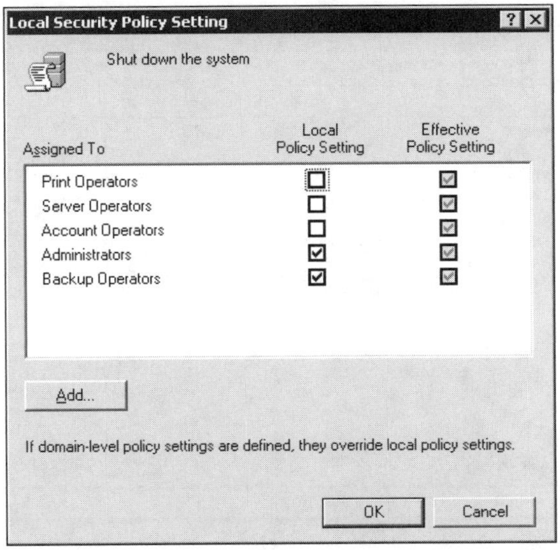

Figure 14-19. Changing a particular group policy at the local level

container, and a group policy template. *Group policy containers* (GPCs) are stored in Active Directory and hold smaller pieces of information that change infrequently. *Group policy templates* (GPTs) are a set of folders stored by default at C:\Winnt\Sysvol\Sysvol*domainname*\Policies\ and have both machine and user components, as shown in Figure 14-20. GPTs store larger pieces of information that change frequently.

You can create and change a GPO linked to a site by opening Active Directory Sites and Services, and you can create and change a GPO linked to a domain or OU by opening Active Directory Users and Computers. See how to do both of these next:

1. Open the Start menu and choose Programs | Administrative Tools | Active Directory Sites and Computers, or Active Directory Users and Computers. The Active Directory dialog box opens. (For this exercise, choose Active Directory Users and Computers.)

2. Right-click the site, domain, or OU that the policy is or will be linked to (use the domain in this example), and choose Properties. The site, domain, or OU Properties dialog box opens.

3. Click the Group Policy tab. If you chose Active Directory Users and Computers and domain as indicated in the preceding steps, you will see a default domain policy listed that you can look at and edit, as shown in Figure 14-21.

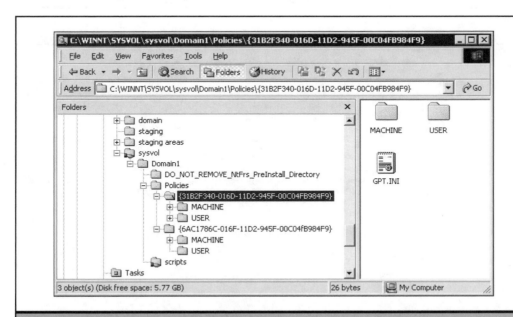

Figure 14-20. The folder structure of group policy templates

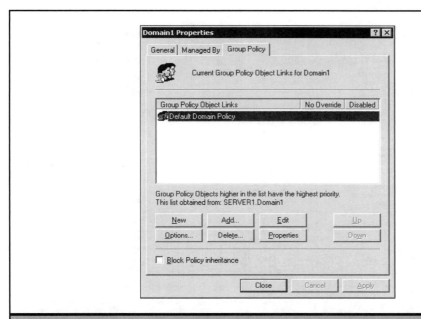

Figure 14-21.   Changing the default group policy linked to a domain

In the Group Policy tab of a domain, you can do the following: create a new group policy linked to that domain; add a link from a group policy in another domain; edit an existing group policy; disable the policy or prevent it from being overwritten using Options; and delete the policy and change its properties.

4. Select Default Domain Policy and choose Edit. The Group Policy window opens.

5. Open several levels of the tree on the left so that you can get down to a level that shows policies and their settings on the right. Notice that there is a great deal of similarity with the group policies at the local computer level, as you saw in Figure 14-18. There are some significant differences, though, as you can see in Figure 14-22.

The icons below Computer Configuration | Windows Settings | Security Settings are different for similar sets of policies: there are some new sets of policies at the domain level; in the default policy at the domain level, all the policies are not defined as it is originally installed by Setup; and there are some differences between the policies at the local and domain levels.

Figure 14-22. Editing group policies at the domain level

6. Double-click several of the policies, and you see that there are no detail policy settings, unlike the policies at the local computer level.

7. As an example of how a policy is set, expand Computer Configuration | Windows Settings | Security Settings | Local Policies | User Rights Assignment and then double-click Back Up Files and Directories. The Security Policy Setting dialog box will open, and if it is still in its default condition, it will be empty. (The default condition is assumed in the remaining steps.)

8. Click Define These Policy Settings and then click Add. In the Add User or Group dialog box that opens, click Browse. The Select Users or Groups dialog box will open.

9. Double-click the users and/or groups that you want to add, and then click OK three times to return to the Group Policy window. You now see that there is a policy setting for Back Up Files and Directories.

10. When you are done making changes to the group policies at the domain level, use the same steps to add and change policies at the site and OU levels.

Employing User Profiles

An individual who is the only user of a computer can tailor the desktop, Start menu, folders, network connections, Control Panel, and applications to their individual taste and needs. If several users are on the same computer, however, they could potentially upset each other by making those changes. The way around this is to create a user profile for each user that contains their individual settings and that loads when the particular user logs on to the computer.

When a new user logs on to a Windows 2000 computer, a user profile is created automatically, and when that user logs off the computer, his or her settings are saved under that profile. When the user logs back on, his or her settings are used to reset the system to the way it was when they last logged off. When Windows 2000 is installed, it establishes the Default User profile that is then used as the default for all new users and saved with any changes under the user's name when the user logs off. A user's profile is a set of folders stored in the normally shared Documents and Settings folder on the hard disk. Figure 14-23 shows the folders within a user profile for a user named Administrator. In the same figure, you can see a folder for All Users, which contains files, folders, and settings applicable to all users, and a folder for Default User.

There are three types of user profiles: local user profiles, roaming user profiles, and mandatory user profiles.

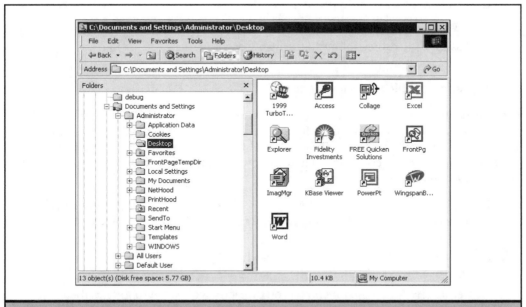

Figure 14-23.   User profile set of folders for Administrator

Creating Local User Profiles

Local user profiles are automatically created when a new user logs on to a computer, and they are changed by the user making changes to his environment, such as changing the desktop or the Start menu. When the user logs off, any changes that were made are saved in the user's profile. This is an automatic and standard process in Windows 2000. A local user account, though, is limited to the computer on which it was established. If the user logs on to a different computer, a new local user profile is created on that computer. A roaming user profile eliminates the need to have a separate profile on each computer.

Creating Roaming User Profiles

A roaming user profile is set up on a server so that when a user logs on for the first time to a computer on the same network as the server, the user is authenticated by the server and his complete user profile is sent down to the computer, where it is saved as a local user profile. When the user logs off the computer, any changes that he made to the settings in the profile are saved both on the computer and on the server. The next time he logs on to the computer, his profile there is compared to his profile on the server, and only the changes on the server are downloaded to the computer, thereby reducing the time to log on.

The process of creating a roaming user profile has five steps:

1. Create a folder to hold profiles.
2. Create a user account.
3. Assign the profiles folder to the user's account.
4. Create a roaming user profile.
5. Copy a profile template to a user.

Create a Profiles Folder   Roaming user profiles can be stored on any server—they do not have to be on a domain controller. In fact, because of the size of the download the first time a user signs on to a new computer, it might make sense to not store the roaming user profiles on the domain controller. There is not a default folder to hold roaming profiles, so you must create one as follows:

1. Log on as Administrator to the server where you want the profiles folder to reside, and open Windows Explorer (Start | Programs | Accessories | Windows Explorer).
2. Click the C:\ local drive in the folder list. Right-click in the right pane and choose New | Folder.
3. In the new folder's name box, type the name you want to give to the folder that will hold your profiles. This should be an easily recognized name, such as "Profiles."

4. Right-click the new folder and choose Sharing. Click Share This Folder, accept the folder name as the share name, and click Permissions. The Everyone group should have Full Control, as well as Change and Read permissions.

5. Click OK twice to close the Permissions and Properties dialog boxes. Leave Windows Explorer open.

Create a User Account   Every user in a domain must have a user account in that domain. You have seen how to create a user account in earlier chapters (Chapters 4 and 9) and we talk about it again in Chapter 15, but as a refresher, here are the steps:

1. While still logged on as Administrator, open the Active Directory Users and Computers window (Start | Programs | Administrative Tools | Active Directory Users and Computers).

2. Open the domain within which you want to create the account, and then open Users. Scan the existing users to make sure the new user is not already a user.

3. Open the Action menu and choose New | User. The New Object – User dialog box will open. Enter the user's name and logon name, and click Next.

4. Enter the user's password, choose how soon the password must change, and click Next. Review the settings that you have made. If you want to change any of them, click Back and make the changes. When you are happy with the settings, click Finish.

For the purpose of these exercises, make a total of five new accounts: one that will have a regular roaming profile, one that will have a preconfigured roaming profile, one that will be a template for the preconfigured profile, and two that will share a preconfigured roaming profile. Leave the Active Directory Users and Computers window open when you are done.

Assign the Profiles Folder to a User's Account   To utilize a roaming profile, the user's account must specify that their profile is stored in the profiles folder that you established earlier. Otherwise, Windows 2000 will look in the Documents and Settings folder of the computer the user is logging on to. The following steps show how to assign the profiles folder to a user's account:

1. In the Users folder in which you added the new users, right-click one of the new users that you added, and choose Properties. The user's Properties dialog box opens.

2. Click the Profile tab. In the Profile Path text box, type **servername**\ **foldername****logonname**. For example, if the server name on which the profile is stored is Myserver, the folder is Profiles, and the logon name is Greatuser, then you would type \\Myserver\Profiles\Greatuser.

3. Close the Properties dialog box and repeat this process for the second and third users you created. Do not assign a folder for the fourth and fifth users you created.

Create a Roaming User Profile　Once you have set up a shared folder on a server and specified in a user's account that the user's profile is in the specified folder on the server, then the actual user profile will be created and stored on the server simply by having the user log on to any computer within the network. Try this with these steps:

1. Log on your user with her own profile to a computer in the network. Make some changes to the desktop and the Start menu, and then log off that computer.

2. Look at the folder you created on the server to hold profiles. You will see a new profiles folder named after the logon name of the user in step 1.

3. Log on this same user to another computer in the network. The changes to the desktop and Start menu will follow you to this computer.

While the preceding technique is fine for someone to whom you want to give free rein to the system and who is knowledgeable about how to tailor it to their needs and desires, if you want to put limits on a user, or on someone who does not have a lot of knowledge about how to change the system, you want to create a template profile and then assign it to one or more users.

To build a template, you simply log on the "template" user that you created to the computer you want to use for the profile, and then make the necessary changes that you want reflected in the profile. If the template will be assigned to several people, be sure that the hardware and applications are the same both among the group that will use the profile and on the computer you used to create the template.

Copy or Assign a Profile Template to a User　You can handle a template in one of two ways. You can "copy" it to create a new profile that you assign to a user, or you can assign the template as is to several users. See how both of these are done in following steps:

NOTE:　The "copying" in this case uses a special technique and cannot use the Windows Explorer or My Computer Copy command.

1. Open the Start menu, choose Settings | Control Panel, and double-click System. The System dialog box opens.

2. Click the User Profiles tab, select the template profile, and click Copy To.

3. In the Copy To dialog box, browse to or enter the path to which you want the template profile copied, and click OK.

4. To assign a template to several users, open the Active Directory Users and Computers window, and open the domain and users in the tree on the left.

5. Scroll the list of users until the first of the users who will share a profile is shown, and then double-click that user.

6. In the user's Properties dialog box, click Profile and enter the full path to the template profile that you created. Click OK to close the Properties dialog box, and close the Active Directory Users and Computers window.

7. Log on each of your new users to one or more computers and make sure they work. One possibility if the logon doesn't work is that there is a typing error in the path of the profile in the user's Properties dialog box.

Using Mandatory User Profiles

A mandatory user profile is a roaming user profile that cannot be changed; it is read-only. This is particularly valuable when several users are sharing the same profile. When a user logs off a computer where a mandatory profile has been used, the user's changes are not saved. The profile does not prevent the user from making changes while they are logged on, but the changes aren't saved. A mandatory user profile is created by taking a roaming user profile and, in the folder with the user's name (for example, the Administrator folder in Figure 14-23), renaming the hidden file Ntuser.dat to Ntuser.man.

CHAPTER 15

Windows 2000 Security Services

Security is one of those topics that is so large that it is hard to get an overall picture of it. One way to try to achieve this overview is to look at the demands for security in a computer network. Once the demands are defined, you can look at how Windows 2000 handles the demands. Security demands include the following:

▼ **Authenticating the user** Knowing who is trying to use a computer or network connection

■ **Controlling access** Placing and maintaining limits on what a user can do

■ **Securing stored data** Keeping stored data from being used even with access

■ **Securing data transmission** Keeping data in a network from being misused

▲ **Managing security** Establishing security policies and auditing their compliance

Windows 2000 uses a multilayered approach to implementing security and provides a number of facilities that are used to handle security demands. Central to Windows 2000's security strategy is the use of Active Directory to store user accounts and provide authentication services, although security features are available without Active Directory. Active Directory, though, provides a centralization of security management that is very beneficial to strong security. In each of the following sections, a security demand is further explained and the Windows 2000 facilities that address that demand are discussed, as are the ways to implement those facilities.

NOTE: Most sets of steps in this chapter require that you be logged on as Administrator.

AUTHENTICATING THE USER

Authentication is the process of verifying that users or objects are as they are represented to be. In its simplest form, computer user authentication entails validating a username and password against a database entry, as is done in a stand-alone computer. In its fullest form, user authentication entails using the *Kerberos* authentication protocol to validate a potential user, possibly using a smart card or biometric device anywhere in a network against credentials in Active Directory. For objects, such as documents, programs, and messages, authentication requires using Kerberos certificate validation. In Windows 2000, all three forms of authentication are available, and both user forms employ a single sign-on concept that allows a user, once authenticated, to access other services within the local computer or the network, depending on their environment, without having to reenter their username and password.

In the normal default installation, when a Windows 2000 workstation or server is started, there is a request to press CTRL-ALT-DELETE. This tells the computer that someone is at the keyboard (and that a cat didn't happen to walk across it). After CTRL-ALT-DELETE is pressed, there is a request to enter your username and password. If the username/ password combination that is entered is not correct, you are given five opportunities to correct it, after which the computer is frozen for 30 seconds. You are then alternatively given one opportunity and then five opportunities, separated by 30 seconds of inactivity, and then the pattern is repeated to correctly enter a username and password. This pattern makes it more difficult to break a password because you can't just repeatedly try a new passwords.

Once a username and password are entered, they must be authenticated. This can be done at either the local computer, where the user will be limited to that computer, or at a server supporting a network, in which case the user will have access to the network.

Local Computer User Authentication

To have a username and password accepted on a local stand-alone computer, a *user account* with that username and password must have been previously entered into the Local Users and Groups database, which is in the Security Account Manager (SAM) file of HKEY_LOCAL_MACHINE in the Registry. Here are the steps to set up a user account:

1. While logged on as an Administrator, open the Start menu, choose Settings | Control Panel, double-click Administrative Tools, and then double-click Computer Management. The Computer Management window opens.

2. In the Tree tab on the left, open System Tools | Local Users and Groups | Users, right-click in the right pane, and choose New User to open the New User dialog box.

3. Enter a username of up to 20 characters. It cannot contain just periods, spaces, or the @ symbol; it can't contain " / \ [ ] : ; | = ,+ * ? < >; and leading spaces or periods are dropped.

4. Enter a full name, a description (optional), and a password with its confirmation, and then select what the user must do with the password, as shown in Figure 15-1.

5. When you have successfully entered the information, click Create and then click Close. You will now be able to log off as Administrator and log on as your new user. Try that to make sure it works.

With the entry of this single username and password, the new user will be able to do anything that is within their level of permission on that single computer. If the computer subsequently is connected to a network, the account has to be reestablished there for the user to be able to use the network.

Network User Authentication

In a network environment, user authentication can be handled by one of several protocols. If Active Directory is not being used, then the authentication protocol on Windows

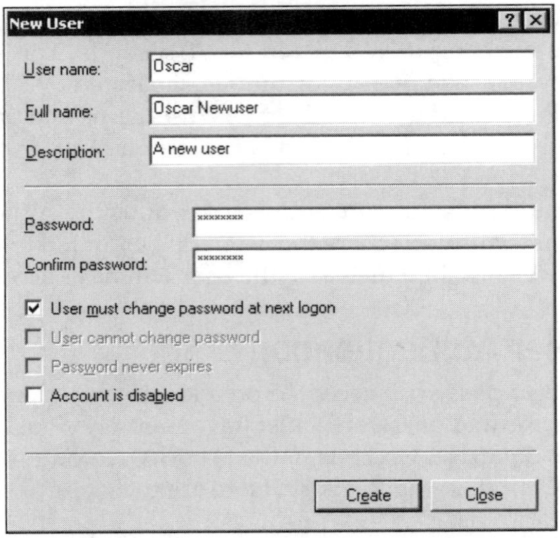

Figure 15-1.   Establishing a user account on a local computer

NT 4 (Windows NT LAN Manager, or NTLM) is the default. If Active Directory is in use, then Kerberos Version 5 is the preferred protocol in Windows 2000. If users are coming in over the Internet, they can use either Kerberos, or certificates and the Secure Sockets Layer (SSL) or Transport Layer Security (TLS) protocols for authentication. In the case of certificates, Windows 2000 can take an authenticated certificate and map it to a user account for integration with the rest of the system (see "Certificate Authentication," later in this chapter).

In all the preceding cases, a user account must first be established on the server before authentication can be accomplished. With NTLM, the procedure for setting up a user account is exactly the same as with the local computer, discussed in the preceding section, except that it must be done on each server in the network, and the Administrative Tools option is probably directly available from the Start menu (Start | Programs | Administrative Tools) without having to open the Control Panel. With Kerberos and the certificate protocols, all of which require Active Directory for full use, the procedure is a little different. Here are the steps:

1. Open the Start menu, choose Programs | Administrative Tools | Active Directory Users and Computers. The Active Directory Users and Computers dialog box opens.

2. In the Tree tab on the left, open the applicable domain and then the user's folder. Open the Action menu and choose New | User.

3. In the New Object – User dialog box, enter the user's name and username, as you can see in Figure 15-2, and then click Next.

4. Enter and confirm the password, choose how you want the user to change the password, and then click Next.

5. Review your choices, use Back if you need to make any changes, and click Finish when the account is the way you want it.

By establishing this one user account in Active Directory, the user can sign on anywhere on the network, which may extend over the Internet, and be authenticated.

Kerberos Authentication

Kerberos Version 5 is the default authentication protocol in Windows 2000, and Kerberos, in several versions, is the default authentication protocol over much of the Internet. This means that the same authentication routines in Windows 2000 can validate both a local Windows 2000 client and an Internet-connected UNIX client. Kerberos was originally developed by MIT for Internet authentication, and an implementation is available for free from MIT (http://web.mit.edu/kerberos/www/). The specification for Kerberos Version 5 is maintained by the Internet Engineering Task Force (IETF) and, along with an overview, is contained in Request for Comment 1510 (see Chapter 6 for a discussion of RFCs), which is available online at http://www.ietf.org/rfc/rfc1510.txt.

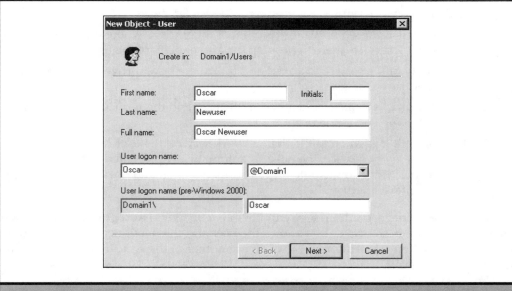

Figure 15-2. Establishing a user account with Active Directory

In addition to commonality with the Internet and numerous systems, Kerberos provides another major benefit to Windows 2000 users. In other authentication schemes, such as NTLM, each time a user attempts to access a different network service, that service has to go to the authentication server to confirm the authenticity of the user. This doesn't mean the user has to log on again, but each service has to get its own confirmation, creating a fair amount of network traffic. That is not the case with Kerberos, which provides each user with an encrypted *ticket* with the user ID and password that network devices can use both for identity and for validity. The Kerberos ticket system also validates the network service to the user, providing mutual authentication between user and service.

NOTE: The Kerberos ticket is also referred to as a *service ticket* and as a *user ticket.* They are all the same object.

Kerberos uses a Key Distribution Center (KDC) on each domain controller that stores the user accounts that have been entered into the network's Active Directory. When a user attempts to log on and use any part of the network, the following process takes place:

1. The username and password are encrypted and sent to the KDC.

2. The KDC validates the username/password combination.

3. A ticket is constructed containing an encrypted username and password plus an encryption key that can be used to transfer information between the user and any network service.

4. The ticket is returned to the user's point of logging on, where it is presented to the network service, thereby proving the authenticity of the user.

5. The ability of the service to accept and utilize the ticket proves the authenticity of the service to the user.

6. Any information transferred between the user and the service is done using the encryption key in the ticket.

7. If, while still logged on to the first network service, the user reaches out to another network service, the ticket is automatically presented to the second service, providing immediate mutual authentication and the ability to securely transfer information.

You can see in the preceding steps another major benefit to Kerberos: the inclusion of an encryption key in the ticket that allows the user and the network service to securely transfer information. This automatically solves another of the security demands, securing data transmission.

Kerberos is a very powerful means for authentication and a major asset to Windows 2000.

Replacements for Passwords

The weakest link in the Windows 2000 security scheme is probably the use of passwords. Users give their passwords to others or forget them, and passwords are stolen or just "found" in many different ways. There is nothing to tie a password to an individual. With someone's password in hand, nothing can stop you from impersonating that person on a password-protected system. Two potential means of replacing passwords are smart cards and biometric devices.

Smart Cards   Smart cards are credit card–sized pieces of plastic that have a tamper-resistant electronic circuit embedded in them that permanently stores an ID, a password, a digital signature, an encryption key, or any combination of those. Smart cards require a personal identification number (PIN), so they add a second layer (smart card plus PIN in place of a password) that an impersonator would have to obtain to log on to a system. Also, smart cards can be configured to lock up after a few unsuccessful attempts to enter a PIN.

Windows 2000 fully supports smart cards and lets them be used to log on to a computer or network or to enable certificate-based authentication for opening documents or performing calculations. Smart cards require a reader attached to the computer through either a serial port or a PCMCIA slot. With a smart card reader, users do not have to press CTRL-ALT-DELETE. They only need to insert their card, at which point they are prompted for their PIN. With a valid card and PIN, users are authenticated and allowed on the system in the same way as they would be by entering a valid username and password.

Currently, Windows 2000 lists seven smart card readers that are Plug and Play–compliant and that Microsoft has tested with Windows 2000. The drivers for these seven devices are included with Windows 2000, and installing them requires little more than plugging them in.

With a smart card reader installed, set up new accounts (as previously described) and then, for both new and old accounts, open the user's Properties dialog box by double-clicking a user in the Active Directory Users and Computers window (see "Network User Authentication" earlier in this chapter for directions on opening this window). In the user's Properties dialog box, click the Account tab and check Smart Card Is Required for Interactive Logon in the Account Options list.

NOTE: In case you wondered, the PIN is encrypted and placed on the smart card when it is made. The PIN is not stored on the computer or in Active Directory.

Smart cards are particularly valuable for remote entry to a network, and can be used by a traveling staff member with a laptop, possibly using virtual private networking (VPN) over the Internet. Smart cards are also frequently used in the issuance of certificates of authenticity for documents and other objects (see the discussion of certificates later in the chapter under "Securing Data Transmission").

Biometric Devices   Smart cards do provide an added degree of security over passwords, but if someone obtains both the card and the PIN, they're home free. The only way to be totally sure that the computer is talking to the real person is to require some physical identification of the person. This is the purpose of *biometric devices*, which identify people by physical traits, such as their voice, handprint, fingerprint, face, or eyes. Often, these devices are used with a smart card to replace the PIN. Biometric devices are just moving from the experimental to the production stage, and nothing is built into Windows 2000 specifically to handle them. Devices and custom installations are available from around $100 for a fingerprint scanner to several thousand dollars for a face scanner. In the next few years, these devices will be everywhere, so, depending on your needs, you may want to keep them in mind.

Certificate Authentication

If you want to bring users into a network over the Internet, but you are concerned that sending usernames and passwords in that public way might compromise them, then you can replace them with a digital certificate. A *digital certificate* (or just "certificate") is issued by a certification authority (CA), who digitally signs it and says that the bearer is who he or she says they are, or that an object and sender are as represented. There are both private and public CAs. An organization can be its own private CA and issue certificates to its employees, vendors, and/or customers, so that those people can be authenticated when they try to enter the organization's network. Also, a well-trusted public CA, such as VeriSign (http://www.verisign.com/), can issue a certificate to a person, object, organization, or web site. A person or organization receiving the certificate, if they trust the CA, can be reasonably certain that the presenter is as represented. Besides a certificate, most CAs provide the bearer with an encryption key in the certificate, so that secure data transmissions can occur.

To set up certificate authentication, these steps must take place:

1. The user must obtain a certificate.
2. A user account must be established for the user.
3. The certification authority must be listed in the Certificate Trust List.
4. The certificate must be mapped to the user account.

Setting Up Certificate Services   The user can obtain a certificate in several ways, one of which is through a Windows 2000 domain controller with Certificate Services installed.

Certificate Services is not part of the default server installation and must be specifically selected. Here are the steps to do that:

1. Open Start, choose Settings | Control Panel, and double-click Add/Remove Programs. The Add/Remove Programs dialog box opens.

2. Click Add/Remove Windows Components on the left and then click Components in the upper right. The Windows Components Wizard dialog box opens. (You may not have to click Components in some instances.)

3. Select Certificate Services, as shown in Figure 15-3, and click Next. Select the type of CA that you want (if it is the first in a domain, it must be Enterprise Root CA, which requires Active Directory), and click Next.

4. Enter the identifying information about this CA and click Next. Accept or change the location of the certificate database and log, and again click Next.

5. If you have Internet Information Services (IIS) running, you must stop it before installing Certificate Services. If you are asked about this, click OK. If you do not have the Windows 2000 Setup CD-ROM in its drive, you'll be asked to insert it. Setup will configure and install Certificate Services as requested.

6. When the installation is completed, click Finish and then click Yes to restart the computer (or, if not prompted, restart it manually).

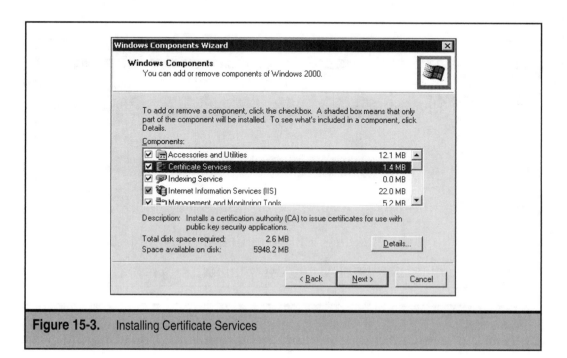

Figure 15-3. Installing Certificate Services

Once you have installed the certification authority, you can review it with these steps:

1. Open the Start menu and choose Programs | Administrative Tools | Certification Authority. In the Tree tab on the left, open the new CA you just created and click Issued Certificates. You should see one or two certificates, as shown in Figure 15-4.

2. Double-click one of the certificates to open it, click the Details tab, and click the various fields to see the details within the open certificate. Click OK when you are done looking at the certificate.

3. Back in the Certification Authority window, click Policy Settings in the Tree tab. On the right, you can see the certificate templates that are available and their intended purpose.

4. Double-click one of the policies to open its Properties dialog box. When you are finished looking at the properties, close the dialog box and the Certification Authority Window.

Requesting a Certificate   With Certificate Services installed, users, computers, and other services can request certificates to identify themselves. Normally, certificates are automatically given to computers and users who are known and trusted entities on the network. Figure 15-4 shows that the two certificates that were automatically created when Certificate Services was installed were issued to the server on which Certificate Services

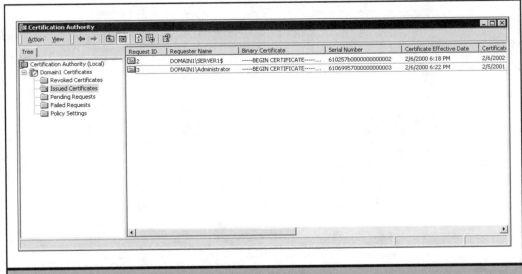

Figure 15-4.   Reviewing certificates in the Certification Authority

resides and to the Administrator who was currently logged on. It is also possible to explicitly request a certificate over either an intranet or the Internet, or on the server with Certificate Services.

Over the Internet or an intranet is the most common way that a user requests a certificate for their use. In doing this, they access a web page that is created and maintained by Certificate Services. Use these steps to request a certificate over an intranet or the Internet:

1. Open your browser and enter the URL or address of the server with Certificate Services. The address should look something like http://*servername*/certsrv/. The page should appear as shown in Figure 15-5.

2. Select the task you want, probably the default Request a Certificate, and click Next. Choose the request type, again probably the default User Certificate Request, and click Next. You may be asked if you want to install Microsoft Certificate Enrollment Control complete with its own certificate from VeriSign.

3. Click Yes. The Microsoft Certificate Enrollment Control automatically collects the necessary information from your computer, and you are told that you can submit your request.

4. Click Submit. If the user and/or computer are already known to the server, a certificate will be issued. Otherwise, you will be told that the request is pending.

Figure 15-5. Requesting a certificate over the Internet or an intranet

5. When you get the certificate, click Install This Certificate. You may be asked if you want to add this certificate to the Root Store, with the certificate displayed in the same window.

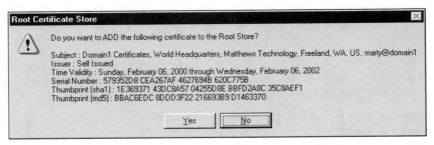

6. Click Yes, given that is what you want to do. You are told that the certificate is installed and you can close your browser.

Directly requesting a certificate from Certificate Services is most commonly done for documents or other objects, or for services. It requires the Certificate console in the Microsoft Management Console (MMC). Here is how to set up the Certificate console (assuming that it hasn't been done before) and request a certificate from it:

1. Open the Start menu, choose Run, type **mmc**, and click OK. The MMC shell opens.
2. Open the Console menu and choose Add/Remove Snap-In. In the Add/Remove Snap-In dialog box, click Add, click Certificates, and click Add again. Select My User Account for where you want to manage certificates, and click Finish.

NOTE: If you choose to manage certificates for My User Account, the snap-in you create will create certificates only for you. If you choose to manage certificates for Service Account or Computer Account, you must pick a service or computer to manage, such as the web server or the local computer, and you will be able to issue certificates for the service or computer.

3. Click Close and then click OK to complete the Add/Remove Snap-In process. In the console Tree tab on the left, open Certificates – Current User | Personal | Certificates, as shown in Figure 15-6.
4. Open the Action menu and choose All Tasks | Request New Certificate. The Certificate Request Wizard opens.
5. Click Next, choose a certificate template to support the purpose of the certificate you want to issue (select Administrator for at least one certificate), and click Next again. Enter a friendly name (call the Administrator certificate **Signature**) and a description and click Next.
6. Review the settings you have selected. If you want to make changes, click Back and make the necessary corrections. When you are ready, click Finish. A new certificate will be issued.

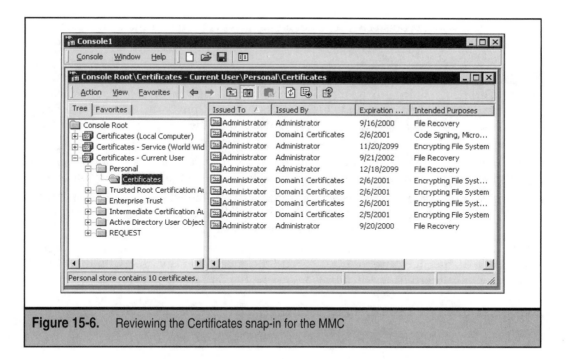

Figure 15-6. Reviewing the Certificates snap-in for the MMC

7. Close the Certificates console and the MMC, saving the settings in a file named Certificates.msc.

Listing Certificate Authorities To accept certificates that are presented to the network, the CA must be known to the network. This is accomplished by being listed as a trusted CA in the Certificate Trust List (CTL), which is maintained as part of the group policy. The following steps show you how to open the group policy, which you worked with in Chapter 14 (see "Using Group Policies"), create a CTL, and make an entry into it (these steps assume that you want to work with the CTL at the domain level, but you could also do it at the local computer level and at the OU level):

1. Open the Start menu and choose Programs | Administrative Tools | Active Directory Users and Computers. The Active Directory Users and Computers window opens.

2. Right-click the domain where the policy will reside, choose Properties, click the Group Policy tab, select the policy you want to use, and click Edit. The Group Policy window opens.

3. In the Tree tab, open Computer Configuration | Windows Settings | Security Settings | Public Key Policies | Enterprise Trust. Open the Action menu and choose New | Certificate Trust List. The Certificate Trust List Wizard opens.

4. Click Next. If you so choose, enter an identifying prefix for the CTL, enter the months and/or days that it is valid, select the purposes of the CTL, and click Next.

5. In the Certificates in the CTL dialog box, click Add From Store. The Select Certificate dialog box opens, in which you can select those certificates whose issuers you want to include in the CTL. At the bottom of the list, you will find the certificates that your new CA issued based on the steps earlier in this chapter.

6. Double-click one of the certificates you created. When it opens, you may find that it is not trusted, such as the one in Figure 15-7, even though it was created on the same computer. You are told that it must be added to the CTL to be trusted.

7. Select the certificates whose issuers you want on the CTL, holding down CTRL while selecting more than one certificate. Click OK. The new list of certificates will appear in the Certificate Trust List Wizard.

8. Click Next. You must attach a certificate, probably your own, for the purpose of a digital signature for the CTL, and the encryption key used with the signature certificate will be used with the file that contains the CTL.

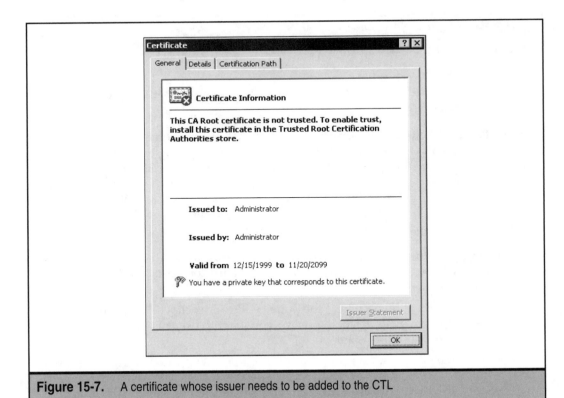

Figure 15-7. A certificate whose issuer needs to be added to the CTL

NOTE: The certificate that you select for the purpose of adding the digital signature to the CTL must be created for the current user with the Administrator template, similar to the Signature certificate you created previously in "Requesting a Certificate."

9. Click Select from Store, select the certificate you want to use, click OK, and then click Next. If you wish, you can add a timestamp; then, click Next again.

10. Enter a friendly name and description for this CTL and click Next. Review the settings you have chosen, click Back if you need to correct something, and then, when ready, click Finish. You will be told whether the CTL was successfully created.

The new CTL will appear on the right of the Group Policy window. If you double-click it, the CTL opens and, in the Trust List tab, you see a list of the certificate authorities that you have added to your CTL. By clicking a CA, you can see some of the details behind a certificate, as shown in Figure 15-8, and if you click View Certificate, you can see the entire certificate.

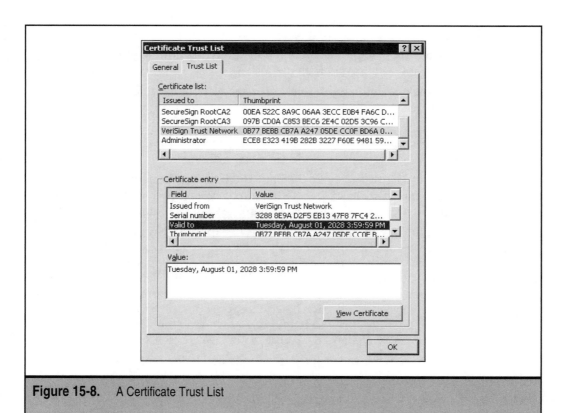

Figure 15-8. A Certificate Trust List

Mapping Certificates to User Accounts   The core of Windows 2000's user-oriented security are user accounts, which require a username and password to log on and are the basis for the permission system that controls access to computer and network resources. When someone comes into Windows 2000 with a certificate, they don't have a username and password to attach them to a user account and the permissions that go with it. The solution is to map or relate a certificate to a user account, so that when someone presents an acceptable certificate, he or she will be attached to a user account and given the permissions they would possess if they had logged on with a username and password. Windows 2000 does certificate mapping in two ways: through Active Directory services, and through Internet Information Services (IIS). Also, mapping can be done from one certificate to one user account (one-to-one mapping) or from several certificates to one account (many-to-one mapping). Mapping through IIS is discussed in Chapter 11.

Certificate mapping through Active Directory services can be done with the following steps (Active Directory Users and Computers should be open from the previous steps; if it is, skip step 1):

1. Open the Start menu and choose Programs | Administrative Tools | Active Directory Users and Computers.

2. Open the View menu and click Advanced Features (if it is not already checked).

3. In the console Tree tab on the left, open the domain with the user account to which you want to map, and then open Users.

4. In the list of users on the right, select the user account to which a certificate will be mapped.

5. Open the Action menu, choose Name Mappings (if you don't see it, redo step 2) to open the Security Identity Mapping dialog box, click the X.509 Certificates tab, and click Add to open the Add Certificate dialog box.

6. Search for and identify, or type, the path and name of the certificate that you want to use, and then click Open. Often the certificates, which have the extension .cer, are in the C:\Winnt\System32\Certsrv\ folder.

    If you don't find a CER file, you may need to export one from the MMC Certificates console. To do so, select Start | Run, type **mmc**, press ENTER. Then open the Console menu, choose the Certificates.msc file, open Console Root | Certificates – Current User | Personal | Certificates, and select the certificate to use. Next, open the Action menu, choose All Tasks | Export, click Next, choose Yes Export the Private Key, click Next, accept the default format, click Next, enter a useful filename, browse to where you want it stored, click Next, click Finish, and click OK when told that the export was successful.

7. The certificate is displayed in the Add Certificate dialog box.

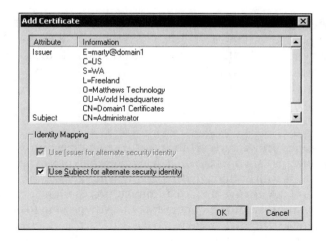

8. If you want one-to-one mapping, both Use Issuer for Alternate Security Identity and Use Subject for Alternate Security Identity should be checked. If you want many-to-one mapping, only Use Issuer for Alternate Security Identity should be checked.

9. Click OK. The certificate is displayed again in the Security Identity Mapping dialog box; click OK. Close the Active Directory Users and Computers window.

Now, when a user presents this certificate, she or he will be mapped to the related user account and given the permissions that are associated with it.

CONTROLLING ACCESS

User accounts identify people and allow them to log on to a computer and possibly to a network. What they can then do depends both on the permissions given to them or given to groups to which they belong, and on the ownership of the object they want to use. Windows 2000, when using the NT File System (NTFS), allows an administrator to assign various levels of permission to use an object (a file, a folder, a disk drive, a printer), as well as assign ownership and the rights of ownership. (You cannot do this with the FAT or FAT32 file system.)

When you initially install Windows 2000, most files, folders, disk drives, and printers give permission for anyone to do almost anything with these objects. There are some files and folders that are related to the operating system that have withheld some permission for users who are not administrators. You can change the initial openness rather quickly by using a property called *inheritance* that says all files, subfolders, and files in subfolders automatically inherit (take on) the permissions of their parent folder. Every file, folder, and other object in Windows 2000 NTFS, though, has its own set of *security descriptors* that are attached to it when it is created, and with the proper permission, these security descriptors can be individually changed.

Ownership

Initially, all permissions are granted by the creator of an object or by an administrator. The creator of an object is called its *owner*. The owner of an object has the right to grant and deny permission, as well as the right to grant the Take Ownership permission to others, allowing them to take ownership. An administrator can take over ownership from someone else, but an administrator cannot grant others ownership to objects the administrator did not create.

You can check the ownership and change it through the object's Properties dialog box. For a file or folder, open the Properties dialog box through Windows Explorer and see how you would change the ownership with these steps:

1. Open the Start menu and choose Programs | Accessories | Windows Explorer.

2. In the left pane, open the disk and folders necessary to see in the right pane the folder or file that you want to look at or change the ownership for.

3. In the right pane, right-click the subject folder or file and choose Properties.

4. In the Properties dialog box, click the Security tab and then click Advanced. The Access Control Settings dialog box opens.

5. Click the Owner tab, in which you can see who the current owner is and the people to whom the ownership can be transferred. When you are finished, click OK twice to close the two dialog boxes still open.

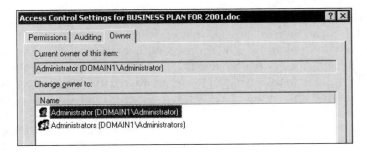

Giving permission to take ownership is described in "Permissions" later in this chapter.

Groups

Groups, or *group accounts,* are collections of user accounts and can have permissions assigned to them just like user accounts. Most permissions are granted to groups, not individuals, and then individuals are made members of the groups. It is therefore important that you have a set of groups that handles both the mix of people in your organization and the mix of permissions that you want to establish. A number of standard groups with preassigned permissions are built into Windows 2000, but you can create your own groups, and you can assign users to any of these.

Look at the groups that are a standard part of Windows 2000 and see what permissions they contain, and then create your own if you need to. Like user accounts, you look at groups differently depending on whether you are on a stand-alone server or on an Active Directory domain controller. (Windows 2000 Professional workstation built-in groups are the same as stand-alone servers.)

Groups in Stand-Alone Servers and Workstations

To view and add groups in stand-alone servers or workstations, you need to use the Computer Management window, as follows:

1. Open the Start menu and choose Programs I Administrative Tools I Computer Management.

2. In the Tree tab, open System Tools I Local Users and Groups I Groups. The list of built-in groups will be displayed, as shown in Figure 15-9.

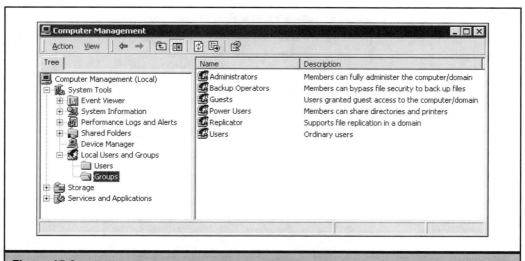

Figure 15-9.   Built-in groups within a stand-alone server or workstation

3. Double-click a few groups to open their respective Properties dialog box, in which you can see the members of that group.

4. Open the Action menu and choose New Group. The New Group dialog box opens.

5. Enter a group name of up to 63 characters. It cannot contain just numbers, periods, or spaces; it can't contain " / \ [ ] : ; | = ,+ * ? < >; and leading spaces or periods are dropped. Enter the description of what the group can uniquely do, and click Add. The Select Users or Groups dialog box opens.

6. Select the users that you want to include in the group. After selecting each one, click Add, and when you have selected all you want to include, click OK. Your new group should look similar to Figure 15-10.

7. When your group is the way you want it, click Create and then click Close. The new group will appear in the list on the right of the Computer Management window. Close the Computer Management window.

Groups in Active Directory Domain Controllers

To view and add groups in an Active Directory domain controller, you need to use the Active Directory Users and Computers window. Within that window, you will find two sets of groups: those in the Builtin folder, which are similar to what you saw in the stand-alone server, and those in the Users folders, which are created by Active Directory. The Builtin groups are limited to the local domain (called a *domain local scope*), while the

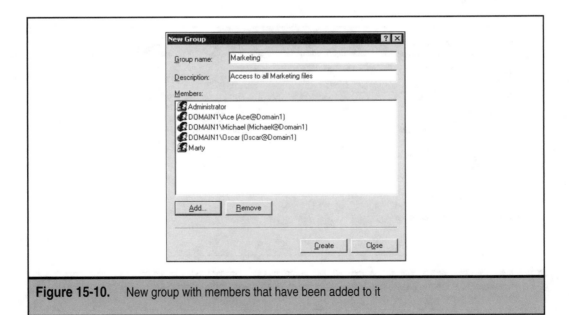

Figure 15-10.   New group with members that have been added to it

Users groups can be either domain-limited or not limited (called a *global scope*). Look at both sets of groups and add a new group to Users with the following steps:

1. Open the Start menu and choose Programs | Administrative Tools | Active Directory Users and Computers. The Active Directory Users and Computers window opens.

2. In the Tree tab, open the domain in which you want to work, and then open the Builtin folder. You will see a list of groups that has many of the same groups that you saw on the stand-alone server.

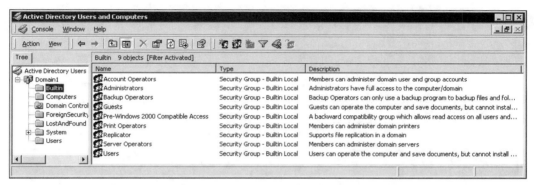

3. Click Users in the Tree tab. You will see a mixture of users and groups, but a different set of groups that are supporting Active Directory and network operations.

4. Open the View menu and choose Filter Options. Click Show Only the Following Types of Objects, click Groups, as shown next, and click OK. Once again, open the Users Folder, and your Active Directory Users and Computers window should look similar to Figure 15-11.

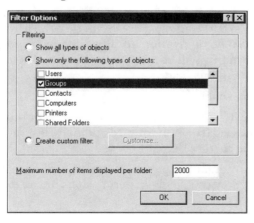

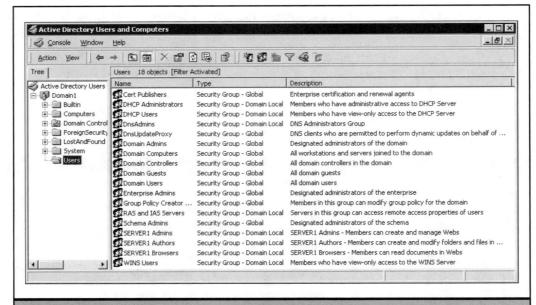

Figure 15-11.   Standard Users groups in an Active Directory domain controller

5. Double-click several of the groups to open them. They contain substantially more information than the groups on the stand-alone servers and workstations.

6. While Users is still selected, open the Action menu and choose New | Group. The New Object – Group dialog box opens.

7. Enter a Group name of up to 63 characters. It cannot contain just numbers, periods, or spaces, and leading spaces or periods are dropped. Notice that the pre-Windows 2000 name is automatically filled in for you. Only the first 20 characters of this name will be used, so if you want, you can enter your own short group name in this field.

8. Choose the group scope. Here are the scope choices:

   ■ **Domain Local**   Can contain users and global or universal groups from any Windows 2000 or Windows NT domain, but their permissions are limited to the current domain.

   ■ **Global**   Can contain users and global groups only from the current domain, but they can be given permissions in any domain.

■ **Universal**   Can contain users and global or universal groups from any Windows 2000 domain, and they can be give permission in any domain, but they are limited to distribution groups.

9. Choose a group type. Distribution groups are used for e-mail and fax distribution, whereas security groups are used to assign permission. Click OK when you are done.

10. Right-click your new group and choose Properties. The Properties dialog box opens. Enter a description and e-mail address, as shown in Figure 15-12.

11. Click Members, click Add, and double-click the user accounts that you want included in the group. When you are done, click OK. Look at the other tabs and make any necessary changes. The Security tab is discussed in the next section.

12. When you have completed the group the way you want it, click OK, and close Active Directory Users and Computers.

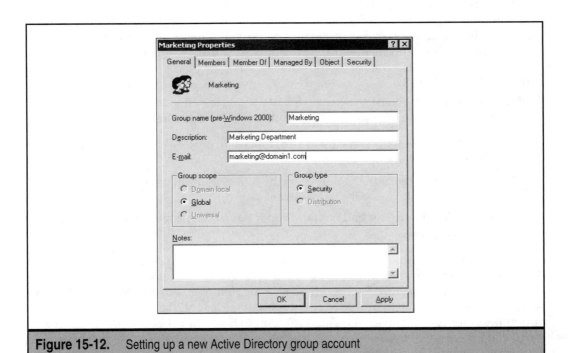

Figure 15-12.   Setting up a new Active Directory group account

Permissions

Permissions authorize a user or a group to perform some function on an object. Objects, such as files, folders, disks, and printers, have a set of permissions associated with them that can be assigned to users and groups. The specific permissions depend on the object, but all objects have at least two permissions: Read, and either Modify or Change. Permissions are initially set in one of three ways:

▼   The application or process that creates an object can set its permissions upon creation.

■   If the object allows the inheritance of permissions and they were not set upon creation, a parent object can propagate permissions to the object. For example, a parent folder can propagate its permissions to a subfolder it contains.

▲   If neither the creator nor the parent sets the permissions for an object, then the Windows 2000 system defaults will do it.

Once an object is created, its permissions can be changed by its owner, by an administrator, and by anybody else who has been given the permission to change permissions. The following sections look at the default permissions for three commonly used objects—folders, shares, and files—and at how those defaults are changed.

Folder Permissions

Folder permissions are set in the Security tab of the folder's Properties dialog box, shown in Figure 15-13. You can open this tab and change the permissions with these steps:

1. Open the Start menu and choose Programs | Accessories | Windows Explorer. Windows Explorer opens.

2. In the Folders pane on the left, open the drives and folders necessary to see the folder for which you want to set permissions.

3. Right-click that folder and choose Properties. In the Properties dialog box, click the Security tab.

You can see that with a default installation, everyone has permission to do everything, so to set specific, meaningful permissions you need to remove the Everyone permission. Do that by selecting Everyone and clicking Remove. If that is done directly, you will be told that Everyone is inherited from a parent folder and that you must turn off the option for inheriting permissions. That is accomplished by unchecking the checkbox in the lower-left corner of the Security tab. When you do that, you are warned that you will prevent any inheritable permissions from propagating to this folder. If you want to continue, which is the only way to set other permissions, click Remove.

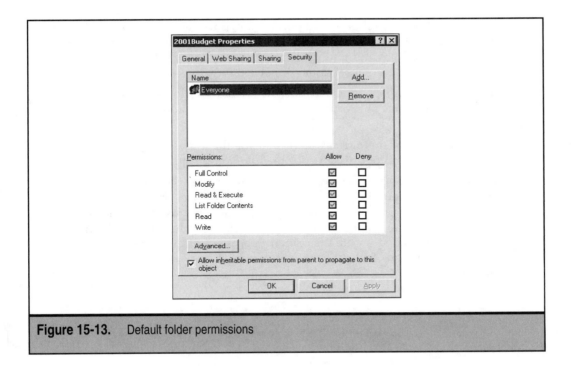

Figure 15-13.   Default folder permissions

To add new permissions:

1. Click Add in the upper-right corner of the Security tab. In the Select Users, Computers, or Groups dialog box, double-click the users, groups, and/or computers to whom you want to grant permissions, and then click OK.

2. Select one of the users, groups, or computers that will be given permission, and then click Allow for the permissions that you want that entity to have, or click Deny to specifically exclude a permission. The tasks that can be performed with each permission are as follows:

   ■ **Full Control**   The sum of all other permissions, plus delete subfolders, change permissions, and take ownership

   ■ **Modify**   The sum of the Read & Execute and the Write permissions, plus the delete the folder permission

   ■ **Read & Execute**   The same as List Folder Contents, but inherited by both folders and files

■ **List Folder Contents**   Read permission, plus view the list of subfolders and files in a folder, as well as execute files, and move through folders to reach other files and folders, where the user may not have permission to access the intervening folders (inherited only by folders)

■ **Read**   View the contents of subfolders and files in the folder, as well as view the folder's attributes (Archive, Hidden, Read-only), ownership, and permissions

■ **Write**   Make subfolders and files inside the folder, plus view the ownership and permissions for the folder and change its attributes

3. After selecting the permissions that you want to use, click Advanced. The Access Control Settings dialog box opens. Select a user or group and click View/Edit. The Permissions Entry dialog box appears, as shown in Figure 15-14. This contains a more detailed level of permissions, called Special Permissions, which are contained within the primary permissions described in step 2. The Special Permissions that are granted by each primary permission are shown in Table 15-1.

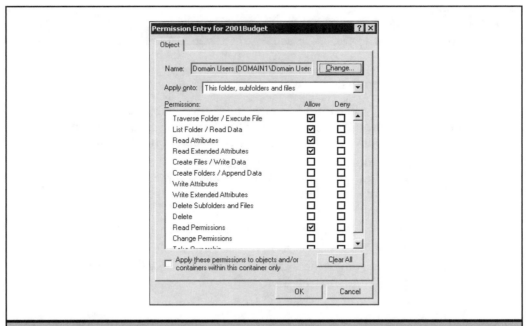

Figure 15-14.   A more detailed level of permissions is available if needed

Special Permission	Primary Permission					
	Read	Write	List Folder Contents	Read & Execute	Modify	Full Control
Transverse Folder/ Execute File			Yes	Yes	Yes	Yes
List Folder/ Read Data	Yes		Yes	Yes	Yes	Yes
Read Attributes	Yes		Yes	Yes	Yes	Yes
Read Extended Attributes	Yes		Yes	Yes	Yes	Yes
Create Files/ Write Data		Yes			Yes	Yes
Create Folders/ Append Data		Yes			Yes	Yes
Write Attributes		Yes			Yes	Yes
Write Extended Attributes		Yes			Yes	Yes
Delete Subfolders and Files						Yes
Delete					Yes	Yes
Read Permissions	Yes	Yes	Yes	Yes	Yes	Yes
Change Permissions						Yes
Take Ownership						Yes
Synchronize	Yes	Yes	Yes	Yes	Yes	Yes

Table 15-1.   Special Permissions Granted by Primary Permissions for Folders

NOTE: Synchronize isn't a default permission unless the folder is set up for it.

4. Make any changes that you want to the detail permissions, check the checkbox at the bottom if you want the permission to be propagated to the subfolders and files of this folder, and click OK three times to close all dialog boxes.

CAUTION: Denying Everyone the Full Control permission prevents anybody from doing anything with the folder, including administrators. The folder is permanently locked from everybody, and the only thing you can do to get rid of of the folder is to reformat the hard drive.

Share Permission

Shares are shared folders, and for those who do not own or administer the folders, a considerably different set of permissions exists. Shared folder permissions are set by clicking Permissions in the Sharing tab of the folder's Properties dialog box, which opens the Permissions dialog box, shown in Figure 15-15. You can open this dialog box and change the permissions with these steps:

1. In Windows Explorer, right-click the shared folder for which you want to set permissions, and choose Properties. In the Properties dialog box, click Sharing and then click Permissions. The Permissions dialog box opens.

2. Remove the Everyone permission by selecting Everyone and clicking Remove. If you are told that Everyone is inherited from a parent folder, click OK and uncheck the checkbox in the lower-left corner of the Security tab. If you are warned that you will prevent inheritable permissions, click Remove.

3. Click Add to open the Select Users, Computers, or Groups dialog box, double-click the users, groups, and/or computers to whom you want to grant permissions, and then click OK.

4. Select one of the users, groups, or computers that will be given permission and then click Allow for the permissions that you want that entity to have, or click Deny to specifically exclude a permission. The following are the tasks that can be performed with each permission:

   ■ **Full Control**   The sum of all other permissions, plus modify other permissions and take ownership

   ■ **Change**   The Read permission, plus add subfolders and files, change data in files, and delete subfolders and files

   ■ **Read**   View the names and contents of subfolders and files in the folder, as well as move through folders for which the user may not have permission

5. After selecting the permissions that you want to use, click OK twice to close all dialog boxes.

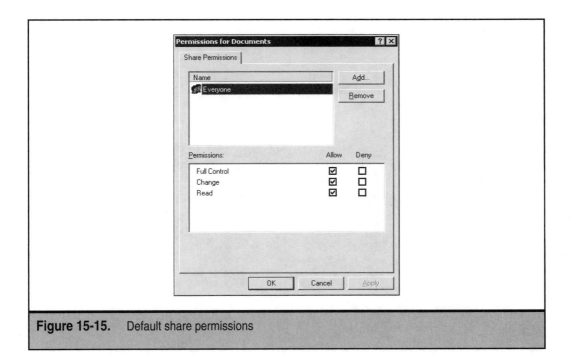

Figure 15-15. Default share permissions

File Permissions

File permissions are set in the Security tab of the file's Properties dialog box, shown in Figure 15-16. You can open this tab and change the permissions with these steps:

1. In Windows Explorer, right-click the file for which you want to set permissions, and choose Properties. In the Properties dialog box, click the Security tab.

2. Remove the Everyone permission by selecting Everyone and clicking Remove. If you are told that Everyone is inherited from a parent folder, click OK and uncheck the checkbox in the lower-left corner of the Security tab. If you are warned that you will prevent inheritable permissions, click Remove.

3. Click Add to open the Select Users, Computers, or Groups dialog box, double-click the users, groups, and/or computers to whom you want to grant permissions, and then click OK.

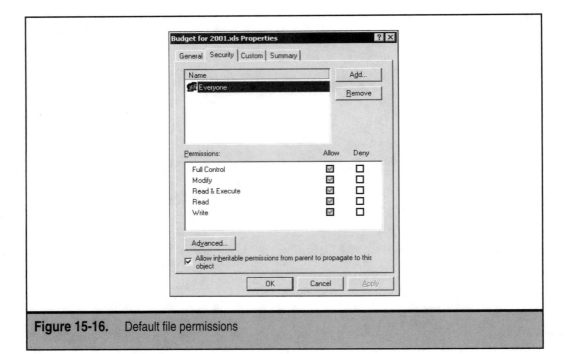

Figure 15-16. Default file permissions

4. Select one of the users, groups, or computers that will be given permission, and then click Allow for the permissions that you want that entity to have, or click Deny to specifically exclude a permission. The following are the tasks that can be performed with each permission:

- **Full Control** The sum of all other permissions, plus change permissions and take ownership

- **Modify** The sum of the Read & Execute and the Write permissions, plus delete and modify the file

- **Read & Execute** The Read permissions, plus execute applications

- **Read** View the contents of the file, as well as view its attributes (Archive, Hidden, Read-only), permissions, and ownership

- **Write** Write to the file, plus view the file's permissions and ownership, and change its attributes

5. After selecting the permissions that you want to use, click Advanced. The Access Control Settings dialog box opens. Select a user or group and click View/Edit. The Permissions Entry dialog box appears. This contains a more detailed level of permissions, called Special Permissions, which are contained within the primary permissions described in step 4. The Special Permissions that are granted by each primary permission are shown in Table 15-2.

Special Permission	Primary Permission				
	Read	Write	Read & Execute	Modify	Full Control
Transverse Folder/ Execute File			Yes	Yes	Yes
List Folder/Read Data	Yes		Yes	Yes	Yes
Read Attributes	Yes		Yes	Yes	Yes
Read Extended Attributes	Yes		Yes	Yes	Yes
Create Files/Write Data		Yes		Yes	Yes
Create Folders/Append Data		Yes		Yes	Yes
Write Attributes		Yes		Yes	Yes
Write Extended Attributes		Yes		Yes	Yes
Delete Subfolders and Files					Yes
Delete				Yes	Yes
Read Permissions	Yes	Yes	Yes	Yes	Yes
Change Permissions					Yes
Take Ownership					Yes
Synchronize	Yes	Yes	Yes	Yes	Yes

Table 15-2. Special Permissions Granted by Primary Permissions for Files

6. Make any changes that you want to the detail permissions, and click OK three times to close all dialog boxes.

SECURING STORED DATA

User authentication puts a lock on the outside doors of the computer, and controlling access puts locks on the inside doors, but if someone breaks through or gets around those barriers, the data inside is available to anyone who wants it. For example, someone may take a disk drive and access it with another operating system, or steal a laptop and methodically break through the passwords. Or, much simpler and more common, an employee either purposefully gets or mistakenly is given access to data they should not have and decides to misuse it.

The answer to all of these scenarios is to make the data itself unusable without a key. This is done by encrypting a file or folder so that no matter how it is accessed, by another operating system or low-level utility, it is encrypted and cannot be read without the key, and the key is itself encrypted so that it is exceptionally difficult to obtain and use.

File and Folder Encryption

File and folder encryption has been built into Windows 2000 NTFS as a new feature and is called the *Encrypting File System* (*EFS*). Once EFS is turned on for a file or a folder, only the person who encrypted the file or folder will be able to read it, with the exception that a specially appointed administrator will have a recovery key to access the file or folder. For the person who encrypted the file, accessing it requires no additional steps, and the file is re-encrypted every time it is saved. All of the encrypting and decrypting is done behind the scenes and is not obvious to the user.

NOTE: Neither system files or folders nor compressed files or folders can be encrypted. You can de-compress a compressed file or folder and then encrypt it.

The Encryption Process

The actual encryption of a file or folder is done with a *symmetric encryption key*, which is the same for both encryption and decryption and is very fast. The symmetric encryption key (also called a *secret key*) is itself encrypted using the file owner's public key that is contained in his or her EFS certificate. (See "Private/Public Key Encryption," later in this chapter.) Therefore, the owner with her or his private key matching the public key is the only one who can open the encrypted file—except for the recovery administrator. When the file is created or re-created and a symmetric key is made, the key is actually encrypted twice, once for the owner and once for the recovery administrator. Then, if the need arises, the recovery administrator can use his or her private key to decrypt the file.

The encrypted symmetric key is stored as a part of the file. When an application requests the file, NTFS goes and gets it, sees that the file is encrypted, and calls EFS. EFS works with the security protocols to authenticate the user, use his or her private key to decrypt the file, and pass a plain text file to the calling application, all in the background, without any outward sign that it is taking place. The encryption and decryption routines are so fast that on most computers that can run Windows 2000, you seldom notice the added time.

TIP: Because many applications save temporary and secondary files during normal execution, it is recommended that folders rather than files be the encrypting container. If an application is then told to store all files in that folder where all files are automatically encrypted upon saving, security is improved.

Encryption Considerations

Several requirements must be met to use file and folder encryption:

▼ Windows 2000 NTFS must be in use. Any other file system, whether Windows NT 4 NTFS or FAT, will not work with EFS.

■ Certificate Services should be installed and running either on a stand-alone computer or within a domain. If Certificate Services is not running, EFS will issue its own certificates, but these are considered "not trusted" by Windows 2000.

■ The user of the file or folder must have an EFS certificate. If one does not exist, it is automatically created.

▲ There must be one or more certificated recovery agent administrators. If one does not exist, a default administrator is automatically appointed and a certificate is issued. The default administrator on a stand-alone computer is the local administrator, while in a domain, it is the domain administrator on the first domain controller that is installed.

CAUTION: If a user encrypts a file on a domain and then attempts to open it on a local computer, the file will not be available, because the public key used to encrypt the file on the domain is contained in a certificate there. When the same user signs on to a local computer (maybe the same physical computer, just disconnected from the network, such as a laptop might be), his or her user account and resulting certificate will be different because it no longer has the domain qualifier, so the private key in the certificate will not open the file.

Recovery Agent Administrators   The reason a recovery agent administrator is required is shown by the situation in which someone leaves an organization, maybe through an accident, and his or her encrypted files are needed. Another situation is one in which a disgruntled employee encrypts shared files before leaving the organization. EFS is disabled without a recovery agent, so that files cannot be encrypted without a means to decrypt them. Several recovery agents may be assigned to an EFS file or folder, but there must be at least one. For each recovery agent, as well as the user, a copy of the symmetric encrypting key encrypted with the person's public key is stored with the encrypted file. Whoever decrypts the file reveals only the data and not any of the other keys.

Copying and Moving EFS Files   Copying and moving EFS files and folders has special significance. Here are the rules:

▼ If you copy a file or folder to an encrypted folder, the item copied will be encrypted.

- If you move a file or folder to an encrypted folder, the item moved remains as it was prior to moving. If it was unencrypted, it remains so, and if it was encrypted, it is still encrypted after moving.

- Copy or moving encrypted files or folders to another file system, such as Windows NT 4 NTFS or Windows 98 FAT32, removes the encryption.

▲ Backing up encrypted files or folders with Windows 2000 Backup leaves the items encrypted.

NOTE: When you back up encrypted data, make sure that both the user and the recovery agent keys are also backed up, which can be done with Certificate Services.

Using File and Folder Encryption

The actual process of encrypting a file or folder is very easy; you simply turn on the Encrypted attribute. Given that there is a certificated recovery agent administrator and that the user turning on the encryption has an EFS certificate, there is very little else to do. Look at the full process, including the certification, in the next sections.

Creating EFS Certificates

Earlier in this chapter, under "Certificate Authentication," there is a discussion of setting up Certificate Services and requesting a certificate. The following steps show specifically how to request an EFS Recovery Agent certificate:

1. While logged on as the administrator who will be the recovery agent, open the MMC by opening the Start menu, clicking Run, typing **mmc**, and clicking OK.

2. Open the Console menu, choose Open, and double-click your Certificates console. In the Tree tab, open Console Root | Certificates – Current User | Personal | Certificates.

3. Open the Action menu and choose All Tasks | Request New Certificate. The Certificate Request Wizard opens. Click Next.

4. Select EFS Recovery Agent as the Certificate Template, as shown in Figure 15-17, and click Next. Enter a friendly name and description, and click Next again.

5. Review your selections, use Back to make any corrections, and click Finish. When displayed, click Install Certificate and then click OK when you're told that the certificate request was successful.

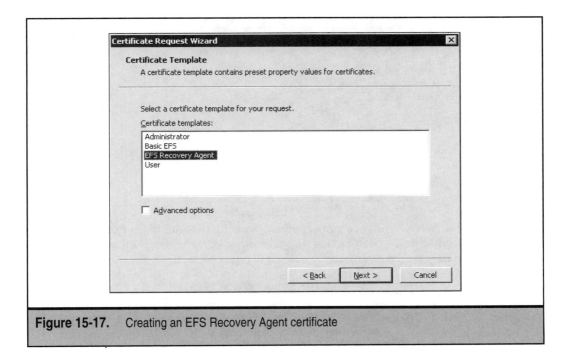

Figure 15-17.   Creating an EFS Recovery Agent certificate

Encrypting a File and a Folder

Encryption of either files or folders can be done from Windows Explorer or from the command prompt.

Encrypting a File from Windows Explorer   Here are the steps to encrypt a file from Windows Explorer:

1. Open Windows Explorer by opening Start and choosing Programs |
   Accessories | Windows Explorer.
2. In the folders tree on the left, open the drive and folders necessary to display
   on the right the file you want to encrypt.
3. Right-click the files and choose Properties. In the General tab, click Advanced.
   The Advanced Attributes dialog box opens.
4. Click Encrypt Contents to Secure Data.

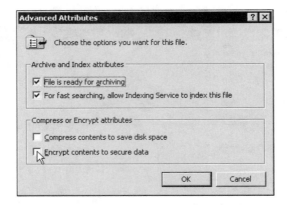

5. Click OK twice. You get an Encryption Warning that the file is not in an encrypted folder, which means that when you edit the file, temporary or backup files might be created that are not encrypted.

6. Make the choice that is correct for you. If you don't want to see this warning in the future, click Always Encrypt Only the File. Click OK.

Encrypting a Folder from Windows Explorer   Encrypting a folder from Windows Explorer is very similar, as you can see in these steps:

1. Open Windows Explorer and display in the right pane the folder you want to encrypt.

2. Right-click the folder and choose Properties. In the General tab, click Advanced. The Advanced Attributes dialog box opens, as you saw in step 4 in the preceding section.

3. Click Encrypt Contents to Secure Data, and click OK twice. The Confirm Attribute Changes dialog box opens.

You are asked whether you want to apply the encryption to this folder only or to the folder, its files, and its subfolders. If you choose This Folder Only, *existing* files and folders in the folder being encrypted will *not* be encrypted, while files and folders created or copied to the encrypted folder after the fact will be encrypted. If you choose This Folder, Subfolders, and Files, existing files and folders, as well as those created or copied in the future, will be encrypted.

4. Choose the settings that are correct for you and click OK.

CAUTION: If you choose This Folder, Subfolders, and Files for a shared folder that has files or subfolders belonging to others, you will encrypt those files and subfolders with your key, and the owners will not be able to use their property.

Encrypting a File and a Folder from the Command Prompt   At the command prompt, you can use the Cipher command to encrypt and decrypt files and folders. The following exercise encrypts a file and then a folder that contains the file plus another unencrypted file, looks at the results, and then decrypts the folder and its contents.

NOTE: Close Windows Explorer before you use the command prompt, and make sure your file and folder names do not have embedded spaces. Failure to follow either of these guidelines can cause problems with the following steps.

1. Open the command prompt by opening the Start menu and choosing Programs | Accessories | Command Prompt.

2. Type **cipher /?** and press ENTER to see the parameters that are available with the command, as shown in Figure 15-18.

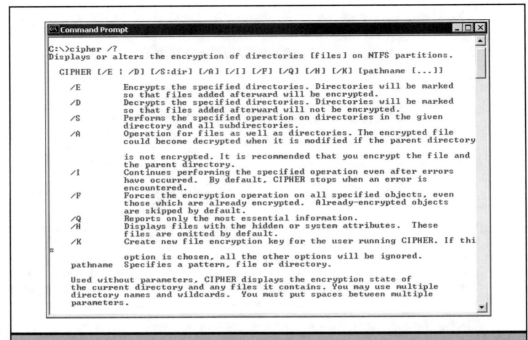

Figure 15-18. Parameters that can be used with the Cipher command

In the Cipher parameters, using /E by itself encrypts only the folder, not the files and subfolders it contains. This is the same as choosing Folder Only in Windows Explorer. If you want to encrypt the folder and its subfolders, you must use both **/E** and **/S** with a space between them. If you want to encrypt the folder, its subfolders, and the files they contain, use **/E /S /A**. To encrypt a file by itself, you must use **/E /A** with a space between them; /E /A will not encrypt the folder.

3. Type **cipher /e /a** *path\filename* and press ENTER to encrypt just the file *filename*.

4. Type **cipher /e** *path\foldername* and press ENTER to encrypt just the folder *foldername*.

5. Open Windows Explorer and look at the attributes for the two files and the folder. (If Enable Web Contents in Folders is turned on in the Folder Options General tab, you see Attributes: Encrypted in the right pane when the file or folder is selected, as shown next. Otherwise, open the file's or folder's Properties dialog box and click Advanced in the General tab.) When you are done looking at these files and folder, close Windows Explorer.

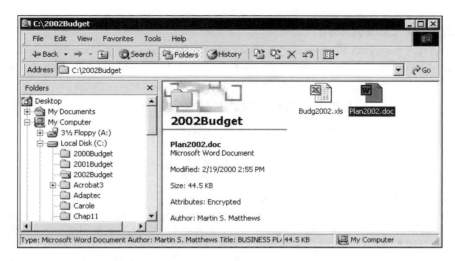

6. Type **cipher /d /s:**_path/foldername_ **/a** and press ENTER to decrypt both the folder and the file it contains, as shown in Figure 15-19.

7. Type **Exit** to close the command prompt and then open Windows Explorer to check out the attributes on the files and folder you have been using.

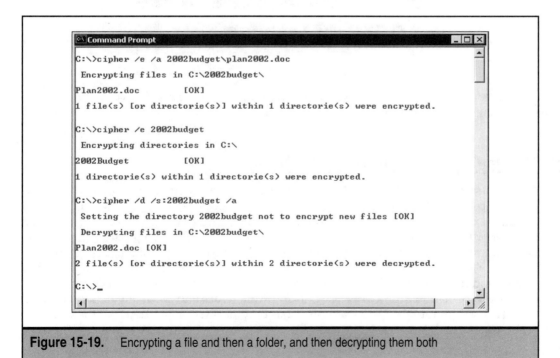

Figure 15-19. Encrypting a file and then a folder, and then decrypting them both

Testing File Encryption

So what happens when someone tries to access an encrypted file? Try it yourself. Log off and log back on as a different user and then try to open the file. It looks like it's going to open, and then this little message appears:

This is purposely understated—"one of those little access problems; call the network administrator and she'll work it out." If access is appropriate, the recovery agent administrator can solve the problem and no one is offended.

Okay, what about copying the file to a non-Windows 2000 NTFS file system, such as a Windows 98 FAT32 machine on the network? The file is no longer encrypted when you do that, correct? Again, try it, first while logged on as the one who encrypted the file. Everything will work as it is supposed to—the file will be copied and will no longer be encrypted. Then, log off and log back on again as someone else and try copying the file. Once more, it looks like it's going to work, and then another little message appears:

This too is understated, and in my case, nothing was using the file. The entire encryption system is meant to be unobtrusive, remaining in the background while doing its job.

SECURING DATA TRANSMISSION

The discussion so far in this chapter has dealt with securing computers and their contents and has been silent about securing the transmission of data among computers, using e-mail, or otherwise transferring information either within a LAN directly or using an intranet or the Internet. Yet, the need to extend a network to outlying parts of an organization and to customers and suppliers is very real and requires secure data transmission. Securing data transmission means the encryption of the information being transmitted so that it cannot be read and misused by those who don't have the ability to decrypt it. Encrypting information is probably as old as the human race and has really blossomed with the advent of computers. Data encryption has become so sophisticated that the U.S. government, worried that it won't be able to decrypt the data (can you imagine that!), hasn't until very recently allowed the better technology to be exported (everyone was getting it over the Internet anyway).

Private/Public Key Encryption

Several encryption schemes for securing data transmission are in use: private key encryption, public key encryption, and combinations of the two. The set of these three schemes and the technology and standards or protocols that surround them collectively is known as the *public key infrastructure (PKI)*. Windows 2000 has made PKI an integral part of the operating system, especially in Active Directory. Windows 2000 has implemented all three encryption key schemes and fully supports them with Certificate Services.

Private Key Encryption

Private key encryption, or *symmetric cryptography* (which is also what is used with file and folder encryption, as previously discussed), is relatively old and uses a single key to both encrypt and decrypt a message. This means that the key itself must be transferred from sender to receiver. If this is done over the phone, the Internet, or even a courier service, an unauthorized person simply needs to intercept the key transfer to get hold of the key and decrypt the message. Private key encryption, though, has a major benefit in that it is much faster (as much as 1,000 times faster) than the alternatives. Private key schemes are therefore valuable in situations where you do not have to transfer the key or can do so with security—for example, for personal use such as data encryption, as just discussed, or sending information to someone that you first met face to face. Several private key encryption schemes are being used with the Internet, including the U.S. government's Data Encryption Standard (DES) and the private RC2 ("Rivest Cipher" or "Ron's Code" [for Ron Rivest] 2) and RC4, both from RSA Laboratories.

Public Key Encryption

Public key encryption, or *asymmetric cryptography,* was developed in the mid-1970s and uses a pair of keys—a public key and a private key. The public key is publicly known and transferred, and is used to encrypt a message. The private key never leaves its creator and is used to decrypt the message. For two people to use this technique, each generates both a public and a private key, and then they openly exchange public keys, not caring who gets a copy of it. Each person encrypts their message to the other by using the other person's public key, and then sends the message. The message can be decrypted and read only by using the private key held by the recipient. The public and private keys use a mathematical algorithm that relates them to the encrypted message. By use of other mathematical algorithms, it is fairly easy to generate key pairs, but with only the public key, it is extremely difficult to generate the private key. The process of public key encryption is relatively slow compared to private key encryption. Public key encryption is best in open environments where the sender and recipient do not know each other. Most public key encryption uses the Rivest-Shamir-Adleman (RSA) Public Key Cryptosystem, called RSA for short, developed and supported by RSA Laboratories.

Combined Public and Private Key Encryption

Most encryption on the Internet actually is a combination of public and private key encryption. The most common combination, Secure Sockets Layer (SSL), was developed by Netscape to go between HTTP and TCP/IP. SSL provides a highly secure and very fast means of both encryption and authentication.

Recall that private key encryption is very fast but has the problem of transferring the key, whereas public key encryption is very secure but slow. If you were to begin a secure transmission by using a public key to encrypt and send a private key, you could then securely use the private key to quickly send any amount of data you wanted. This is how SSL works. It uses an RSA public key to send a randomly chosen private key using either DES or RC4 encryption, and in so doing sets up a "secure socket" through which any amount of data can be quickly encrypted, sent, and decrypted. After the SSL header has transferred the private key, all information transferred in both directions during a given session—including the URL, any request for a user ID and password, all HTTP web information, and any data entered on a form—is automatically encrypted by the sender and automatically decrypted by the recipient.

Several versions of SSL exist, with SSL version 3 being the one currently in common use. SSL 3 is both more secure than, and offers improved authentication over, earlier versions.

Another combination of public and private key encryption is Transport Layer Security (TLS), which is an open security standard similar to SSL 3. TLS was drafted by the Internet Engineering Task Force (IETF) and uses different encryption algorithms than SSL. Otherwise TSL is very similar to SSL and even has an option to revert to SSL if necessary. Both SSL 3 and TLS have been proposed to the World Wide Web Consortium (W3C) standards committee as security standards.

Encryption Keys and Certificates

The PKI in Windows 2000 and in general use on the Internet depends on digital certificates to issue, authenticate, and maintain encryption keys. (See "Certificate Authentication," earlier in this chapter, for a discussion of certificates and how to issue and use them.) To get an encryption key, you get a certificate, of which the key is a part. To authenticate the key, you use the certificate that it is a part of. The key is stored in a certificate, which is the means by which keys are maintained in an organization. Certificate Services in Windows 2000 provides all of these services.

Implementing Data Transmission Security

You may be thinking that SSL and TLS sounds great, but also sound complex to use. In fact, both are easy to use, either across the Internet or internally in a LAN.

Implementing Secure Internet and Intranet Transmissions

To implement secure Internet and intranet transmissions, you need a web server that supports SSL or TLS, such as Microsoft IIS 5, plus a supporting web browser, such as Microsoft Internet Explorer 5, both of which are included in Windows 2000. From the browser, to visit a web site that has implemented SSL or TSL, you simply need to begin the URL with **https://** rather than http:// (see Chapter 11 on IIS for details on how to implement secure web sites). SSL will then kick in, and without you even being aware that it's happening, the browser and server decide whether to use DCS or RC4, use RSA to transfer a private key, and then use that key and the chosen private key encryption scheme to encrypt and decrypt all the rest of the data during that session. The only thing that you see is a message saying you are about to begin to use a secure connection, similar to this:

Once you are connected using SSL, your browser will indicate that a secure connection is established. Netscape and Microsoft display an icon of a padlock in the browser's status bar.

NOTE: Even though the combination of public and private encryption is relatively fast, it is still significantly slower than no encryption. For that reason, it is recommended that you use SSL only when you send sensitive information, such as financial or credit card data, and not for an entire web site.

Implementing Secure LAN Transmission

Although SSL can be used within a LAN and in an intranet, it requires a security server (which function IIS fulfills) and can get in the way of applications that are working across a LAN. The answer to this is *Internet Protocol Security* (IPSec), which works between any two computers over a network to supply encrypted transmission of information without a security server and without getting in the way of applications. IPSec is a part of IP and works at the third (Network) layer, below any applications, and therefore seldom interferes with them (see the discussion of networking layers in "The OSI Model" in Chapter 6).

The IPSec Process   IPSec is almost totally automated, and once group policies are established for its operation, network users don't realize that their network communication is taking place securely. The process for establishing and carrying out IPSec is as follows:

1. Domain or local computer policies are established that specify what network traffic needs to be secure and how that security will be handled.

2. Based on the policies, IPSec establishes a set of filters to determine which network packets require secure transmission.

3. When IPSec receives from a sending application a series of network packets that require secure transmission, the sending computer passes this fact to the receiving computer. The two computers exchange credentials and authenticate each other based on IPSec policies.

4. Given authentication, the two computers work out an algorithm whereby each computer can generate the same private key without having to transmit the key over the network, again based on IPSec policies.

5. The sending computer uses the private key to encrypt the packets it is transmitting, digitally signs them so the receiving computer knows who is sending the packets, and then transmits the packets.

6. The receiving computer authenticates the digital signature and then uses the key to decrypt the packets and send them on to the receiving application.

Setting Up IPSec   To set up and use IPSec, you need only establish or revise default IPSec policies. You can do that through the IP Security snap-in to the MMC with these steps:

1. Open the Start menu, choose Run, type **mmc**, and press ENTER. The MMC shell opens.

2. Open the Console menu, choose Add/Remove Snap-In, click Add, scroll down, and double-click IP Security Policy Management.

3. Select whether you want to manage security policy for a domain or a computer, select which domain or computer, and click Finish.

4. Close the Add Standalone Snap-In dialog box and click OK to close the Add/Remove Snap-In dialog box. Open the Console Root and select IP Security Policies on Active Directory, so that your MMC looks like this:

5. Right-click Secure Server and choose Properties. In the Rules tab, you will see a list of IP Security Rules, as shown in Figure 15-20.

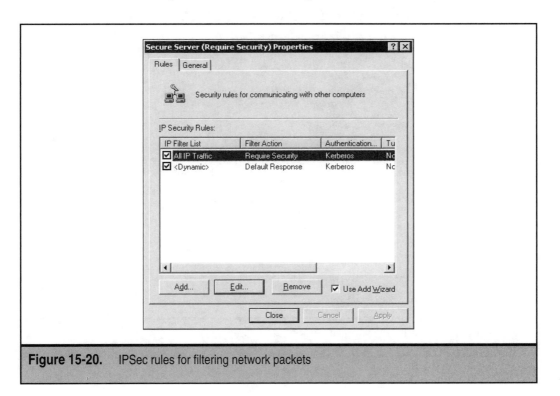

Figure 15-20. IPSec rules for filtering network packets

6. Select the All IP Traffic rule and click Edit. The Edit Rule Properties dialog box opens. Look at each of the tabs and then return to the Filter Action tab.

7. Select Require Security and click Edit, which displays a list of security methods similar to the list in Figure 15-21. You can select each of these and click Edit again to select the particular security method you want for a given situation.

8. When you are done, click OK twice and then click Close twice to return to the IPSec console, where you can also click the Close button, answering Yes to save the console settings with the name IPSec.

You can see that the Windows 2000 IPSec default is to require security on all IP traffic. This is a safe default; your data will be better protected. The negative side of this default is

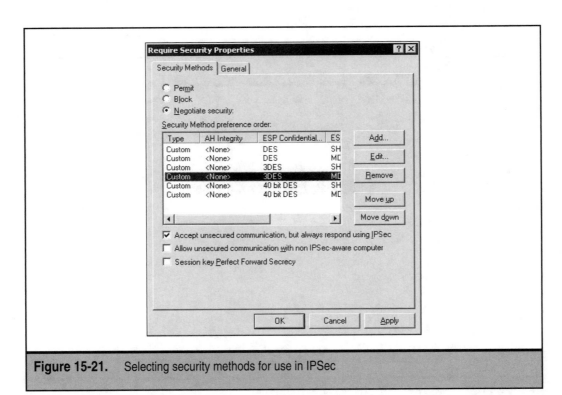

Figure 15-21. Selecting security methods for use in IPSec

that the security negotiation between the computers, encrypting and decrypting the data, and the extra bits to transmit all take time. It also uses a lot more bandwidth on the network. Only you and your organization can determine which is more important—time and bandwidth, or security. The point is that Windows 2000 gives you the choice, enabling you to make the determination of which networking aspect has a higher priority.

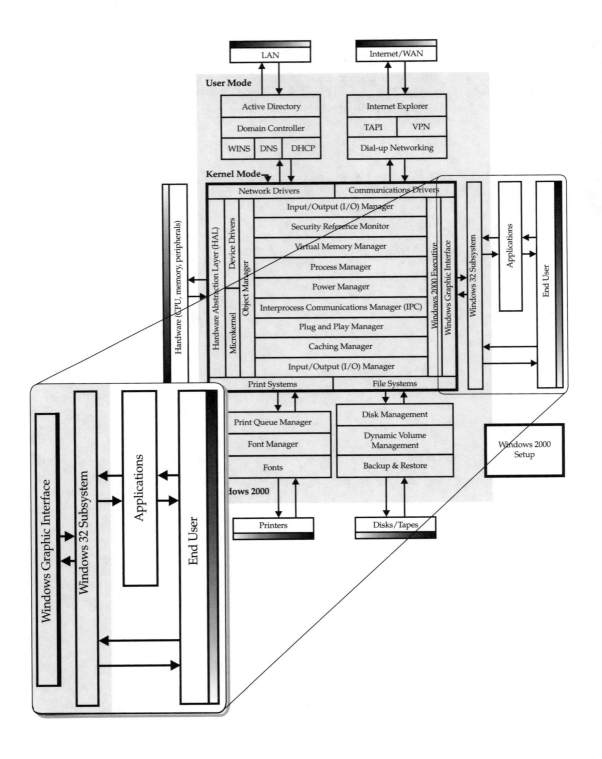

PART VI

Using Windows 2000 Professional

Windows 2000 Professional is a combination of the best parts of Windows NT Workstation and Windows 98. The ease of use and user friendliness of Windows 98 is joined with the robustness, reliability, and security of Windows NT. Windows 2000 Professional gives business users a computing platform to handle their applications, communications, and processing needs. Whatever business need, Windows 2000 provides a powerful, reliable, and secure operating system to accomplish it.

Chapter 16 takes you on a tour of Professional and describes how to use the major components. Chapter 17 shows you how to customize Windows 2000 to your needs and then how to set up and install applications to fit your requirements. Chapter 18 explores the powerful features that Windows 2000 has for laptop and notebook computers.

CHAPTER 16

Working with Windows 2000 Professional

W indows 2000 Professional is the operating system of choice for business users. In this chapter, you'll find out how best to set up Windows 2000 Professional to meet your needs and to utilize its resources.

STARTING WITH START

Although Microsoft was the target of many snide remarks when it introduced the Start button with Windows 95 (why do you click Start to shut down your computer?), it has outlasted most of its naysayers. At first glance, you won't notice much difference in Windows 2000 Professional compared to earlier Windows OSs, but there are some pearls if you look deep enough.

Expanded Menus

Expanded menus allow you to incorporate additional functions in the existing Start menu tree. An example is the Control Panel.

How do you typically open the Control Panel? Most users open the Start menu, click Settings, click Control Panel, and wait while the Control Panel window opens onscreen. Then, they double-click the icon of the individual control panel they want to use, wait for that dialog box to display, and then perhaps choose a subcomponent. You might lessen the pain of this process by creating a shortcut on your desktop or on the Quick Launch toolbar, but there's still a lot of clicking and waiting. With an expanded Start menu, you generally can get where you want with two clicks and a few hovers. See how with these steps:

1. Open the Start menu and choose Settings | Taskbar & Start Menu. The Properties dialog box of the same name opens.

2. Click the Advanced tab and select the Expand Control Panel checkbox under Start Menu Settings.

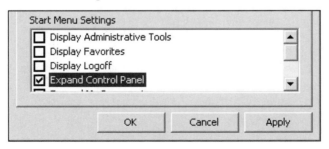

3. Click OK to close the dialog box.

TIP: To open the Control Panel window after you've expanded it, open the Start menu, click Settings, right-click Control Panel, and choose Open.

Now, to open a control panel, simply open the Start menu, point to Settings, point to Control Panel (notice the rightward-pointing arrow next to its label), and click the control panel that you want to open, or point to one that has a submenu, as shown in Figure 16-1, and make your selection from there. You can see that this is a faster and easier way to get to Control Panel (or any of the other expandable choices, such as My Documents, Printers, and Administrative Tools).

TIP: To expand the Favorites folder and the Administrative Tools control panel, you must first check their corresponding Display checkboxes in the same Start Menu Settings list, located in the Taskbar and Start Menu Properties dialog box, described in the previous numbered list.

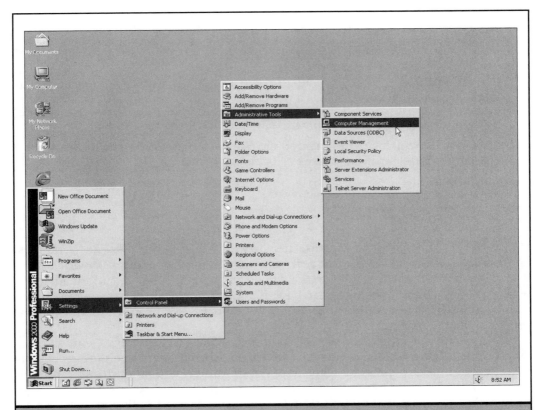

Figure 16-1.   Get where you want to go faster with expanded menus

Personalized Menus

If you've used Office 2000, you have probably developed an opinion on the merits of those truncated menus that appear when you click a menu bar item such as File, Edit, or Format. Windows 2000 offers the same concept, referred to as *personalized menus,* out of the box on the Programs menu. Only those menu items that you have used recently appear on the Programs menu. All items on the menu can be exposed by clicking the double down arrow at the bottom of the list, shown next, or by leaving the menu open a few moments.

I find this feature a bit annoying and turn it off as soon as I install a product that offers it by default, such as Windows 2000. Here's how:

1. Right-click an open area of the taskbar and click Properties.
2. On the General tab of the Taskbar and Start Menu Properties dialog box, clear the checkbox next to Use Personalized Menus.
3. Click OK.

Help

HTML Help is no longer a new feature; it's used in Windows 98, Office 2000, and most applications released in the last few years, and though it has no radical changes in Windows 2000, it is certainly becoming more refined and makes getting the information you want more convenient. In doing research for this book, I used Help extensively and found it to be a much better resource than earlier attempts by Microsoft to wean us off the printed reference material it used to supply.

A really neat new aspect to Help is the addition of the Favorites tab, as you can see in Figure 16-2. Whereas remembering how to navigate to Help topics you use repeatedly was always a burden in previous versions of Windows, now you simply display the topic once, open the Favorites tab, and click Add to have it ready the next time you want to go there. Either double-click the topic title in the Topics list or select a title and click Display. The Overview and Glossary topics are especially handy, because they provide a springboard to other links with related information.

Much work has been done by Microsoft to assist us in finding the topics that contain the information we seek. Microsoft has done usability studies over the years to determine how

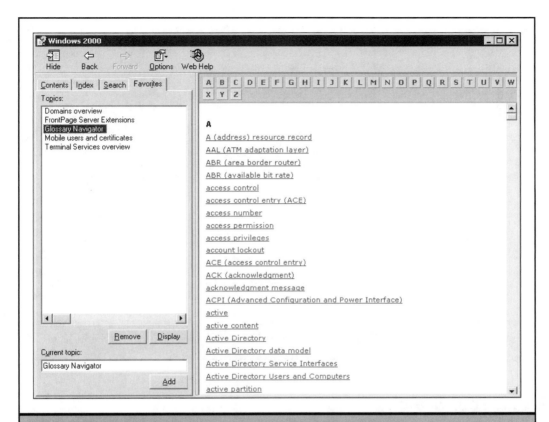

Figure 16-2.   Easily return to often-used Help topics from the Favorites tab

people search for information. Help provides three basic methods, besides the logging of Favorites, to cover as many personality types as possible. If you are the sort of person who is used to opening a table of contents and drilling down the major headings to peruse the information offered and ultimately find the topic you seek, you will be comfortable with the familiar Contents tab. If you are a more ordered type, you will probably find the Index tab more to your liking. However, for the most direct access and comprehensive topic listings, you can't beat the Search tab. Compare the results of a keyword search for the network protocol X.25 in the three tabs, shown in Figure 16-3. In the Contents tab, you might never find it; in the Index tab, you get something to work with; but using Search gives you everything Help has to offer.

NOTE: For a really comprehensive Help topic search capability, check out the Search tab in Windows 2000 Server. You can add Boolean criteria such as AND, OR, and NOT to narrow or broaden your search, you get a ranking of the topics found, and you have access to Find features such as Match Similar Words and Search Titles Only.

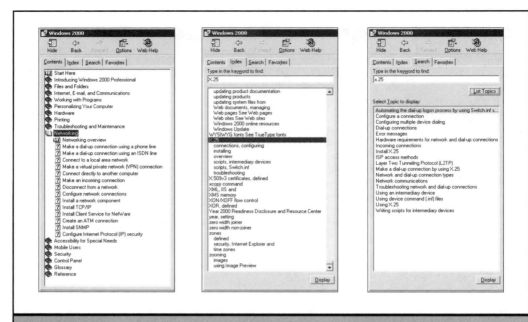

Figure 16-3.   The Search tab provides the most comprehensive and direct way to get help

Indexing Your Search

In addition to having a new verb to tell us how to locate items (we now "search for" items rather than "find" them), how we do that is much improved. The much-used Search Results dialog box, shown in Figure 16-4, provides a clean set of controls to locate files and folders by name, text, date, type, size, or more advanced criteria, such as case and whether to search removable (albeit slow) storage media such as tape.

TIP: When selecting Search Slow Files to search removable media, you might have to copy the files to a faster media for the search to be performed.

Perhaps the most exciting feature of the search capability in Windows 2000 is the ability to use the built-in Indexing Service to improve its performance and add other enhancements. The Indexing Service is not enabled by default. To add indexing to your searches, follow these steps:

NOTE: The Indexing Service is especially useful if you use Internet Information Services (IIS) to host web sites. With web creation software, such as Microsoft FrontPage, you can create the web controls to tap the search capabilities of the Indexing Service and allow users to find information on your web site. See Chapter 11 for more information on IIS.

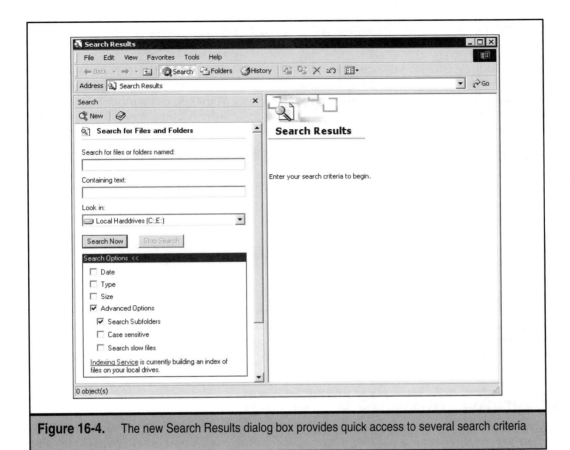

Figure 16-4.   The new Search Results dialog box provides quick access to several search criteria

1. Open the Start menu and choose Search | For Files or Folders.

2. In the Search Results dialog box, click Search Options and then click the Indexing Service hyperlink.

3. In the Indexing Service Settings dialog box, select Yes to enable the service, and click OK.

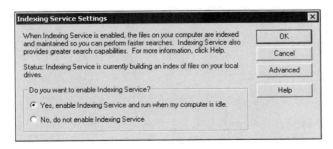

4. The label next to the Indexing Service hyperlink will change to let you know it's building a catalog of your files.

The index particulars are displayed in the Indexing Service window, shown next. You can open this window by clicking Advanced in the Indexing Service Settings dialog box, or you can see the same information in the Computer Management window (Start | Settings | Control Panel | Administrative Tools | Computer Management | Services and Applications | Indexing Service).

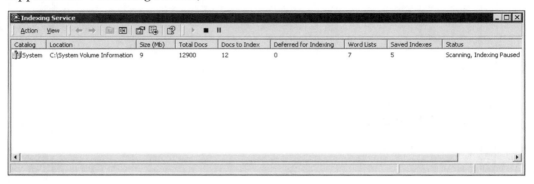

Catalog	Location	Size (Mb)	Total Docs	Docs to Index	Deferred for Indexing	Word Lists	Saved Indexes	Status
System	C:\System Volume Information	9	12900	12	0	7	5	Scanning, Indexing Paused

TIP: Wondering where the Browse button went that allowed you to focus your search for files and folders anywhere in a drive's hierarchy? Open the Look In drop-down list and scroll to the bottom of the list.

EXPLORING WINDOWS EXPLORER

The venerable Windows Explorer, which used to be easily accessible on the Start | Programs menu, has migrated down a layer to the Accessories menu (along with Command Prompt). I suppose it makes more sense to consider these two icons of Windows as accessories, but in this instance I think Microsoft might have just left well enough alone. In any case, Explorer remains, but contains a few tweaks that keep life interesting.

TIP: If you use Windows Explorer a lot and find its menu placement awkward, you can drag its icon from the Accessories menu to the Quick Launch toolbar next to the Start menu. But if you do that, the icon will disappear from the Accessories menu. A better approach is to drag a copy from the C:\Winnt folder to the Quick Launch toolbar, which leaves the icon intact on the Accessories menu.

The features described in this section are all available from Windows Explorer, but many appear in other areas of Windows 2000 as well. When you get right down to it, Explorer is really just a folder with some added properties.

My Documents

Windows 2000 takes the constantly evolving "My" model that started in Windows 95 and makes it even more pervasive. You probably noticed where things were headed when you first looked at the Windows 2000 desktop and saw that Network Neighborhood has transformed into My Network Places This paradigm is most evident with the My Documents folder. Notice that My Computer, which had always maintained the position of prominence at the top of the default desktop icons and in the Explorer Folders bar, has now been usurped by My Documents. Microsoft seems to be making a very strong statement that we as users should organize our folders and files into the My Documents folders. To encourage us to do this, Microsoft makes it very convenient.

To see this new arrangement, just open a new instance of Windows Explorer. The My Documents folder opens by default as the first item under Desktop, displaying its contents, including any default folders such as My Pictures and My Webs.

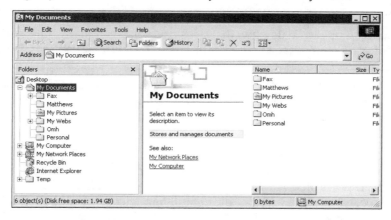

 NOTE: My Network Places is described in Chapter 7 of this book, and the My Webs folder is created when you save a new Web from Microsoft FrontPage.

Finding Your Documents the Old-Fashioned Way

So, if you want to copy a file in your My Documents folder, where would you go to find it? If you open My Computer and then open the disk drive on which Windows 2000 is installed, you probably won't see a My Documents folder at first glance. Windows 2000 assumes there will be different user accounts on a single machine and thus sets each up with its own collection of personalized folders and files under the \Documents and Settings folder. Typically, you'll have a folder for the Administrator account, an All Users folder, and folders for each individual who has a user account on the machine. Opening a user's folder displays several folders that contain unique files and settings, including Cookies, Desktop, Favorites, Start Menu, and My Documents. When you open the My Documents folder for your user account, you can finally locate and copy that file referred to at the beginning of this paragraph. There has to be a better way, and fortunately there is—several in fact.

 NOTE: If you are upgrading from earlier Windows versions, you will probably find your personal profile data in a different location—for example, upgrading from Windows NT places data in Winnt\Profiles*username*\\.

Finding Your Documents in Windows 2000

Here are places and techniques you can use to quickly access your My Documents folder:

▼ The desktop icon installed by default

■ In folders that are set up with the default Web view of My Computer, you can click the My Documents link under the folder description

■ In Open and Save dialog boxes from newer applications, you can click the My Documents icon on their respective toolbars along the left side of the dialog box

■ From the Outlook bar's Other Shortcuts group

▲ When you open a dialog box that performs some action on a file, such as opening or saving, the Look In location generally defaults to My Documents

TIP: You can change the location of your My Documents folder by right-clicking the folder icon and choosing Properties. Under Target Folder Location, click Move to browse to the new location where you want the folder stored.

My Pictures

Along with guiding you to document storage, Windows 2000 holds your hand when working with graphics files. The My Pictures folder under the My Documents folder is really nothing special, except instead of the default Large Icons view of other folders, it displays Thumbnails view, shown in Figure 16-5, so that you can more easily find that picture you took of Aunt Mable at the family picnic.

Like My Documents, when you perform some action on a graphics file, the application's dialog box typically displays the My Pictures folders as the location to open or store the file.

While the folder itself is not terribly exciting, the Thumbnails view (available to any folder from its View menu) is pretty cool. As you can see in Figure 16-5, each graphics file is displayed with enough clarity to distinguish a photo from a screen capture, and the selected file is enlarged and provided with a toolbar for viewing and printing options.

Working with Files and Folders

Many of the basic file manipulation actions haven't changed since the Windows 3.*x* days, but Windows 2000 offers a few new twists.

Where Are Cut, Copy, and Paste?

Following in the Windows tradition of providing the user with several methods to perform similar actions, Windows 2000 Professional now provides another method to use when working with files. The venerable Cut, Copy, and Paste toolbar buttons have been replaced by Move To and Copy To buttons. More interesting than just a name change, now you have the ability to easily navigate to a new location for the file without having to open and close folders in Explorer (which usually meant losing the view you originally had in the right pane of the Explorer window).

Figure 16-5. My Pictures displays thumbnails and provides tools for viewing and printing graphics files

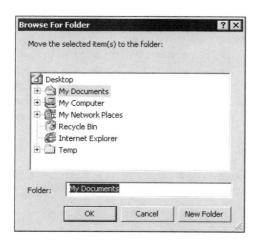

But what about when you want to cut a file to *remove* it (rather than simply move it somewhere else) from your hard disk, and then want it stored on the Clipboard as a temporary depository in case you quickly realize you made a mistake? Well, that's what Delete is for, and because you have the Recycle Bin as a safety valve, you really don't need to worry about changing your mind and inadvertently deleting a file. And, if you really prefer the Cut, Copy, and Paste trio, you can still use a file's or folder's context menu (opened by right-clicking the file or folder), or use the CTRL-X, CTRL-C, and CTRL-V key combinations.

Open With

An overdue feature is the ability to open a file from Explorer with a program other than the one that's associated with its file format. For example, a JPEG graphics file is generally associated with and opened with Iexplore.exe, but what if you want to open the file in a drawing program, such as Adobe PhotoDeluxe? The most recent attempt to get around this problem worked fine, but you had to know the "trick" to get the Open With command displayed on a file's context menu. Now, simply right-click a file and choose Open With from the context menu and you'll get a list of programs you can use.

NTFS Options

The NTFS file system, described in Chapter 12, provides several enhancements over FAT32. Two areas that can be accessed through Explorer are setting permissions for others to view or modify the file (described in Chapter 15) and setting user-defined values for several attributes of a file. Assuming you have the proper permissions, you can change or create the values for many properties of a file. Similar to the capability to add keywords to Word files to assist in locating them during a search, you can now do the same with any file and also tag it with other properties, depending on the file's type. Follow these steps to fully document a file:

1. In Windows Explorer, right-click a file's icon (other than a web link file) in the right pane and choose Properties.

2. Click the Summary tab and you will see a basic set of properties you can modify.

3. Click the Advanced button to see a file's basic properties and other properties you can modify, as shown in Figure 16-6.

4. Click to the right of a property to expose a drop-down text box in which you can add your own text.

Folder Options

The Folder Options dialog box has several changes. The first is that it is opened from the View menu instead of the Tools menu (just as Internet Explorer's Options dialog box is now opened from the Tools menu and is renamed Internet Tools). Select View | Folder Options and you'll see both new settings and retooled legacy settings you can choose from. Also, a new Offline Files tab enables you to set up your computer to use files when you're offline from a network connection, and then synchronize them when the connection is reestablished. This is used in conjunction with the Windows Explorer Tools menu's Synchronize command and is described in Chapter 18.

NOTE: The Briefcase also handles synchronization of files, but is generally not preferable to using offline files and folders, except in a few special circumstances. This feature is also covered in Chapter 18.

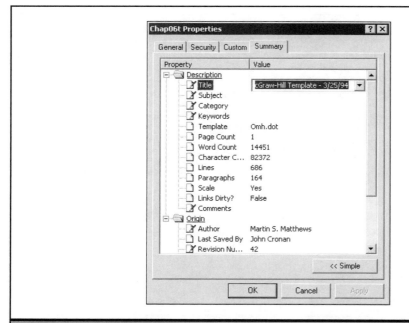

Figure 16-6.   Advanced properties add more ways you can categorize a file

The General tab, shown in Figure 16-7, should look very familiar to Windows 95/98 and NT 4 users. Use this tab to change the view of your desktop (that is, how many Web view features you want) and to choose whether you want folders to open in their own windows or continue to use the same window. If you frequently drag and drop files between windows, you'll want folders to open in their own windows; otherwise, the clutter of separate windows might lead you to use a single window.

After installing a new version of Windows, the View tab, shown in Figure 16-8, is the first place I go to start customizing. Starting at the top of the dialog box, I click Like Current Folder after I've changed my Explorer view to Details so that all folder file lists show up with their associated information. Under Advanced Settings, the other default setting that I cannot live with is the Hide File Extensions for Known File Types, which hides 99 percent of the file extensions, making it at best difficult, and at worst dangerous, to open a file without knowing explicitly its type. A few other checkboxes are interesting, especially if you're not used to some of the features provided by an NT-based operating system:

▼ **Display Compressed Files and Folders with Alternate Color**   If you take advantage of the capability to choose compression selectively for individual files and folders, you will want to be able to easily identify them.

■ **Display the Full Path in the Address Bar/Title Bar**   One of these options is most helpful in figuring out which folder you are in and where that folder is located.

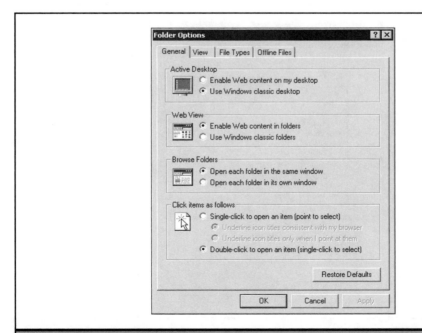

Figure 16-7.   The Folder Options General tab is where you determine how your desktop will look

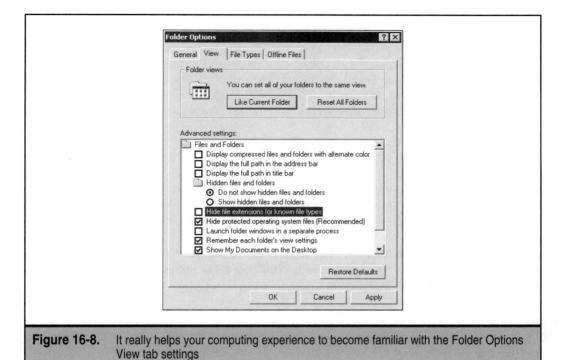

Figure 16-8. It really helps your computing experience to become familiar with the Folder Options View tab settings

- ■ **Hidden Files and Folders** If you're like me, you can't stand to have things hidden, even if you don't use what is hidden. I therefore select Show Hidden Files and Folders and uncheck Hide Protected Operating System Files even though its use is recommended.

- ▲ **Launch Folder Windows in a Separate Process** This option uses the underlying Windows 2000 architecture to segregate the actions of folder windows into separate memory spaces.

There's nothing terribly exciting about the File Types tab. It serves the same basic function it has in several Windows versions—to associate a file type to the executable file that will open it when needed.

ACCESSORIES

Windows 2000 Professional continues the Windows tradition of offering a little something for just about anything you might need to do with a computer, from writing a memo, to sending it by fax, to playing a game while you're waiting for it to transmit. Although third-party programs are available that provide more robust offerings for just about every accessory Windows provides, you really can't beat the scope of what you get for one price (takes some of the sting out of the sticker price if you look at it this way). This section gives you a glance at the features that you've seen before and a more detailed look at the newer features. Access the accessories by pointing to Accessories on the Start | Programs menu.

Accessibility

The features in Windows 2000 for those with difficulty in seeing, hearing, and hand movement are split between the Accessories | Accessibility menu and the Accessibility Options control panel. However, you can enable most of the control panel settings as well as the Accessibility menu utilities from the new Accessibilities Wizard. (See Chapter 17 for those settings found in the Accessibility Options control panel.)

Accessibility Wizard

To start the Accessibility Wizard, follow these steps:

1. Open the Start menu and click Programs | Accessories | Accessibility Wizard. Click Next after reading the opening narrative. Note that if you have trouble using a mouse, there are alternative ways to make a selection, as described in the wizard dialog boxes.

2. In the second dialog box, Text Size, take a vision exam by choosing the line whose smallest text you can read. Windows 2000 will adjust display settings to match the choice you make, as shown in Figure 16-9. Click Next.

TIP: If you choose the last line, Microsoft Magnifier, described in the next section, will start so that you can use it throughout the remainder of the wizard.

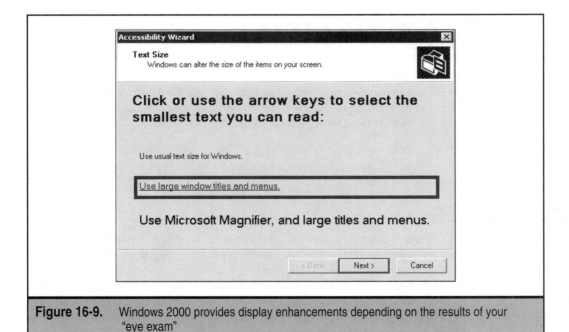

Figure 16-9.   Windows 2000 provides display enhancements depending on the results of your "eye exam"

3. Select how Windows 2000 will handle your choice of text size and other settings in the Display Settings dialog box. Click Next after verifying the settings are correct for you.

4. In the Set Wizard Options dialog box, select the type of impairment, if any, that you have. Subsequent wizard dialog boxes are tailored based on your choices here. Click Next.

5. Select the options you want, using the Back button to adjust your choices, as necessary. Eventually, you will see the Save Settings to File dialog box, shown next, which lets you save your settings to a file (with an .acw file extension) so that you can transfer it to other computers. Click Next after making your choice.

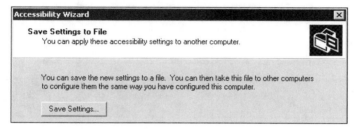

6. In the final dialog box, review your selections and click Finish when satisfied.

Accessibility Utilities

Three programs are included in Windows 2000 that are designed to benefit those with vision, hearing, or mobility impairment, but they might also be useful in other applications. Each utility can be opened from the Accessibility menu in either of two ways:

▼ Directly click Magnifier, Narrator, or On-Screen Keyboard

▲ Choose Utility Manager and start the utility from there, as shown in Figure 16-10

The three utilities are described next.

NOTE: When opened, each utility displays an informational dialog box that provides a caveat stating that the utility provides a minimum level of functionality and that for day-to-day use by a person with an impairment, a more robust program is recommended.

Magnifier   The Magnifier allows you to dedicate a portion of the desktop to display an enlargement of the area under the mouse pointer, what the keyboard currently has its attention focused on, or what text editing is in progress. You can adjust the size of the area by dragging a border, by dragging the area from the default location at the top of the desktop to another side, or by dragging away from the screen sides and making a floating window, as you can see in Figure 16-11.

In the Magnifier Settings dialog box, you can choose from nine magnification levels, select what is tracked, and configure how the Magnifier is displayed.

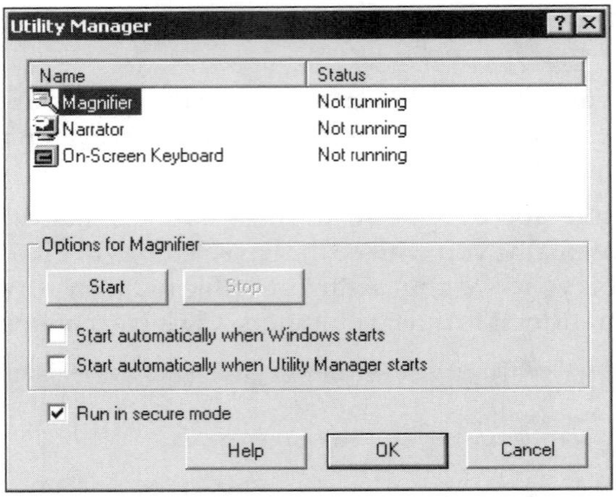

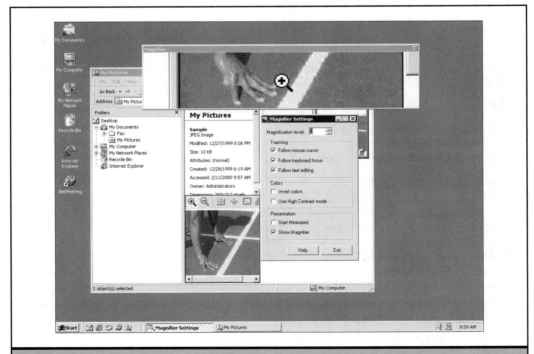

Figure 16-10. The Utility Manager lets you run and manage accessibility utilities from a single interface

Figure 16-11. You can easily enlarge a screen object by using the Magnifier

Narrator The Narrator provides an audio indication of what's happening on your screen. If you have difficulty determining what a particular window, dialog box, or other object is, the Narrator might provide an additional clue. For example, if you want to save a new document in Word and are not 100 percent sure whether you clicked the Save button or the Open button, the Narrator will say something regarding the name of the dialog box that is displayed.

On-Screen Keyboard Onscreen keyboards have been around for some time for multilingual use, but they are also useful for enabling people to enter text using a pointer device instead of the keyboard. The On-Screen Keyboard, shown in Figure 16-12, provides an almost exact replica of the enhanced 101-key keyboard that most of us use. The layout can be changed using the Keyboard menu. Other options are available from the Settings menu, with three of the four options easily understood at first glance. The Typing Mode option opens a dialog box of the same name, shown next, that lets you choose how a character is typed. You can enter a character in three ways:

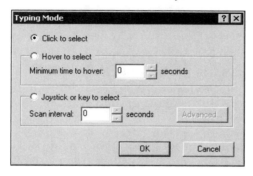

▼ **Click to Select** Requires a pointing device, such as a mouse, be used to click the character you want (this is the default choice).

■ **Hover to Select** Permits you to point to a character and, after a user-defined interval of time, the character is entered.

▲ **Joystick or Key to Select** Uses a continuous scan, a row at a time, and then a character at a time within a row, left to right, in which you then select the character you want by pressing a keyboard key or by using a joystick or mouse. The methods of actuation and execution are found by clicking the Advanced button and selecting one or both checkboxes in the Scanning Options dialog box, shown here:

Figure 16-12. The On-Screen Keyboard lets you type characters using a pointing device or a single character from a conventional keyboard

Communications

The Communications accessories provide utilities that let you connect to other computers in several different ways. The following list looks at these accessories as they relate to the progression of communications technology, starting with the oldest technology and continuing to those that are still breaking ground. More details about their actual workings follow this list.

▼ **Phone Dialer** In its basic form, assists in making basic voice telephone calls. New in Windows 2000 is the ability to quickly place calls using "modern" technologies, such as video conferencing.

■ **Network and Dial-up Connections** Manages how your hardware is set up to connect to other computers, through a LAN or over phone lines (discussed in Chapter 7).

■ **HyperTerminal** Provides for the transmission of digital data between computers using older (pre-Internet) protocols. Though still useful for connecting to bulletin board services (BBSs) and certain remote applications, this form of data communications software has little use today for most people.

■ **Fax** Uses POT (plain old telephone) wire to transmit data in the form of a graphic; became popular in the 1970s, and still is today for businesses to send and receive documents.

■ **Internet Connection Wizard** Assists in configuring the necessary settings to connect to the Internet and the World Wide Web.

▲ **NetMeeting** Provides the leading edge of communications, using live video, audio, and other collaborative methods over the Internet. The "next best thing to being there" has come a long way toward making the experience of interacting with people thousands of miles away similar to having them in the room with you.

NOTE: The Internet Connection Wizard and Network and Dial-up Connections accessories are basically shortcuts to these utilities that are accessed more directly in other ways in Windows 2000. They are described in Chapters 10 and 7, respectively.

Fax

Windows 2000 provides a straightforward fax utility that can handle basic send and receive functions. The options on the Fax menu let you manage the fax service and send a cover page, while documents are faxed from their respective application's Print dialog box. This service uses the Control Panel to handle a majority of its setup options.

HyperTerminal

In the days before we all became enamored with the Web, data transfer between computers was handled quite effectively with data communication software (and still can be). However, the ease with which the average computer user can use the Internet to access information and transfer files has relegated data communication software to mostly specialized tasks, such as the following:

▼ Manually sending dialing instructions to your modem

■ Configuring devices such as routers either remotely using a modem or locally using a null modem cable

■ Transferring files between computers using serial ports and a null modem cable

■ Sending and receiving files using modems and a direct phone connection

■ Saving onscreen text to a text file, or "capturing" text

▲ Printing onscreen text

You start using HyperTerminal by setting up a connection in the Connection Description dialog box, shown next, which opens automatically when you start HyperTerminal. After entering a name, selecting an icon, and clicking OK, a wizard-like set of dialog boxes obtains the necessary information from you to make the connection.

After you create a connection, it appears on a second Accessories | Communications | HyperTerminal menu, where you can in one click both open the HyperTerminal window and establish the connection.

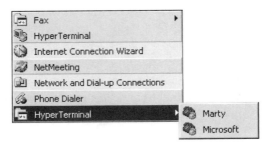

NetMeeting

The most comprehensive suite of services offered by any of the communication accessories is found in NetMeeting. Within a NetMeeting session, you can do these tasks:

- ▼ Send files
- ■ Videoconference
- ■ Audioconference
- ■ Use Chat to send and receive real-time typed messages
- ■ Collaborate using shared applications or a drawing whiteboard
- ▲ Share a desktop remotely for troubleshooting or to gain access to a home or office computer when on the road

Of course, to be able to fully utilize all of NetMeeting's features, you need a few other whistles and bells besides Windows 2000:

- ▼ The fastest connection to the Internet that you can get. Moving streaming video and audio bits requires lots of bandwidth to ensure smooth appearance and dialog. For anything but casual use, cable, DSL, or ISDN speeds are really the minimum to consider, with corporate LAN or Tx lines even better.

- ■ A video camera on each end of the connection for videoconferencing. You can get by with unilateral camera use, but obviously only one party will see the other party. Several good cameras are available for around $100, and most come without the need for a separate video card.

- ▲ A microphone, speakers, and a sound card, which now generally are standard features of a computer system.

TIP: For better audio performance, consider using a headset with a boom microphone instead of the stand-alone components. This prevents the microphone from picking up what is coming out of the speakers, and keeps the microphone a constant distance in front of your mouth no matter where you move your head.

The first time you start NetMeeting, a wizard appears that configures several aspects of the software, including personal data such as your name and e-mail address, whether to log on to a directory service when NetMeeting starts, your connection speed, and audio component's tuning and acceptability. A *directory service* allows you to list yourself and find others, to easily make connections. Windows 2000 uses Microsoft's Internet Directory by default, which requires you to install the latest MSN Messenger and have a Microsoft Passport account (which you have if you use Hotmail). You can also use other directory services that may not require as much collateral work.

You do not need to use a directory service. You can establish a connection with another user through several other methods, such as the computer name (assuming you're connecting over a LAN), other computer's IP address, or telephone number.

After you finish the wizard, the NetMeeting window opens, as shown in Figure 16-13, from which you control all aspects of what NetMeeting can do. Get started by placing a call: click the Place Call button, type the address of the other computer in the Place A Call dialog box, shown next, and, after you're connected, choose which features of NetMeeting you want from the buttons on the bottom of the NetMeeting window or from the Tools menu.

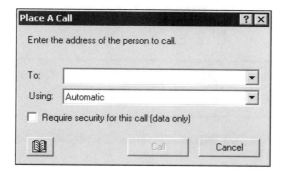

Phone Dialer

Although you might think of Phone Dialer as a rather simplistic applet that allows you to maintain a list of frequently called numbers and quickly place a call using a speed dialer, you'll want to give it a second look, because Windows 2000 has given it quite a makeover. Not only can you still speed dial, but you can speed dial the following:

▼ A normal voice call

■ A call over the Internet

▲ An Internet conference call

Using a voice phone number, an IP address to an individual computer, or a directory server on your corporate network or somewhere on the Internet, you create connections that are saved for future use. The left pane in Figure 16-14 shows where you add directory

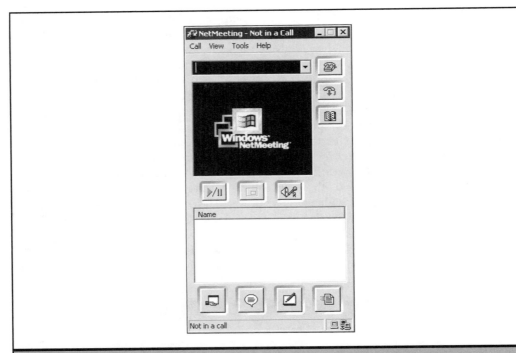

Figure 16-13. The NetMeeting window provides everything you need to collaborate online

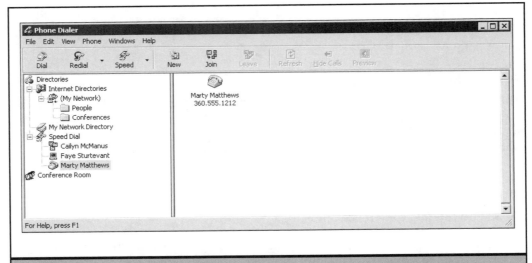

Figure 16-14. The Phone Dialer lets you quickly connect to other people individually or in conference

servers, access Speed Dial accounts, and set up Internet conference calls. The three Speed Dial accounts show the icons used to distinguish between conference calls, Internet phone calls, and normal telephone calls.

Entertainment

The four applets that comprise the Entertainment group probably will not be new to you; they've all been around since at least the Windows 95 days (Sound Recorder was available in Windows 3.*x*!), but at least one applet has gotten a radically new look and enhanced functionality:

▼ **CD Player**   The CD Player wins the prize for the most improved look; the interface has taken on the appearance of a real CD player, unlike a basic dialog box. Though functionally much the same (how many different ways can you play a CD?) as it's always been, the new feature to download album information from Internet music sites is quite neat, as you can see in Figure 16-15. I also like spinning the volume knob with the mouse pointer and being able to shrink the window to the height of a title bar and toolbar.

■ **Sound Recorder**   The Sound Recorder operates much like a tape recorder, enabling you to record and play back digital sounds from several sources, such as a microphone, CD, MIDI (Musical Instrument Digital Interface) devices, and other audio input devices. Limited mixing capabilities are also available, with which you combine sounds from multiple sources into one sound file with a .wav file extension.

▲ **Volume Control**   Designed to appear like a mixer, Volume Control, shown in Figure 16-16, allows you to set playback and recording levels for your available devices. The default window shows five parameters, but you can modify the number of output and input parameters (the quantity of parameters is generally determined by the features offered by your sound card) that appear from the Volume Control Properties dialog box (open the Options menu and click Properties).

TIP: You can open the Volume Control window by double-clicking the speaker icon in the taskbar's tray; single-clicking the icon opens a slider for the volume output level.

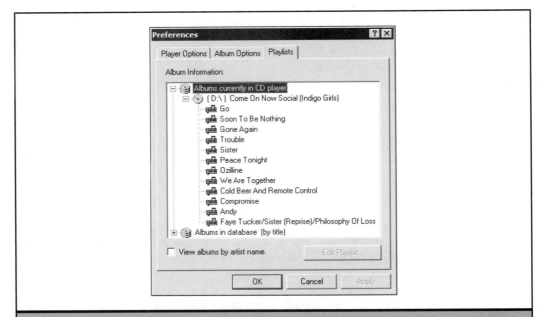

Figure 16-15. CD Player can automatically download your CD play list from Internet music sites

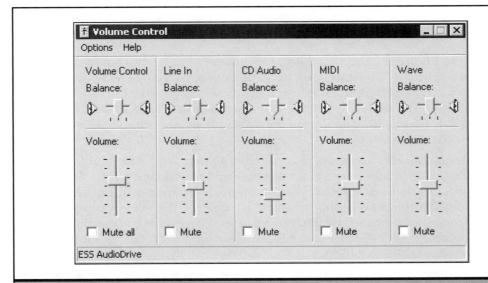

Figure 16-16. Volume Control lets you adjust playback and recording levels

▲   **Windows Media Player**   A constantly evolving applet, the Media Player is
    Microsoft's program for handling Internet (or intranet) audio or video, such as
    streaming video, live radio broadcasts, and live concerts and speeches, as well
    as saved media files, such as the same WAV files that Sound Recorder can
    record. To get an idea of the breadth of material you can view and/or hear
    with Media Player, open it and choose one of the Favorites from the menu of
    the same name. Often, you will not see the presentation open in the Media
    Player window itself, as shown in Figure 16-17, but it will be the Media Player
    software at work. Unfortunately, if you try to run media over the Internet, it
    might open in Windows Media Player or it might not. There is better than a 50
    percent chance you will need a player from RealNetworks (the basic model is
    free and available from http://www.real.com), because RealNetworks is
    currently the trendsetter in Web-based audio and video media presentation.
    Windows Media Player is discussed further in Chapter 11.

TIP: Microsoft is serious about overtaking RealNetworks players with Media Player as the format of
choice for online media. Periodically open the Help menu in the Windows Media Player window and
click Check for Player Upgrade to download the latest weapon in the arsenal.

Figure 16-17.   Windows Media Player works in the background

Games

The following four games provided by Windows 2000 are not new and have been offering computer users a break from their normal day's activities long before the Web took over as the top offender to computing productivity:

▼ **FreeCell**   Similar to Solitaire, the goal in FreeCell is to place the card deck into four stacks, referred to as *home cells*. You use four other "free" cells to temporarily store cards while you are arranging the deck in columns.

■ **Minesweeper**   A game of sleuth, you try to locate hidden mines spread throughout the matrix without actually uncovering them. By clicking a square, you get information on how many mines surround it. By getting information on the location of mines around an individual square, you can deduce the actual location of the mines.

▲ **Pinball**   This is the gee-whiz game of the bundle, as you can see in Figure 16-18. Space Cadet provides 3-D graphics, action sounds, constant music to give you that cacophony experience of an arcade, and keyboard controls to

Figure 16-18.   Pinball launches Space Cadet, an exciting replica of the favorite arcade game

activate pinball actions such as flipper movements, table nudges, and ball releases. You can enlist up to four players to see who will come closest to advancing from Space Cadet to Fleet Admiral.

▼ **Solitaire**   The grande dame of computer games, Solitaire provides a perfect representation of the card game of choice for those who have extra time on their hands and no company. This game of strategy and chance is a fast-moving endeavor to align as many of the four suits in order as you can.

System Tools

Windows 2000 has significantly trimmed the number of applets that appear in the Systems Tools group. Several more system-like tools are available now than ever before, but they are more broadly categorized, and are distributed throughout the operating system, mostly in the Administrative Tools group. These tools, as well as some of those on the System Tools group, are covered in other chapters of this book. The few that are not given significant coverage elsewhere are described here:

▼ **Character Map**   A veteran of the Windows 3.*x* days, Character Map provides an overview of the characters in each font family that Windows 2000 supports. It is useful for copying characters into documents, typically foreign, that are not available on the English keyboard. You can also find out the key combination to add many of the same characters in the future without opening the window. The Advanced View provides a search capability to locate characters in several character sets supported by Windows 2000 besides the default Unicode standard. Figure 16-19 shows the information provided by Character Map for a selected character.

▼ **Scheduled Tasks**   Used primarily as a scheduling tool to run disk maintenance programs, such as Disk Defragmenter and Check Disk, when the computer is not being used (for example, Saturday night at 2:00 A.M.), you also can choose to run any executable program file. You add tasks by double-clicking the Add Scheduled Task item in the Scheduled Tasks window. The Scheduled Task Wizard walks you through selecting a program to schedule, as well as its periodicity, time, and user account that will run it. After a task is created, you can use its Properties dialog box to make more specific settings, as shown in Figure 16-20.

▼ **Getting Started**   This is where you can revisit the information that was offered when you first installed Windows 2000 (such as online registration and a Windows overview) if you cleared the Show this Screen at Startup checkbox in the Getting Started with Windows 2000 dialog box.

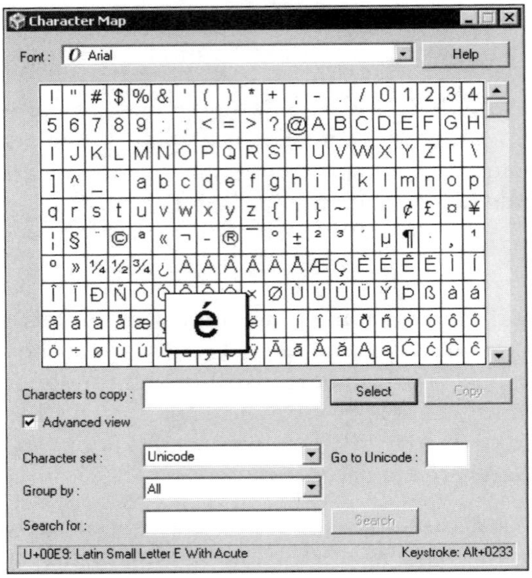

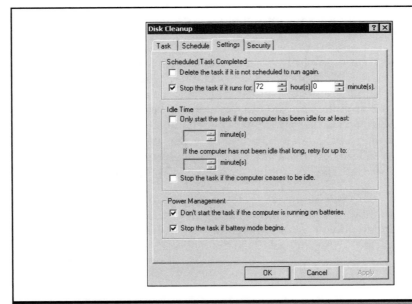

Figure 16-19.   Character Map provides an enlarged view and descriptive information on selected characters

Figure 16-20.   The Settings tab of a Scheduled Task's Properties dialog box provides more options than the Scheduled Task Wizard

Miscellaneous

Finally, the following table briefly describes those uncategorized accessories that are probably used most often, especially the new additions to the Accessories menu, Command Prompt, and Windows Explorer:

Accessory	Description
Address Book	Used by many programs, including Outlook Express and NetMeeting, for contact information such as e-mail addresses and directory services
Calculator	Provides online versions of arithmetic and scientific handheld calculators
Command Prompt	Runs DOS commands and other command-line–executed programs and utilities
Imaging	Provides basic editing of graphics, including photos and scanned images
Notepad	Provides a no-frills text editor
Paint	Provides a simple but effective drawing program for bitmapped graphics
Synchronize	Ensures version control of documents that are used on more than one computer (described more fully in Chapter 18)
Windows Explorer	Provides comprehensive file and folder management
WordPad	Provides basic word processing using several easily converted formats

CHAPTER 17

Customizing Windows 2000 Professional

Windows 2000 Professional offers a number of ways to set up a computer for an individual's needs, some of which are new and others that are enhanced from earlier Windows versions. The first part of this chapter covers the choices you have to create just the right working environment for your needs; the second half of the chapter focuses on adding applications to Windows 2000 Professional—the real purpose of a desktop operating system.

PERSONALIZING THE DESKTOP

Microsoft desktop and server operating systems have been on a convergent path almost from the time Microsoft had one version of each (Windows 3.*x* and Windows NT). The closer Microsoft gets to a single operating system (rumored to be code-named Whistler), the more cross-pollination of kernel, features, and appearance you are likely to see in any newly released version. Windows 2000 Professional typifies this progression, especially in the areas of user friendliness and a customizable desktop, by bringing forward the best of the Windows 98 user interface and adding a few new "gee whiz" aspects to the experience. Whereas Chapter 16 introduced some new features found on the desktop, such as personalized and expanded menus, this chapter digs a bit deeper and looks at the rest of the new features.

The Desktop

By default, Windows 2000 Professional provides a rather austere although fully functional display to greet you, as shown in Figure 17-1. You can install dozens of applications and successfully connect with people and organizations both locally on a LAN and worldwide on the Internet by doing word processing, filling in a corporate online form, preparing a graphics design, and buying parts from eBay without ever changing the appearance of your desktop. To many, that is just fine. To others, computing is not possible without photos of their kids or grandkids displayed as wallpaper, moving stock tickers giving up-to-the-minute stock prices, and icons arrayed across the desktop for every program, document, or link they have. One of the beauties of Windows 2000 Professional is that it doesn't matter what approach you take—you can be equally successful in your computing experience whether you're left- or right-brained.

The desktop essentially is just a slate on which all the screen elements of Windows reside. Figure 17-1 shows two elements: icons in a column along the left side, and the taskbar (described in the next section) along the bottom edge. Additionally, you can add more icons (which open folders or are shortcuts to open files or other objects, such as Internet addresses) for various installed applications, icons that represent URLs to favorite web sites, single or multiple windows that contain applications, and background patterns or graphics to replace the default sky blue. You also can make the desktop "active" by using a majority of the available real estate to display a web page, as shown in Figure 17-2.

Figure 17-1. An out-of-the-box Windows 2000 Professional desktop

NOTE: If your desktop doesn't seem to match the "normal" set of items and applications presented here, it might be governed by *group policies.* As described in Chapter 14, group policies are set up by an administrator to standardize (and often restrict) machine settings throughout an enterprise.

You can modify how your desktop appears and behaves through its context menu. Options available include the following:

▼ **Active Desktop** Provides a flyout menu of further options with which to customize the desktop, which includes, among other things, adding graphics available on the Web. The Active Desktop is more fully described in the section "Active Desktop," later in this chapter.

■ **Arrange Icons** Allows you to sort icons into columns by several categories. You can also ensure icons stay in their correct order by choosing Auto Arrange from the flyout menu.

■ **Line Up Icons** Moves icons from their current position to the nearest column in the invisible grid that covers the desktop.

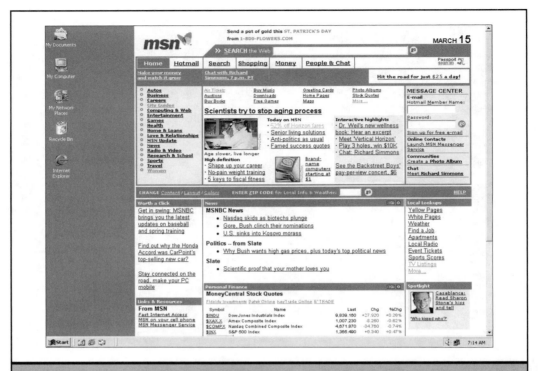

Figure 17-2. The Active Desktop can add a web page as a partial background

- **Refresh** Updates the desktop for any changes you've made.
- **Paste/Paste Shortcut** Places an item on the desktop that had been added to the Clipboard through a copy or cut.
- **Undo** (appears situationally) Allows you to reverse an action, such as a delete or rename.
- **New** Provides a quick means to add folders and shortcuts to the desktop, and open documents from installed applications such as Word or Paint.
- ▲ **Properties** Opens the Display Properties dialog box, shown in Figure 17-3, which offers detailed options to control how you see and interact with your desktop.

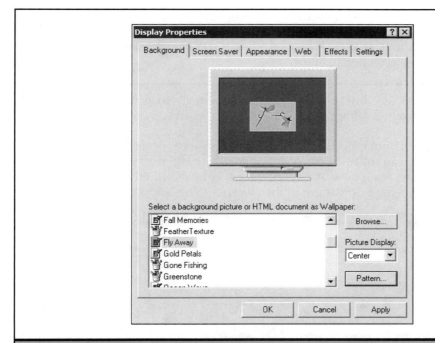

Figure 17-3.   The Display Properties dialog box provides full customization of the desktop

Display Properties

The options in the Display Properties dialog box are categorized among six tabs, described in the following sections.

Background Tab   The Background tab provides a familiar set of features going back to Windows 3.*x*, including a selection of graphics you can use to replace the default blue background. The backgrounds come in two varieties: wallpapers and patterns.

The Windows-provided wallpapers are graphics comprised of JPEG or BMP files, but you can browse for any supported graphics file or even a favorite HTML file. Wallpaper graphics may or may not completely cover the entire desktop. If not, you have a few options. You can change the Picture Display option from Centered to Tile or Stretch, which will either cover the desktop with multiple copies of the graphic (Tile) or size it to fill the desktop (Stretch). Some graphic formats size better than others. For example, JPEGs size well, whereas BMPs don't. To fill in areas of the desktop that aren't covered by wallpaper, you can use a pattern, as shown in Figure 17-3.

TIP: To use JPEG, GIF, or HTML files as wallpaper, the Active Desktop feature must be turned on. Windows 2000 will prompt you and perform the enabling for you if you try to use any of these files.

Patterns are small, bitmapped designs that are tiled to create a sort of "elevator music" background. You can cover the entire desktop with a pattern or, as mentioned earlier, cover areas around any wallpaper. A pattern can easily be modified by using the Pattern Editor, opened by clicking Edit Pattern in the Pattern dialog box.

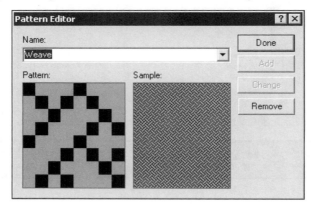

Screen Saver Tab Another Windows legacy tab whose name is somewhat deceiving, Screen Saver, actually provides three disparate features:

▼ **Screen savers** Used to serve a real function—to prevent screen phosphor burn in older monitors—but today they are really more just for show, since most monitors aren't as susceptible to screen phosphor burn and now shut down after a period of inactivity. There are twelve screen savers you can pick from, or you can add commercially sold ones that will appear in the list after they're installed. Set the number of minutes of computer inactivity before the screen saver displays using the Wait spinner.

■ **Security** You can lock the screen after the screen saver is activated, by selecting the Password Protected checkbox. You use your logon password to unlock the screen and resume working with the computer. This is best utilized when you are temporarily away from your desk and don't what to log off of your computer.

NOTE: Windows 95/98 users will find that you no longer enter a separate password for the screen saver, which is a double-edged sword, because although you don't have to remember another password, you cannot use a simpler password than the one provided by your IT department.

▲ **Energy savings** Offers a path to the Power Options Properties control panel, in which you not only can set a power scheme for the monitor, but also can control the power to hard disks, configure an uninterruptible power supply (UPS), enable hibernate support, and configure other advanced options. Power options are described fully in Chapter 18.

Appearance Tab The settings on the Appearance tab control the color, font, and size of the screen elements that make up dialog boxes, icons, and windows. You simply click the screen element in the preview area or choose it from the Item drop-down list box and set its properties. Two color settings are available for title bars, so you can fade one color into another. A less tedious approach to setting screen colors is to choose one of the preset appearance schemes that already have a coordinated design. After making any changes, it's best to save them under a new scheme so that the original scheme is not altered.

Web Tab The Web tab, in combination with the desktop context menu Active Desktop flyout menu, controls properties for the Active Desktop. The Active Desktop is fully described later in this chapter.

Effects Tab The Effects tab, shown in Figure 17-4, has evolved into a "catch-all" location for several desktop appearance options that used to be scattered among several dialog boxes. Some of these features are still also controlled in other locations, but are worded differently. For example, the Use Large Fonts checkbox, normally cleared, becomes selected if you either choose Use Large Window Titles and Menus in the Accessibility Wizard or choose Large Fonts in the monitor and video card Properties dialog box, described later in this chapter.

TIP: The Change Icon dialog box provides a very limited number of alternate icon examples for the standard Windows 2000 icons. Browse to Moricons.dll in the System32 folder to see many additional choices.

Settings Tab The two desktop settings that most affect how your desktop (and all of Windows) looks are found on the Settings tab. These are the number of screen colors and the screen resolution, or Screen Area as it's labeled.

The number of colors you can choose from is dependent on your video card. Generally, more is better (up to a point of diminishing return), especially if you have the video RAM to handle the processing demanded by the greater numbers of color. I cannot see much, if any, onscreen difference between True Color (24 bit) and True Color (32 bit), so I opt for the smaller number to enhance performance.

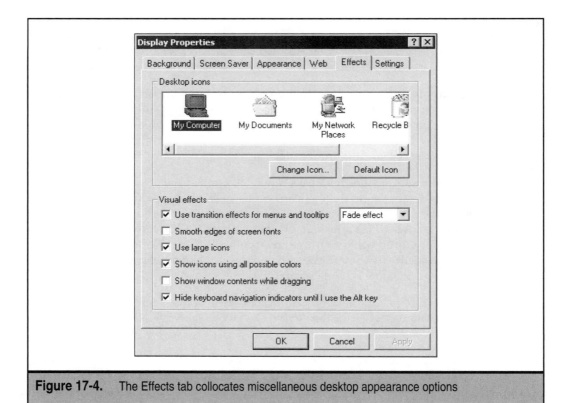

Figure 17-4.   The Effects tab collocates miscellaneous desktop appearance options

The screen area defines how many pixels are projected onto the screen, represented by a width times height value. At the lowest screen area value of 640 × 480, screen objects are at their largest, take up the most "real estate," and appear grainier. Conversely, at your highest resolution, objects are smaller, consume less acreage, and are sharpest. The preview area on the Settings tab provides a representation of the screen appearance as you change resolution. Also, you may find that you cannot choose the high number of colors you want at the higher screen resolutions, because the processing power and memory on your video card cannot handle higher values of both colors and screen resolution. What's the best compromise? Get the largest, sharpest monitor you can and use the highest resolution that allows you to see clearly text and small objects, such as icons, permits a high numbers of colors, and has the highest refresh rate (described later in this section).

TIP: Many manufacturers refer to a screen's resolution in terms other than numerical values. The more common are VGA (640 × 480), SVGA (800 × 600), XGA (1024 × 768), XGA+ (1280 × 1024), and SXGA+ (1400 × 1050).

Clicking Advanced on the Settings tab opens a Properties dialog box for your monitor and video card. An example is shown in Figure 17-5. This dialog box reflects your monitor and video adapter and varies from one set of equipment to another. The tabs in the Properties dialog box and their contents for a typical monitor and adapter are as described next (yours may be different).

▼ **General** Allows you to modify the font size of screen text and choose how you want Windows 2000 to handle changes made to screen settings.

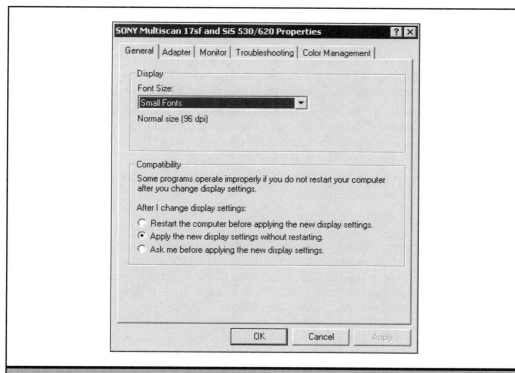

Figure 17-5. The Properties dialog box for your monitor and video card is opened by clicking Advanced in the Settings tab of Display Properties

■ **Adapter**   Provides a shortcut to the video card's Properties dialog box (the same one you see going through the Device Manager) and lists the resolution, color, and refresh rates supported, as shown next.

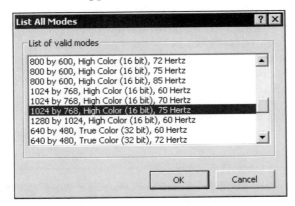

■ **Monitor**   Provides a shortcut to the monitor's Properties dialog box (the same one you see going through the Device Manager) and lets you choose a refresh rate. A higher refresh rate is generally easier on the eyes and produces less flicker.

■ **Troubleshooting**   Provides settings (which are video-card dependent) that you can modify, although you generally shouldn't make changes unless you're having problems. Use in conjunction with the Display Troubleshooter, opened from the Troubleshoot button on the Settings tab.

▲ **Color Management**   Provides color profiles that affect how colors are displayed on your monitor.

Active Desktop

What is "active" about a desktop? Microsoft's definition centers on a connection to a web server, either on the Web or locally on an intranet. By placing dynamic content on your desktop, such as a stock ticker, you are updated with its latest information, assuming that you have a TCP/IP connection in place. Obviously, an Active Desktop is of much greater benefit to users with a dedicated connection who receive updates as they occur; dial-up users receive updates only while online.

The main avenue to set up an Active Desktop is through the Display Properties dialog box's Web tab. Open the dialog box by right-clicking an open area of your desktop and choosing Active Desktop | Customize My Desktop.

Selecting the Show Web Content on My Active Desktop checkbox turns on the controls in the dialog box, as shown in Figure 17-6. By default, your browser's home page is available to use as an active item; however, you can easily add more exciting content by

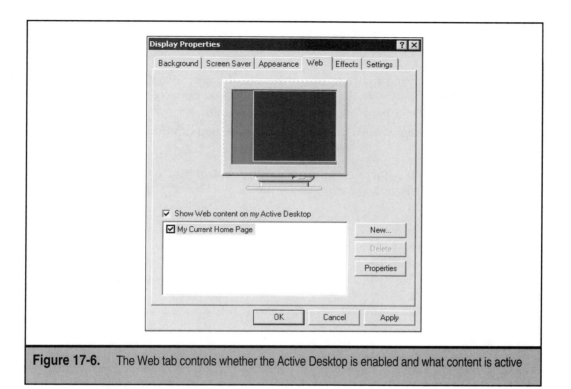

Figure 17-6. The Web tab controls whether the Active Desktop is enabled and what content is active

clicking New to open the New Active Desktop Item dialog box, which gives you three ways to add content, as described in more detail next.

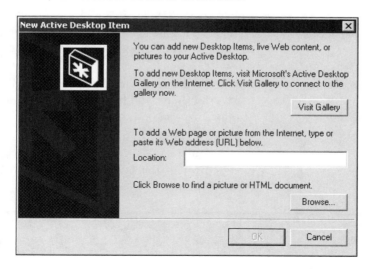

▼ **Microsoft's Active Desktop Gallery** By clicking Visit Gallery, you are connected to a Microsoft-hosted site that provides categorized lists of available content.

■ **URL** By entering a URL from a web page of your choosing—from either the Web or an intranet—in the Location text box, you can access any available content.

▲ **Local machine/network** By clicking Browse, you can find a graphic or HTML file.

Once your desktop is "active," you can further control it by using new options that appear in the desktop's context menu, under the Active Desktop option, as described in Table 17-1.

Taskbar

From this one innocuous gray toolbar on the desktop, you can control almost your total Windows experience. Actually, the taskbar is a supercharged toolbar insofar as it con-

Option	Description
Customize My Desktop	Opens the Display Properties dialog box's Web tab
New Desktop Item	Opens the New Active Desktop Item dialog box, shown earlier
Show Web Content	Enables web content on your desktop; this is the same as selecting the Show Web Content on My Active Desktop checkbox on the Web tab
Show Desktop Icons	Provides a toggle to show or hide desktop icons that might superimpose themselves on your web content
Lock Desktop Items	Ensures web content (and standard icons) is not inadvertently moved from its original placement
Synchronize	Updates web content from its sources
Active content list	Displays web content items that you have added and that are listed on the Web tab; items with a checkmark next to them are displayed; for example My Current Home Page and Microsoft Investor Ticker

Table 17-1.   Active Desktop Options

tains three permanent residents—the Start button, tasks area, and notification area—as well as other toolbars, such as the Quick Launch toolbar, which is added by default.

Start button   Tasks area   Notification area

Quick Launch toolbar

Start Button

Several of the newer features that appear on the Start menu were described in Chapter 16; this chapter looks at the Start button itself. Although you are familiar with using Start as a portal to various program shortcuts located on the Start menu or the layered Programs menu, how often do you think of the button as a means to access other Windows features? As with any other item in Windows 2000, the Start button has a context menu where the Open option provides access to the Documents and Settings folder containing each user's personalized Start menu settings, or profile. (See "Employing User Profiles" in Chapter 14 for a more detailed description of user profiles.)

The options shown in Table 17-2 are available when you right-click the Start button.

The Start button is also used as a "drop point" for any shortcut you want to appear on the top section of the Start menu. For example, you can just drag the CD Player shortcut

Option	Description
Open	Displays the Start Menu folder in a window for the currently logged-on user.
Explore	Opens Windows Explorer with the Start Menu folder open for the currently logged-on user. This is the most useful view to see and manage shortcuts on the Start and Programs menus.
Search	Opens the Search Results window set up for searching for files or folders in the Start Menu folder belonging to the currently logged-on user.
Open All Users	Displays the Start Menu folder showing the program shortcuts that are available to any user that logs on to the machine.
Explore All Users	Opens Windows Explorer with the Start Menu folder open for All Users.

Table 17-2.   Start Button Context Menu Options

from the Programs | Accessories | Entertainment menu, drag a shortcut's icon from the desktop, or drag a shortcut from Windows Explorer, and drop any of them on the Start button. Also, you can drag and drop a program's executable (EXE) file to the Start button, which automatically creates a shortcut on the Start menu, leaving the program file at its current location.

TIP: To add more shortcuts on the Start menu without having to scroll it, click Start, choose Settings | Taskbar & Start Menu, and select the Show Small Icons on Start Menu checkbox.

Quick Launch Toolbar

Directly to the right of the Start button is a toolbar included on the taskbar that provides one-click access to applications (and at least one feature). You can add applications to the Quick Launch toolbar by dragging and dropping their EXE files onto it. Though your desktop icons are often covered by one or more windows, you always have ready access to the taskbar, whether it's visible at the bottom of your screen or becomes visible when you move the mouse pointer to the bottom of the screen. Even if you don't add shortcuts to the Quick Launch toolbar, clicking its Show Desktop icon (the one feature alluded to earlier in this paragraph) quickly minimizes all open windows so that you can access a desktop icon. Clicking Show Desktop a second time restores the desktop as it was with all the windows reopened that were open prior to clicking Show Desktop the first time.

If you right-click an open area of the Quick Launch toolbar, you see an expanded taskbar context menu that provides options at the top that allow you to change how the Quick Launch toolbar and its icons appear (View Small and Large, Show Text, and Show Title). If you choose Open, the Quick Launch toolbar folder for the logged-on user opens. This is a much faster way to reach the contents of the toolbar in a folder window than navigating to c:\Documents and Settings*username*\Application Data\Microsoft\Internet Explorer\Quick Launch.

Tasks Area

Any open window, such as a folder's contents or a running program such as Word, has a "task" associated with it that appears on the taskbar. The tasks area serves two major functions: you can see how many windows are open or how many applications are running even if they are hidden, and you can quickly "bring to the top" any of the open windows by clicking its task. A *task* is a visible representation of the function, provided by the four icons in a window's title bar: the context menu icon on the far left, and Minimize, Maximize/Restore, and Close on the far right. A task's context menu, opened by right-clicking the task, provides the same options as the menu opened from the window's context menu icon. As more windows are opened, more tasks are added to the taskbar, and they may become indistinguishable. Placing your mouse pointer on top of a task provides a screen tip that identifies it.

Notification Area

The rightmost element of the taskbar goes by several names, such as "notification area" and "taskbar tray." Regardless of its name, it provides icons for easy access to certain aspects of available features. For example, the Task Manager, when running, provides an icon that shows a graphical view of CPU usage. Also, screen tips, which are displayed when pointing at an icon in the notification area, provide information, such as, the Internet connection icon provides the connection speed, and the clock provides the date. If you find that the less-used icons in the notification area take up too much valuable taskbar real estate, you generally can remove them by using their context menus, or by double-clicking them and finding an option in the dialog box that opens. One exception is the clock; it is removed by using the Taskbar and Start Menu Properties dialog box.

Taskbar Properties

Other properties of the taskbar, such as adding additional toolbars, are controlled through the taskbar context menu or its Properties dialog box. For example, you can add a toolbar with these steps:

1. Right-click an empty area of the taskbar and point to Toolbars on the context menu.

2. Choose one or more of the four listed toolbars, shown next, or click New Toolbar to open a dialog box of the same name that allows you to browse for a folder to place on the taskbar. The folder's contents will become icons from which you can open subfolders or documents.

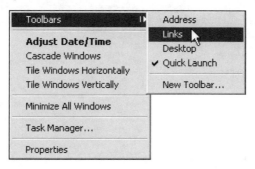

As part of the Active Desktop features described earlier in this chapter, you can add toolbars that access Internet Explorer web pages. Using either the Address or Links toolbar opens your browser to the address or link you specify. The Address toolbar provides the same functionality as the Address boxes you see in folder windows and Internet Explorer itself, including AutoComplete. This handy feature is found throughout Windows 2000 wherever you have the opportunity to type the name of a file, folder, web address, or other resource. AutoComplete "remembers" prior entries, and as you begin to type, it offers suggestions based on the characters you type. For example, if you have already visited the web sites www.aadvaark.com, www.acme.com, and www.altavista.com, and then type an "a" in the Address toolbar, you are presented with all three choices; if you type "ac," Windows 2000 presents only the second choice, www.acme.com.

APPLICATIONS

Windows 2000 Professional is designed to run on desktops and laptops where people do work. The work is done by using any one of thousands of applications, and each of these applications, although written to be used on a Windows OS, has the potential for causing conflicts with other running applications or the OS itself. A major cause of the past general protection faults (GPFs) and "blue screen" errors in Windows (which necessitate a subsequent reboot) was the interoperability of applications and their interaction with the OS. Windows 2000 and the underlying NT architecture have made great strides in producing a reliable and stable platform, and full-on system crashes are almost nonexistent. Along with improvements made to memory management and application handling, Windows 2000 uses a component first introduced in Office 2000 called the Windows Installer service that centrally manages application installation, configuration, repair, and uninstall, as shown in Figure 17-7. Windows Installer is covered next.

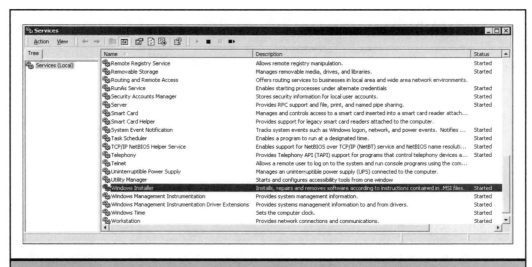

Figure 17-7.   The Windows Installer service manages applications behind the scenes

Windows Installer

Windows Installer allows the Windows 2000 operating system to manage application installation and configuration through several key areas:

▼ Version checking of shared components (allowing applications to coexist better)

■ Self-repairing installations that "fix" themselves without user intervention

■ Full uninstall capability, including checking component use by other applications before removal

▲ Interoperability with Windows 2000 IntelliMirror for group policy use over a network

Windows Installer evolved from the necessity to provide a standardized setup environment under which programmers could write applications. Using guidance provided by the Windows Installer SDK (Software Development Kit) and Windows Installer Programmer's Reference, programmers create Windows Installer-based *packages* that must conform to several levels of acceptance. For example, packages must pass validation testing, observe componentization rules, identify shared components, install to the Program Files folder by default, and support handling by the Add/Remove Programs control panel.

Additionally, Windows Installer views all applications as being comprised of three fundamental units: components, features, and products. *Components* are collections of application files, Registry keys, and other resources that are always grouped together during installation and removal; that is, if one subcomponent is removed, they all are removed. Components are transparent to typical users (nonprogrammers). *Features* are those options that you can select when you choose a Custom install instead of a Typical install. A *product* represents an application or a family of applications (such as Office). The product is defined by an MSI file, whose database format Windows Installer interprets to determine what features need to be installed and whether any are already available on the machine.

Applications written prior to Windows Installer's implementation also can run on Windows 2000. They use legacy installers that can cause problems, especially by overwriting newer files with older files and not referencing shared components. Windows Installer overcomes these deficiencies and provides the following tangible benefits to users:

▼ **Self-repair of damaged application files**   When an application is started, Windows Installer verifies whether the installation is correct; if it is not, Windows Installer makes repairs as needed.

■ **On-demand installation**   Features are installed when needed by the user. This is possible because programmers can code application features to be installed in one of four ways: installed on the local hard disk; installed to run from the source, such as from a network share or CD; installed on demand as the user needs them; and not installed at all.

- **Interrupted installation** If an installation is interrupted, Windows Installer can return to the previous successful installation.

- **More stable installation/removal** Few problems are encountered with other applications during application installation and removal.

▲ **Unattended installation** Allows installation packages to be set up so that no user intervention is required; that is, all communication necessary for the installation is between Windows Installer and the computer.

The most visible way to recognize that an application meets the requirements of the Windows Installer service is that it displays a "Designed for Windows 2000"-type logo. This is your assurance that the application not only meets Windows Installer needs, but also has been rigorously tested for operating system interoperability and stability.

Installing Applications

Applications can be installed from a variety of sources and media. As long as you can access the drive or establish a network connection (or even an Internet connection), you should be able to successfully install the application on your machine. Of course, this assumes you have the security permissions to access the files at their source location. Once you know you are able to get to the files, there are several methods you can use to start the setup routine of the application to be installed. Each application has an executable file, which Microsoft applications typically name Setup.exe, that will start the process. How you execute this file is determined by the different methods available; there are five alternatives:

NOTE: Some older Windows, and especially DOS, applications use Install.exe as their setup routine executable file.

▼ Use the Add/Remove Programs control panel

■ Use autorun CDs

■ Use the Run command

■ Use Windows Explorer

▲ Use the Internet

Using the Add/Remove Programs Control Panel

The Windows 2000 preferred method of installing applications is to use the Add/Remove Programs control panel. Though more direct methods are available, as described next, this method ensures that the correct files are initially executed for setup and helps prevent associated problems. Install a new application with these steps:

1. Open the Add/Remove Programs control panel by clicking Start and choosing Settings | Control Panel | Add/Remove Programs. The control panel opens with a listing of currently installed applications.

2. Click Add New Programs on the left side of the dialog box to view the installation options, as shown in Figure 17-8.

3. If you're installing from a drive, either local or network, click CD or Floppy. If using removable media, insert it into its drive and click Next. Windows 2000 Professional will try to access the drive it's in. If Windows is unable to find a Setup executable file, you can browse to the correct local or network location.

4. If you have a server that is set up for network installation, choose the application from the list under Add Programs from Your Network. If a large number of applications are listed, try narrowing your search by choosing an appropriate category from the Category drop-down list.

5. Follow any prompts that the setup routine presents, and select the default or typical installation, or customize the features you want installed.

6. After the installation is successfully installed and your machine is rebooted (if necessary), you will see the application registered under Currently Installed Programs, as shown here.

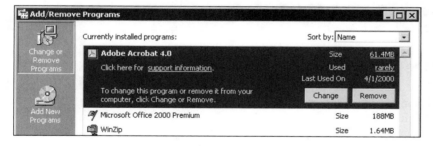

Using Autorun CDs

Most newer programs have CDs that automatically welcome you to the setup routine when you place the CD in its drive, as shown in Figure 17-9. After selecting features you do or do not want installed, clicking a button, such as Continue, generally is all that's required.

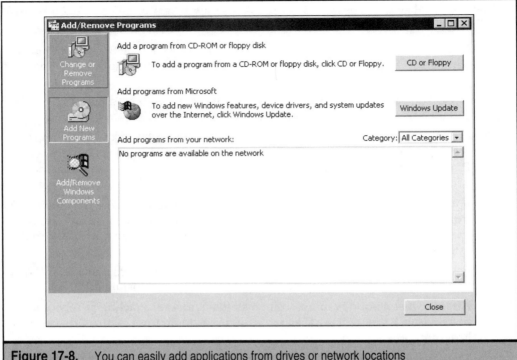

Figure 17-8.   You can easily add applications from drives or network locations

Using the Run Command

You can use any one of several manual methods to execute an application's setup file, as you would to run any executable file. Clicking Start and then Run from the Start menu opens the Run dialog box, which lets you enter the path to the Setup.exe in one of three ways:

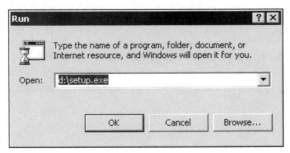

▼   Type the path in the Open text box; for example, \\aardvark1\office2k\ setup.exe or d:\setup.exe

■   Select a previously used address by clicking the down arrow at the right end of the Open text box and choosing from the list

▲   Click Browse and navigate to the file

Using Windows Explorer

If you started your Windows experience with the 3.*x* versions and Program Manager, it's hard to break the habit of doing as many file manipulations as you can from within a folder/file hierarchical structure, such as Windows Explorer. From within this one interface, you can quickly view and open drives, create new mapped drives to networked computers, and manually locate the Setup.exe file in the folder where it's located. Then, you simply need to double-click it.

Figure 17-9.   Installing applications with autorun CDs means simply inserting the CD into its drive

Using the Internet

As the Web increasingly replaces many of the functions formerly relegated to desktop computers, more and more applications are being made available on the Web. After you find an application that you want on the Web, and provide any information the site requires from you, you generally are presented with a File Download dialog box, shown in Figure 17-10, that offers you two options:

▼ Run the setup routine and install the application over the Web

▲ Download the files, usually as a single file compressed by a "zipper" such as WinZip, copy them to your local machine, and then manually run the application's Setup.exe file

Whether you should choose to run the setup routine or download the files and then run the setup routine locally (see the next section) depends on many factors, such as application size, your connection speed, the number of computers that will install the application (download once, install many across a faster LAN), and how often the application is updated.

NOTE: The latest phenomenon of the Web involves "renting" applications (such as Microsoft Office), which does not require the application files to be downloaded to your local machine—much like using a networked version in a corporate setting. One such service on the horizon involves using software such as the client version of Windows 2000 Terminal Services on your Windows 2000 Professional computer. You would then connect via the Internet to a machine running the server version of Windows 2000 Terminal Services. In a standard window, you would see the desktop of the server and be able to run applications installed on it, such as Word, bypassing any true installation of application files on your local machine.

Starting Applications

Just as you have several ways to install an application, as many (if not more) ways exist for you to start, run, execute, or launch an application. As the previous section demonstrated, setting up an application really just involves "running" its Setup.exe file. The same is true when starting an application, except now you are running the application executable file, generally named something similar to the application itself, such as Winword.exe for Microsoft Word for Windows, or Acrobat.exe for Adobe Acrobat Reader. Some methods of starting applications are more automated and generally preferred over others.

Using the Programs Menu

The final dialog box you often see when installing a program offers to place a shortcut on the Programs menu for you (some don't offer, they just do it). I recommend you accept

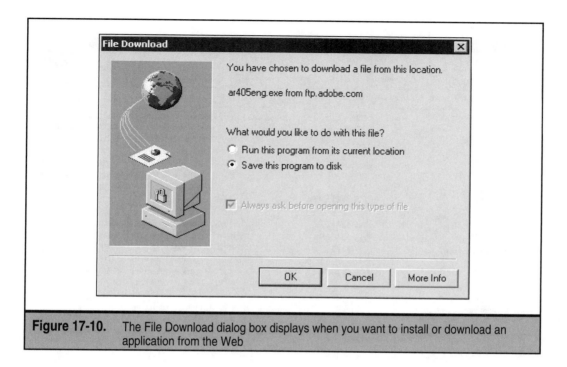

Figure 17-10.   The File Download dialog box displays when you want to install or download an application from the Web

the offer, because occasionally the executable file you need to run is buried in a mass of folders and is named something that you'd never associate with the application. After a shortcut is placed on the Programs menu, you can "reverse engineer" it to find out exactly what the application executable file is and where it's located. To find the path:

1. Click Start, choose Programs, and then right-click the application's shortcut on the submenu.

2. On the context menu, choose Properties; in the application's Properties dialog box, click the Shortcut tab.

3. You can read the path to the executable in the Target text box or you can open a folder window with the file selected by clicking Find Target, as shown in Figure 17-11.

Placing Shortcuts

After you identify the application's executable file, you have all the shortcut placement options described in the early sections of this chapter. If you have a shortcut on the Programs menu, you can drag and drop it to the desktop, the Quick Launch toolbar, or the Start menu.

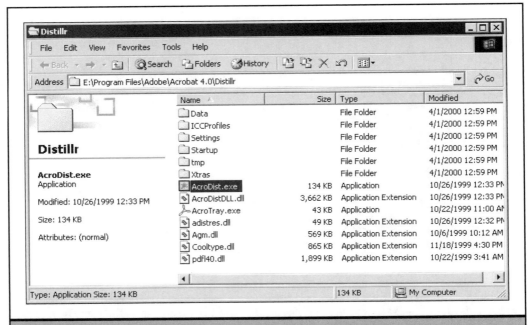

Figure 17-11. Find an application's executable file from its shortcut's Properties dialog box

TIP: Dragging a shortcut from the Programs menu to the desktop or the Quick Launch toolbar removes it from the Programs menu. It's always safer to right-drag a shortcut to its new location, which opens a context menu with the options to Move or Copy. Dragging a shortcut to the Start button always copies it.

You also can drag an application executable file directly from a window, such as Windows Explorer, to another location, which causes a shortcut to be copied there automatically. Or, you can first create a shortcut by right-clicking the file and choosing Create Shortcut from the context menu, and then drag the shortcut to the location you have chosen.

Application Maintenance

One of the primary benefits of Windows Installer is its ability to fix applications on-the-fly. If the source files are accessible, you might not even realize a repair is happening. If you need to insert a CD or reestablish a network connection, Windows Installer will prompt you for the action necessary. There are also several manual repair methods you can access if you find that an application is not behaving properly. For example, on the Help menu of newer applications, you can find a Detect and Repair option (or something similar) that starts the process.

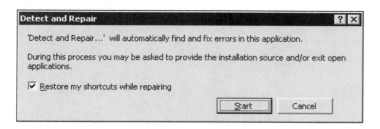

Another location for application repair help or information is the Add/Remove Programs control panel. Supported applications in the Currently Installed Programs list will have a Support Information link that provides product information, and links to technical support and reinstallation procedures.

Another class of maintenance falls under the auspices of updated information. You can find maintenance releases that correct problems found since the original release of the application, and any improvements that have been added since release. Again, the Help menu on many applications provides an option that links to the company's web site for file downloading, such as the Office On the Web options for Office 2000 products, shown in Figure 17-12.

Figure 17-12.   Microsoft provides a wealth of updated information for its Office suite of applications

CHAPTER 18

Mobile Computing with Windows 2000

Windows 2000 Professional was conceived and created with the needs of the mobile computer user in mind. Unlike its predecessor, Windows NT, which you really wouldn't consider installing on a portable computer unless you had a specific need to, Windows 2000 Professional provides features and enhancements that make you want to seek it out for use on laptops and notebooks. Many of these features, such as the power management supported by Advanced Configuration and Power Interface (ACPI), were designed specifically for the mobile computer user and thus are introduced in this chapter. Other Windows 2000 services, such as file compression and encryption, also have application in a desktop environment, and although they're covered in earlier chapters, they are discussed in this chapter from the perspective of mobile use. Regardless of your intended use of each Windows 2000 Professional service, support, or feature, you will find this chapter an invaluable resource as a professional, or even casual, "road warrior."

NOTE: Installing Windows 2000 Professional on a portable computer is no different from performing a desktop installation. Unlike earlier Windows versions, you don't have to choose a specific Mobile or Compact installation option to receive features intended for mobile computing (or remove those that were deemed unwieldy for laptops). See Chapters 3 and 5 for information on setting up Windows 2000 Professional.

USING FILES IN A MOBILE ENVIRONMENT

Many file management features introduced or enhanced in Windows 2000 have the mobile worker in mind. Three of the most relevant file-usage areas pertaining to portable computers include synchronization, compression, and encryption. These topics are discussed next.

File Synchronization

The problem of working on files at the office, at home, and on the road and keeping track of changes has been a version-control headache since the first worker brought a report home to work on over the weekend. A new Synchronization Manager uses a feature referred to as Offline Files, which enables you to "check out" a file from a network storage location and make changes while disconnected from the network, and then it compares your local copy with the copy on the network when you resume your connection. You can resolve any disparity in the versions through the Synchronization Manager. Also, the Briefcase, a legacy synchronization tool introduced in Windows 95, is still available for users who exchange files predominately by a removable disk, such as a 3.5"-inch floppy or Zip cartridge, instead of a network connection.

Setting Up Offline Files

Before you try to use Offline Files, it's best to check whether your computer has this feature enabled and whether it's set up properly. Verify Offline File settings with these steps:

> **NOTE:**   Windows 2000 Professional turns *on* the Offline Files feature by default; Windows 2000 Server turns it *off* by default.

1. Open Window Explorer or My Computer and choose Tools | Folder Options.
2. On the Offline Files tab, select the Enable Offline Files checkbox (if not already checked), as shown in Figure 18-1.

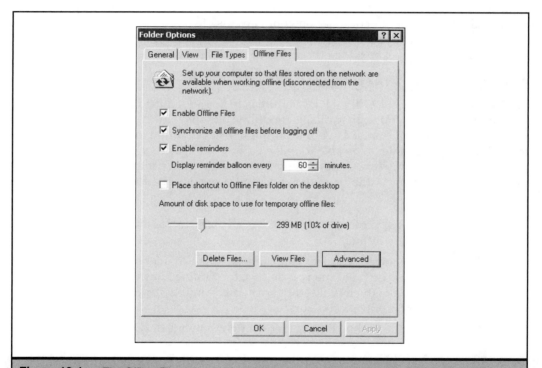

Figure 18-1.   The Offline Files tab provides settings that manage how network files are used

Enabling Offline Files makes available the remainder of the options on the tab:

▼ **Synchronize All Offline Files Before Logging Off**   Enables an automatic final synchronization each time you leave your current computing session.

▲ **Enable Reminders**   Provides a visual indication at a preset interval that you are disconnected from the network and are working offline, as shown next.

You can also choose to have an Offline Files folder shortcut placed on your desktop, and can allocate the amount of space on your hard disk to use to temporarily store offline files. The only change you might want to make to the default settings is to select the Offline Files folder checkbox; the others should work fine as is.

Downloading Files for Offline Use

The next step in using the Offline Files feature is to download the files or folders located on your network that you want available for offline use. Remember, these are shared, networked objects, so you must have the permission level commensurate with your intended use. For example, to be able to make editing changes to a Word document, you must have Write permission. Contact the owner of the shared component if you are having problems accessing a file or folder. Follow these steps to download files to your Offline Files folder:

1. Using Windows Explorer or My Network Places, locate the networked files you want to use offline.

2. Right-click the object you want and choose Make Available Offline from the context menu. The first time you do this, the Offline Files Wizard opens and asks you to make the initial settings you made in the previous section. Then, an initial synchronization occurs.

3. Double-click the Offline Files folder shortcut on your desktop, or open the Offline Files tab and click View Files, to see the files you have elected to use offline, as shown in Figure 18-2.

The Offline Files window provides several columns of information regarding the files it contains. You can modify the columns that are displayed by selecting View I Choose Columns.

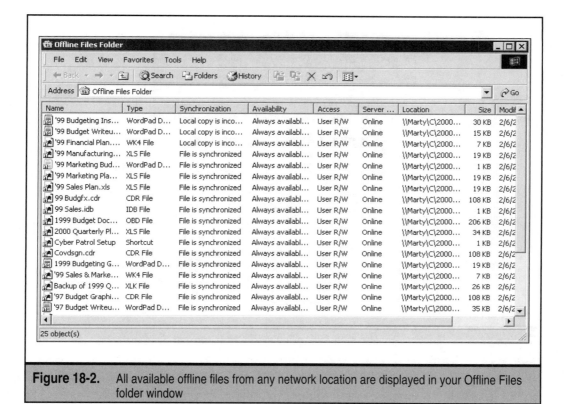

Name	Type	Synchronization	Availability	Access	Server ...	Location	Size	Modif ▲
'99 Budgeting Ins...	WordPad D...	Local copy is inco...	Always availabl...	User R/W	Online	\\Marty\C\2000...	30 KB	2/6/2
'99 Budget Writeu...	WordPad D...	Local copy is inco...	Always availabl...	User R/W	Online	\\Marty\C\2000...	15 KB	2/6/2
'99 Financial Plan....	WK4 File	Local copy is inco...	Always availabl...	User R/W	Online	\\Marty\C\2000...	7 KB	2/6/2
'99 Manufacturing...	XLS File	File is synchronized	Always availabl...	User R/W	Online	\\Marty\C\2000...	19 KB	2/6/2
'99 Marketing Bud...	WordPad D...	File is synchronized	Always availabl...	User R/W	Online	\\Marty\C\2000...	1 KB	2/6/2
'99 Marketing Pla...	XLS File	File is synchronized	Always availabl...	User R/W	Online	\\Marty\C\2000...	19 KB	2/6/2
'99 Sales Plan.xls	XLS File	File is synchronized	Always availabl...	User R/W	Online	\\Marty\C\2000...	19 KB	2/6/2
99 Budgfx.cdr	CDR File	File is synchronized	Always availabl...	User R/W	Online	\\Marty\C\2000...	108 KB	2/6/2
99 Sales.idb	IDB File	File is synchronized	Always availabl...	User R/W	Online	\\Marty\C\2000...	1 KB	2/6/2
1999 Budget Doc...	OBD File	File is synchronized	Always availabl...	User R/W	Online	\\Marty\C\2000...	206 KB	2/6/2
2000 Quarterly Pl...	XLS File	File is synchronized	Always availabl...	User R/W	Online	\\Marty\C\2000...	34 KB	2/6/2
Cyber Patrol Setup	Shortcut	File is synchronized	Always availabl...	User R/W	Online	\\Marty\C\2000...	1 KB	2/6/2
Covdsgn.cdr	CDR File	File is synchronized	Always availabl...	User R/W	Online	\\Marty\C\2000...	108 KB	2/6/2
1999 Budgeting G...	WordPad D...	File is synchronized	Always availabl...	User R/W	Online	\\Marty\C\2000...	19 KB	2/6/2
'99 Sales & Marke...	WK4 File	File is synchronized	Always availabl...	User R/W	Online	\\Marty\C\2000...	7 KB	2/6/2
Backup of 1999 Q...	XLK File	File is synchronized	Always availabl...	User R/W	Online	\\Marty\C\2000...	26 KB	2/6/2
'97 Budget Graphi...	CDR File	File is synchronized	Always availabl...	User R/W	Online	\\Marty\C\2000...	108 KB	2/6/2
'97 Budget Writeu...	WordPad D...	File is synchronized	Always availabl...	User R/W	Online	\\Marty\C\2000...	35 KB	2/6/2

25 object(s)

Figure 18-2.   All available offline files from any network location are displayed in your Offline Files folder window

Files or folders that have been chosen for offline use can be identified by a set of opposing arrows, located in the lower-left corner of their icons. All files in the Offline Files window are tagged with this icon. This identification comes in handy when you are looking at networked folders and can quickly spot those files that have been set up for offline use.

Synchronizing Files

At any time that you want to ensure updates are propagated from your machine or to your machine, you can request synchronization. A synchronization manager, shown in Figure 18-3, provides a single point of contact from which you can synchronize any shared files that have been set up for offline use. See what options are available by following these steps:

1. In Windows Explorer, choose Tools | Synchronize. The Items to Synchronize dialog box opens and lists the folders in which you have offline files.

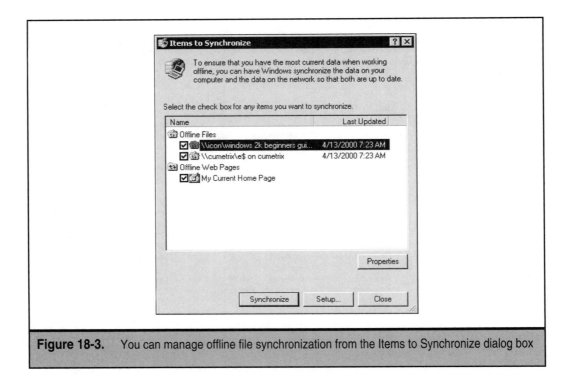

Figure 18-3. You can manage offline file synchronization from the Items to Synchronize dialog box

2. Clear the checkmark in any folder listed that you don't want synchronized, and click Synchronize. Any discrepancies are reported, as shown next, and you can decide what action to take.

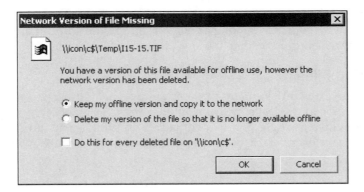

3. Click Properties in the Items to Synchronize dialog box to open the Offline Files folder listing all of your offline files. Close this folder to return to the Items to Synchronize dialog box.

4. Click Setup to open the Synchronization Settings dialog box, shown in Figure 18-4, where the three tabs provide options on how you want to handle synchronization during various events or scheduled times.

The Logon/Logoff and On Idle tabs are similar to each other and enable you to choose the type of connection to your offline files, such as a LAN, VPN, or dialup, and choose the items to be synchronized. Other options pertain to logon and logoff events and how to synchronize when your computer is idle for a specified period of time.

Clicking Add on the Scheduled tab allows you to establish a periodic timetable for synchronization tasks through the Scheduled Synchronization Wizard. You simply identify the offline items and when to perform the update. As in most Windows 2000 wizards,

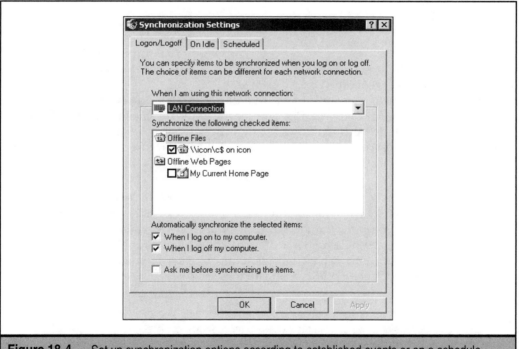

Figure 18-4.   Set up synchronization options according to established events or on a schedule

you are shown the results of your wizard choices in the final dialog box, for review prior to clicking Finish, as shown here:

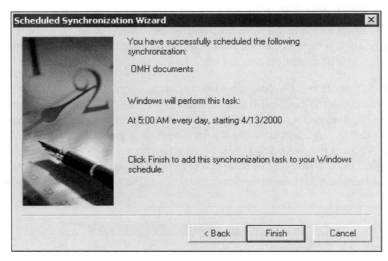

Click OK to close the Synchronization Settings dialog box, and then click Close to close the Items to Synchronize dialog box.

If you just need to synchronize individual files, simply locate the networked files in Windows Explorer or My Network Place, or locally in the Offline Files folder, right-click the individual or selected group of files (using CTRL- or SHIFT-click to select noncontiguous or contiguous files, respectively), and choose Synchronize from the context menu.

My Briefcase

Offline Files has no equal for keeping files in "synch" in a networked environment where file sharing is extensively used, but if you predominately exchange files between a single desktop and portable computer, an alternative to Offline Files is available with the Briefcase. The transfer of files between the two machines can take place through a standard network connection, or using a direct cable connection, or by using removable media, such as a floppy disk. See how to set up a Briefcase with these steps:

NOTE: Creating network connections is covered in Chapter 7. Chapter 10 discusses making direct cable connections and dial-up Remote Access Service (RAS) connections.

1. On the computer that contains the original files (generally your desktop machine), locate a folder (or your desktop) in Windows Explorer where you want the Briefcase to reside, and right-click to open the folder's or desktop's context menu.

2. Click New | Briefcase to create the Briefcase. Double-click the Briefcase to open the Welcome to the Windows Briefcase informational dialog box and the New Briefcase window. After reading the Welcome message, click Finish.

3. Drag the files you want to work on outside the office from their current folder to the new Briefcase (either the icon or the window that opened in step 2). The files will be copied, not moved, as in a typical intra-machine drag operation.

4. Drag the Briefcase to either a floppy or another removable disk that you can take to the other computer, or drag the Briefcase directly to the other computer over a network, RAS, or direct cable connection. You can continue to work on the files that were placed in the Briefcase either from their original location or from the copy in the Briefcase.

5. Open the Briefcase in Windows Explorer and choose File | Update to determine when files in the Briefcase are not identical to the original. The status of each file is displayed under the Status column, as shown next.

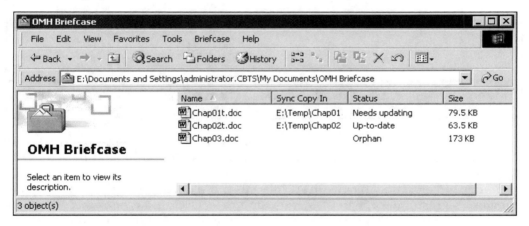

6. Right-click any file that displays Needs Updating and choose Update from its context menu. The Update dialog box provides the action that Windows 2000 thinks you want to take, as shown in Figure 18-5. If the action indicated between the two files is not what you want to happen, right-click the action and choose an alternative.

7. Click Update to synchronize the files. Copy the updated Briefcase to the portable machine through any of the methods mentioned in step 4.

8. Make any changes to the files in the Briefcase on your portable computer and save them when done. Copy the Briefcase back to the original computer. Any files that are not identical will be flagged as needing an update, as described in step 5.

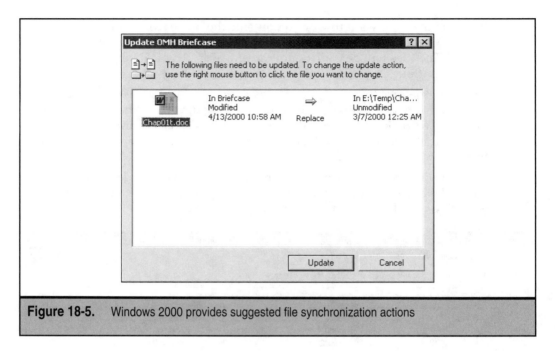

Figure 18-5.   Windows 2000 provides suggested file synchronization actions

There are a few things to keep in mind when working with briefcases. You should always copy the entire Briefcase between computers, not individual files, and the Briefcase has to be closed before it can be copied. Also, you need to be careful about renaming or relocating files that are placed into a Briefcase. Any path or name changes will result in orphan files in the Briefcase. *Orphans* are files that Windows 2000 cannot match with an associated file, and therefore cannot synchronize.

File Compression

Older mobile computers typically have a hard disk that is one third to one half the size of the hard disk in a comparable desktop system, so file size can become a factor. You can compress the entire disk or individual files and folders. The following are several factors that determine which method of compression is best for you:

▼ **How close are you to reaching the maximum size of the hard disk?** A nearly full disk indicates the entire drive needs compression.

■ **Do you move files to removable media?** If you use floppy disks, you are limited to file sizes of 1.44MB. If you use Super Disks (a new high-density 3 1/2" floppy disk–like device), you can have file sizes up to 120MB.

■ **Do you plan to use the machine in a dual-boot situation?** If so, it's probably time to look at buying a larger disk, because only NTFS (NT file system)

formatted drives support compression, and NTFS is not recommended for
dual-boot systems.

▲   **How much file maintenance are you willing to do?**   An entire disk compression
is a one-shot event, whereas file and folder compression requires manually
identifying the items to be compressed.

TIP: You can easily determine whether a drive is NTFS-formatted and able to support compression.
Right-click a folder or file and click Properties on the context menu. If an Advanced button appears on
the General tab in the lower-right corner of the dialog box, it's NTFS-formatted.

No matter which direction you choose, you can find detailed information on drive
and folder/file compression in the "Data Compression" section in Chapter 12.

File Encryption

Portable computers are highly susceptible to theft and are being targeted as much for the
information they contain as for the value of the hardware. If you depend on a laptop computer for work, you probably have a plethora of files that contain sensitive information
about your organization. And this same dependence probably carries over to your personal information. How many credit card numbers, passwords, usernames, Social Security numbers, and other vital information could be found on your laptop? I would rather
have my wallet stolen than my laptop. At least I have a good idea of the number of items
in my wallet. I cringe at the thought of what personal data someone could find scattered
across my hard disk.

To this end, file encryption is a strong defense against the potential nightmare of a stolen computer. However, you should consider the following facts concerning the Windows 2000 File Encryption System (EFS):

▼   As with compression, your drive must be formatted with the NTFS file system.

■   You cannot have both compressed and encrypted files and folders, nor can you
encrypt system files.

■   You cannot share encrypted data, because only you have the necessary security
credentials to open the file.

■   Moving and copying encrypted files requires a bit more thought. Cutting and
pasting will move encrypted files into an encrypted folder, dragging will move
them but will not encrypt them.

▲   You should encrypt folders instead of individual files and encrypt temporary
folders so that any temporary files created are also encrypted.

For a complete discussion of file encryption, including how to encrypt items, see "File
and Folder Encryption" in Chapter 15.

POWER MANAGEMENT

A computer cannot run without power, and mobile computers are not always connected to a steady source of it, so power can become a show-stopper when there isn't much left. Fortunately, this is one area of computing that has gotten a lot of attention in the last few years, and Windows 2000 has kept right in step with the latest enhancements and developments to conserve what battery power you have available. Power management is also applicable to desktop machines, but in a more "green" sense of not wasting it. Laptop users generally are more concerned about not running out of it.

The core power features provided in Windows 2000 are byproducts of an industry-wide standard known as Advanced Configuration and Power Interface (ACPI) that defines the hardware interface for the computer. This interface allows computer engineers to design mutually understood power management features for the operating system, hardware, and applications.

ACPI

To take advantage of the power features provided by Windows 2000, your computer's BIOS (basic input/output system) must support ACPI. Prior to installing Windows 2000 Professional, you can access your BIOS settings during the initial booting process by pressing a designated key or key combination (DELETE in many computers). If the BIOS has a Power area and settings for options such as suspend, standby, and times before hard drives and video displays turn off, you're probably in luck. If you want absolute knowledge that you have ACPI, you can contact the computer manufacturer and inquire about receiving the latest BIOS upgrade for your laptop. My laptop is a late 1997 Micron with a Phoenix BIOS, and it has support.

After Windows 2000 Professional is installed, you can check whether the Shut Down Windows dialog box has a Hibernate and/or Stand By option. If either one is there, you're okay; if they're not there, all is not lost yet, because you might simply need to enable them, described later in this section.

ACPI also provides support for the new hardware "hot swapping" feature. This is described in "Hardware Support," later in this chapter.

Power Options

The Power Options control panel provides the venue for setting all power-related features in Windows 2000 Professional. The tabs that are displayed and the options that are available on a tab vary from one computer to another, depending on what power management features are supported by the computer and whether a battery is used to run the computer. Compare one laptop's selection of tabs and options, shown in Figure 18-6, with those offered by a desktop system, shown in Figure 18-7.

Since this chapter is directed toward mobile computers, the following sections address power management in Windows 2000 Professional from a laptop computer's perspective.

TIP: If you have an older laptop that doesn't support ACPI, you may still have many power management features available through the legacy Advanced Power Management (APM) standard. To enable APM on your computer, make sure that the Enable Advanced Power Management Support checkbox is selected on the APM tab of the Power Options Properties dialog box.

Power Schemes

The Power Schemes tab of the Power Options Properties dialog box, shown in Figure 18-6, provides several schemes that dictate how power is managed by the monitor and hard disks, and whether and how the standby and hibernate features operate. (Display the Power Options Properties dialog box by opening the Start menu, choosing Settings | Control Panel, and then double-clicking Power Options.) You can change to any of the built-in schemes in the Power Schemes list box and see if the settings work for you. If you need to modify a setting, you can save it under a new name and have it available from the same list. The default settings for Portable/Laptop are a good starting point to see how the compromise of inconvenience versus battery life works for you. Having your screen set to turn off after one minute gets quite distracting, because every time you stop clicking or pressing keys for a minute, the desktop goes blank. But if you are on a transcontinental flight and really need to get that report done, any extra time you can get out of that battery is probably worth the inconvenience. Besides being able to turn off your monitor and hard disks, two other features in a power scheme assist in saving power: standby and hibernate.

In the hierarchy of power savings, you generally first turn off your monitor and hard drive. If your machine is going to be idle for an extended period, you should put it in *standby*, whereby, in addition to the monitor and hard disk turning off, your entire computer is put into a low-power state. When you come out of standby by pressing a key or moving the mouse, your desktop is instantly restored to the configuration it had before you selected Stand By from the Shut Down Windows dialog box. Additionally, you can add a level of security to your system by password-protecting the screen so that your Windows password must be entered before the desktop will display. Choose this option, if available, by selecting the Prompt for Password When Computer Goes Off Standby checkbox on the Advanced tab. The main drawback to using standby is that nothing is saved to your hard disk, so if there is a power interruption, your screen configuration and unsaved work might be lost.

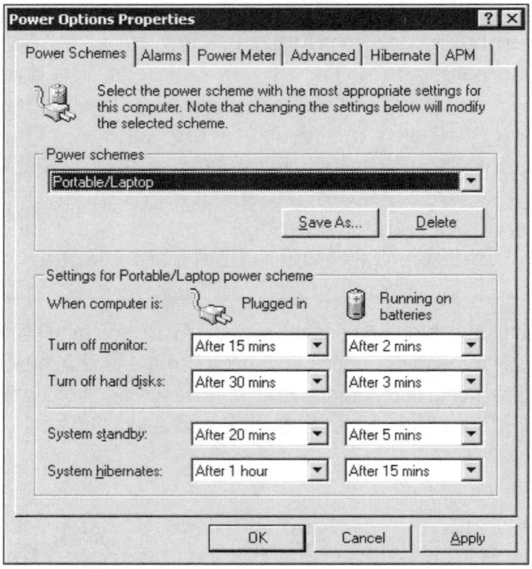

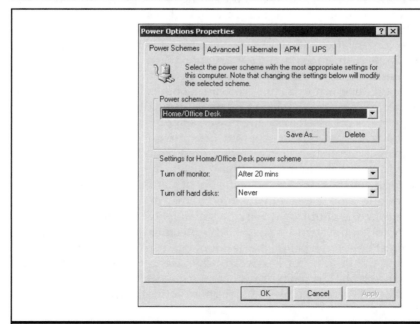

Figure 18-6. A robust offering of power features is available for mobile computers, including battery management

Figure 18-7. Desktop computers use power settings predominately to control hardware

The *hibernate* feature does what standby offers but does so by saving the state of the computer to your hard disk. The upside is that a computer in hibernation can experience a power loss, such as a battery running out of power, and all unsaved data and desktop settings will appear as they were before "going under." The downside is that it takes longer for the system to come back up. You have to turn the computer back on to "Resume Windows" instead of "Starting Windows" and supply your password to "unlock" it. This shouldn't be a big concern, since hibernation is really meant for lengthy idle periods, such as overnight. Another benefit of hibernate is that if you are in the middle of a project, you can leave the applications and files open when the computer goes into hibernation, and they will be open when the computer "wakes up."

TIP: If you do not seem to have the hibernate feature, verify on the Hibernate tab that the Enable Hibernate Support checkbox is selected.

Battery Management

Many people judge a laptop not by gigabytes, megahertz, or nanoseconds, but by hours and minutes of battery life. Windows 2000 Professional provides a host of information and settings to better observe and manage battery life. The Alarms tab, shown in Figure 18-8,

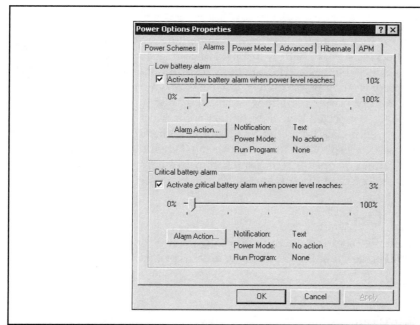

Figure 18-8.   With the quantity and sophistication of alarms available, you can easily avoid draining a laptop's battery completely

provides two levels of alarms to let you know when things are getting interesting, powerwise. First you receive a low-battery alarm, and then a critical-battery alarm follows. You can adjust the amount of minutes of battery life left for each alarm.

Additionally, you can set what actions should take place when the two alarm thresholds are reached, as shown next for the low battery alarm, from displaying a message, playing a sound, placing the computer in a suspended state, or running a program.

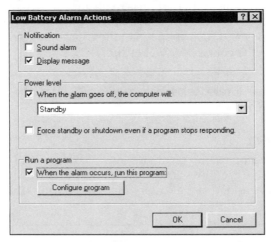

You can also monitor the amount of battery life remaining by opening the Power Meter tab and checking on each battery installed in your laptop, as you can see in Figure 18-9. By clicking a battery's icon, you can get additional information, such as whether the battery is charging or discharging. A faster way to get a quick look at the amount of battery power remaining is to place your mouse pointer over the battery icon (or AC-connected icon, if the battery is charging) in the notification area. You can also right-click the battery icon in the notification area and choose Open Power Meter to display the Power Meter tab. When a laptop is connected to AC power, an icon indicating so appears in the notification area if the Always Show Icon on the Taskbar checkbox is selected on the Advanced tab.

HARDWARE SUPPORT

Mobile computing benefits from the overall enhanced level of hardware support provided by Windows 2000 Professional. The following areas are of particular interest to mobile computer users:

▼ Hardware profiles

■ PC (or PCMCIA) cards

▲ Hot docking/undocking

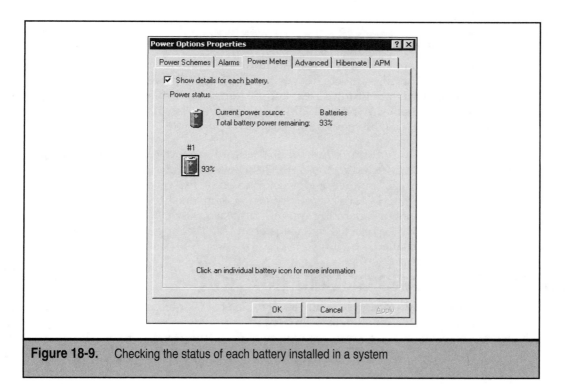

Figure 18-9.   Checking the status of each battery installed in a system

Hardware profiles are instructions that let Windows 2000 know what devices are to be started and what settings those devices are to use. On a desktop computer, you probably only have the default profile called Profile 1, since your device inventory generally is static. Every time you boot your computer, it sees the same modem, CD-ROM drive, and other devices. Unless you specify otherwise, any new hardware is added to the same profile, and all devices are started on each boot. Mobile or laptop computers might have several different profiles, depending on how they are configured. If you have a docking station, you might have a network card and CD-ROM drive built into the station. When away from the desk, you probably use a network PC card. PC cards are those credit card–sized components that expand a laptop's ability to add devices, typically requiring you to open the back of a desktop case and insert an adapter card or drive. Windows 2000 "remembers" these configurations and saves them for future reference. Windows 2000 is generally very good at determining which profile to use when booting, but some device combinations may cause it problems. You can have Windows 2000 Professional present the list of profiles and choose which one to use, and manage other aspects of hardware profiles from the System control panel/System Properties dialog box. See how with these steps:

1. Right-click My Computer on the desktop and choose Properties to open the System Properties dialog box.

2. Click the Hardware tab and then click Hardware Profiles under the section of the same name.

3. In the Hardware Profiles dialog box, shown in Figure 18-10, you can view properties of profiles and create new profiles from existing ones in the Available Hardware Profiles area; under Hardware Profiles selection, you can choose whether Windows 2000 Professional starts with the first profile listed or gives you the opportunity to select a profile first.

Other handy hardware features for mobile users are supported by the ability to "hot swap" devices, including the laptop itself in and out of a docking station. Essentially, you can remove a device, such as a PC card, from the computer without having to turn the device off, or, conversely, you can add a device without having to reboot the operating system—unheard of behavior until very recently. PC cards can be removed or ejected by means of an icon that appears in the notification area when they are installed.

CONNECTIVITY AND COMMUNICATION

A mobile worker using a laptop typically must return to his or her primary office at some point and upload or download data to or from the organization's network. The ways in which that process could be accomplished used to be pretty straightforward. If you were

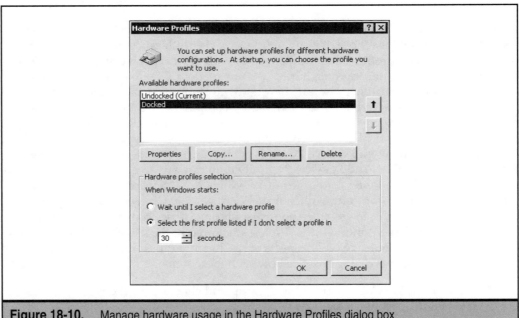

Figure 18-10.   Manage hardware usage in the Hardware Profiles dialog box

physically out of the office, you would use RAS to connect to a server by dialing a number, and establish a connection that exposed that portion of the network to which you had access. Not a bad way to transfer data, except for the long-distance telephone charges. If you were at the office, you would probably find a network jack and, through either the network card in your docking station or a PC network card, log on to the network and bring things up to date. In the Internet era, there seems to be an ever-increasing number of ways you can connect to a network (the Internet being one itself), and laptop or portable computers use most if not all of them. In addition to RAS and plugging in directly to a network, you can connect using direct cables, infrared, cell phones, and satellites.

Although Windows 2000 Professional doesn't yet have a satellite connection option, you can find the other options in its networking repertoire. Network connections are created in the Network Connections Wizard, shown in Figure 18-11, and are managed in the Network and Dial-Up Connections dialog box. Open this dialog box by right-clicking My Network Places and choosing Properties. These and other communication links are fully covered in Chapters 7 and 10.

If you have any hesitation to upgrade your current computers to Windows 2000 Professional, leave those doubts behind if you own a laptop or notebook computer. Just satisfy the processor, disk space, and memory requirements outlined in Chapter 3, and begin using the operating system of choice for the person computing on the go—you won't be disappointed.

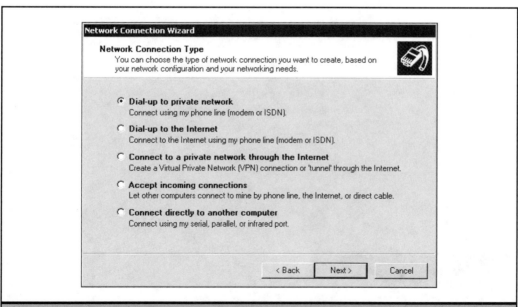

Figure 18-11.   The Network Connection Wizard displays several ways mobile computer users can stay in touch with the home office

Index

B

D

▼ E

▼ F

G

▼ **H**

I

K

L

M

N

Q

R

V

W

XYZ